Common

Also available from Bloomsbury

How to Be a Marxist in Philosophy, Louis Althusser
On Resistance, Howard Caygill
Alienation and Freedom, Frantz Fanon
From Communism to Capitalism, Michel Henry
The Politics of Aesthetics, Jacques Rancière
Disparities, Slavoj Žižek

Common

On Revolution in the 21st century

Pierre Dardot and Christian Laval

Translated by
Matthew MacLellan

Preface by
Imre Szeman

BLOOMSBURY ACADEMIC
LONDON • NEW YORK • OXFORD • NEW DELHI • SYDNEY

BLOOMSBURY ACADEMIC
Bloomsbury Publishing Plc
50 Bedford Square, London, WC1B 3DP, UK
1385 Broadway, New York, NY 10018, USA

BLOOMSBURY, BLOOMSBURY ACADEMIC and the Diana logo are trademarks of Bloomsbury Publishing Plc

First published in France as Commun. Essai sur la révolution au XXIe siècle

First published in Great Britain 2019

The translation of this work was partially funded by the Department of English and Film Studies at the University of Alberta, Canada

Cover design by Irene Martinez-Costa

A catalogue record for this book is available from the British Library.

A catalog record for this book is available from the Library of Congress.

ISBN: HB: 978-1-4742-3860-1
PB: 978-1-3500-2121-1
ePDF: 978-1-4742-3861-8
eBook: 978-1-4742-3862-5

Typeset by RefineCatch Limited, Bungay, Suffolk
Printed and bound in Great Britain

To find out more about our authors and books visit www.bloomsbury.com and sign up for our newsletters.

"The common day and night—the common earth and waters,
Your farm—your work, trade, occupation,
The democratic wisdom underneath, like solid ground for all."

Walt Whitman, "The common place"
Leaves of Grass

"Advice to non-Communists;
Everything is communal, even God."

Charles Baudelaire, "My Heart Laid Bare"

"Mlash said: 'There is nothing common in me.'
'And for you, what might it be?'"

Alexis Pelletier
Pensées inédites et commentées de Mlash

Contents

Acknowledgments

Our study of the principle of the common is greatly indebted to all those who participated in the collective work of the research group *Question Marx* and the seminar "Du public au commun" ("From Public to Common") that we co-hosted with Antonio Negri and Carlo Vercellone at the Collège international de philosophie and the Centre d'économie de la Sorbonne between 2010 and 2012.

We would like to thank all those who offered contributions during our working sessions and who participated in the public discussions we organized, in particular: Philippe Aigrain, Laurent Baronian, Saïd Benmouffok, Alain Bertho, Yves Bonin, Philippe Chanial, José Chatroussat, François Chesnais, Serge Cosseron, Nathalie Coste, Thomas Coutrot, Patrick Dieuaide, Jean-Michel Drevon, François Duchamp, Giorgio Grizotti, Nicolas Guilhot, Laurent Jeanpierre, Mathieu Léonard, Anne Le Strat, Danièle Linhart, Alberto Lucarelli, Jason Francis Mc Gimsey, Éric Martin, Ugo Mattei, Jean-Marie Monnier, El Mouhoub Mouhoud, Gabriel Nadeau-Dubois, Paolo Napoli, Jorge Novoa, Bernard Paulré, Jérôme Pelisse, Pascal Petit, Frédéric Pierru, Franck Poupeau, Anne Querrien, Judith Revel, Hossein Sadeghi, Christophe Schneider, Andrée Steidel, Ferhat Taylan, Bruno Théret, and Olivier Weinstein.

We also want to thank those who provided us with invaluable pieces of documentation, notably Gilles Candar, Guy Dreux, Louise Katz, Jean-Louis Laville, Alexis Pelletier, Pierre Sauvêtre, and Valentin Schaepelynck. And we cannot forget Corine and Thierry Richoux, for whom the noble and ancient craft of winemaking is also an art of the common.

The book would not have been possible without our editor, Rémy Toulouse, who provided us with unwavering support from the beginning, and whose many suggestions helped make our analysis as clear as possible.

And we thank, once more, Anne Dardot and Évelyne Meziani-Laval, our respective spouses, whose support, confidence, and advice was essential, as always.

Preface

Imre Szeman

The world, it seems, is a disaster. The relentless drive for profits and unfettered consumerism are eating up the planet's resources and poisoning it in the process. The rich are getting richer, and richer, and richer still. The poor and the precarious have, in turn, given up on even the fantasy of class mobility, knowing full well that the game is rigged. Global warming will violently impact human, animal, and plant communities over the remainder of this century, and indeed, centuries still to come. Nowhere are the true desires and capacities contained in the ideal of democracy to be found in actually existing politics. Nothing is going right, or, for that matter, ever has. We're living in the remnants of a teenager's house party, held when parents are away for the weekend. Even if it means we might get in trouble, we're now expecting them to return to clean up the broken glass and adjust the angles of the crooked picture frames. Except they won't be returning; there never were any parents in the first place.

Given the state we're in, what is to be done? Critics and theorists of all stripes have proposed innumerable political prescriptions. If the present is a disaster, they say, then let's live and work together differently. Let's move beyond capitalism to a more just and equitable social and economic system. Let's change our understanding of and relation to nature. Let's figure out a truly democratic way of being in relation to one another. Out of the billions of individuals that make up the planet, let's come together to craft new processes and practices, actively and collectively, that would allow us, finally, to inhabit a common. The evidence before our eyes today suggests not only that all this is far easier said than done, but also that we've likely been heading down the wrong path for far, far too long.

Pierre Dardot and Christian Laval's *Common: On Revolution in the Twenty-First Century* proposes we take a new direction. "All the efforts since the nineteenth century that tried to renew both political thought and social theory in order to more effectively confront capitalism have failed to produce a fully coherent politics of the common," they write. The fundamental aim of *Common* is nothing less than to succeed where all these others have failed. Through the extensive and multifaceted overview of the history of the communal ideal carried out in its pages, *Common* lays the foundations for a politics tailored to the challenges of this new century. This is possibly the best account of the communal idea that exists in a single book, beginning with the ideas of old standbys likes Plato and Aristotle, through to Proudhon and Marx, and up to such strange bedfellows as Nobel Prize-winning economist Elinor Ostrom and political theorists Michael Hardt and Antonio Negri. Even those who might at times take exception to their arguments will find this book to be an ideal place from which to start their own assessment of where we go from here to transform the common from idea into reality.

The labor of moving through the history of the common, testing out and checking in on varied articulations of it, isn't intended by Dardot and Laval as an exercise in compiling a new recipe of the political out of the bits and pieces of old ideas and practices (a pinch of Proudhon, a dash of Marx). The critical exploration undertaken here is meant instead to grapple with the political and conceptual missteps that have hitherto impeded the development of the common. There are two key insights that emerge as central to Dardot and Laval's understanding of how, moving forward, we should better conceive of the practices and processes shaping the common. The first and most critical point is the need to stop theorizing the common as a socio-political formation produced by capitalism. This is, of course, the contribution made to political thought by Marx, and affirmed (if in distinct ways) by the various Marxisms that have followed in his wake. The common (or, in the case of Marx, communism) has to pass through capitalism, it has been imagined, because of the way in which capitalism assembles those collective forces of labor that will eventually bring about its demise. Dardot and Laval are generous readers of Marx (and indeed of all the thinkers whose work and ideas they explore). However, they view any theory of political transformation that cedes political struggle to the motors of history as limited in the extreme. *Common* owes a debt to the groundbreaking work of Hardt and Negri, whom Dardot and Laval see as the first thinkers to directly take up the challenge of systematically re-imagining the common for the twenty-first century. Yet if they see Hardt and Negri's theory of the common as problematic, it is because they see it as repeating a spontaneism endemic to the left thought: the view that history will generate those new modes of cooperation and socialization that will bring about the conditions necessary for a new common. "We freely admit that capital creates an objective antagonism between itself and its workers," Dardot and Laval write. "Yet given the various forms capital has taken since the mid-nineteenth century, we're less sure about the proposition that the capitalist institution of forced cooperation and mechanization will ultimately produce a fully socialized individual who has developed all his faculties as a result of an increase in free time." The common has to be fought for in the present, by those living in the present, who want to bring about a different social order than the one in which they currently find themselves.

The second insight that emerges from Dardot and Laval's analysis concerns the limit of approaches that view the common negatively or defensively, whether knowingly or unknowingly. One of the tendencies for left politics today is to view the commons as something that once existed, but is now quickly being eaten up by an ever-expanding capitalism. The description of the common or commons as over time being absorbed by capitalism (as spelled out in the "tragedy of the commons"), with neoliberalism constituting the most ferocious attack yet on anything and everything common, has the misfortune of positioning the common (once again) in relation to capitalism. The common becomes imagined as what capitalism isn't and does so on the terms first established by the latter. Dardot and Laval draw our attention to how this view of the common ultimately affirms the legitimacy of the state as it is currently exists, and also positions property (i.e., ownership, however construed) as central to the common, too.

Though they find a great deal of merit in David Harvey's description of neoliberalism as being engaged in a practice of "accumulation through dispossession"—dispossession of common or public property—Dardot and Laval argue that this view of capitalism misses "a more general accumulation through an expanded and deepened subordination of all elements of the population's existence—consumption, transportation, leisure time, education, health, the use of space and time, social and cultural reproduction, and ultimately subjectivity itself." Any politics of the common that views it as something lost that needs to be recovered (as in Peter Linebaugh's account of the long process of the "enclosures of the common") can only generate a defensive politics, one that positions the people as endlessly running after the capitalist state in the hopes of undoing its work or taming its more aggressive tendencies.

So just what is it that Dardot and Laval understand as the common? In many ways, *Common* constitutes a sequel to *The New Way of the World: On Neoliberal Society* (2009; English translation 2013). In that book, Dardot and Laval provide an overview of the operations of "neoliberalism reason," and end with a call for the necessity of the construction of an alternate form of reason—what they call the "reason of the common." *Common* takes up this project, announcing in its opening pages, "The common (singular) is a political principle through which we are able to build the commons, maintain the commons, and sustain the commons. It is, as such, a political principle that defines a new system of struggles on a global scale." It is essential to understand that for Dardot and Laval, the common needs to be understood as a *verb*, rather than a *noun*—as a practice or process of commoning. The common is not simply a situation of co-belonging (as might be the case if one participates in an off-grid community) or co-ownership (property divvied up in equal measure), which are evoked by the use of the plural term "the commons." Rather, the common is activity, the collective process of fashioning a new political subjectivity; it is a task that has some clear aims (bringing about the end of property, for instance), but which in most ways is as interminable as history itself. Against political views that look to the state to defend the people, or to the unfolding eschatology of socio-historical form (à la Marx), Dardot and Laval insist on the active, affirmative character of collective practices and struggles that take up the challenge of generating new political forms. Throughout their investigation of the history of common, they reiterate this point with more and more certainty and clarity: the common is about coming together and creating, equally and collectively, a new world from the old.

One of the challenges for any theory proposing political change is that, inevitably, it becomes important to provide an account of how one gets from here to there—from neoliberalist reason to the common. If not via the social contradictions generated by history, or by the sudden, unexpected burgeoning into life of political energies thought to be dormant, then what? What might come as surprise to many readers is Part 2 of *Common*, in which Dardot and Laval offer a second archaeology to go along with the first on the common—an overview of property rights in Western history, as a way of mapping the dialectic of the law of property and the law of the common. "If the common isn't directly immanent to the social itself—or even a 'tendency' of the social that we need only stimulate to bring into existence," they write, "it's because the common is first and foremost a matter of law, and therefore a determination of what *must* be." Neither *res communis* in Roman Law nor Anglo-Saxon common law provide the resources for the constitution of a law of the common; in each case, the legal apparatus of the existing sovereign determines what might constitute the commons as opposed to private property, a distinction that can be (and is) changed as needed. Dardot and Laval argue that the common has to be organized around a radical challenge to and elimination of private property. Drawing on the insights of Marx's defense of customary law (which he undertook as a journalist working at the *Rheinische Zeitung* early in his life), they outline a process they name "instituent praxis." Nether a recognition of laws that already exist, nor a creation of laws from scratch, instituent praxis generates revolutionary social and political change on the basis of what exists. When it comes to social change, this is a process that circumvents the creaky old opposition between reform and revolution, and does so in a manner that is attentive to the principles of co-activity and of the unappropriability (of property) that will constitute the basis of a new politics. As with the insights about the political principles of the common, Dardot and Laval's original investigation of the law in the constitution of new political communities takes us down paths we've yet to go down. Like the work of other critics in recent years, *Common* announces the need to conceptualize and develop durable structures to confront neoliberalism and to advance left politics. The law need not be imagined (as it often has been in French thought) as limiting, violent and dangerously determinate; indeed, only a law of the common can radically challenge and overturn the reign of the law of property.

However extensive the account offered here of the communal ideal and the law of the common, some might still feel that there are missing elements of this account of the conditions for twenty-first century politics. The common is produced through practices of co-creation and co-development that are the basis for genuine, expansive social and political transformation. The political principle of the common outlined here, Dardot and Laval take pains to emphasize, isn't an invention, a matter merely of political theory, but "reflects the aspirations of those hostile to capitalism and its machinations." Be that as it may, it has to be noted that even if hostility to capitalism today is widespread, found in those myriad anti-globalization and environmental groups from which they draw inspiration, only a minority of the planet's inhabitants are engaged in active challenges to the political and economic status quo. The question that looms over these pages, and indeed, the pages of any theory of revolutionary transformation, is how we get from where we are now to a situation in which people everywhere are engaged in the work outlined in the provocative and useful political propositions with which *Common* ends. There are blockages and limits to the activity of the common that go beyond limits in how we have framed it conceptually or in relation to law—impediments that are at once social, political, and psychological.

In imagining the coming into being of the common, one might have thus expected to find here an account of what can only be called ideology. Perry Anderson famously castigates Western Marxism for its turn from economics and politics to philosophy, which brought with it a constituent pessimism about political change that it has found hard to shake. Yet even Anderson understands (at least at times) the reasons for this turn: the necessity of mapping cultural and social forms and structures "in relationship to the maintenance or subversion of the social order" (78). From Louis Althusser's analysis of the work of the Ideological State Apparatuses that make subjects "go" all on their own (without the state or the police standing over their shoulder), to Herbert Marcuse's investigation of the dynamics of affirmative culture, to Lauren Berlant's articulation of the "cruel optimism" with which the majority of us manage the disappointments of living in capitalism, the work of a great deal of left thought over the past century has been to understand why political change has, at least in some parts of the world, ground to a halt. Capital has indeed taken various forms since the mid-nineteenth century; free time hasn't produced a fully socialized individual because free time—indeed, even sleep time, as Jonathan Crary has argued—has become an ever more important part of the operations of capital. No wonder the tendency is for a defensive reaction to capitalism! And if there continues to be faith in the fact that capitalism might bring about its own demise, it is in part because the operations of ideology have meant that the subjects of capital don't always seem very interested in or capable of doing it themselves.

Dardot and Laval don't express any fears about how the subjects of capitalism might become the subjects of the common. They don't imagine the need for the right kind of subjects, ones no longer beholden to the structures and practices of the ideologies that support capitalism (which might require the intervention of something like a political party to bring about). The subjects of the common, it seems, are produced through the very activity of the making of the common, but how these subjects begin their transformation in the first place is somewhat of a mystery. Dardot and Laval do what they can to move past these limits by placing their faith in the inhabitants of the planet to, in common, generate the principles and prospects of a collective planetary life. For them, the operations of ideology may be real enough (however much some of the left might want to wipe their hands of it, or of related concepts like hegemony); however, the idea that one needs to get things right in how one views capitalism before one can act on it, can only impede the project of the common, setting things aside indefinitely and tragically.

Fears about the confusions and misdirections introduced by ideology, as have been expressed recently in relation to the rise of violent populisms across the globe (e.g., Modi in India, Orbán in Hungary, Erdogan in Turkey), might lead one to be cautious about any politics that appears to orient itself toward "the people." But this kind of worry can come perilously close to the view that there must be a "correct" mode of the political, judged as correct by political experts (including "experts" on the left) who somehow stand outside of ideology, and so can measure the right way to behave politically. The reign of experts who (as Jacques Rancière has pointed out) hate real democracy and substitute for it "appropriate" modes of technocratic governance has ensured that there is in fact less and less opportunity for democratic decision-making within official politics. And when people do get to participate, it is on terms dictated by experts, via "yes" and "no" votes that contain and limit genuine political expression. Dardot and Laval believe that the self-government of the common is accessible to everyone, everywhere, and now. We shouldn't look for the capacities of "the people" in faux games of democracy, like the vote over the exit of the United Kingdom from the European Union, but in challenges to the status quo that emerge when publics are actually allowed to openly voice their opinions. In an online poll, publics named a

British Antarctic Survey vessel *Boaty McBoatface*—a humorous challenge to military protocol and self-import, as well as to the pretense of democracy extended by the poll itself. Such a decision might be a better index of political will (however comic or irreverent), of the capacities that exist today for the co-activity of the common, than the outcomes of elections that have recently granted power to dangerous, autocratic, and racist leaders around the world. Change is possible and waiting to happen. (Note: the ship was renamed *RRS Sir David Attenborough* by the British government—the people were not allowed to speak).

The world is a disaster. Yet there *are* more and more people around the world engaged in a process of collectively re-shaping the world into something other than a disaster. The activity of creating the common today, however dispersed and small it might sometimes appear to be, *is* producing subjects who no longer have any faith in existing social and political systems. The tents of the Occupy movement might have been taken down around the world, but the remnants of the politics articulated at each site continue to animate how many understand just what needs to be done. Through the rigorous analysis and argument they offer on behalf of a new idea of the common, and the energy of political principles they provide us, Pierre Dardot and Christian Laval's *Common* promises to contribute substantially to the process and practice of generating a new world, lived in common, and operating by laws that no longer celebrate property above all else. A new global society is coming.

Works Cited

Althusser, L. (2014), *On the Reproduction of Capitalism*, trans. G. M. Goshgarian, New York: Verso.

Anderson, P. (1976), *Considerations on Western Marxism*, London: New Left Books.

Berlant, L. (2011), *Cruel Optimism*, Durham, NC: Duke University Press.

Crary, J. (2013), *24/7*, New York: Verso.

Dardot, P. and C. Laval (2013), *The New Way of the World: On Neoliberal Society*, New York: Verso.

Hardt, M. and T. Negri (2005), *Multitude: War and Democracy in the Age of Empire*, New York: Penguin.

Harvey, D. (2005), *The New Imperialism*, Oxford: Oxford University Press.

Linebaugh, P. (2009), *The Magna Carta Manifesto: Liberties and Commons for All*, Berkeley, CA: University of California Press.

Marcuse, H. (1988), *Negations: Essays in Critical Theory*, trans. J. J. Shapiro, London: Free Association Books.

Rancière, J. (2006), *Hatred of Democracy*, trans. Steve Corcoran, New York: Verso.

Introduction

The Common: A Political Principle

The future looks bleak. We are living in a strange, disquieting, and worrisome moment, where nothing seems possible. But the cause of this despair is no mystery. It is not because of capitalism's eternity, but rather arises from the fact that capital has yet to encounter sufficient counter-force. Capitalism continues to deploy its relentless logic despite the almost daily evidence of its profound inability to proffer even the slightest solution to the various crises and disasters it creates. Indeed, capital's hold over society seems to strengthen the more its consequences and crises continue to unfold. Public bureaucracies, "representative democracy," and experts of all sorts are increasingly constrained within theoretical frameworks and practical *dispositifs* from which they cannot escape. The collapse of what was once called the "socialist alternative" – which since the nineteenth century helped contain or correct the more destructive effects of capitalism – only deepens the feeling that effective political action is impotent or impossible. The failures of state communism, the neoliberal replica that no longer deserves the name "social democracy," the sovereigntist turn across much of the Western left, the weakening of organized labor, the rise of xenophobic hatred and nationalism, it all makes one wonder whether or not there are still social forces, alternative models, modes of organization, or critical concepts that offer some hope for a life *beyond capitalism*.

The Tragedy of the Non-Common

The situation in which humanity finds itself is becoming increasingly intolerable. The true "spirit of capitalism" was never better rendered than by that famous expression attributed to Louis XV: "*Après moi, le deluge*."[1] By continually constructing the basis for its expansion on an ever-broadening scale, capitalism is destroying the conditions for life on the planet and threatening humanity's self-destruction.[2] After the Second World War, capitalism's drive was more or less channeled by redistributive policies that were thought to obviate the return of the manifold social, political, and military disasters that befell the West since the turn of the nineteenth century. In the 1980s, however, neoliberal capitalism deployed an entire arsenal of public policies designed to lead us down a completely different path by disseminating the logic of competition throughout the whole of society.

The result has been a new system of norms that has transformed our working lives, behaviors, and even our thoughts. This new system transformed the social into a generalized field of competition wherein our relationships to ourselves and to others now function according to a logic of continual self-overcoming and unlimited performance. This competitive normativity did not arise spontaneously from within, as if it were a natural part of our psychology or biology, but is rather the predictable outcome of deliberate policy. It is with the support of a very active state that the unlimited accumulation of capital exhorts the transformation of our societies, social relations, and subjectivities in an increasingly imperative and intensifying manner. We live in an age of "cosmo-capitalism," in which not only our working lives, but all our institutions, activities, and leisure time have been re-shaped and redirected by a general normative logic that is geared toward the goals and pace of capitalist accumulation. This new normative system is fuelling today's generalized economic warfare, underpinning the powers of market financialization, creating increasing inequality and social vulnerability for a growing majority, and accelerating democracy's obsolescence.[3]

This normative logic has also precipitated today's ecological crisis. In the words of Joel Kovel, neoliberal capitalism turns everyone into an "enemy of nature."[4] For years, the United Nations Development Programme (UNDP) and the Intergovernmental Panel on Climate Change (IPCC) have issued report after report describing climate change as the most important and urgent problem humanity has ever faced.[5] While it is the world's poorest peoples who will be the first to suffer the effects of climate change, every new generation born after the mid-twenty-first century will suffer the increasingly disastrous effects of climate disruption. In his lucidly argued *Climate Wars*, Harald Welzer argues "the impact of climate change on global inequalities and living conditions [will] vary enormously from country to country," and he predicts the twenty-first century will witness "not only tensions over war and mining rights but also *resource wars*."[6]

Yet it is not only the ecological crisis that threatens the futures of entire populations around the world. Indeed, there is a certain danger in thinking that only the climate crisis is worthy of mass mobilization, while corporations, dominant classes, and the state continue to compete for wealth, power, and prestige as usual, as if nothing dangerous is happening. But this crisis, more than others undoubtedly, is especially symptomatic of the impasses we are facing. For the world can no longer be saved by creating isolated sanctuaries for nature's "common goods" (land, water, air, forests, etc.) that might "miraculously" protect these resources from the continuous and indefinite expansion of capitalism. Today, more than ever, every activity and every locale is interconnected: saving the world today it is not therefore so much a matter of isolating and protecting some natural "good" or "resource" considered fundamental to human survival, as it is a matter of profoundly transforming the economy and the society *by overthrowing the system of norms* that now directly threatens nature and humanity itself. In other words, effective political ecology can only come from a radical anti-capitalism.[7] Yet how is it that a looming disaster, pronounced by the entire scientific community, does not arouse (outside of a small minority) the kind of mass movement we might have expected? The extremely grave diagnosis proffered by the UNDP, the IPCC, and numerous other institutions thus raises the difficult question about the underlying conditions for collective action sufficient to respond to the climate emergency. Neither the corporate sector nor the state offers anywhere near an adequate response to deal with the serious climatic processes already underway. The repeated failures of the various international summits on climate change only underscore the fact that our economic and political leaders remain ensnared within the logic of global economic competition. The idea that humanity now shares a common destiny has failed to take hold, and the paths toward indispensable cooperation remain blocked. We are living the *tragedy of the non-common*.

This tragedy does not arise from humanity's ignorance of its looming future, but arises from the fact that humanity is currently dominated by economic groups, social classes, and political castes that refuse to yield their power and privilege, and are instead trying to prolong their domination by perpetuating forms of economic warfare, blackmailing the unemployed, stoking hatred of foreigners, etc. The impasse at which we find ourselves is thus a testament to our state of political disarmament. At the same time that we are forced to pay the price for capitalism's refusal to accept limitation, our societies are in the midst of a considerable deterioration of "democracy" – inasmuch as this term designates the few means, however rare or limited, by which it is possible to contain the globe's dominant economic logic, maintain life-worlds outside the market, support those institutions that operate according to principles other than sheer profit, channel or mitigate the effects of the "law of global competition," etc. The "responsible politicians" who alternatively succeed each other in election after election have, by now, almost entirely forfeited their freedom to act and have instead submitted themselves to the economic forces they have encouraged and strengthened. The rise of nationalism, xenophobia, and all manner of paranoia about our "security" is a direct consequence of the decline of the democratic state, whose sole function today is merely to properly adapt society to the demands of the global market.

It is illusory to continue to wait for the nation-state to wake up and protect its population from financialization, outsourcing, or climate change. There is no doubt that many important social movements have, in recent decades, attempted to salvage what they could in terms of public services, social protections, and labor law. But it is clear that the nation-state framework, and the state lever as such, is insufficient and inadequate for coping with today's social regressions and mounting environmental risks. We have seen firsthand how the state's form and function have shifted along with the intensification of global capitalist competition: the state's role is no longer to administer to the population and improve its well-being, but rather to impose the harsh law of neoliberal globalization. For if the concept of the common has indeed become a central political issue today, it is precisely because it brutally undermines belief in the progressive promise of the state. This criticism is obviously not meant to echo the neoliberal condemnation of various social, cultural, or educational state interventions, but is rather a call to recognize the state's inherent bureaucratic limitations and thereby submit the state form to social activism and truly democratic political participation. In fact, it was paradoxically neoliberalism itself that turned political thought in the direction of the common by shattering the false, mirror-like alternative between the state and the market. Neoliberalism showed that it was now pointless to expect the state to re-anchor the capitalist economy in republican law, social justice, or even liberal democracy. Neoliberalism thus put an end to the idea that the state could function as society's best recourse to the disastrous effects wrought by capitalism itself. From this perspective, Ugo Mattei is perfectly right to insist that the meaning of "privatization" – property that has been transferred from the state to private, oligarchic groups – can also be seen as the fruit of common work or property reserved for common use.[8] Public ownership, in this sense, is not the protection of the common, but rather a form of "collective" private property reserved for the ruling class, which it can dispense where it sees fit, and deprive from the population according to its desires or interests. That so-called leftist governments around the world have been so zealous in this plunderous activity tells us much about why there is such massive disenchantment with electoral politics all over the world today.

Collective action, generally speaking, seems increasingly impractical wherever one looks. The administration of the social is characterized by overwhelming bureaucratic domination, and everyday life is saturated with mass consumerism, as either a form of psychological compensation or a semiotics of prestige. And this is in addition to the extreme individualization of contemporary labor-management policies, the objective – and effect – of which has been to destroy the collective character of labor. Becoming an "entrepreneur of the self," to "take responsibility," to "exceed one's objectives" are all injunctions that do not predispose workers, who are already in a position of dependence and subordination, to adopt collective forms of resistance. Those who "win" know very well how to collectively defend their interests, while those who lose remain isolated within the generalized field of competition and are ultimately reduced to powerlessness. This rampant "decollectivization" – that most seriously affects low-skilled workers – is a major cause of the veritable social vacuum we all feel. It is a contemporary version of what Hannah Arendt called "desolation."

In the face of such overwhelming odds, the most common response has been to simply deplore the lack of political alternatives, the ruin of collective ideals, and the weak echoes of concrete utopias. This is why it is especially important today to work toward producing new vistas on capitalism's beyond, to theorize the conditions and possible forms of collective action, to formulate new principles that can guide our struggles, and to link dispersed actions in such a way that a new, generalized model of society can be rebuilt. While we do not want to overestimate the importance of this work – it will not be enough itself because, quite simply, there is no substitute for committed activism – we think such theoretical work nonetheless has an important role to play.[9]

The Strategic Emergence of the Common

The emergence of the "common" as a political rallying cry initially grew out of dispersed social and cultural struggles against the capitalist order and the entrepreneurial state. As the central term used to denote an alternative to neoliberalism, the common became the effective principle for struggles and movements that, over the past two decades, have resisted the dynamics of capital and given rise to original forms of activism and discourse. In other words, the common is far from a purely conceptual invention: the common is rather the concrete product of social movements and various schools of thought dedicated to opposing the dominant tendency of our era, namely the extension of private appropriation into every sphere of our societies, our cultures, and our very lives. In this sense, the term "common" does not so much refer to the *resurgence* of the eternal Communist Ideal, but rather designates the *emergence* of a new way of challenging capitalism and imagining its transcendence. In other words, it is a term that helps us turn our back on the strategy of state communism once and for all. By appropriating and operating the means of production in its entirety, the communist state methodically destroyed the prospects for real socialism, which "has always been conceived of as a deepening – not a rejection – of political democracy."[10] For those dissatisfied with the neoliberal version of "freedom," the common is thus a means of opening up a new path. It is precisely this context that explains the thematic emergence of the common in the 1990s. It was a shared political demand that could be found in the most local and concrete struggles, as well as within the largest national and international political mobilizations.

The call for the common gained its initial prominence in the alter-globalization movement and the ecological movement. The older notion of the "commons" was chosen for its ability to oppose what these movements viewed as a "second wave of enclosures." This expression – "enclosure" – refers to the centuries-old process of appropriating collectively used lands and the concomitant suppression of the customary rights of the European peasantry through the erection of various enclosures in the European countryside. The general spirit of the contemporary anti-enclosure movement is aptly summed up activists in the Cochabamba "water war": "we own nothing, and yet we are victims of a great theft."[11] This conception of the commons, in its various guises, has since become the object of intense theoretical scrutiny. Numerous empirical analyses, many at the behest of Elinor Ostrom, have dealt with the institutional forms, functional rules, and legal instruments that allow communities to communally manage shared resources – both natural or material resources as well as immaterial "intellectual commons" – outside of the framework of the market or the state. The rapid expansion of the Internet into every dimension of our lives over the past two or three decades has also shed light on new opportunities for intellectual cooperation and reciprocal exchanges within digital networks, as well as the risks to intellectual freedom that are posed by the ongoing concentration of digital capitalism and the increasing police controls exercised by states. Analyses of the common by philosophers, legal theorists, and economists have multiplied over the past decades, and scholarship in what is now a veritable field of "commons studies" has grown increasingly rich. Michael Hardt and Antonio Negri, for their part, provided the first systematic theory of the common. Their analysis of the common had the great historical merit of shifting discrete reflections on various concrete experiences of the *commons* (plural) toward a more abstract and politically ambitious concept of the *common* (singular).[12] In short, we are living in a moment in which the "common" is a term that designates a regime of practices, struggles, institutions, and research all dedicated to realizing a non-capitalist future.

The purpose of this book is to contribute to this larger effort by *re-casting* the concept of the common in a more theoretically rigorous fashion. This re-conceptualization proceeds both by re-articulating contemporary practices that ground their meaning in the concept of the common, as well as through an examination of a series of Western categories and institutions (sometimes very old) that have periodically made the common a concept both valorized and cursed: valorized – and even sacralized – because the common maintains a great affinity with that which *exceeds* profane commerce, and cursed because the common is an idea that always *threatens* the legitimacy and enjoyment of private or state property. The analysis we offer here is thus an attempt to "get to the bottom of things," all the way down to the genealogical roots of Western law and political economy. We interrogate the meanings of terms like "wealth," "value," "property," and "thing" (*res*). We question the philosophical, juridical, and economic basis of capitalism, and we try to illuminate what this political edifice has repressed, and what it forbids us from thinking and instituting. The institution of individual private property, the control and exclusive enjoyment over a thing (*res*) – according to the ancient Roman figure of *dominium* – is the decisive piece of this whole edifice, and this despite its relative dismemberment and doctrinal crisis since the end of the nineteenth century. This institutional aspect of property, whose fundamental principle consists in removing some object or resource from common use, negates the underlying forms of cooperation that are the basis of all production, and it ignores the accumulated forms of communal wealth from which all new wealth finds its condition of possibility. But while this "proprietary fiction" extends its influence over a vast domain of culture, ideas, technology, life, etc., it also increasingly reveals its limitations and negative side effects. Far from constituting its opposite, state-owned property ownership is rather the public transposition and complement of property as such, especially insofar as the state has not merely internalized property's norms but now takes the initiative on behalf of the latter to its own detriment: it was the state, in Brazil, that abandoned public transport to the private sector in its major cities; it was the state, in Istanbul, that privatized urban spaces in the interests of large real estate companies; and it was the state, in Ethiopia, that conceded sole land ownership to multinational corporations for ninety-nine year leases. The institution of private property was momentarily but badly shaken in the nineteenth century by the great socialist protest, and it struggled to justify its appropriation of the fruits of the workers' labor. Today it is exposed to another critique, one that reveals how property is not merely a carefully designed apparatus for deriving enjoyment from the collective work of others, but that private property is now a general threat to the very conditions of all collective life itself.[13] Herein lies the basis of a radical political reversal: whereas the common was hitherto conceived as a great threat to property, which was propagated as both the means and reason for living, it is this same institution of private property that has now become the most serious threat to the very possibility of life itself.

The aim of this book is to show the political principle of the common already at work across a range of contemporary political movements, struggles, and discourses that are opposing the hegemony of neoliberal rationality across the globe. Today's struggles for "real democracy" – such as the movement of the occupation of squares (15M, Occupy, Gezi, etc.), the numerous regional "springs," student struggles against the capitalist university, mobilizations for popular control of water distribution, etc. – are not random and chaotic events. They are not accidental and transitory eruptions, nor scattered and aimless revolts. These struggles are all based on the political rationality of the common. They are all collective experiments in new democratic forms.

This political dynamic is clearly manifest in the relationship between the "Commune" and the "commons" in the occupation of Gezi Park in Istanbul during the spring of 2013, one of a series of occupations in parks and squares around the world since 2011. The "Commune" was the name given to political form at work in Gezi Park (i.e., a highly localized form of self-government), while the "commons" was the name given to the various urban spaces that Erdogan's neoliberal policies tried to confiscate for the profit of private interests. It is also the name of a group, "Our Commons," formed in February 2013, that opposed "the loss of that which is common."[14] For ten days, from June 1 to 11, behind the barricades that read "Taksim Commune," Taksim Square and Gezi Park were turned into a living environment (*un espace de vie*) where experiments in common practices and forms of action took place. It is in spaces like these that we find the essence of the common: while treated as "thugs" by state power, "the urban activists defended their living spaces, created a common wherever they were isolated by physical force, and took care of both the collective space and themselves."[15] Political commentary on the Commune desperately tried to pin down the proper political actor or subject of the Occupy Gezi movement, as if it were necessary, at all costs, to assign this resistance to a "someone" in particular, as if the irreplaceable political value of the event did not derive from the fact that the collective subjectivity at work shattered all prior identity categories or silos (Kemalist versus Islamist, privileged "White Turks" versus poor Turks from the provinces, etc.).[16] It is precisely the aim of this book to explore the political significance of these types of contemporary collective struggle against neoliberalism.

Our introductory chapter (Chapter 1) specifies what we mean by the term "common": if the "commune" is used to name a specific, local, self-governing polity, and the "commons" is the name given to a diverse array of objects or resources managed by the activities of individuals and collectives, "common" is more properly the name of the principle that both animates and guides this activity. The analytical fine-tuning of this term is especially important, we argue, given both the diverse theoretical contexts in which the term is used, and the high degree of philosophical, juridical, and religious overdetermination the concept has experienced over the course of its long discursive history. In the first section of the book, "The Emergence of the Common," we re-construct the specific historical context that gave rise to the new principle of the common, and we critique, as far as is necessary, the limitations of the concept as it has been proposed by various economists, philosophers, legal theorists, and activists. In the second section, "Law and the Institution of the Common," we will more directly re-shape the concept of the common by deliberately situating it within the discourse of law and institutions. For nothing could be worse than abandoning the law to those who profess to enact it. In our view, every system of norms is always a site of conflict, and the law is no different. Thus, in contrast to the misunderstanding that the concept of the common is new, our analysis does not start from scratch. Rather, we will build on a long history of institutional and juridical creativity that has defied bourgeois society and its proprietary logic, and we will draw from multiple contributions in the fields of history, legal theory, political philosophy, as well as the socialist tradition, that seek to formulate a new conception of the common, one that is capable of illuminating the meaning of contemporary struggles by more accurately determining their context and the specific challenges they face. And lastly, in the final part of the book, we sketch the broad outlines (as opposed to a detailed "program") of what we call the "politics of the common."

1

Archaeology of the Common

Identifying the political principle of the common amongst contemporary anti-capitalist struggles all over the world requires some prior explanation of what we mean by "common." The extensive adjectival use of "common" in expressions like "the common good" or "common goods" (in terms of property) might suggest the word can, in fact, mean almost anything, and that anyone may lay claim to it. It would, in this case, be little more than what Auguste Blanqui referred to in his discussion of "democracy" as a "rubber word."[1] Perhaps we are dealing, then, with an insignificant word, a null-concept, or a baseless and uninteresting term. The term is, in fact, often used as if it designated a kind of *lowest common denominator*, as if it were a middling term that unifies "men of good will" of all classes and perspectives. Unfortunately, neither good intentions nor sudden pangs of conscience will ever pose a serious political threat to capitalism. And if the common only referred to vague notions of a "good life" in "harmony with nature," or to some shapeless notion of the "social bond," there would be very little to say about it, and moral treatises about the evils of capitalism would more than suffice. For what else might we say about contemporary struggles if we are only dealing with movements of moral indignation that are merely seeking to introduce a little more attention and care for others in a world increasingly ravaged by the self-interest of dominant oligarchies? For who cannot recognize themselves, at least rhetorically, in the aspiration to create a more "common world," to re-establish forms of "rational communication," and more positively re-define what it means to "live together"? Such generalized aspirations are rich soil for everything from the most intransigent republicanisms to all those particular communitarianisms that call for a return to our roots, origins, traditions, and beliefs.

Our re-conceptualization of the common is intended to break with all the colloquialisms about the common that are rarely subject to serious reflection and can be somewhat amnesic, to say the least. But before we can begin to theorize a new "reason of the common,"[2] we need to do some archaeological work: for even the most recent of political struggles emerges out of a pre-established context and is inscribed in a specific history. And it is precisely a careful exploration of the long history of the common that will allow us to dispense with the many platitudes, confusions, and misinterpretations of the subject. The aim of this introductory chapter, then, is to identify the initial discourses from which the concept of the common emerged, in order both to determine what the common is not as well as begin to introduce the specific concept of the common we want to develop in this book.

Co-Activity as the Basis of Political Obligation

The etymological root of the word "common" provides us with an initial bearing and direction for research. Émile Benveniste indicates that the Latin term *munus* belongs, in the Indo-European languages, to a vast anthropological record of the gift, while at the same time designating a very specific social phenomenon: according to this root, the term designates a particular type of performance and counter-performance concerning honors and benefits associated with an office or a position of status. The term thus speaks to the inseparability an office, a function, a job, a task, or a charge, and that which is reciprocally given in the form of gifts and rewards. What we find in the term's etymological meaning is thus the Janus-face of the debt and the gift, of obligation and recognition. The term is thus bound up with the fundamental social fact known as symbolic exchange, which – at least since the work of Marcel Mauss – ethnological and sociological literature has documented in almost every form of human society. The term designating reciprocity – *mutuum* – is likewise a derivative of *munus*, yet *munus* is not reducible to this formal requirement for reciprocity alone. Rather, its singularity resides in the collective and often political character of the remunerative duty (in the etymological sense of the verb *remuneror*, meaning to offer a gift or a reward in return). In other words, *munus* does not, first and foremost, refer to gifts and obligations exchanged between family members or between friends, but designates the various benefits and counter-benefits that concern the symbolic existence of the community as a whole. We find the significance of this root in the later Latin term for the public spectacle of the gladiators – *gladiatorum munus* – as well as in the term that expresses the political structure of a city (*municipium*) as constituted by citizens of a municipality (*municipes*). From this perspective, we can also see the manner in which the term *immunitas* refers primarily to an exemption from a duty or a tax, and may on occasion refer, in moral terms, to the conduct of one who selfishly wishes to escape his duties toward others. This root also demonstrates how the terms *communis*, *commune*, *communia*, and *communio* are all formed through the same articulation of *cum* and *munus* (*cum-munus*) that not only designates that which is pooled or "shared in common" (*mis en commune*) but also, and perhaps especially, designates those subjects who have "duties in common." The common – or the Latin *commune* – therefore always implies a certain obligatory reciprocity related to the exercise of public responsibilities.[3] The term "common" is particularly apt, then, for designating the political principle of *co-obligation* for all of those engaged in the same *activity*. It resounds the double meaning contained in *munus* – obligation *and* participation in a shared "task" or "activity" – and should be understood in a broader sense than the narrower concept of "function." For us, then, *common activity* refers to the act in which people collectively engage in the same task and thereby produce, through their activity, the moral and legal norms that regulate their collective actions. In a strict sense, then, we define the *political principle* of the common in the following terms: "obligation only exists between those who participate in the same activity or the same task." We consequently hold that such relations of obligation do not exist on the basis of mere belonging or membership that is independent of such co-activity.

If we look back even further than the Latin etymology, this conception of the common is also suggested somewhat in the ancient Greek – the political language *par excellence* – and more precisely the ancient Greek as fixed in the Aristotelian lexicon. The Latin origin of "common" resonates with the conception of the institution of the common (*koinôn*) and of the "putting or sharing in common" (*koinônein*) we find in Aristotle. According to the Aristotelian take on the concept, it is the citizens who collectively deliberate in order to determine what is appropriate for the city and what constitutes a just course of action.[4] For Aristotle, "living together" is not simply a matter of "sharing the same pasture," "as in the case of grazing animals," nor is it merely a matter of pooling everything together. "Living together" is more fundamentally based on the "sharing of conversation and thought": it is to produce, through deliberation and legislation, similar customs and rules of living for all those who pursue the same end.[5] The institution of the common (*koinôn*) is the effect of a "pooling" (*mise en commun*) that presupposes a shared mode of existence. And for Aristotle, that which holds for a small community of friends pursuing a common purpose also holds, at a larger scale, for a city oriented toward the "sovereign good." While it is not necessary to delve further into an analysis of the Aristotelian conception of the activity of "sharing in common" here, suffice it to say that Aristotle's *koinônein* constitutes the fundamental matrix for our own conception of the common: it makes the practice of "sharing in common" the basic pre-condition for every common, in both its normative and affective dimensions.[6] Yet the primary limitation of this Aristotelian perspective, which we cannot ignore, is its advocacy for the private ownership of property under the condition that what is privately owned is put to common use.[7] For while the distinction between *ownership* and *use* is theoretically useful – as we will argue throughout the book – the reality is that the common use of private property always depends on the "virtue" of legislation and education,[8] and thus such an arrangement seriously underestimates the real force of an institution like private property and its ability to compel certain kinds of conduct.

The concept of common activity we have drawn from Aristotle is absolutely irreducible to much of the recent discourse that makes use of the adjective "common." Browsing through the contemporary political literature, one cannot but be struck by the mess of mixed traditions, superimposed meanings, and confused concepts. By and large, most authors adopt virtually the same syncretic concept of the common: one that is characterized by a politics that tries to bring about the "common good" through the production of "common goods" that are viewed as the "common heritage of all humanity."[9] An ancient theologico-political notion of the "common good" is thus re-articulated and re-deployed alongside an economico-juridical category of "common goods" and an often very essentialist conception of a common human nature, wherein the latter functions as the basis for an understanding of the "vital needs essential to humanity" or some notion of the "natural social co-existence of men." Thus whomsoever today attempts to theorize new uses for the category of the common immediately runs up against this triple tradition that continues to shape, more or less consciously, our contemporary representations of the common. The first tradition, whose origin is essentially *theological*, conceives of the common as the highest end of our political and religious institutions: the superior norm of the "common good" (in the singular) ought to be the principle that guides the action and conduct of those who are burdened with both bodies and souls. The second tradition is *juridical* in character and manifests as an extension of a certain economic discourse concerned with the classification of "goods" (plural): this discourse tends to reserve the qualification "common" for a certain types of material "things" (*chose*). This tradition is especially active in the alter-globalization movement which, for example, advocates for the creation of various "global commons" such as the atmosphere, water, knowledge, etc.[10] The third tradition is *philosophical*: it tends to identify the common with the universal (that which is common to all), and any aspects of the common that resist this universalist identification are jettisoned into the insignificant margins of the ordinary or the banal. We will now briefly examine each of these traditions in order to better show how this muddled agglomeration of ideas hinders the development of a truly *political* concept of the common.

The Common: Between Statism and Theology

The resurgence of the theologico-political notion of the "common good" raises a number of important questions that are not generally addressed in most contemporary political literature. Who, for example, is in a position to define what counts as the "common good," and who precisely controls the means by which a given mode of politics can be said to conform to this notion of the "common good"? The fact is that this theological notion of the "common good" is burdened with a number of fundamentally anti-democratic postulates in terms of endowing the state, the "wise," "ethical experts," or the Church with the power to determine the definition of the common.

This theological notion of the "common good" has, of course, a very long history that we are unable to exhaustively trace here. It should suffice for our purposes, however, to unearth several notable aspects of the concept's history in order to highlight certain difficulties inherent in its contemporary resurgence. The expressions the "common good," the "common benefit," and the "common utility" are all derived from Latin, but the corresponding Latin roots of these terms are themselves derived from Greek philosophy, and specifically from the manner in which Greek philosophy conceives the relationship between the just and the advantageous. They are derivations of the Greek term used by Aristotle to signify the "common benefit" or "common advantage": *koinê sumpheron*. It was, however, principally through the intermediary of Cicero that the expression *utilitas communis* – a translation of Aristotle's *koinê sumpheron* – passed into the political and ethical discourse of the West (though the term was further modified as it was subsequently transmitted by the Fathers of the Church, especially Augustine). For Cicero, the term is meant to emphasize the civic duty expected of magistrates in the exercise of their respective offices. All those who hold an office are forbidden from serving their own interests at the expense of the common benefit (*utilitas communis*) considered coterminous with human society, insofar as this *utilitas communis* is both the framework for the reciprocal obligations that are a natural or universal aspect of human society as such and, at the same time, works toward some concept of specifically "public" utility (*utilitas rei publicae*), from a republican perspective. To betray the common utility for one's own selfish interest, as tyrants are wont to do, is unnatural for Cicero, and for this reason must be extirpated from the human community: "to neglect of the common benefit is . . . contrary to nature; for it is unjust."[11] City officials must aim for the utility of everyone, as a whole (*utilitas universorum*), though the latter is itself only ever tautologically identified with the common utility (*utilitas communis*). The common utility is thus conceived as the utility of man as man (*utilitas hominum*): "if nature prescribes that one man should want to consider the interests of another, whoever he may be, for the very reason that he is a man, it is necessary, according to the same nature, that what is beneficial for all (*omnium utilitas*) is something common."[12] Suffice it to say that man, as part of the cosmos and a member of humanity, must ensure his interests conform to the obligations of life in society by struggling against the destructive *cupiditas* (avarice) of the human community. To this end, however, the Ciceronian conception of the *utilitas communis* also authorizes the wise to confiscate the property of the injurious man who acts as a parasite on the community.[13]

We should recall that, in the context of Cicero's Stoic philosophy, it is nature that ultimately prescribes the common utility and thus dictates the conduct of the one who is entrusted with the political responsibility to ensure the utility of public affairs (*utilitas rei publicae*). In other words, it is still the honest and wise man who determines the "common benefit" that, for Cicero, is constitutive of human society as such. Through the subsequent transmission and cultivation of classical texts throughout the centuries, servicing the common utility continues to fall to the virtuous man who must always subordinate his own interests to the *utilitas communis*. It will not be until the rise of utilitarianism in the eighteenth century that this Ciceronian model will be upended and self-interest will be transformed into the very definition of human nature itself, and thus the basis of an entirely new system of norms.

For Cicero, legislation and government action must always aim "for the common benefit" (*communi utilitati*). That said, Cicero distinguishes between the benefit of the "public thing" (*chose publique*) that imposes itself on everyone, and "public" utility in the narrower sense of the interest of the state. Cicero certainly sees no need to justify the actions of the state to those who defend specific interests that run contrary to the utility of society as a whole: "those cases are splendid in which the appearance of public benefit has been despised out of regard for honourableness."[14] This strictly republican opposition is not found in all Roman political doctrine, and in fact it disappears entirely during the Imperial era. We should also emphasize, at this point, the relative lack of distinction, which will persist for some time, between the *common* utility and the *public* utility (*utilitas publica*), wherein all that is considered "public" and the obligations constitutive of human society (*societas hominum*) are intertwined. This confusion is due to the fact that the term "public" has two different meanings,[15] a duality that persists in multiple languages today. Public is opposed to private, as the common is opposed to what is individual.[16] On the one hand, the "public" is opposed to everything that belongs to the private sphere, but this does not mean the "public" is synonymous with the state. We speak, for instance, of a "public lecture," which refers to something said in front of everyone, and we still speak today of "public opinion," which is obviously not the opinion of the state. On the other hand, the term "public" also designates state institutions and functions: the *publicum* is the wealth of the state, and the *bona publica* is the property of the state. In other words, Roman political doctrine bequeathed a term that refers to the community of citizens but which can also be used to magnify and augment the domination of state institutions over its political subjects.

It is especially remarkable to observe how the term "public benefit" is increasingly attested in the codes and institutions of the Late Empire for signifying the specific interests of the state as distinct from society. During this period, the term began to function as a practical "principle of political action for Emperors."[17] After the fall of the Roman Republic and the multiple crises that threatened the Empire, the *Salus Rei publicae* became a lever of imperial absolutism. The Ciceronian opposition between "the utility of public affairs" and "public utility," in the narrow sense, disappears the more Roman statism becomes the norm. It is significant, as can be inferred from Jean Gaudemet's very precise analysis of the Roman juridical tradition, that under the reign of Theodosius I (fourth century) the term *utilitas communis* no longer designated the "deliberations of provincial assemblies, which was considered less a state service than a body representative of collective interests."[18] Once the interests of the community were subordinated to the interests of the state, the doctrinal landscape shifted in the fourth and fifth centuries to oppose the "public utility" and the "individual utility" (*utilitas privatorum*) while still affirming the pre-eminence of the former.

But history is never linear. On the basis of sixth-century re-constructions in the legal compilation known as the Justinian Code, the Eastern Christian Empire restored the doctrine of "common utility" as distinct from the "utility of the state," but it did so in order to affirm the notion that care for the good or the *koinôn* was now entrusted to the Emperor by God. According to Jean Gaudemet, the Byzantine revival of Ciceronian formulations was only in part due to the influence of the Church Fathers. Augustine, as we know, borrowed Cicero's definition of the Republic as based on the double fundament of law and the common utility.[19] But it is more likely that it was the durability of the Aristotelian doctrine of *koinê sumpheron* that was the real basis of this revival. This point is very important for the posterity of the theme in Christianity up to the present day.

These concepts, of which all subsequent political doctrine will make extensive use, then splits off into two major modes of thought in which the Greek sense of the common is still manifest: the first of these directions is the *statisization* of the common in Roman political doctrine, and the second major evolution of the term involves its *spiritualization* in the context of Christianity.

The first adaption of the Greek concept eventually leads us toward the modern doctrine of sovereignty, wherein the state is granted a monopoly over the common will. The substitution of public utility (in the statist sense of this expression) for the common utility will become one of the fundamental features of the history of Western political philosophy. Sovereignty, as that which defines the full powers of the state, was placed at the very center of public law, especially after Jean Bodin: "a commonwealth is a just government, with sovereign power, of several households and of that which they have in common."[20] This same notion of sovereignty was then re-cast by Rousseau in order to make the "common good" the singular concern of *la volonté générale*. Rousseau identifies the "common good" with the "common interest," wherein the latter refers to "that which is common" amongst all particular interests and which therefore "forms the social bond." To say the common good forms the social bond is tantamount to saying social connectivity itself is "effectuated" by the general will, which effectively means the latter is tasked with "direct[ing] the powers of the state in accordance with the purpose for which it was instituted."[21] We can see here how the notion of the "common good" is conceived as a state institution.

But of course this statisization of the common good did not emerge in a single day. Countless historians explain how Roman notions continued to circulate amongst the ruling elite in the Merovingian and Carolingian periods.[22] The *res publica* as *persona ficta,* an abstraction embodied or represented in a public personage, made its great return in the twelfth century when Cicero and Roman law were re-discovered. But it was also during this period that the common good was transformed into a major theological category. Pierre Abélard, in his *Theologia Christiana*, aptly illustrates the statist usage of the concept when he defines the *res publica* as "that whose administration is assured by virtue of the common utility."[23] But the reality is that Abélard re-interprets Roman categories by relating them to the model of the early Church communities,[24] wherein the primacy of the common benefit is now identified with the ideals of Christian society. Everything that one possesses must contribute to the common utility,[25] which is just a way of saying one's possessions must always remain subject to the needs of the common. Abélard's pupil, John of Salisbury, argues in his *Policraticus* (1159) that the Prince's *potesta*, his capacity to act, must be grounded in the "utility for each and all." But of course the hierarchy of laws and principles in the Christian context is very different from its classical Roman predecessor. If there is no power except that which comes from God – according to the words of St. Paul in his Epistle to the Romans (Romans 13: 1–2) – the Prince is never anything more than the mediator between the Divine Law and the human community. Legitimating the administration of the *res publica* by reference to the common utility thus logically produces a very different understanding of the common utility in this new Christian paradigm.

The second major evolution of the common good, however – its "spiritualization" – gave the Church a virtual monopoly over the definition of the supreme good. In the thirteenth century, and more in reference to Aristotle than Cicero, the common good (*bonum commune*) became a core ethical and political concept, the *locus communis*, of canonists and jurists. The common good – as the ethical basis for politics and the core criterion for good government – is increasingly used as an argumentative weapon by partisans on both sides of the Western Schism (between the Empire and the Pope).

The Christian iteration of the common good is of course very different from the supreme good in Aristotle. In its Christian version, the ultimate goal is not happiness in the earthly realm, but joy in the experience of God. While it is certain that there was a great dissemination of Aristotelian texts in the thirteenth century,[26] it is undoubtedly an exaggeration to speak of an "Aristotelian Revolution": in the first place, Aristotle was far from the only classical source that influenced medieval thought, but the great medieval commentators of the *Ethics* and the *Politics* also read these texts in a very particular way. If the Scholastic conception of the common good is the principle by which the Prince is evaluated, it is nonetheless a metric that belongs to the City of God; the common good is inscribed within a Divine Order in which everything has its place, and where everyone must assume their proper station and pursue their proper end.[27] The great Aristotelian commentators – Albertus Magnus and Thomas Aquinas – prioritized the salvation of the soul as the highest end, thereby superseding the good in the City of Man. Humanity's supreme good lies in God, and any necessary dedication to public service is but one progressive step toward the Creator.[28] The *civitas perfecta* is itself inscribed upon the path toward the common good, which is God. This dissociation of man and citizen is clearly far removed Aristotle's version of this concept, as is the morality that proscribes the "continuous impulse of the earthly creature toward heavenly bliss," not to mention the idea of the Christian community as a mystical body.[29] This spiritualization of the common good is characterized by a celebration of hierarchy and submission to the Divine Order. In this sense, the Thomistic conception of the common is a "re-ordering" according to God's plan, a responsibility that falls to the spiritual and temporal authorities. It is not hard to understand why this Christian theory of the common good was so well suited to the theory of terrestrial sovereignty – provided the latter always remains subject to Divine Law.

On the basis of this invariably circumscribed account, the double fate of the common in the West should be relatively clear. While the state and the Church disputed each other's monopoly over the common good, they gradually came to a consensus on a division of powers. We can see, then, the degree of thoughtlessness involved in careless contemporary efforts to re-deploy this theologico-political notion of the "common good." Most authors who use the term are generally unaware of the concept's heritage: for the source of its normativity is nothing less than the repression of human praxis itself. Far from serving as an emblem of emancipation, the concept shields and justifies archaic forms of domination, to the extent that institutions like the Church are still able to claim exclusive knowledge of the common good and thereby command authority over social relations. We see this today in the Church's tyrannical pronouncements on matters of sexuality, marriage, and the family. We should also recall that the "social doctrine of the Church," which has always taken the "common good" as its first principle, has unproblematically managed, alongside Thomistic Scholasticism, to accommodate the theory of the divine origin of the universal destination of earthy goods and property rights, on the condition that property is used for the common good.[30] Given the steady march toward capitalism that took place in the subsequent centuries, the doctrine's historical record is not particularly encouraging.

But we have also argued that the authors who seek to theorize the common today are not content simply to revive old Scholastic notions of the common good. They also intend to articulate the common good in economic terms. This time, however, the revival of the commons comes at the cost of its reification.

The Reification of the Common

The second major problem faced by contemporary theories of the common concerns their tendency to endow external things or objects with an essence that prohibits humanity from appropriating them. We refer to this second problem as the "reification" of the common, insofar as the common is viewed as possessing certain inherent properties. And the concept that largely facilitates this reification of the common is the concept of "common things" or "things in common" (*res communis*) found in Roman law. It is this legal concept that we need to examine first.

Our initial point of departure will be Virgil's *Aeneid*, and the episode we are concerned with appears in Book Seven. The Trojans, led by Aeneas, finally reach the shores of Latium after many misadventures. They send an envoy to the aged King Latinus and offer him gifts so he may peacefully welcome the Trojans. The King receives the Trojans in his palace, and he addresses them and asks them what they seek. Ilioneus, one of the Trojan spokespersons, responds by recalling a terrible hurricane they were forced to endure: "escaping that flood and sailing here over many barren seas, now all we ask is a modest resting place for our father's gods, safe haven on your shores, water, and fresh air that's free for all to breathe (*cunctis . . . patentem*)."[31] The fact that air and water are qualified by one of the Trojan ambassadors as "free for all" deserves our attention. For it is precisely by means of this qualification that the Trojans attempt to convey their peaceful intentions to Latinus: we ask very little, only an encampment on the riverside, along with air and water.[32] Of course we know the events that follow: the uprising of the shepherds gives way to the general outbreak of a war in which the Italians, led by Turnus, take up arms against Aeneas and his companions. There is no *a priori* reason to suspect Ilioneus and company of a ruse, for they truly consider water and air to be "free to all." How exactly, then, should we understand this expression?

Both air and water each seem to belong to a singular legal category, that of "things in common" or *res communes*. In her book *Les Chose Communes* (2006), Marie-Alice Chardeaux writes, "in Roman law, the category *res communes* includes the air, running water, the sea, and the sea shore."[33] After observing how *res communes* is often confused with unowned property (*res nullius*), Chardeaux specifies the distinction in the following terms: "things in common are unappropriable by their very nature, which should not be confused with things that are simply unowned and have not yet been appropriated, and can therefore be appropriated by the first claimant."[34] In terms of the genealogical distinction between *res communes* and *res nullius*, it was the Roman jurist Marcian (first half of the third century) who introduced this new class of objects into Roman law: specifically, those things produced "in the first place by nature and which do not belong to anyone." Marcian distinguished between two types of objects belonging to this general class:

> Some, which go by the name *res nullius* (things unowned) are factually vacant: they are destined to belong to the first occupant who seizes them. Wild animals are one such example. The other class, called *res communes omnium*, are those things which, by their nature, cannot belong to anybody and whose usage is open to all. Examples include the air, running water, the sea and the seashore, extending up to the high-water mark of the high tides of winter.[35]

The fact is *res communes* was one of the more problematic statutes complied and listed in Roman law. For such objects were effectively confined "to the margins of the divisions commonly applied to all legal objects," such as the distinction between patrimonial[36] and extra-patrimonial property, or the distinction between objects of Divine Law and objects of earthly law. A famous passage from the *Institutes* of Gaius (as re-cast in the *Institutes* of Justinian) explains this second distinction in the following terms:

> objects of Divine Law include sacred objects (objects and places dedicated to the celestial gods), religious objects (places and graves reserved for the devotees of the gods) and holy objects (urban enclosures)[37]; that which falls under human law includes all things public (unappropriable and outside the realm of legal commerce) and all things private (appropriable and within the realm of legal commerce). Like objects of Divine Law, the non-appropriable objects of public law are designated by the term "*res nullius in bonis*," which is to say objects of public interest that belong to no one.[38]

This conceptual separation did not, however, prevent a certain imprecision as regards the distinction between that which is public and that held in common. The seashore, for instance, is often referred to as both "common" and "public."[39] Nevertheless, it is possible to differentiate between the two classes of objects according to three criteria. First, their respective catalogs do not overlap. Secondly, the cause of their unappropriability is not the same: that which is public is subtracted from the domain of appropriability by a public act of law, whereas things held in common have no owner as a result of their inherent nature. And third, the intensity of their unappropriability is not the same. Public property is rendered as such in an institutional and permanent manner, which thus allows any citizen to contest any private appropriation of that which is public; that which is common, however, is much more susceptible to falling under the temporary *dominium* of an occupant. As Marie-Alice Chardeaux puts it:

> He who constructs a building on the seashore is its owner as long as the building subsists. But this act of appropriation is necessarily temporary, because nature is inalienable. As soon as the building falls, the soil recovers its original condition as held in common. Marcian, accordingly, compares this law of nature to a human law provisionally suspended, such as when a prisoner of war recovers his original condition of freedom once he returns across the border."[40]

In the final analysis, the juridical segregation of *res communes* highlights the difficulty Roman law encountered when trying to conceptualize these types of commons within the sphere of law as such. Indeed, *res communes* tended to be conceived more like an "original enclave" – a holdover from a more primitive age of humankind in which all property was held in common, rather than a fully legal category in its own right.[41] *Res communes*, in a sense, constitutes a kind of "pre-juridical enclosure" inside of which the law allows an autonomous state of nature to subsist, as if in a "fossilized state."[42] At the same time, we must not ignore the extent to which this pre-juridical enclave fulfilled a very specific legal function – namely, it was the model for the management of much that was "publically" held, such as rivers, roads, squares, and theaters. The paradigm of things held in common, whose use is open to all,[43] was therefore used to classify things rendered public as well. Again, the only difference between the two was the nature of their legal compartmentalization: whereas that which is "public" was extracted from the sphere of appropriation by a public act of law, the common attains its status by virtue of its inherent nature. Yet it is precisely this irreducible difference that is most significant: "if *res communes* is conceived as unappropriable *by its nature*, it is precisely because it cannot be fully integrated into the juridical sphere. Conversely, were *res communes* somehow compelled to become a fully legal category, the justification for its unappropriability would probably not have been based on its essence."[44] We can see, then, how the legal model can only work if we completely disregard the very reason for the unappropriability of the commons. The conclusion is thus self-evident:

> Nothing that is, by its nature, unappropriable fully belongs to a legal category in Rome. Objects of Divine Law and that considered to be public escape the domain of appropriation and commerce, but their unappropriability is the result of a public act of law or a sacred convention that qualifies their use, for humans and gods. We can see, then, given these conditions, why things held in common were conceived in Roman law as inherently unappropriable objects. They are viewed this way precisely because they fail to achieve the status of a fully legal category."[45]

Indeed this conclusion fits perfectly with Roman law's peculiar concept of an "object" (*res*) as such. As Yan Thomas has clearly established, the modern metaphysical opposition between subject and object is foreign to Roman law: there are not, on the one hand, free subjects who are the holders of rights and, on the other hand, exterior objects upon which these rights are exercised.[46] Consequently, *res* is not imagined as existing within a passive natural world, nor as a purely external materiality. The semantic kernel of the concept refers, first and foremost, to a trial, or a process of dispute, and it is from this kernel that we proceed from the contested "issue" at hand to the actual "object" over which the disagreement arose to begin with:

> the original sense of *res* thus oscillates between litigious concepts, the context of the litigation itself, and the object that furnished the contentious dispute from the start. Hence, by extension, the concept denotes a situation that must be ruled over by a judgment or governed by a law. But, in any case, the core meaning of *res* emerges out of the dispute, and is determined according to the interchange of the debate: *res in controversia posita*.[47]

In this context, then, *res* is not an inert object upon which the violence of the law is imposed, nor an object dominated by a unilateral subject: "if *res* is an object, it is primarily an object of debate or dispute, a collective object that both opposes and unites two protagonists within the same relation."[48] While virtually all juridical meaning related to goods or public objects was derived from interpretations formed in the late third century BCE,[49] it is unclear how the notion of something that is unappropriable by nature (*res communes*) could constitute a fully legal category within this context, since everything that might be recognized through this legal notion is in fact constituted only in relation to a dispute or a trial of some kind. The concept is thus conceived as a "sort of receptacle" for lumping together anything considered unappropriable by nature. What we see here again, then, are the "continual difficulties involved in juridically qualifying natural entities that pre-exist the law."[50]

There is not a lot to learn, then, from this fringe legal category, and so our political futures should not be based on the expansion of *res communis* as we have inherited it from Roman law. Indeed, we must renounce the very idea, once and for all, that there are natural objects that are unappropriable by their nature, and that it is this essential nature that grounds legal unappropriability as such.[51] Yet many exponents of the commons today are determined to pour new wine into this old bottle. In addition to the air, running water, the sea, and the seashore, new potential objects include the moon, outer space, the seafloor and its subfloor, the human genome, natural landscapes, the airwaves, intellectual property in the public domain, certain forms of information, solar radiation, animal and vegetable life, and even the tranquility of nature itself.[52] NGOs linked to the United Nations are, for instance, determined to codify many of the above objects as belonging to the "heritage of all humanity." Yet this inflation of the category only leads us toward a pernicious naturalism, which is precisely what we refer to here as the *reification* of the common – and this is precisely because the word *res* is no longer understood according to the technical Roman meaning of a "dispute" or a "conflict" but is habitually understood as an inert material object embedded in a relation of pure externality. What we get, then, is a categorical expansion in which legal recognition is bestowed upon more and more phenomena that are thought to escape the mastery of the subject as a result of their intrinsic natural properties.

Yet when we examine the question more closely, we see there are really two sorts of arguments invoked to anchor unappropriability in the intrinsic nature of objects: some phenomena fall under the category *res communis* because their inexhaustibility renders the very idea of ownership nonsensical, or a given object is subsumed within the category because it is either elusive or impossible to capture. According to the first explanation, *abundance* explains why a common object or resource can be simultaneously used by everyone. As nineteenth-century legal thinker Charles Comte put it, "some phenomena, such as the light of the stars, the atmosphere of the earth, and the water contained in the seas and the oceans exist in such great quantities that men cannot create any perceptible increase or decrease; each one can appropriate as much as he needs without detracting from the enjoyment of others or causing them the least harm."[53] And we often find the very same idea, more or less, in much more recent commentary: "the physical properties of the air and the water, their seeming inexhaustibility, ensures that their use by a subject in a particular place or time does not preclude another subject making similar use under the same conditions and in the same place and time."[54] While these phenomena are all very useful, they are also worthless due to their abundance, and it is their inexhaustibility that renders any claim of ownership over them nonsensical.

The second rationale for natural or intrinsic unappropriability is the physical impossibility of appropriation as such. It is because of "their remoteness or their fleeting nature" that such phenomena "revolts against exclusive enclosure": "we do not enclose the light, we do not enumerate the clouds." This argument holds that the air "resists all attempts at real or permanent ownership" by its ubiquity, or that the water, "fluid and mobile, escapes as soon as one attempts to retain it."[55] As the legal theorist Jean Domat put it, "the heavens, the stars, the light, the air and the sea are goods that are so common to the whole world that none can master them, or deprive others of them.

And, furthermore, the nature and situation of all these things is in all proportion to suit their common use by all."[56] Grotius speaks of the sea in the same spirit:

> there is . . . a natural reason which forbids that the sea . . . should become a private possession. The reason is that occupation takes place only in the case of a thing which has definite limits . . . 'Water,' says Aristotle, 'is not bounded by a boundary of its own substance.' Liquids therefore cannot be taken possession of unless they are contained in something else.[57]

Similarly, Joseph Ortolan describes the category of the "common things" as found in the Roman jurists in the very same terms: "it is the nature of these things that places them in this class: it is physically impossible for anyone to own the sea, the air, the sun or the stars."[58]

What is especially striking about these two different conceptions is, firstly, the singular relation they presuppose between the law and the reality to which the law relates. It is a relation that betrays a pronounced naturalism: the law "merely endorses a reality over which it is powerless"; it does not proscribe the unappropriability of common things, but simply *observes* it.[59] The law, in this case, is thus reduced to cataloging a pre-existent reality that bears its own legal standard, rather than creating its own reality through the development of its own legal categories. Against this naturalism, we must insist that there is no natural standard of unappropriability, and any such norm can only be a legal norm: "the sea is not something that is held in common simply because it is abundant. Nor is the human genome something that is held in common because of its common character."[60] What is striking, however, is how an entire discourse of contemporary political economy has revived these old naturalistic chestnuts and dressed them up in new terminological garb. As we discuss in more detail later in the book,[61] the criteria for classifying property (rivalry, exclusivity, etc.) upon which this discourse is built often tend to merely reiterate the ideas of the Roman jurists,[62] with one major difference: some of the goods this new discourse of political economy tries to integrate into an expanded sphere of common goods are goods that Roman law did not consider to be goods at all. By viewing the inherent characteristics of goods as the basis for a politics grounded on these "common goods," we actually condemn ourselves, without realizing it, to a very circumscribed number of phenomena defined by criteria that only the law and political economy – i.e., specialists rather than co-participants – can provide.

It is from this perspective that the idea of a "common heritage of humanity," which emerged in the sphere of international law only a few decades ago, deserves radical re-examination. It is well known that the idea was intended to create special legal status for removing certain phenomena from the sphere of state sovereignty, such as Antarctica, outer space, or the deep sea, and the category has since been subject to proposed expansion to include the genetic make-up of plant life as well as the human genome itself.[63] We encounter here, again, the same naturalistic fallacy: never mind the fact that the concept neglects the complexity of a genome that is simultaneously individual and collective, such efforts amount to an assertion that what is common to the entire species from a biological point of view should necessarily be common in law, as if one could simply infer *de jure* commonality from *de facto* commonality.[64] Moreover, the notion of "heritage" is not without its own legal problems, the most obvious of which is that the very notion of heritage or an inheritance (*patrimony*) necessitates a subject. In this instance, it is of course humanity itself that is purported to constitute the relevant legal subject. But humanity as such has no legal standing: "because it is not a subject of right, humanity is not the owner of common inheritance. Thus we have an inheritance without a subject." The juridical notion of a subjectless inheritance is sufficiently incoherent that we need not press the issue further at this point. Though we might briefly note that it is precisely because of this confused notion that the very subtraction of certain phenomena from the sphere of appropriation is paradoxically justified by the obligations arising from this subtraction: "the expression is thus merely metaphorical: it refers simultaneously to an act of conservation and transformation."[65]

Given the obvious limitations of this naturalistic approach, it becomes tempting to ground a new politics of the common in the universalistic essence of humanity itself – and, indeed, it is precisely this route that has been chosen by those who would make the essence of humanity the basis of both a new universalism and a new humanism.

The Common: Between the Vulgar and the Universal

But could the common not simply be defined as coterminous with the human by virtue of its belonging to humanity as a whole? Is all that we "share in common," beyond our differences, not enough to form the basis of new global politics? Once more, for NGOs, legal theorists, and sectors of the alter-globalization movement, humanity is precisely the essence from which "another world" can be built. As we have seen above, the ancients did not disregard the foundation afforded by the universal. In Ciceronian philosophy, the common is grounded in a sociability that is unique to humankind. Christianity later extended this identification between the common and the universal in its own particular way: it is as a creature of God and a rational animal that humanity aspires toward heavenly joy. And the Western philosophical tradition has persistently posited the common as providing the basis for co-belonging. As Judith Revel aptly observers, "from the perspective of political philosophy, the common always precedes the community; it represents bedrock, soil, rootedness, essence, and nature."[66] And there is certainly no shortage of attempts to come up with a modernized notion of the common good in the social sciences, such as psychoanalysis, for instance. In contrast to its ancient counterpart, then, this inverted iteration of essentialism substitutes the material identity of things for the inner identity of the human.

Yet at a certain moment in its history, philosophy also sought to dissociate the common and the universal, even going so far as to devalue the former in favor of the latter. Indeed, heaping contempt upon the word "common" was accepted philosophical practice for much of the Western philosophical tradition. In the French language, the term "common" begins to denote the idea of the "ordinary" around 1160, and its pejorative significance is further underscored by its proximity to the adjective "vulgar," which is used during the same period to refer to "the people."[67] This association is still evident in the manner in which different sections of the bourgeois household are hidden from sight as a result of their association with domesticity. As Judith Revel again observes, these are:

> the spaces that are removed from the gaze of potential visitors, who are contrarily channeled toward rooms with a more 'representative' function. These spaces include all the household functions that do not contribute to the pure theatre of social relations (kitchens, bathrooms, pantries, laundry), and it is behind these closed doors we find those who are excluded despite – or precisely because – they ensure the ongoing daily operation of the household.[68]

Embedded in the language of philosophy (especially in the classical age), the word "common" was associated with the word "vulgar," which is an echo of the Latin *vulgus,* which refers precisely to the "common people" or the "common man." The derogatory term "common man" emerges in the seventeenth century and is quickly enshrined in the language of philosophy. For instance, at the end of the second of Descartes's *Metaphysical Meditations,* in the context of his analysis of a piece of wax, the Latin term *vulgus,* which appears twice in the same sentence, is rendered into "common" in its English translation: "but one who desires to know more than the common herd [*supra vulgus*] might be ashamed to have gone to the speech of the common herd to find a reason for doubting."[69] And quickly afterward, in his discussion of the moment when he first saw the wax, Descartes states, "[I] believe that I knew it by external senses, or at least by what they call the 'common sense,' that is, the imaginative power."[70] We must therefore distinguish "good sense" or understanding from "common sense" (*sensus communis*) or imagination in this philosophical discourse: specifically, "good sense" is good so long as it is not common.[71] To fully appreciate this epistemological devaluation of "common," one need only recognize that the expression "common sense" or "common sensation" (*koinê aesthesis*) comes from Aristotle – yet, for Aristotle, the concept of common sense does not designate some sixth or special sense in addition to the other senses at all, but rather signifies the common or simultaneous perception of an object by the different external senses at once.[72]

In any case, the term "vulgar" long continued its association with the term "common" in the language of philosophy. In §40 of the *Critique of Judgment*, Kant deplored the fact that the understanding of the sound, but as of yet uncultivated, mind has

> the unfortunate honor of being endowed with the name of common sense (*sensus communis*) and indeed in such a way that what is understood by the word common (not merely in our language, which here really contains an ambiguity, but in many others as well) comes to the same as the *vulgar*, which is encountered everywhere, to possess which is certainly not an advantage or an honor.[73]

What Kant conveys here, through the expression *sensus communis* or the "idea of a sense that is common to all," is the ability of the subject to "set himself apart from the subjective private conditions of the judgment, within which so many others are as if bracketed, and reflect on his own judgment from a universal stand-point (which he can only determine by putting himself into the stand-point of others)."[74] Contrary to the more widespread usage, then, we see that Kant dissociates the common from the vulgar and, in what amounts to a kind of semantic ennobling, relates the common to the universal. The maxim "enlarged mentality," or "thinking that puts itself in the place of the other," is a command for thought to elevate itself to the universal, rather than settling on a generality that applies to greatest number of people. It is on this condition that taste, as a faculty of aesthetic judgment, "can bear the name of a communal sense,"[75] even if this common sense does not claim to produce objectively binding rules. *Gemeinsinn* is, in this sense, a subjective principle of orientation that assists in the formation of the aesthetic judgment.

The Kantian rehabilitation of *Gemeinsinn* no doubt owes much to the concept of "common sense" developed by Shaftsbury in the eighteenth century, but it differs significantly from Shaftsbury's version of the concept at the same time. For Shaftsbury, common sense is understood as the sense of the community, a "sense of public good and common interest."[76] In other words, it is not so much a distinctive cognitive faculty, but rather a social and political *moral sense* that forms adequate representations of the moral good. While *good sense* designates a natural faculty for distinguishing between right and wrong, *common sense* refers to a disposition to form representations adequate to the public good, or what we might call a "disposition to the common good."[77] We may observe, in this context, how the social and political import of the term is very different from that promoted by Thomas Reid. For the latter, common sense is actually close to good sense, and acquires a genuine capacity for developing knowledge by becoming the source of natural judgments common to all men. While the Kantian notion of common sense does retain something of this meaning, we must also insist, with Gadamer,[78] that Kant's version of the concept is almost totally void of any social or political significance, inasmuch as it is a singularly aesthetic judgment. Hannah Arendt, for her part, tried to endow the common sense of §40 in the third *Critique* with some measure of social and political force. Specifically, she translated the German *allgemein* as "general" rather than "universal," and then spoke of a "general point of view" in order to understand political judgment itself in this light, though without really determining the nature or boundaries of this (political) community of judgment itself (Arendt did not seem to think this community included all of humanity as such, nor did it designate some particular political community). But as she herself admits, the actual point of view Kant refers to when he speaks of "the enlargement of the mind" or "enlarged thought" is really nothing more than the spectator who judges: "it does not tell one how *to act*. It does not even tell one how to apply the wisdom, found by virtue of occupying a 'general standpoint,' to the particulars of political life . . . Kant does not tell one how to take others into account; he does not tell one how to combine with them in order to act."[79] The important thing, in any case, is that while Kant has the merit of rehabilitating the common by linking it to the formal requirements of the universal, the concept remains almost entirely dissociated from the dimension of activity (collective or otherwise).

This polarization of the term "common" can be seen even more clearly if we pay close attention to the manner in which the common was, early on, *distinguished* from the universal. In fact, the distinction between the two is much older than is often believed. Aristotle, for instance, very clearly distinguished between the common (*koinon*) and the universal (*katholou*).[80] While the universal is determined by the limits of a *genus* ("man" or "animal" for example), the common denotes that which is common to several *genera*. If we look strictly at the breadth of the two terms, the common is here superior to the universal. This explains why that which is most common, or that which is most "transgeneric" or similar across most genera, is also that which is most indeterminate: for instance, *being*, in general – which is "common to all things" since all things *are* – cannot constitute a border or delineation for a genus (and without which the genus could not exist). There is nothing that being excludes, and there is nothing superior to being, no superior category to which being would belong. In this sense, being is a common term, but not a universal term. But, on the other hand, the universal is superior to the common in the sense that the universal gains in comprehension in proportion to its delineated extension. In other words, the universal is aligned with determination while the common is always threatened with indeterminacy: the more common something is, the more indeterminate it is. What emerges from Aristotle, therefore, is that ontology is *stricto sensu* that which is most common, and thus the discourse of being is also the emptiest discourse. In general, then, we have a situation here where the common is either identified with the universal and thereby becomes the object of the most positive discourse – i.e., the discourse of science – for there is no science without the universal, as Aristotle liked to repeat; or, on the other hand, the common suffers from the empty generality of that which exceeds the universal, in which case there is precious little to say about the common that is not purely negative.

In what way, then, does this philosophical framework impact the discourse through which the human relates to itself and, consequently, the manner in which relation between humans is grasped in thought? In the first instance, it is not likely that that which is most common or general amongst all humans will constitute a durable political or affective relation: for how might the commonality of being in itself produce such relations? Yet a persistent and Aristotelian-influenced philosophical tradition depreciated the common underneath the universal, particularly when it came to reflecting on the relation between humans and their own essence. It is precisely at this point that we find ourselves again speaking the language of political philosophy. What is specifically at issue this time, however, is that which is common to those *of the same genus*, which is to say between all the individuals of a particular genus (in this case, humanity) rather than what is common to several genera and, *et fortiori,* to every genus (*being* as transgeneric).

Two *Additions* to Hegel's *Encyclopedia of the Philosophical Sciences* attest to this very clearly. The first addition (Add. 1 of §163) makes an adjustment with respect to the nature of the concept-as-such. In Hegel's view, we generally misunderstand the genesis of a concept, such as that of the plant for example, when we imagine it to be an operation that places a particular plant beside many different plants in order to determine "what is common to them": "it is of the most enormous importance as much for knowing as for our practical comportment that the merely common (*das bloss Gemeinschaftliche*) is not confused with the truly universal factor (*dem wahrhaft Allgemeinen*), the universal."[81] After taking the example of the principle of personality as constitutive of the universality of man, which for Hegel becomes historically manifest with the emergence of Christianity, Hegel then references Rousseau's social contract: in Rousseau's famous text, Hegel views Rousseau's distinction between the "general will" and the "will *of all*" as a particularly pertinent example of the "difference between the merely common and the truly universal." Indeed, as Hegel puts it, the "general will is the *concept* of the will."[82] In other words, the general will is the universal, whereas the will of all is merely the common. And this, as Hegel points out, is precisely because of the definition provided by Rousseau himself: the will of everyone is "the sum total of individual wants."[83] Yet here Hegel offers a criticism. In his view, Rousseau "would have accomplished something more thorough, in relation to the theory of the state, had he always kept this distinction in mind."[84] Hegel thus critiques Rousseau for misunderstanding the distinction between the common and universal, despite the fact that it was he himself who disclosed it. What is at issue here is nothing other than the ability to positively ground the state upon the universality of the human essence. By making the state the result of the contract, Rousseau failed to realize this foundation precisely because he misunderstood the difference between the universal and the common: by grounding the state on the contract, he did not ground it on the essence of humanity, but on the free will and consent of individuals, which is to say the "'general' will which proceeds from this individual will as from a conscious will."[85]

Hegel's second *Addition* (Add. 2 §175) establishes the same distinction between the common and the universal, but does so through an examination of the form of judgment Hegel calls the "judgment of the set of all." For example: "all human beings are mortal," and "all metals are conductors of electricity."[86] In these judgments, we encounter the most familiar and habitual form of universality, namely that which proceeds from the subjective point of view by which we collectively assemble individuals in order to re-define them as an "all" of some kind or another: "the universal appears here only as an external bond which encompasses the individuals subsisting for themselves and indifferent to it. The universal is, nevertheless, in fact the ground and basis, the root and substance of the individual."[87] The "will of all," as the sum total, is precisely this kind of exterior link. Hegel then opposes the true universal (the true basis of the individual) to the superficial universality that unifies individuals in an external manner: "if we consider, for example, Caius, Titus, Sempronius, and the other inhabitants of a city or a country, then the fact that they are collectively human beings is not merely something common to them, but their *universal*, their *genus*, and all these individuals would not be at all without this, their genus."[88] What all these individuals "have in common" then, is a purely nominal universality, as Hegel demonstrates through the example of the earlobe:

> it has been noted that human beings, in contrast to animals, have this in common with one another, that they are equipped with ear lobes. It is, meanwhile, apparent that if, somehow, one or the other should not have ear lobes, the rest of his being, his character, his capacities, and so forth would not be affected by this. It would, by contrast, make no sense to assume that Caius could somehow not be a human being but be brave, learned, and so forth.[89]

Through this example, we get a pretty clear sense of the Hegelian opposition between that which is common to all men – or that which is common between them – and the universal that is constitutive of their genus (human essence): a man deprived of his earlobe does not cease to be a man, for man is "in the universal," and it is only as a result of this *internal essence* that he has the power to be courageous and learned, to the extent that these particular qualities belong to him and "insofar as he is, above all, a human being as such." In short, that which is simply common to men (like the earlobe) is in fact accidental and external to them, while that which is truly universal (their humanity) is their essence and determines them internally. In light of his opposition, one can understand Hegel's dissatisfaction with Kant's "universal point of view" and Rousseau's "will of all': the former because it is merely a subjective point of view that does not proceed from humanity's essence, and the second because Rousseau is only dealing with a sum total of individual wills.

The only way to escape from both naturalism and essentialism is to hold to the principle that it is not from our common characteristics that certain things are, or ought to be, "in common"; nor is it due to the essence of our identity or our membership within the same genus that humans have something truly *in* common, rather than simply something common between them. In the sense that we understand the term, the common must not be confused with specific properties that all humans share (reason, will, perfectibility, etc.). Nor is the common derived from some concept of humanity as a collective, what Kant called the "whole of mankind." It is not some interiority that we *have* in common, even with the qualification that this commonality "should not be interpreted in terms of belonging." In the words of Catherine Colliot-Thélène, "the individual human does not belong to humanity in the way that one belongs to a family, a tribe, a caste, or a Nation-State. The individual is its humanity, which it shares with the rest of its species, which is an entirely different thing."[90] It could be said that that humanity, understood as an aggregate or collective, corresponds to a "universal state of men," but the notion of "state" here could only be supra-sensible at best.[91] Ultimately, the common is neither humanity as essential morality or dignity (*Menschheit*), nor humanity as species (*Menschengattung*), nor humanity as the aptitude for sympathizing with other humans (*Humanität*) that arises from our ability to think and put ourselves in the place of others, as described above.[92] As we will argue throughout this book, the common must rather be thought of in terms of *co-activity*, and not co-belonging, co-ownership, or co-possession.

It is for the same fundamental reason that we part ways with Nietzsche when he depreciates the universal by reducing it to a median standard to which everyone conforms – which of course Nietzsche only does in order to more sharply contrast the "noble" and "rare" minority he so adores. We reject this approach not only because Nietzsche differentiates the common *qua* "vulgar" from the common *qua* "universal" only to provocatively conflate these terms again by rendering the definition of the former the truth the later, but mainly because our understanding of the common is not *a priori* defined in terms of some kind of personality type – psychologically or socially – independent of the actual practices of individuals themselves. In §43 of *Beyond Good and Evil*, Nietzsche argues that there can be no "common good" (*Gemeingut*) because that which is truly good can never be common:

> My judgment is *my* judgment: other people don't have an obvious right to it too – perhaps this is what such a philosopher of the future will say. We must do away with the bad taste of wanting to be in agreement with the majority. "Good" is no longer good when it comes from your neighbor's mouth. And how could there ever be a "common good"! The term is self-contradictory: whatever can be common will never have that much value.[93]

For Nietzsche, a judgment's value is essentially indicative of a certain personality type, insofar as a judgment of real value is one that does not seek agreement with others. Unlike the Kantian idea of the *sensus communis,* Nietzsche's judgment derives its value from its rarity, and the rarity of the personality type who boldly enunciates such judgments.

Common and Praxis

Against these essentializing conceptions of the common, and against all those critiques of the common (Kantian or Nietzschean) that reduce the common to the quality of a judgment or a personality type, we forcefully assert that *only practical activity* can make the common, just as it is only practical activity that can produce a new collective subject (which is a far cry from the idea that a rights-bearing subject can somehow pre-exist collective activity). If there is some "universality" to the common, it can only be the *practical* universality that arises when each individual, at any given time and under any given conditions, engages in the same task. The common can only be re-thought by breaking with the metaphysical confrontation between the free subject and the inert material object offered up to this subject's sovereign grasp. This is why we have opted for the noun when we speak of the common, rather than settling for the more common adjectival form. This is not to say that one should not use the adjectival form to describe the objects constructed and maintained by this kind of co-activity (in fact, this is already itself a form of nominalization), but rather that one should avoid, at all costs, speaking of "common goods" or even "*the* common good" in general. *The common is not a good*, and the plural changes nothing in this respect, because the common is not an object of the will, whether as a possession or as that which is constituted by the will. The common (singular) is a political principle through which we are able to build the commons, maintain the commons, and sustain the commons. It is, as such, a political principle that defines a new system of struggles on a global scale.

We also refuse, for this very same reason, to link the common to some vague and mysterious sense, which is already clearly manifest in public opinion today, that things are not as they should be. We prefer to use a concept like the "the moral economy of the crowd" or the "moral economy of the poor," as coined by historian E.P. Thompson, to signify the set of practices and values aimed at defending the interests of the community against aggression by the dominant classes.[94] For the common is no more an abstract moral principle than a personality type. Those who would work to construct a common cannot allow themselves to be defined in advance by an identifiable psychological type, nor a social category with pre-defined contours: *they are what their practices make them*. Generally speaking, and in accordance with one of Marx's most profound ideas (from his Six Thesis on Feuerbach), we insist on the idea that practices make people what they are. For it is on the basis of practices that we are able to account for the very development of societies as such, insofar as society is, as Marx put it, "the product of men's reciprocal activities."[95]

We do not, therefore, conceptualize the common as the equivalent of the abstract principle of "solidarity" that is only permitted in childhood games and military combat.[96] Nor should it be confused with the sociological idea that, since August Comte, locates the foundation of moral obligations and the rationale for political organization in the general functional interdependence of all our social activities. This grand idea – which is really just a "social" re-interpretation of the economistic representation of the division of labor – was rendered systematic by Émile Durkheim along with the legal theorist Léon Duguit, for whom a society is a "great cooperative."[97] This interpretation of the social, which viewed the cooperation of labor in the workshop as the model for re-organizing society as one great "association," was socialism's initial inspiration, prior its double degeneration into totalitarianism and twentieth-century social democracy. But neither sociology nor socialism, despite some remarkable insights that have since fallen into almost total obscurity, have been able to draw out all the political implications from their underlying intuition that human activity is always co-activity and co-obligation, cooperation and reciprocity. And it is no great mystery why: the political trajectory of the West, which eventually granted the state a complete monopoly over the "common utility," led to the bureaucratic management of production, on the one hand, and an insurance industry approach to the management of the "social," in which the latter exists somewhere between the state and the market. In other words, all the efforts since the nineteenth century that tried to renew both political thought and social theory in order to more effectively confront capitalism have failed to produce a fully coherent politics of the common.

And finally, we refuse to exclude the domains of the "social" and the "economic" from the institution of the common, as is characteristic of many strains of "republican" or "democratic" political philosophy. For these political traditions, rational political praxis should not mingle with the activities of production or exchange: the latter tend to be viewed as animalistic or mechanical proclivities that either belong to a sphere of sheer necessity or are dominated by a form of instrumental rationality, as if the supposed imperviousness of politics from economics bore any resemblance to actual realities of our contemporary neoliberal societies. This approach should therefore be viewed as a profound regression in relation to the remarkable achievements of nineteenth-century socialism and feminism: namely, the sudden irruption of workers and women onto the political scene, subjects who had been hitherto excluded from the "common." These movements disrupted political theory by making work, social activities, and social relations direct objects of public debate. Of course, the separation of the economic from the common (i.e., from politics), as we find in both Hannah Arendt and Jürgen Habermas, tends to be explained by the experience of twentieth-century totalitarianism. For these authors, then, the only possible alternative left open, given the ongoing demise of rational deliberation, seemed to reside in the rather desperate attempt to protect some separate sphere of "action" or "communicative action" outside a surging wave of economic colonization. Today, however, the sheer scale of capitalist expansion has put an end to any such hopes. The very nature of our epoch obliges us to start over, but this time to start at the root of things.

Part I

The Emergence of the Common

The principle of the common emerged out of various democratic struggles and social movements at the beginning of the twenty-first century. Its emergence signals a new era of emancipation. A new theoretical discourse is in the process of being formed, one that is closely connected to a range of alter-globalization movements and informed by multiple theoretical sources. The first part of this book articulates the historical context of this emergence and critically maps the initial theoretical articulations of the common.

Every movement opposing capitalism is invariably affected by the tragic fate of the twentieth century's revolutions. State communism continues to burden future alternatives, and there is a real danger that we will see a more or less sophisticated revival of regimes calling themselves "communist" as the disasters produced by capitalism continue unabated. Yet despite the weight of this historical burden, we are currently witnessing a marked tendency toward invention – or more precisely, a tendency toward the creation of a common that is more than mere rhetoric. As a first step in this larger process, the proceeding chapter (Chapter 2) re-examines a series of different communist models that have historically functioned as so many ways of repressing the common, insofar as the latter is understood as a form of co-obligation that people adopt for themselves (as we described in Chapter 1). In the next chapter, we insist that the supposed "realization" of the common through the model of state ownership consistently led to the destruction of the common by the state.

The destruction of the common eventually resulted in the collapse of the communist states and ushered in the triumph of neoliberal reason around the world in the 1980s. Since then, neoliberal orthodoxy has relentlessly hammered home the message that capitalism is the only imaginable form of society. During the 1990s, however, new groups of militants and intellectuals from around the world picked up the thread of protest against the dominant order and began to challenge capitalism's "appropriation" of natural resources, public spaces, and state properties. According to this renewed critique, our epoch is characterized by a generalized predation of the common by organized oligarchies. These oligarchies gorge themselves on our collective wealth through an extension of property rights that subsumes everything within their field of accumulation, including knowledge, the natural world, and even life itself. This new critical discourse speaks of "expropriation" and "dispossession" as the singular and defining feature of contemporary capitalism, and it is in this context that the common has become a recurrent theme of these new protest movements. But despite its many iterations, the concept of the common that has emerged within this discursive framework is very specific: it speaks of various "commons" that are increasingly subject to new "enclosures." In what ways, we must ask, has this analogical relationship to capitalism's pre-history impacted our contemporary concept of the common, and what are the specific theoretical and political consequences of adopting this historical analogy?

As we describe in Chapter 3, this theme of "plunder" and "theft" is a discourse that appears to be essentially negative, reactive, and defensive, and its critique, logically speaking, seems to demand little more than widespread resistance to stop the ongoing forms of "robbery" perpetrated by an increasingly unbridled capitalism. A more positive vision of the common has, however, also coalesced around a new political economy of the common, and the work of Elinor Ostrom in particular. Ostrom's empirical research, combined with her institutionalist theory of collective action, shows how the market and the state are not the only possible systems of production: very diverse institutional models, from all over the world, are entirely capable of providing their members with sustainable resources in sufficient quantities through the institutional creation and renewal of rules of communal management. Ostrom's work has been disseminated throughout the United States and beyond, and now serves as a major reference for movements all around the world trying to build new models of collective action and thought. Movements inspired by her work have especially sought to expand upon the new technological commons in information and knowledge. Yet while we recognize the importance of Ostrom's work, we are also critical of some aspects of its political economy, especially in terms of its reification of "goods." This reification seems to be constitutive of virtually all economic discourses on the commons as such, and in our view it parasitizes and paralyzes the discourse's ability to genuinely theorize the institutional aspects of the common. Without detracting from the major historical significance of Ostrom's work, we are compelled to point out its important limitations. And for us, these limitations cannot be overcome by a theory of the *commons*, but only by a theory of the *common* (Chapter 4).

Of course, it was precisely this task – of translating a theory of the *commons* into a theory of the *common* – that was systematically undertaken by arguably the most important theorists of the common, Michael Hardt and Antonio Negri (alongside the work of a number of other economic and legal theorists working on similar topics). The theory of the common Hardt and Negri offer in their trilogy – *Empire* (2000), *Multitude* (2004), and *Commonwealth* (2009) – constitutes a landmark event in the history of critical thought. Unfortunately, their theory was compromised, in our view, by a number of fundamentally untenable premises – specifically, the essentially "rentier" nature of contemporary capitalism, the growing empowerment of "immaterial labor," and their views on the spontaneous development of an informational and reticular communism. While Hardt and Negri frame their theory of the common around an analysis of the most recent and advanced information and communications technologies, their theory of the common is only modern in appearance. As we argue in Chapter 5, their theory of the common is better viewed as a return to Joseph-Pierre

Proudhon's concept of the "collective force." While this concept, like much of Proudhon's thought, has been virtually forgotten today, Proudhon's ideas about the collective force were an essential part of nineteenth-century socialist debates, particularly in terms of (negatively) shaping Marx's competing conception of capital as the fundamental driving force of the common. The series of genealogies and analyses offered in Part 1 (Chapters 2, 3, 4, and 5) thus have a singular purpose: to clear a path for the new theory of the common we take up in Part 2.

2

The Communist Burden; or Communism Against the Common

Bureaucratic state communism progressively blocked the possibility of another society long before the collapse of the actually existing "socialist systems," and to a much greater extent than is usually imagined. We have not yet been fully able to process the practical and theoretical consequences of the birth, development, and decline of the communist states, many of which included some of the worst regimes in history, such as those under the cultist control of Stalin, Mao, and Pol Pot. Faced with the criminal regimes with which the names of these leaders are now virtually synonymous, and the overwhelming evidence of the near total destruction of the workers' movement within the various historical forms and projects of state communism, disarray on the left has often prevailed: many leftists defected to the winning side, while others continue to revel in denunciations of the "capitalist conspiracy against socialism." How many excuses have been invented in order to stave off the "cognitive dissonance" (to borrow Leon Festinger's formula[1]) between the ideal of emancipation and the sinister realities of state terror?[2] There is, however, another path open to us, but this path requires a lucid examination of what the history of communism teaches us, so we may create a new and different future for emancipatory struggles.

Any genuine politics of the common must confront the doctrines and practices that were the purview of twentieth-century communism. What exactly was the nature of the "common" in the various forms of communism? And, more precisely, what is the relationship the various forms of state communism maintain with what, from time to time, could be understood as a really existing common? Our first clues come from the term's lexical genesis, which speaks volumes about the connections between the very different historical periods that have contributed to contemporary understandings of communism. We know the word appears in a text written by Victor d'Hupay de Fuveau in 1785. In this text, the term was used to designate a "community of a moral-economic regime" that would be "feasible in small groups" and would be comprised of "a diversity of talents" designed to replace the monks of the then depopulated monasteries.[3] As it turns out, the author of this text was a friend of Restif de La Bretonne, who penned the expression "communism of the community" in his autobiography (*Monsieur Nicholas*) in order to designate one of several new modes of government.[4] It can hardly be viewed as a matter of chance that the word acquired its political significance in the 1790s: while the term was already charged with memories of the peasant insurrections of the twelfth century, it would eventually be linked to the revolutionary events of the Paris Commune, to François-Noël Babeuf's "Conspiracy of Equals," while simultaneously signifying the survival of rural communities and customs.[5] How can we not be intrigued by a term that was first used to designate the officers of the urban communes, the members of rural communities, and various religious communities, and which became, at the end of the eighteenth century, the name for a more general political aspiration that sought "real equality" and the "abolition of property"? The words pronounced by Sylvain Maréchal in his *Manifesto of Equals* echoes into the ages: "the moment has come to found the *Republic of Equals* – that grand asylum open to all human kind. The days of general restitution are come. Weeping families, come and seat yourself at the common table provided by nature for all her children."[6] For Babeuf's community of supporters, it is nature that ultimately makes possible their shared existence, the realization of "collective well-being," and the community of goods, all of which were considered absolutely synonymous:[7] "we aim at something more sublime, and more equitable; we look to *common property*, or the *community of goods!* No more individual property in lands. *The earth belongs to no one.* We claim – we demand – we *will* the communal enjoyment of the fruits of the earth: *the fruits belong to all.*"[8] And achieving this "holy enterprise," in Babeuf's words, demands nothing less than the sacrifice of a deceitful civilization: "perish, if needs be, all the arts, provided real equality abides us!"[9] This statement echoes both Rousseau's passionate speeches and writings as well as the mid-eighteenth-century codes of nature.

Immediately following this term's inaugural period, as indicated by historian Jacques Grandjonc, the European states were suffused with a lexical proliferation forged from the Latin root *communis* – common, *commun*, *gemein* – and this proliferating vocabulary soon penetrated the revolutionary vocabulary of the 1830s–1840s. But how, exactly, did the word "communism" – which for Restif was meant to designate the "excellence of the community" – end up denoting a form of state absolutism that became the governing paradigm for the organization of economic and political power across vast swaths of the planet a century later? Today, of course, the main features of bureaucratic communism are well known. In this respect, Victor Serge was one of the first to summarize these features using a lapidary phrase that, at least, has the merit of concision: "the bureaucratic and police – it would be more accurate to say terrorist – monopoly of power."[10]

For many, the hopes born of the Russian Revolution, the illusions it spread, the debates it generated, and the divisions it sowed are now behind us. We have definitely moved on to other matters, and there is no need to revisit the past. In China, for instance, state capitalism continually claims the country's communist and Maoist heritage for itself; many of today's opponents of capitalism remain strangely silent when it comes to the sordid history of "actually existing socialism"; supporters of Castro are by no means lacking; and we might wonder whether certain intellectuals, who claim to be critical thinkers, are not more or less ashamed of the nostalgia they feel for the happier times of their youth when they could believe, in good conscience, in the virtue of the communist states. A new and curious silence seems to have spread amongst these intellectuals following the "Solzhenitsyn Shock," the capitalist conversion of the Chinese economy, and the fall of the Berlin Wall.[11] In contrast to the din and denunciations of today's neoliberal partisans, the silence on the left about the failures of bureaucratic communism is a conspicuous black hole within contemporary political thought – and thus it is no coincidence that our present is marked by the paucity of futurity. This is perhaps the major symptom of the disorder that has overtaken the intellectual and political world, and arguably the principle reason why political theory has shied away from the search for alternative politics, and why it has proved so incapable of producing any credible forms.

No genuinely new thought about the future will be possible unless we agree to re-examine the major forms of twentieth-century communism. We must critically assess the entire array of doctrines and practices that adopted the term, laid some claim to this rather old tradition, or modified the term to suit the needs of a radically different doctrinal project. In our view, there have been three great conceptions of communism that have historically succeeded one another. The first conception of communism is associated with the supreme value of the community, and its principle is unity by and through equality. The second major conception of communism, and that most associated with Marx, replaced the notion of "community" with "society," wherein the latter was understood as a *sui generis* reality defined by its capacity for self-organization, the dynamism of its immanent forces, and the faculties and energies of its members who insist on democratic coordination as the only way to ensure this mode of life succeeds. And the third major conception of communism corresponds to the birth of the twentieth-century communist states, and it is a form of communism characterized by the power of a single party over the administration of society. This form of communism was only rhetorically related to the communist doctrines that preceded it, for its preferred mode of governance was not the principle of democracy but the principle of terror. But beyond this tripartite periodization, we think it is especially important, for this aspect of our analysis at least, to identify what Max Weber called "ideal types" – i.e., models of intelligibility that can help us distinguish between the mix-forms and hybrids history invariably gives us. To this end, then, our task is to isolate the most significant aspects of these historical forms of communism while disregarding the less pertinent aspects of these admittedly ideal types.

Communism as "Community of Life"

In a classical text that seeks to provide a sociological definition of socialism, Émile Durkheim constructs such a definition by opposing socialism to communism. In Durkheim's view, these two doctrines are confused much too often. Communism is an ahistorical – or at least transhistorical – utopia that aspires toward the creation of a community of equals who share all goods in common. And for Durkheim, communism's principal, if not founding, source is Plato's *Republic*.[12] Unlike socialism, which is concerned with a specific mode of economic organization that appears at a precise moment in history, communist utopianism is singularly concerned with the morality (or immorality) of private property in all contexts. Against the reign of private property, which it views as the ultimate source of immorality – "the vicious basis of society" in the words of Restif le Breton[13] – communism posits the "excellence of the community" as based on reciprocity. Communism is thus the practical expression of true morality, and the sole source of true, communal happiness. As Durkheim thus writes:

> The fundamental communist idea – everywhere the same under scarcely different forms – is that private property is the source of selfishness and that from selfishness springs immorality. But such a proposition does not strike at any social organization in particular. It is true, it applies to all times and to all countries; it fits equally the system of large or of small industry. It does not aim at any economic fact, for the institution of property is a juridical part of it. Finally, communism holds to a common authority of abstract morality, which is of no one time nor of any one country."[14]

This type of communism seeks to organize collective existence on the basis of communal goods and communal practices of consumption. It takes the form of a collective asceticism in which personal property is renounced for reasons of moral improvement and/or preparation for salvation. By sharing everything in common, the individual merges into the unity of the community and thereby purifies and perfects itself. Making everything common changes the individual: it leads to moral improvement and spiritual progress. Communism is thus entirely oriented toward the rejection of wealth, to the extent that economic self-interest is posited as a kind of solvent that corrodes the integrity of the group. Conversely, the practice of sharing, especially when it comes to the collective consumption of collectively owned goods, is a means of purgation, a vector of moral health, just as it leads to religious salvation in early Christian theology.

This ideal of community life based on a community of goods undeniably finds its principal source, as Durkheim suggests, in Plato's *Republic*. For Plato, the community of goods is primarily a means of saving the city from the mortal danger of dissension and civil war by prohibiting the guardians of the city from owning private property, on the grounds that such possession diverts them from their task of defending the city against its enemies: "if they acquire property in land, houses, or money, they will become farmers and men of business instead of Guardians, and harsh tyrants instead of partners in their dealings with their fellow citizens."[15] In Plato's city, the leaders are "protectors and defenders," they refer to each other as "Fellow-Guardians," while the rest of the population "provide their pay and livelihood."[16] The former thus receive their subsistence from the latter as remuneration for their protection, and it is distributed amongst them communally. We see, then, that the community of goods is thus relatively restricted in that it only applies to the guardians, due to the nature of the official function that is entrusted to them; it does not apply to laborers and artisans, who remain private owners, and the equality between the guardians presupposes, as its essential condition, inequality between the guardians and the producers. What kind of unity is created by this underlying presupposition? The *Republic* is absolutely saturated with the word "community" (*koinônia*). Speaking of the guardians, who are forbidden from touching gold or silver or from possessing private houses, Plato writes: "they shall eat together in messes and live together (*koinê zên*) like soldiers in a camp."[17] But the strongest expression of this mode of unity is without a doubt that of the "community of pleasure and plain" (*hedônes te kai lupês koinônia*), featured in a passage in which Plato describes the community of women and children as the best form of community. Within such a community, argues Plato, all the citizens collectively rejoice and grieve in the same manner for their gains and losses. Under these conditions, everyone says "this is mine" or "this is not mine" in relation to the same object at the same time. In this way, a unity is realized that effectively transforms the entire city into a unified person: in the same manner that the pain felt from an injury to one's finger is felt throughout one's entire body, so too does the entire city suffer when one of its citizens is injured.

The Platonic ideal is therefore based on a structural homology between the political community and the communion of the body and the soul within a single individual. It is this homology that truly makes the unity of the political community a substantial unity. This homological conception of unity is that which separates Plato's doctrine of "life in common" (*koinê zên*) from Aristotle's notion of "living together" (*suzên*).[18] In fact, almost all of Aristotle's criticism of Platonic communism in Book II, Chapter 2 of the *Politics* is based on the objection that excessive unity brings ruin to the city precisely by returning it to the state of the family and the individual. Aristotle explicitly targets Plato's claim that a perfect city is one in which all citizens say "this is mine" and "this is not mine" at the same time about the same thing; for Aristotle, Plato commits a paralogism based on the double meaning of the word "all" (*pantes*): it can be applied to each individual in particular (its distributive sense) just as much as it can designate all the citizens taken together (its collective sense). But since the term is only used in its second meaning by those who possess women and children in common, they should be saying "this is us" rather than "this is mine."[19] What is at stake in this criticism, for Aristotle, is the irreducibility of the unity of "we" to the unity of the "I": because the city is necessarily composed of different elements, the city is unable to maintain the same rapport with one of its parts that an individual person maintains with one or another of its parts. But for Plato, however, the inverse is true: the unity possessed by the city is a substantive unity that is indivisible in character, which implies that the relation between the whole and its parts is indeed reducible to the relation between the individual and its parts.

From this perspective, the community of goods is absolutely not inscribed within a comparative typology of different forms of property; it is not a case of "common property" as opposed to "private property," but rather a condition of communal living that is first and foremost about the creation of a moral community. It is precisely this idea that will exert a profound attraction on the first theorists of communism. However, it would be a mistake to see the early utopian communities proposed by early communist thinkers as mere replicas of Plato's Republic, as is Durkheim's view. The origins of the communal ideal, in both the West and the East, are heterogeneous, and the origins of some its iterations are both anterior and external to the Greek heritage of Plato entirely. Religiously inspired communities, which Durkheim strangely ignores, deserve particular attention given the central role religious ideas played in early-nineteenth-century forms of communism.[20] The communism of the 1830s–1840s often directly referenced religious texts – the Old Testament just as much as the *Acts of the Apostles* – to legitimize the suppression of private property, which in their eyes was responsible for all injustice and inequality. The centrality of the theme of sharing, the renunciation of personal property, and the community of goods suggests the first movements claiming to be communist were strongly rooted in a long Judeo-Christian tradition that Durkheim writes about elsewhere.[21] The egalitarian revolutions of the future are in many ways modeled on the Christian form of the pre-constituted community.[22]

Samuel, "the first of the prophets," was the first Judeo-Christian figure to establish religious communities outside of the cities that were based on the sharing of goods. Indeed, many such communist-like movements appeared before the advent of Christianity, such as the Essenes, for example.[23] According to the *Acts of the Apostles*, the first Christian community, established in Jerusalem around 35–37 CE, was based on the renunciation of private property and the sharing of goods. Indeed, the *Acts of the Apostles* contains many of communism's most canonical doctrines, and these doctrines extended well beyond the confines of Christianity:

> And they continued steadfastly in the apostle's doctrine and fellowship, and in breaking of bread and in prayers . . . And all that believed were together, and had all things in common. And sold their possessions and goods, and parted them to all *men*, as every man had need; and they, continuing daily with one accord in the temple, and breaking bread from house to house, did eat their meat with gladness and singleness of heart.[24]

And further:

> And the multitude of them that believed were of one heart and of one soul: neither said any of *them* that ought of the things which he possessed was his own; but they all had things in common. And with great power have the apostles witness of the resurrection of the Lord Jesus: and great grace was upon them all; neither was there any among them that lacked: for as many as were possessors of lands or houses sold them, and brought the prices of the things that were sold; and laid them at the apostles' feet: and distribution was made unto every man according to as he has need.[25]

The *Acts,* written by the author of the Gospel of Luke, transmitted this communal ideal to both Eastern and Western Christendom. For the author of Luke, the communal ideal was a necessary part of the search for God, and it demanded certain doctrines and rites, such as the communal meal (which persists to this day).[26] One of the principles that eventually passed into Christian doctrine by way of the Fathers of the Church – Augustine in particular – is the idea that God created the world according to the principle of communal unity, and this means wealth must be shared in common. This is the foundational doctrine of the entire monastic movement, for instance. According to the *Rule of Saint Basil* (fourth century), the sharing of goods was the norm: "let all things be in common for all, and let no one own anything of their own: not clothing, not shoes, nothing of any bodily use." Communion is thus both a spiritual and material doctrine, as is symbolized by the common meal. And this notion is also forcefully expressed in the sixth-century *Rule of Saint Benedict* (Benedict was greatly inspired by Saint Basil). In Chapter 33, the *Rule* explicitly states "*all things should be the common possession* of all [omniaque omnium sint communia], as it is written, *so that no one* presumes to *call anything his own.*"[27] Indeed, the rule decrees the repression of almost any desire for property whatsoever:

> Above all, this evil practice must be uprooted and removed from the monastery. We mean that, without an order from the abbott, no one may presume to give, receive, or retain anything as his own, nothing at all – not a book, writing tablets, or stylus – in short, not a single item, especially since monks may not have the free disposal even of their bodies and wills. For their needs, they are to look to the father of the monastery, and are not allowed anything which the abbot has not given or permitted.[28]

The difference between Christian communism and the Platonic *koinonia* (as discussed above) is clear enough. In order to ensure all are but "one heart," it is no longer sufficient for everyone to say, at the same time and about the same thing, "this is mine" – it is now forbidden for *anyone* to say "this is mine" at all! This crucial inflection corresponds to Michel Foucault's distinction, in the *Hermeneutics of the Subject*, between the Platonic *epistrophe* and Christian *metanoia*. While the Platonic conversion consists in turning away from the world of appearances in order to attain true knowledge of being, Christian conversion is all about a rupture in the subject's mode of being, whereby the latter renounces itself.[29] The city in the *Republic* does not require each guardian – i.e., each leader – to renounce their will; rather, knowledge of the truth is obtained through self-control. The monastic "community of life," on the other hand, requires that each "sheep" definitively and completely renounce his will through complete submission to one's personal pastor, akin to the apprentice's obedience to the master. It is in this sense that pastoral governmentality produces a mode of individualization that involves an annihilation of the self through the mortification of the will.[30]

This principle of total renunciation, as a means of searching for God, is founded on a major theological principle: God's gift of creation to man, as stated in a famous passage from St. Ambrose and influentially cited by the French economist and socialist Constantin Pecqueur in the 1840s:

> The earth was created in common for all, rich and poor alike. Why then, the rich, do you arrogate for yourselves the right of ownership? Nature does not recognize the rich . . . The earth was given in common to all men, and no one can claim to be the proprietor of anything except the portion of the whole that suffices his needs, anything more can only have been obtained through violence. Nature furnished all goods to all men in common. God created all things such that their enjoyment might be common to all, and that the earth should be the common possession of all. Nature thus begets the law of community, and it is only usurpation that begets private property.[31]

Returning your personal property to the community is to repay one's debt – it is to return those goods that belong to God because God created them in the first place. Sharing one's goods is to acknowledge one's debt to the Creator. This is the message of Christ. This ideal of the total community has, therefore, two dimensions: it simultaneously exemplifies and intensifies the constitutive human bond as founded on symbolic debt (a principle that stretches back to the most ancient societies) and, at the same time, salvation through the perfection of life is promised by this type of community. In other words, the absolute unity of the community in which everyone merges together does not in fact exclude individualization, but is actually its means. Put differently, individualization is the paradoxical result of self-renunciation. This voluntary act of personal dispossession detaches one from the world: it breaks old ties and creates a whole new community on the basis of personal salvation. It is not about creating paradise on earth, but about preparing one's future entry.

A number of more or less heretical movements also claimed this communal ideal (up until very recently, in fact) out of a desire to protest a hierarchical pastoral governmentality in the name of the principle of absolute equality between all members of the community. In *Security, Territory, Population*, Foucault spoke of these egalitarian communities as characterized by various forms of "counter-conduct" – that he includes "asceticism" and "mysticism" as two such forms of counter-conduct suggests these communal movements, for Foucault, were clearly religiously oriented, and were not based on the mere economic renunciation of personal property.[32] As Foucault puts it, "each is a pastor, a priest, or a shepherd, which is to say that nobody is."[33] Foucault's discussion of the Taborites is particularly illuminating in this respect. The Taborites represent the radical wing of the Hussite movement, which recognized the right of every individual, layman or priest, to interpret the Holy Scriptures according to his own lights, and advocated the abolition of private property, taxes, and all forms of human authority in general ("everyone lives together as brothers, and no one is subject to another"). After the defeat of the Taborite army in 1434, the tradition survived in the sect of the Moravian Brethren, the defenders of the rural communes.[34] This doctrine of absolute communal equality is also found in the Diggers (led by Gerrard Winstanley in the seventeenth century), the Christian Communist Republic of the Guaranis in Paraguay, and the Brethren of the Common Life in Holland (which developed the "small schools" in Europe). This ideal permeated the eighteenth and nineteenth centuries as well. Morelly, in his *Code of Nature*, saw Jesus as the personification of the communist ideal, and Cabet called him the "prince of the communists." A number of nineteenth-century communists believed they were Jesus's direct successors. Cabet, for instance, doesn't hesitate whatsoever to assert the "community of goods" was "proclaimed by Jesus, by all his apostles and disciples, by all the Fathers of the Church, and all the Christians of the first centuries."[35] It was even the doctrinal basis of the German communists in the League of the Just (against whom Marx and Engels struggled in the 1840s). In short, this mode of communism, which extols the "community of goods, work, and pleasure," in the words of Philippe Buonarroti (and we ought to add the community of education to this list), is historically grounded in the model of the moral community. By creating equality and destroying individual property, this moral community is a means of eradicating all the social sources of selfishness and envy. And if this moral imperative isn't grounded in God, it's grounded in nature. In the first article of his analysis of Babeuf's doctrine, Buonarroti states: "nature has given to each individual an equal right to the enjoyment of all the goods of life"; and in Article Three he writes, "nature imposes on each person the obligation to work; nobody could, without committing a crime, evade his share of the common labour."[36]

This is not to say, however, that the egalitarian and proletarian communism of the late-eighteenth and early-nineteenth century should be solely viewed as a kind of

Christian heresy, despite both its obvious religious character and the hostility of these movements toward the official Church (which these movements accused of having abandoned and betrayed the message of Christ). And while it is certainly true this ancestrally religious form of communism remained highly influential until the nineteenth century (in both France and Germany), authors like Restif, Babeuf, Buonarroti, and even Cabet incorporated new dimensions into these movements that completely escape Durkheim's attention. There is, firstly, its revolutionary dimension: the community of ownership is to be established by a revolutionary government that settles at last the conflict between the rich and the poor. In other words, this dimension offers a definitive solution to the class conflict. This form of communism is no longer merely conceived as a sharing of goods and property that morally renews humanity, but also as a collective and egalitarian organization of work guided by a concern for social justice and the material well-being of every member of the national community.[37] While collective well-being is undoubtedly still based on the morality of sharing and the search for real equality, the communal form now adopts a "materialistic" character insofar as it insists on satisfying the needs of the great mass of the population through the re-organization of social relations – primarily through the abolition of private property, but also through the collectivization of work and the equal distribution of goods. For these early communisms, mass de-privatization of property is the only pathway to equality, and it means the nation will be transformed into a community writ large that will be managed by a state administration. If the "communalists" idealize the community as the means of achieving equality, the revolutionary communists merely alter the vision's scale. Article 1 of Babeuf's *Fragment of a Draught of an Economic Decree* declares, "there shall be established in the Republic a grand national community" whose communal property will be exploited by all its members and whose fruits will be shared by all according to legal rules.[38] Work will be regulated by a "supreme administration"; it will organize the members of the community according to class, establish the list and modalities of work to be carried out, and determine the quantities of goods to be consumed.

It is not that the concern for morality suddenly disappears – it is, in fact, always a central preoccupation – but rather the challenge now facing those claiming the term "communism" has decisively shifted toward questions of production, consumption, efficiency, and economic well-being at a national level. And work, importantly, is now used as an argument against private property. Everything comes from labor: everyone works just as much as everyone else, all property is communal, everything belongs to all, and all the pleasure of consumption must be equally distributed: "and as each, in entering society carries with him an equal stake and contribution (the totality of his strength and means), it follows that the burdens, the productions, and the advantages, ought to be equally divided."[39] Work is organized according to a division of labor, public stores distribute goods, public transportation moves goods, and the community now functions at the level of a nation, if not the world. The communists of the first half of the nineteenth century may well still be imbued with the older model of moral community, but they combine this vision with the organizational rationality of an emergent industrial society. And even if they seek to effectively apply the traditional model of the community of goods at the national level – through the use of a "supreme authority" charged with administering the entire economy and society by means of ascetic and severe police powers – it would be a mistake to call these communists "archaic" or "retrograde."

Like many socialists of this era, these early theorists tried to conjoin two singular concerns: they wanted to adhere to a long-standing religious and moral tradition but, at the same time, they wanted to respond to the social and economic disruption they were all experiencing. During the 1830s and 1840s they begin to break with the moral and religious model by making the "happiness of a regenerated humanity" (Cabet) depend on egalitarian social organization and economic prosperity. This exigency was based on a new model that links social volunteerism ("associationism"), and its associated economic efficiencies, with its beneficial aspects for worker morality. The eternal inspiration of the "community of goods" can be achieved much more easily by the effects of "industrial progress" than by the mere sacrifice of personal wealth, as was the case for the ancient forms of communism.[40] For the Icarians,[41] the workshops are strictly disciplined, and everything is ordered in the interest of efficiency, exactitude, and punctuality. In the first model – the moral community – the superior administrator regulates both daily life and economic production without any separation between the two. But it is difficult to reconcile the requirement for absolute equality with the functional distribution of individuals by a superior administration.[42]

Communism as "Association of Producers"

In contrast to the moral community, the second model of communism we have enumerated in this chapter inherits most of its traits from modern socialism. We observed above how Durkheim opposes "communism" and "socialism." Socialism, for Durkheim, is a uniquely modern phenomenon: its goal is the collective organization of economic production. Unlike utopian communism, socialism, for Durkheim, is entirely contemporaneous with industrial capitalism: its *raison d'être* is to repair and re-constitute a social fabric that has been torn apart by the market order. And its means of reparation is a mode of production based on a division of tasks and a hierarchy of "capacities." Socialism should not therefore be viewed as an extension of the "communist ideal" as found in the Bible or in Plato. Its fundamental feature, for the majority of its representatives, is neither the sharing of goods nor collective consumption, but the re-organization of industrial labor according to the model of "association."[43] Instead of the old moral model of the "community of goods," what we now have is a new "association of individuals."[44] If the older mode of communism was ultimately a derivation of the most ancient expression of the "community of goods" – i.e., the logic of symbolic debt – modern socialism is, contrastingly, a society of individuals: it is a doctrine of immanent social energy to be organized, social forces to be coordinated, and an inherent power that its members must reclaim from the clutches of private property.[45] In this sense, the difference between the two models stems from the fact that socialism, like sociology, views modern society as a *sui generis* reality: it is a site of autonomous interactions or "motion" that calls for a specific, original, and rational form of organization. Socialism is a doctrine that strives to arrange immanent social forces by giving them an associational form adequate to their nature. Socialism and sociology are thus the heirs of the inventors of "civil society." But the "society" of the socialists eschews the political management of the economy, which seems too much like government by "experts" or "lawyers." Rather, the artificial separation of political powers from society (from its socio-economic core) is dissolved in socialism's "association of producers," such that politics itself is doomed to outright extinction.[46] The best definition of socialism in this respect is given by Pierre Ansart:

> For Saint-Simon, as for Marx and Proudhon, the task of the revolution is to liberate previously oppressed social forces, destroy the powers of alienation and objectification, and make the free development of social activity possible. But it's not only a question of increasing the possibilities of social realization for all individuals and enhancing the development of the productive forces. The socialist revolution will also restore, to all members of society, total mastery over their activity, thus making possible a society that is freed from all internal obstacles, a society "*en acte*" in the words of Saint-Simon or Proudhon. The revolution will ensure the transition from a society governed by relations of political obedience to a society entirely devoted to administrative activity, activity directed toward objects devoid of relations of domination. The class of industrial workers, or proletarians, who were previously dominated by political power or by capital, will undertake a movement of re-appropriation that will give them complete control over themselves and their actions. It will substitute the empowerment of institutions with the dynamism of its own forces and the immediacy of its needs.[47]

In their own way, Marx and Engels participate in this socialist and associationist turn by re-defining communism as a "free association of producers." From this perspective, Durkheim's opposition between socialism and communism loses its relevance: for Marx and Engels, communism is not at all "archaic" but fundamentally modern. For them, the relevant opposition is not between socialism and communism, but is rather internal to communism itself, between "utopian communism" and "scientific communism." In this respect, Marx and Engels endow communism with an additional and completely original dimension. They want to replace the older moral and religious aspects of communism, which are still very active in the socialism of Owens and Saint-Simon, with a new understanding of historical development that is entirely scientific. Of course, the idea that science should replace politics is certainly not new – indeed, the very notion of "scientific socialism" came first from Proudhon, not Marx. For the latter, however, this new communism is scientific because it is based on knowledge of the evolutionary laws of societies. More specifically, it is based on objective knowledge of the end goal of all historical development as such, a goal that must be consciously attained by the masses through the experience of struggle. Communism thus no longer designates the project of an ideal city, but the "real movement that will abolish the present state of things" or, as Marx writes in the *1844 Manuscripts*, "the necessary pattern and the dynamic principle of the immediate future."[48] Yet unlike Cabet, Marx and Engels are not merely content to say that the community of goods has never been easier to create because industry enables unlimited abundance. Rather, they more ambitiously attempt to deduce the necessity of communism from the development of capitalism itself, and to make class struggle the means by which capitalism will give birth to a superior social form. For Marx, it is the very motion of private property and capital, as based on "a wholly empirical analysis,"[49] that is the basis of communism. Communism is therefore both a scientific theory (a theory of motion) and a form of revolutionary practice geared toward the conscious transformation of the conditions of life that have been imposed upon man. This is precisely Marx's meaning in another definition found in *The German Ideology*:

> Communism differs from all previous movements in that it overturns the basis of all earlier relations of production and intercourse, and for the first time consciously treats all natural premises as the creatures of men, strips them of their natural character and subjugates them to the power of individuals united.[50]

Communism is depicted as a harmonious accord between history's "objective tendencies" and its "subjective dimension," as if the consciousness of historical necessity, inscribed in its real movement, inevitably gives rise to economic contradictions and class conflicts, thus rendering the utopian project itself meaningless.[51]

From this perspective, it is the critique of political economy that will show how the development of capitalism's contradictions itself engenders the historical conditions through which communism becomes a necessity. This is the theoretical logic that allows Marx to scientifically establish the law of historical transformation that will abolish capitalism. This is the explicit meaning of numerous passages in Marx's various works and correspondence, one of the most well known of which appears at the end of Chapter 25 of *Capital* (vol. 1) – the chapter on the so-called "primitive accumulation." If capitalism destroys the small, individual, and independent producers, as Marx explains in this chapter, capitalism will in turn be destroyed by the same mechanisms of its own development, "with the inexorability of a natural process."[52] Marx and Engels ground their logic on a simple historical pattern. Capital expropriates workers as a condition of its expansion. The workers that are organized by capital become, one day, stronger and more numerous and they in turn expropriate capital. History's denouement is thus the "expropriation of the expropriators."[53] The question that Marx poses is ultimately this: how does capitalism itself create the conditions for communism or, put differently, how does capital generate the common out of itself – i.e., from the internal logic of its own processes? Such, for Marx, is the famous logic of the "negation of the negation": the most thoroughgoing integration of the workforce into the great, mechanized industries of capitalism produces a socialization of labor and the concentration of capital. This in turn constitutes the conditions for passage into another regime of ownership based on new relations of production. Capitalist socialization is thus posited as the condition for the association of workers. Through a strange act of faith, that which made worker control over the production process impossible now becomes its "presupposition."

Of course, history has not confirmed the ineluctable character of the "expropriation of the expropriators." History has not shown us how capital's planned and organized association of workers creates the conditions for the collective management of production and trade. Marx, it seems, remains a prisoner of the false symmetry he established between the transition from feudal society to bourgeois society, on the one hand, and the passage from bourgeois society to communism on the other. For Marx, revolution is like a kind of "birth," according to the metaphor he continually employs, wherein the superior form of society is always contained in the form that precedes it, and capitalism, accordingly, itself creates the material conditions for its own transcendence. Yet the conditions of communism, which Marx thinks are produced by capitalism, do not in fact at all resemble the conditions that permitted the consolidation of the economic power of the bourgeoisie. As Cornelieus Castoriadis observed in 1955, while reflecting on his increasing distance from Marx's thought, if capitalism is defined by the production of factories, mass proletarianization, the concentration of capital, and the application of modern science to production, these features really have very little to do with the underlying condition of the bourgeois revolution:

> But where can we find already realized in this society socialist relations of production as bourgeois relations of production were in "feudal" society?' Now, it is obvious that these new relations of production cannot be merely those realized in the "socialization of the labor process," the cooperation of thousands of individuals within the great industrial units of production. For these are the relations of production typical of a highly developed form of *capitalism*.[54]

For Castoriadis, capitalist "socialization" should in no way be confused with the association of workers: it is characterized, as Castoriadis points out, by the antagonism between the "mass of executants" and a "stratum of directors." Thus, whereas the bourgeois revolution was essentially "negative" for Castoriadis, in the sense that it "limit[ed] itself to erecting into law a state of fact by abolishing a superstructure that in itself already is unreal,"[55] the socialist revolution is "essentially positive" because "it has to construct its regime – constructing not only factories but new relations of production for which the development of capitalism furnishes merely the presuppositions."[56] Castoriadis's critique can thus be summarized by the following formula: "the capitalist transformation of society *ends* with the bourgeois revolution; the socialist transformation of society *begins* with the proletarian revolution."[57] In other words, Marx did not think of the construction of socialism as the establishment of new relations of production because of his confusion between "socialization" and "association."[58] For Castoriadis, this confusion was not a matter of chance, but strictly corresponds to Marx's notion of a quasi-natural law of evolution leading societies toward communism. Put differently, Marx's thesis – which has been adopted by all manner of Marxisms right up to the present day – is that there is a kind of objective production of the common by capital, which itself is the material condition of the conscious production of the common by the association of workers.

Yet this ostensibly scientific communism is everywhere in crisis. Its faith is exhausted, and only a few old believers still swing the censer that blesses the glorious march of its history. How can we still believe that the development of capitalism is a necessary, if somewhat painful, phase in the ultimate appearance of a new mode of production? The fact is we have moved on from our faith in objective human progress. We no longer believe in the narrative of the inexorable emancipation of humanity, which presupposes and even justifies all manner of slow births and difficult deliveries.

The exhaustion of this old belief is especially apparent in the recent transformation of communism, by some of its heralds, into a Kantian "regulative idea," which of course completely breaks with the Marxian theses of a "real movement that dissolves the current state of things." Communism, in this register, seems to have acquired the strange status of a "moral belief," not unlike the famous "postulates of practical reason" in terms of the effects the latter produces on the will:[59] in the same way that "I want to believe" in God because I need this presupposition in order to work toward the realization of sovereign good, I now "want to believe" in communism because I need this presupposition in order to act in the here and now for the cause of emancipation. Suffice it to say that this latter version of belief, unlike the former, means one has effectively renounced the idea of historical necessity and is, in a sense, but one more manifestation of this older narrative's demise and the futility of trying to resurrect it. There's no need to deplore or rejoice in its demise: it is simply a fact.

Of course, this doesn't mean that communism has been reduced, in the words of François Furet, to "the passing of an illusion." Rather it means that a certain moment has ended and, perhaps, a new era of emancipation is opening up, one that has little to do with its previous historical forms. But creating new historical forms demands an examination of each of communism's historical instantiations, especially that form dominated by the figure of the party-state. And no clever subterfuge – especially not the specious analogy that renders communism a kind of mathematical "hypothesis" in need of demonstrable proofs – must distract us from this task.[60] For it should be understood that the attempt to test a political hypothesis is itself part of the hypothesis, just as the attempt to demonstrate a mathematical hypothesis is part of that hypothesis as well. The only goal of this deplorable paradox is its ability to cancel out the hypothesis's empirical failure as a criterion of invalidation – which is just a way of making its failure only an "apparent failure"[61] – such that even the hypothesis' failure is paradoxically its validation. But what is most worrisome is the revolting conclusion drawn from this self-justifying rationality: can we reduce the terror of the Stalinist or Maoist state to a mere "demonstration" of the communist hypothesis, thus passing off millions of victims in the name of "justifying" this hypothesis?

State Communism, or the Bureaucratic Capture of the Common

Despite the last redoubts of China or North Korea, the cycle of state communism that began in 1917 has effectively drawn to a close. While we have already discussed certain aspects of Marxism and social democracy, we must, above all, be completely frank about the nature of state communism: the communist states of the twentieth century were, by and large, terrorist states that not only monopolized arbitrary violence but also insisted on a discursive monopoly over the social world, thought, art, culture, and the very future of human societies. The circumstances out of which these states emerged has usually been used to justify a whole series of infamous crimes, including the suppression of the Kronstadt rebellion, the concentration camps and the trials, and – right up until the collapse of these states – arbitrary police espionage and the highly conservative nature of the state bureaucracies. Trotsky, for instance, who was a firm believer in state terror, justified its use to Karl Kautsky in the following manner: "the degree of ferocity of the struggle depends on a series of internal and international circumstances. The more ferocious and dangerous is the resistance of the class enemy who have been overthrown, the more inevitable does the system of repression take the form of a system of terror."[62]

This is not to say, of course, that historical circumstances did not play an important role in the emergence of justifications of this kind: civil war, military encirclement, the famine, and industrial disorganization seem to have forced a number of decisions onto leaders that very quickly led to the establishment of the dictatorship of the Party, and foreclosed the type of society that both Lenin and Trotsky wanted to build before the revolution (which was something closer to the Paris Commune writ large).[63] However these "internal and international conditions," as Trotsky puts it, do not explain everything. Most decisions were undertaken according to a widely shared premise (including those who were subsequently dispatched by Stalinism): the party that builds, controls, and governs the new state is always right because it alone is enlightened by the "science of communism." In the case of the Soviet Union, the democratic ideal of the free association of producers was ultimately supplanted by forms of domination and servitude that had absolutely no relation to the culture of critique, the objective analysis of facts, and the refusal of dogma that was the fundamental basis of Marx's intellectual ethic.[64]

Early on, the complete nationalization of industry and trade, the weakening of institutions of workers' control, co-optation of unions within the apparatus of production and government, the creation of the Cheka, the establishment of a single-party monopoly and the refusal to tolerate any dissident tendencies sowed the seeds that allowed Stalin, after the defeat of the European revolutions and the rise of fascism, to ascend within the Party, eliminate all opponents and possible rivals, and implement forced collectivization of agriculture and bureaucratic planning. The great Stalinist turning point thus occurred when, as the despotic head of the state administration, Stalin implemented a terrorist policy of "primitive socialist accumulation" that was based on a double logic of excessive exploitation of manual labor placed under state control, alongside the threats of the firing squad or deportation to forced labor camps.

This was a period of so-called "socialism in one country," which had almost nothing to do with the hopes of revolutionary Marxism, as noted by Victor Serge in his assessment of the revolutionary experience: "the essential fact is that in 1927–1928, following a coup carried out within the party, the revolutionary State-party becomes a reactionary bureaucratic police State on the social structures created by the Revolution."[65] It bears mentioning, given Marc Ferro's remarkable analysis of the 1917 Revolution, that the Party, in the first years of the regime, was sociologically very dissimilar from the revolutionary organization in 1917. The Party integrated hundreds of thousands of plebeian youths who made up a social group with specific interests and a unique mentality that rendered them an easily manageable political instrument.[66]

Yet the ultimate destiny of the communist revolutions of the twentieth century was not a foregone conclusion. While there were decisive bifurcations and specific conditions that led to a degree of bureaucratization that caused even Lenin himself to begin to worry (though much too late of course), these conditions were not insurmountable. And while it is both stupid and vain to blame Marx for the Gulag, it is nonetheless important to identify exactly what aspects of the socialist and communist movement, even before the October Revolution, promoted the development of these administrative practices in the Party and, ultimately, in the state.

The ideal of obedient militants and soldiers, the creation of ruling oligarchies, and the dogmatism of party officials all play an important role in the constitution of bureaucratic organizations. But we fundamentally misunderstand the tragic history of "Soviet" bureaucratization if we do not grasp the institutional logic that, even before October, made the Party the central apparatus for attributing legitimacy upon the "political direction of the masses" and for assigning the plurality of organizations representing the working class (the soviets, trade unions, cooperatives, etc.) only fictive place.[67] After lending initial tactical support to the autonomous organs representing the working class and the Russian population at large that developed between February and October of 1917 – the factory committees, neighborhood committees, militias, etc. – the Bolsheviks very quickly eliminated them. Marc Ferro's extensive archival research has shown how the Party "bureaus" (or cells), as early as February 1917, controlled the Petrograd Soviet, how Party delegates replaced the representatives of various factory committees and neighborhood committees (whose composition was genuinely popular), how a new stratum of Party apparatchiks took control of decisive positions of power in the new administration in a matter of months, and how, finally, all remaining proletarian institutions were bolshevized, or progressively taken over by the state.[68] Democratic activity was thus rapidly eroded by two forms of bureaucratization: from the top, the Party colonized what were hitherto autonomous popular workers organizations, and from below, the Party developed an apparatus designed to replace the general assemblies. This double "bureaucratic capture" of the democratic committees and the soviets at the very beginning of the revolution triggered a monopolization of the revolution by the Party that was effectively irreversible.[69]

The State-Party and the Imposition of a Productivist Logic

As we can see, the imposition of certain practices, under specific historical conditions, can lead to the statist capture of democratic energies and the confiscation of real power by a party destined to become the singular ruling institution of the state.[70] This leads to an impressive inversion of the socialist project, and it is not difficult to understand how it led to the collapse of the workers' movement. Instead of *recuperating* the forces of society that had been appropriated by the state and by capital, the revolution led to the creation of a party-controlled state – or, rather, a "state-party" that tried to direct all social forces and interactions from above. The role of the working class in this situation, then, is merely to blindly obey and work. As Trotsky crudely pointed out in *Terrorism and Communism:* "the worker does not merely bargain with the Soviet State: no, he is subordinated to the Soviet State, under its orders in every direction – for it is *his* State."[71] In this conception, the common is purely and simply identified with state property itself.

The most current term for his type of regime is "totalitarianism." According to Hannah Arendt, the essence of this type of regime is the denial of individual rights and the "rule of law," insofar as the latter is the only way to truly protect the former. For Arendt, then, liberalism is the only philosophy capable of blocking this modern pathology that absorbs all aspects of social, economic, and cultural life into the state apparatus. For us, however, this characterization of totalitarianism as the negation of the individual, or as the rejection of plurality within society, is insufficient.[72] It misses the historical singularity of the phenomenon, which is not merely the statist appropriation of the means of production, but also the creation of various instruments for controlling the population in the name of the "leadership of the society by the Party." In other words, in this type of regime, state organs exercise terrorist powers over the population to the extent that they are the eyes and ears of a Party enlightened by the science of history, a Party that pretends to be the source and the wellspring of all collective and individual life but which in fact reduces the life of the worker to a programmable economic function.

In order to properly account for this larger process, we need to return to the Marxian illusion of the objective production of the common by capital. This idea, which is linked to definite evolutionist tendencies in Marx's thought, led many Marxists to think that socialism in economically backwards countries must first wait for the development of bourgeois forces of production before these countries could proceed toward their socialist future. But, of course, the socialist revolutions of the twentieth century broke out in almost entirely economically backwards countries. As Castoriadis put it, "the wicked irony of history was that the first victorious revolution took place in a country where the population had been anything but 'disciplined, united, organized by the very mechanism of the process of capitalist production itself.' And the task of unifying and homogenizing Russian society had to be accomplished by the Bolshevik party and Stalin's totalitarian terror."[73] Under these conditions, the state-party thus became the principle agent of industrialization and the apparatus that imposed discipline upon the population. It was this apparatus that laid the groundwork for forced collectivization and exploited the collective workforce it directly organized. In other words, where the production process itself was not able to "organize, unify and discipline" the working class according to the mechanisms of its internal logic, the state-party was forced to take it upon itself to "organize, unify and discipline" the working class by violently subjecting workers to the worst forms of productivism. "Proletarianization" was thus accomplished through the iron rule of a state that used the forced march to produce its own form of "primitive accumulation."

Yves Cohen has very effectively articulated the nature of this bureaucratic mode of production and the original characteristics of the social relations it entailed. Simply put, the state apparatus stifled any possibility of genuine politics: "the state provided everything; it was the voice of the proletariat and the people. The Party is the site of truth and law, and the latter is always subordinated to the state." In other words, politics is eliminated because it is monopolized by a party that brooks no dissent or discord: "everyone has a 'formal' voice – every proletarian, every worker, any part of the people, in fact all the people, because the Party speaks for them all." Thus, as Cohen puts it, the "disqualification of politics leaves only administration."[74] We can in fact see something of an unexpected and paradoxical realization of the old Saint-Simonian prophecy in this form of administrative rationality, in the sense that the monolithic party violently realizes Saint-Simon's substitution of the "administration of people" for the "administration of things," insofar as state communism did in fact administer people as if they were things. This administration thus becomes the site of potentially unlimited power when, for one reason or another, personal or oligarchical authority is able to impose its will upon the Party and upon the larger administrative state.

Rather than explain everything by the long history of the Russian state, we should ask instead if this process of bureaucratization is not just as much – if not more so – the logical outcome of a party rationale that was imposed upon the workers' movement and which has largely escaped critical interrogation. These so-called bureaucratic "distortions" or "degenerations" have often been explained and sometimes even justified by historical "circumstances," as in Domenico Losurdo's highly symptomatic project of relativizing Stalin's crimes and rehabilitating his personality. But the first signs of bureaucratization appeared before the civil war and foreign intervention. The fact is that these signs point to very old organizational practices of the social democratic parties that were merely taken to extremes in the case of the Bolsheviks. If Lenin, as far back as 1902, became the central theoretician of the ruling party, it was because he considered this kind of party necessary to make successful revolution in a country where capitalist social relations were undeveloped (if not entirely absent). Lenin's iron discipline was firstly justified by the need to produce proletarian unity by imposing class consciousness on the proletariat from the outside, since it could not be internally generated by the mechanisms of capitalist production itself. By framing itself as the underlying condition and guarantor of the consciousness and unity of the working class, the Party also claimed exclusive representation of proletarian interests since, after the revolution, the "socialist state" would itself be the representative of the working class and would ensure the unity of the entire population as a means of legitimizing the state's absolute monopoly of bureaucratic power.[75] By claiming to both possess and embody historical knowledge, the Party and the state granted itself the right to impose historical truth upon society by force. In other words, the logic of the Party re-introduced the old representative relation between the sovereign and the people, wherein the unity of the people is a function of the monolithic nature of its singular representative (i.e., the state). In this sense, Hannah Arendt was right to see the dictatorship of the Party as the "last stage of government in the nation-state."[76] Yet this was not a question of just any party, but a very particular form of the Party that sought to produce the unity of the proletariat through the capture of state power. And once this objective was achieved, the Party continued to produce this unity through the ongoing organization of labor and production.

The Democratic Common versus the Common of State Production

The logic of the Party quickly imposed its unique institutional dynamic. As mentioned above, the monolithic Party acted as the sole instrument for creating a commons of production given the underdevelopment of capital. These conditions in particular explain why the uprisings that tried to disrupt the state monopoly of the common have been based on the claim to create a democratic common, in its most direct form, within the sphere of production, which is to say the terrain upon which this monopoly exercised its greatest violence in the ordinary lives of millions of people.

This was particularly true of the Hungarian revolution of 1956. In his 1976 essay "The Hungarian Source," Castoriadis underscored the radical character of this revolution:

> The purest, total, most extreme form of bureaucratic capitalism has been achieved in Russia, China, and the other countries masquerading as 'socialist.' The Hungarian revolution of 1956 has been the first and, until now, the only total revolution against total bureaucratic capitalism – foreshadowing the content and orientation of the future revolutions in Russia, China, etc.[77]

Why precisely, was the Hungarian Revolution a "total revolution"? Its total character was based in its intent to destroy the division between a circumscribed "political" sphere reserved for government, and the rest of social life devoted to production and work. In other words, the Hungarian Revolution aimed at a "de-professionalization of politics," or the abolition of the political as a special sphere of competence, in favor of the "universal *politicization* of society."[78] The workers' councils were thus especially important for three reasons: (a) the establishment of "direct democracy" – i.e., "true political equality" or "equality as to power"; (b) their "rootedness in existing concrete collectivities" that were not limited to the factories; and (c) "their demands relative to *self-management* and the abolition of work norms."[79] Just as the watchword of the emergent bourgeoisie was "no taxation without representation," the emergent principle of the Hungarian workers' councils was: "*no execution of decisions without an equal part played by all in the making of decisions.*"[80] What we see in this slogan is, in fact, the principle of the common in the purest form: only co-participation in decision-making produces co-obligation in the execution of decisions. The demand to abolish all work norms should thus be viewed in especially positive terms. It means, in effect, that "people charged with the implementation of a task are the ones entitled to make decisions concerning the rhythm of the work,"[81] and the only body authorized to make rules in this regard is the collective of those that will have to follow these rules. This demand, in itself, breaks with the belief in a purely technical organization of production, and at the same time overturns the habitually recognized primacy of specialists in favor of the primacy of the operators of the instruments of production themselves.[82]

Maoist China offers another striking example of popular resistance to capitalist-productivist norms imposed by the state-party. In a short but illuminating essay, sinologist Jean François Billeter suggests, "the famine that Stalin organized in Ukraine from 1933 to 1934, which caused the deaths of millions (8 million in 1933, according to one estimate) was not just a step toward industrialization. It was an exercise in the 'class struggle' that Mao Tse-Tung directly inspired."[83] Billeter distinguishes between four great moments within the "chain reaction" that led to the gradual acceptance of a market rationality in China: the first period extends from 1920 to 1949, the second from 1949 to 1957, the third from 1957 to 1979, and the fourth from 1979 to today. Lingering on the third period, Billeter shows how the "Great Leap Forward" was driven by the objective to create an industrial power capable of rivaling the countries of the West "at any cost and as quickly as possible." This merciless logic, that prevailed in capitalist countries in a different form, requires all social relations and all human existence itself become subject to the imperatives of production." Referencing historian Jasper Becker, who estimates that 30 million people died during the 1959–1961 famine,[84] Billeter argues that it was "the largest famine not only in the history of China, but in the history of the world as such." Furthermore, Billeter adds that these victims did not die from fatigue or illness, "but solely of hunger, in silence, under the supervision of a regime in complete control of the entire situation." Far from seeing the Great Leap as merely the temporary irruption of governmental irrationality, Billeter forcefully shows how Chinese leaders

> were determined to break productivity records in order to make China an industrialized nation. To this end, the peasantry was subject to brutal and irreversible proletarianization. Even family life had to be abolished, since it acted as a brake on the pace of transformation. Like the Nazi camps, the Great Leap is extremely revealing, and it should be placed at the very heart of contemporary history, not its margins.[85]

What we have here is another exemplary instance of the way in which state communism made up for the absence of a spontaneous process of the production of the common by capital with unprecedented levels of state coercion: the state took it upon itself to create a "common of production" from scratch by internalizing a hyper-productivist logic that could produce a "new man" capable of beating capitalism at its own game.

After being sidelined in the wake of the catastrophic Great Leap, Mao did everything he could to regain power between 1962 and 1966. To this end, Mao experimented with a number of methods between 1966 and 1968. "In 1966," writes Billeter, "Mao failed to achieve his ends by regular means, so he opted for others." Aware of the frustration of the youth, and of the student youth in particular, Mao mobilized the youth against those who resisted him within the party apparatus. Having previously secured the support of the army through Lin Piao (Lin Biao), Mao intervened every time the student rebellions deviated from his desired course or exceeded the objectives he had implicitly assigned to the students. And when the military tried to impose its will upon Mao, he revived the uprisings and directed them against the military itself when necessary. There is no question Mao was playing with fire: he took the great risk that these rebellions might mutate, then and there, into a genuine movement for social and political emancipation, especially once the students became involved; Mao would then have to violently crush the beginnings of a true revolution that he himself had started. And this, of course, is what he would finally have to do with the help of the army in 1968.[86] Billeter's analysis does a remarkable job of condensing the lesson of Hua Linshan's insightful book *Les Années rouges* (*The Red Years*).[87] As a schoolboy in Guilin when the Cultural Revolution erupted, Linshan recounts how he found himself caught in an incredibly violent civil war, and he speaks of the doubts that plagued him at the height of the fray, as well as his general state of mind. Beginning in January 1969, when the Central Committee started attacking the "leftist ideological tendencies" in the rebels, which was when the first massacres began, Linshan was increasingly tormented about the real reasons for the Cultural Revolution.[88]

What becomes increasingly apparent is that the student and working-class youth took the democratic principles invoked by the leadership at face value, especially its claim to model itself on the Paris Commune. We know that, for Mao, implementing the popular "right to elect and dismiss managers" was completely out of the question. Yet nowhere was Mao's cynicism more apparent than in his original proposal for a "Shanghai Commune" in March 1967. This creation of a Shanghai Commune was originally intended to create a power structure that could centralize, in a single organization, the functions that were previously divided between the Party and the government. However, Mao's decision to change its name was ultimately based on his view that a "commune" was an insufficiently strong form of organization to ensure effective control of power.[89] However, from the perspective of the actors involved in the rebellion, the principles of control over leaders (especially their recall), which were at first brandished in the name of Chairman Mao himself, now appeared to many to be incompatible with the very nature of the regime. As Jean François Billeter observes (and as we have mentioned above), Linshan shows that "Chairman Mao risked triggering a genuine revolution in order to achieve his ends." But Linshan also shows that "the students, the workers, and others seized this occasion to act according *to their own objectives*, which they discovered through the course of their activity, and the more they became autonomous, the more their efforts portended the negation of the regime."[90] Linshan was subsequently sent to the countryside for re-education after the crackdown, and he informs us in the final pages of his moving testimony of the conclusion he finally reached:

> I now understand why Chairman Mao triggered the Cultural Revolution. He wanted to implement measures he considered necessary but which ran counter to the will of the population. In order to implement these measures, he had to wield absolute power. This is where we come in. He used us to launch an attack against the organizational basis of the Party. It was an immense deception. Mao had no intention of ever applying these principles.[91]

If the Cultural Revolution was thus a contradictory phenomenon, it was not because of a "political experience that saturates the form of the party-state."[92] It was rather because the students and workers clashed with the state on behalf of the political nature of the kind of common the Cultural Revolution would produce: for the students and the workers, the goal was to extend the communal logic of the Paris Commune to the sphere of economic production. The name "Mao," therefore, does not designate the invention, "in the space of the party-state," of a "third recourse" of "mass political mobilization" that is beyond "formalism" and "terror";[93] rather, the name "Mao" signifies a combination of cynical manipulation, deception, and terror that scarcely has any equivalent. In this sense, Mao is nothing other than the name of one of the greatest political criminals of the twentieth century, alongside Stalin and Hitler.

Liberating the Common from its Statist Capture

We can now take better stock of the strange inversion of the original socialist project. "Socialism" or "scientific communism" was not merely an imperative to rationalize and coordinate economic activities through a central organ, as in Durkheim's reductive definition. Taken in this restricted sense, there is no doubt the socialist project inspired productivist policies designed to promote industrial centralization. But communism has also been the bearer of democratic ambitions: specifically, the project was an attempt to extend democracy into the economic and professional world; it is an affirmation that democracy does not stop at the doors of the workshop, factory, or farm. For many of its advocates, communism was not a project to re-establish a "community" in which the individual submitted to a whole embodied in a leader or a party, but a project that re-organized society according to managerial and legislative principles that gave real power, remuneration, and recognition to all those who participated in communal work. This form of associationist, economic democracy refuses to be coordinated by the market, but it also does not entrust all its command functions to the state-form either – unlike the *babouvistes*'s (followers of Babeuf) preference for a "supreme administration." And insofar as socialism is all about democratically organizing cooperative workers who perform different functions, it is not a negation of social diversity or professional differentiation. Indeed, many of its principle theoreticians viewed economic and social democracy as the solution to the very problem posed by this emergent industrial diversity. Jaurès, in this respect, speaks of a "communism of energies." In other words, socialism's defining problem or challenge is the creation of institutions for economic and social cooperation, and its preferred solution to this problem is a consensual association that is collectively managed by workers – even to the point of thinking, like Proudhon, that the "workshop will dissolve the government." The experiments in collective management, self-governance, and workers' councils that have occurred since the nineteenth century all bear the stamp of this aspiration for economic democracy.

We've also attained a better understanding of the distinctive logics animating the three dominant forms of communism: the community of goods, the association of producers, and the bureaucratic state. The first model presupposes an originary unity that it seeks to re-discover through perfect equality and the outright refusal of property. The second model – what Durkheim calls "socialism" and Marx calls "scientific communism" – inversely presupposes a state of social and economic differentiation that must be coordinated according to principles of justice and merit that only some form of economic democracy can realize. The Marxian variant of this second model is thought to develop almost automatically out of capitalism itself, what we have called the objective development of the common by capital. The third mode of communism tries to organize a society conceived as a passive material to be informed, distributed into classes and categories, and completely directed by "scientific knowledge" that belongs to, and is embodied in, a superior organization. Distinguishing between these three forms or "ideal types," over and above the empirical hybridizations that history actually produces, seems essential to us for theorizing a contemporary alternative to capitalism that does not condemn us to repeat the past.

Of all three models, the first and the second are the most incongruent: the concept of a free association of individuals violently clashes with the authoritarian distribution of individuals within the community whose functions are determined in advance.[94] Some articulation is possible between the second and the third models, due to their shared notion of a communal sphere in matters of production, but only to a certain extent: while the second model views the common as emerging from the process of production itself, the third makes it the job of the state to create the common by force. And, finally, there is a certain proximity between the first and third models by virtue of the role each entrusts to a "supreme administrator" for coordinating the distribution of individuals within their respective functions. This is what ultimately explains the plural meanings of Alain Badiou's notion of the communist hypothesis, even if these various meanings are difficult to reconcile with each other. We have already seen how this notion can refer to both a Kantian moral precept – communism "as if" – and a mathematical theorem – communism as "verified by its failures." But we must not forget the third meaning of the term: communism as the eternal idea that determines the actions of the philosopher-kings in the *Republic*: this is communism as "*sub specie aeternitati.*" These philosopher-kings described by Plato are artists who work according to a "divine pattern" in order to trace the outline of the political constitution. The individual and city are their subject matter: they must "wipe the slate of human society and human habits clean," and then draw again, "until [they] have made human nature as acceptable to God as may be."[95] Legislators of this kind endeavor to relate the human to the divine by means of a "cleansing of the soul." We can now see the importance of this exercise: Badiou is drawn to both the Platonic community of goods and the model of state communism, but completely bypasses the second model, the free association of producers. It is in this respect that Badiou's criticism of the "party-form"[96] is entirely superficial. It misses that which is most essential: the use of coercion and terror to change the human soul. And it is also in this sense that Badiou's Platonism makes perfect sense: it rescues the hard core of state communism while denying everything in this model that speaks of a material common within the sphere of production.

Why, one might ask, is the construction of these models, these "ideal types," a necessary pre-condition for theorizing what we will refer to in the rest of the book as the "common"? Its principle benefit is its ability to help us distinguish the true common from its false pretenses: the common, in the sense of a co-obligation that we all impose on ourselves, cannot be thought of as an original state to be restored, nor something that spontaneously emerges out of the process of production, nor something that is imposed from the outside, from above. The last part of this conclusion is worth repeating: the so-called "realization" of the common in the form of state ownership can only lead to the destruction of the common by the state. And if some aspects of the common may have survived, in subterranean forms, within societies dominated by this form of state property, it is only through active resistance to this suffocating form of state control.[97]

3

The Great Appropriation and the Return of the "Commons"

The collapse of state communism did not bring the struggle against global and financial capitalism to an end. The new dominant order that emerged in the 1990s was almost immediately contested by new militant groups and new ways of thinking from all over the world. These new forms of resistance emphasized the invasive and destructive effects of neoliberalism, and spoke of the need to build a new world order based on principles other than competition, profit, and the excessive exploitation of our natural resources. By the end of twentieth century, the emergent alter-globalization movement testified to the energies of a re-constructed and global anti-capitalist movement made up of ecological activism, traditional social movements, and a range of more specific grievances prompted by neoliberal policies. In all the manifestos, platforms, and declarations that were published for the better part of a decade on behalf of the "anti-globalization" struggle, the terms "commons" or "common goods" frequently appeared as a means of articulating various struggles, practices, rights, and ways of life opposed to the intensification of privatization and commodification that has plagued the world since the 1980s. Whether as an adjective or a noun, singular or plural, the term "common" became a movement flag, a watchword of resistance, and a guiding principle for almost every alternative to neoliberal capitalism. It is in this sense that the contemporary convergence of movements opposed to neoliberalism, in the name of the commons, marks a new and distinctive moment in the history of social struggles against global capitalism.

It is above all the reference to the "commons," in its various forms, that *the* common, in the singular, began to emerge as the central category of contemporary anti-capitalism. Given the historical antiquity of what in French goes by the name *les communaux*, the sudden appearance and importance of the term at the dawn of the twenty-first century may seem somewhat curious. Yet the reasons for its recent emergence are aptly summarized by Indian activist Vandana Shiva in the context of the "water war" in Bolivia: "if globalization is the ultimate enclosure of the commons – our water, our biodiversity, our food, our culture, our health our education – then reclaiming the commons is the political, economic, and ecological agenda of our times."[1]

Let us recall that by the "commons" we mean, first of all, the collection of rules and customs that allowed peasants of the same community to collectively use roads, forests, pastures, etc.[2] During the late 1990s and early 2000s, however, the content of the term was greatly expanded to include anything that might become either the target of privatization or commodification, or anything that has been stolen or destroyed in the name of, or under the guise of, neoliberalism. As a result, the term became politically and critically charged anew: it is a signifier that is diametrically opposed to the great appropriation of wealth, over the past few decades, by the narrow oligarchy referred to as the "1 percent" by the occupants of Zuccotti Park in New York in 2011. At the very least, the term is the germ form of a broader and more universal struggle against neoliberalism, one which demands the collective and democratic reclamation of resources and spaces that have been captured by private oligopolies and governments. "The water is ours," declared the irrigation farmers and the members of the Cochabamba cooperatives; "the city belongs to everyone," declared the occupants of public squares in Madrid, Cairo, New York, and Istanbul. The idea of the common has thus become global in a double sense: it encompasses extremely varied types of resources, activities, and practices, and it also concerns the entire population of the planet.[3]

The "paradigm of the commons" is also hegemonic within the environmental movement, even if the valence of the term is altered somewhat in this context. For various environmental movements, it is not so much a matter of defending free access to community resources confiscated by private interests, nor a matter of protecting public property from privatization. Rather, the goal of the environmental movement is to protect natural "common goods" from unrestrained exploitation. The term "commons," in this context, is more about prohibiting or restricting access or use. In this context, this updated notion of the commons encompasses two types of property that the Roman legal tradition tended to keep separate: "common" and "public" property.[4] The ecological movement, then, defends the commons, defined as "common natural resources," against predation and destruction at the hands of a mere fraction of the world's population, while the anti-neoliberal and anti-capitalist movements are more focused on the neoliberal fire sale of "public goods." Yet these different meanings of the "commons" circulating in today's political lexicon are not necessarily opposed, but can in fact be reconciled. This is clearly manifest, for instance, in the case in the Cochabamba "water war," which pitted populations struggling to make access to water a fundamental human right against powerful economic groups advocating its private exploitation and commodification.[5] What unifies the different valences of the commons under the same conceptual umbrella is the demand for a new form of "communitarian" management, a form of communal resource democracy, that is more responsible, sustainable, and just than today's dominant order.[6] According to several authors, the paradigm of the commons thus signals a major shift in the way in which political action is conceived, both in terms of its ends and its means: it is a new "revolution in the revolution."[7] The old statist solutions, which saw public property as the best solution to the economic and social problems of a given national population, are either rejected outright by today's popular movements – as was the case concerning struggles over nationalization of oil and gas in Bolivia – or are viewed with great suspicion given the extent to which governments everywhere have sold off public services and utilities and formed close alliances with large multinational corporations.

How should we measure the theoretical accuracy and political scope of this newly re-introduced concept of the "commons" in contemporary critical thought? What do we gain, in terms of our understanding of contemporary capitalism, by analogously interpreting the commons as the historical repetition of the widespread dispossession of communal lands across the European countryside in the Middle Ages? We also need to ascertain whether the practices and spaces of the common that were characteristic of pre-capitalist societies can help us grasp the originality of new practices and spaces like the Internet. As we shall see, this analogy is useful, but it also has its limits. Put differently, the great appropriation is both one of the major tendencies of our era and the dominant frame of reference that explains the analogous recourse to the historical commons. But to interpret today's global transformations in the singularly negative register of expropriation invariably leads to partial interpretations of ongoing processes, and it confines our theorization of the common to an essentially defensive strategic mode.

The New Global "Enclosures"

The emergence of the "commons" is a direct response to one of the most striking aspects of neoliberalism: the "theft," perpetrated by the partnership between private oligopolies and the state, of that which previously belonged to the public domain, the welfare state, or local communities. The immense transfer of property and capital from the state to the private sector, especially the "shock therapies" and the "transitions toward a market economy" forced upon the former communist countries during the late 1980s and 1990s, is arguably one of the defining aspects of this great appropriation. But this trend was hardly confined to the East. Capitalist countries in both the "center" and the "periphery" have opened up all manner of social and economic activity that had otherwise been exempt from capital's direct domination since the end of the nineteenth century: publically owned railway companies, national coal, steel, and shipbuilding industries, the production and distribution of water, gas, electricity, the postal service, and the telephone and television industries; the partial privatization of social security systems, retirement plans, elementary, secondary, and post-secondary education, healthcare; and the introduction of competitive mechanisms and the profit motive throughout the public services. The social effects have been immense. Over the course of the past thirty years, inequality has increased, the proportion of wealth accumulated by the richest has exploded, and financial speculation has accelerated divisive forms of urban segregation. Past mechanisms for integrating the working classes into the national society have been overwhelmed, workers' organizations and leftist parties have lost their mediating function, and while the apparatuses of redistribution have not entirely disappeared, their scope has considerably narrowed. In short, society has become polarized, fragmented, and depoliticized.

While these tendencies differ from one locality to another, they share a universal character insofar as they are all linked to the generalization of neoliberal policies in the 1980s. The "Washington Consensus," as theorized by John Williamson in 1990, aptly delineates the different components of the policies that were first implemented in Latin America and then spread to the rest of the world. The great neoliberal turn has often been simplified as the triumph of the "total market." And while it is true that the official ideology of Thatcher and Regan is in accord with this description, the fact is that the actual imposition of competitive logics across every social sector was not solely achieved by private actors. As Marx recognized early on, and as Karl Polanyi would subsequently remind us, the state has always been a very active agent in the construction of markets. And this new cycle of appropriation is, perhaps more than ever, a joint venture of public power and private force, especially the larger multinational corporations from around the world. This partnership has resulted in the re-composition of the dominant classes: half private, half public, simultaneously national and global, its members occupy a wide range of powerful positions within the state apparatus, the media, and the economic system. They have monopolized the senior positions in the parties of the traditional right as well the "modern" left, and they are increasingly shuffled through the "revolving door" between the market sector and the public administration, all the while developing an awareness of their common interests under the guise of economic "realism" and "serious" management. This "public-private" neoliberal hybridization has necessitated a new concept of power – "governance" – which has only exacerbated the confusion surrounding the increasingly misleading opposition between public and private ownership.

By focusing on the practices of appropriation and dispossession, the demand for the commons tries to revive a tradition of struggle against the long-term expansion of the logic of property, or the hegemonic legal superstructure that corresponds to capitalism's economic actuality. The current expansion of private property and the intensification of commodification are thus conceived by numerous authors as a "second enclosure movement," to borrow James Boyle's phrase.[8] This second enclosure movement repeats and generalizes, in every domain – and especially the domains of biodiversity and intellectual and scientific creation – the first enclosure of the Western European countryside between the fifteenth and nineteenth centuries.

The paradigm of the commons is expressly defined against the expansion of the logic of property and the expansion of the market (which is commonly identified with neoliberalism). According to David Bollier, who has compiled arguably the most extensive catalog on the subject, this "silent theft" concerns every example of the commons, including natural resources and public spaces, cultural heritage, educational institutions, and communications infrastructure.[9] This general "enclosure" movement is led by large multinationals and supported by governments who are themselves increasingly subject to the logic of the market. The intensification of commodification, the increasing power of global corporations (corporatization), and the pressures exerted by the logic of property (propertization) are all reinforcing tendencies, and they undermine any attempt to erect political or moral limitations on the market's expansion. What has occurred in the United States is occurring in every other region of the world today as the result of the power of large multinationals supported by national governments: namely, a new expansion of capitalism (even if some advocates of the commons do not use this term) accompanied by the formidable global enhancement of property. A number of examples of this expansion are particularly significant: the theft of seeds from indigenous farmers by large multinational agribusinesses like Monsanto, the development of patents on life as a result of pressure from the biotech sector,[10] and the monopolization of patents on the most used software in the world by computer giants like Microsoft.

To denounce these "new enclosures" is to accentuate a series of inseparable tendencies characterizing contemporary capitalist globalization. In the first place, the term "enclosure" refers to the seizure of natural resources and lands that still takes place on a large scale throughout the world. Let's take two particularly telling examples of this practice, the first of which relates to land, and the second to water. The first example concerns so-called "land grabbing," which aggravates the destructive effects of free trade, agribusiness, and biotechnologies on peasant farmers throughout the world. It is a practice that seizes arable land in countries of the global South – sub-Saharan Africa, Indonesia, Philippines, Brazil, Argentina, Uruguay, etc., – largely through long-term leases (usually twenty-five- to ninety-nine-year leases).[11] This practice of land grabbing, which already represents close to 2 percent of all arable land on the planet, is the work of multinational corporations and states in both the global South (China or India) and the global North (the United States or Great Britain), who are eager to secure supplies of food and energy while simultaneously boosting the profitability of their corporate and financial industries through speculation on land and agriculture prices.[12] This phenomenon has accelerated since the food crisis of 2007 and continues to accelerate as a result of ongoing financial speculation. In 2011 alone, eighty million hectares of land were seized in this fashion. These transactions usually occur between national states and investors without the involvement or consultation of local populations. This has been the case in numerous African countries. The effects on peasant agriculture, on crop production, and on the diets of local populations suggest this direct and brutal application of the power of global capital to the agricultural lands of poor countries is a repetition of the commodification of European lands several centuries ago, and it is producing similar consequences (though on a much vaster scale). Rising land prices, prohibitions on access to former communal land, the seizure of the most fertile lands, preference for export crops, and the diffusion of genetically modified organisms (GMOs) and the associated use of herbicides and pesticides has led to the widespread expropriation of peasants, who are forced to live in the slums of various Third World megacities. It has also led to increased food prices for the population as a whole. While this speculation-based seizure of land only compliments the range of instruments and practices that already restrict food production in favor of export crops, it has dramatically accelerated the capitalist transformation of agriculture and the destruction of peasant communities.

The appropriation of agricultural land is also directly linked to the seizure of water for the benefit of these major export crops. Generally speaking, the capitalist control of water is another example of a contemporary practice that rather closely resembles the historical expropriation of the "commons" in Europe.[13] While water management in the world's largest cities is still largely under public control, the trade in water has grown significantly since the 1980s. The global market in private water is dominated by a handful of oligopolies, including two French companies: Suez environnement (formerly Lyonnaise des eaux) and Veolia (formerly Compagnie générale des eaux). They operate in dozens of countries on every continent, with the active support of the World Trade Organization (WTO), the World Bank, and national governments, but also the United Nations Educational, Scientific and Cultural Organization (UNESCO), a member of the World Water Council, which lobbies for the privatization of water. Advocates of water privatization justify their efforts by speaking of the need to invest in water infrastructure to keep up with increasing urban populations, to provide access to potable water to more than one billion people, and to meet the basic sanitary needs of more than 2.5 billion people. From their point of view, states and municipalities are not capable of raising sufficient funds to construct, renovate, and maintain networks for the production and distribution of drinking water, and so private companies are said to be the only organizations with sufficient means to do so, so long as they are free to allocate water – now understood as a normal "economic good" or commodity – according to a remunerative price. The result of the privatization of water management, wherever it has been implemented, is usually an increase in the price of water for users, who are considered "rational consumers," and so it is the poorest populations who suffer most restrictions on access. The technological race initiated by the "giants" of the industry to propose new solutions to growing demand – recycling used water, desalination, etc. – suggests that water's marketization, despite the numerous struggles that have taken place since the 1990s, is far from over.[14] Amongst all the struggles against water privatization, the struggle in Cochabamba, Bolivia is undoubtedly most emblematic. In October 1999, the Bolivian government passed Law 2029, which the farmers and the people of the barrios famously fought against. Law 2029 was an act of expropriation and confiscation from top to bottom: in addition to the privatization of municipal water ownership, it forbade autonomous neighborhood cooperatives from digging wells, and it even outlawed local farmers from using reservoirs to collect rainwater.[15]

Yet while these specific examples are especially illustrative, we must bear in mind that our entire "environment" – both the natural environment and the built environment – is being affected by this extension of property and the market in multiple ways. Essential goods, such as food and medicines, are increasingly restricted by market logics and global oligopolies. Cities, streets, squares, and public transit systems have been transformed into commercial and advertising spaces. Cultural institutions, sporting facilities, and places of leisure and rest are rendered increasingly difficult to access as a result of rising user fees. Public services such as hospitals, schools, and prisons are built and co-managed by private business. Public research institutions and universities prioritize profitability. The forests, seas, rivers, and the subsoils are increasingly submitted to intensive industrial exploitation. And our entire cultural heritage, which belongs to the "public domain," is re-defined as a form of "capital" to be developed within museums and libraries. This great appropriation, in all its various manifestations, has of course led to massive economic inequality and exclusion. It accelerates ecological disaster, it turns forms of culture and communication into commercial products, and it increasingly dissolves society into individual consumers who are indifferent to their common fate.

The Paradigm of the "Enclosure of the Commons"

Under these conditions, one of the interpretive frameworks most frequently used to grasp the nature of this new "great transformation" is the historical analog with the "enclosures against the commons." One of the best examples of this is Peter Linebaugh's book dedicated to the Magna Carta.[16] Beginning with a 1994 reference by

Subcomandante Marcos to the great English Charter of 1215, Linebaugh proposes the following interpretation of neoliberalism and the movements opposing it: all around world we are currently re-witnessing a history that Europe, and especially England, experienced from the thirteenth century onwards, namely the destruction of the "commons" by enclosures.[17] It is through this seductive analogical reasoning that all forms of anti-capitalist resistance have been articulated as a struggle in defense of the "commons," and thus practices and knowledge rooted in the distant past are thereby put into direct relation with the most sophisticated communication and information technologies used by today's Internet "commoners."

Yet the analogy proffered by Linebaugh is merely the scholarly echo of a more diffuse reference to the commons that emerged in the mid–1990s, perhaps most famously within the Zapatista movement, but also across a range of struggles and movements in North and South America, India, and Europe. According to David Bollier, the "paradigm of the commons"[18] was initially forged as a polemical and strategic weapon that directly targeted the domination of a market-based economic model and its concomitant ideology of property rights, which was framed as the only way to improve economic efficiency and overall prosperity. "The commons," argues Boiller, "is a new (i.e., newly recognized) cultural form unfolding in front of us."[19] As the basis of a social movement that resembles the ecological movement in many respects, the commons has three dimensions: *scientific*, *normative*, and *activist*. In particular, the commons makes it possible to re-think political action, re-define the objectives of political action, and re-consider its forms. It is also worth noting, in this respect, that the category of the "commons" also emerged during this period within the academic discourse of American political science through the work of Elinor Ostrom and her collaborators. Ostrom's work showed the extent to which collective management of communal resources was still practiced in many parts of the world, and how this management escapes the logic of the market and the administrative state without sacrificing economic efficiency in the least.[20]

The "paradigm of the commons" is both defensive and offensive. It is defensive, in the first instance, in that it conceives of the "commons" in terms of all those existing "communal resources" that ought to remain at the disposal of either a restricted community or society as a whole. For Bollier, strategies to protect the "commons" from the invasion of the market (and other practices of appropriation constituting the "silent theft" of what belongs to everyone), can only be developed if we are first able to realize that the landscape, the water, the air, ideas, science, radio waves, the Internet, and also social relations, education, and civic engagement are all "communal resources" that belong to everyone.[21] But this paradigm is also offensive insofar as it promotes practices of sharing in relation to already existing "communal resources." "The commons," writes Bollier, "constitutes a new breeding ground in which new social practices of 'commoning' are born; these practices provide us with useful ways of rethinking our social order, our forms of political governance and our ecological management. The commons enables emergent new energies capable of redesigning our political institutions."[22] This new political culture helps us understand that wealth is not created solely by the owners and managers of capital, according to the vulgar neoliberalism universally shared by governments of the right and the left; rather, wealth is created by communities or societies whose members pool their knowledge and competencies to create prosperity. The rise of the Internet and the formation of digital communities over the past thirty years demonstrate the extent to which the creation of value is increasingly dissociated from market metrics. Collaborative practices developed on the Internet have also led to achievements as important as the free software movement or the creation of encyclopedias like Wikipedia. These achievements testify to the emergence of another political economy and another conception of wealth associated with networks (much of which has been explored in detail by theorists like Yochai Benkler).[23]

The "paradigm of the commons" has also been developed by authors closely connected to global social movements. One of the most emblematic texts in this canon is undoubtedly Naomi Klein's "Reclaiming the Commons," which was drafted in 2001 after the first large-scale "anti-globalization" mobilizations in Seattle and the inaugural World Social Forum in Porto Alegre. In this article, Klein defines the alter-globalization movement as fundamentally based on the reclamation of the "commons."[24] If, as Klein argues, the movement is based on a "coalition of coalitions," the central task of the movement is to interlink a series of protests motivated by seemingly disparate concerns. According to Klein, sustaining this kind of movement depends on an awareness of the two distinctive threats to the commons: "the privatization of every aspect of life, and the transformation of every activity and value into a commodity."[25] The movement's slogan – "the world is not for sale" – precisely expresses the need to defend and promote the commons as an inalienable resource. Whether the struggle concerns the protection of public spaces, the refusal of GMOs controlled by multinational agribusiness, the struggle against the marketization and commodification of health and education, the fight for universal access to water, protests against industrial activity or agricultural pollutants, etc., all these struggles share the same "spirit," which for Klein is the need to "reclaim the commons."[26] As Klein and others argue, the alter-globalization movement is not a movement opposed to "globalization" as such; it is, however, opposed to unlimited privatization and, in turn, the movement fights for democratic control of trade and the exploitation of communal resources. These struggles are not about defending national industrial apparatuses or protecting local cultural or social particularities. They subscribe to a "global" interpretation of evolving conditions and struggles. This, for Klein, is one of the major features of the "anti-globalization" movement. As she ironically points out, the struggle's global orientation was made possible by the very actions of the multinationals, whose imperialistic ambitions created the conditions and imposed the necessity of an international and intersectoral coalition of diffused resistances. It is the very process of globalization itself, led by the large oligopolies and international organizations who drafted today's global laws of commerce and finance, that promotes awareness of the interdependence of ecological, social, and economic issues.

This is precisely what we mean when we speak of the general and abstract character of the category of the commons. The category has the advantage of encapsulating every aspect of reality, every practice, every institution, title, and statute that is potentially threatened by the logic of property and the "market," which is itself encapsulated in the general and abstract metaphor of "enclosure." In other words, the category makes it possible to unite disparate forces that all find themselves combating the same adversarial logic. As David Bollier underscores:

> By evoking the commons, we are able to start building a shared vocabulary that designates what we collectively own and what we must manage in a responsible manner. We can reclaim control of an international endowment that extends from the atmosphere to the oceans, from the human genome to the Internet, and throughout public space and the public domain. All these collective goods have become the object of exploitation, privatization and aggressive commercialization.[27]

The new paradigm of the common thus draws its strength from the coalition it seems to promise between diverse struggles – the gathering of trade unionists, ecologists, and alter-globalizationists in Seattle in 1999 was, it seems, just the beginning. In the Gramscian vocabulary of Ernesto Laclau and Chantal Mouffe, we could say the concept of the "commons" is one of those terms that produces a "chain of equivalences" between struggles in different domains.[28] The concept's strategic value is also highlighted by those, like Pillippe Aigrain, who have long advocated for a "coalition of common goods" that unites ecologists fighting in defense of the "physical commons" and computer scientists struggling for the promotion of an "informational commons."[29]

Yet Naomi Klein's call to re-claim the category of the commons was also a call for a new connection between "local welfare" and the most abstract global processes, a veritable fusion of movements dedicated to defending or creating a more fulfilling, democratic, and autonomous way of life, and the struggle against the omnipotence of giant corporations.[30] What is especially attractive about the paradigm of the commons is therefore its ability to create connections between struggles against the most harmful aspects of neoliberalism (commodification, privatization, climate change, etc.) and struggles for a new form of social organization based on principles of solidarity, sharing, and respect for the environment and biodiversity. The defense of the commons is therefore inscribed in Klein's larger vision of a democracy completely re-grounded in the practice of local self-governance.[31] This is one of the most fundamental aspects of the return of the commons: it is no longer a question of appealing to the state to defend the people, but it is about promoting forms of democratic control over common resources. As Oscar Olivera, one of the Bolivian leaders of the "water war," cogently puts it:

> At the heart of the struggle over the privatization of water in Cochabamba was who would decide the present and the future of our population, who would control our resources and the conditions in which we live and work. We wanted to decide these questions by and for ourselves.[32]

A Renewed Struggle Against Neoliberalism

The emergence and global diffusion of the call to reclaim the commons is linked to a series of overlapping struggles in the 1990s, all of which were concerned, in one way or another, with the most harmful and intolerable aspects of neoliberal reform. And while the category of the "commons" was not always used by activists participating in struggles that took place between the end of the 1990s and the early 2000s, particularly in Latin America, a retroactive reading nevertheless reveals the presence of the category in these movements; the category can be symptomatically detected in the emergence of new organizations and movements that challenge both capitalist social relations, founded on the private ownership of resources, *and* traditional modes of managing "public goods" through state bureaucracies. This makes it possible to identify both the unity of this movement as well as its great variety, its constitution as a global field of struggle and its tendency to be localized and singular. In terms of this articulation between the "local" and the "global," the Zapatista movement is especially illustrative. The Zapatistas were especially known for the close links they sought to forge, both theoretically and practically, between the expropriated and exploited indigenous communities in Chiapas and a more general "struggle for humanity against neoliberalism." This is why the movement exerted such great influence on numerous intellectuals and activists, from the beginnings of its insurrection on January 1, 1994 – the day that the North American Free Trade Agreement (NAFTA) went into force – up until the beginning of the 2000s. The Zapatista's search for a new practical form of universalism, and their refusal to adopt the older organization forms of the Leninist or Guevarist types, soon became a globally resonant feature of all anti-neoliberal movements, and their preoccupation with the procedures for conducting discussion and decision-making became one of the hallmarks of anti-neoliberal and alter-globalization movements of the early twenty-first century.[33]

Because Latin America was the first region of the globe to be subjected to the harshest and most notorious neoliberal policies, such as the International Monetary Fund's (IMF) "structural adjustment programs," it was the region in which the first great popular movements contesting neoliberalism arose, and the region in which their first successes were won. The December 2001 insurrection in Buenos Aires, which ousted President Fernando de la Rua, comes immediately to mind. This insurrection inaugurated a period of extremely powerful mobilization across a diverse range of sectors in the Argentinian capital. The people gathered in hundreds of popular assemblies in the capital, alongside the unemployed "piqueteros" and other employees who occupied almost two hundred so-called "recuperated industries," which is the term used to denote industries placed under "worker management." But it is without doubt the Bolivian "water war," followed by the "gas war," that really began to popularize the "return of the commons" (even before the struggles in Italy over the re-municipalization of water) and provided hope for other victories elsewhere. Of all the events in Bolivia between 2000 and 2005 that led to mass protests over the privatization of water distribution in the city of Cochabamba (for the benefit of the American Bechtel corporation), as well as the national gas export treaty between the Bolivian government and a multinational consortium, we will only mention some of its more notable episodes and lessons. If, as Franck Poupeau has shown, the popular mobilization in Cochabamba did not create a completely new and durable political form,[34] it nonetheless produced practices and institutions of self-governance that deserve careful attention. The establishment of participant assemblies transformed water consumers into genuine "actors" invested in the management of their resource; these assemblies re-invigorated and re-activated older forms of community deliberation that were then combined with urban and unionist forms of democracy. What is especially striking is the compatibility between the struggle's objectives and the subjectivities of those mobilized by the movement, a compatibility that arose from the fact that the struggle's organization for the recuperation of the communal resources already laid the groundwork for its future management. For the struggle was not only economic and social, but concerned the general political form of society as such. Yet however advanced this Bolivian political process may have been, it was ultimately blocked by the prevalence of the "developmentalist" model, which ultimately endows the state with centralized control over resource management.

In the context of today's struggles, there is no doubt that statist solutions based on centralized administration, which massively informed leftist politics during the twentieth century, are still very powerful. But, at the same time, the re-configuration of the corporate state (i.e., its increasing alliance with economic oligopolies), and its subordination to the organizations and imperatives of the Washington Consensus and the European Union, has pushed left politics in new directions. Despite a variety of hesitations and confusions, the need to chart a new path was clearly manifest in the alter-globalization discourses and struggles of the 2000s. Eight years after the publication of Naomi Klein's article, the call to reclaim the "commons" was echoed in the "Reclaim the Commons" manifesto launched at the 2009 World Social Forum in Belem, Brazil:

> Humankind is suffering from an unprecedented campaign of privatization and commodification of the most basic elements of life: nature, culture, human work and knowledge itself. In countless arenas, businesses are claiming our shared inheritance – sciences, creative works, water, the atmosphere, health, education, genetic diversity, even living creatures – as private property. A compulsive quest for short-term financial gain is sacrificing the prosperity of all and the stability of the Earth itself. The dismal consequences of market enclosures can be seen in our declining ecosystems: the erosion of soil and biodiversity, global climate change, reduction of food sovereignty. Aggressive intellectual property politics harness those suffering from neglected diseases or who can't purchase patented medicines, reduce cultural diversity, limit access to knowledge and education, and promote a global consumerist culture.[35]

This manifesto echoes the themes found in the "Universal Declaration of the Common Good of Humanity," drafted by François Houtard and proposed at both the World Forum for Alternatives (which took place during the Rio+20 conference in June 2012) and at the World Social Forum in Tunis in 2013.[36] What is notable in this second manifesto, however, is that the common goods in question do not need to be identified one by one, but are rather collectively grouped within the general category of the "common good," whose natural foundation is Mother Earth. This is a discursive shift inspired by the indigenous movements of Latin America and was designed to "serve as the basis for the convergence of social and political movements."

The successful spread of the category of the commons, which by now is completely entrenched in the anti-globalization lexicon, was thus due in large measure to its seductive and "floating" character. All these manifestos and texts vacillate between the plural "commons" or "common goods" and the singular the "common good," as we pointed out above.[37] But what ultimately unites all of these terminological variations is the critical charge each iteration of the concept carries: they all communicate a rejection of the great neoliberal project of appropriation, and they even touch on the very justifications of capitalism itself. In short, to challenge the commons' enclosure is to question private property as the absolute condition of social wealth.

Property Rights and Competition Through Innovation

The debate concerning private property has undoubtedly shifted over the course of the last two centuries. Where the argument was once largely theological and moral in character,[38] it has gradually turned into an argument based on economic efficiency, and more specifically an argument about the role of the state in economic activity. During the first half of the twentieth century, Ludwig von Mises and Friedrich Hayek, amongst other theoreticians of contemporary capitalism, thoroughly and relentlessly attacked the practice of centralized state planning; the Friedmans, and others, subsequently attacked forms of state coercion exercised over our economic choices in their bestsellers.[39] In *Wealth and Poverty,* George F. Gilder paradigmatically explained how free-market capitalism is the best means to reduce poverty. All of this apologetic literature tried to ground capitalism's superiority over socialism in its increasing productive capacity and its superior potential for satisfying the population's needs. But these were not the most original texts when it came to defending private property and renewing the debate concerning the "commons." The article that played the leading role in this respect was American biologist Garrett Hardin's famous article "The Tragedy of the Commons," published in the journal *Science* in 1968. According to Hardin, the "commons" – a term that encompasses everything from the air we breathe, to national public parks, to social insurance mechanisms – are inevitably overexploited by rational individuals eager to maximize their personal gains at the expense of others. For Hardin, this behavior is the major reason why the prior rights and practices of the commons were abandoned in favor of individual property. It is one of the more interesting paradoxes of intellectual history that Hardin's aggressive attack against the commons was one of the central reasons for the "return of the commons" in later theoretical and political debates.[40]

But there was another theme that made it possible to re-invigorate the justification for property rights as well as broaden and reinforce this discourse over the past thirty years: the theme of *innovation*. The pioneer in this field was undoubtedly Joseph Schumpeter. For Schumpeter, the entrepreneur played a central role in all aspects of economic life. The entrepreneur was the premier agent of technological progress and the agent responsible for the cycles and inherent instability of capitalism. The "re-discovery" of Schumpeter's theses on the entrepreneur in the 1980s corresponded to a period of intensifying innovation-based competition amongst large multinationals. As Schumpeter had already observed, businesses invariably attempt to capture technological rents through the possession of patents, since the latter provide temporary monopolies of exploitation within a given market. Instead of condemning monopolies in the name of pure and perfect competition in ideal markets, Schumpeter urges us to consider the positive and beneficial effects of "practical monopolies" within the "perpetual storm" of "creative destruction" that is capitalism's dynamic.[41] We would do well to follow Schumpeter in understanding how competition between large corporations always presupposes the "organic" implementation of protection and restriction, which constitutes the very conditions of their dynamism. For it is precisely the protections provided by patents or other practices of secrecy that enable investment and innovation. To put it differently, as the risks produced by the competition these firms face invariably intensifies, firms are forced to consolidate various forms of monopoly practice to weather these storms.[42]

The revival of this economic argument was accompanied by a new historical discourse that views the strengthening of property rights as one of the most important factors in the West's economic take-off. Douglass C. North and Robert Paul Thomas are two such "neoinstitutionalist" economic historians who have re-read the development of Western economic growth as a function of property rights. North and Thomas propose an "exhaustive explanation" of economic history "consistent with and complimentary to standard neo-classical economic theory."[43] Their explanation is based on a simplified utilitarian hypothesis: "economic growth requires only that some part of the populace be acquisitive" and "if a society does not grow it is because no incentives are provided for economic initiative."[44] Economic growth, therefore, relies heavily on institutional arrangements that encourage personal enrichment. In contrast to much contemporary economic history, in which technology, economies of scale, or human capital are cited as the decisive factors in material progress, North and Thomas argue that institutions and property rights are the crucial criteria that explain the near-simultaneous economic trajectories of various European countries since the Middle Ages. Their rationale, which they suggest comes directly from Bentham, tells us that if we want to promote growth, "individuals must be lured by incentives to undertake the socially desirable activities."[45] The legal codification of property rights makes it possible to more directly link the gains and losses of economic activity to the individual who worked and invested. If the individual does not reap the fruits of his own activity, his desire for enrichment will not be encouraged.

The lesson to be drawn from this neoinstitutionalist scholarship is that only exclusive rights over land or production can incite individuals to act. As in Hardin's thesis, this rationale supposes individuals are responsive to only one type of motivation – financial motivation – and, more profoundly, it presupposes a universal "economic man" who can only realize his desire for enrichment through institutions and rights adequate to his nature. The error of this utilitarian "institutionalism" does not, however, lie in its overevaluation of the effects of institutions, but in conceiving of institutions as the result of a cost/benefit analysis and, in turn, as a reflection of the self-interested nature of the individual. The birth of the nation-state is thus analyzed as a consequence of the expansion of the market. Public goods like justice and the protection provided by the state are desired and paid for by taxes because they are more "profitable" than private protection and private justice.[46] Douglass and North, in this respect, offer a perfectly tautological definition of institutions:

> Throughout history, institutions have been devised by human beings to create order and reduce uncertainty in exchange. Together with the standard constraints of economics they define the choice set and therefore determine transaction and production costs and hence the profitability and feasibility of engaging in economic activity . . . Institutions provide the incentive structure of an economy; as that structure evolves, it shapes the direction of economic change towards growth, stagnation, or decline.[47]

North and Thomas do indeed admit that very particular historical conditions were necessary for the development of these exclusive rights and public protections; amongst these conditions, they especially cite demographics as a decisive variable. But the essence of North and Thomas's reasoning lies in the postulate of egoistic man, and so the differences in growth between countries are explicated by the attitude of the states that favor, in very different ways, the establishment and strengthening of property rights. For example, North and Thomas argue that the economies of France and Spain were stagnant for long periods because of their incapacity to create a system of rights that stimulated economic productivity, in contrast to the economies of England or the Netherlands.[48] And North and Thomas attach great importance to the creation of new kinds of property rights in the seventeenth century, namely patents and their subsequent integration into common law. They speak especially highly of the ability of patents to guarantee inventors a greater and greater portion of the profits drawn from the economic exploitation of their inventions.[49] Without overestimating the impact of these neoinstitutionalist theses – which the authors describe as "revolutionary"[50] – it is worth observing the extent to which these kinds of readings are manifestations of a marked modification of the classical understanding of the industrial revolution: it was neither the eighteenth nor the nineteenth centuries that "invented" capitalism, according to such revised interpretations, but it was the transformation of institutional frameworks during the previous centuries that led to economic growth. The political conclusion to be drawn from such analyses is clear: prosperity is always dependent on the organization of productive property rights and, in particular, a "system of property rights to define the gains of innovation and to see that they accrue to the individuals who undertake such innovation."[51]

Neoliberal historians seeking to re-write economic history from the perspective of property rights have thus, from a certain point of view, adopted the same position established by Bentham two centuries earlier. If an individual is born with certain dispositions that lead him to pursue his own self-interest – even if only out of concern for his own physical preservation – it is only in society, and by virtue of the juridical guarantees society offers, that he truly becomes an economic man capable of rationally pursuing his own calculated self-interest. And of course the rise of this new economic institutionalism was not a matter of sheer happenstance. Its arguments were formulated at the same time as patents – the insurance instrument of large corporations *par excellence* – were beginning to become a major strategic tool in global economic competition, as is amply demonstrated by the sharp rise in the number of patents granted around the world over the last three decades. This shift in economic theory and practice is also illustrated by series of related policy changes in the United States during the 1970s and 1980s, such as the extension of patentability into new domains, particularly in the arts, literature, and intellectual life generally, but also into the field of biological life. New commercial processes, software, and even the substances contained in plants have since become patentable by categorizing these scientific "discoveries" as marketable inventions. Similarly, the rights of patent holders have not only been strengthened, both at the national and international level, but the duration of patents have been extended, and the courts adjudicating disputes are increasingly sympathetic to those complaining about counterfeit or fraud. And lastly, public institutions seeking more funding – universities and public research institutions in particular – are now required to file patents under the regulations enacted in the Bayh-Dole Act (1980) in the United States.[52]

The Demand for the Commons Against "Intellectual Property"

We mentioned above how the return of the commons paradigm corresponded to the recognition of the enormous theft perpetrated by economic oligopolies actively supported by governing elites. We should take note, however, of the fact that the critique's attack is in fact more precise: the strategy of the commons focuses on one of the major tendencies of past three decades, namely the strengthening of property rights in the fields of information, knowledge, and culture, and by extension over the elements of life itself – in short, the strengthening of "intellectual property" by neoliberal governments. On this point, American legal theorist James Boyle's commentary is particularly enlightening. According to Boyle, the first enclosure movement concerned land, while the second concerns the "intangible commons of the mind." The increased number of patents filed in the United States and elsewhere testifies to the accelerated pace of juridical enclosures within the intellectual domain. The result has been a global market in property rights pertaining to knowledge. Or, more exactly, patents have made it possible to create markets in knowledge by legally classifying knowledge of a specialized, codifiable, and marketable type. The argumentative basis for the extension of this type of market, and the concomitant transformation of knowledge this type of market requires, is grounded in the language of *competition*: the countries or businesses that do not establish such enclosures are condemned to lose ground in the world market.

The enclosure of the intellectual domain has opened entire fields of life and culture to the lucrative activities of private business. Patents granted to sequence the human genome, the extension and prolonged duration of copyright law, and the enhancement of trademark protections are just a few examples of the much larger trend whereby developed countries are engaged in a veritable war to blanket the globe's economic, social, and cultural terrain with exclusive patents. This conflict is evident in the regulatory and organizational changes that now subject public research institutions and universities to the trade secrecy laws, and it is manifest in the establishment of international accords aimed at generalizing restrictive re-interpretations of property laws. The 1992 NAFTA, followed by the Agreement on Trade-Related Aspects of Intellectual Property Rights (TRIPS) in 1994 – both of which coincided with the creation of the WTO – were two watershed moments that led to a whole series of other bilateral accords promoting trade liberalization. These accords were expressly directed against the "developmentalist" tendencies of post-colonial states in the 1960s and 1970s, particularly in terms of the sweeping legislation passed in these states to accelerate transfers of technology and establish systems of public health. Since the 1980s, however, the most powerful countries in the global North have reversed these trends by acquiring an array of mechanisms designed to exert pressure and impose sanctions on developmentalist states, largely through rules that prioritize remuneration on technological rents and corporate brands for wealthy states.[53]

Yet it is precisely this strategic alliance between multinational corporations and governments on the matter of "intellectual property rights" that unifies the various movements reclaiming the commons. By extending the reach of property to include new objects, and by transforming the theory and practice of property rights, these efforts compelled a response as universal as that of the commons. The term "intellectual property" was first introduced during the founding of the World Intellectual Property Organization (WIPO), a United Nations dependent organization, in 1967. But it was during the Uruguay Round negotiations, which led to the creation of the WTO and the signing of TRIPS in 1994, that numerous leisure and mass entertainment industries, along with pharmaceutical, agro-chemical, and information technology and biotechnology firms, all agreed to make "intellectual property" a major focus of international trade agreements, over and above their various differences of opinion and the competitive nature of their economic interrelations. As has been well documented, this corporate alliance successfully fused together two distinct kinds of rights that were previously inscribed in distinctive registers as a result of their distinctive histories: "literary and artistic property," which protects the "right of the author" – the Anglo-Saxon version of which is copyright – and "industrial property" which is protected by patents.[54] This fusion between what had hitherto been the purview of artistic creation and that which had been associated with industrial manufacturing was made possible by an increasing number of discourses that articulated scientific discovery, academic and traditional knowledge, trademarks, etc. as all belonging to the relatively new category of "information." These new forms of "information" account for an increasingly large share of the value produced in the "knowledge economy" and consequently it must be protected with increasing vigor. The creation and subsequent strengthening of intellectual property rights has extended the logic of value into vast "immaterial" domains by invoking the need for a system of legal restrictions and temporary reservations that are increasingly numerous and narrowly defined. As Maurice Cassier argues with respect to the patent:

> The justification [for these rights] is no longer the author or the inventor, it is the investor. Lawyers have observed that the patent is an economic tool for market manipulation, one that it makes it possible to create, extend, and protect markets. It is a new model that is being put into place. Research investments must be recuperated according to the problematic of return on investment, rather than the older model that rewards the inventor.[55]

Mikhaïl Xifaras has similarly documented the multiple phases involved in the creation of copyright (rights of the author) that were not immediately assimilated into intellectual property statutes. In his view, a veritable "theoretical revolution" occurred when these temporary privileges were transformed into property:

> Property now means exclusive ownership rather than physical control, and creator's rights have become archetypal. And as purely nominal as the term may be, the triumph of the term "intellectual property" was of great practical importance. It is now generally agreed that it contributes considerably to the extension of these rights to new objects, it helps to strengthen the prerogatives of their owners, it brings about a convergence of the different legal regimes dealing with various types of creator's rights, and it provides ideological support for the legitimacy of these rights ("property" sounds a lot better than "temporary monopoly").[56]

The most striking example of this converged and reinforced regime of intellectual property rights is the private appropriation of life itself. It was traditionally considered self-evident that living beings were not patentable because patents, save rare exceptions, only applied to technical creations of an industrial nature. The basis for this traditional interpretation, as Maurice Cassier points out, is the conviction that "nature that develops outside of human activity belongs to the common good; it is inappropriable, it is the domain of discovery."[57] The first ruptures with this traditional approach occurred in the interwar years with regards to seeds, but it was in the 1980s that the traditional interpretation was substantially overruled after the United States Supreme Court granted a patent on a bacterium, on the pretext of human modification. This new interpretation shattered the distinction between discovery and invention, and a path was cleared for the patentability of all life, since, as Cassier again puts it, "everything that is in nature that is extracted, isolated, rendered accessible and even made better by the inventor may now be subject to patents." The most famous and the most controversial case involves Myriad Genetics, which held a monopoly on the genes responsible for breast and ovary cancer, and accordingly enjoyed a monopoly over testing and research concerning at-risk populations. The American Supreme Court eventually revoked this monopoly in June 2013, and thereby permitted competitive research concerning these specific genes, though this decision hardly challenged private genetic ownership as such.

The race for patents is based on the principle of "biopiracy," whereby firms from the global North exploit the "biological and genetic reserves" of the countries of the global South, and file patents on substances or genes to ensure ownership over any marketable applications arising from these resources. This patenting involves the transformation of indigenous knowledge into the inventions of Western firms, such that local populations are prohibited from using the properties of plant life by international trade agreements. One of the most exemplary cases of this practice concerns neem, a plant that has been used in India for thousands of years, and whose applications include agriculture, medicine, and cosmetics. Communities in India have used neem for varying purposes for many centuries, but in the past few years the properties of neem have been subject to sixty-four exclusive patents owned by several private corporations.

The agricultural giant W.R. Grace, which holds a patent on the fungicidal properties of neem, installed a neem seed-processing plant that captured a large portion of available neem seed. This drove up prices and restricted free uses of the plant. Yet the massive mobilization of Indian society, which received global media attention, successfully resulted in the patent's annulment by the European Patent Office. The patent was annulled on the basis of a Vedic manuscript that showed that the virtues of the fungicide had been known in India for centuries. Unfortunately, as the French Collective Against Biopiracy points out, "most traditional knowledge is without written record, and thus it finds itself in a difficult situation in the legal world of patents."[58]

One of the most remarkable aspects of this appropriation of life is without doubt the manner in which firms like Monsanto have, since the 1980s, become veritable "Gods of Life," in the words of Vandana Shiva, for millions of farmers who have become dependent on patented and commercialized seeds. These patented seeds have the extraordinary characteristic, as spelled out by the international legal framework for intellectual property, of not being able to be renewed or re-used by farmers. These patents thus deprive farmers of their knowledge, experience, and ultimately any sovereignty over their production. By favoring monocultures, the commercialized seeds of Monsanto – along with three other firms that have cornered the world seed market – have fundamentally altered agriculture in numerous countries. In India, for instance, Monsanto controls 95 percent of cotton production. Rising costs, which are a consequence of royalties owed to these multinational firms, have pushed numerous peasants into debt and ruin. This extreme dependence resulted in a wave of suicides that eventually compelled the Indian authorities to question the deregulation of the seed market.[59]

The "Grand Narrative" of the Expropriation of the Commons

We have just seen how the return of the commons paradigm corresponds to a very precise historical conjuncture in which the control of strategic resources – such as "knowledge" – by private business has become an essential competitive asset. What remains to be seen, however, is the usefulness of this historical reference to the commons that forms the basis of this new paradigm. Can we be sure the overall transformations of capitalism we are witnessing are best understood through past historical experiences such as the enclosure of communal lands?

In order to arrive at a conclusion, we would do well to recall some of the classic expositions dedicated to the birth of agricultural capitalism in Europe. These accounts are especially useful for highlighting the social violence wrought by the enclosure movement and the expropriation of peasant land.[60] The first exposition we should consider is the famous passage from Thomas More's *Utopia* (1516) in which More denounces all the groups and individuals whose behavior brings harm upon one's country. Alongside the pestering nobility and the carnivorous mercenaries and brigands, More speaks of the greedy monopolization of the land for the purposes of sheep breeding. The greatest evil, as he conveys to one of his interlocutors, comes from the flocks of sheep blanketing England: "'your sheep,' I said, 'that are commonly so meek and eat so little; now, as I hear, they have become so greedy and fierce that they devour human beings themselves. They devastate and depopulate fields, houses and towns."[61] More proceeds to describe this race to monopolize land in the following terms:

> For in whatever parts of the land sheep yield the finest and thus the most expensive wool, there the nobility and the gentry, yes, and even a good many abbots – holy men – are not content with the old rents that the land yielded to their predecessors. Living in idleness and luxury without doing society any good no longer satisfies them; they have to do positive harm. For they leave no land free for the plough: they enclose every acre of pasture; they destroy houses and abolish towns, keeping the churches – but only for sheep-barns.[62]

In More's view, this practice of land hoarding is one of the worst acts of violence committed against the peasantry, and has the most sinister of consequences not only for the peasants but for society as a whole:

> Thus, so that one greedy, insatiable glutton, a frightful plague to his native country, may enclose thousands of acres within a single fence, the tenants are ejected; and some are stripped their belongings by trickery or force, or, wearied by constant harassment, are driven to sell them. One way or another, these wretched people – men, women, husbands, wives, orphans, widows, parents with little children and entire families (poor but numerous, since farming requires many hands) – are forced out.[63]

Four centuries later, Karl Polanyi described the consequences of enclosure in essentially the same terms:

> Enclosures have appropriately been called a revolution of the rich against the poor. The lords and nobles were upsetting the social order, breaking down ancient law and custom, sometimes by means of violence, often by pressure and intimidation. They were literally robbing the poor of their share of the common, tearing down the houses which, by the hitherto unbreakable force of custom, the poor had long regarded as theirs and their heirs'. The fabric of society was being disrupted; desolate villages and the ruins of human dwellings testified to the fierceness with which the revolution raged, endangering the defences of the country, wasting its towns, decimating its population, turning its overburdened soil into dust, harassing its people and turning them from decent husbandmen into a mob of beggars and thieves.[64]

These passages, by More and Polanyi, are all the more remarkable insofar as one might be forgiven for believing that they were not, in fact, denunciations of the invasion of English lands by sheep, but accounts of the destructive effects of genetically modified maize and soybeans and their associated herbicides on peasant communities in India or Latin America.

Marx likewise described some of the most striking examples of this form of expropriation in Chapter 26 of *Capital* (vol. 1). Given the fact that widespread theft was necessary for the development of capitalism, Marx describes, in great detail, the historical process that deprived small landowners of the collective use of common lands and facilitated their expulsion from rural communities. Before the economic violence of the modern factory began to absorb and oppress England's "free laborers," Marx explains how these workers first had to be cut off from the possibility of working and subsisting in their rural communities and villages. In order to "liberate" workers from their dependent relationship on their family, clan, village, artisanal gild, or the land – thereby producing "the fundamental conditions of capitalist production"[65] – it was first necessary to destroy older forms of feudal and communal existence. Marx recounts how, from the fifteenth and sixteenth centuries onwards, mass populations of independent peasants, farmers, and agricultural workers were driven from their lands by the concentration of landed property and the replacement of feudal property rights with modern property rights. One of the consequences of this economic and social transformation was the abolition of communal lands and customs, along with the appropriation of Church land during the Protestant Reformation and the capture of other lands by the state. The enclosure of communal lands and the introduction of large-scale pastures are cited by Marx as amongst the most important factors for spurring on the economic revolution that created the underlying conditions for modern capitalism.

In contrast to the idyllic narratives of the bourgeois economists, who imagined capitalism as arising from the wisdom of the most meritorious and prudent laborers, Marx insists that the "so-called" original accumulation, as favorably described by these economists, in fact arose through violence and dispossession. "In actual history," writes Marx, "it is a notorious fact that conquest, enslavement, robbery, murder, in short, force, play the greatest part."[66] This plunder initially proceeded by sporadic and "independent methods" but, by the eighteenth century, it was a large-scale and entirely legal operation.[67] Based on historical documentation, Marx recounts the "whole series of thefts, outrages, and popular misery that accompanied the forcible expropriation of the people, from the last third of the fifteenth century to the end of the eighteenth century."[68] This theft continued in an entirely legal fashion well into the nineteenth century through the "clearing" of the countryside, which is to say the removal of the now-unproductive inhabitants that remained on the land. As Marx underscores, the consequences of this theft of communal land were numerous: lower wages for day laborers, the impoverishment of small landowners and farmers, rural exodus, the desertification of the countryside, and the creation of a superfluous population without house or home. The usurpation of communal lands allowed large-scale farmers to convert their smaller holdings into much larger herds of livestock, which increased the amount of fertilizer necessary for land cultivation and this in turn increased yields and incomes.

All of this, for Marx, is a form of "expropriation . . . written in the annals of mankind in letters of blood and fire."[69] The implementation of new relations of production in both the countryside and the city constituted a mode of "extra-economic force" that preceded the development of the capitalist system – yet once the latter was sufficiently developed, it exercised its own "economic" violence over those it subdued and this, in general, sufficed to maintain social order: "the silent compulsion of economic relations sets the seal on the domination of the capitalist over the worker."[70] During the phase preceding the development of capitalist relations, however, it was the most naked private and government violence that reigned over and oppressed the poor, the beggars and vagabonds, as well as the urban workers who tried to maintain professional workers' associations. The social relation between capital and labor, which rests upon a vast market in which workers are compelled to buy the products of their labor, now contrarily assumes an air of justice and equality: the peaceful exchange of equivalents according to contractual rules. The initial theft that first subdued the masses was thus repressed and erased from history. It was precisely with this historical process in mind, and within the limits of this context, that Marx took up Proudhon's famous assertion: "Property is theft!"

Yet unlike Proudhon, Marx did not idealize or lament the passing of this prior state of communal property. What Marx was more interested in was the "historical process of divorcing the producer from the means of production."[71] What was fundamentally important for Marx was the suppression of the peasantry's private property, which was a form of private property that only existed in the form of the commons:

> What does the primitive accumulation of capital, i.e., its historical genesis, resolve itself into? In so far as it is not the direct transformation of slaves and serfs into wage-labourers, and therefore a mere change of form, it only means the expropriation of the immediate producers i.e., *the dissolution of private property based on the labour of its owner*.[72]

The historical sequence of Marx's argument is based on a succession of three discrete moments linked together by the logic of the "negation of the negation": in the first instance we have private, individual ownership of the means of production based on labor itself. This initial moment is then followed by capitalist private property based on the expropriation of small proprietors, and then the third moment in this logical sequence concludes with the social ownership of the means of production.[73] The mass expropriation from which capitalism was created was thus based on the destruction of the direct link between labor and property. Unlike Proudhon, Marx did not defend this direct relationship between the small proprietor, his means of production, and the fruits of his labor. For, on the contrary, preserving this direct relationship would amount to curbing the historical tendency toward the concentration of capital and the socialization of the workers – and thereby delay the ultimate moment in which "the expropriators are expropriated." The logic of Marx's thinking is essential here: capitalism is far more a social product than the prior mode of production it destroyed (and which was condemned by history in any case). Only the myopic economists believe capitalism is the reign of private property in general. For Marx, capitalism is more fundamentally defined by the *destruction* of private property for the immediate producers. The destruction of the commons is thus not, in itself, an historical aberration. These commons were residual sites harboring older modes of social relations of production; while they allowed small peasants to subsist on their land, they also keep them economically stagnant and even condemned them to intellectual and political idiocy. Suffice it to say that Marx naturally viewed the ostensible improvement of cultivating methods made possible by the enclosure movement as a fallacious argument for its justification.[74] Nonetheless, for Marx, the development of the forces of production historically justifies the disappearance of the commons and, along with it, a rural way of life condemned by the subsumption of older communal goods within the market and the transformation of peasants into proletarians.

The concept of the "commons" thus hardly appears in Marx's conception of historical evolution (or at least within his more theoretical work). The communist revolution does not attempt to "return" to the commons condemned by the forward march of history. For Marx, the traditional commons have no place in future societies because their suppression played a decisive role in the process of historical evolution he narrates: this great act of *predation* was, indeed, a condition of expropriation. The idea that the suppression of the commons was necessary will remain a key element of Marxism, at least in its more orthodox versions.[75] Other authors, however, have since challenged this view, such as Karl Polanyi in *The Great Transformation*. While Polanyi linked the expropriation of the peasants to the creation of a market in land, he nonetheless broke with Marx's linear conception of historical development. By interpreting the great political upheavals of the twentieth century as reactions against the commodification of both humanity and nature within the context of a market society, and essentially as attempts to build firewalls that would impede capitalism's spread, Polanyi gave socialism a completely different meaning. And even Marx himself seems to have at least partially repented in this respect. In his famous letters to Vera Zassoulitch, he argued that the vestiges of communal property in Russia could serve as the basis of a communist revolution, which of course runs completely counter to the historical schema of successive modes of production he persistently defended throughout his life.[76]

Imperialism as the Exacerbation of Capitalist Violence

Marx was not, however, content to confine this vast exercise of plunder to capitalism's beginning alone. Colonization, for Marx, entailed the same process of generalized theft, though now on a global scale, and re-focusing on the extraction of precious metals, the transfer of raw materials to industry, and of course the slave trade. While Marx thus anticipated much of the anti-colonialist and anti-imperialist literature of the second half of the twentieth century,[77] he nonetheless maintained a distinct division between these two phases of capitalist development. The first phase is marked, as we have just described, by the predominance of "extra-economic violence" necessary for the mass expropriation of small, independent producers. The second phase is characterized by the prevalence of economic violence issuing from the relation between capital and labor within a matured capitalist economy. In *The Accumulation of Capital* (1913), Rosa Luxemburg challenges this evolutionary chronology by arguing that capitalism continues to plunder resources from non- or pre-capitalist zones alongside the everyday extraction of surplus value.[78] For Luxemburg, capitalism can only expand by subordinating regions or groups outside itself not yet composed of workers or capitalists. Put differently, the destruction of the peasantry and artisan industry, colonization, and territorial conquest are not confined to the early phase of capitalist development: they are permanent features of capitalism as such. This is why imperialism is necessary and why the developed capitalist powers are compelled to take control of territories, through acts of brutal violence, that are not yet structured by the mechanisms of capitalist exploitation. This also explains the domestic colonialism carried out in the rural territories controlled by each capitalist nation-state. For Luxemburg, all of these processes are merely a temporary stop-gap delaying the inevitable collapse of capitalism: for once all these territories are conquered, there will longer be any "outside" in which capital can offload its products and make a profit.

Luxemburg's work thus shifts analysis away from the historical roots of capitalism and compels us to look at the ongoing conditions of its continued expansion. Capitalism can only continue to prosper, argues Luxemburg, through its connection with the "non-capitalist milieu": "capitalism in its full maturity also depends in all respects on non-capitalist strata and social organizations existing side by side with it."[79] The means to achieve this end are manifold: selling goods, stealing local resources, or uprooting populations and transforming them into new proletarians. This leads to a continuous destruction of the patriarchal peasant economy: "the second condition of importance for acquiring means of production and realising the surplus value is that commodity exchange and commodity economy should be introduced in societies based on natural economy as soon as their independence has been abrogated, or rather in the course of this disruptive process."[80]

Louis Althusser similarly described the importance of this theme when he wrote about Marx's discussion of primitive accumulation in *Capital* (vol. 1).

> This means was the most brutal violence: the thefts and massacres, which cleared capitalism's royal road into human history. This last chapter contains a prodigious wealth which has not yet been exploited: in particular the thesis (which we shall have to develop) that capitalism has always used and, in the 'margins' of its metropolitan existence – i.e., in the colonial and ex-colonial countries – is still using well into the twentieth century, *the most brutally violent means*.[81]

In his attempt to renew Marxian analyses of the "extra-economic violence" in the 1960s and 1970s, Althusser mainly trained his attention on capital's colonial "peripheries." His analysis was thus much more restrictive than that of Luxemburg, whose consideration of the processes of domination and destruction also included all that which is not yet capitalist within the capitalist countries themselves.

"Dispossession" as a Typical Mode of Accumulation for Financial Capitalism

The arrival of the neoliberal phase of capitalism has led numerous authors and activists to describe the increasing commodification of social and cultural life, and to describe neoliberal privatization as a new form of domestic colonization that is strikingly similar to that described in Luxemburg's analysis. One of the more prominent of these authors is David Harvey. Harvey, who is associated with the alter-globalization movement, developed a theory of "accumulation by dispossession" that is especially relevant to our discussion. While Harvey is wary of analogies with "enclosures" and "commons" – he rightly argues that all "commons" are not analogous to the pastures described by Garrett Hardin[82] – he is nonetheless inclined to use the analogy of the enclosure of the commons to describe neoliberal privatization,[83] particularly in terms of the importance of dispossession within the neoliberal phase. Harvey even goes so far as to describe neoliberalism as a specific mode of accumulation that, alongside exploitation, characterizes the extended process of reproduction analyzed by Marx in his major critiques of political economy. For Harvey, then, dispossession is not a form of primitive accumulation confined to capitalism's past, but a permanent form of capital accumulation. And during the current era of financial capitalism, dispossession tends to become a dominant mode of accumulation, which explains the "new wave of 'enclosing the commons.'"[84]

Let's examine Harvey's thesis in more detail. The predatory logic signified by the concept of "dispossession" is not characteristic of early capitalism alone. Rather, it is the continuous effect produced by the expansion of capitalism in the natural environment, in culture, and in social relations. Following Luxemburg, Harvey distinguishes between two "aspects" of an "organic process": "accumulation by enlarged reproduction" – i.e., extracting profit through normal economic activity – and "accumulation by dispossession" – i.e., theft facilitated by financial speculation and manipulation under the combined aegis of financial institutions and state power. Harvey refers to this partnership as the "state-finance nexus" and it acts, in his view, as the "central nervous system for capitalist accumulation.[85] In other words, finance is empowered by its association with the state and through its ability to overaccumulate as a result of extended reproduction, and it is under these conditions that dispossession becomes a dominant mode of accumulation.

In fact, Harvey argues that dispossession is one of the most generalized processes in human history, and thus extends well beyond the framework of capitalism alone. But it nonetheless plays a major role in the evolution of capitalism, insofar as it allows the system to expand and accelerate the concentration of ownership and the centralization of capital. Accumulation by dispossession continues to function at the periphery through the theft of resources and the destruction of cultures, and it is also exercised at the very heart of the global economic system through the elimination of the smallest and weakest proprietors, as is manifest during economic crises when smaller shareholders and individual owners are plundered *en masse* by hedge funds and banks. This predatory logic is also facilitated by governmental actions, such as when public-sector pensions are replaced by private insurance schemes, or when public universities are weakened in order to benefit private institutions. And accumulation by dispossession is realized through the private appropriation of public spaces, natural resources, and scientific research. In short, accumulation by dispossession is at work wherever capital is not merely content to reproduce itself, but seeks to extend and deepen its control over nature and society through the combined pressures of competition and profitability.

Accumulation by dispossession thus denotes an increase in value that is not realized by the classical, endogenous mechanisms of capitalist exploitation, but by a combination of political and economic means that allow the ruling class to seize, free of charge if possible, that which was not previously owned or that which was formerly public property or part of the collective cultural or social heritage. The great interest in the concept of "accumulation by dispossession" is therefore not merely a function of its ability to renew Rosa Luxemburg's analysis; it is also due to the fact that it accounts for the specific neoliberal practices of privatizing state-run services, bureaucracies, insurance institutions, and healthcare and educational institutions. Indeed, enlarging the domains of possible economic predation is, for Harvey, the principle characteristic of neoliberalism. If capitalism needs to constantly reproduce itself outside the geographical territory or social groups already under its domination, as Luxemburg already showed, it must also renew, deepen, and strengthen its grip within the countries already under its control. And the stage of financial capitalism is precisely characterized by the necessity of this new process of dispossession: any aspect of social life that has hitherto managed to escape capitalist domination is now experiencing some form or another of economic colonization.

In Harvey's account, crises of capital are not so much crises of the overproduction of goods in the context of underconsumption by mass exploited workers, as Rosa Luxemburg argued, but crises of the overaccumulation of capital. On this point, Harvey remains entirely faithful to the Marxian analysis of the contradictions of capitalism: neoliberal practices of global dispossession are the direct response to the problem of endemic surpluses of capital that lack sufficient outlets for profitable investment:

> What accumulation by dispossession does is to release a set of assets (including labor power) at very low (and in some instances zero) cost. Overaccumulated capital can seize hold of such assets and immediately turn them to profitable use . . . Privatization (of social housing, telecommunications, transportation, water, etc. in Britain, for example) has, in recent years, opened up vast fields of overaccumulated capital to seize upon. The collapse of the Soviet Union and then the opening up of China entailed a massive release of hitherto unavailable assets into the mainstream of capital accumulation. What would have happened to over-accumulated capital these last thirty years if these new terrains of accumulation had not opened up?[86]

While Harvey recognizes great diversity in the concrete acts of dispossession, as well as the contingent character of many of the events that have contributed to the development of this process, he nevertheless observes the coherence of these processes as collective response (i.e., market liberalization and privatization) to an underlying economic contradiction. At base, then, that which seems most original in Harvey's theory of "accumulation by dispossession" is in fact that which is most consonant with traditional Marxist theory: the state is certainly able to act in a great many ways, yet it acts more or less as the visible hand guiding the logic of capital.

If Harvey insists so forcefully on the global dimension of neoliberalism, it is because he is primarily concerned with strategy. The weakening of the labor movement means there is no pre-defined social or political subject that will lead large-scale anti-capitalist struggle. Hence Harvey's interest in theorizing the capacity of the "dispossessed" in all walks of life to collectively take on neoliberal capitalism – especially in a post–2008 period of aggressive political austerity that is accelerating this global process of dispossession. Might we witness a grand alliance of all the victims of neoliberal dispossession? Could such an alliance repeat the popular struggles against the enclosure movement described by historians such as Thompson, Hill, or Tilly? We will not enter into this debate here, nor will we spend much time analyzing the very orthodox manner in which Harvey describes dispossession as "positive" whenever it happens to hasten the arrival of socialism.[87] It will suffice here simply to take note of the manner in which the theme of theft and predation has "crystalized" in contemporary Marxism. Yet this thematic also poses a fundamental problem: the analogical framework of the expropriation of the "commons" tends to analytically privilege practices of "theft" and "pillage" while downplaying the classical analysis of worker exploitation under neoliberal conditions.

The Limits of the "Enclosure" Paradigm

New forms of political action always need to invent their own language and rhetoric, and this is often accomplished by re-connecting with past experiences and prior analyses. There is nothing inherently wrong with this as such. However, we should always interrogate what kinds of thoughts a borrowed vocabulary permits and, accordingly, what kinds of thoughts it prevents. There is no doubt that the thematic of "theft," "plunder," and "enclosures" dominates contemporary critical analyses of neoliberalism. And while the more productive aspects of "commoning" are not ignored entirely (as is largely the case above), they are often relegated to the background, given the obvious difficulty of foregrounding these aspects within an essentially negative discourse of the commons. Harvey is undeniably an excellent interpreter of this new critical spirit. His analysis is undoubtedly one of the more theoretically sound accounts of the present but, nonetheless, are we sure it is completely adequate to the reality with which we are currently dealing? Harvey's account suggests we are largely confronted with financial capitalism's conquest of the public domain and other common goods as a result of the overaccumulation of capital within the systemic core of finance capital. Yet this type of analysis is not particularly good at making concrete connections between these practices of privatization and what is going on within the so-called normal sites and processes of capitalism – in private businesses, in labor relations, in the labor market, and even within public services under attack by New Public Management (all of which is described at length within an abundant sociological and economic literature). At base, the idea that the enclosure movement is the principle form of capitalist accumulation today corresponds to a very specific conception of capital that tends to privilege urban, ecological, and cultural struggles, especially insofar as these struggles portend greater hope – or at least more radical activism – than modes of resistance to new forms of capitalist exploitation within businesses and bureaucracies themselves. It also corresponds to a historical moment more marked by the defense of all those aspects of quotidian life not yet completely subsumed by capital, rather than an offensive mobilization waged by those directly dependent on capital's logic – namely private-sector wage earners and, increasingly, public-sector workers under the thumb of neoliberal management. And third, this specific conception corresponds to a moment in which public ownership of the economy no longer appears to offer the solution it once did during the heyday of socialism and the labor movement. On all these points, Harvey's work is terrifically lucid. He is also particularly aware that the new struggles, the diversity of which testifies to the scope of contemporary dispossession, are searching for an alternative vision other than the socialism or communism of the past two centuries. But he fails to see how the essentially negative approach, grounded in a discourse of dispossession or enclosure, is insufficient to constitute a new alternative vision.[88]

The ultimate question that arises, then, is whether we have not simply replaced an exhausted alternative to capitalism with another paradigm that will only lead us toward another theoretical and political impasse. The first paradigm, as described above, was the logic of Marxism in its dominant version, wherein the common is conceived as an objective product of capital. This path that takes us beyond capital from *within*. The second paradigm of thought subscribes to the notion that the common can only be recovered, *stricto sensu*, from capital's outside. In this view, defending and developing the commons that exists outside of capitalism is sufficient to overcome capitalism. This is the path of *diffusion from the outside*. For many, the latter option is the only alternative path that is conceivable today, given how so-called "collective" property has only resulted in bureaucratic state capitalism. As Naomi Klein argued, the anti-globalization movement seeks to protect the world from generalized privatization and defend local resources and spaces: protecting the world means defending small, isolated commons. But should the strategy of the "commons" be reduced to the creation of small, isolated pockets – which undoubtedly echoes both the Zapatistas and online hacker communities – in the hopes that practices of sharing and solidarity will begin to take root outside the dual logic of property and the state? As John Holloway aptly put in in his famous phrase, this strategy amounts to an attempt "to change the world without taking power."[89] As seductive as this formula is, it nonetheless fails to interrogate the domination of capital over labor and the effects of statism on society, and how these modes of power might be overcome. For it is far from certain that, in order to theorize new forms of struggle and conceive new alternatives, we should ignore the manner in which capital currently exercises domination over labor in private business and in a state sector increasingly subject to the logic of competition and corporate management. The fact is that neoliberal capitalism simply cannot be reduced to processes of "enclosure" and "dispossession." While there is no doubt such phenomena should not be relegated to the pre-history of industrial capitalism, they are by no means the only new forms of domination and exploitation at work within private businesses and the state sector. We must recall, in this respect, that the job of theoretical critique is to establish connections between contemporary processes of appropriation and subjectification, not dissociate them.

We have seen how appropriation has intensified as the result of increased competition between states and oligopolies all vying for control over sources of profit and rent. Seizing control of sources of rent and reinforcing property rights to ensure monopolistic rents are, in the hands of capitalist actors and other forms of power, instruments of war waged against society as a whole. The geographical extension and local intensification of capitalist relations now go hand in hand, and this is undoubtedly why analyses of primitive accumulation are still important and useful. As soon as we recognize that primitive accumulation is not merely one phase within a larger periodization of capitalism but an intrinsic characteristic of capital's ongoing reproduction, accumulation can then be seen as a continuous process designed to separate individuals from the conditions and means of production they have inherited – or developed through struggle – for living in a relatively autonomous fashion from the capitalist apparatus of production and consumption.[90] Marx understood primitive accumulation – the inaugural separation of individuals from the means of production – as the underlying historical condition necessary for the development of capitalism and its indispensable condition as it continues to reproduce and expand. Marx thus considered this process to be a continuation of the initial historical rupture introduced by primitive accumulation.[91] We can see today how this process of separation has expanded toward a whole array of conditions that allow people to live in relative autonomy from capital: the means and conditions for insuring against the risks of everyday life, consumption, healthcare, education, entertainment, communication, etc. But we must also recognize that this process of separation is not only a form of dispossession: it also introduces new relations of dependence and submission and, as a result, produces a more general modification of our social bonds, identities, and subjectivities. And this is precisely what Marx meant by the extended reproduction of capital: once capital begins to function according to its own laws of unlimited accumulation, it never ceases to produce the conditions of its own reproduction.[92] And amongst these conditions, capitalism produces the type of individuals it requires, in this case the "free laborer" forced to sell his labor power. As we will see below, one of the conditions of capitalism's continued reproduction today is not so much the "theft" of that which is outside it – whether we call it "life" or "knowledge" is not particularly important – but rather the imposition of a more complete submission, and radical transformation, of society and subjectivity in relation to capital.

At the same time, however, we must take note of the significant rupture the paradigm of the commons introduces into the Marxian conception of primitive accumulation. Marx only considered the expropriation of small, independent producers by capital, which is to say small private property based on individual labor. The commons, for Marx, were never anything more than the collective condition of individual independence, the very independence that the abolition of the commons destroyed in the process of creating the "free laborers" necessary for capitalism to function. This is not the situation we face any longer. The relative autonomy that has been won by workers, which is to say by the workers already separated from their means of production, does not only concern small individual proprietors, but what Robert Castel refers to as the "social property" of workers within the context of a "wage society."[93] The social struggles of the nineteenth and twentieth centuries led to the creation of a set of bureaucratically administered rights, titles, and services concerning education, healthcare, workers rights, social housing, etc. What we call the "social" denotes this network of apparatuses designed to either satisfy collective needs on a basis other than that of the market, or to ensure work is not entirely commodified. This vast domain, which ensures a certain collective and organized independence of individuals in relation to capital, is under attack today on behalf of the primacy of competitive logic and market efficiencies. We could even more fundamentally say that what we aptly call the "crisis of democracy" – i.e., the direct domination of economic and financial power within the process of political decision-making – is but one aspect of the separation of individuals from the political means and conditions of their collective autonomy.

The central question here, of course, is what exactly do we mean by neoliberalism? The apparatuses of power that govern neoliberalism and shape our behavior such that it conforms with the generalized norm of greater and greater accumulation do not only function according to a negative logic of dispossession, resignation, and dismantlement. Neoliberal policies, which impact all aspects of social life, are not only designed to provide financial capital with cheap assets or to facilitate the revenge of the ruling class for the losses incurred during the Keynesian-Fordist period. The very term "dispossession" presupposes the theft of something one once owned, whether this is a good, a right, a power, or an essence. Neoliberalism's essential trait, however, is to completely transform social relations, beginning with the relationship between people and things. Its singular feature is its attempt to systematically submit every component of social reproduction – wage work, family life, politics, culture, history, subjectivity, etc. – to capital's imperative to reproduce on an expanded scale. Dispossession is only one moment of this more general process in which capitalism attempts to metabolize social reality itself, a process Marx refers to as "subsumption under capital." Political elites are not, therefore, merely the "straw men" of financial capital: they act within their proper domain and use their own techniques – legal or otherwise – to bring about the great symbiosis of capital and the state that is arguably the fundamental characteristic of neoliberalism.[94] By instilling more and more competition into every aspect of social life, and by adapting the various social and political spheres to this new norm of generalized competition, neoliberal policies attempt to make the reproduction of society and the reproduction of capital virtually synonymous. And this is not to say that the former is merely the reflection of the latter: more accurately, the former is both its result and the underlying condition of the latter.

In summary, then, we argue that dispossession should not be interpreted as a specific mode of accumulation in itself. Rather, dispossession is one part of the continuous reproduction of the social, cultural, political, and subjective conditions necessary for broadening the accumulation of capital, or the "world-becoming" of capital by way of neoliberal governmentality. If nature, culture, and society are interiorized by capital as so many immanent conditions of its own development, then we increasingly come to view capital – according to an inversion of the radical imaginary – as the unavoidable and insurmountable condition of life in all its aspects, and we begin to feel as if capital is a kind of "cosmos" from which there is no escape. Neoliberalism does not therefore only strive toward "accumulation by dispossession," but rather promotes a more general accumulation through an expanded and deepened subordination of all elements of the population's existence: consumption, transportation, leisure time, education, health, the use of space and time, social and cultural reproduction, and ultimately subjectivity itself. We must also understand, therefore, how struggle has likewise spread: it not only concerns sites of production but also urban spaces, modes of circulation and exchange, education, training and research systems, leisure activities, and consumption practices. Given the suffocating logic of this "cosmo-capitalism," which seems to develop according to a kind of self-generation, the struggle itself is compelled to globalize: it adopts a coordinated and federated sectorial structure and it organizes gatherings or meetings of all those affected by neoliberalism in various city centers (the "square"). We can see then how the very practical necessities of global resistance to neoliberalism explain the emergence of the category of the "commons" in the 1990s. The commons both designates and federates the most diverse modes of resistance against the subsumption of society, subjectivity, and life under capital. The "commons" is thus a watchword, or an emblem. But, as we discuss in the next chapter, because this category always seems to designate that which already exists in nature, in society, or in our own intelligence, the concept of the commons is in fact limited by the heterogeneity of the "goods" or the "contents" that are increasingly the objects of today's new enclosures.

4

Critique of the Political Economy of the Commons

The dissemination of the paradigm of the commons in the 1990s, as we have just seen, was closely linked to the rise of resistance movements challenging neoliberalism in Latin America, the United States, and Europe. But the commons paradigm also came to prominence during this period in an academic literature produced by researchers – principally Americans – who were determined to formulate a new theory of political economy. The issue at stake in this research was not trivial: it sought to overcome the otherwise constitutive distinction in legal and economic theory between private and public goods, private and public ownership, and between the market and the state.

There is no question this orthodox opposition is still alive and well in contemporary protest movements. In this respect, denunciation of widespread *commodification* often leads to a reflexive defense of national or *public* services and a call for expanded state interventionism. Whatever its merits, such demands are counter-productive at best insofar as they refuse to challenge an opposition that codes *the market as the rule and the state as the exception.* Conceptualizing the state as a mechanism for resisting the invasion of the market thereby doubly justifies this division of labor between the market and the state, since it concedes a "proper" sphere of activity to each entity. Since at least the 1950s, standard economic theory fully accepted the legitimacy of public or government production on the pretext that certain goods are *inherently* suited to private ownership while others are *naturally* suited to state management. In this respect, standard political economy is merely obeying the basic principles of political philosophy that, at least since Hobbes, assigned the state a dual function: to protect private property and furnish public goods that society's egoistic atoms are incapable of furnishing on their own. Adam Smith himself adopted this same framework. In both political philosophy and classical economics, the "market" and the "state" are viewed as necessary and sufficient poles for ensuring a properly run society. The aim of the political economy of the commons, however, was precisely to depart from this consensual opposition between the state and the market, both practically and theoretically.

This theory of the commons, whose best-known representative is Elinor Ostrom (Ostrom was awarded the Nobel Prize in Economics in 2009),[1] focuses on the practical and *institutional* conditions for managing common resources. This school of thought thus distanced itself (albeit incompletely) from standard economics insofar as the latter assigns the production of goods to different apparatuses (i.e., the state or the market) based the intrinsic nature of the goods themselves. By revealing the institutional dimension of resource management practices, Ostrom's work led to a theoretical breakthrough whose importance cannot be underestimated. That said, Ostrom's ability to reveal the importance of institutional analysis was nonetheless limited by her dependence on the dominant naturalistic framework of standard economics, wherein particular resources are viewed as more (or less) suited to collective management based on their intrinsic properties. The "common," within this strain of institutional political economy, is thus a qualifier that applies to resources that are naturally "common": because of their intrinsic character, such resources are more rationally managed through collective action than by either the market or the state.[2] By adopting this economic framework, the commons becomes inscribed in a typology of goods based technical criteria: there are goods that are "common" by their nature and consequently conducive to collective management, just as other resources lend themselves to public or private management according to their intrinsic particularities. After studying numerous cases of collectively managed natural resources at a micro-social level, Ostrom and her team used these technical criteria to develop a research program on today's emergent digital "knowledge commons" on a much larger scale.

The consequences of adopting this naturalistic framework are not insignificant and they tend in opposite directions. If the common is a natural property of certain goods, this justifies the creation of a special economy designed to meet the special needs of these "common goods" in between – or outside of – the vast economies of market-produced goods and state-produced goods. In this respect, then, there is nothing revolutionary about this thesis at all; in fact, it is rather conservative. But, in a very different sense, if this political economy of the common succeeds in showing, or in making us believe, that our most essential economic and social goods are naturally "common," then this school of thought would seem to have solved the million-dollar question vis-à-vis our exit from capitalism. Indeed, much contemporary critical theory takes precisely this view. André Gorz's chapter titled "The Exit from Capitalism has Already Begun" from his book *Ecologica* (2010) – in which Gorz explains how "the sphere of what is free is extending irresistibly" within the "knowledge economy" – is a perfect example of this interpretation:

> Information technology and the Internet are undermining the reign of commodities at its foundation. Everything translatable into digital language and reproducible or communicable at no cost tends irresistibly to become private property, if not indeed universal property, when it is accessible to – and useable by – everyone ... This is a revolution that is undermining capitalism at its base.[3]

As we will argue, however, adhering to this naturalistic typology of "goods" cannot help us identify the specific characteristics of the common – indeed, the special nature of the commons can only be revealed by critiquing this naturalistic framework. And yet, we must stress here that our critique of economic naturalism is only possible because of the theoretical opening produced by Ostrom's research on the *governance* of the commons. Indeed, when all the implications of this new problematic are properly unfolded, it collapses the naturalistic rationale of standard economics in two senses: by undermining the supposed natural egoism of the human agent and by undermining the classification of goods according to their intrinsic nature.

"Private Goods" and "Public Goods"

Standard economic discourse so permeates both public debate and theoretical discussion that its categories are still the dominant terms used to express and articulate our understanding of the "common" today. Political economy, much like legal theory, tends to think in terms of "goods" (even if the definition of a "good" differs between the two disciplines). In the legal sphere, goods are defined as objects that are appropriable. In standard economics, on the other hand, an economic good is defined by its ability to satisfy some need, by its mode of consumption, and by the method of its production (market or otherwise). Within this framework, then, the commons is considered a property of goods themselves rather than a property of institutions. As we argue, however, the "commons" are not reducible to "common goods."

We must first begin by understanding more precisely what is meant by the expression "common good." The term is often confused with synonyms like the "collective good" or the "public good." But what distinguishes a public – or collective – good from a private good? According to standard economic doctrine, most goods must be produced by private firms operating in competitive markets because of the intrinsic technological and economic properties of the goods themselves.[4] There are, however, a handful of goods whose specific characteristics make them "naturally" suited for production by the state or other social organizations (churches, unions, parties, associations, etc.) that are capable of exercising discipline over their members, in one way or another, to ensure the production of non-market goods. In short, the reason public goods aren't produced by the market is because the needs they satisfy aren't suited to a market logic of production based on voluntary individual payment.

Private goods, on the other hand, are defined in standard economics as "excludable" and "rivalrous."[5] A good is said to be "excludable" when its owner or producer is able to restrict right of ownership over the good to any person who refuses to buy the good at the price the owner demands. A good is said to be "rivalrous" when its purchase or use by one individual diminishes the quantity of the good that can be consumed by others. A "pure" public good, then, is a good that is both non-excludable and non-rivalrous. A good is said to be non-excludable when its owner cannot restrict its use on the basis of payment; and a good is said to be non-rivalrous when it can be consumed or used by large numbers of people without additional production costs because the consumption of the good does not diminish the overall store available to others. Classical examples of these goods include street lighting, fresh air, fireworks, light from lighthouses, or national defense. The fact that there are certain needs that can only be satisfied by public goods accordingly justifies state intervention in the economy, as is described in classic works in economics produced by Richard Musgrave and Paul Samuelson in the 1950s.[6] According to Richard Musgrave, one of the functions of the state is to ensure optimal allocation of economic resources. This means the state must subsidize or directly produce those goods that cannot be produced by the market as a result of their intrinsic properties. Public goods are thus defined negatively as goods that cannot be spontaneously produced by a market in which private interests are satisfied by an act of voluntary purchase. Public goods, in other words, are "market failures." It is because certain goods are somehow defective or deficient in the context of standard market norms that they must be produced by the state or non-profit institutions (insofar as they are deemed sufficiently necessary for economic efficiency or the well-being of the population). If no one can be excluded from the consumption of a good, and if the consumption of a good by one individual does not diminish its availability for others, it means the good is both non-excludable and non-rivalrous. Accordingly, then, the production and financing of such goods can only be realized on the basis of a certain compulsion – a moral compulsion in the case of a church or a non-profit association, or a political compulsion in the case of the state. Of course, the mere fact of a market failure does not, on its own, oblige the government or any other local authority to intervene in the economy, but in some cases the intrinsic properties of certain goods may justify such an intervention.

Any justification for political intervention in the economy is always closely linked to the so-called "free-rider" problem. A free rider is a calculating individual who willingly leaves the burden of payment for a good (from which he profits) to others on the basis of the good's non-excludability. A free rider can also be someone who refuses to assume of the costs of his own activities (as in the case of a polluter). It is important to observe, at this junction, that the entire logic governing this intrinsic or naturalistic distinction between goods rests upon a very elementary utilitarian foundation: namely, the premise that the "rational" individual is egoistic, calculating, maximizing, and singularly motivated by personal self-interest. In other words, the whole model is underpinned by the postulate of economic man. This hegemonic figure can only enjoy goods selfishly and is incapable of producing or consuming in common with others. In *The Logic of Collective Action* (1965), Mancur Olson showed that an individual of this kind has no motive to collectively produce a good that others might consume without paying for it, and so it is contrarily better to allow others to bear costs in one way or another, since benefit from the collective outcome is the same for those who do not pay as for those who do.[7] Compulsory taxation, or some other form of political or moral compulsion, is therefore the only means of providing collective goods. And this is precisely why, in a great many cases, "public goods" are goods provided by the state. It is also true, as Olson pointed out, that regular interaction between individuals within groups had a tendency to reduce instances of free riding.

Since the 1950s, the theory has been refined to show how the classic examples of public goods actually constituted a very specific category of "pure public goods" that had to be integrated within a more general theory of "externalities" – i.e., beneficial or detrimental communal effects produced by private actions. The market, for example, may produce too few positive externalities on its own – such as the benefits of education when it is entirely paid for by users – and, inversely, the market may produce too many negative externalities – such as atmospheric pollution without any public regulations governing greenhouse gas emissions. What is at issue here is not the way in which these goods are consumed, but rather the general consequences for society as a whole. But whether it is because of the particularities of public goods or in order to correct for externalities, public intervention in the economy is always justified by *market failures*. And market failure, in turn, is always a function of the intrinsic characteristics of goods, whether it concerns the manner of their consumption or the general social effects involved in their production.

A public good is therefore defined negatively within the framework of a theory in which the market is the default mechanism for allocating resources. While our aim here is not to exhaustively examine the characteristics sufficient for justifying public intervention, we should, however, stress the fragility of the boundaries established between the public and private by the theoreticians of the public economy in the 1950s. Indeed, the neoliberal theorists have very cunningly preyed on this fragility in order to argue that even if certain goods are of a special nature, their production does not necessarily require production by the state. The European Union's doctrine, to take one example, no longer uses a vocabulary of "public goods" or "public services," but rather opts for terms like "service of general interest" because this terminology leaves space open for private companies to produce previously public goods or services (albeit within regulatory frameworks still determined by public authorities). And we have seen in the previous chapter how the theory of property rights provides further intellectual legitimacy to such policies aimed at greater privatization and commodification.

The orthodox economist thus reasons on the basis of a double postulate concerning the intrinsic nature of goods and the behavior of economic man, and this rationale justifies the shared distribution and production of goods and services between the state and the market. But the reality is that the production of goods does not conform to a reductive economic rationale that excludes politics or ethics. The reason why a given good or service is produced or provided by the state or the market is never solely due to the natural properties of the given good or service, but is rather a more complex outcome of a variety of political, cultural, social, and historical factors that we must not ignore (as is often the case in standard economic doctrine).[8]

The Discovery of "Common Goods"

Despite the rigor of the economic theory mentioned above, numerous economists have since discovered that one cannot exhaustively classify all economic goods through such a reductive framework that delegates the distribution and production of goods between the market and the state on the basis of technical considerations – such as exclusivity or rivalry – or by distinguishing between purely public and private goods. It was from the recognition of the failures of this prior model to exhaustively account for all goods that Elinor Ostrom's research on common resource management was born.

For instance, if we combine (as was done during the 1970s) the two properties of economic goods – exclusivity and rivalry – we in fact distinguish between *four*, not *two*, types of goods. In addition to "purely private goods" (excludable and rivalrous) – such as donuts purchased at the supermarket – and "purely public goods" (non-excludable and non-rivalrous) – such as public lighting, national defense, or the light emitted from lighthouses – there are also "hybrid" or "mixed" types of goods. There are also what are called "club goods," which are both excludable and non-rivalrous – such as tolled bridges or highways, or artistic and sporting performances. While there is a cost of consumption in each of these cases, the consumption of these goods by one individual does not diminish the quality of consumption by others. There are also other goods referred to as "mixed goods" – which we will refer to as "common goods" – that are non-exclusive and rivalrous, such as fishing grounds, open pastures, or irrigation systems. These goods are "mixed" because it is difficult to restrict access to such goods, except by establishing rules of usage. It is these mixed goods that Ostrom refers to in her work as "common-pool resources" (CPRs). While these goods can be individually exploited, there is a risk that the overall quantity of the resource will be diminished or even exhausted if everyone tries to maximize their own personal utility. Mixed goods, or CPRs, can also be provided by state authorities, as in the case of national parks. For Ostrom, however, the use of these goods does not necessarily presuppose a rigid choice between individual property or public ownership. On the contrary, these goods can be effectively sustained by forms of collective management, as is demonstrated by the empirical studies carried out by Ostrom and her team in Switzerland, Japan, Spain, and the Philippines. What was most novel about Ostrom's approach was that she focused on the *institutionalization* of these resources, and on this basis she worked toward a systematic theory of self-organizing and self-governing collective action.[9] And while her approach was indeed novel in relation to standard economic theory, it was based on extensive historical inquiry into centuries- and even millennia-old communal practices that have long been the object of systemic denigration in the field of modern economics.

The "Tragedy of the Commons" Debate

In order to understand the true stakes of Ostrom's political economy of the commons, we must situate her work within the context of the larger debate that developed around Garrett Hardin's famous article "The Tragedy of the Commons."[10] In his 1968 article, Hardin believed he could show how communal land, even before the enclosure movement, was destroyed by overexploitation at the hands of sheep-breeders driven solely by self-interest.

Hardin's rationale is based on the premise of economic man's rational behavior, and the inability or unwillingness of economic man to consider the larger effects of unrestrained exploitation of a common resource. Hardin's driving concern in his famous essay is the issue of overpopulation, which the Malthusian Hardin viewed as the most distressing problem facing humanity as a whole. Hardin's objective was thus to critique the idea that a given population will reach an optimum population under conditions in which everyone decides on matters of procreation based solely on self-interested motives. For Hardin, humanity will surely be led to ruin if families are permitted the freedom to have as many children as they want: given the finite nature of the world, freedom in matters of procreation is simply impossible. Hardin thus returns to Malthus as a means of critiquing Smith: for Hardin, any hope in the population's capacity to spontaneously self-regulate, as if by a kind of "invisible" demographic hand, is folly. It is in this respect that Hardin (likely without realizing it) actually revives a long-standing historical debate about communism. That idea that everything in the natural world belongs to everyone, that the world is a banquet open to all, was one of the central communist themes in Étienne-Gabriel Morelly's *The Code of Nature*: "the world is a table sufficiently stocked for all the guests. Sometimes the dishes belong to everyone, because everyone is hungry, while sometimes they belong to only a few, because others are satisfied. No one is the absolute master, and no one has a right to pretend to be."[11] Morelly's gesture is a refusal, on behalf of the priority of satisfying our most basic and primary needs, of the notion of scarcity when it comes to the most basic goods. He therefore rejects the claim that there is not a place at the table for everyone on earth. This is of course a position that is diametrically opposed to Malthus's view, which Hardin cites in his article:

> A man who is born into a world already possessed, if he cannot get subsistence from his parents on whom he has a just demand, and if the society does not want his labour, has no claim of right to the smallest portion of food, and, in fact, has no business to be where he is. At nature's mighty feast there is no vacant cover for him. She tells him to be gone, and will quickly execute her own orders.[12]

There is no such thing as a "free lunch." This is the fundamental idea behind what Hardin calls the "tragedy of the commons."

In order to illustrate his thesis, Hardin imagines the exploitation of an open pasture. All the "rational" herders are self-interestedly compelled to increase the number of livestock they place on the pasture without limit, and this invariably leads to the overexploitation of the communal lands. In effect, then, if every herder directly pursues their own personal utility by augmenting the number of livestock they place on the pasture, the "disutility" wrought by the overexploitation is suffered by all. This is why Hardin opts for the term "tragedy," which he uses according to the strict definition provided by philosopher Alfred North Whitehead[13]: tragedy, for Whitehead, is an irreversible and inevitable process, and this is precisely the nature of a logic that compels each herder to maximize his own profit without worrying about the cost of his or her collectively supported behavior:

> Each man is locked into a system that compels him to increase his herd without limit – in a world that is limited. Ruin is the destination toward which all men rush, each pursuing his own best interest in a society that believes in the freedom of the commons. Freedom in a commons brings ruin to all.[14]

Hardin's assertion, as we can see, is not as simple-headed as his critiques often suggest. What he is questioning is not the existence of the commons as such, but rather the "freedom" to exploit the commons in an unlimited fashion.[15] The fundamental lesson Hardin wants to convey in his parable of the "rational" herders is thus the exact opposite of the lesson Bernard Mandeville conveys in his "Fable of the Bees": by allowing each individual to maximize their individual utility without limit, humanity does not achieve "the greatest happiness for the greatest number" – to borrow Hardin's dearly held Benthamite formula – but rather courts collective ruin.

But what kind of "commons" is Hardin talking about in his article? One of the defining features of Hardin's famous article is in fact the manner in which he indiscriminately collapses every form of common resource within a single generic category. Are overexploited pastures the same as oceans depleted of fish or whales? Are they the same as polluted air and water? And are oceans, rivers, and urban air pollution the same as social programs and national parks? In a certain number of these cases, it is obvious that limited access, an operating quota, taxation, or some other forms of control would be sufficient to avoid the destruction of most of the natural resources Hardin mentions. It has been amply shown, for instance, that unhindered access to groundwater in India during the "Green Revolution" accelerated water depletion. Indian states actively encouraged their wealthiest farmers to tap into wells without limit and at the expense of other uses of water, such as irrigation, canals, or reservoirs. One group of experts has estimated that half the country's water needs will no longer be met within twenty years.[16] The probable consequences of this overexploitation of water thus correspond fairly well to Hardin's warning about the "ruin of the common." On the other hand, it is worth noting that Hardin's conclusion does not sufficiently account for the extent to which this destructive process was also due to the total absence of public regulation, along with the fact that unfettered access for well drillers – i.e., the richest farmers who sell water to the poorest farmers as well as to intermediaries who truck water to urban centers – was carefully planned. The behavior of these calculating and maximizing egoists, in other words, did not arise spontaneously: it was a product of social planning and, in this specific case, arose directly from a very water-intensive form of capitalist agricultural development.

The fact remains, however, that Hardin's examples of the "commons" are really a confused amalgam of very heterogeneous cases. He confuses what Roman law called *res communis* – that which belongs to no one and is unappropriable, such as the sea or the air – and *res nullius* – that which has no owner but can be appropriated, such as fish caught in the sea.[17] But above all, he confuses these categories with the unrestricted exploitation of goods taken from a limited stock. Hardin's argument thus rests on a sophism in which he introduces economically "rational" behavior – i.e., behavior driven entirely by the logic of self-interest – into a normative context that precisely excludes such behavior, since virtually every instance of common resource management in history has been based on rules that were precisely designed to prevent such cases of overexploitation. In other words, Hardin's fable completely ignores the existence of a "moral economy" – to borrow E.P. Thompson's phrase – that informs customary-use rules for common resources. This is a major historical error, insofar as it allows Hardin to conclude that the destructive consequences wrought by free access to common resources can only be avoided by individual privatization, or nationalization/centralization of the common resource. In other words, Hardin's analysis leaves no room for a third term between the market and the state.

Despite these problems, an abundant neoliberal literature has since spawned from Hardin's famous analysis. This literature uses Hardin's thesis to bespeak the advantages of private property while emphasizing the inefficiencies of any form of public or collective management. Public services or social insurance systems fail, so argues this literature, due to the fact that they all fall prey to "free riders" who enjoy all the benefits while paying none of the costs. If Hardin's thesis was principally interpreted in neoliberal terms, it was because it resonated with powerful currents within dominant economic theory that were renewing arguments in favor of private property and which were violently opposed to all forms of communal or state property (which were accused by the neoliberals of transferring costs onto the community and risking resource depletion). The theory of property rights accordingly emphasizes the idea that only private ownership is able to "internalize externalities" – whether positive or negative – while all other forms of property simply fail to weigh the negative externalities imposed upon others while preventing those who justly accrued wealth through meritocratic effort from enjoying the full benefits of their wealth.[18]

The Institution as the Heart of the Commons

The principal contribution of the new political economy of the commons was precisely its ability to sort out the widespread confusion that is clearly manifest in Hardin's article between completely free access, on the one hand, and collective organization and management on the other. In other words, its core insight is to have recognized that the commons were originally based on self-organized, collective regulation. Elinor Ostrom thus showed (though often without sufficient explication) that these natural commons should not be defined as physical "things," pre-existing the practical uses made of them. Nor, for Ostrom, should these commons be defined as natural spaces that are merely overlaid with additional rules. These communal resources should rather be understood as a product of social relations between individuals who exploit certain communal resources based on rules of use, sharing, or cooperation. To borrow Yochai Benkler's very apt phrase, these communal resources are "institutional spaces."[19] This revised understanding is undoubtedly at the root of the crucial terminological shift from "common goods" to the "commons."[20] The major contribution of this new political economy of the commons resides in this insistence on the necessity of diverse practical rules for enabling the production and reproduction of common resources. As David Bollier writes, "the commons paradigm does not look primarily to a system of property, contracts, and markets, but to social norms and rules, and to legal mechanisms that enable people to share ownership and control resources."[21] This emphasis on the collective establishment of rules of practical action, which is what Ostrom conceives as an institution, introduces a *governmental* conception of the commons in which the latter is conceived as an institutional system of cooperative incentives.

For Ostrom, an institution is "simply the set of rules actually used (the *working rules* or *rules-in-use*) by a set of individuals to organize repetitive activities that produce outcomes affecting those individuals and potentially affecting others."[22] As Ostrom continues, "working rules may or may not closely resemble formal laws that are expressed in national legislation, administrative regulations, and court decisions ... working rules are those actually used, monitored, and enforced when individuals make choices about the actions they will take in operational settings or when they make collective choices."[23] A "successful" institution is one that is capable of adapting to changing circumstances and is able to regulate internal conflicts. For Ostrom, then, there is a close link between the sustainability of a common, the adaptability of its internal regulations, and the "institutional diversity" that relates to the ability of members to adapt diverse conditions of production. Communal resources may be exploited by groups of varying sizes, but in order to endure, these groups must obey a system of collective rules concerning their productive operations, group boundaries, and the procedures by which rules are elaborated and modified. The latter, which constitute "constitutional rules," are the institutional parameters in which "operational rules" are elaborated and discussed. As Oliver Weinstein aptly writes, "the hierarchical system of rules that regulates a common and its governance thus appears to be a genuine political system." In short, the commons are institutions that allow for communal management according to several levels of rules established by the "appropriators" themselves. Benjamin Coriat, for instance, defines "common lands" according to the following resonant formula: "collective resources managed by means of a governance structure that ensures a distribution of rights between members participating in the common ('commoners') in order to facilitate the orderly exploitation of the resource while ensuring its long term sustainability."[24]

There is thus no need to privatize the commons by imposing exclusive property rights upon it, as the neoliberal institutionalists would have it; nor is there any need to appeal to a Leviathan in order to control individuals and force them to obey the sovereign, who is the sole source of information. There are many collective ways to agree and create cooperative rules that are not reducible to the market or state control. And this has been empirically demonstrated in the numerous cases wherein groups have completely bypassed statist constraints or private ownership in order to avoid the well-known "tragedy of the commons."

The "Analytical Framework" of the Commons

Ostrom outlined the framework for the institutional analysis of commons management in most detail in her 1990 book *Governing the Commons*.

While she examines the management of communal resources in very different settings in this book, each case is similar insofar as they all feature a small group of people who establish collective rules for the use of some form of communal property. Managing the production of communal natural resources – such as pastures, fisheries, forests, irrigation systems, etc. – functions according to a certain number of institutional principles foregrounded in Ostrom's theory. Ostrom's approach doesn't, therefore, try to find a single model at work in every situation. Instead, it posits an analytical framework comprised of variables that interact and condition the codification of various forms of activity. In other words, there is no one single or proper way to manage a commons that is transposable everywhere. And while it is true that Ostrom's theory places great emphasis on the dynamic diversity of the institutions she studies, the main thrust of her analysis is to identify a number of fundamental issues that need to be resolved if any given system of collective exploitation hopes to be sustainable. For instance, the common must always have clearly definable limits in order to be able to identify the specific community concerned with the common in question; institutional rules must be well adapted to local needs and conditions and must be consistent with community objectives; the individuals governed by these rules must regularly participate in the committees charged with modifying them; participants' rights to determine and modify these rules must be recognized by external authorities; a member-oriented self-monitoring apparatus must be established, along with a graduated system of sanctions; community members must have access to an inexpensive system of conflict resolution; and, finally, the positions for overseeing the various regulatory functions must be adequately distributed amongst the group.

This list of principles for managing the common might seem somewhat underwhelming at first glance. Nonetheless, these requirements reveal an essential aspect of the common that standard economic theory systematically ignores: namely, the close connection between the norm of reciprocity, democratic management, and active participation in resource production. This is because a common does not bring consumers together within the context of a market, nor does it rely on an administration unconnected to the actual production process. Rather, a commons involves "co-producers" who work together by giving themselves collective rules. In this sense, then, the paradigm of the commons not only challenges the economy of private goods but also its complimentary opposite, the economy of public goods (as we have seen above), by analyzing forms of activity and production, outside the market and the state, that are shaped by productive communities that political economy has been radically unable to account for (up to this point). Ostrom's approach has also been verified through empirical examination of various "knowledge commons," whereby production corresponds to very specific social and political conditions. Within these commons, the economic production of resources is inseparable from civic engagement: production is closely linked to norms of reciprocity and presupposes both relations between equals and democratic frameworks for establishing and implementing rules. It is worth noting, in this respect, how this political economy of the commons is not entirely dissimilar to an earlier tradition of socialism, which also made cooperation the antidote to the capitalist logic of competition.

But above all, the theory of the commons is all about the *constructed* character of the commons. There is nothing in the theory that suggests – as some libertarians are tempted to believe when it comes to the expansion of the Internet – that a common can operate without established rules, or that it could be viewed as a natural object whereby "free access" is synonymous with absolute legal and economic "laissez-faire." Spontaneism will simply not do: reciprocity is not an innate biological fact, and democracy is not an eternal datum of human existence. Instead, the common must be thought of as the construction of regulatory frameworks and democratic institutions that organize reciprocity and thereby avoid both Hardin's "free rider" problem and the tendency of market societies to produce passive consumer citizens.[25] In a certain sense, then, the theory of the commons is perfectly contemporaneous with neoliberalism, insofar as the latter theorizes, supports, and promotes the commodification and the construction of markets through the development of property rights, contractual forms, and constructed modes of competition. In other words, the theory of the commons is based on a similar theoretical constructivism, but it turns in the opposite direction: it encourages, at a practical level, the establishment of regulatory frameworks for enabling collective action.

This regulatory system of the commons is a collective invention that is transmissible while, at the same time, being susceptible to change according to circumstances and constraints; it is also a series of incentives that orients individual behavior. In this strict sense, Ostrom is herself inscribed within the paradigm of neoliberal governmentality insofar as her work is all about guiding individual behavior through institutional incentives and disincentives:

> Institutions shape the patterns of human interactions and the results that individuals achieve [through incentives]. Incentives are the positive and negative changes in outcomes that individuals perceive as likely to result from particular actions taken within a set of working rules.[26]

Ostrom's approach should therefore be viewed as a form of dissident neoinstitutionalism. Its methodology is based on an analytical framework that similarly understands economic phenomena as arising from the institutions that guide behavior and "shape human interaction," according to North's definition.[27]

But Ostrom's work, of course, does not extol the virtues of property rights in the same manner as North and the other neoinstitutionalist theorists. On the contrary, Ostrom's work is all about showing how a set of rules can encourage individuals to renounce opportunistic behavior and adopt cooperative conduct. Or even better, Ostrom's work in fact shows that it is often the rules themselves that produce "perverse incentives" that compel individuals to act opportunistically and "ruin the commons." For Ostrom, accordingly, the dilemma of the commons is best interpreted as a variant of the famous "prisoner's dilemma." The prisoner's dilemma tells us that in a situation in which individual decisions are interdependent, but where these same individuals cannot communicate or deliberate on the basis of a common plan, non-cooperative strategies tend to prevail. But of course this outcome is largely derived from the structure of the situation as imposed by game theorists themselves. The reality is that whenever individuals are able to assemble, talk amongst themselves, and make collective decisions, cooperative strategies become possible and agreement – one that is not imposed from the outside – is often the result. Of course this is not always the case, as Ostrom points out: it may be the case that individuals interested in protecting a common resource find they are unable to do so because "the participants may simply have no capacity to communicate with one another, no way to develop trust, and no sense that they share a common future."[28] And while it is not an insurmountable obstacle, Ostrom also adds that such agreements are often undermined by relations of force and structures of domination operating within groups: "alternatively, powerful individuals who stand to gain from the current situation, while others lose, may block efforts by the less powerful to change the rules of the game."[29]

Generally speaking, Ostrom appropriates a number of the central tenants of neoliberal doctrine, from Hayek and Public Choice Theory, and inflects them in a new way. Two aspects of these doctrines are especially operative in her analyses: first, she adopts the idea that rational individuals are best suited to creating institutions that promote interaction by diminishing uncertainty[30]; and second, she adopts the thesis of "adaptive efficacy," found in both North and Hayek, that tells us that the only institutions able to survive are those best able to adapt to changing internal and external conditions.

Ostrom's hypothesis concerning individual rationality as a basic premise of *ad hoc* solutions is, however, balanced by an insistent reference to a social reality that conditions the governance of the common. Unlike North, who tries to unify all the social sciences by rendering rational, individual behavior the sole behavioral concern of institutional constraints, Ostrom argues that social conditions favoring or hindering the establishment of practical rules must always be taken into account. For the ability to collectively develop rules of use is itself dependent on a community-specific system of norms and on the possibility of establishing communicative exchanges between individuals. From this perspective, then, Ostrom's institutionalism veers away from mainstream methodological individualism by borrowing sociology's model of the socialized individual and cognitive psychology's theory of experiential learning.[31] Ostrom's work focuses on a social art she calls "crafting": the term refers to the skilled work of an artist or craftsman, and in this respect differs greatly from the mere application of a system of rules imposed from above or outside by experts or scholars. The "artisanal" character of crafting, as Ostrom explains, stems from the fact that every commons has its own unique mode of government and, therefore, "crafting institutions ... requires skill in understanding how rules, combined with particular physical, economic, and cultural environments, produce incentives and outcomes."[32] When it comes to the commons, there is simply no "one best way." The creation of institutions presupposes an extended process of imagination, negotiation, experimentation, and correction of the rules whose practical effect on behavior changes over time:

> Rules governing the supply and use of any particular physical system must be devised, tried, modified, and tried again, and considerable time and resources will be invested in learning more about how various institutional rules affect participants' behavior. Thus, the choice of institutions is not a 'one-shot' decision in a known environment but rather an ongoing investment in an uncertain environment.[33]

By using the same methodological tools of the rational choice theorists, Ostrom theorizes institutions in terms of "social capital." For Ostrom, social capital is just as important as physical capital when it comes to the creation and maintenance of the commons.[34] Yet despite Ostrom's use of standard economic vocabulary, the process of institutional "crafting" she describes is, in fact, profoundly sociological and political. These cooperative incentives that constitute the institution mobilize all the knowledge belonging to the social group in charge of the common, and often presuppose external political conditions that permit and encourage self-governance of the commons. As Ostrom accordingly remarked concerning the creation of an irrigation system:

> The crafting of irrigation institutions is an ongoing process that must directly involve the users and suppliers of irrigation water throughout the design process. Instead of designing a single blueprint for water-user organizations to be adopted on all irrigation systems within a jurisdiction, officials need to enhance the capability of suppliers and users to design their own institutions. Involving

> suppliers and users directly will help ensure that development institutions are well matched to the particular physical, economic, and cultural environment of each system.[35]

The Limits of the Institutional Analysis of the Commons

Elinor Ostrom's analysis undeniably breaks with many of the dominant presuppositions of neoclassical economics: her work shows how the commons requires voluntary engagement, dense social ties, and clear, durable norms of reciprocity. On the other hand, however, Ostrom's theory of the commons was never meant to be a general principle for re-organizing society as a whole. Her theory is rather a pragmatic appeal that advocates a plurality of forms of activity, property rights, and economic regulations. For Ostrom, there is no one single correct way to organize production, since the conditions of production always differ so greatly. While the construction of the commons is necessary in particular situations and for specific goods, it in no way questions the rationality of the market or the state as such. Her pluralism is linked to her analytical preference for individual rationality, which is the underlying method for selecting the best solutions in heterogeneous situations. According to Ostrom, rational and egoistic individuals may create markets, they may call for state intervention, and they construct a commons; it simply depends on the demands of different situations. Does she not understand how institutions shape subjectivities and, as Olivier Weinstein points out, what is most interesting about the common is not its productive efficiency but its capacity for creating new ways of life and new subjectivities?" [36] The fact is, Elinor Ostrom is not an anti-capitalist or an anti-statist: she's a liberal. Given her preference for institutional diversity, she believes individuals should have the freedom to invent, on their own (and without governmental constraint), contractual arrangements that they find most beneficial.[37] In reality, then, her theory is essentially a critique of the theory of exclusive property rights as well as a critique of the state's authority when it comes to imposing solutions "from above." From this perspective, then, her analysis constitutes a kind of academic protest against the systematic devaluation of social cooperation both by apologists for property rights as well the "socialistic" justification for centralized state intervention. That said, her implicit argument that an archipelago of commons might survive within the icy waters of the market and the state as a result of the superior rationality of the commons (as inferred from a number of specific cases) suggests she may have underestimated the gravity of the larger economic and political context in which these commons are forced to exist. What reason is there to think such local institutional arrangements, and their organization forms, would not be heavily constrained by the imperatives of capital? Reading Ostrom, we are forced to assume that the individuals populating these commons will not, somehow, also be immersed in the global economy, will not suffer its effects, and will not import the logic of capital into their communities or workplaces.

The reality is that Ostrom's concepts limit her analysis. Her concepts are drawn from the standard corpus of economics and game theory, and they struggle to account for real relations of power and exploitation. By obfuscating relations of power in each "community," her approach's inability to grapple with the great historical conditions that have led to the destruction of innumerable traditional commons is all the more conspicuous in her overall theory. By failing to deal with relations of power within groups themselves, Ostrom's theory is also unable to consider the effects of systemic domination on behavior. And by restricting her analyses to local arrangements alone, her theory is unable to examine hierarchical relations that may exist amongst different forms of production and different types of social relations. Ostrom's approach simply says nothing about the social system as a whole,[38] despite the fact that institutions are always "embedded" in society, and its stakeholders are always a product of history.[39]

Ostrom's guiding premise of institutional diversity forbids her from considering the political possibility of constituting the common as a generalizable alternative rationality.[40] It *a fortiori* ignores the question of how other institutions might develop according to the principle of the common. In short, there's no inquiry at all about how we might pass from the *commons* to the *common*. Ostrom doesn't propose any generalizable principle of organization, and she deflects criticism on this point by falling back on a "polycentric" analysis of economic reality. From this perspective, then, Ostrom's work falls far short of the ambition of, say, regulation theory, which tries to understand how "the founding institutions structuring contemporary society" evolved.[41]

The limits of this new institutional economy of the commons ultimately lie in the fact that it has not completely freed itself from the fundamental hypotheses underpinning the theory of private and public goods.[42] It never adequately divorces itself from the postulate that the form and the framework in which goods are produced ultimately depend on the intrinsic qualities of the goods themselves. From this point of view, the critique her economic theory of the commons mounts against Hardin's thesis remains, unfortunately, problematic. While natural resources of limited stock may be compatible with the various institutions described in its empirical studies, many other goods are still "naturally" assumed to be more efficiently produced by the market or the state. Of course, were economists to take historical reality into account in a serious way, they would immediately see that the enclosure movement did not arise from the landowners' sudden realization that land is "naturally" an exclusive and rivalrous good – rather, they would see that the enclosure movement was in fact the product of changing social relations in the English countryside (as Ellen Meiksins Wood's remarkable work has recently shown).[43] Ostrom's theory of the commons is thus, at best, a refinement of the theory of public goods developed in the 1950s. It extends and reproduces the same limitations that plague every naturalism bent on classifying goods according to their intrinsic properties.

And lastly, even if her analysis does indeed culminate in a new conception of the individual as socially committed to the management of the commons, Ostrom never jettisons her premise about the rational actor who always acts on the basis of a cost-benefit analysis. Her work thus reproduces the figure of the calculating individual who chooses the institution of commons in order to arrive at a strictly private advantage. The fact that collective norms always exert pressure on individual choices and norms, not to mention the importance of such norms for conditioning situational variables – especially in terms of a given country's economic and political structure – merely underscores the insufficiency of this basic neoclassical postulate.[44] Thus, despite all her empirical realism, Ostrom's work falls prey to the "error that consists in presenting the theoretical view of practice as the practical relation to practice," as Pierre Bourdieu aptly put it.[45] To suppose that the decision to adopt forms of collective management stems from the calculation of rational individuals is to forget that the common is no more decreed from the outside than it is the aggregate result of isolated individual decisions. The common is rather a social process with a logic all its own.

From One Common to Another

The language of the commons is not only "descriptive and performative," as David Bollier emphasizes, but it is above all extremely inclusive. That is to say that it provides a singular frame of reference for theorizing modes of activity, protest movements, and other social relations that, at first glance, appear to have very little to do with one another. As early as the mid–1990s, it was becoming apparent to Elinor Ostrom and the various researchers associated with her approach that the spread of digital technologies, the rapid extension of the Internet, and the concomitant growth of online communities and other forms of networked exchanges were opening up a new domain in which the framework for analyzing the dilemmas of collective action could be applied. But, at the same time, it was necessary to grasp the singularity of these "new commons," and the ways they differed from the "natural commons" (water, forests, fish, fauna and flora, etc.) that had been the previous object of Ostrom's analyses.[46] What, then, are the implications of extending this political economic concept of the "commons" into "cognitive," "digital," or "informational" activities that have little to do with the management of natural resources? Are the naturalistic limitations of her analyses overcome once our attention is shifted to goods with very different characteristics?

In the first place, we must emphasize that the conception of knowledge we are dealing with here is situated within the specific context of economic theory, and in this particular domain, the meaning of the term "knowledge" is exceptionally loose. It is defined as a resource that can be produced and shared, regardless of its purpose, relevance, or use. "Knowledge," in economics, designates ideas or theories just as much as it designates information or data in any form whatsoever. For instance, Charlotte Hess and Elinor Ostrom consider "all intelligible ideas, information, and data" as forms of knowledge, and they even extend this definition to forms of intellectual and artistic creation.[47] Economics, even in its most standard version, has long viewed cognitive and informational resources as strategic factors when it comes to competitiveness and growth, which is why it developed the now largely trivialized notion of the "knowledge economy." To claim knowledge as a common, in this context, thus exceeds mere academic concern. The claim is a "global" counter-strategy that, in the works of some authors, means the "knowledge economy" must be re-founded on a completely new basis and, as envisioned by André Gorz, as a new non-capitalist society.

Sharing-based practices, such as disseminating scientific or artistic works, creating free software, constructing collaborative encyclopedias, etc., are all contemporary examples of the "new knowledge commons" that is based on values of social commitment and reciprocity. This type of commons, which has become an object of growing interest in the United States, has specific features that distinguish it from so-called "natural" commons. The first distinguishing feature is that knowledge commons are not necessarily confined to small communities, as was often the case when dealing with the collective exploitation of common natural resources. Open virtual communities, vast networks of international researchers, and all manner of extended and prolific universes populate the blogosphere, and so it is clear we are no longer dealing with the same phenomenon, or the same types of problems. In this respect, Ostrom's analysis is not all that dissimilar from Mancur Olson's, for whom the problem of "free riding" could be neutralized by restricting the size of the group. Size, for Ostrom, is likewise one of the decisive criteria for predicting whether the co-production of communal rules is likely to take hold or not. Indeed, Ostrom argued that the non-cooperative models described by Hardin, Olson, or the prisoner's dilemma were "useful for predicting behavior in large-scale CPRs in which no one communicates, everyone acts independently, no attention is paid to the effects of one's actions, and the costs of trying to change the structure of the situation are high."[48] This is the core theoretical issue when it comes to studying practices of cooperation that are far more extensive: it compels us to ask whether a change in scale forces us to modify our analysis of the "commons." In a text dedicated to the "future of the commons," David Harvey emphasizes how Ostrom's typical case studies were never larger than one hundred co-owners. For Harvey, the restricted size of the communities managing common property promotes a rather idyllic image of the commons that obscures all hierarchical dimensions through its focus on direct interpersonal relations. In Harvey's view, the nature of the problems and their concomitant solutions necessarily changes once we move from one scale to another, and this especially applies in the transition from the local to the global: "lessons gained from the collective organization of small-scale solidarity economies along common-property lines cannot translate into global solutions without resorting to nested hierarchical forms of decision making."[49] Perhaps we are right, then, to be skeptical about the ability of a category like the "commons" to be able to account for very different phenomena – from the family management of the refrigerator, to a municipal library, to scientific knowledge, or to the planet's atmosphere – under the pretext that these are all cases of "shared resources." One the one hand, Harvey certainly has good reason to critique the radical left's phobia of hierarchy – if not its phobia of organization as such – as well as its problematic idealization of "horizontalism." This phobia has led to political impasses and demoralizing failures as a result of the left's inability to create durable organizational models that are adequate to the object of the left's demands and the size of its movements (Occupy Wall Street, Indignados, etc.). On the other hand, however, Harvey misunderstands the extent to which the work of Ostrom and her collaborators are interested in practices and communal norms governing much larger groups. This is precisely the aim of Hess and Ostrom's research on the "new knowledge commons," whereby the two theorists attempt to come up with an analytical framework capable of transposing the characteristics of natural commons onto new these objects.[50]

Is Knowledge Naturally Common?

According to Ostrom and her collaborators, creating use rules are fundamental to governing every kind of commons. But these rules can vary from one type of common to another. "Traditional commons," to use Ostrom's terminology, are primarily threatened by the kind of human overexploitation that results from competition and the accumulation of private wealth. Collective use rules are therefore designed to achieve an equitable and collectively optimal system of sharing that does not exhaust but rather renews resources like water, fish, and pastures. The same, however, is not true for knowledge. In fact, we could even say that the problematic is inverted when we pass from natural commons to knowledge commons. In the case of knowledge, use rules must be designed to prevent the artificial depletion of the resource as a result of property rights, patents, entry barriers, etc. – in other words, all those devices now known, thanks to the work of James Boyle, as "new enclosures." Whereas natural resources are scarce resources – i.e., both non-exclusive and rivalrous – a knowledge commons involves non-rivalrous goods: their use by one individual does not merely fail to diminish its utility for others, but in many cases actually augments it. To put it in Hess and Ostrom's terms, the difference between a knowledge commons and natural resource commons is that whereas the latter is "subtractive" (i.e., rivalrous), the former is not. Once produced, new technologies allow knowledge to be disseminated at a marginal cost that is exceptionally low, sometimes zero. And the more that useful knowledge is shared, the more knowledge is subsequently produced on a network or in a community of knowledge, and the more said knowledge increases in value.[51] This property of knowledge – which is nicely articulated by the French expression "*plus on est de fous plus on rit*" – leads to a form of the commons that is a veritable "cornucopia." In other words, knowledge is not "subtractive" (as are natural commons) but is rather aggregative or cumulative: not only does knowledge not lose value when it is consumed, but it actually acquires additional value and, above all, allows more knowledge to be produced. Knowledge is thus an essentially productive good, insofar as its consumption by others not only fails to diminish the knowledge of others but, by favoring the production of new knowledge, produces a general augmentation. In this respect, one often encounters the well-known remark by Thomas Jefferson:

> If nature has made any one thing less susceptible than all others of exclusive property, it is the action of the thinking power called an idea, which an individual may exclusively possess as long as he keeps it to himself; but the moment it is divulged, it forces itself into the possession of every one, and the receiver cannot dispossess himself of it. Its peculiar character, too, is that no one possesses the less, because every other possesses the whole of it. He who receives an idea from me, receives instruction himself without lessening mine; as he who lites his taper at mine, receives light without darkening me.[52]

It is not difficult to imagine why so many movements and authors are interested in this "natural" characteristic of knowledge. For it would seem, according to this view, that this dynamic is, in itself, capable of subverting the very foundation of the market economy. But again, we must be careful not to adopt an overly naturalistic position (as is clearly manifest in Jefferson's remarks). Far too often, analysis of the knowledge commons rests upon the supposed intrinsic properties of knowledge as a purely public good – i.e., its natural productivity and its cumulative character. The economic categorization of knowledge is undoubtedly seductive: it casts any barrier erected within the domain of knowledge an unnatural intervention. Indeed, it inverses the prior liberal naturalism by interpreting all enclosures of knowledge as so many anti-natural, and therefore anti-productive, constructions. The reality, however, is that neither the enclosures nor the knowledge commons themselves are "natural." They are governed by legal systems, regulatory frameworks, and institutions that sometimes favor the restriction of knowledge to the point of reserving exclusive access for a select few, while at other times they may favor the freest and widest dissemination possible. It is not the "nature" of knowledge that makes it so productive: it is the juridical rules and social norms that determine the scope of its extension and its corresponding fecundity. As Nancy Kranich has shown in her research on the strategies and methods used by private publishers to profit from American libraries and universities, there is nothing in the nature of knowledge itself that naturally makes it a shared resource.[53] Digital technologies alone are not enough to make knowledge "naturally" open and available. This is evident, according to Kranich, by the development of commercial or governmental enclosures that limit or even prohibit access with increasing frequency. This limitation or prohibition on access is, of course, nothing new. This form of control always crops up whenever knowledge is reserved for elite castes or favored classes. It takes specific institutions such as schools, public libraries, scientific institutes, and universities to disseminate knowledge and stimulate research. But it is precisely these institutions that have been weakened or transformed by the spread of the logic of intellectual property. By codifying this legal category and extending it to an ever-increasing range of immaterial goods – as we saw in the previous chapter – lawyers and legislators have enabled the proliferation of increasingly long-lived monopolies dedicated to protecting economic rents that are ostensibly designed to encourage innovation. Yet exclusive property rights have undoubtedly yielded largely detrimental effects when it comes to creativity and the dissemination of works and ideas, while most digital commons have contrastingly demonstrated a marked ability to encourage creativity and innovation. What is more, the digital commons allow large communities of contributors to form more open, innovative, and productive online communities. Yet such collaborative productivity is only possible through the invention of technological and social rules, as well as through legal apparatuses that favor cooperative practices and convey an ethic of sharing. As Benjamin Coriat emphasizes, an informational commons is only ever the result of "foundational and constituent acts."[54]

According to Hess and Ostrom, the fundamental problem of knowledge can be reduced to the problem of digital capture. If, according to these authors, knowledge is a purely public good – i.e., if it is both non-exclusive and non-rivalrous – there are nonetheless technical means of transforming knowledge into a good that is the exclusive property of a title holder who can refuse to transfer ownership except through payment. And it is precisely because knowledge can be captured by new technologies that knowledge commons can be assimilated into the same framework as a natural commons, and why knowledge "must be managed, controlled, and protected into order to guarantee its sustainability and preservation."[55] It is in this precise sense that we ought to speak of a "knowledge commons" or "informational commons." To be clear on this point: it is because knowledge has *ceased* to be a purely public good that it *must* be regarded as a common good, which is to say that it must be placed within the same analytical framework as the "natural commons." The productivity of knowledge must be secured by rules similar to those that ensure the sustainability of natural resource stocks. Failure to establish such social rules would lead to what Michael Heller refers to, in the context of property rights in biomedical research, as the "tragedy of the anti-commons."[56] The purpose of such rules is to prevent the depletion of creativity and innovation that would result from the imposition of property rights and commercialization. For Hess and Ostrom, knowledge commons are much more vulnerable than is often thought. The centralization of information on private or public websites raises fears that informational resources might disappear altogether. But, perhaps above all, the creation of enclosures by both the market and the state (as Boyle and Bollier have emphasized) can restrict access to information and cause informational flows to dry up. As Hess and Ostrom thus argue, "the challenge is how to blend systems of rules and norms related to this new commons to guarantee general access to the knowledge that empowers humans while ensuring recognition and support for those who create knowledge in its various forms."[57] Knowledge commons are not, therefore, common by virtue of the "non-subtractive" nature of the resource, but because of the apparatus that protects the production of knowledge from enclosure and commercialization. In other words, the emphasis is once again on the social rules that govern the resource, rather than the technical aspects of the resource itself. New technologies can create very different types of objects when it comes to knowledge. They can produce contradictory objects, and sometimes they even do so within a single institution. American universities, for instance, systematically apply for informational patents while, at the same time, developing open-access online courses.

This is the lesson that Hess and Ostrom draw – again according to their very naturalistic perspective – from their analysis of the knowledge commons framework. It is diametrically opposed to the spontaneous ideology of hackers, for whom freedom within digital networks presumably necessitates the absence of rules. If important domains of knowledge have already been restricted or threatened by market elements, it should also be noted, according to the advice of Ostrom and her collaborators, that these domains can be re-organized as legal commons in order to protect knowledge from the logic of property or from the direct control of capital and commercial exploitation. Indeed, the researchers that developed the notion of a "knowledge commons" initially modeled these commons on self-organized academic communities, who took advantage of the opportunities for collective work that these new information technologies promoted by developing a set of rules that governed the operation of these communities.

The "Constitutional Basis" of Knowledge Commons[58]

Intellectual innovation and productivity depends on strong rules and norms that ensure the free circulation and growth of knowledge through the sharing of research and results. The validity of this assertion can be immediately verified by considering several "canonical" examples of a knowledge commons, beginning with the Internet. We know that the "network of networks" was born out of a series of initiatives and discussions largely conducted amongst a small community of researchers who established a system of egalitarian and reciprocal exchanges. The primitive Internet, which was academic and non-commercial, was established using public funds within the context of public research, and its purpose was explicitly outlined in a document written by the creators of the Arpanet – the Network Working Group – during the late 1960s and early 1970s: "we hope to promote exchange and discussion to the detriment of authoritarian proposals." Twenty years later, one of the founding members of the group again wrote, "the result was to create a community of network researchers who believed strongly that collaboration is more powerful than competition."[59] As Patrice Flichy put it, it was not the technology that allowed academic research to become networked, but quite the opposite: it was the decision to work cooperatively through the open exchange of information that, in an unintended manner, disclosed the potentialities of networks. This cooperative model, which merely responded to the demands of its designers, has informed practices and shaped techniques that have subsequently spread far beyond scientific and research circles.

With the growing success of peer-to-peer networks, it is evident how much the academic community has significantly shaped, up the present day, cooperative and exchange-based practices. If academic institutions were indeed the midwives of the network revolution, it was because of the dual values of a cooperative ethic amongst scholars and the series of rules, explicit or implicit, which prohibited private appropriation of the result of common research. Thus, while the Internet may appear to be recent development, it is in fact the offspring of a rather old tradition of "open science." In the 1940s, American sociologist Robert King Merton enumerated a certain number of conditions that defined the "scientific ethos," and that leads, in his view, to the production of knowledge. Amongst such ethical components – which include universalism, disinterestedness, moral integrity, and organized skepticism – Merton listed "communism," admittedly a strange term to flow from the pen of a sociologist who was not particularly sympathetic to the political regime of the same name. What Merton meant by this term had to do with the idea that science presupposes an organization of relations between scientists that truly renders knowledge a kind of global and communal heritage, which is incrementally enriched by all scientists as their work advances, and from which they can draw to continue their research. "Communism," in other words, was an essential aspect of open science, for Merton. And it could only develop if researchers remained independent from political and economic powers, and were satisfied with symbolic remuneration and regular career advancement.[60] For Merton, then, science was incompatible with the norms of capitalism, as he asserted in the most emphatic way. Accordingly, the financing for scientific work could in no way be dependent on the anticipation of results, as if it were a kind of private investment. Rather, science should be supported by society as a whole or, failing this, funded by philanthropic means devoid of any contractual obligations.

The centrality of this scientific ethos in the rise of collaborative networks also played a major role in the creation of free databases for researchers in the 1980s. Faced with rising prices for scientific publications, American academics created digital systems designed to disseminate research and create journal portals and databases that implemented the principles of "open science" on a vast scale, in contravention of the commercial practices of publishers and "university entrepreneurs" who tried to monopolize the results of scientific work through patents. And it was this same spirit that permeated the free software movement. By permitting free access to source code, the free software movement operates through the creation of "rules of freedom" that allows each participant to study how a given program works in order to improve its design and redistribute new copies.[61] This movement was an ethical revolt against the imposition of proprietary software (as opposed to free systems), and it prompted a computer scientist at the Massachusetts Institute of Technology (MIT) artificial intelligence laboratory, Richard Stallman,[62] to create a new regime of legal protection for classifying "open" common property, based on open source code.[63] In 1985, Stallman created the Free Software Foundation, whose explicit goal, according to Philippe Aigrain, was to "build a set of software tools to meet the needs of general computing and to ensure these tools remained available under a common property regime."[64]

After years of effort, the free software movement currently mobilizes hundreds of thousands of developers and involves users numbering in the tens of millions. The GNU/Linux operating system, which is used in most websites today, is the direct result of this collaboration, along with other very successful projects such as Firefox, Apache, or Debian. As Aigrain again emphasizes, Stallman's major contribution to these successes was the protection of the GNU system through a GPL (General Public License).[65] The GNU GPL was released in 1989 and created a genuine commons by defining rights and duties for users.[66] The community of users and producers is protected by a legal regime of communal intellectual property titled "copyleft" – a term created by Don Hopkins, a friend of Stallman's, to emphasize its opposition to traditional copyright. It is a general concept that defines a series of principles applicable to software distribution licenses, and it is designed to protect the rights of user-producer communities, rather than individual authors. The central idea of copyleft is to give anyone permission to run a program, as well as to access, distribute, and modify the source code.[67] Anyone can draw from the results accumulated by the community, including for commercial uses, in order to make new contributions (but without appropriating developmental results, which must remain common).

In short, copyleft inverts the logic of copyright in order to meet the opposite end copyright was intended meet: as opposed to restricting the use of software, copyleft is a means of allowing it to be "free" – which is to say not exclusively appropriable – "for the benefit of the entire community." Copyleft actively excludes exclusion, which differs from the simple abandonment of software into the public domain, insofar as it imposes explicit rules on users to ensure free access to any subsequent modifications. Copyleft is not, therefore, a negation of property, but a paradoxical use of the rights of creators over their creations: the user is free to use the software as he wishes, except when it comes to its mode of distribution. This is intended to ensure the continued enrichment of the commons."[68] As Pierre-André Mangolte points out, "the copyleft clause creates an egalitarian and durable institutional framework that is conducive to the prolonged development of free software and the establishment of cooperative forms of production."[69] The range of licenses offered by the creative commons movement has henceforth made it possible to produce commons in multiple domains, by disseminating systems of rules created but computer experts and lawyers that allow cultural, scientific, artistic, and intellectual works to be made available to anyone through these special licenses. These licenses create a particular form of copyright that, for example, obliges disclosure of the origin or paternity of a work while prohibiting its commercial use. And it is worth noting how much the free software movement has drawn its strength from the close ties it forged between computer practitioners and legal theorists who have become increasingly interested in new technologies, such as James Boyle, Eben Moglen, Lawrence Lessig, and Yochai Benkler. This alliance between computer scientists and legal theorists only confirms the assertion that a knowledge commons presupposes a legal and normative architecture that is resistant to commercial strategies and the logic of property.

The use of free software has, of course, been vigorously opposed by the great tech oligopolies who attempt to impose their particular standards on software – with the notable exception of IBM, which, starting in 1999, partnered with the movement in a commercial context. Stallman and many others involved in the movement prioritize freedom of use and creation, as is evident in the very expression "free software." In their view, if property is legitimate in matters of material goods, it is not so when it comes to intellectual creations, which pose specific and very diverse problems (depending on the specific case at hand). It is always counter-productive to extend the category of property to immaterial goods, such as software, because the latter are not "objects" but collective processes of creation that are by definition unfinished. As Mikhaïl Xifaras emphasizes, it is in the name of a "particularly altruistic and civic utilitarianism" that Stallman has fought against the imposition of copyright onto software. And the social offshoots of the free software movement are also very interesting. Digital co-production communities can now be found in all shapes and sizes. The rapid and continuous development of Wikipedia, which since 2001 has been the most visible of the new types of collaborative resources, contains millions of articles written by hundreds of thousands of authors, and is visited by hundreds of millions of users. Wikipedia's founding principle is of course well known: it is a "freely distributed encyclopedia that everyone can improve," according to the website's slogan. We can clearly see the principle of digital cooperation in the example of Wikipedia: the latter presupposes the establishment of rules to facilitate the free dissemination of content, as well as rules to stimulate article writing and the establishment of an organized mechanism for collectively monitoring any modifications. We might also cite, as another example, the rapid expansion of open educational resources, which is fuelled by institutions or teachers who are contributors to a communal education apparatus through online courses, lectures, exercises, or educational games that are freely shared under a "creative commons" license.

In addition to these classic and perhaps overcited examples, we should also include some more recent developments, such as the transformation of knowledge commons into "common manufacturing." Since the mid–2000s, the "maker" movement has transferred the principles of digital cooperation into the world of material production.

It combines desktop technologies that enable digital autofabrication (especially 3D printing) with the online collaboration of members of the maker community.[70] Certain authors like to imagine a profound re-composition of the conception and production of material goods that aligns with the production of digital services, and which would no longer require the large-scale mobilization of fixed capital. This would, indeed, be a new individualized form of production – it would be free of patents and entail a "free" mode of product design. Not only could the rules of the free software movement govern the vast field of the "Internet of Things," but they would also apply to traditional products through the digital re-making of these objects and the collaborative "mixing" of the two domains. But beyond these few examples, which fuel imagination and prophecy alike, we should not overlook all those online practices of sharing data, information, or works, the birth of participatory media, and all the smaller-scale cooperative and collaborative practices that cluster around particular interests. These smaller efforts have been especially aided by digital communications technologies and the incredible growth of social networks based on the shared content of their users (even if this content is captured by a market logic).

Through its profusion, and the multiplicity and diversity of its contributors, the Internet is undoubtedly a collection of resources that are produced and shared by users who give and receive on the basis of reciprocal giving. But is it, as Mikhaïl Xifaras asks, a liberated and emancipated space that will deliver us from private property and move us from cognitive capitalism to "informational communism"? What is most characteristic of these movements, and of the free software movement in particular, is their ability to create a range of legal processes in order to avoid the negative effects of the exclusivity of "intellectual property," which tends to impose itself as a common right over the entire field of immaterial production. Free and open-source licenses also form the "constitutional basis" of the knowledge commons in all its various forms, from *l'Art libre* up to open access for academics and researchers, and they constitute the background condition for the creation of collective wealth by a community of users.[71] Yet the question remains as to whether the resistance posed by the supporters of free and open-source software to the extension of intellectual property is a generalizable model for challenging the domination of the logic of property, not only in the digital and informational domain, but in all sectors of production, and thereby serving as a model for a new type of society.

A New General Ethic?

The theorists of the "hacker ethic" are one of the best examples of the practical extension of the ethos of open science to software creation and its protest against the new enclosures.[72] For numerous commentators who often tend to extrapolate observable trends from this movement and apply them to the larger society, the ethic and aesthetics of hackers are currently in the process of altering the economy and our society as such. A "hacker" – a term that designates both a programming enthusiast and a computer-savvy practitioner – should not be viewed as a kind of "lone wolf" who is merely out for their own self-interest. Neither are hackers simply "geeks" who are obsessed with computer technology.[73] According to the jargon, "the term 'hacker' . . . tends to connote membership in the global community defined by the net . . . It also implies that the person described is seen to subscribe to some version of the hacker ethic."[74] The hacker ethic, as described in a number of books, has several dimensions. It is based on a certain ethic of enjoyment, a commitment to freedom, and a relationship to the community geared toward "generalized giving." According to the work of American anthropologist Gabriella Coleman, the ethic does not come from the influence of a guru, but was rather a gradual construction that emerged as collaborative practices on the net were extended, and as these practices began to encounter very real obstacles created by the logic of property. At the same time, however, this ethic was not cut from whole cloth. It inherited many of its values from the counter-culture of the 1960s, and this helped transform cyberspace from an essentially technical tool into a social and political project.[75] More often than not, it was older Californian hippies that fed the imaginations of these "virtual communities" created on the basis of encounters in which anyone is free to partake from his or her own personal computer. These communities are thus no longer merely based on academic interests, as was the case in the early days of the Internet, but are now largely formed on the basis of common interests such as music and literature, for example.

According to philosopher Pekka Himanen, the hacker ethic is a new work ethic that shifts the quest for efficiency and profit to a search for passions and for solidarity.[76] Indeed, some theorists have gone so far as to describe the hacker as an "anti-*Homo oeconomicus*."[77] Unlike the alienated industrial worker, the hacker is an ordinary artist who is very different from the inspired and solitary genius of European romanticism. The hacker inscribes his practice within a collective aesthetic dynamic, and the hacker's somewhat idealized worldview is reminiscent of the discourse of the artistic avant-garde of the twentieth century.[78] If we follow Himanen, this new work ethic is in the process of supplanting the puritan morality of sacrifice and renunciation, and is gradually spreading through the entire economy and giving rise to a new general spirit capable of forging a new type of economic system.[79]

Gabriella Coleman summarizes the hacker aesthetic as follows: "Hackers . . . tend to value playfulness, pranking, and cleverness, and will frequently perform their wit through source code, humor, or both: humorous code."[80] This was certainly true of Richard Stallman, who often emphasized the dimension of shared joy in the practice of hacking.[81] Creative play is the principle motivation of the hacker. The hacker must demonstrate self-deprecation, mischief, and skill in order to be recognized in his or her community. This dimension lends the activity of the hacker characteristics that are diametrically opposed to the forced work that predominates in capitalist society. The activity of hacking – which is founded on passion rather than constraint – breaks the boundary between work and leisure and renders the latter no longer a space of passivity and isolation but a site of collective action.

If humor – which is always linked to "performances" in the aesthetic sense of the term – is one of the principal characteristics of these communities, they are also unified by their radical liberal beliefs: freedom of expression, freedom of association, and the freedom to access information and culture are fundamental and intangible principles of the hacker community. In other words, the hacker movement resists neoliberalism and the ideology of intellectual property by returning to the principle of freedom of individual expression that lies at the foundations of liberalism itself. The hacker slogan "code is speech" means software developers must enjoy the same freedoms as any other citizen. Yet if private appropriation prevents this expression, it is because speech is not free. As Himanen puts it, "freedom of expression and privacy have been important hacker ideals."[82] It is in this sense that we should view the hacker spirit as a resurgence of American movements that favor the protection and extension of fundamental civil liberties, liberties that are threatened or violated by state surveillance or Internet oligopolies. The creation of the Electronic Frontier Foundation (EFF) by Mitch Kapor and John Perry Barlow in 1990 was one of the key moments in the definition of cyber rights and the defense of cyberspace's independence. The movement became increasingly politicized as state power (whether totalitarian or "liberal") became increasingly interested in controlling the Internet. The close alliance between large Internet companies and the state has made cyberspace a space of intense surveillance where there are potentially no limits to how much these entities can intrude into our personal data or exchanges.[83]

The hacker ethic therefore constitutes an actualization of the ideas of the most traditional form of moral and political liberalism, rather than a prefiguration of informational communism. It especially inherited certain libertarian sensibilities from the counter-culture of the 1960s and 1970s. From this perspective, true creativity is only possible in the least regulated and least hierarchical context possible. This sentiment is clearly evident in the examples furnished by Eric Raymond in his classic text of hacker literature in which he opposes the creativity of the cooperative "bazaar" to the "cathedral" of the classical computer companies. As is very common in hacker literature, horizontalism, equality, and the greatest possible individual freedom are touted as the primary assets of collaborative networks and are regularly opposed to the obsession with prescription and control by businesses and administrations.[84] Undoubtedly things are not so simple, and quite often the coordination and selection of contributions to projects is directed by an informal hierarchy, or even a "benevolent dictator," according to the term used to designate leaders of cooperative projects, such as Linus Torvalds. If these idealized conceptions of the hacker community and its practices are to be taken with caution,[85] we must also ask ourselves if this ethic, which is nourished on a literature that simultaneously describes and constructs this ethic, does not in fact reflect the existence of a set of diffuse norms of mutual help and solidarity that strongly inhibits the opportunistic behavior of "free riding." In this sense, then, the hacker ethic plays a role that is at least partially similar to the collective norms established in the institutions and rules of natural commons. In any case, and however accurate these various commentaries on the hacker ethic may be, the practices developed in the fields of free software, participatory media, collaborative sites, data sharing, etc. have demonstrated that social, civic, and ethical factors play a major role in the intellectual and aesthetic creativity required for the digital production of certain goods and services. And, above all, they provide us with practical evidence that refutes the dominant neoliberal view that the only effective incentive in the domain of knowledge, as guaranteed by the logic of property, is monetary reward.

"Freedom" and the "Common"

Freedom must be understood, according to Richard Stallman's now-famous phrase, not in the sense of "free beer" but in the sense of "free speech." Many authors in the field, such as American legal theorist Lawrence Lessig, describe freedom – defined as the absence of regulation by the market or the state – as the ultimate value of the free software movement and, more generally, of the larger movement in favor of a creative Internet viewed as an "innovation commons."[86] According to Lessig, free resources "are those available for the taking."[87] Lessing – and Stallman, for that matter – thinks the struggle is no longer between the market and the state, but between the exclusive ownership of information and knowledge and free access to these resources. The Internet is the best example of such a "free resource," which is to say a resource "held in common." Does this mean that the knowledge commons, in contrast to the natural commons, exists in a universe that need not be governed by any norms or laws? Of course, surfing from one site to another by clicking on what you want is not really the same as co-producing knowledge and information. Many authors, in this respect, stray quite far from Ostrom's lesson when they describe open access in cyberspace as a new "terra nullius" that can be accessed by anyone for any use.[88]

It is worth wondering whether the insistence within the free software movement on freedom of use, freedom of diffusion, and freedom of modification, which is in turn supposed to give rise to a free culture, does not tend to overshadow the principal feature of the movement – namely the constitution of communities of co-users and co-producers. For the *libriste* movement, in this respect, is not merely a reiteration of the utopian idea of free circulation of information and the generalized transparency made possible by computer technologies. To make sure the fruits of collaboration between hundreds or even millions of Internet users cannot be exclusively appropriated by any one member of the community, but can, on the contrary, be used and modified by all, requires a specific form of "freedom" and "openness" that is created by constructing institutional rules.

In short, a knowledge commons always presupposes rules, and these rules are determined according to the collective tasks being performed, the required competencies, and the size of the community. The selection of members, the coordination of contributions, the raising of necessary funds, the preservation of archives, all of these tasks demand real work if a commons is to be durable and productive. We should add, furthermore, that the rules about the "openness" of any given community may change from one cooperative project to another. For instance, if Wikipedia authorizes large-scale open collaboration, there are other projects in which developers are more strictly selected according to competencies and their adherence to the philosophy of free software. This is what stands out in Sébastian Broca's description of the development of the Debian operating system, which is very similar in its architecture to the natural commons analyzed by Ostrom and her colleagues – for instance, the distinction drawn in the Debian system between constitutional rules and operational procedures, or the establishment of a conflict resolution body (the "Technical Committee").[89]

What is undoubtedly the most misleading interpretation of Internet "freedom" is the tendency to overlook the series of rules incorporated by the technological system as such, which is of course a system that facilitates or hinders certain modes of exchange or communal work. As Lessig put it, cyberspace's "code is its law."[90] The code, or architecture, of cyberspace includes all the principles and instructions contained in the infrastructural hardware and software that constitute the structure of the web. During the early decades of the Internet, these infrastructures were not centrally controlled and consequently were able to be developed according to the applications and contents of any given contributor. According to Lessig, "the system is built – constituted – to remain open to whatever innovation comes along."[91] As Lessig put it in his first book, published in 1999, there is nothing "natural" in cyberspace: everything is a choice, everything has been constructed according to a certain logic favoring the free flow of information.[92] That said, the code, which is of course the system's true regulator, is always susceptible to change.[93] One of the Internet's most important architectural principles is the TCP/IP protocols, which allow data to be exchanged without its contents being reported or disclosed on the network. This initial elementary architecture made it impossible for a powerful agent – such as the state or large telecommunications corporations – to regulate the interactions between Internet users. The protocol was based on the end-to-end principle, according to which the development of data exchanges – and the entire Internet in general – can be accomplished without central interference. The other important defining principle of the Internet was "net neutrality," which is a principle that concerns the circulation of "packets" of data within networks. To say the Internet is built on a principle of net neutrality means all these "packets" are treated in a strictly equal fashion, regardless of their content.[94] This essential condition is, today, greatly threatened by the growth and power of Internet oligopolies. By concentrating and allying themselves, these oligopolies could radically transform cyberspace through a market logic that accumulates data on Internet users and uses this data in order to maximize advertising profits.

By the late 1990s, Lessig had begun to see how governments and large corporations were transforming the Internet's code in order to better manage cyberspace according to their increasingly overlapping interests. The identification of the Internet user, the collection of personal information, and generalized espionage by businesses and intelligence agencies was overwriting the "primitive code" and altering the nature of cyberspace. To fight for freedom on the Internet is to defend personal liberty against the double menace of corporate influence and state surveillance. But it is also a fight to defend a shared space that is not governed by either the logic of the market or by state censorship.

The Illusion of "Technological Communism"

A number of commentators, usually based on partial observations and a very general understanding of knowledge, have begun to see the incarnation of a generalized informational communism in the expansion of the Internet. In a text that skillfully parodies the *Communist Manifesto*, Eben Moglen, a professor of law at Colombia

University, argues that the class struggle has been displaced onto the terrain of knowledge and now pits the "creators," who are allied with the workers, against the property-owning class. One of the more interesting aspects of this text is its reproduction of the Marxian tension between a historical law that necessarily leads to an emancipated society and an analysis of the antagonistic relations between classes that does not, in itself, allow one to pre-emptively designate a victor before the struggle comes to completion. As Moglen puts it:

> the advance of digital society, whose involuntary promoter is the bourgeoisie, replaces the isolation of the creators, due to competition, by their revolutionary combination, due to association … The network itself, freed of the control of broadcasters and other bandwidth owners, becomes the locus of a new system of distribution, based on association among peers without hierarchical control, which replaces the coercive system of distribution for all music, video, and other soft goods.[95]

Internet communities are thus viewed as the prefiguration of a new mode of social and political organization based on generalized cooperation enabled by networked computers.

Yet this whole notion is, in our view, overly optimistic. Whenever one reads an author who advances this thesis, one should always ask the following: does the advent of communist society depend on a social movement that has equipped itself with the instruments of struggle and created new institutions that correspond to the principles of a society founded on cooperation? Or does the transformation of capitalism and the passage to the reticular communist society rest entirely on the new forms of value created in the knowledge economy? It is not entirely uncommon to find both logics, usually in a confused state, in works by the same author. There is no question, for instance, that Hardt and Negri's description of the future society as an extension of the free software movement, wherein "open source" becomes the matrix of this coming society, is an attempt to avoid the more problematic versions of technological determinism:

> We might also understand the decision-making capacity of the multitude in analogy with the collaborative development of computer software and the innovations of the open source movement … When the source is open so that anyone can see it, more of its bugs are fixed, and better programs are produced.[96]

For while there is still significant risk here of trying to solve political problems with technological solutions, it is nevertheless conceivable that the future society, as Hardt and Negri envision it, will indeed emerge through a political struggle that tries to impose "freedom" and "openness" onto closed systems.[97]

For other authors however – and sometimes for Hardt and Negri as well, at different moments – the cooperative model will smoothly triumph by virtue of the immanent logic of capital itself, a logic that operates on the basis of networks and creates value by capturing the free cooperation of the hive mind while it produces collective knowledge.[98]

According to this thesis, contemporary firms strive to capture the positive externalities generated by social communication and cognitive cooperation, which have recently become the principle source of economic value. By taking the exploitation of collaborative work in the context of free software as a kind of economic prototype, this "cognitive capitalism" begins to spread as firms become increasingly aware of the economic importance of online, virtual communities. This new "mode of production," based on interconnected intelligence in the network, begins to then create the conditions for capitalism's overcoming.[99] André Gorz, at times, falls prey to this technological determinism when, for example, he argues, "the computer emerges here as the universal and universally accessible tool through which all forms of knowledge and all activities can theoretically be pooled."[100] What we find here is utopian thinking – which is often quite old – whose recurrent theme consists in extrapolating the effects of certain systems of organization or technical infrastructures into full-blown models of social organization. Whether it was the industrial system for Saint-Simon, or the development of cybernetics a century and a half later for Norbert Wiener, in each instance economic and technological forms serve as points of support for futuristic projections of complete social re-organization.

The "Knowledge Commons" from Capital's Perspective

If one consults contemporary managerial discourse, one realizes that connectionist capitalism (*le capitalisme connexionniste*) has had its eyes on the common for over a decade and a half, and capitalism's grip over the economy is in fact enhanced by its use of new technologies and by the commercial necessity to assemble, communicate, and invent in common. Not only is this literature in total discord with the thesis on the ineluctable emergence of the democratic commons from today's cognitive capitalism, but rather it testifies to the private sector's ability to stop at nothing to construct, both internally and externally, managerial and commercial quasi-commons. There is, by now, an abundant business literature that describes, in detail, the efforts that are being made today to re-think the corporate business model along network lines, and to identify and develop the mechanisms for creating an "ersatz" common in the direct interests of capitalist accumulation.[101] If cooperation within the firm does not happen on its own, it must be the primary task of new managers to create the conditions for cooperation, argues Oliver Zara. Collective intelligence and the management of this knowledge are now viewed as the two fundamental resources that determine business performance.[102] The management of collective intelligence "favors a new art of collective work based on sharing, intellectual assistance, and co-creation," argues Zara benignly.[103] It is all a matter of substituting "command and control" with "connect and collaborate."[104]

The management of cooperation, which is an exemplary manifestation of what Luc Boltanski and Eve Chiapello call the "new spirit of capitalism,"[105] obviously runs up against the ultimate goal of any business – profitability – and the strictly individualistic incentives that determine career advancement and make higher pay the sole purpose of one's employment.[106] Accordingly, then, Zara argues that interfirm cooperation is never spontaneous: it requires incentives, tools, specific modes of organization, an entire "art" the manager must master with increasing refinement. Of course, it goes without saying that this intra-business organization of cooperation has nothing whatsoever to do with democracy: "businesses are not democracies (some exceptions aside) and for their survival and sustainable development, *it is preferable for businesses to remain undemocratic*."[107] Instead, this new mode of capitalist governance creates "in-house" commons that mobilize the ideas and knowledge of collaborators, but without ever suggesting that employees might participate in collective decision-making. The novelty of this transformation is therefore more apparent on the marketing side of business, which tries to create communities of consumers that, depending on their volume and the density of their interconnections, may play a very important role in the financial value of the business.

Marketing professionals have long been in the habit of collecting personal information to make customer profiles and construct consumer databases in order to either target advertising to individuals directly or to sell or lease this data to other businesses. Yet these marketing practices are becoming increasingly important for organizing the "constitutional basis" of the firm as such. Firms are no longer only concerned with attracting a market made up passive consumers that do not know each other and do not trade amongst themselves. Today, firms must build "consumer capital" – i.e., a community of consumers who are invited to enter into the universe of brands themselves, who participate in the development of products, and who even innovate as co-producers. Far from the naïve vision of capital as a mere parasite feeding upon open networked connections, what we are witnessing now are increasingly sophisticated marketing strategies designed to organize the free cooperation of consumers. The goal is to retain these customers and to endow their consumption with collective meaning, but also to increasingly exploit the information they provide about themselves and the employees with whom they interact – or, even better, to elicit creativity from a group of people of varying skills and, ultimately, to profit from their largely voluntary work. This is the basis of crowdsourcing, for instance, which relies on the free and spontaneous collaboration of users to elicit opinions about products and to propose new or improved sales techniques or after-sales services. With the rise of the Internet, "ordinary people," argues Jeff Howe, "who use their free time to create content, resolve problems, and even contribute to institutional R&D [research and development] have become a new reservoir of labor, cheap labor."[108]

If we take the new management gurus at face value, then the key to managerial success now lies in the ability to construct a commercial commons. According to John Hagel and Arthur Armstrong, firms must now rely on the organization of "virtual for-profit communities," which have become the true vectors of profit in the new economy. Virtual communities are no longer simply spaces of freedom and sharing as imagined by the heirs of the counter-culture. They are now new commercial forms. A winning business strategy now consists in not only informing customers about products on websites, but in creating communications between customers on the basis of common interests related to the products being sold, or in providing a service that allows customers to sell to each other through a for-profit intermediary. The construction of such communities by corporations is increasingly necessary due to the law of returns that says, "the more you sell, the more you sell" – a principle that ensured the success of both Microsoft and Facebook.

In emerging markets such as these, it is crucial to be the first to fully benefit from an extremely lucrative monopolistic dynamic; a good example of the profitability of organizing such social networks is Twitter.[109] Examples like Twitter show how much the community of consumers determines the value of a business – or, better, how much the virtual community allows companies to reduce production costs through the use of free labor. The capitalization of the community is a perfect example of the manner in which the logic of the network has been instrumentalized by marketing. The larger the network, the greater the financial value for the firm. According to Hagel and Armstrong, the name of the game is all about organizing the virtual commercial community in order to "capture value from members."[110]

And, of course, consumers do not merely supply corporate websites and other forums with their opinions, advice, or information – they also participate in the R&D of products. Under networked conditions, consumption becomes the production or co-production of goods. Consumer-users are transformed into voluntary co-producers of innovation, according to Eric von Hippel[111]: innovation is increasingly created by composite communities of people with differential competencies, and this diversity is an important source of creative fecundity for firms. According to some authors, the online collective project model will, at least partially, substitute the classic business model when it comes to the development of a product, because it enables substantial cost reductions in R&D by using the voluntary labor furnished by a community formed on the basis of a passion or interest. In the age of "wikinomics," a neologism created by Don Tapscott and Antony D. Williams, consumers have become "'prosumers' by co-creating goods and services rather than simply consuming the end product."[112] This opens up a new era in which billions of people voluntarily participate in the production of wealth that is then appropriated by firms. As Tapscott and Williams rather naïvely assert, we "can now actively participate in innovation, wealth creation, and social development in ways we once only dreamed of."[113]

Firms are now faced with a situation in which they must "harness the new collaboration or perish,"[114] and this means radically modifying their organizational structure. Capital's extension over the field of cooperative organization is aimed at making productive use of the time and motivations that exceed the normal parameters of the salaried labor force. Employees' free time or the activities of retirees or students now become productive voluntary time, and consumption and leisure are increasingly integrated into the production of goods. Yann Moulier-Boutang is thus mistaken when he argues, "entrepreneurial intelligence consists in converting the wealth already present in virtual digital space into economic value."[115] All indications suggest that "entrepreneurial intelligence" is now a matter of constituting the free cooperation of consumers and thereby producing collective knowledge that will be directly incorporated into the production cycle at minimal cost. The common is thus already a managerial category that compounds the classical exploitation of workers with the unprecedented exploitation of consumer-users.[116]

One cannot but wonder if the businesses associated with these online communities, who "are already discovering the true dividends of collective capability and genius," will be able to continue to profit from this free workforce and continue to develop this model of exploiting free collaborative work.[117] The proponents of capitalism's digital revolution seem convinced that powerful motivations are yet to be exploited. For the consumer becomes the cooperator not by economic constraint, as is the case with the employee, but by seduction, a taste for sharing, a valorization of skills, the recognition one receives from others, the passion invested in a voluntary activity, etc. Of course, integration within a community of consumers is not in itself new. It was already at work within the logic of "branding," which makes each consumer wear a corporate insignia or logo and thereby become a voluntary marketer. It is because the commodity is a signifying mark for the consumer that a symbolic community becomes desirable and functions as a means of identification. But marketing is now in pursuit of something more than mere unremunerated participation in the sales department: it now wants unpaid labor in the productive force, a free and voluntary labor force in the service of the firm. It is a matter of putting consumers to work: making them co-producers of goods and co-producers of their own subjection. And, to momentarily draw on the psychological categories of human resource management, this is only possible by taking advantage of all the dissatisfactions associated with compelled labor (i.e., wage labor) and by overcoming monetary or "extrinsic" motivations in order to better exploit non-monetary or "intrinsic" motivations and the workers' aspiration for collective work. From the skewed perspective of capital, then, the commercial commons of digital capitalism is leading us toward a more democratic future:

> We are becoming an economy unto ourselves – a vast global network of specialized producers that swap and exchange services for entertainment, sustenance, and learning. A new economic democracy is emerging in which we all have a lead role.[118]

As we can see, then, waiting for the spontaneous cooperation of individuals in computer networks, or for the "production of knowledge by knowledge" that flows from the cognitive dynamic itself, is an illusion.[119] Today, it is the firm that builds the commercial quasi-common by constructing an interactive framework for creating profit: businesses are "monetizing" the ecosystems they have designed and made available for their creative clients. In other words, it is primarily capital that is in the business of producing the "knowledge commons."

In summary, then, it is hard not to notice similarities between the advocates of informational anarcho-communism and those extolling the merits of digital capitalism. We find the same arguments in each discourse, and the same technological illusions propped up into absolute truths. But if there is one aspect of the new, networked firm that is continually emphasized by its advocates, it is the constructed character of the commercial quasi-commons. Is this merely a case of vice paying homage to virtue? Whichever way one looks at it, it should be clear that the transition from cognitive capitalism to informational communism will not happen naturally or spontaneously. Knowledge is no more naturally rare than it is naturally abundant. Its production, circulation, and use depend entirely on the institutions that order and shape its related practices. Contrary to the claims of a certain techno-spontaneism, "network effects" do not naturally arise as a result of the simple act of connecting computers together: they are generated by a system of rules (including technological rules) that favors sharing, discussion, collective creation, passion, enjoyment of the game, etc. Developing the potential of digital technologies is not synonymous with rapt fascination or naïveté. Authors like Stallman and Lessig have sufficiently shown that certain characteristics of any given technological architecture may favor the constitution of communities, whereas other characteristics might very well destroy these communities.[120]

In his attempt to develop a new "political economy of the information network," Yochai Benkler shows the fragility of web structures in the face of the mechanisms now used by large corporations to control, often in alliance with state security and politic agencies, today's information and communications environment. While the dissemination of the personal computer and the achievement of increasingly dense interconnections between Internet users may pose a material obstacle to the concentration of the means of communication and the production of information, there is no guarantee that this technical and economic condition, which is essential to the constitution of a new public space, will be sufficient in itself to ensure the future of informational democracy and a culture of communal production. If, as Benkler maintains, the Internet has indeed given rise to a new informational environment that is much more suitable to the vitality of political democracy, or even the collective creation of a "more critical and self-reflexive culture,"[121] this is undoubtedly due to the "political ownership" of the technology, which permits direct contact between Internet users, the pooling of resources, and cooperation in the production of information.[122] But like Stallman and Lessig, Benkler also points out that Internet technology alone does not determine a particular social and political form; at most, it facilitates such a form and makes it possible. However, "different patterns of adoption" can serve very different strategies and induce very different social relations.[123] The question of common knowledge must therefore be addressed in terms of a "battle" that spans the whole field of these new technologies. In other words, we must categorically reject those prophesies that forecast the inexorable arrival of a free society as a result of nothing more than the dissemination of digital technologies.[124]

To avoid these kinds of errors, it is crucial to draw on the major lessons of the Elinor Ostrom's political economy of the common. The analysis she developed with her collaborators at the University of Indiana broke with the naturalism of orthodox economics while, at the same time, giving theoretical expression to the actuality and efficacy of collective practices, most of which were very old. Her approach emphasized the "institutional dimension" of the emergence and management of the commons, and this led her to the conclusion that it is not so much the intrinsic quality of a given good that determines the "nature" of the common, but rather it is the organized system of management that institutes an activity and its object that creates a common. While one may get the feeling from the literature on the commons from the 1980s that only "natural resources" can be governed as a common, subsequent developments concerning the production, dissemination, and maintenance of knowledge and information have shown, in the view of Ostrom and her team, that while the institutional character of a given commons depends, of course, on considerations related to economic efficiency (and hence an adequate relationship between the nature of the resource and the rules governing its production), the institutional character of the commons is not about economic efficiency alone: it is also based on "normative choices." It is through the recognition of the normative character of the commons and its associated institutions that Ostrom's work offers a two-fold critique of reigning economic orthodoxy.

Ostrom thus responds to the reigning economic dogma with a double argument. First, she shows that an institutional system for communal organization may be much better suited to the "sustainability" of resources – or to the production of knowledge – than the market or the state. But more than this, Ostrom decisively shifts the question of the commons into the terrain of collective action and its political conditions. This displacement in favor of rules of governance made it possible to put so-called natural commons and knowledge commons on the same plane, and it allowed her to broaden her analysis, especially near the end of her career, in order to deal with important questions concerning the environment and democracy at a global level.

In this sense, then, the emergence of the "commons paradigm" owes much to Ostrom's work. By showing how threats to the environment or threats to our ability to freely share intellectual resources are all linked to systems of rules – whether explicit or implicit, formal or informal, or actual or potential – that can destroy a commons or prevent its development, Ostrom's work made it possible to fully appreciate the dangers of economic behavior guided by the logic of appropriation, particularly in terms of the latter's tendency to irredeemably deplete natural resources. On the other hand, her work also emphasizes the risk of intellectual and cultural underproduction wherever knowledge is privatized, and how privatization threatens creativity and communication by restricting intellectual co-production by hindering the use of our public inheritance. In both cases, her analysis encourages an examination of the rules that make it possible to counter these dangers. On this point, Ostrom cannot have failed to see the potential political impact of her work (though she remained extremely cautious about the practical applications that might be drawn from her studies). Ostrom allowed us to see how Hardin's dilemma of the commons was about more than the use of local resources in small communities. It showed us that many of the political, social, ecological, and military problems facing nation-states and the world as a whole conform to the terrible logic of the "prisoner's dilemma," which locks us into a rigidly individualistic rationality rendering us incapable of arriving at collective solutions. "Much of the world is dependent on resources that are subject to the possibility of a tragedy of the commons"[125] – though, of course, Ostrom showed that the tragedy of the commons is really just a tragedy of impossible cooperation whenever individuals are imprisoned by their own self-interest. In any case, by shifting the discourse from *production* to *institutions*, Ostrom initiated a profound critique of economic naturalism – but she did not complete it. She fundamentally transformed the common from a natural phenomenon into an activity-based principle and institution, and thereby uncovered a new logic that, in turn, calls for a new theoretical approach.

5

Common, Rent, and Capital

As we indicated at the beginning of the book, we are indebted to Michael Hardt and Antonio Negri for first introducing the concept of the "common" – in the singular – to both critical political theory and activist discourse. The substitution of the singular "common" for the plural "commons" was a decisive theoretical achievement, and it accordingly warrants special recognition and careful study. Within the parameters of this new theoretical universe,[1] we are no longer compelled to conceptualize capitalism's present as a continual repetition of its origins. Indeed, as Hardt and Negri parenthetically admit in the Preface to *Multitude,* they were reticent to use the plural concept of the commons at all, precisely because the

> term refers to pre-capitalist-shared spaces that were destroyed by the advent of private property ... The more awkward [term] "the common" highlights the philosophical content of the term and emphasizes that this is not a return to the past but a new development.[2]

The common now designates the hidden dimension and the obscured condition of capitalism in its most modern form. The common is not what capitalism destroys but what it exploits, and to a certain extent the common is what capital produces:

> Our communication, collaboration, and cooperation are not only based on the common, but they in turn produce the common in an expanding spiral relationship. This production of the common tends today to be central to every form of social production, no matter how locally circumscribed.[3]

More importantly, Hardt and Negri's analysis of the commons, unlike the paradigm of the commons described in the previous chapter, does not ignore the capital–labor relation – though as we will see, Hardt and Negri's understanding of contemporary capital–labor relations is not without its problems. For us, the common is the philosophical principle that makes it possible to conceive of a future beyond neoliberalism, and for Hardt and Negri the common is the only possible path toward a non-capitalist future. The common is also a category tasked with undermining any residual nostalgia for state socialism, particularly in terms of the state's monopolization of a bureaucratized public service. In other words, the common is a category that transcends public and private. There is no doubt Hardt and Negri's use of the concept of the common can be a little blurry around the edges and rather ill defined at times; nonetheless, their work represents a fundamental step in the right direction in terms of the common's capacity for explaining the contemporary machinations of capitalism and the struggles striving to push us beyond the neoliberal present.

Hardt and Negri's concept of the commons is, in many ways, the polar opposite of the "paradigm of the commons" we discussed in the previous chapter. Instead of the negative framework of "destruction," Hardt and Negri theorize the commons from the perspective of "production": the commons is less something we need to defend from attack, and more something we need to promote and institute. And while we should not underestimate some of the theoretical advances made by Hardt and Negri, one of the central claims we make in this chapter is that the theory of the commons Hardt and Negri produce in their trilogy – and especially in *Commonweath*, the third volume of the trilogy, which is entirely devoted to the concept – inadvertently revives an older socialist and anarchist doctrine. To put it bluntly, Hardt and Negri's modern theory of the commons repeats the most striking aspects of the work of Pierre-Joseph Proudhon. In their own way, as Lorenzo Coccoli observes, Hardt and Negri make *theft* a central mode of accumulation that is independent of capital itself (as did Proudhon).[4] As Hardt and Negri put it, "scholars who critique neoliberalism often emphasize that capitalist accumulation is an increasingly predatory operation that functions through dispossession."[5] For Hardt and Negri, it is not so much the privatization or market subsumption of natural resources, urban spaces, or public services that constitutes capital's principle means of appropriation, but rather its financial rents that act as capital's principal lever for capturing the common products of immaterial labor. What is especially interesting or strange about Hardt and Negri's revival of the Proudhonian doctrine of "theft" is, however, that it is formally expounded through constant references to Marx.

Theorizing the common today first requires a clear view of the two discourses that have traditionally divided socialism. The purpose of this chapter, then, is to illuminate contemporary debates on the common through an archaeological exposition of this bifurcated socialist discourse. The first of these socialist discourses describes the common as a socially immanent dynamic that Proudhon refers to as the "collective force," and it is this immanent and spontaneous force that is subsequently stolen through the institution of property. The second socialist discourse is born from the work of Marx and argues that the common is not produced spontaneously at all, but is rather the direct product of capital – more specifically, it is a product of capital's power of command over labor and its imperative to organize productive cooperation. Capital, in Marx's view, produces the common out of its frenzied drive toward its own enrichment, through its organization of the collective force of the workers into the collective force of capital.

We refer here to the first of these discourses as the *spontaneous social force of the common*. This is undoubtedly Proudhon's take on the commons, and its correlative is an analysis based on exploitation as "theft." For Proudhon, that which individuals and societies produce spontaneously is subsequently subtracted for the benefit of private individuals or classes through various types of legal or political mechanisms, though the primary mechanisms of theft are private property and the state. For Proudhon, who follows and modifies the Saint-Simonian tradition, the common is nothing other than the *spontaneous nature of the social itself.* In this respect, Proudhon belongs to the same tradition as the classical political economists, especially Smith, who make labor the source of all wealth and who can accordingly only justify rent and profit as something that was extracted after the fact.

Marx's very different conception of the common was in fact a direct response to this sociological and anthropological model. And while, at a passing glance, Marx seems to borrow much from Proudhon, closer examination discloses how different Marx's analysis really is. While Marx undoubtedly views humans as fundamentally "social" creatures, he insists that the social character of humanity is not an eternal essence, but is historically developed and is therefore always manifest in historically different forms. In the capitalist mode of production – and here we should think especially of Marx's analyses in *Capital* (vol. 1) of labor's cooperation in the context of large-scale industry – it is capital itself that organizes the common and puts it to work producing the surpluses necessary for accumulation. For Marx, the concept of capital is the foundation of bourgeois society. Capital is that unique form of value that valorizes itself by producing more labor and hence more value. There is no economic activity, and thus no work for the workers, unless there is profit to be had for the capitalist. Capitalist appropriation does not therefore take place after the fact, but production itself is always already organized around the pursuit of private profit – indeed, through a typical ideological inversion characteristic of employers, the wage itself appears to be an illegitimate tax on the capitalist's income (the famous "cost of labor"). For Marx, the productive cooperation implemented by capital is the objective foundation of communism, and thus the explanatory scheme Marx offers is the *historical production of the common by capital.*[6] The historical gestation of the common within capital is the foundation of progressive Marxism, which sees the conditions of a superior type of society in germ form within the capitalist productive forces themselves.

Within the first of these socialist discourses, cooperation precedes labor's submission to capital, and so the entire problem can be resolved by organizing new relations between workers that simply bypass the appropriative powers of property. And for Proudhon, these new relations are to be organized on a strictly professional basis. In the second socialist discourse, the solution to the problem resides in the expropriation of the property owners themselves: the appropriation of capital by individual workers leads to the creation of a great collective worker, and cooperation is thus no longer directed by capital but organized by the workers themselves. A clear understanding of this older socialist debate is essential for adequately dealing with the challenges of theorizing the common today. It is not a question of choosing one discourse over the other, but of properly identifying the way in which this great debate has re-emerged within contemporary discourses of the common, which in turn raises two crucial questions: to what extent is the "rentier" theory of contemporary capital, which speaks of capital's ability to capture rents from the common, compatible with our understanding of the current organization of labor and the subjective mutations characteristic of neoliberalism? And secondly, to what extent does the doctrine of capital's production of the common allow us to account for the transition to a post-capitalist world? We suspect these questions are not just theoretically important, but have strategic bearing as well.

Defining the Common

The concept of the common that Hardt and Negri initially proposed in *Empire* and expanded on greatly in *Multitude* refers, in the first place, to the historically specific productive activity of "multitudes" within the context of late-twentieth-century globalization. By producing new interactions of all kinds, by creating multiple communicative networks and circulatory flows, globalization allows previously isolated individuals to produce the common: "insofar as the multitude is neither an identity (like the people) nor uniform (like the masses)," write Hardt and Negri, "the internal differences of the multitude must discover *the common* that allows them to communicate and act together."[7] Hardt and Negri see the "production of the common," through social interaction, as the dynamic and ultimately subversive force within empire. It propels empire forward and constantly overflows it. This is what Negri refers to elsewhere as the "power of multitudes." However, in the third volume of their trilogy, *Commonwealth*, the concept of the common becomes increasingly syncretic: it begins to encompass very heterogeneous objects and processes within the intellectual architecture of "alter-modernity," while it simultaneously condenses and projects a philosophical position onto capital's contemporary trajectory and its concomitant social struggles.

The common's first definition relates to what Hardt and Negri call "the common wealth of the material world – the air, the water, the fruits of the soil, and all nature's bounty – which in classic European political texts is often claimed to be the inheritance of humanity as a whole, to be shared together."[8] There is nothing especially original here. While Hardt and Negri rightly recall how many conceptions of the common have been influenced by this theological framework, which conceives of the common as a gift to all of humanity from God, it is unclear what benefit is derived from preserving this theological account of the "natural common," especially since it takes us some distance from our contemporary concerns about theorizing an alternative to neoliberalism. The second "more significant" definition of the common Hardt and Negri offer refers to the "artificial common"[9] – i.e., "those results of social production that are necessary for social interaction and further production, such as knowledges, languages, codes, information, affects, and so forth."[10] According to this definition, the commons is not a gift of the divine, nor even a gift from nature, but rather it designates both the condition and result of human activity in all societies. In addition to its prior theological meaning, the common is now endowed with anthropological significance as well. Human activity in any form always presupposes common conditions and resources. We all adopt various social "habits" as a result of social interaction, and this activity produces, reproduces, and transforms these initial conditions and resources.[11] The common, in this view, is both a set of conditions and the results of human activity – both "common resources" and "common products." This generalized anthropology of the commons tends to reduce the "production of the common" to notions of "communication" associated with the study of linguistics, notions of "habits" as understood by the American pragmatists, and even the concept of "culture" as used in the social sciences in the most general sense.

Hardt and Negri are, however, not entirely satisfied with these older and heterogeneous descriptions of the common, and so they develop a third definition of the common that is more original and more in line with the subject matter these two authors have long studied, namely the rise of "cognitive capitalism" and "immaterial labor." On the one hand, capitalist production is compelled to exploit everything that belongs to the common – including all the contents of the two previous definitions – and, in general, to subject all of social life to its own ends. But, on the other hand, it also increasingly requires free access to the "immaterial" resources of the common that have expanded in the new form of "biopolitical" production.[12] This is because "the hegemony of immaterial labor creates common relationships and common social forms in a way more pronounced than ever before."[13] If the common, in this sense, is increasingly the underlying condition upon which contemporary capitalism operates, and the common itself is based on immaterial labor, then the common is therefore the most promising development for the realization of the future communist society. In lockstep with the dominant Marxist tradition, cognitive capitalism itself is said to generate the conditions of its own transcendence:

> The content of what is produced – including ideas, images, and affects – is easily reproduced and thus tends toward being common, strongly resisting all legal and economic efforts to privatize it or bring it under public control. The transition is already in process: contemporary capitalist production by addressing its own needs is opening up the possibility of and creating the bases for a social and economic order grounded in the common.[14]

Intensely cognitive forms of immaterial labor function as the universal and spontaneous driver of the commons. This is Hardt and Negri's theory of the common.[15] It is based on the hegemony of the network as a "common form that tends to define our ways of understanding the world and acting upon it," and on the essence of knowledge as non-appropriable and uncontrollable, both of which intrinsically challenge the logic of value and its subsequent measure.

And finally, Hardt and Negri offer a fourth definition of the common, one which belongs to the register of social and political struggle and is defined as a collective act of the multitude. A new form of democratic social organization, in germ form, is latent in the struggles of today's cooperative and immaterial workers, as well as in the struggles of the poor multitudes all over the world. The "common wealth" (two words) produced by workers is translated into a political form that inaugurates the "commonwealth" (one word). This new commonwealth is no longer the "republic of property" but the political institutionalization of the common.

While these four definitions of the common are undoubtedly part of an ambitious project to endow the concept with an expansive scope, Hardt and Negri often struggle to articulate between them. In fact, it seems to us that the unity of the concept is almost purely rhetorical, especially when Hardt and Negri speak of a "biopolitical reason" that tends to function as a kind of vitalist inspiration for making all different aspects of the concept coalesce.[16] By collapsing theologico-juridical, anthropological, economic, and political dimensions into the same concept of the "common," Hardt and Negri hardly help develop the clarity of the concept, much less elaborate a new politics based on the concept they are trying to construct. Suffice it to say that their definition includes everything given in nature, all universal aspects of social life, the products of immaterial labor in the historically dominant era of cognitive capitalism, and finally all that which most characterizes contemporary struggles. We think this expansive amalgam needs to be unpacked.

The fact is that the unity of the concept of the commons is not really based on the realities the concept tries to describe, but rather derives from a "communistic" reading of Spinoza that functions something like a universal key. Being is the affirmation and self-development of power: nature, social life, immaterial labor, and political struggles are all manifestations of this power and the modes through which this power is affirmed. It then suffices merely to say that power and production are identical, and that being and the common are synonymous, in order to justify a concept of the common as a transhistorical principle that has operated since the beginning of time, all the way up to the immanent emergence of the superior society we are currently witnessing.

One of the more problematic contradictions Hardt and Negri encounter emerges out of their attempt to create a positive concept of the common as *production*, but without abandoning the natural, social, and intellectual definitions of the term. Yet these disparate elements only find their unity through the operations of capital, and capital, we are told, captures the common wealth in all its immensity and diversity from the outside. In this sense, then, the common only seems to exist as a resource confiscated by capital so that the latter can achieve profitability. In short, then, Hardt and Negri remain beholden to a negative definition of the common as the object of "theft" and "capture." Their communized Spinozism is combined with a neo-Proudhonism that can only conceive of exploitation as the "*a posteriori* illegitimate capture of the products of labor" – an assertion that could have easily come from Proudhon's *First Memoir on Property*.[17] This approach not only represents a profound regression in relation to Marx's analysis of capitalism, but also a profound blindness to contemporary forms of worker exploitation, the transformations of social relations and subjectivities under neoliberalism,[18] and the significance of struggles being waged today. What is ultimately most important, for Hardt and Negri, is not so much that they give voice to a revolt against the unbearable oppression of neoliberalism – the most negative aspects of which, especially in the workplace, are largely neglected – but that they openly testify to the "power of the multitudes" in accordance with the historical ontology upon which their analysis ultimately rests.

The institution of the commons is thus understood not as a determination of the second by the first but, inversely, as a determination of the first by the second. In other words, the common is thought to exist and develop independently of its institutional substrate, which is to say its status as "property," under conditions of biopolitical production. Its future institutionalization is conceived as the long-awaited coincidence between its prescribed political form and the nature and dynamism of its productive activity, which supersedes the old and outdated politico-juridical forms that paralyzed its essential productivity and hampered the production of the common throughout the centuries. The institution of the common, for Hardt and Negri, is thus a classic case of "adequacy" and "correspondence," in the sense that neither the institution of private property nor the public institutions that assert state control over the means of production are properly adapted to today's biopolitical production. Unlike the scholastic model, then, the "legal-political superstructure" now descends into the base in order to, as it were, "rise above it." Yet one cannot but wonder whether all of this does not ultimately promote a certain quietism: why the bothersome struggle to invent another world if cognitive capitalism necessarily produces its own transcendence as a result of its internal logic, and if "nature constitutes the wealth of the common that is the basis of human activity."[19]

Cognitive Capitalism: Rent and Theft

It may seem strange to place Hardt and Negri's analysis alongside such an "outmoded" nineteenth-century thinker as Pierre-Joseph Proudhon. Does Hardt and Negri's work not deal with the most recent transformations of our capitalist economies and societies? This unlikely pairing raises another question: can we reconcile the manner in which Hardt and Negri radicalize a certain Marxist optimism that tells us the objective conditions for the overcoming of capitalism have already been achieved, along with their profound (if unconscious) proximity to Proudhon? The answer to our question, and the underlying reason Hardt and Negri revive Proudhon's critique, ultimately lies in their specific diagnosis of the relations between immaterial labor and capitalism. To put it in Marxian terms, Hardt and Negri's thesis is based on the hypothesis of a certain *regression* of the direct control exercised by capital over workers, in the sense that capitalism will revert (in terms of one of its tendencies at least) from the "real subsumption of labor under capital" to conditions of "formal subsumption" and, eventually, from conditions of formal subsumption to the non-subsumption of labor under capital.[20] Hardt and Negri are not unaware of this aspect of their thesis: "the return movement from real to formal subsumption corresponds, in certain respects, to the recent reappearance of many antiquated, parasitical forms of capitalist appropriation."[21] This is the crux of their entire analysis: labor has already emancipated itself from the command of capital because the latter is incapable of organizing the most creative and fertile forms of intellectual cooperation. And, unsurprisingly, the conclusion to this process nicely accords with Negri's earlier work: communism already exists as the shrouded verso of contemporary capitalism itself.

Let us recall that, for Marx, capital first subsumed "free labor" – which is to say, labor separated from the conditions of production – but left the pre-existing traditional labor process unchanged. In other words, capital took control of the pre-existing trades, skills, and tools and integrated them into its reproductive cycle without re-organizing, re-defining, or re-shaping them (as it will at a later stage of its development). By continually reproducing the conditions of its own expansion, capital is forced to ceaselessly revolutionize its relations with its subsumed workers. It increasingly subjects workers to its logic of accumulation and transforms them, purely and simply, into nothing more than "ingredients" or "variables" in its operations. It imposes new gestures, rhythms, movements, behaviors, etc. onto the workers. The living labor of the worker is no longer incorporated into the process of self-valorization of capital as the work of a more or less qualified individual, but as an element of "socialized labor" or "common labor" (*vergesellschafteter* or *gemeinsamer*). This socialized labor is adapted to the mechanized system through the "appliance of chemical and other natural agencies, shortening of time and space by means of communication and transport, and every other contrivance by which science presses natural agencies into the service of labour."[22] Hardt and Negri's central thesis, along with the other theorists of cognitive capitalism, is that cooperation is no longer an effect of the direct domination of capital over living labor, but, on the contrary, is an external social or communal process, in the sense that it develops within society, outside of the process of production: "cognitive and affective labor generally produce cooperation autonomously from capitalist command, even in some of the most constrained and exploited circumstances, such as call centers or food services."[23]

The idea, today, that value is ultimately created outside and prior to the capitalist organization of labor is a return to the notion of a spontaneous collective force that is subject to a process of subtraction from the outside of an essentially rentier type. This thesis proceeds from the contemporary observation that the productive process increasingly mobilizes knowledge. The whole notion thus builds upon Marx's famous passage from the *Grundrisse*, though it inflects Marx's commentary in a very singular fashion (if not inverting its meaning altogether).[24] Industrial capitalism is becoming "cognitive": value is no longer created from fixed capital but derives from the shared knowledge possessed and embodied in the workers themselves. This is also why it is not only labor that is transformed, but the objects of labor as well. Production has become "biopolitical" in the sense that the production of immaterial goods (knowledge, images, affects, etc.) is also the production of human subjectivity as such. Yann Moulier-Boutang defines this new mode of capitalism as follows:

> The cognitive capitalist mode of production, if one wants to provide a concrete description of it that is sufficiently general to cover all its varieties (the production of material goods, services, signs and symbols) is based on intellectual cooperation networked by means of computers.[25]

"Rent" becomes the central mechanism of accumulation when capitalism enters its "cognitive" phase, but not because so-called bad financial capital leeches off so-called good productive capital, but because cognitive capitalism can only accumulate by imposing enclosures around knowledge and extracting revenue in a parasitic fashion.[26] This "becoming rent" of capitalism follows from the fact that workplace cooperation is no longer organized by capital. Instead, capital only functions by capturing and distributing incomes because "intellectual cooperation" is now the direct, determining factor in contemporary production: "in fact, rather than providing cooperation, we could even say that capital *expropriates cooperation* as a central element of exploiting biopolitical labor-power."[27] In short, the core proposition here is the idea that the "locus of surplus-value" is the common: "exploitation is the private appropriation of part or all of the value that has been produced as common."[28] The hegemony of immaterial labor in the creation of value, the expropriation of the common, and the predominance of rentier-style appropriation by finance capital are intertwined phenomenon. By detaching itself from the production process, capital takes on the more liquid and volatile form of financial capitalism. Confronted with an autonomous intellectual and productive common, capital is now nothing more than a rentier and parasitic power that preys on the actual sphere of production from the outside. This analysis remains faithful to Marx, who explained how capitalist rent "no longer appears here as the normal form of surplus-value."[29] Carlo Vercellone, one of the premier theorists of cognitive capitalism, puts it this way: "in sum, rents functions as a claim or right of ownership over material and immaterial resources that enables the extraction of value from a position of exteriority in relation to production."[30] If capitalist profit is no longer derived from the extraction of surplus value produced through the organization of cooperation, this is due to the new centrality of knowledge in the productive process, combined with the fact that knowledge is embodied in individuals (not in fixed capital). In other words, knowledge is on the side of "living labor," and it can no longer be encoded or controlled by capital.

According to this view, capital is in the process of abdicating its command over production and instead creates artificial conditions of scarcity by erecting "new enclosures." These enclosures slow down or block the production and circulation of knowledge in order to collect rent. A contradiction thus arises between a rentier-style capitalism that exploits cognitive cooperation and the "collective worker of the general intellect," and a knowledge society that develops outside these relations of exploitation (i.e., outside the factories and offices) through the support of welfare-state institutions.[31] In any case, knowledge is not ultimately generated in those sites in which labor is directly exploited. This is, unfortunately, a subject about which Hardt and Negri have very little to say, aside from merely emphasizing how "the core phenomenon is no longer the accumulation of fixed capital by the capacity of learning and creativity within the workforce." Almost nothing is said about all the studies dedicated to ongoing changes in the labor force and the highly ambiguous nature of the "autonomy" employees have achieved today.[32]

For these theorists, cognitive labor "is at the center of capitalist valorization and thus it possesses the power to break with the mechanisms of capitalist production."[33] Everything now transpires as if the hegemony of knowledge within the productive process has already given birth to a common that, by virtue of its progressive expansion, is destined to explode the capitalist integument confining it. There are several ways in which this argument is postulated. One of these ways emphasizes the fact that labor is no longer managed by outdated Taylorist methods, but through negotiation on the market – either through negotiations that involve the parent businesses and subcontractors or through relations between businesses and independent workers: "the Talyorist logic that proscribes specific tasks thus gives way to a results-oriented cognitive logic,"[34] and this logic involves an indirect relation of monetary command, whereby discipline is supplied by the market. Ronald Coase's theory, which tells us that the primary reason why firms are created is to reduce transaction costs, would therefore be at least partly overcome.[35] This new organization of work also grants greater autonomy to increasingly creative and independent employees: "the principal source of value now resides in the creativity, the polyvalence, and the innovative force of employees, not in fixed capital and not in the routinized execution of work."[36] As Negri and Vercellone put it:

> The rise of the cognitive dimension of labor correspond to the emergence of a new hegemony of knowledge mobilized by labor in relation to the knowledge embodied in fixed capital and in the managerial organization of firms. Moreover, living labor increasingly supplants many of the functions formerly fulfilled by fixed capital. Knowledge is thus more and more collectively shared, and this disrupts both the internal organization of firms and their relations with the outside world.[37]

The "knowledge economy," which is the terminological inverse of "cognitive capital," is based on a free and diffuse intellectuality that directly produces the common and which is exploited by capital as if it were "a gift from nature." The reality, however, is that the knowledge economy is the product of welfare-state institutions that ensure the ongoing collective reproduction of society as a whole – i.e., healthcare, education, public and university research, etc.[38] – through the establishment of deferred and socialized wages. Indeed, one of the effects of welfare-state planning is precisely the removal of knowledge, in terms of its creation and dissemination, from the exclusive domination of capital. Because knowledge has become independent of the fixed capital controlled by the bourgeoisie, labor and capital have thus become independent of one another, and capital's revenues are not so much profit as rent obtained from "privatizing the common" – i.e., by establishing multiple forms of property rights. This process explains the precipitous rise of patents over the past few decades, but also the precipitous rise in shareholder earnings as well as the proliferation of "access rights" for services and means of communication. We can see, then, how the category of "enclosures" plays an increasingly essential role in this analogical reasoning. As Carlo Vercellone asserts, if rent is what is accrued to an owner through the expropriation of the common, we are therefore entitled to insist on the fact that "the original land enclosures and these 'new enclosures' of knowledge and life belong to a single logic."[39]

It is indisputable that this thesis is based on a number of important transformations to labor processes and consumer access to goods and services. The problem, however, is that its account of these transformations is incomplete. The principle failures of this approach to cognitive capitalism are its tendencies to seriously underestimate the ongoing management and exploitation of labor through new forms of neoliberal governmentality in the private sector, and to confuse worker autonomy with new forms of power through which capital shapes cognitive labor and its corresponding subjectivities. It is not that these theorists ignore what they call the "prescription of subjectivity" by capital, but that they fail to see them for what they really are – namely, new forms in which capital subsumes labor by re-orienting its conduct in a flexible and indirect way. In other words, they fail to see how their thesis on the autonomy of immaterial labor completely contradicts their concomitant account of the transformations of labor under neoliberal capitalism:

> The new prescription of subjectivity – which includes attempts to internalize firm objectives in workers, the shift to results-oriented workplace, the rise of project-based management, pressures related to customers service, as well as the pure and simple constraint posed by a rise of work precarity are all mechanisms adopted by capital to deal with an "unprecedented" situation, namely, the importance of

> mobilizing the knowledge and subjective involvement of employees who are the bearers of collective knowledge.

And Negri and Vercellone argue further:

> The various forms of precarity now built into the wage relationship are, above all, instruments capital uses to try to enlist (and freely profit from) the total involvement/subordination of workers, without recognizing or paying a wage that corresponds to labor time that is not integrated into (and hence not measurable by) the official work contract.[40]

Their error is not, therefore, a function of their ignorance of new forms of neoliberal labor, but it lies in their insistence on viewing them as "external to production," instead of mechanisms by which capital subsumes intellectual labor in a manner that is perfectly immanent to contemporary forms of capital valorization.

It is precisely because capital increasingly needs to extract value from intellectual sources that it deploys "psychological" techniques of control that offload all the burden and the responsibility for economic objectives onto the employee. Labor, especially intellectual labor, is not "free": on the contrary, it is increasingly constrained by market pressures and disciplinary controls that continually measure its performance through various forms of evaluation. Firms do not passively wait for their cognitive rents to simply fall into their laps; rather, they try to codify and exploit everyday know-how by re-shaping knowledge and language, and all while organizing and directing the "cooperation competition" of their employees to elicit maximum productivity.

The analogical reasoning behind this work on cognitive capitalism thus fails on two points. The first error resides in the belief that diffuse intellectuality exists outside the control of firms and is produced outside the sphere of capital's influence and action. Quite the contrary: that our educational systems are increasingly subject to the narrow logic of the market has never been so obvious,[41] to say nothing of the powerful apparatus of distraction and mass leisure geared toward producing neoliberal subjects. While it is true that capitalist production may increasingly depend on knowledge, capital has also successfully transformed knowledge into information that can be reduced to commodifiable units and then fully incorporated into the process of capital valorization. "Knowledge" is "human capital," one of the most essential dimensions of capitalist subjectivity. And this process is not confined to knowledge; language has also undergone a similar mutation (which is obvious to anyone familiar with the abundant "operational" literature in the fields of management, marketing, and finance).

Their second and related error lies in the idea that capital no longer has an active and structuring role in the organization of cognitive labor and the development of knowledge. The opposite, in fact, is the case. The theorists of cognitive capital confuse the new modalities by which intellectual labor is subsumed by capital with an increase in labor "autonomy," as if capital had become entirely financial, and as if the principle function of management consisted in "exercising essentially financial and speculative functions" while "the actual organization of production has increasingly devolved to employees."[42] In sharp contrast to this diagnosis, the sociology of labor has shown over the past few decades that it is rather the scope, intensity, and means of hierarchical control that has changed. Corporate management increasingly tries to produce a more "internalized" mode of subordination, one based on "motivation" and commitment to corporate objectives. We could even refer to this as a more advanced stage of subjective subsumption of labor under capital than the mode of "real subsumption" analyzed by Marx. If "formal subsumption" corresponds to the extraction of absolute surplus value through the extension of the working day, the extraction of surplus value under conditions of "real subsumption" is made possible by increasing productivity. Accordingly, the subjective subsumption of labor under capital extracts surplus value by imposing a particular mode of "ultra-subjectification" onto labor, the principle of which is the limitlessness of capital and an almost innate submission to the imperative to continually produce and consume "surpluses" (some of the more immediate consequences of which include the repeal of labor laws, especially when it comes to legal limits concerning work time).

As El Mouhoub and Dominique Plihon have shown,[43] the Taylorist division of labor is far from disappearing from even the most "cognitive" businesses or production systems. The intellectual work of conceptualizing and developing products and services – work in the fields of design, marketing, management, and manufacturing – have almost nothing in common with the idealized and narcissistic image of the "worker-artist-inventor" who is not dependent on fixed capital. As for the fields of academic research, publishing, and teaching, it is hard to see what might compel one to believe today that "the production process is increasingly devolving to employees." What we are witnessing instead is the increasing dominance of quantitative evaluation methods, as well as increasing reliance on management procedures designed to impose bureaucratic proscriptions concerning the objectives of research activities. In contrast to the principle thesis conveyed by the theorists of immaterial labor, the wage relation has not been relaxed because knowledge is now embodied in workers (as opposed to fixed capital); on the contrary, the wage relation has hardened and constricted as capital introduces a whole raft of mechanisms designed to target worker subjectivity itself. Capital is doing everything it possibly can to prevent the emergence of anything like the "collective worker" of the general intellect. The techniques capital has deployed are designed to govern subjects like individual capitals who must enter into hybridized cooperative-competitive relations (as is touted in contemporary management literature) in order to produce maximum economic performance. These are not neutral techniques, nor are they *post hoc* devices implemented after the theft of what is created in the pure productivity of the common. These techniques actively proceed from the underlying self-valorizing logic of capital.

Proudhon: The Common as Spontaneous Social Force

When reading these theorists, one gets the sense that this conception of the common as the immanent product of immaterial labor is a new idea, especially insofar as the whole idea orbits around today's most advanced technologies and its associated activities. The reality, however, is that the thesis on cognitive capitalism is in fact a strange combination of two rival conceptions of history's dynamic, namely those provided by Proudhon and Marx. The former's conception of history has all but fallen into oblivion, despite some recent research and some notable publications on the subject, while the undeniable magnitude of the latter's theoretical and political posterity goes without saying. A thorough exposition of the contemporary relation between capital and the common thus demands we re-visit the theoretical dispute between these two influential theorists of the common.

As we mentioned in the chapter's introduction, the Proudhonian model subscribes to a notion of the common as a *spontaneous social force*, while Marx views the common as the *historical product of capital.* Proudhon's approach is based on the analytic of exploitation that is also a principle of social re-organization. Proudhon calls it the "collective force" in order to distinguish it from the power of individuals. The collective force is the fundamental source of *aubaine* – "increase" or "surplus" – a term Proudhon uses to designate the exploitation of the collective work made possible by the institution of property. The principle of this collective force, which he proffers as his great discovery, is also the basis for one of the great critiques of communism – or at least a certain paradigm of communism as the community of goods. Proudhon's intent was to open up a third path between the "regime of property" and the "communitarian regime" (which was the term he gave to the communism of his day).[44] In *La Solution du problème social* (*The Solution of the Social Problem*), Proudhon unambiguously summarized his project: "between property and community, I will build a world."[45] For Proudhon, both property and the community – i.e., capitalism and communism – exploit the collective force. Proudhon thus argues that individualism and collectivism are equally deficient when it comes to understanding the nature of society's intelligence. Both the absolutism of the state and the absolutism of the individual – i.e., communist and individualist solutions respectively – lead to the destruction of social life. Unity – whether of the communist state or of the individual in the framework of the individual property owner – always overpowers the plurality of individuals in a society and dampens the plural composition of individuals themselves: "man is man only through society, which is supported, for its part, by the balance and harmony of the powers which compose it."[46] What, then, is the basis of society? For Proudhon, it is an immanent force that proceeds from the plurality of social beings who are themselves plural, and the establishment of their collective power, which is always greater than the sum of its parts.

Proudhonian sociology is thus based on a primordial discovery: the irreducible "collective force" that arises out of the sum of all individual forces. Proudhon's sociology was especially influenced by the economists in this respect, chief amongst them Adam Smith and his famous analysis of the manufacture of pins,[47] which is especially manifest in Proudhon's Smithian analysis of the division of labor: "therein lies the whole problem of social transformation."[48] Yet for Proudhon, Smith was mistaken in making the division of labor his first and defining principle. Smith failed to see, argued Proudhon, that the "association of several men who pool their industry in common" is the principle of increased productivity. This collective force, born out of the "association of forces" not only concerns "workers who are presently employed," which is to say those who produce collectively at the same time, but "also every successive operation undertaken with a common goal and for an identical object."[49] The association from which this collective force is derived is "the indissoluble chain that unites the workers: all contribute to a singular goal, social wealth."[50] It is precisely this wealth that is stolen from the workers by those who own property, and it is this wealth that the new order must return to the workers.

In his *First Memoir on Property* of 1840, Proudhon argued the following:

> "The capitalist," they say, has paid the labourers their "daily wages"; more precisely, it should be said that the capitalist has paid as many times "one day's wage" as he has employed labourers each day, which is not at all the same thing. For he has paid nothing for that immense power which results from the union and harmony of labourers and the convergence and simultaneity of their efforts. Two hundred grenadiers stood the obelisk of Luxor on its base in a few hours; do you suppose one man could have accomplished the same task in two hundred days? Yet according to the calculation of the capitalist, the amount of wages paid would have been the same. Well, a desert to prepare for cultivation, a house to build, a factory to run – they are all obelisks to erect, mountains to move. The smallest fortune, the slightest establishment, the beginning of the lowest industry all demand the combination of so many different kinds of labour and skill that one man could not possible execute them all.[51]

This collective force arises from the "interdependence" of many individuals of differing talents and roles, all organized according to a plurality of possible arrangements. If Adam Smith, and others before him, illuminated the productivity of the division of labor and the coordination of tasks, Proudhon uses the example of the Obelisk of Luxor to emphasize how the collective force can also productively work when the shared capacities of many individuals are simultaneously applied to the same object or task. The collective force undoubtedly depends on the sheer number of arms and brains at its disposal, but it chiefly arises from the relations established between individual forces, the diversity of its associated functions, and the harmony established between individual relations. There are, accordingly, many ways in which this collective principle can be economically established. In *La Capacité politique des classes ouvrières* (*The Political Capacity of the Working Classes*) Proudhon demarcates, within the "economic forces" in general, the division of labor, machinery, competition, workers' associations, credit, and the union of simultaneous forces, all of which constitute but one mode of economic organization: "what I refer to as the economic forces are specific modes of activity, the effect of which is to multiply the power of hard labor beyond what it would be capable of if economic activity were left entirely to individual freedom."[52] It is in this sense that we can clearly see how Proudhon's condemnation of property is due to the manner in which he views property as the legal instrument by which the fruits of common labor are privately appropriated. Property and the collective force are antagonistic, at least up to a certain point, since there are artists and peasant proprietors who do not steal the output of the collective force but, on the contrary, augment the collective force through mutual exchange and competition. For Proudhon, then, not all property is theft: only that property that makes it possible to receive an income without work is theft, because it is a right not to one's own labor – in concordance with Locke's principle – but to the labor of someone else.

Proudhon extends this fundamental principle of production to all social life, and to all political activity. Economic analysis provides the key to understanding society, insofar as it shows how the combination of individual forces that produce a result greater than the sum of its parts is the secret of all human activity as such. For Proudhon, it is the social bond itself that is the source of all wealth: it is the principle of economic productivity and the principle of intellectual and spiritual fecundity. As Pierre Ansart observes, "Proudhon replaces the centrality of technological or material force with the social relation as the basis of the collective force."[53] The collective force is social being itself. Social being is the heart of his ontology, and the focus of his sociology. Every form of social relation is a force multiplier of all the individual forces it encompasses. Proudhon posits an active and creative power of the group as such, which derives from the fact all activity and all production is co-activity and co-production (the workshop being but one particular example). As soon as individuals group their isolated forces together, they constitute a collective force: "the end result of these agglomerated forces, which must not be confused with their sum, constitutes the force of power of the group."[54]

While the collective force is indeed immanent to the social bond, social relations are nonetheless differentiated: there are simultaneous or successive relations of cooperation in production on the one hand, and relations between differentiated independent producers, on the other. The workshop functions according to a simultaneous cooperative force, while society as a whole is structured through a division of specialized labor. In both cases, a certain combination of work generates a productive effect that translates into a surplus of wealth over and above a simple addition of individual forces. For Proudhon, then, the productivity of the collective force is based on the simultaneous pooling of all forces. Everyone, working together, is able to achieve a goal that could not be accomplished by a succession of individual efforts. This notion of a compositional effect – the "cooperation of forces" – is very similar to the division of labor in the workshop (which is also an effect of the organization of labor, albeit of a different kind) insofar as it is dedicated to ensuring the coherence of a series of successive operations to be carried out. And lastly, Proudhon extends this analysis of the social division of labor, based on specialized functions and the various exchanges that result from the division of labor, to the larger scale of society itself. For Proudhon, the whole of society should be viewed as a space in which individuals cooperate on the basis of commutation or reciprocity. And everything that facilitates these types of exchanges amplifies the collective force.

This collective power is not the outcome of choice, nor is it the expression of the rationality of the self-interested individual, nor still is it the result of an external power. The collective force is not produced by the individual or the state: it is society itself that possesses its own dynamism and thereby generates these productive effects. Proudhon rejects the individual nominalism that denies the reality of the social as much as he rejects the realism that reifies the individual at the expense of the social (which is then viewed as an entirely separate entity). Society consists of relations that can neither be reduced to their elements nor constituted as an entity that is detached from its elements.

The *sui generis* reality of the collective force is not only economic, it is also social. And it is all of these things in a double sense: society is both produced and productive as a result of the activity of labor: "labor is the bonding force of society." It shapes society and determines its movement. It is the collective worker who shapes society. But it is also the social composition of activities and functions that concretely produces "social wealth." This is not only due to the fact that it is always a group of workers who carry out all productive labor, nor because production presupposes a division of labor, but above all because all work, even if it is seemingly individual work, is in reality social or collective. Viewed in this light, Proudhon even goes so far as to question whether there can really be said to be, from this perspective, a purely individual force at all – a claim that would fundamentally negate our spontaneous perception of society as a composite of individual and collective forces: "as soon as man works, he embodies society . . . in the working society . . . there are no workers, only one worker, unique, and infinitely diversified."[55]

To be in society is to be a "collective man." All individuals are always already plural, always already involved in community activity, and always indebted before being creative. Our so-called individual force is already part of the collective force because everyone is a combination of multiple components drawn from our education and our continuous socialization: is individuality itself not merely the superficial effect of an underlying multiplicity of sources and factors? For Proudhon, we are singularly deceived whenever we believe the individual to be an atom, believe the individual is the source of wealth, or believe all the merit and talents of some atomistic individual are rightly its own:

> Just as the creation of every instrument of production is the result of collective force, so also the talent and knowledge of a man are the product of universal intelligence and general knowledge slowly accumulated by a number of masters and with the aid of many inferior industries.[56]

While it may seem as if this Proudhonian notion of "human capital" bears a family resemblance to neoliberal theories (which are based on an homonymic concept), Proudhon's approach is in fact diametrically opposed to the neoliberal position insofar as he insists that capital cannot be viewed as a form of personal property that gives one the right to a corresponding income (and in this sense Proudhon's approach is closer to what Marx calls the "general intellect" in the *Grundrisse*):

> Talent is a creation of society rather than a gift of nature; it is an accumulated capital of which the recipient is only the guardian. Without society, without the education and powerful assistance which it gives, the finest nature would be inferior to the most ordinary capacities even in the areas where it ought to shine.[57]

This perspective lies at the heart of Proudhon's disagreement with the "capacitive" and inegalitarian theorists like the Saint-Simonians and the Fourierists.

True social science begins with the discovery that the collective force is stolen by both the proprietary class and an alienating state.[58] Instead of allowing those engaged in direct cooperation and exchange to determine economic arrangements, external powers have monopolized the surplus of social wealth (whether produced through exchange or cooperation) for their own benefit. The totality of the collective force, and the fruits of its production and exchange, is alienated by private property and the state. Proudhon's first analyses were focused on the exploitation of labor by private property, and then he later extended this analysis to state alienation. The exploitation of man by man, and the exploitation of the government of man by man, manifests the same logic of usurpation and theft. In his famous 1840 text *What is Property?*, Proudhon tries to show how the collective force is the source and target of exploitation, and he directly points the finger at the property-owning class: "for when you have paid all the individual forces, you have still not paid the collective force. Consequently, there always remains a *right of collective property* which you have not acquired and which you enjoy unjustly."[59] It is the collective force that is the real substance of profit or the *aubaine*, as Proudhon calls it. The capitalist appropriates the collective force at no cost and, accordingly, Proudhon's theory of exploitation is actually very simple: the individual wage corresponds to maintenance of the worker, the satisfaction of its elementary needs, while accrued profit is the expropriation of the fruits of the collective force. Capital, writes Proudhon, is therefore "accumulated, concretized, solidified labor,"[60] and its capture is facilitated by private property. As Proudhon further explains:

> The collective strength of a hundred workers is incomparably greater than that of a worker raised a hundred-fold, and so this force is not properly paid by the wages of a hundred workers; consequently, there has been an error in accounting between the workers and the masters.[61]

And for Proudhon, the state's political alienation of society follows the very same logic. Economic exploitation and political exploitation operate according to the same mechanism, namely the alienation of the collective force. This is what accounts for the great unity and coherence of Proudhon's remarks. Historical reality, as Proudhon argues, is the appropriation of the output of social power by the state.[62] The power of society is monopolized by an individual or a class that seizes the collective force of a people who are then rendered incapable of governing themselves. The state is an imposter. Its power, while real, comes from the totality of forces that comprise society.

But why, then, do people tend to both submit to the state and respect private property? For Proudhon, this is not an aberration or a normative departure. Rather, he argues that there is a logic in enslavement, and a truth in our consent to our exploitation. Our acceptance of external power over us is due to the perception that the establishment of each is integrated into the collective force, which is then embodied and represented by these forms of social power. We are nothing without others: since we must integrate ourselves into the whole in order to produce this collective force, we must also submit to the authority that embodies this collective force, whether this is the authority of the property class or the state. As Proudhon puts it:

> Workers and citizens do not really submit to an exploiter or to a tyrant: they do not submit because of seduction or terror. It is rather the representative of the *social*

> *power* to which they submit. While this is a power that is ill-defined in their thoughts, it is nonetheless a power they feel they cannot live without. It is a power, whatever its principle may be, that shows them its seal, and they tremble to break it through their insurrection.[63]

To attack capitalist property would thus be to attack the productive force itself, and to attack the state would be to attack society itself. In both cases it would be to attack social power – i.e., the power of association, whether in its commutative or cooperative forms. In short, it would be to attack their own social being.

Usurpation or theft by political authority is based on the idea that if social power is the product of relations between groups of workers and members of the society, then these relations must be regulated and balanced by the law.[64] This is the indispensable role of the judiciary – it legitimates the usurpation of power. It is thanks to the legal apparatus' ability to regulate exchange and cooperation that states and capitalists are maintained. Justice – a core concept in Proudhon's reasoning – is the regulation, or more exactly the self-regulation, of social relations without which there would be neither common activity nor social productivity. Yet justice has been monopolized by castes of lawyers, in the pay of property owners, so that they may legally "justify" their unjust appropriation. The law produced by the sovereign legislator is therefore never true justice. Real justice can only arise from all those concrete and varied ways in which equilibrium between parties is regulated – i.e., by the contractual management of their relations in order to ensure the equity of exchanges according to the "true value" of goods and services. In other words, justice is immanent to economic and social activity, and economic and social law is nothing other than the shaping of these relations between individuals themselves. By purporting to endow these rights with the "force of law," the legislator has been able to pass itself off as a transcendent entity over and above these individuals. This is the basis of Proudhon's double refusal of individualism and communism.

These views led Proudhon to produce a systematic critique of communism, which Marx repeats almost word for word in his *Economic and Philosophical Manuscripts of 1844*. Communists believe state property is a vehicle for overcoming the economic exploitation rooted in capitalist private property. Yet, for Proudhon, even if community ownership expropriates capitalist private property, it does not fundamentally change the relationship between workers and their products. Rather than seeing a solution in the regulated association of multiple and diverse forces, the communists opt for the communal ownership of capital as the singular source of wealth, which Proudhon views as symmetrical to the "individual hypothesis," adopted by the liberals, whereby all wealth is derived from the isolated individual. But as Proudhon showed (before Marx), property still prevails over free activity in this type of communism. As Proudhon once exclaimed, "communism is still property!" And as he wrote elsewhere, "it is very curious that systematic communism, the deliberate negation of property, is conceived under the direct influence of the prejudice of property, and it is property that is to be found at the root of all communistic theories."[65] Indeed, Proudhon believed alienation would become even more intense under communism, since the community not only owns the means of production and its products, but it owns individuals as well. The community is thus the apex of property, since everything belongs to the community *qua* moral person.

The socialists and the communists remain committed to the program of community property because they have fallen prey to the illusion that capital and the state are the only sources of wealth. In his *System of Economic Contradictions*, Proudhon attacks the socialists for wanting to seize capital and the levers of state power without realizing that these forms are merely derivative organs of more primordial forces:

> Capital and power, secondary organs in society, are always the gods whom socialism adores: if capital and power did not exist, it would invent them. Through its anxieties about power and capital, socialism has completely overlooked the meaning of its protests.[66]

The communists and the socialists are thereby trapped within a false symmetrical opposition: they advocate communal property over individual property, yet the former is merely the property of those who control the community. What they call "emancipation" is actually absolute political oppression and a new form of exploitation. The communists hypostatize the collective force by making it the prerogative of the state, as if the state itself was the origin of the collective force. It is because they think power and force come from the center and the top, and not from the activity of individuals, that they assent to this exploitative logic. In the final analysis, however, there is only one kind of state organization for Proudhon, and that is the state as a generalized police force, a reactionary state, and a state of pure constraint. For Proudhon, then, we must take a very different path, one based on economic law, industrial democracy, and communistic federalism. It is this path that has been all but abandoned, if not in practice than at least in theory, and it is a path that must be reopened.[67]

Marx: The Historical Production of the Common by Capital

To his great merit, Proudhon foresaw the intimate connection between the collective force and the law and, as we will see later, he anticipated the crucial relation between the common and institutional activity. But, nonetheless, he still viewed the law as outside and prior to the collective force. The law is merely the *acknowledgment* of a social bond that precedes it. The collective force is spontaneous and free, and its products are stolen by private property and the state, such that both private and public property performs an essentially *rentier* function. Property (private or public) does not organize the collective force, and it creates nothing itself. It is fundamentally negative. Property denies the *spontaneous nature of the social*. The Marxian analysis, on the contrary, completely opposes the view that all profits are essentially rent, or that rent ought to be the dominant paradigm through which all forms of social exploitation should be thought.[68] It was undoubtedly this fundamental divergence that was at the root of Marx's hostility to Proudhonian thought in the second half of the 1840s. That said, we sometimes forget how much Marx borrowed from Proudhon, especially from his concept of the collective force, and at times he even seems to adopt some of its central features.

As early as 1842, Marx read and eloquently commented on *What is Property?* A year later, in *The Holy Family* (1843), Marx wrote, "Proudhon's treatise *Qu'est ce que la propriété?* is as important for modern political economy as Sieyès work *Qu' est-ce que le tiers état?* for modern politics," and he even went so far as to call Proudhon's book "a scientific manifesto for the French proletariat," which is no small compliment.[69] It is well known that the two men participated in lengthy exchanges in Paris in 1844, and while Marx later recalled how he sought in vain to explain Hegel to Proudhon, he is less forthright about how much his nascent thought was indelibly marked by what Proudhon taught him. Indeed, there was a time when the two marched lockstep toward a common end, and Marx even acknowledged his debt to Proudhon, in *The Holy Family*, concerning the idea about the negation of property through the revolutionary action of the proletariat. And while Marx may distort things somewhat on this point, it is nonetheless the case that it was in Proudhon's *First Memoir on Property* that we find the idea that the workers must necessarily destroy property: "all human labour being the result of collective force, all property thereby becomes collective and undivided; in more precise terms, labour destroys property."[70] This inevitable conclusion is not fundamentally different from Marx's famous phrase mentioned above, according to which "capitalist production begets, with the inexorability of a natural process, its own negation."[71] Now is not the time, however, to dive deeper into the quarrel between these two men, nor to detail the battles led by Marx against the Proudhonians within the First International.[72] Instead, we want to look a little closer at the uses Marx made of the Proudhonian concept of the collective force, especially as regards worker cooperation.

In contrast to the maxims of bourgeois political economy, capital is not a form of private property that magically generates profit, but is rather the product of cooperation amongst producers. As Marx and Engels asserted as early as their 1848 *Manifesto*, "capital is a collective product, and only by the united action of many men, nay, in the last resort, only by the united action of all members of society, can it be set in motion. Capital is, therefore, not a personal power, it is a social power."[73] While this notion of "social power" is reminiscent of Proudhon, it is far from a spontaneous form. Social power, in Marx's view, must be precisely shaped by capital in order to be integrated into the production process. Chapter 13 of *Capital* (vol. 1), titled "Cooperation," provides a very clear exposition of Marx's view on the matter. Borrowing from Proudhon, Marx argues that the collective force of cooperating individuals is always greater than the sum of its individual workers. Indeed, Marx argues that it is a trait unique to the species, insofar as man is a "social animal." Even before the advent of large-scale industry (characterized by the planned and rationalized organization of cooperative work), the simple union of several workers within the same factory led to a "spirit of cooperation" that increased productivity. But it is only once capital succeeds in systematizing the cooperation of the "global worker" (*travailleur global*), who then becomes an appendage of the machine, that the species fully arrives at "the creation of a new productive power, which is intrinsically a collective one."[74] In other words, capital makes it possible for the human species to take a giant leap forward by enabling "the social productive power of labour" to achieve a degree of power unrivaled in all human history: "when the worker co-operates in a planned way with others, he strips off the fetters of his individuality, and develops the capabilities of his species."[75]

The social nature of man thus finds its most historically advanced instantiation (as of yet) in capitalist cooperation. The "global worker" is the "social animal" whose socialization is now systematized and planned by capital. Capital, in other words, embraces the social nature of the species and pushes it to its fullest extent. Through concentration, capital "socializes" the growing mass of proletarians:

> [The] concentration of large masses of the means of production in the hands of individual capitalists is a material condition for the co-operation of wage-labourers, and the extent of cooperation, or the scale of production, depends on the extent of this concentration.[76]

But this cooperation demands direction, command, and modes of supervision. These are the tasks that constitute the specific function of capital once work becomes cooperative. This task is not only technical, but is also a response to the structural antagonism between "the exploiter and the raw material of his exploitation."[77] If it is capital that constitutes and organizes cooperation, it does so – as Proudhon had already shown – in order to profit from the fruits of this collective force without having to pay for it in full: "[the capitalist] pays [the worker] the value of 100 independent labour-powers, but he does not pay for the combined labour-power of the 100."[78] When the capitalist compels worker cooperation, it is no longer one hundred individual labor powers with which the capitalist deals, but labor power that has "ceased to belong to themselves" and is "incorporated into capital,"[79] such that the collective force organized by capital always appears to the workers as the effect of the authority of the capitalist, as the heteronomous power of capital. The productive force of social labor appears to be "a power which capital possesses by its nature – a productive power inherent in capital."[80]

The workers thus become mere variables in the larger production process. They are elements of a capital that unwittingly self-develops by subsuming the force of living labor within itself:

> As co-operators, as members of a working organism, they merely form a particular mode of existence of capital. Hence the productive power developed by the worker socially is the productive power of capital. The socially productive power of labour develops as a free gift to capital whenever the workers are placed under certain conditions.[81]

The division of labor in manufacturing, and the machinery that corresponds to large-scale industry, only deepens the incorporation of the worker into capital. As cooperation develops, the worker enjoys less and less independence from capital. The worker's individual labor power counts for nothing; he is absorbed into capital as a "global worker."

Marx's analysis thereby revealed what Proudhon failed to see: cooperation is anything but spontaneous. It is produced by capital, and the scale of cooperation always depends on the amount of capital deployed by the capitalist (even for the simplest forms of cooperation). It follows, then, that exploitation cannot be analyzed as the mere theft of something that previously existed or that which was produced outside the capital–labor relation in the form of an autonomous collective force, because the collective force is, in fact, organized by capital according to its needs and its further development. It is capital that gives rise to systematic cooperation, and it is capital that produces forms of organized labor that make it possible to increase the rate of exploitation through a combination of cooperation and mechanization. In short, what Marx calls the "theft of the labour of others" is much more than simple theft: it presupposes the submission and incorporation of the victim into the system of organized labor.

Marx thus "assimilated" and transformed Proudhon's analyses of the collective force and integrated these analyses into his own conception of capitalism's singular dynamic. But it is not only in Marx's economic writing that Proudhonian ideas can be found: the same assimilation-transformation of Proudhon is also manifest in Marx's commentary on French political history. Marx, in a sense, "digests" Proudhon in order to articulate the specific historical dynamics through which the Paris Commune is interpreted as the antithesis of the French Empire. For instance, Marx's description of the French bureaucracy as a "parasitic" state (as opposed to the active society) is very Proudhonian.[82] For Marx, the centralization of the state serves exactly the same function as the economic concentration of capital. In the course of successive revolutions, the state increasingly represses society as it becomes more and more centralized, isolated, and external in relation to the larger society, to the point that the conscientious revolution (*la consciencieuse révolution*), by perfecting and concentrating executive power, "sets it up against itself as the sole target, in order to concentrate all its forces of destruction against it."[83] And nineteen years later, in his address to the First International titled *The Civil War in France*, Marx recognizes the "Communal Constitution" as the original and inaugural feature of the Paris Commune, though he completely dissociates the Constitution from its Proudhonian roots. In any case, communism, for Marx, can only arise from a specific historical dynamic that creates the necessary conditions for communism's emergence. The economic common and the political common, the free association of the producers and the political federalism of the communes, can only be realized upon the conflicted terrain created by capital and the state themselves. Capital and the state contribute to producing, right in front of themselves, the collective forces that will be their eventual destruction.

Capital's Common and the Worker's Common

We have written elsewhere about the problems inhering in the dialectical theory Marx opposes to Proudhon's approach. Are we really to believe that the development of large-scale, mechanized, automated industry will give rise to a unified and polyvalent individual capable of fully developing all his faculties? And can we really believe that the constricted and domineering socialization of the workers by capital necessarily leads to a free association of individuals? We freely admit that capital creates an objective antagonism between itself and its workers, and we will also admit that workers' struggles to limit their exploitation express a nascent desire to re-appropriate the fruits of their labor (as is clearly demonstrable through an analysis of the history of workers' struggles). Yet given the various forms capital has taken since the mid-nineteenth century, we are less sure about the proposition that the capitalist institution of forced cooperation and mechanization will ultimately produce a fully socialized individual who has developed all his faculties as a result of an increase in free time.

If the common, in the form of social labor, finds its most developed form in the "technological application of science"[84] to production, as Marx explains in the *Grundrisse* and in Chapter VI of *Capital* (vol. 1), then we are dealing with a form of historical necessity that will invariably lead to the "expropriation of the expropriators." This is the logic of Marx's famous "Fragment on Machines," from the *Grundrisse*, that has been so central to the theorists of Italian *operaismo* ("workerism"). In this influential passage, Marx describes capital's tendency toward a progressive reduction of social or communal work, and a concomitant shift away from cooperative production in favor of mere supervision and regulation of an "*automatic system of machinery*" in which workers are but cogs endowed with intellect.[85] This tendency allows the workers to largely liberate themselves from manual labor, wherein they are subsequently able to completely devote themselves to their own development and fulfillment. Given its importance for many contemporary theories of the common, this passage warrants close and careful examination. For this famous "Fragment on Machines" is not merely a rough draft of the more precise analysis found in *Capital*, but rather constitutes a singular theoretical moment in itself within Marx's work.[86] In these writings, Marx dares a rather precise prognostication on the basis of certain tendencies already at work in capital's present: specifically, in this case, capital's tendency to assimilate scientific advances toward its own ends and the contradictory effect of this assimilation in terms of capital's control over its workers. At the outset, we should observe how Marx's prognostication is completely at odds with Hardt and Negri's thesis concerning knowledge and autonomy: as Marx clearly indicates, scientific knowledge does not reside in the worker, but rather it is "concentrated" in fixed capital, such that capital increasingly relies on a combination of the forces of production to the detriment of direct labor power. Living labor thus loses all its independence: "the worker's activity, reduced to a mere abstraction of activity, is determined and regulated on all sides by the movement of the machinery, and not the opposite."[87] Intellectuality, in other words, is completely monopolized by capital.

Once science is objectified in the mechanisms of the productive apparatus, it makes the total domination of capital over labor possible:

> The science which compels the inanimate limbs of the machinery, by their construction, to act purposefully, as an automaton, does not exist in the worker's consciousness, but rather acts upon him through the machine as an alien power, as the power of the machine itself.[88]

Reading this passage, one might think Marx was actually describing the effects of industrial Taylorism. The reality for Marx, in any case, is that this "automatic system of machinery" is merely the continuation of the tendency, already at work in manufacturing, that leads to an increasingly radical division between the worker and the means of production. This tendency then leads to the domination and transformation of the worker through a simple combination of natural forces: "[it is,] hence, the tendency of capital to give production a scientific character [and] direct labor is reduced to a mere moment of this process."[89] Of course, as Marx rightly asserts, it is in no way science itself that is responsible for technological progress; rather, the entire productive apparatus is the result of the logic by which capital develops techniques and mechanisms precisely designed to extract surplus value. In accordance with the ideas of Adam Smith and Charles Babbage, Marx articulates technological production as a phenomenon that decomposes and re-composes direct labor in the manufacturing process, and then again, but now in a more systemic fashion, in large-scale industry. The division of labor and cooperation in capitalistic form is what makes machinery possible, through a combination of natural, scientific forces and the planned coordination amongst machinery. Capitalism, as Marx explains in almost inexorable terms, transforms "the production process from the simple labour process into a scientific process, which subjugates the forces of nature and compels them to work in the service of human needs."[90] This reduces direct labor power to a state of near powerlessness "in the face of the communality [*Gemeinsamkeit*] represented by and concentrated in capital." Labor is no longer productive save "[those] common labours which subordinate the forces of nature to themselves."[91] As a result of capital's frenzied drive to accumulate, cooperation, once restrained by the capital's command, is transformed into a combination of natural forces subject to applied science and its mechanized objectification. Centralized cooperative labor is painfully supplanted by scientific activity, and the common is thereby "concentrated" in fixed capital. In the final analysis, the automatic system of machines is nothing but the "capitalist common" in its most advanced form.

But where does the knowledge objectified in fixed capital come from? Marx's answer on this matter is ambiguous, insofar as his response takes on certain Proudhonian features. And it is undoubtedly the case, in our view, that it is precisely these Proudhonian features that lie at the root of Negri's interpretation of Marx's 1857–1858 writings. Capital appropriates the social development of the general intellect "free of charge," as Marx puts it,[92] and this then amounts to the theft of that which is derived from generalized social progress that capital neither produces nor organizes. Yet Marx understands very well that if science – much like value – is one of capital's historical "pre-conditions," it also becomes, as a condition of its subsequent development, one of capital's "results." Far from remaining unmoored or free floating within society, science is transformed into a sphere of professional activity that is increasingly subject to specific economic imperatives and is increasingly rationalized and "objectified" in fixed capital: "invention then becomes a business, and the application of science to direct production itself becomes a prospect which determines and solicits it."[93] While we might reproach Marx for being somewhat positivistic here, it is worth noting that "science," for Marx, is an index of advanced social development and one of capitalism's most important creations. Marx explicitly tells us how machinery really only develops once "all the sciences have been pressed into the service of capital."[94]

The fact is that it is only after the development of the general intellect, or rather general intellectuality – a phenomenon born from social life and which in turn nourishes social existence – that knowledge truly supplants the exploitation of labor as the source of wealth. The total domination of living labor is thereby dialectally transformed into the condition of labor's emancipation. Let us not forget that capital is a "moving contradiction" that "works toward its own dissolution as the form dominating production."[95] If capital employs machinery to produce ever more labor power, it unwittingly produces, despite itself, the foundation of a completely different system of wealth, one that is not based on the quantity of labor stolen from workers, but on the development of science and technology to continuously create more disposable time. This contradiction pits capital's tendency to continually increase labor productivity for the benefit of the capitalist against its concomitant tendency to produce free time for the benefit of the worker, and for the society as a whole. In a very illuminating passage, Marx writes:

> What capital adds is that it increases the surplus labour time of the mass by all the means of art and science, because its wealth consists directly in the appropriation of surplus labour time; since *value [is] directly its purpose*, not use value. It is thus, despite itself, instrumental in creating the means of social disposal time, in order to reduce labour time for the whole society to a diminishing minimum, and thus to free everyone's labour time for their own development.[96]

The development of the social individual, which is enabled by the augmentation of disposable time as a result of this new foundation of wealth, is not a unilateral tendency for Marx, even if he describes it as ineluctable: production, for Marx, increasingly issues from the "the *combination* of social activity [which] appears, rather, as the producer."[97] Society – which is to say "individuals in mutual relationships, which they equally reproduce and produce anew" – now appears as the true subject of production (its "producer"), and it now appears as if capital was only a necessary moment in this larger process. Society thus takes the form of the "social individual," "the human being in the process of becoming [and] in whose head exists the accumulated knowledge of society."[98] Only at the conclusion of this process does the "general intellect" become the real wealth of individuals (not capital) and the basis of the "real life process."[99] Emancipation is thus ultimately grounded in the movement of capital:

> In this transformation, it is neither the direct human labour he himself performs, nor the time during which he works, but rather the appropriation of his own general productive power, his understanding of nature and his mastery over it by virtue of his presence as a social body – it is, in a word, the development of the social individual, which appears as the great foundation-stone of production and of wealth. The *theft of alien labour time, on which the present wealth is based*, appears as a miserable foundation in face of this new one, created by large-scale industry itself.[100]

This process irrevocably leads to the polarization between the "*surplus labour of the mass*" – which is the "condition for the development of general wealth" and the "*non-labour of a few*" – and the "development of the general powers of the human brain."[101] It is through this polarizing process that another logic, or another future, becomes possible, one based on the "free development of individualities, and hence not the reduction of necessary labour time so as to posit surplus labour, but rather the general reduction of the necessary labour time to a minimum, which then corresponds to the artistic, scientific, etc., development of the individuals in the time set free, and with means created, for them all."[102] In other words, the reduction of necessary labor proportionally extends non-labor to the whole society as such, which can now devote itself to the pursuit of true wealth – i.e., "the developed productive power of all individuals."[103]

Marx's anticipatory vision of the future in the *Grundrisse* is by no means original within the socialist tradition. One need only think, for example, of the conferences organized by William Morris. For Morris also developed a vision of a socialist future, in which the creative and aesthetic qualities of individuals are able to flourish because machines have freed workers from the most immiserating labor.[104] Marx's vision of the future, however, involves an account of capitalism's development that is rather astonishing and, we must admit, not very historically credible. Marx exaggerates capital's tendency to develop the productive forces – which appear to him to be "the material conditions [that will] blow this foundation sky-high"[105] – to the point that he fails to consider how an increase in productive power might also modify the composition of subjective consumption and needs. In a word, Marx underestimates the capacity of capital to continue to subject the "real life process" to its own imperatives.

Finally, there is one more point that merits further discussion: namely, Marx's conception of science, knowledge, and/or the intellect. On the one hand, one has to admit Marx's talent for anticipatory analysis when he emphasizes, more than a century ahead of the development of genetically modified seeds, how agriculture "becomes merely the application of the science of material metabolism."[106] However, by overemphasizing the liberating potential of knowledge, Marx reciprocally underestimates capital's ability to subsume intellectual activity and its products. Knowledge seems to be embodied in fixed capital, but without substantially affecting the individual – other than through the potentially liberating character that it exerts on necessary labor time and its ability to contribute to the "combination of human activities and the development of human intercourse."[107] Now, if there is a lesson to be learned from the movement of capital, it is that the progress of knowledge in the fields of management, organization, commerce, or communication – which has been considerable as a result of capital's intensive interest in these fields – are not at all "sciences" that capital has captured by extracting them from a rich social milieu in order to extend the independence of wealth vis-à-vis labor time. In other words, this whole normative and descriptive dimension of knowledge about man and society seems to have largely escaped Marx.

We have already seen, in numerous instances, how much Marx believed in the "historically necessary" conversion of capital's forced *socialization* into voluntary free *association*, and how the cooperation coerced by capital is converted into free cooperation.[108] But this belief runs counter to all the historical work documenting the ways in which a class constitutes itself through the conscious creations of institutions and the subsequent struggles it leads. While Marx insightfully analyzed capital's development of a common as a result of the former's gradual detachment from living labor, he did not, however, undertake a comparable analysis of the progressive autonomy of the workers' movement, of the class constitution of the workers, or the formation of a proper *workers' common* that is independent from the development of capital. On this point, at least, Proudhon deserves to be recognized as the more prescient of the two. More astutely than Marx (and before him too), Proudhon theorized the workers' struggle for autonomy in institutional terms.[109] While Marx's inadequacy was partly remedied by the lessons he drew from the Paris Commune, he nonetheless continued to emphasize the fetishistic development of a vanguard party amongst most of his followers.

What we get in Marx is precisely the idea that the conditions produced by capitalism make worker organization possible and, concomitantly, they produce the conditions for their unification, solidarity, and eventually their struggle against exploitation. Increasingly sophisticated forms of subjection, which are more concerned with increasing productivity than with lengthening the working day, are simultaneously linked to new forms of cooperation that generate a "collective worker." This collective worker is accordingly able to organize itself on its own foundation, develop organizational independence, and, by increasingly engaging in resolute struggle against capital, constitute itself as a new historical subject. By integrating workers into its great mechanisms for extracting surplus value, capitalism simultaneously creates a new terrain upon which the class struggle will be fought *and* ushers in a new antagonistic subjectivity. While Marx never wavered from his narrative of historical finality based on an implacable structural necessity, he was admittedly one of the theorists who, at times, most precisely analyzed the concrete conditions of the worker struggles unfolding on the new terrain he theorized. It is this latter dimension of Marx's work that we are most interested in expanding upon throughout the rest of this book. Rather than continue to theorize the objective creation of the common by capital in one way or another, we want to look at the creation of a different kind of common, a common the workers' movement gives itself by creating its own institutions independent of the strict laws governing the reproduction of capital.

Beyond the Two Models

This analysis of the theoretical divergence between Proudhon and Marx allows us to establish a fundamental axiom for *theorizing the common anew*. This confrontation between Proudhon and Marx helps us grasp several contemporary illusions about the genesis of the common. While Hardt and Negri's recent theory is clearly both original and ambitious, their work looks a little different once it is seen as a revived version of an older discourse on the spontaneous production of the common. And while Hardt and Negri describe Marx, rather than Proudhon, as the more important source of inspiration for their work, this intellectual lineage can only be sustained by extracting both theorists from their proper context and rather drastically re-interpreting Marx's remarks on knowledge and science. By turning Marx into a visionary who anticipated the supposed autonomy of knowledge under conditions of immaterial labor, Hardt and Negri actually attribute Proudhon's ideas to Marx – for example, the very Proudhonian assertion that "production thus relies ... on workers who immediately cooperate together prior to the discipline and control of the capitalist."[110] And if Hardt and Negri really are the true heirs of Proudhon, it is because of the scant attention they pay to the actual organization of intellectual labor, and their refusal to consider the forms of submission to which intellectual labor is rigorously subjected. At base, this oversight grows out of their naturalistic conception of the common, according to which knowledge is naturally unappropriable because it is naturally non-exclusive. In other words, by adopting the view that goods are "naturally" common, Hardt and Negri are able to claim cognitive capitalism is doomed by a boundless expansion of knowledge: "when I share an idea or image with you, my capacity to think with it is not lessened; on the contrary, our exchange of ideas and images increases my capacities."[111] Formulations such as these are precisely what we find in the typology of goods characteristic of the new institutional economy of the commons.

But, on the other hand, Hardt and Negri never abandon their Marxian historical optimism. We might even say, on this point, that they are perfectly orthodox Marxists. What we find in their work is thus a strange and rather obscure logic: while capital may be essentially parasitic, it is nevertheless "creative" in terms of the conditions necessary for communism. In an attempt to overcome Marx's false equivalence between the passage from feudalism to capitalism and the passage from capitalism and communism, Hardt and Negri write, "we can already recognize – in the autonomy of biopolitical production, the centrality of the common, and their growing separation from capitalist exploitation and command – the makings of a new society within the shell of the old."[112]

The reality is that "biopolitical production" does not inherently expropriate a fundamentally creative common – as if cooperation in cognitive or affective work were inscribed into new forms of production that have become autonomous in relation to a purely parasitic mode of capitalism. Capital's organization of production, of knowledge, and of life has in fact never been so direct, so detailed, and so totalizing.[113] What we are encountering instead is a real subsumption of intellectual labor that replaces outdated, artisanal, irregular, and discontinued means of expropriating our cultural inheritance and intellectual work.

By affirming an overly simple and factually erroneous theory about the intrinsic and irreversible autonomy of intellectual labor, Hardt and Negri eschew more fundamental questions concerning the concrete forms through which the common is produced and reproduced today.[114] A careful consideration of this question necessarily requires a more detailed interrogation of the new conditions of struggle that workers and citizens face today. It also, and perhaps more importantly, demands an examination of the types of practices workers and citizens are implementing and the types of institutions they are creating to escape, as much as possible, from capital's grip on their activities and their existence. This is work that needs to be done, and it demands a perspective that pushes beyond the dispute between Marx and Proudhon, and which refuses any of the more or less confused hybridizations of these two models. It requires a perspective that is not limited to the sociological or economic discourse that theorizes the common as "naturally" emerging from either social life itself or from the accumulation of capital. We must conceive of a different theoretical model of the commons, one that better accounts for our historical creativity and is accordingly more "operational" when it comes to political strategy. This new theoretical model must be based on collective practices and political struggles. It must put these practices at the center of its analysis, and not as negative acts of "resistance" to domination, or "protests" against the neoliberal order, but as the positive basis for new institutions and new laws. For us, it is time to systematically theorize the institution of the common in these terms.

Part II

Law and Institution of the Common

The approaches we have examined in the first part of this book have tended to theorize the common as (a) entirely immanent to "biopolitical production," in the case of Michael Hardt and Antonio Negri; (b) as involving threatened public services or goods produced by the state, as in the case of the alter-globalization; or (c) as the intrinsic qualities of certain goods or resources, as in the case of standard political economy and, to a lesser extent, the work of Elinor Ostrom. However varied these three approaches may be, they all either explicitly link the common to state property or at least leave open the possibility of anchoring the common in the property form, even if the form of property itself is left indeterminate (which is to say dependent and adaptable to the various "common goods" in question). This is why we now need to more explicitly confront the relation between the common and the law of property. If the common is not directly immanent to the social itself – or even a "tendency" of the social that we need only stimulate to bring into existence – it is because the common is first and foremost a matter of law, and therefore a determination of what *must* be. The challenge here is to substitute a new law by rejecting the claims of the old law. In this sense, then, it is a confrontation of *law against law*: either we accept the law of property as an exclusive and absolute right, in which case the common will never be more than a residual phenomenon eking out an interstitial existence in the margins of society left unoccupied by property, or we assert the common as the principle of a new law that will re-organize the whole of society by radically challenging and overturning the reign of property.

To this end, Chapter 6 traces a genealogy of the law of property in order to show how property rights were in fact a rather recent construct in Western history. We also show how the supreme Western legal dichotomy between public and private law is also a recent invention, despite spurious claims that the latter is rooted in Roman law. The true opposition facing us is not therefore between common property and private property, but between unappropriability and every form of property as such (whether private or state owned).

In Chapter 7 we then examine the history and scope of Anglo-Saxon "common law," especially the latter's claim to limitless self-improvement through the continual adaptation of older customs. As we argue in this chapter, the law of the common cannot be based on English common law (or customary law), insofar as common law is constituted of a body of experts, lawyers, and judges, all of whom are continually concerned with selecting laws that respect, and are compatible with, private property.

In Chapter 8 we theorize the law of the common as a law that directly and immediately asserts itself as the exclusive law of the poor against the law of the privileged (rather than a mere customary law that ignores the reality of social conflict altogether). Our inquiry in this chapter will be guided by Marx's articles on the famous "theft of wood" debate from 1842, which will help us interrogate the very notion of "poverty" itself.

In Chapter 9 we look more closely at the emergence of the idea of a "proletarian law" at end of the nineteenth century. We show how this idea partially evolved out of the older laws of the guilds and early trade unions, but also how it was based on the creation of new institutions designed to meet the challenges of the historically original experience of the nascent industrial labor movement. By focusing on the legal creativity involved in the creation of workers' institutions and laws, we reveal the inadequacy of a workers' law based solely on the unconscious transmission of prior customs. As we argue, the law of the common can only be produced by a conscious act of institutionalization.

Chapter 10 will be entirely devoted to an examination of the nature of the institution as an activity, in contrast to the sociological tendency to privilege the already "instituted" at the expense of the act of "instituting." Our aim here is to outline the distinctive features of the specific practice that creates institutional rules, or what we call "instituent praxis." Instituent praxis, for us, is not a matter of *post facto* recognition of that which already exists, nor an act of creation *ex nihilo*, but a form of practice that creates the new through the transformation of that which already exists. In order to have any chance of success, the law of the common must proceed from this type of praxis rather than solely relying on the spontaneous diffusion and transmission of customary rights.

6

The Law of Property and the Unappropriable

Re-thinking the common means interrogating the concept at its root. In order to proceed with what we refer to as a "methodological reversal" (*renversement dans la method*), which is in many ways the essence of our project here, we must re-examine the long history, stretching back all the way to the Greeks, that literally stifled or snuffed out the notion that the common is an irreducible dimension of social life. Property, whether public or private, has been continually imposed as a kind of natural mediator between both people and "things," as well as between people themselves. Through its centuries-long disconnection from direct activity, the common tended to become little more than a nominal or enveloping community, whose members were viewed as integrated parts of a natural, mystical, or political body of some kind or another. The central lesson to be drawn from our archaeological investigation is the fact that there are many ways to think about "living together" and about acting in common, and there are many ways of reading the history of our societies other than through the bipolar narratives of the glorious advent of "civilization" via the invention of individual property, or the anticipation of the final return of communal property. Re-reading the Greeks and Romans from this perspective is not, then, an attempt to find the "origin" of the common. Rather, it is an inquiry that tries to re-construct the way in which the constitutive "collectivity" of every political community has been repressed in Western thought, across multiple historical periods and authors, beginning, first and foremost, with Aristotle. Our "return" to these older texts should not be seen, then, as a kind of "detour." Rather, contemporary political theory and activity is in the process of re-connecting, from today's completely different historical circumstances, with a concept of the common that Greek philosophy and Roman law allows us to both grasp and potentially extend: the common, as the principle that binds us together, *is the unappropriable as such*. Hence our central thesis: *if the common is to be instituted, it can only be done on the basis of unappropriability, and in no case can it become the object of property.*

The Activity of "Commoning" (*koinônein*) as the Institutionalization of the Common (*koinôn*)

In *Governing the Commons*, Elinor Ostrom cites Aristotle's critique of the Platonic community of women and children from Chapter 3, Book 2, of the *Politics*:

> That which is common to the greatest number (*to pleistôn koinôn*) has the least care bestowed upon it. Everyone thinks chiefly of his own (*tôn idiôn*), hardly at all of the common interest (*tôn koinôn*); and only when he is himself concerned as an individual.[1]

The distinction between the personal and the common is immediately posed in terms of *property*: what is common to a large number of people is what they all possess in common – i.e., women and children, in the Platonic city – just as what is proper to each individual is what each individual owns – i.e., one's wife and one's children, in most other cities. What is at issue here is the quality or intensity of the care (*epimeleia*) the possessor endows upon that which he owns in common with many others: if one takes less care of that which is owned in common, it is largely because one "principally" takes care of what is one's own (in terms of priority), and not because care or attention is diluted overall in direct proportion to the number of owners. Hence the question Aristotle poses in Chapter 5 of the *Politics* concerning the optimal political constitution: "What is the proper system of property for citizens who are to live under the best form of constitution? Should property be held in common, or not?"[2]

Aristotle poses three possible solutions: (a) "plots of land are owned separately, but the crops ... are brought into a common stock for the purpose of consumption," (b) "land may be held in common ownership, and may also be cultivated in common and worked in common, but the crops may be divided among individuals for their private use," and (c) "the plots and crops may both be common."[3] Assuming those who cultivate the land are citizens who work on their own account – as opposed to slaves working on behalf of their owners – Aristotle argues that unequal distribution of profits and penalties will inevitably occasion frequent disputes. Aristotle thus makes the following general remark: "but indeed there is always a difficulty in men living together (*suzên*) and having all human relations in common (*koinônein*), but especially in their having common property."[4] As we can see, then, the issue here is grounded in the disadvantages associated with "common property" (*koinas tas ktêseis*). Common property arises from the act of pooling resources together, and solely and exclusively concerns goods (literally "acquisitions"). The difficulty Aristotle identifies is thus based on the dissonance between living together and sharing resources together. As we have already learned,[5] Plato's mistake, according to Aristotle, was to have confused "living together" (*suzên*) and "living in common" (*koinê zên*), and Plato's justification for community property (at least for the guardians) arises out of this confusion. But if, as in Aristotle, the difference between the *sun* (the whole) and the *koinê* (the common) is irreducible to the point that it affects the very the nature of living (*zên*) itself, then it may well begin to appear that the imperative for all citizens of the same city to share goods in common will no longer square with the particularities of "living together." For we should recall that Aristotle's underlying premise is that a city should not have the same degree of unity as a family or, *a fortiori*, as an individual, and so for these reasons it is preferable, for Aristotle, to combine the common use of goods with their private ownership.[6]

Does this mean, then, that "living together" is fundamentally distinct from "sharing resources in common" (*koinônein*)? This clearly contradicts the basic fact that "living together" is the fundamental prerogative of those who live in a political community (*koinônia*) as such. This type of community, as Aristotle puts it, is based on "liv[ing] together and shar[ing] conversation and thought."[7] As Pierre Aubenque observes, the verb *koinônein* "does not refer to passive participation within an already existing order, but describes the active and reciprocal communication that makes such an order possible."[8] In other words, the term designates "participation" not in the sense of belonging, but in the sense of "equality in taking part." The fundamental Aristotelian lesson, then, is the recognition that it is not the pre-constituted political community that enables forms of sharing or pooling to occur, but it is rather the fact of this sharing or pooling itself that makes the common *qua* political community itself possible. This is not to say we are dealing with the exercise of a "constituent power" in the modern sense of the term,[9] but simply that the activity of sharing in common is the activity that brings the common into existence and which continues to sustain it throughout its existence. To put it more generally, and beyond Aristotle's particular concerns, *every true political common owes its existence to a sustained and continuous activity of collective sharing.*

For us, this point is absolutely fundamental. It touches on all the essential aspects of the common as an institution, and therefore gets to the essential nature of the institution as such. In this respect, Hannah Arendt's interpretation of Aristotle merits attention, insofar as she understands the "collective sharing of words and actions" as an activity that only takes place within a preliminary framework established by a lawmaker, understood as a constitutional "architect." Arendt is concerned with separating the "making" (*poiesis*) of the lawmaker from the "activity" (*praxis*) of the political subject who acts within the constitutional framework. The founder, in her view, is like an artisan or a craftsman who makes the laws, and the politician is the one who acts within the boundaries of the law. For Plato and Aristotle, the act of constructing this constitutional framework (as well as producing laws) is considered to be a "pre-political activity," and is therefore a more privileged activity than politics or political action properly speaking, because the former is a matter of craftsmanship, which is to say poiesis rather than praxis.[10] Yet Aristotle's privileging of "making" at the expense of "action" runs counter to a passage in the *Nichomachean Ethics* in which Aristotle distinguishes between two modes of "politics": the first, which Aristotle calls *nomothetikè*, is "legislative" inasmuch as it refers to the laws ("legislative science"), and the second, which Aristotle calls *politikè*,[11] refers to communicative action and deliberation and leads to the adoption of "statutes" designed to govern over particular and temporary issues. Immediately after marking this distinction, Aristotle states the following: "hence these people are the only ones who are said to be politically active; for these are the only ones who put [political science] into practice, as hand-craftsmen put [a craft] into practice."[12] Thus, while Arendt makes it very clear that only "legislators and architects belong in the same category,"[13] Aristotle says precisely the opposite in this case: it is the "administrators," or those who deliberate with a view to adopting decrees, that act as craftsmen. In other words, the legislators or lawmakers are more comparable to chief contractors who direct the craftsmen. There is nothing in this passage that suggests Aristotle viewed "*poietic*" legislative activity as pre-political; rather, administrative activity is subordinated here to legislative activity, inasmuch as the particular (the statute) is subordinated to the universal (the law). In the very same text, Aristotle even goes so far as to say that laws are "works of politics" (*politikès erga*), which would of course be nonsensical if he viewed legislation as a pre-political phenomena. For Aristotle, then, the legislative does not possess its own justification, but rather acts as a framework for political deliberation.[14] The rules of justice, which are laws, are instituted at the level of the political community, which means that the law is both the effect and the cause of this community: it is effect inasmuch as "there is no legislative activity except within a polis," and it is cause inasmuch as the law differentiates the *polis* from the non-political aspects of social life.[15] In this sense, legislation is fully political and categorically *koinônein*. At base, and as strange as it may seem, Arendt's biased reading merely revives the figure of the great, anti-democratic *nomothète*, or the creator and giver of the law (on the model of Lycurgus, Solon, or Numa). As such, any theory based on the principles of emancipation and autonomy must absolutely reject these kinds of mythological figures, and the foundation for politics they create.

Our reading of Aristotle thus suggests we ought to distinguish between two very different types of sharing in common: the sharing of "goods" that compromises or prohibits the political common as "living together," and the sharing of "speech," "thought," and "actions" that is inversely irreducibility of the political common. In the first instance, the decisive difference between the two is that the second form of sharing does not concern acts appropriation: there is no such thing as communal property when we are dealing with "speech and thoughts," whereas there may be common property in relation to "goods," even if this property is undesirable insofar as it imposes an excessive and harmful degree of unity onto the city (as is Aristotle's interpretation). As we know, Aristotle's solution is not to adopt common property as such, but to opt for the common use of private property.[16] If we take an overall view of the problem, however, it is difficult to avoid the following conclusion: the form of sharing that constitutes the political common does not deal with appropriation because the political common is neither common property or private property: it is not property of any kind at all. In other words, the political common is radically outside of property as such precisely because it does not involve a good, and there can be no property – private or common – unless we are dealing with a good of some kind. While there may, in short, be such things as "common goods," *the common itself is not a good*, at least in the sense of something one could freely acquire and dispose of (what the Greeks call *ktêsis*).

But there is more. The political common – no matter what type of constitution governs a particular city – is always ordered according to a specific determination of the "common advantage" (*koine? sumpheron*). This means that every political common is based on a certain concept of "justice": indeed, as Aristotle puts it, "the good in the sphere of politics is justice; and justice consists in what tends to promote the common interest."[17] In a well-constituted political community, this is determined through collective deliberation – i.e., a collective deliberation as "sharing of conversation and thoughts" described above – about what is just and what is unjust.[18] Belonging to such a community presupposes each individual is endowed with "the will and the capacity to communicate, share, and participate."[19] In other words, only a subject who realizes this capacity for sharing with other subjects can partake in a political community. Indeed, this activity of sharing, and actualizing this capacity through deliberation, is precisely what founds the community in the first place, rather than the reverse: "belonging is the consequence, not the cause, of this participation."[20] Only the activity of sharing determines whether or not one belongs to the political community. But insofar as this deliberation also determines what is just and unjust, this also implies that the activity of deliberation concerning the political good constitutes the political common, which makes the latter an "order." As Aristotle puts it, "justice is an ordering of the political association."[21] This is not to say that justice is a kind of order that emanates from the political community, but rather that justice is itself the activity that "constitutes the political community."[22] Deliberate and rational discussion about the rules of justice thus directly proceeds from the active participation of citizens engaged in collective deliberation. The political common, in other words, must be actively instituted through the actualization of our "natural" capacity to share in common.[23]

This Aristotelian exegesis singularly illuminates the importance of our "methodological reversal." It shows the necessity of returning to the idea of *common activity* as the fundamental principle of the common, rather than construing the common as a natural datum that is independent of human activity, like a substance one could possess and exchange. It is crucial to recognize that the common is established by an *act* of sharing in common that that is literally law-producing – in the sense of Aristotle's notion of "justice" – while necessarily excluding the possibility of this law becoming a right of ownership over the common. Unlike Aristotle, however, we shall not restrict the political common to the sphere of the "city" – in either the ancient Greek sense of the *polis* or the modern sense of the "state." We refuse this conceptual limitation not only because participation in any form of commons always involves a political dimension, but also because the only form of politics capable of restoring the term's foundational sense of *koinônein* – the sense of "equality in taking part"[24] that is the essence of sharing in common as such – is that which makes the common its object, its principle, and its center of gravity, whatever its scale (the nation-state form has no particular priority in this respect). To repeat our fundamental thesis: *the common can only be instituted on the basis of complete unappropriability; under no circumstance can the common be the object of the law of property.*

The "Illusion of Archaic Collective Property"[25]

To better articulate our thesis, let's move on to an examination of the anthropological idea that "communal property" lies at the origin of human history and, concomitantly, that humanity's fundamental mission is to "re-establish" this form of communal property – as if history itself posits a right of re-appropriation over the common that humanity need only consciously realize. This concept of history profoundly informed the development of "historical materialism," insofar as the latter relied on specific historical data to establish successive modes of production characterized by different forms of ownership – from "primitive communism" all the way up to "advanced communism." It is well known that Marx described "communal property" as the original form of property amongst the Romans, the Germanic tribes, the Celts, the Slavs, and in India.[26] Indeed, Marx's passion for history and ethnography (which he frequently discussed with Engels) was largely motivated by his search for "primitive communism." Matters become much more complex, however, when it comes to understanding exactly what Marx meant by "communal property," and how he understood the relation between communal property and individual property. For Marx is careful to never straightforwardly articulate these terms as opposites. This is evident, for instance, in the well-known passage from Chapter 32 of *Capital* (vol. 1), wherein the "negation of the negation" does not re-establish "private property" but rather re-establishes "individual property" based on cooperation and communal ownership over the land and the means of production.[27] Marx's refusal to see communal property and individual property as opposites is perhaps even more evident in the section of the *Grundrisse* that discusses "pre-capitalist modes of production," wherein Marx compares Roman public property to the communal property of the ancient Germans.

Let's look more closely at the historical material Marx drew from to formulate his notion of revolution, and carefully consider his interpretation of this data on the basis of his contrast between Roman and German forms of communal property. First, Roman communal property is specifically based on a distinction between the *ager publicus* (public domain) and private family property. Indeed, the institution of the *ager publicus* played a significant role in the history of the Roman Republic, from its archaic origins until the rise of the Empire.[28] During the conquest of Italy, Rome confiscated part of the land it conquered and transformed it into the property of the Roman people, and these lands were then colonized by plebeian settlers. The Romans decreed "everything immovable belongs to the Roman state and is therefore inalienable and imprescriptible, although allocated as part of the public service."[29] This property was then doled out in parcels to plebeian citizens as "possessions" but not as "property" (*dominium*), which meant the Romans only recognized a citizen's right to use and enjoy the plots of land, but not the right to divide or sell them.[30] The state subsequently became accustomed to handing over large tracts of land to its creditors – i.e., members of the nobility – who were permitted almost unlimited enjoyment of these public tracts. According to the perspective adopted by Marx in the *Grundrisse*, Roman antiquity is thus characterized by a rather unique configuration between communal property and private possession: specifically, it was a relation in which state ownership was the prerequisite for private possession. Only state ownership enabled private appropriation of the soil: "the private proprietor of land is such only as a Roman, but as a Roman he is a private proprietor of land."[31] For Marx, then, the Roman question *par excellence* is: "what mode of property creates the best citizens?" The best citizen is precisely the citizen for whom state citizenship is the guarantor of his private ownership. This arrangement, in Marx's view, is especially advantageous insofar as it is based on a certain equality between free and independent peasants, each of whom has the same right to possess a particular plot of public land.

When we then look closely at the passages in which Marx compares the Germanic form of property with its Roman counterpart, however, we find that the Germanic form is actually the inverse of the Roman: "among the Germanic tribes, the *ager publicus* appears rather merely a complement to individual property," whereas, for the Romans, the public domain is viewed as a "particular economic presence of the state as against (*neben*) the private proprietors."[32] How should we understand Marx's notion of "as against" (*neben*) here? Private owners who are private "in truest sense of the term" – i.e., they are "deprived" of partaking in the *ager publicus* – are the most wealthy citizens. They are deprived of the *ager publicus* because they already possess an *ager privatus*. This is a simple consequence of the fact that land in the public domain was originally created for those citizens who did not already own their own parcels of land. Private owners, "in the truest sense of the term," are not therefore plebeians to whom the state concedes possession of a plot of land, but patricians who are literally "excluded from the *ager publicus*." There are, therefore, two forms of private ownership: "possession" and "property." The former is obtained through the allocation of common land, while the latter exists outside the ambit of common land entirely. Under these conditions, affirming the idea that the public domain only exists amongst the Germans as a "compliment to individual property" means affirming the idea that "individual property" is only recognized as such in relation to communal property. For the Germans, individual property designates the family household ("independent houses"), and these households are considered to be "independent organisms" separated from other households by "long distances." If there is, then, an *ager publicus* for the Germans, it takes the form of "communal land" or the "people's land," and is generally reserved as "hunting land, grazing land, timber land, etc."[33] Far from belonging to the public domain in the sense of a Roman "prerequisite" or "pre-condition" for the private appropriation of land, individual or family property for the Germans presupposes simultaneous access to communal goods. The latter, in this case, is the communal property of multiple families who recognize themselves as members of the same "tribe" (*Stammwesen*). This is the inverse of the Roman configuration: that which was the pre-condition in the Roman system is the "result" in the case of the Germans. For the Germans, communal property is the product of mutual relations between individual owners or, as Marx put it, "their effective assembling for common purposes." In other words, it is a "communal accessory" of individual land ownership rather than the latter's pre-condition.[34]

What is most significant in Marx's analysis of communal property amongst the Germanic tribes is ultimately the separation between the common and the state: indeed, it is precisely this separation that allows Marx to project communal property back to the origins of human history itself. In the case of the German *ager publicus*, one may say there is a public, but there is not yet a state. And for Marx, the prior existence of this configuration alone makes it possible to conceive of the "common of the future" as a form of non-state public that emerges after the fated post-revolutionary withering of the state form. In any case, what also merits particular attention here is how this "original common" gives rise to an important distinction between that which is merely individual and that which is privately individual: for this common, in effect, merely extended a form of individual appropriation that was not exactly "private," in the sense of a *dominium* or an exclusive and unlimited right over a given object. It is undoubtedly still possible to talk of "possession" of the common, but only on the condition that this possession had the peculiar feature of being neither facilitated nor guaranteed (in the legal sense) by the state (unlike the Roman *possessio* enjoyed by the plebeians). In fact, the German is, in this respect, both an individual owner and a member of a tribe, and so his access to common land (for hunting, grazing, etc.) is premised on him already being an individual owner. His property is not "private" in the sense that the latter is primarily defined by what it *excludes*: if, in Rome, the wealthy proprietor "excludes" others while at the same time being himself "deprived" of access to the common, the German individual owner has access to the common only because he is already an individual owner.[35] Marx thus feels justified in saying, "it is really the common property of the individual proprietors, not of the union of these proprietors endowed with an existence separate from themselves, the city itself."[36] The Germanic form as an originary prototype thus offers us a double example of (a) communal, *non-state* property and (b) individual, *non-private* property. It is no surprise, then, why this configuration garnered so much attention from the pioneers of the materialist conception of history.

Historically and anthropologically, however, it is an open question as to whether the ancient Germanic form of "communal property" was really as Marx repeatedly asserts. In his book *Avant l'histoire* (*Before History*),[37] for instance, Alain Testart maps the flow of history as an evolution from the first forms of social life up until what he refers to as the "invention of wealth." Testart observes how the ethnographic societies of the Neolithic period (in Melanesia and North America) recognized wealth has having only one "advantage," namely the social consideration or esteem its possession provides. There was no wage labor in these societies and therefore no power over those who are forced to work for a wage, and, above all, there was no possibility for wealth to produce further wealth by investing in land, for instance. What was completely absent in these societies, then, was some means of differentiating amongst social classes: land could not be "rented by a landlord and transformed as income in the form of rent, what we could describe as 'land rent'"). Ownership status was based on the actual use of an object, which in turn meant prolonged disuse led to the loss of status or title. Hence Testart's distinction between two very different types of property: he refers, on the one hand, to the oldest historical form of property as "usufund property" because it is "founded on continuous temporal use and only so long as this use can be demonstrated."[38] This kind of use-based qualification on property makes modern modes of land ownership nearly impossible, insofar as the farmer and proprietor are always the same person. Contemporary property, on the other hand, is referred to by Testart as "fundiary property" because it is "founded on the basis of funds [i.e., money] independent of the work it creates or the uses to which it is put": whether the landowner uses the land himself, leases it, or leaves it uncultivated has no bearing on his proprietary status or title."[39] What this means is that wealth cannot play the same role in both systems of property: in the fundiary property regime, wealth constitutes the basis of economic power insofar as land becomes a source of income through investment; in the usufund property regime, excess wealth cannot be invested and so instead it is converted into social prestige, through sumptuous feasts, for example.

From this essential distinction, Testart advanced the general hypothesis that Neolithic societies were largely organized according to usufund property regimes, and from this premise he sketched a more general model of social evolution comprised of three great periods he referred to as "worlds": "world I" includes every "society without wealth" organized on the basis of usufund property regimes; "world II" designates societies that combined the accumulation of wealth with usufund regimes; and lastly, "world III" includes societies with wealth organized on the basis of fundiary property regimes. The historical succession of these three worlds – from world I to world II, then from world II to world III – defines, for Testart, the flow of history (*sens de l'histoire*) as based on the increasing importance of wealth. It should be noted that these worlds only approximately correspond to established archaeological periods: thus, while most Neolithic societies belong to "world II," the Neolithic period is not entirely coincidental with world II insofar as certain Iron Age societies also belong to this world, as do certain hunter-gatherer and sedentary-storage societies, such as those in California (though the latter were not agricultural).[40] Testart's hypothesis undermines the presupposition that hunter-gatherer societies were – like the Neolithic societies that followed them and inherited their property conventions – societies in which property did not exist (or perhaps only in the form of collective ownership). The conspicuous obstacle we encounter here, then, is the categorical confusion between usufund property and collective property. For while usufund property may not lead to the expropriation and immiseration of workers, nor produce masses of landless peasants, it is certainly not immune to inequalities and hierarchies:

> [Usufund property] is a real form of property – and not, as has been said, merely a usufruct – and is indeed a form of property that is part of the means of production, capable of generating inequalities and powerful dependencies. But *it does not permit the expropriation of the worker*, nor does it allow, in Marxian terms, the separation of the worker from his means of production. So long as the worker works his field, it cannot be taken from him.[41]

We should not, therefore, hastily assume that just because the means of production are collectively owned, and the worker is not separated from the individual means of his own production (and reproduction), that inequality is absent as well. While it may be true that "misery was born from fundiary property" and thus Neolithic societies were not "societies of luxury and misery," they were not "egalitarian societies" either. For Testart, at least, the notion of an "egalitarian society" at the origin of history is largely contradicted by contemporary anthropological evidence.

Since the Germanic tribes were such an important historical datum for Marx's analysis of property, the topic deserves a little more attention. These barbarian peoples belonged to the Iron Age and were part of "world II" (wealth alongside usufund property). Relying largely on classical sources that describe land ownership – specifically excerpts from Julius Caesar's *The Gallic Wars* and Tacitus's *Germania* – Testart arrived at very different conclusions from most contemporary commentators, who tend to see "evidence of the collective or public ownership of land" in these sources.[42] Yet neither Caesar nor Tacitus uses the term *ager publicus* to describe land ownership, nor do they speak of the *populous* or the *civitas*. They talk instead about an "absence of property," which simply designates their lack of any adequate notion for more precisely accounting for the real differences between the German property regime and the Roman model with which they were familiar. For Testart, however, only the notion of usufund property can precisely account for the German system, and for at least two reasons. The first reason is that cultivated land is clearly distinguished from uncultivated arable land in these sources: it is the abundance of the latter which renders their dispersed allocation practical,[43] because "what is not cultivated is not property" and can be shared, whereas that which is cultivated, and is currently being used, cannot. This is exactly what we find in usufund property regimes. And the second reason is that both Caesar and Tacitus speak of an "annual re-distribution of land," a practice that usually corresponds to usufund property: "if no one has right to land he has not cultivated, everyone therefore as a right to land to cultivate it."[44] Land is thus allocated on the basis of need, but what counts as "need" of course varies according to the social status of each individual (what Tacitus calls *dignatio*), or the number of clients or slaves who depend upon a given individual. Distribution is not, therefore, egalitarian, but the land is also not yet a "means of social domination" because the powerful cannot accumulate land by stripping the weak of their property. It should be pointed out, moreover, that in the case of the Germans, usufund property was not inherited (whereas it otherwise generally is). In summary, then, what we are dealing with is a profoundly inegalitarian society that was not, however, a "class society" in the classical Marxist sense. That is to say that it was not a society in which workers were separated from the means of production which then became the exclusive property of non-workers.

What about the "political system" in these types of societies (world II) and amongst the ancient Germanic tribes more specifically? Following the general consensus, Testart argues that the whole of Neolithic Europe consisted of "societies without a state," but he is careful to distinguish between three main categories within this general framework.[45] The first category (or society) is characterized by an "absence of functional power," meaning power is not derived from political function but from ostentatiously spent wealth; the second type of society is characterized through the use of "councils" that function as sovereign assemblies at all levels of social life (village, tribe, confederation) – such as the "primitive democracy" of the Iroquois, as described by British anthropologist Lewis Morgan. And the third type of society is structured by lineage (as is typical of Africa), wherein authority is always derived by referencing a founding ancestor and is exercised through solidarity or co-responsibility. The leader in these societies is usually the eldest in the line of succession. The institutional politics of the Germanic tribes is best described as a kind of "military democracy," as Engels puts it,[46] which places the German peoples in the second of Testart's categories. For the command exercised by the German generals did not derive from an acknowledged political or military position that guaranteed obedience: "warriors only participate in wars" if the chief, and the chief's planned expedition, pleases them. In other words, "military service is not compulsory."[47] Accordingly, the Germanic armies were "small, private armies who sustain[ed] themselves through pillage" and whose structure depended on the personal ties of "warrior companionship." Germanic societies also tended to be governed by an "assembly of people" (which was called the *concilium*) to whom affairs previously discussed by the "chiefs" were usually submitted.

The political organization of the Germanic tribes thus not only differed from the Romans, but also from the Gauls during the same epoch. The Gauls levied troops from the population *en masse*, convened assemblies of armed subjects, and collected taxes, all of which seems to attest to the existence of a state. "The difference between the Germans who only participated in wars if it pleased them and those who are compelled to fight is the difference between a society without a state and one with a state."[48] The antiquity of peoples' assemblies in Europe, the close resemblance between the Germanic popular assemblies and the *thing* in medieval Scandinavia and Iceland, the absence of any traditions analogous to those of the Near or Far East, and many other convergent factors led Testart to posit the "hypothesis of very old examples of the common since the beginning of the Neolithic period, including primitive democratic regimes."[49] From this perspective, then, the Greeks did not "invent" democracy, but rather tried to "perfect a very old form" by altering its institutions to suit the needs of a new *polis*-based regime.[50] A striking contrast thus emergences between the East of the fourth and third millennia and barbarian Europe in the second and first millennia: whereas the invention of bronze, the city, writing, and the state all coincided in the East, barbarian Europe welcomed the invention of bronze but refused the other three innovations. One explanation for this refusal, as articulated by Pierre Clastres, is "a sort of prescience about the horrors of despotism" alongside anxieties about social division. But perhaps there is a more plausible "political" explanation: these innovations were refused because of a several-thousand-year-old tradition of "primitive democracy," characterized by an "assembly that appoints generals and confers upon them the power of delegation, and which are therefore equally capable of removing them." In short, these democratic institutions (as opposed to lineal modes of organization) did not create hospitable environments for the emergence of the state.[51] Yet, at the same time, it is clear that the example of the Germanic tribe is in no way an ideal image of an egalitarian society based on "individual possession of collective property." Germanic society was rather based on a combination of usufund property, sometimes very stark social inequalities and hierarchies, and a "military democracy" in which the powers of chiefs were constrained by assemblies. If it was a "non-state common," it was not one that was based on the land, but one whose commonality was embodied by the assembly: the assembly was no one's property, it could not be confiscated by any of the chiefs, and it was based on some conception of "equal participation."

What are we to say, then, about the nineteenth-century thesis on ancient collective or communal property? This was a widely held and shared anthropological belief in the second half of the nineteenth century, and Marx and Engels avidly adopted it for their own purposes (which are not too difficult to discern). In retrospect, the popularity of this thesis appears to be linked to the hegemony of political individualism during the nineteenth century.[52] In the strictest sense, property rights are the most "absolute" of any right (*plena in re potestas*), in that their holder enjoys the following prerogatives: the right of use (*usus*), the right to the property's fruits (*fructus*) – which is also called the right of enjoyment and includes both "natural fruits" and "civil fruits" (i.e., income from the property) – and finally the right to abuse (*abusus*) or dispose of the property, by destroying it, altering its substance, or selling or giving it away.[53] It is obviously this last right, the right to dispose of a thing – whether by destroying it or by transforming its substance – that is most central to the definition of property rights, and it is on the basis of this definition of property rights that we are able to clarify the often imprecise notion of "collective ownership."

Like Testart, we can immediately distinguish three kinds of ownership rights in French law: "undivided ownership," the typical case of which is inheritance; the ownership of legal personhood (such as an abbey in the Middle Ages or a corporation today); and lastly, public property. With respect to the first, there is no doubt we are dealing with a form of private property that is subject to agreement by other members of the community (albeit very limited). In the case of legal persons, we are dealing with a form of collective ownership, but the collective is only a "nominal" form in the sense that it merely references the group or collective that manages the otherwise private property. And public property is, of course, almost entirely conceived as the property of the state, and this must not be confused with the property of the citizen, since public property is not always accessible to citizens; it may sometimes be accessible to citizens (road, communal spaces, etc.), but it is still nonetheless not the property of the citizens as such. The conclusion is clear: "public property is never the property of all."[54] If we examine the situation in Africa (where the practice of collective land ownership at the village level is still relatively common) in the light of these qualifications, the hypothesis is still untenable, despite the often-made comparison between the Russian *mir* and rural communes in the West. While the African "village" is perhaps the only serious candidate for true collective ownership of the land, the example is still problematic insofar as a village does not enjoy all the rights that are usually constitutive of ownership: it does not enjoy the right of use, nor the right to the property's fruits, nor finally the right to dispose of or alienate the property.[55] The village leader distributes vacant land amongst the family heads, but this does not mean that the "village" is the owner of the land. In fact, these vacant lands tend to be the only lands that are actually managed or controlled by the municipality, and so they are not really collective property but more like "non-property": these lands are not a "good" in the usual sense and they are often not susceptible to appropriation (otherwise they would not be vacant). They are, in this sense, *terra nullius*.[56] Moreover, the category of usufruct – and only individuals can be usufructuaries – does not work with this example either, because this category only has meaning in relation to the context of a true owner or a "bare owner," which is precisely what is lacking here.[57] We are forced to conclude, then, that it is actually the "men and their families who are the true owners of the land in Africa."[58]

The Advent of Proprietary Individualism

How then, under these conditions, do we account for the advent of "possessive individualism" – to use C.B. MacPherson's phrase – and the re-imagination of human civilization as an association of private proprietors? Its arrival may have begun in a theological re-interpretation stretching back all the way to the Book of Psalms (as mentioned previously),[59] wherein the earth was conceived as the gracious gift of God to his creatures. While God may be the original and only master (*dominus*) of the earth, the advent of sin compelled humanity to make arrangements that would allow them to lead their lives according to the natural order, one of the first of which is of course the preservation of life itself. Thus, enjoying the fruits of one's labor, and ensuring the continuation of a dignified life through thrift and by building up a personal estate, necessitates a rational system of property rights, as Thomas Aquinas argued in his

Summa Theologica. In his discussion of Saint Basil and Saint Ambrose's theses on the community of goods, Aquinas distinguishes between property as such – which only applies to God's absolute sovereignty over his creation – and the human uses of the earth. The latter is organized through positive law and is an expression of human reason that renders the possession of external goods lawful:

> Community of goods is ascribed to the natural law, not that the natural law dictates that all things should be possessed in common and that nothing should be possessed as one's own: but because the division of possessions is not according to the natural law, but rather arose from human agreement which belongs to positive law, as stated above ... Hence the ownership of possessions is not contrary to the natural law, but an addition thereto devised by human reason.[60]

While private property is not therefore exactly "natural," as was subsequently established in the Catholic dogma of Pope Leon XIII in his *Rerum novarum* of 1891 (which was entirely and explicitly directed against the socialist doctrine of collective property),[61] possession to the end of supporting oneself is nonetheless lawful because it is necessary for life. Drawing inspiration from Aristotle's remarks on the problems posed by collective property, Aquinas argues in favor of private property by referring to the incentives it provides in terms of personal advantage:

> [Possession] is necessary to human life for three reasons. First because every man is more careful to procure what is for himself alone than that which is common to many or to all: since each one would shirk the labor and leave to another that which concerns the community, as happens where there is a great number of servants. Secondly, because human affairs are conducted in more orderly fashion if each man is charged with taking care of some particular thing himself, whereas there would be confusion if everyone had to look after any one thing indeterminately. Thirdly, because a more peaceful state is ensured to man if each one is contented with his own. Hence it is to be observed that quarrels arise more frequently where there is no division of the things possessed.[62]

Human reason is thus the basis for the practical necessity of the division of possessions and its guarantee by positive law. If this shift in scholastic ideology begins in Aquinas, it becomes even more entrenched through the later remarks of Pope Leo XIII:

> It is the mind, or reason, which is the predominant element in us who are human creatures; it is this which renders a human being human, and distinguishes him essentially from the brute. And on this very account – that man alone among the animal creation is endowed with reason – it must be within his right to possess things not merely for temporary and momentary use, as other living things do, but to have and to hold them in stable and permanent possession; he must have not only things that perish in the use, but those also which, though they have been reduced into use, continue for further use in after time.[63]

This scholastic argument thus broke with the older ideal of the community of goods propagated by the first Christians and the Fathers of the Church by "naturally" – i.e., in conformity with the essence of man's rational being – giving man not merely the right but the *duty* to "dominate nature." This doctrinal shift was based on the notion that man, as "master of his own acts, guides his ways under the eternal law and the power of God, whose providence governs all things," and this is because "it is in his power to exercise his choice not only as to matters that regard his present welfare, but also about those which he deems may be for his advantage in time yet to come," in the words of Leo XIII. This justification for property through man's rational nature was then used to undermine the frequent references made by nineteenth-century communists and socialists to the Gospels and the Fathers of the Church:

> The fact that God has given the earth for the use and enjoyment of the whole human race can in no way be a bar to the owning of private property. For God has granted the earth to mankind in general, not in the sense that all without distinction can deal with it as they like, but rather that no part of it was assigned to any one in particular, and that the limits of private possession have been left to be fixed by man's own industry, and by the laws of individual races. Moreover, the earth, even though apportioned among private owners, ceases not thereby to minister to the needs of all, inasmuch as there is not one who does not sustain life from what the land produces. Those who do not possess the soil contribute their labor; hence, it may truly be said that all human subsistence is derived either from labor on one's own land, or from some toil, some calling, which is paid for either in the produce of the land itself, or in that which is exchanged for what the land brings forth.[64]

This justification for property is perhaps best understood on the grounds of work and need. In this respect, the Reformation significantly influenced this doctrinal shift by extolling the great merits of the worker and denouncing the vices – and even the crimes – of idleness, social parasitism, and decadent lust. Calvin, accordingly, argued that it was not so much nature but private property that was God's true gift, the latter of which is said to be necessary for the good of the community. This shift was tantamount to a revolution in Christian thought: it is not merely the earth that God has given to man in common, but also the faculty of reason, the taste for work, the consciousness of oneself and one's body – in short, everything that makes private property an authentically scared right. These arguments cleared the way for Catholics and Protestants alike to naturalize capitalism and the social inequalities it produced.

But the scholastic argument itself was not enough to transform civilization into an association of private proprietors. In the political philosophy of John Locke, for instance, we go far beyond merely depicting private property as a natural right. In Chapter 5 of his *Second Treatise on Government*, Locke strives to found property on the natural right of self-ownership: ownership of one's body and faculties, and thus of one's work, which is nothing other than the application and objectification of one's faculties.[65] For Locke, then, the right to ownership over the natural world is fundamentally and incontestably a function of the ownership of one's self. In other words, property is no longer justified through mere convenience or utility (as conceived by human reason), but is now a fundamental right that everyone possesses in themselves. We know Locke describes property in various ways. In a very general sense, property is a concept that encompasses "life, liberty, and property." In contrast to the absolutist thesis that endows Adam's successors with property rights over the earth, Locke argues that the earth was originally owned by everyone. Locke thus interprets the primitive community as a "positive community," as opposed to the notion of the "negative community" defended by Grotius and Pufendorf – i.e., God made all men co-possessors of the earth and all the fruits of nature (as opposed to the negative notion that there was no possession or belonging as such).[66] For Locke, however, God did not give the earth in common to man so it could remain fallow; it must be put to productive use. It is therefore labor that legitimates property and allows it to take shape. The first form of property, as mentioned, is the ownership of oneself. The first right of property, then, is the right to self-preservation, which, by association, justifies the ownership of everything that issues from the application of one's body and one's personal efforts. Personal property is like a form of corporeal extension and a means of personal self-preservation. The axiom of this new normative regime is the idea that the individual owns his mind and body. This axiomatic premise of self-ownership *cum* individual property will be continuously repeated to render property rights both a natural and sacred right, and a fundamental condition of the commodious life.[67] Locke's notion of proprietary individualism is one of the defining features of modern economic dogma that has persisted largely unchanged all the way up to contemporary neoclassical economics. As Leon Walras puts it:

> Personal faculties are by natural law the property of the individual. In other words, every person belongs to himself, because every person – that is to say, every free and rational person – has the right and the duty to pursue his own ends, to achieve his own destiny, and is responsible for this pursuit and its accomplishment. The principle of inequality applies here, which means we should enjoy in proportion to our efforts ... Moreover, since the individual is the owner of his own personal faculties, he is also the owner of his work and his wages, and thus owner of the products, consumable income, or new capital he acquires through his wages.[68]

Such bourgeois apologetics were particularly refined and honed during those crucial periods when the proprietary class felt most threatened. In the face of the socialist menace, Adolphe Thiers went so far as to evoke a "natural instinct in man, child, animal whose sole end is the indispensible reward for work," in his 1848 argument for property.[69] In a very "laborious" manner, as he admits, Thiers attempted to justify property by virtue of its social universality and its corporeal naturalness in order to ward off the dangers threatened by society's enemies. Wherever we find society, argues Thiers, there is property: it is a "general and universal fact, without exception."[70] For Thiers, the proprietary instinct is part of a universal faculty that produces a sensation and consciousness of one's spiritual and corporeal individuality: "consciousness of self, firstly, then my faculties, both physical and intellectual: my feet, my hands, my eyes, my brain, my soul and my body."[71] This universal instinct is then overlaid with the social conventions derived from humanity's adoption of a sedentary lifestyle, which in turn produces firmer and more developed laws:

> Thus, in proportion as man develops, he becomes more attached to that which he possesses. In a word, he becomes more proprietary. In a barbarous state, property hardly exists; in a civilized state, man is passionate about his property. It has been said that the idea of property is weakening everywhere. This is a factual error. It regulates itself, becomes more precise, and grows stronger, not weaker.[72]

To undermine this natural and conventional fact would be to commit civilizational regression, for civilization itself is nothing but the generalization, strengthening, and refinement of property rights: "amongst all nations, however crude, we find property – first as a fact, and then as an idea, an idea that is more or less clear according to the degree of civilization that has been attained, but it is always invariably present."[73] From Thier's perspective, then, anyone who questions property rights is no better than the barbarian, who must therefore be crushed, as the French bourgeoisie did in June of 1848 and May of 1871. All these bourgeois arguments are based on the idea that property is a function of individual faculties alone, and on the idea in particular that individual labor is the ultimate source of wealth. It is impossible for these bourgeois writers to imagine man as something other than an independent worker – "he works for himself," as Thiers repeats – and proprietor. And if there are inequalities, if there is predation, all of this can be justified by the fact that nature did not evenly distribute faculties amongst men.

In addition to this natural rights argument (whose theological basis is never far removed), Thiers proffers a utilitarian argument concerning the incentive for personal advantage very similar to that already formulated by Aquinas: it is because of labor and property that humanity managed to escape misery and achieved well-being and prosperity: "man, thrown naked upon the bare earth, passes from misery to abundance through the exercise of the powerful faculties endowed by God," as Thiers eloquently explains.[74] Property is the guarantor of prosperity, and its beneficial consequences are more than enough justification. Hume and especially Bentham likewise managed to free themselves of natural rights and its associated theological yoke – a yoke that still hung from Locke's head, despite the fact that he sought, above all, to reconcile natural law and utility, which, according to him, have gone hand in hand since the beginning of the world.[75] Indeed, Bentham's fight with William Blackstone – one of the great defenders of absolute property rights – was motivated by Bentham's desire to purge the legal system of any basis other than utility. For Bentham, all law is an "imaginary creation," a "fictive entity" that ought to be entirely shaped by political authority and established with a view to the effects it is capable of yielding in terms of human motivation and action. What is still described by Locke as a natural right, a right grounded in the Almighty Being who is its absolute origin, is for Bentham something to be imputed by terrestrial authority alone – and all as a result of philosophical arguments that are remarkably similar to those which Locke develops in his *Essay Concerning Human Understanding.*

Bentham developed a close connection between the definition of juridical and political legal fictions and the possibility of the "greatest happiness for the greatest number."[76] Bentham's doctrine is concerned with explaining how the individual proprietor is not at all some generic being who follows a God-given drive for self-preservation, but is rather an effect of political constructs that correspond to human activity governed by the impulse to seek out pleasure and avoid pain. For Bentham, the institution of property is only justifiable through reference to its utility, which alarmed many liberals who were especially attached to the sanctity of property rights. For, as Karl Polanyi demonstrated, it was precisely on the basis of these utilitarian arguments that numerous limitations on property rights were established as early as the mid-nineteenth century, limitations that have henceforth given rise to welfare-state initiatives, such as the taxation of inheritance and labor law. The same arguments were made by certain economists who wanted to restrict agricultural rents in order to promote industry and trade, even to the point of envisaging the nationalization of land in order to abolish the nefarious and even parasitic influence of the landed aristocracy.[77]

There is little doubt that the utilitarian approach, especially as the field of political economy developed, ultimately prevailed over the theological and juridical discourse on natural property rights, and property has subsequently been defended primarily on the basis of economic efficiency. Private property is an institution that is inseparable from the market, and the latter is viewed as the best system of resource allocation ever invented. Personal possession generates more productivity than any other form of property – especially collective or communal property – because the individual devotes himself to it more attentively; he puts more of himself into it, and expects to keep the results from himself. This is why Locke, and then Condillac, argued that while America might have the most fertile lands, they could only become fruitful if a real regime of property rights was introduced. Utilitarianism thus divorced natural notions of morality, based on fraternity and compassion, from the proprietary, market economy.

One of the most significant outcomes of this nineteenth-century intellectual transformation is the treatment given to the notion of *res communes* by juridical defenders of absolute and exclusive property rights. Amongst those who viewed primitive communities as "negative communities" – i.e., a *lack* of ownership as opposed to co-ownership – we see, right away, an attempt to reconcile this notion of the negative common with those goods or resources that Roman law considered naturally common in themselves. An illustrative example of this can be found in Robert-Joseph Pothier's *Traité du droit de domaine de propriété* (1777):

> The first men held all those things God gave to mankind in common. But this community was not a positive community, such as that which is established between several persons who partake, in common, the dominion of a thing by each having a share; rather it was a community that, according to those who have studied these matters, is called a negative community, because it consists of a resource that is common to all but which belongs no more to one of them than to any of the others ... But as the human race has since multiplied, men divided the earth amongst themselves and most of the things on its surface; and what befell each of them began to belong to them privately ... this is the origin of the right to property. Yet everything was not divided, and many things remained, and many things remain still to this day, in their former state of negative community. These things are referred to by the jurists as "*res communes*."[78]

The question that persists, however, is why certain things remained, and must remain, outside this great division that established private property. As Mikhaïl Xifaras observes concerning the argument put forth by Jean-Baptiste-Victor Proudhon, the notion of *res communes* "is weakened by the adoption of the theological premise of the negative community."[79] For the very notion of the negative community does not mean that everyone co-possesses some undivided content, but rather that nothing yet belongs to anyone: the objects or resources in question, then, are, strictly speaking, *res nullius* (without master) and not *res communes.* These objects or resources are merely vacant and awaiting a master, which of course poses no problem whatsoever for the subsequent establishment of private property. But from this perspective, the domain abandoned to mankind from God should logically include the sea, the air, and fire, as well as all things material, since the four elements cannot, in this view, be considered superior to man. "In other words, it is difficult to see why the rationale that moves us from the unappropriability of the four elements – i.e., earth, water, air, and fire – to the appropriability of one of them – i.e., the earth – cannot be reproduced for the other three."[80] Put differently, why is it only the water, air, and fire that remain "common" under the presupposition that their status is consistent with the negative community thesis?

In the work of Charles-Bonaventure-Marie Toullier, however, the category *res communes* encompasses not only that which is unappropriable by nature, "but also that which is appropriable but not yet appropriated, such as fish, for example, whose status is held in abeyance until they are actually fished."[81] And according to Charles Demolombe, the otherwise rigid distinction between *res communes* and *res nullius* is significantly relativized by the prospect of the indefinite augmentation of mankind's power; the only real difference between the two categories is that, while the former "also belongs to the negative community, its unappropriability is only due to the current status of mankind's power," while the latter is immediately and directly unappropriable.[82] But it is above all in the work of Augustin-Charles Renouard that the reversal of the classical approach to this distinction is most successful: since, according to purely human law, all that is appropriated is (by definition) appropriable, *res communes* are considered appropriable up "until the factual evidence to the contrary is provided; that is to say, until they are no longer so."[83] To gauge the extent of this reversal, one need only recall Domat's position on *res communes* (the heavens, the stars, light, air, and the sea).[84] Renouard writes as follows:

> This passage exposes the final cause behind the great fact of unappropriability [Domat] observes. The sovereign harmony presiding over creation has placed out of apprehension, in particular domains, principle things without which the enjoyment of life would be impossible for those excluded, whenever such things are appropriated. It essential that everyone breathes air, and that the sun shines for everyone. We must therefore reverse the terms of Domat's proposition if we want to shore up his legal explanation. It is not because some goods are common that no one is able to master them; *it is because no one is able to master them that they are common to all.* The community of their use, if it is, according to the providential laws, the cause of their unappropriability, is the result of human law."[85]

The conclusion is obvious: the day on which mankind is able to appropriate these goods, they will *ipso facto* cease to be commons.

The *Summa Divisio* (Supreme Division) Between Public Law and Private Law

The erasure of the common and its restriction to certain "naturally common goods" is also connected to the bifurcation in legal doctrine and political thought concerning the "public" and the "private," which was then extended into the field of political economy in the form of the opposition between the state and the market.

If the division of law into public and private is a relatively recent occurrence in the West, it is precisely because this division is based on the fundamental presupposition of possessive individualism. It is often asserted that the distinction between public property and private property already existed in ancient Rome. The question we are concerned with, however, is whether this distinction already involved the partition of law as such into separate public and private domains. What is most characteristic of Roman law, as we saw in Marx's comparison between the Germanic and Roman systems, is a very particular articulation between private family property and public property. Public property is state property insofar as it is identified with the *populous romanus*. It is this legal fiction that legitimates both the distribution of the *ager publicus* amongst the plebeians and the exclusion of patricians (who already have their own private land). Public property, in the Roman system, thus has a double relation with the "private": it guarantees private "possession" for the plebeians while negatively externalizing the exclusive private property of the patricians. But what should we make of the public itself? For the notion of an inalienable and imprescriptible public domain, comprised of land parcels allocated to individuals, in no way exhausts the content of the term. Since this public domain is the property of the state, should we conclude, then, that the *publicum* and the state are, in general, identical? Should we be satisfied with a conception of the public as the pure negation of the private property of the *dominus*? And if so, do we not run the risk of reifying a strictly legal opposition? And must we understand this legal partition, this legal *summa divisio* (supreme distinction), as extending beyond Roman law, as is characteristic of modern Western legal discourse?

The reason why this reductive and simplified definition of the category "public" in Roman law became so prominent is doubtless due to the fact that juridical attention in the West, over the years, has been disproportionately focused on the figure of the individual proprietor (*dominus*), and the absolute power he exercises over the things he possesses (*res*), particularly when it comes to alienating objects in the course of mercantile exchange. In other words, the irreplaceable value of Roman law was its ability to anticipate the development of market exchange in Western modernity. Marx's attitude in this respect is representative of widespread opinion in the nineteenth century. What explains the relative continuity and persistent vivacity of Roman law outside the society in which it was born was the fact that Roman law was the first legal system to formalize equality and freedom as the basic "presuppositions" that orient exchange between proprietary subjects. For instance, a *servus* (slave) is defined as someone who cannot acquire goods through exchange, which negatively verifies that one must be free in order to engage in exchange.[86] In other words, this right was able to isolate the abstract determinations of the "juridical person" insofar as they correspond precisely to the "individual of exchange." This is why Roman law "anticipates" the legal framework of industrial society despite the fact that it was born out of conditions in which trade was very rudimentary.[87] Teleological criticisms of this interpretation aside, Roman law, for Marx in any case, was at the very least notable for its unusual degree of autonomy in relation to an economic infrastructure dominated by forced labor rather than exchange value.

More generally, however, our concern here lies rather in the "uses" of Roman law, or rather the "different uses" that have been made of it, and can still be made of it, today. In the present context of globalization, the insistence on the atemporal continuity of Roman law is used to justify the current revival of "pandectism" in the form of a *usus modernus pandectarum*.[88] It is the high degree of categorical abstraction that is typical of Roman law that, above all, allows the latter to be transposed onto contemporary legal systems, regardless of national context. According to Reinhard Zimmerman, for example, the latent principle of European contract law, which delineates how contracts based on informal consent have binding force, is nothing more than "Roman law in modern clothing."[89] The revival of Roman law was, essentially, all about establishing a "common European law" to be developed by legal scholars (professors, judges, lawyers). For instance, the expression "common law" (*jus commune*) was previously used to describe the canon law of the Roman Catholic Church that arose after the papal revolution of the eleventh and twelfth centuries. It was the legal framework of a pan-European organization that, in effect, became the "first modern state."[90] Many of the rules of this "new" European common law were borrowed from Roman law as recorded in a series of texts compiled between 529 and 534 on the order of Byzantine Emperor Justinian (and heavily glossed by subsequent academic jurists since the end of the eleventh century).[91] But, to confuse matters, this revived Roman law was often referred to as *jus commune* insofar as it was applied by the Church across Western Europe.[92] Canon law and Roman law thus constituted two legal codes operating under the common denominator *jus commune* – they were sometimes designated by the expression *utrumque jus* ("the one and the other law").[93] Viewed from this historical perspective, Zimmerman argues that the subsequent articulation of Roman law as *jus commune* constituted an "analogical precedent of globalization,"[94] a view which is further bolstered by the retrospective connection made between the renaissance of Roman law in the twelfth century and the renaissance of imperial politics. While this analogical reasoning purports to strive after a merely technical and ahistorical conception of law, what we are really dealing with here is an "exercise of power" whose purpose is clear: the valorization of the contractual form inherited from Roman law corresponds perfectly to the logic of globalized markets, which similarly tends to contractualize social relations at the expense of the rigidity of the "law."[95]

We should also note how this "neopandectist" endeavor very precisely privileges the categories of Roman private law. This shows the extent to which neopandectist ideas have influenced the division between public and private law, or rather, the extent to which it privileges, in its own way, the primacy of private law under conditions of globalization, and thereby actively reinforces the latter. As it turns out, however, the division between public and private law is actually a rather recent creation, and is by no means a principle derived directly from Roman law itself (contrary to the claims of this well-established tradition). One of the first jurists to use the expression "civil law" in reference to property law, contracts, and, more generally, all the branches of law that deal with relations between individuals, was Johann Apel in his book *Methodica* (1534), a work that effectively founded German legal science. Originally, Roman *jus civile* included all the rules that governed Roman citizens, and not merely what we have referred to as "private law" since the sixteenth century; it also included constitutional law, administrative law, criminal law, ecclesiastical law, and every other branch of "public law." As Harold Berman puts it, "a sharp division between public law and private law . . . and the treatment of *jus civile* chiefly (though not exclusively) as private law, became characteristic of Western legal thought only in the sixteenth and succeeding centuries."[96]

The work of Apel was further deepened and systematized by his colleague Konrad Lagus, who published his own *Methodica* in 1543. Lagus's text parsed multiple legal classifications based on Aristotle's delineation of four "causes." According to the criterion of "material causes" – which in this context refers to the object of each type of law – Lagus subdivides "civil law" into "public law" and "private law." This division between public and private is essential for determining "final causes," which is to say the purpose or the end of the law as such: public law is said to relate to public interests (*res publicae*) and private law is said to relate to private interests (such as contracts or injuries).[97]

In the final decades of the sixteenth century, Nicolas Vigelius and Johannes Althusius were determined to systematize the legal codes they had inherited from their predecessors. In his *Methodus universi iuris civilis* (1561), Vigelius completely emancipated civil law from the order imposed on it by the various collections of Roman law, such that "the entirety of civil law" was no longer identified with "Roman law as such" but with "law as such," which is to say the totality of law in force in the Empire, and in the cities and territories of Germany. He then divided civil law into two categories – public law and private law – and then subdivided each of these two categories further: public law was divided into legislative, executive, and judicial functions, and private law divided into personal law, property law, inheritance law, law of obligations, etc. Althusius, who worked within the tradition of both Lagus and Vigelius, in turn divided the entire legal code into public and private law in *Jurisprudentia romana* (1586) and *Dicaelogica* (1603). This new legal science, the foundation of which was built by these German Protestant legal scholars in the sixteenth century, "constituted the basis of the new European *jus commune* of the sixteenth to eighteenth centuries."[98] This new legal system was something like a third *jus commune* that was distinctive from both canonical law and Roman law according to the Justinian Code, but which borrowed from these two legal systems as well as from royal and princely law, feudal law, city law, and commercial law. As we can see from this account, the division of the totality of law into public and private law is not at all the supreme division within Roman law itself, but rather dates back to the middle of the sixteenth century. Civil law was either drawn into private law without being entirely assimilated into it – as in Apel – or extended to the entirety of law under the designation "civil law as a whole," as in Lagus and Vigelius.[99]

Public Domain, State Property, and Res Nullius

We have seen above how terms such as *utilitas publica, utilitas rei publicae* or *utilitas communis* co-existed within the works of classical Latin authors and later legal theorists for quite a long time.[100] What, then, are we to make of this notion of *publicum* within the context of a legal system that had not yet established the division between public and private as its guiding legal principle? We are indebted to Yan Thomas in this endeavor, insofar as his article "La valeur des choses. Le droit romain hors la religion" ("The Value of Things: Roman Law Outside Religion") sheds important light on this question.[101] By viewing the sovereignty of the individual proprietor over his possessions as the foundation of Roman law, Thomas emphasizes the derivative and completely unoriginal character of [modern] private law: the categorization of "things" (*res*) within the sphere of appropriation and exchange was accomplished by means of a "detour" which allowed certain objects that had been previously "entrenched" within the sphere of appropriation to be removed and "assigned to the gods or to the city." The jurisprudence of the Imperial epoch designates these things as "*res nullius in bonis*."[102] This compound expression may sound rather strange if one accepts the notion that goods transmitted from parents to their descendants – i.e., an "inheritance" – must be something that belongs to someone (*alicuius in bonis*) and cannot be something that belongs to no one (*nullius in bonis*). The difficulty, then, lies in understanding how something that is inherited (*in bonis*) can, at the same time, be devoid of a property title (*nullius*), but this is precisely the case when it comes to the gods and the city. Concerning such things, the law expressly states that alienation is prohibited and trade is not allowed. In Paolo Napoli's view, Yan Thomas showed us that the distinction between that which is "appropriable" and "unappropriable" is "not by virtue of their objective nature, but as a result of *institutional decision*."[103] We could not put it better ourselves. The institution of the unappropriable occupies a central place "in the general economy of Roman law" by negatively carving out a set of common objects or things (*res*) that were previously accessible, measurable, and appropriable. "It is through contrast, then, that the institution of sacred and reserved objects, transforms everything else into objects of private law. In this domain, everything is appropriate, alienable, and subject to various measures of civil procedure."[104] In short, this "reservation" of sacred objects had the side effect of "freeing everything else."[105]

But what exactly are these "things" (*res*) that the law inscribes within the realm of the "sacred," the "religious," or the "public" as a means of allowing the former to escape the juridical space of market exchange? One Roman source cited by Thomas states that no one could buy a thing whose "alienation is forbidden, as with sacred and religious places or things that cannot be traded, *not because they belong to the city, but because they are destined for public use*, like the Champ du Mars."[106] The Roman text thus clearly distinguishes between the "property of the city" and that which is for "public use" only. This distinction penetrates into the very interior of public space, and this is where its importance lies: there is, on the one hand, "a public domain in which the state disposes of objects freely, by allocating or selling public land, for example." And on the other hand, there is a "zone of 'public use' (squares, theaters, markets, porticos, roads, rivers, waterways, etc.) whose unappropriability was absolutely necessary"; the objects subject to this custom were exempt from all forms of private appropriation, "not as a result of state ownership, but because of their institutional assignment."[107] It was precisely through this assignment or designation that such objects or resources were made "freely accessible to all," as if each member of the *populous* enjoyed a right of use as a very condition of their status as citizens. Of these things – which also included basilicas and temples – jurists said they were *res usibus publicus relictae*, which is to say "things left to public use," and they often went so far as to say they were to remain public "in perpetuity."[108] On the other hand, property that merely belonged to a city could be alienated in the event of indebtedness. In other words, "public" should not be understood in the strict sense of those things intended for public use, but rather "in the sense of what belongs to the patrimony, so to speak, of the cities (*si qua civitatium sunt velut bona*)." What makes this distinction interesting is that it shows us how there were two very different concepts of "public" operating simultaneously within Roman law: "public" in the sense of public use and "public" in the sense of state property. Indeed, the city or the state was not permitted to appropriate the first type, while the second type was explicitly viewed as part of the state's holdings. Recall, for example, what was said above about the lands belonging to the *ager publicus*: if the state could allocate these lands to individuals as private possessions, it was precisely because they were not intended for public use, but were rather public property intended for private use, which is a very different matter. Official documents even go so far as to differentiate between a consecrated place – such as a temple – and the landed estate attributed to it (i.e., the lands upon which a temple sits). Whereas the consecrated place is absolutely unappropriable, the property attached to it is. So definite was this distinction that the combination of these two properties did not alter the original legal structure of the sacred space: "the thing constituted as sacred, and to which other property was subsequently added, remains the only part of the whole that is perpetually unappropriable. It is, one might say, legally immortal."[109] The thing or space is inherently unappropriable and is "represented by the public administrators of the sacred."[110]

We must therefore be careful not to confuse these two kinds of *res nullius*: on the one hand, *res nullius in bonis* designates that which is unappropriable and inalienable. And on the other hand, there is the category of "things without a master," "which is also designated by the term *res nullius*." Despite their similarities, this latter expression refers to a "strictly inverse" juridical regime insofar as it "designates a state of things that are factually vacant but can be possessed by the first occupier." The latter, in other words, "has not yet become the property of anyone," but can be appropriated by the first master, who is also the first occupant. It is with respect to this category that the law refers to the qualities of the natural world. It speaks of "wild animals that hunt and fish, stones or pearls picked up along the beach, found treasures, islands that are born in the sea or in river beds."[111] Conversely, the seabed itself is absolutely unappropriable, and the regime with which it is associated is "compared with public roads or religious or sacred places."[112] The difference between these two kinds of *res nullius* is that the *res nullius in bonis* is institutionally subtracted from the private sphere, which implies "a suspension of the subject – object relation involving complete mastery of the latter by the former," where *res nullius* as such is intended to enter this same sphere, thereby becoming objects in a relationship of mastery.[113] But whether an object is able to "exit forever" from the sphere of appropriation (*res nullius in bonis*) or initially enter the sphere of appropriation (*res nullius*), "these objects are only ever considered from the point of view of their legal constitution, which is to say the fundamentally political manner in which these goods are categorized."[114]

These "things" are not, therefore, inscribed in a discourse that concerns their being, which is to say their ontology. The question "what is a thing?" is simply not applicable here. Generally speaking, Roman law says nothing about what things are – i.e., in themselves, or based on their intrinsic nature prior to and independent of the law – but is rather almost exclusively concerned with their qualification in law and by the law. The term *res* must not be understood, then, in the sense of a "designation" that extends to everything in the "external world, both natural and social"; rather, the term is, from the outset, a kind of "qualification" that implies a whole series of procedures by which things themselves are evaluated. We should recall, here, that the original meaning of the term *res* is derived from the procedural trial or debate surrounding the object, or the dispute *qua* object: "the Roman *res* was not conceived as a *Sache* nor as a *Gegenstand*, but more precisely as an 'affair' (*res* corresponds in this sense to the Greek *ta pragmata*) or a process involving the qualification or the evaluation of the litigated object (*res*)."[115] It is only on the basis of this conception that we can understand the difference between patrimonial objects and commercial objects: such litigious processes either determined the value of an object (in terms of its price) or determined the uses of objects that were not appropriable and hence not property.[116] For the latter objects, no fine would be able to compensate the city for its loss; even if penalties were demanded in criminal proceedings, what prevailed in civil court was a compulsion for restitution in kind, or the replacement of "the same thing" (*res ipsa*).[117]

But how does this internal distinction between public "use" and public "property" help us theorize the specificity and irreducibility of the common? Simply put, the Roman designation concerning the public use of an object or resource is perhaps the closest historical precedent for our conception of the "institution of the common." For anything that falls under this designation is not at the free disposal of the state, because such objects or resources are not susceptible to appropriation as such, state-based or private, and this is the essential point. As we have already described in the context of the ostensible "communal property" of Germanic tribes, the common is nothing other than a *non-state public* – along with the additional condition that the object or resource is not an object of property, but is absolutely outside the realm of property as such. What makes the Roman precedent so interesting is that it achieves a singular "combination between an institutional designation and its use by the many, which is to say the multitude of citizens," to borrow Paolo Napoli's apt phrase.[118]

While this prohibition – which applies equally to the city and to private individuals – "does not mark the victory of the state over the individual," it is more debatable whether this combination of a *non-state public* successfully liberates a "sovereignty of praxis."[119] Indeed, this question raises the further necessity of clarifying the often confused and generic notion of "praxis" itself: for while a "non-state public" can be used by all, its institutional designation is only ever made by a relatively small and restricted caste of legal professionals. While this legal designation is undoubtedly the pre-condition for collective use, should we not also demand that the designating act be itself collective? Is the collective use of the common not compromised when the manner of its institutionalization is reserved for a minority of experts and specialists? We readily agree that the opening of a public space that can be used by all has the advantage of "displacing the transcendental problem of subjective ownership" "through the force of institutional designation":[120] by opening up such a space, no subject is able to claim a right of ownership over the space, whether the state or the individual, and the citizens who collectively enjoy a *right of use* over the common are also deprived of any *rights of ownership*. In this sense, then, the predominance of a "right of use" cancels out the possibility of a rights-holding proprietary subject. But what about the designating act itself? Should it continue to be the prerogative of a narrow caste of lawyers, legal experts, and judges, rather than the community of users themselves? And what about the status of the "administrators of the sacred" who are responsible for administering objects deemed unappropriable? Can we dissociate the act of designating or institutionalizing the common from its collective use without re-introducing relations of mastery?

The Use and Administration of the Unappropriable

Paolo Napoli suggests a promising way of surmounting this difficulty by sparing us from having to theorize a subject of the common who enjoys particular rights within common. *This is because there is not, and cannot be, a subject of the common.* More specifically, if the use of the common, as a form of collective practice, produces its own kind of subject, it stands to reason that this subject is not the subject *of* the common since it did not pre-exist the very practice that produces it. It is not, therefore, a question of opposing a "good" subject (of collective use) from a "bad" subject (of proprietary mastery). To fully grasp this notion, we must first re-consider the old and oft-decried concept of "administration" and properly articulate its relation to the concept of "use" we have been discussing up to this point. By doing so, we hope to arrive at a concept of "administrative use" or even "common administrative use" that would not only "displace" but would more radically "transcend" the "abstract, rights-bearing subject."[121]

There are two main ways of defining the concept of administration in the modern Western philosophical tradition, and each articulates administration alongside the notion of government, albeit in opposite ways. One such definition comes from Rousseau's article "Political Economy" from the *Encyclopédie*. Rousseau's central concern is to demarcate the family or domestic economy from political or public economy. "Government" is the name Rousseau gives to the public economy. It belongs to the "executive power" and must be subordinated to the "supreme authority," known as "sovereignty," because it is the "owner" or "rights holder," so to speak, of "legislative law." The principle of this form of governmental power is outlined under the first rule of political economy: "to follow in everything the general will" and "ensure the observance of the laws" is the rule that must be imposed by the public administration, which is to say the "executive power." The second rule, which deals with the "government of persons" is to "establish the reign of virtue" – especially as regards public education – and the third, which concerns the "administration of property," is to provide for public needs and ensure the subsistence of citizens.

Rousseau thus gives us a classical exposition of the way in which administration is identified, pure and simple, with government or executive power, such that the "ministers" are merely the "servants" of the sovereign.[122] The second, and antithetical, way of conceptualizing administration in the Western philosophical tradition comes from Saint-Simon, for whom administration is defined through its opposition to government in the classical political sense. Saint-Simon principally sketched out his conception of administration in *L'Organisateur* (1819–1820), and it revolves around a few key ideas: in an industrial society, politics is nothing more than the "science of production," and industrialists and scientists are correspondingly the only qualified political representatives. The regulating organs of the society must, therefore, be composed entirely of industrialists and scientists, since all collective affairs require as much specialized skill as does private enterprise. In a completely industrialized society, then, questions about the form of government will simply fade away: the reason for this is that governmental action, for Saint-Simon, is necessarily arbitrary in that it always consists in exercising command over others. This is the opposite of the form of control exercised by the boards of directors of the great industrial companies: here you have administration, not government. Humanity, for Saint-Simon, is destined to pass from a "governmental or military" regime to an "administrative or industrial" regime. The "government of men" will thus irrevocably give way to an "administration of things."

In the first instance, then, administration *is* government: it is the activity that applies and enforces the law. In the second instance, however, administration is antithetical to government: if the essence of government is command and control, administration consists in strict rational management on the basis of scientific truth. In short, administration consists either in the execution of the general will (which is a form of command) or in the scientific management of production. Giorgio Agamben's genealogy of these modes of governmentality in the West unfortunately does little to clarify this distinction (to the extent that it is concerned with this distinction at all). In fact, Agamben's "genealogy" only minimally resembles Foucault's methodology, despite Agamben's claim to "understand the internal reasons why [Foucault's genealogy of governmentality] failed to be completed."[123] Agamben's objective is to trace two branches of political modernity back to their roots in the two great paradigms of first-century Christian theology: the modern theory of sovereignty, for Agamben, is derived from the paradigm of the "political theology" of the unique and transcendent God, and modern biopolitics is derived from the "economic theology" of the Trinitarian God.[124] Agamben's analysis at least has the merit of clarity: it is part of his overall project to advance, once again, the so-called "theory of secularization," according to which all modern innovations are really nothing more than transpositions of older theological frameworks.[125] Within this framework, it does not really matter much whether the government of men was thought at one point to be either a matter of execution (of laws) or management (of industry): the theological origin of the concept of government prevents this kind of dissociation by more powerfully reducing both the "administration" and "efficient management" of men and the world to the same theological concept. This operation traces every school of "modern economics" (the physiocrats, Smith, etc.) back to the "theological model of the government of the world,"[126] and reproaches Rousseau for mistakenly conceiving of government as executive power without realizing that the real problem of politics is not that of sovereignty but of government.[127] And despite all Saint-Simon's efforts to overcome the alternative between the "legalists" (Rousseau) and the "economists" (Smith), the "administration of things" is really little more than the best-kept secret of the Trinitarian mystery.

In contrast to Agamben's theological interpretation of governmentality, we argue that the "real problem" of politics lies in subtracting the concept of administration from this genealogical opposition and thereby freeing it from all these various historical instantiations. In the first instance, technocratic modes of representation tend to correspond to both sides of this opposition. The Weberian concept of instrumental rationality, for instance, which involves the careful calculation of the necessary means to achieve a certain end, is clearly a form of administration that has next to nothing to do with active and participatory deliberation. For it is precisely ends-oriented deliberation, which is absolutely essential to any real form of political activity, that both sides of this opposition *a priori* exclude: either the ends are always prescribed from outside and from above – as in the case of sovereign legislative power – or because ends are already neutralized by scientific and statistical evidence – as in administration as the mere management of production.

Instead of relating the "servitude" of a *ministrare* to an external will (*ad-ministrare*, or "working under someone's orders") or the impersonal necessity of science (*ad-ministrare* as "serving scientific truth"), we want to think of administration in terms of a collective practice linked to the uses of unappropriable objects or resources. Administration, for us, is neither a form of sovereign governance nor scientific management, but rather the active and collective "co-production of non-state juridical norms."[128] The common, as that which is defined by its unappropriability, is fundamentally a "practical category" for us,[129] which is the very antithesis of a "theologico-political" category. On this condition, and only on this condition, would it be possible to turn to Christian theology to help theorize something like the "administrative use" of the common. Indeed, as Napoli points out,[130] Christian theology has, from its origins, been based on the need to think about the specific kind of relation that each Christian has to maintain with the so-called "deposit of faith" entrusted to his custody: for this act of maintenance is precisely an "administrative" activity as opposed to a "proprietary" relation, since it is a matter of preserving this theological deposit, not appropriating it. This custodial practice is thus homologous to the definition of "depositary" in civil law[131]: as an administrative practice, it authorizes all uses intended to preserve the integrity of the deposit, "excluding acts of proprietary availability." Such a fundamental exclusion suggests a re-reading of the history of the Church as "a series of struggles to safeguard the collective indivisibility of the common deposit over which no one can have control" by aiming for a "cooperative use of the deposit."[132] We are still in theological terrain here, but are now talking about the "theologico-administrative," rather than the "theologico-political" as in Agamben. The use of the unappropriable and the administration of the unappropriable may, however, be confused insofar as they both exclude any relation to a proprietary subject and, in some cases, can even produce a radical "de-personalization of belonging" at the level of the juridical.[133]

The Primacy of Creative Legal Practice Against the State

In order to dispel this kind of misunderstanding, we must additionally insist that the administrative use of that which is unappropriable formally excludes appropriation only according to *one* of the two principle meanings of the term "appropriation." Our discussion of appropriation has, thus far, only been concerned with one – though undoubtedly the most widespread – of two meanings of the term: namely, appropriation as property or possession – either property that already belongs to one or several persons (which implies ownership by expropriation or through exchange) or property that is vacant, available, and belongs to no one (i.e., *terra nullius*). This is the meaning that is manifest in the term's etymology, in which *proprius* is derived from *pro privo*, or "a specific title." But we have neglected the second meaning of the term, even though it is often linked to the first, especially in the discourse justifying ownership or possession. For a thing can also be appropriated for the purposes of meeting a certain end; for example, appropriating land in order to satisfy certain human needs through its cultivation. What is central to this meaning of the term is, of course, its purpose or "end." Each of these meanings thus involve two very distinctive relationships: In the first sense, the relation involved is a relation of belonging that links an object to one or many people while excluding all others: that which I possess cannot belong to someone else insofar as it is mine alone. In the second sense, however, the relationship in question is not one of belonging but of purpose: it is about the correspondence between an object or resource and its *uses* by one or many persons.[134] We can, of course, combine the two senses of the term without much difficulty by, for example, arguing that it is ultimately the specific form of the relationship of belonging that, in the final analysis, determines its purpose. For instance, it is only because a collective of peasants owns the land that the latter can be used for specific collective ends (whereas private ownership of the same land would likely yield different ends as far as the land is concerned).

It is more or less implicitly assumed that an object's purpose is a function of its natural properties, and that certain forms of property hinder the ability of the object to fulfill its natural end. This type of rationale opens a whole Pandora's box of quarrels about the best form of property (private, statist, cooperative, communal, etc.). On the other hand, however, we could also radically dissociate these two forms of relation by approaching the question of appropriation (in the sense of suitability or purpose) obliquely. Instead of speaking of unappropriation directly (in the sense of those things that cannot enter into proprietary space), we could pose the question in terms of the forms of *human activity that unappropriation is designed to fulfill*, in which case the end in question is resolutely social rather than "natural." This approach has the merit of shifting our attention toward questions of *use* as a collective practice: once a thing (*res*) has been removed from proprietary space, whether private or state-based, how might it be collectively used so that everyone benefits? In particular, what are the rules this kind of subtraction must then invent in order to prevent such goods from being diverted from their social purposes by predatory forms of appropriation? The rules of collective use, in this case, thus become rules that regulate behavior in relation to the unappropriable object or resource. It is therefore toward the *legal and normative dimension of productive use*, and not the dimension of subjective belonging, that this dissociation of the term directs our inquiry. Focusing our attention on the dimension of productivity (rather than belonging) has, in fact, other implications in terms of the relationship between use and the institution itself: by focusing our attention on the end or purpose of the equation, use or administration takes on an essential *instituting* function. We would even say that focusing on practices of common use is that which most fundamentally ensures the *continued institutionalization* of the common.

This "practical" conception of the institution of the common, or rather this conception of practices *as* institutionalization itself, radically differs from the concept of "institutionalization" developed by Pierre Legendre. For Legendre, symbolic or "dogmatic" apparatuses – i.e., "institutions" – bind societies together through a specular-type logic in which institutions function as "mirrors" in which subjects are able to recognize themselves according to the status reserved for them. And it is ultimately through this process that subjects reciprocally interpellate the legitimacy of the institutions to which they belong. This form of institution is founded on a mythological "founding referent" that generates a certain "image" of humanity that is not fundamentally mimetic (in the sense of reproducing an image of something already found in nature). Through the construction of a normative mirror that is indispensable for humanizing the subject, the institution, for Legendre, belongs to the realm of the "imaginary" rather than the "imagination." Legendre forcefully insists on the fictional character of the great social subject, a mythical figure and the great Author of the Text: these symbolic institutions literally make society "speak" and, as such, rely on a series of rites, arts, and other commemorations designed to maintain belief.[135] This fiction of a great Subject that speaks, an imaginary Author of the spoken word who is the absolute Other for every particular subject, guarantees subjective identification by grounding the legitimacy of places and names, insofar as this fictional Author is understood to be the custodian of all the constituent categories of social and political life.

In modern Western societies, it is the state (supported by the discourse of science) that serves this logical function insofar as it is the entity that legitimately "speaks" as both the origin and guarantee of the juridical system. It is the system that distributes and classifies things and people in civil law, and it is the state that functions as the actor and director of a "theater" aesthetically staging the foundation of this normative discourse. In this respect, the state undoubtedly serves a subjective function. "Institutionality" – the state being merely its Western instantiation – is a fundamental anthropological dimension of social life. It is the material manifestation of the human animal's capacity for complex speech. From this perspective, institutionality appears to be both a pre-condition and the result of an operation designed to "institute life" (*vitam instituere*), in the sense of the phrase Legendre borrows from the Roman canonical tradition used to designate the city codes that organized the lives of city residents (the phrase originates with Demothenes, but Legendre uses the third-century jurist Marcian's translation, which the latter inserted into the Justinian Digest of the sixth century).[136] The principle effect of this "institutionality" – in terms of institutions that construct identity on a specular or "mirror-like" basis – was its ability to render the Western normative tradition seemingly immune from practice-based transformations, insofar as practices are themselves already derived from the basic juridical frameworks that make up this institutional tradition. Legendre is, on the one hand, careful to note the divergence of theology and the law in the twelfth century, which he views, alongside Harold J. Berman, as the fundamental bifurcation that eventually led to secularization in the West. But it cannot have been the sole purview of lawyers to realize this kind of transformation of tradition; one of the most remarkable traits of the West was the transfer of the power of legitimation from theology to the sciences in general, and the humanities in particular, such that it simply will not do to reduce the advent of modernity to scientism, economism, or even capitalist management, as is often the case. Far from constituting a homogenous mass, the Western normative tradition has always been pulled in two directions at once, given its simultaneous commitment to capitalist *efficiency* and the ideal of juridical (*nomos*) autonomy – and this is only one of the major fault lines. This and other innumerable fault lines continually threaten to capture practices that strive toward social transformation and juridical innovation (*fictio legis*).

The Common as "Being-in-Common" and the Common as "Acting-in-Common"

We have seen how Roman law was not, in fact, based on a supreme partition between private law and public law. Rather, Roman law produced an internal public space that escaped the influence of both the state and the market, and it was through the creation of this non-statist public space that an autonomous sphere of commerce was first brought into relief. We then argued that the positive feature of this non-state public (its negative feature being its exclusion from the sphere of commercial trade) was its orientation around the right of use. And lastly, we pointed out that the exercise of these rights were based on social practices, and only those practices that were independent of the state were capable of generating laws. We must now ask ourselves to what extent the primacy accorded to these practices that create and orient the common are still frustratingly tethered to a persistent discourse of "being-common" or "being-in-common" – in other words, an *ontological* discourse of the common at work in a number of different approaches to the common today.

One of the most valuable lessons of Yan Thomas's account of the Roman jurists, in this regard, is to have shown that the Roman political and legal construction of *res* leaves no room for ontology. Contrary to the claims of the Catholic Neothomistics, the institutional designation of an object or resource for public use was not derived from the supposed natural or inherent nature of the object or resource, as if the nature of things simply spoke for themselves. The legal designation of something as public was always based on procedures implemented by magistrates. Insofar as the common is exclusively based on practices of collective use, we likewise insist that the common categorically excludes *ontological* considerations as the basis for its institutionalization.

One example of this *ontology of the commons* is of course the familiar discourse that grounds the latter in the being or ontology of spontaneous social production.[137] But the ontological dimension of the commons is even more prominent in that contemporary discourse which, under the guise of exempting the "being-in-common" from any form of substantialization or community reification, actually achieves a "decoupling of the political from being-in-common,"[138] the effect of which is to discourage any politics of the common whatsoever. In his genealogy of the word "communism," Jean-Luc Nancy places special emphasis on the "*I*":

> [Communism] does not belong to the political. It comes before any politics. It is what gives to politics an absolute prerequisite to open the common space to the common itself – neither to the *private* or the *collective*, neither to separation or totality – without permitting the political achievement of the common itself or an attempt to turn it into a substance. *Communism* is a principle of activation and limitation of politics.[139]

The common as "being-in-common" is here turned against the common as "being-common" – the latter of which "communism" had justly assumed to be its political project, which led to all the consequences we need not repeat here. This communism of "being-in-common" is made up of two complimentary aspects: on the one hand, it is the "principle of the activation of politics" insofar as being-in-common is that which makes politics itself possible; on the other hand, it is the "principle of the limitation of the political" in that it defines the limit beyond which politics denies itself as politics by denying the "being-in-common."[140] What, exactly, is the ontological dimension of being-in-common? For Nancy, the "with" (the *co-* or the *com-* of communism) does not designate a property that is superimposed into the individual being, but rather constitutes the very existence of the latter as a form of "co-existence," "being-with," or "being-together": "*Communism* is togetherness – the *Mitsein*, the being-with – understood as pertaining to the existence of individuals, which means, in the existential sense, to their *essence*."[141]

Is there any originality in Jean-Luc Nancy's ontology of "being-in-common" in relation to that of Heidegger? The term *Mitsein* ("being-with") appears in Chapter IV, §26, of *Being and Time*, following Heidegger's analysis of "world" in Chapter III. Heidegger's consideration of "being-with-another" is thus an extension of his analysis of world. For Heidegger, it is because I am in the world that I share the world with others, not the other way around: if I were not first and foremost in the world, the world would not be a "*with-world*" (*Mitwelt*) for me.[142] As Pierre Sauvêtre clearly observes,[143] Nancy radicalizes Heidegger here insofar as the determination of "being-with" no longer proceeds from the "being-in-the-world" of *Dasein*, but rather constitutes the fundamental determination of being itself: "'with' as the essential trait of Being,"[144] or "Being is to be *cum*."[145] "Being-in-the-world" no longer precedes "being-with," but rather the latter is recognized as coming absolutely first. In *communism*, then, neither *-ism* nor *commun-* are worthy in themselves: all that remains is "*cum:* the Latin preposition *cum* taken as universal preposition, the preposition of any existence."[146] We can see then how Nancy grounds his project in a "co-ontology" or a "co-existential analytic." It is precisely for existential reasons that the *co-* of communism has a completely different meaning than the *co-* of collective:

> The *with* is no external link, it is no link at all. It is *togetherness* [*être-ensemble*] ... The *with* has nothing to do with what is called *collective* ... The *co-* of *collective* is not the same as that of *communism*. This is not only a matter of etymology (*munire* versus *ligare*). It is a matter of ontology: the *co-* of *collective* is a mere external "*side by side*" which implies no relationship between the sides or between the parts of his "*partes extra partes*."[147]

The emphasis Nancy puts on the *cum*, independent of any relation to the world, logically leads toward the quasi-essentialism of the Heideggerian existential. This explains why, as we have seen above, "being-with" must be understood "as pertaining to the existence of individuals, which means, in the existential sense, to their *essence*," and thus communism, for Nancy, is ultimately about coming into contact with the *essential-existential*.

In the work of Roberto Esposito, we find a very similar emphasis placed on "being-with" in the sense of "being of *cum* and as *cum*," which is to say being "between" or "in relation," but with the distinction that the community is theorized on the basis of an opposition between "proper" and "immunity."[148] In contrast to the "proper," in the sense of "authentic" or "belonging," the common is "improper."[149] As opposed to "immunity," in the sense of a form of exemption or exoneration, the common is understood as a "task," "duty," or "law" that is imposed on all.[150] The result is that the community is not based on the sharing of property, but is based on a shared "duty" or "obligation." This *munus* is therefore understood as an "original debt" that references our existence as mortal beings, i.e., our finitude: the community it founds is not a fated community or a complete community, but it is a "flawed community," inasmuch as it is only our mortal finitude that makes us beings-in-common or beings-with.[151] In this sense, finitude is a lack that is common to us, in such a way that this "lack-in-common," far from undermining our togetherness, is "what holds us together, what constitutes us as beings-in-common."[152]

In contrast with this unilateral conception of "being-with" independent of any relation to the world, Hannah Arendt's reading appears to be more faithful to Heidegger's thesis on the primacy of "being-in-the word": the world, which Arendt refers to as the "public realm" or "common world," is "related ... to the human artifact, the fabrications of human hands." It is "a world of things" existing "between those who have it in common," an "in-between" that "relates and separates men at the same time."[153] As such, "it is what we have in common not only with those who live with us, but also with those who were here before and with those who will come after us."[154] While the world is made up of fabricated objects, on the one hand, its status as a "public realm" is not merely a function of the temporal duration of these objects, but is based on the plurality of perspectives through which the public realm is conceived by people living in different circumstances, a plurality that is irreducible to a "common measure" or "common denominator." For Arendt, this plurality of perspectives is the essential condition of politics as such: politics is man's recognition of the fact that he must deal with the same world seen from different points of view. It is precisely when this plurality is effaced that humans are threatened with the "worldlessness" that gives rise to totalitarianism. And no specious reference to some "human nature" can guarantee against the destruction of the common world: "under the conditions of a common world, reality is not guaranteed primarily by the 'common nature' of all men who constitute it, but rather by the fact that, differences of position and the resulting variety of perspectives notwithstanding, everybody is always concerned with the same object."[155] What carries away the common world and, with it, politics itself, is a normative uniformity of perspectives that destroys the identity of the object by destroying the plurality of perspectives from which this object is grasped.

There is no "being-in-common" inscribed into the very constitution of existence itself. Only man's active interest in that which lies "in between" them endows the world with its simultaneously precarious and precious commonality.

There seems to be an undeniable coherence, from this point of view, between Arendt's ostensible Heideggerian "anti-biologistic prejudice" or "anti-naturalism" and the necessity of re-thinking the notion of human nature, or man's *humanitias*, beginning with the base "natural reality" of the *bios*.[156] The entire question is a matter of knowing whether politics is ultimately derived from an ontology of "being-in-common" or from "life" as such. To pose the question rather abruptly: is there a politics of "being-with" or a politics of "being-in-common"? In Nancy we find an allusive reference to the kind of "praxis" that emphasizes the exigency of "being-in-common" on the basis of the "inequality" of the singularities that are "with," as opposed to the equality of the market as universal equivalence. However, this assertion is expressly accompanied by an essential proviso: the affirmation of the inequality of the singularities "can be almost anything you like – existential, artistic, literary, dreamy, amorous, scientific, thoughtful, leisurely, playful, friendly, gastronomic, urban, and so on: politics subsumes none of these registers."[157] In other words, the sole function of politics is to open a space in which the affirmation of the common of "inequivalence" can take place. According to this definition, there is no space of political praxis of the common. We could make an analogous claim about the work of Roberto Esposito, for whom the community by default is an "impolitical form" of community. The *im-* of "impolitical" is not meant to designate negation, as in the sense of apolitical, but rather suggests the inverse of the complete form of political community. The question that arises, then, is how a form of politics could be derived from a conception of the community as a kind of defect? Once again, Esposito's thoughts on the matter are allusive, if not discordant. In the third section of *Terms of the Political* we find Esposito's most precise formulations on the matter. Beginning with a discussion of the "reversal," whereby Nazism represents the complete inversion of biopolitics into "thanato-politics," Esposito suggests the possibility of another biopolitics, an "affirmative biopolitics" that is "no longer a politics over life, but a politics of life."[158] He does, however, also recognize that knowing "where to look for, how to think, what a biopolitical democracy, or a democratic biopolitics, that is capable of exercising itself not on bodies but in favor of them might mean today is quite difficult to identify conclusively."[159] We must emphasize here the difficulty involved in squaring this affirmation of the positivity of life with the existential "being-with" Esposito initially invoked in order to ground his concept of the *communitas*. How, indeed, are we to pass from a condition of "being-with" which "determines us at a distance and in difference from our very selves" as an "infinite lack," an "unpayable debt" or even an "irredeemable fault,"[160] to a life that is "the indivisible point at which man's being corresponds perfectly with the way in which the form (life) takes the shape of its own content"?[161]

All these efforts effectively run up against the same principle difficulty: once one affirms the primacy of ontology, the passage from ontology to politics can only ever be a leap of faith, simply because deducing a form of politics from an ontology is an impossible wager.[162] And on this point, it will not do to simply cite Deleuze and Guattari's assertion that "politics precedes being."[163] We must go further and assert that the only ontology that is possible is what Foucault referred to as the "ontology of the actuality."[164] Such a task demands grasping the historical character of our "today" in terms of the points of support it offers for an emancipatory praxis. There is no "existential" dimension that exempts us from the work required to constitute the common as an instituting activity: as a determinate of action, the common cannot be instituted on the basis of a misleading alternative between being and having, between being-in-common (in the sense of being-with others) and having-in-common (in the sense of "property" as both "possession" and "characteristic").

In accordance with our terminology from the preceding chapters, "common activity" is the term we use to designate the forms of action that institute the common and support it. "Common activity" is not merely "acting in common": it is not in fact a matter of what is done together, whether in terms of a journey or an act of protest, but rather it designates that specific mode of action that is based on the form of co-obligation signified by the Latin *munus*. The notion of a "task" or an "activity" contained within this term – and which Esposito erroneously subordinates to the imperative of a "law" or "duty" – is especially applicable here. In this respect, the primary meaning of *communis* warrants priority, insofar as it privileges humans over things, and it does so to the extent that human agents share common duties and tasks: *communis* was, first of all, the name used to describe a shared task between subjects (*communis* as the "sharing of duties") before designating those things that are shared by all (*res communes*). It is therefore necessary to posit the principle that co-obligation arises from the sharing of tasks or activities; co-obligation is not primary or foundational because it is inherent in our "existence," our "condition," or even our "life." If common activity is a form of action that "institutes," it is precisely because it consists in the co-production of legal norms and obliges all co-producers as co-producers in the course of their work. This is why the activity of instituting the common can only be done in common, such that the common is both a qualitative form of human activity and the result of this activity itself. In this respect, the model of the ancient legislator, who is a foreigner to the city over which he endows its inhabitants with a constitution created from whole cloth, is in fact a "counter-model"; so too is the model of a separate body in charge of *auctoritas* to which the task of perpetuating the foundational act necessarily reverts.[165] And since the central aspect of the common to be instituted is its unappropriability – rather than its "inequality," its "improperness," or its "impersonality" – the co-obligation of "actors of the common"[166] is that which compels them to manage the unappropriable object or resource in such a manner that it is preserved and transmitted into the future. In these terms, then, common activity is nothing but the "common use of the common" of which we have already spoken.

7

Law of the Common and "Common Law"

The next question concerns the nature of the law that common activity must produce as a result of its exercise, such that all co-actors or co-participants are bound by collective co-obligation. We have just seen how the right of use and its concomitant institutionalization were identified with creative or generative legal practices. We might consequently assume, then, that the law of the common should be a form of customary law rather than a legislative law – in the sense of a law emanating from a sovereign authority or the will of a legislator – insofar as customary rights are a form of law more readily associated with the *common* or common people. In the English legal system, for instance, common law is based on custom or precedent, whereas law that is derived from the decree of a sovereign authority is categorized as statute law. In this sense, then, law produced by common activity would logically be more similar to common law, even in terms of its content, insofar as common activity qualitatively transformed into law would ultimately remain dependent on the underlying activity from which the law arose in the first place. But this presupposition immediately raises an important question: how does the "customary" become "common"? What exactly is the nature of the "common" in common law, such that anything consecrated by custom comes to be identified with the common, or even *of* the common?

In the first instance, one could just as easily argue that custom is merely the contingent, which is to say the local or the particular. In this respect, there could be nothing less "common" than the customary, since all manner of arbitrary, bizarre, and absurd customs are equally capable of receiving the seal of tradition. From this point of view, only the universality of law would seem to be compatible with the common. Indeed it is precisely in this manner that those who favor legislative law over customary law tend to praise the former's rational and universal character. Hegel, for instance, distinguishes between a simple collection of custom, which he characterizes as "formless, indeterminate, and fragmentary," and modern legal systems that assume the rational form of a "code" – the exemplar of which, for Hegel, was the Code Civil of 1804 or the Napoleonic Code – grounded in universal legal principles.[1] From this point of view, Roman law is not a straightforward example of legislative law, at least in the historical form in which it has been transmitted to us, insofar as it also takes a largely non-rational form (consider, for instance, the *Corpus Iuris Civilis* of the Justinian Laws).[2] What is essential, for Hegel and others, is the universality that law acquires only by becoming "law," in the strongest sense of the term. The most ardent defenders of common law, on the other hand, are inclined to articulate the latter as the result of a historically spontaneous process of accumulation that is by definition irreducible to this kind of formal codification. This kind of law is more closely identified with the English "constitution" as a form of *lex non scripta* (or "unwritten constitution") that is enriched through the generations by successive contributions that do not alter its fundamental substance and are independent of formal processes of enactment or promulgation.

Friedrich Hayek is undoubtedly the neoliberal theorist who draws the sharpest distinction between law as posited (*positus*) by a legislator and customary law. In his discussion of seventeenth-century English intellectual history, Hayek contrasts the "rational constructivism" of thinkers such as Francis Bacon and Thomas Hobbes with a much "older tradition," still alive in England, "survived chiefly. . . in the works of the great common law lawyers, especially Sir Edward Coke and Matthew Hale, the opponents of Bacon and Hobbes."[3] Hayek also includes thinkers such as Bernard Mandeville, Adam Ferguson, Adam Smith, and David Hume within this "sometimes described as 'anti-rationalist'" tradition.[4] What distinguishes this specific "type" of rationalism, according to its practitioners, is a preference for a legal system that arises through a "decentralized" or spontaneous process, a process analogous to Darwinian natural selection.[5] In the nineteenth century, the German historical school associated with Friedrich Carl von Savigny was "largely based on the conception of the spontaneous order elaborated by the eighteenth-century Scottish philosophers."[6] There is therefore direct theoretical continuity between the great English common law theorists and the German historical school, particularly in relation to their respective notions of "natural law": what this intellectual tradition rejects is precisely "natural right as derived from natural reason," but not "discovered natural right." In other words, natural law cannot be "made" or "decreed" because it is the product of a process of "natural growth," which is to say accumulated practical experience.[7]

The problem with this legal confrontation is that both sides view the dichotomy between legislative law and customary laws as both unavoidable and insurmountable: for the one camp, customary law is wholly rejected for being formless and irrational in comparison to positive law; for the other camp, customary law is inversely celebrated as law without a legislator, a law whose production has nothing whatsoever to do with the deliberation and decision of a will. Upon closer examination, however, this dichotomy is both artificial and unfounded insofar as the dichotomy presupposes a rather homogeneous notion of customary law, as either an empirical collection or an uninterrupted growth. This conception of common law seems rather problematic for us, particularly in terms of the profound transformation of the English legal system during the seventeenth century.

The confrontation between these two legal systems is, we should add, more than an academic debate between historians or legal theorists: it touches on the controversial idea of creating a kind of global common law. For the evolutionist school of common law, which is profoundly influenced by Hayek, the current development of international jurisprudence, in the field of commercial contracts or investment rights, is indeed a welcome development: it is seen as the pure and simple extension of juridical and cultural advances (which themselves issued from more or less spontaneous economic and social interaction) that produce and maintain the competitive market. The extension of common law practices, from this perspective, would therefore create a "spontaneous order" at the level of the global market as well. "Common" law, then, according to the neoliberal interpretation, is simply the spontaneous legal framework for the codification of property rights, the contract, and profit. Yet as we have discussed, it is precisely in opposition to this vision of the world that the opponents of neoliberal globalization have called for the defense and rehabilitation of the "commons." Just as the concept of the "common" is an object of tremendous dispute today, so too did the "commons" play an absolutely decisive role in the interpretation and development of English common law. Rarely has a matter of legal history been so central to the major conflicts of our time.

A National Myth: The "Organic Continuity" of Common Law

We are indebted in this respect to Harold J. Berman, whose second volume of *Law and Revolution* (2006) expertly parses this decisive transformation in the history of Western law.[8] Following his analysis of the "papal revolution" of 1075–1122 – through which a new legal code, canon law, was established by the Roman Church as a means of emancipating itself from the stewardship of emperors, kings, and feudal lords by re-constituting itself as a kind of pan-European "modern state" – Berman turns to the legal impacts of the English and German revolutions. In his account, Berman argues that the dominant thesis on the national opposition between English law (which is a continuation of German customary law in its purest form) and the absolutist model that issues from the Roman legal tradition, is largely a retroactive projection, to say the least. In particular, Berman observes how the thirteenth-century English jurist Henry de Bracton, the author of a famous treatise on the laws and customs of England, is unduly appropriated by the proponents of this conventional thesis: in their view, Bracton is a source of English "national" hostility toward the "foreign" law – i.e., Roman or canon law – whereas "Bracton, in his great treatise on English law, quoted Roman law favorably in at least five hundred different places."[9]

What is at stake in Berman's re-construction is nothing less than the very ideology of the English Revolution itself, insofar as the "organic community of English history from early times" – which was "broken only by Tudor-Stuart despotism" – was maintained by virtue of an "English 'common law' superseding the 'foreign' legal regimes that once coexisted with it."[10] And it would seem certain Calvinist religious beliefs also played an essential role in this ideological struggle. Calvinist influence was firstly manifest in the idea that God plays a direct role in historical development, especially "through his elect nation, England," which in turn gave rise to the conviction that "the English common law had unfolded over many centuries, gradually perfecting itself, and that it was peculiarly English and superior, at least for England, to any 'foreign' law."[11] The influence of Calvinism was secondly evident in the idea that God is a legislator whose followers are inspired to translate his will into laws and institutions: "the historical jurisprudence of Coke, Selden, and Hale found a secular equivalent of biblical law in the pre-sixteenth-century heritage of the English common law."[12] In Berman's view, the insistence on the historical continuity of English law in the seventeenth century was ultimately linked to "the emergence of the aristocratic parliamentary state, with its party system of Whigs and Tories and its guilds of judges and barristers," in the same way that the emergence of the bureaucracy in the service of the monarchy, the Prince, and his advisors in sixteenth-century Germany was linked to the conceptual coalescence of German legal science.[13] In contradistinction with this ideological notion of legal continuity, Berman reveals the profound and lasting "innovations" introduced into English law during the "revolution of 1640–1689," thereby undermining the insistent English ideological self-valorization that "disguis[ed] radical change as continuity with the past."[14]

One of the most important of these innovations concerned the organization of the courts and the introduction of judges who were independent of the Crown. To get a proper sense of the scope of this innovation, it is worth saying a few words about the Tudor system of government. At the same moment in which the Tudors rendered the King's Council and Parliament (the House of Lords and the House of Commons) instruments of royal power, they also created new courts that were more directly responsive to royal prerogative than were the traditional common law courts. The common law courts – specifically the courts of Common Pleas, the King's Bench, as well as the Court of Exchequer – "were the first professional royal courts to have been created out of the King's Council in the twelfth century," and as such were "distinguished from ecclesiastical courts, manorial courts, feudal courts, urban courts, and mercantile courts."[15] Unlike these older judiciaries, the new courts created by the Tudors, which were called Prerogative Courts, "operated to some extent, though by no means entirely, according to doctrines and procedures derived in part from the earlier canon law of the Roman Catholic Church and in part from the secular Romanist law which had been studied for some centuries in the universities of Europe, including Oxford and Cambridge."[16] During the course of the sixteenth century, a growing share of the judicial affairs of the country was transferred from the common law courts to the Prerogative Courts, and this created a growing antagonism between the two legal systems. During the reign of James I, for instance, this antagonism erupted in open conflict, wherein Edward Coke prominently affirmed the supremacy of common law over every other legal system or tradition. Parliament thus passed several laws after the English Revolution of 1641, two of which abolished the Star Chamber, the High Commission, and other Prerogative Courts, thereby making the common law courts sovereign over civil and criminal affairs.[17]

By the end of the sixteenth century, however, King James I appropriated the theory of political absolutism as outlined in Jean Bodin's *De la République* (1576) in order to justify the consolidation of his power, especially in the judicial domain. James's absolute power was, in his view, derived from "his lack of accountability to anyone other than God himself":[18] not only can the king revoke the authority and competence of a magistrate, but, in the mere presence of the king, the magistrate's authority and competence becomes completely null and void. According to this approach, any judicial review of royal laws and proclamations was reduced to a "mere administrative function"; the work of Parliament was re-interpreted as merely "advisory" or "corroborative"; and all the charters and other commitments English kings had previously entered into were construed as merely "conditional and temporary."[19] "When the seventeenth-century English common lawyers invoked as an 'inheritance' judicial or parliamentary powers to limit the royal prerogative," writes Berman, "King James would reply that they were merely granted by earlier monarchs as a 'toleration' and could therefore be revoked at his discretion."[20]

It was under these conditions that Sir Edward Coke, first as chief judge of the Court of Common Pleas, then as a member of the Court of the King's Bench (from 1606 to 1616), and finally as a parliamentarian, waged a long struggle to restrict the powers of royal prerogative and subordinate the latter to both common law and Parliament. The core of the conflict revolved around the ongoing but questionable validity of the laws introduced by James I's predecessors: were they an "inheritance" to which subsequent monarchs were bound, or were such laws simply a "toleration" that could be revoked at the behest of a ruling monarch? Coke's view was that laws currently in force constituted a "memorial of the past," by which Coke meant the following: "the Tudors, the Plantagenets, and the earlier Norman and even Anglo-Saxon rulers, who in and through their councils and their parliaments and their courts had, over the centuries, created a legal system that had duration in time and carried with it meanings remembered from the past."[21] What is especially remarkable about Coke's position is that he does not oppose absolutist theory with an alternative general theory of the law, but rather argues for a unique conception of "English" law that can only be understood in the context of its national specificity. Indeed, Coke was the most vocal and successful proponent of identifying English law with common law as such, despite the fact that the latter was merely one of the branches of English government: canon laws, or Roman laws, which were in force at the time in a large number of English courts, were considered "foreign laws" by Coke.[22] It was largely on the basis of Coke's efforts that it soon became customary to identify the "law of the land" with English common law, or the law that was applied in the courts of the Common Pleas, the King's Bench, and the Exchequer.

It is only with a view to these developments that the multiple meanings of the adjective "common" in the characteristically English expression "common law" can begin to be properly parsed. In the first place, "common" is of course understood to mean a law that unifies all the laws relating to everyday uses and practices, to the point of guaranteeing that all subjects of the kingdom may "benefit from a uniform justice."[23] Second, and this is an essential point, the term applies to the reason and experience upon which common law was founded. What kind of "reason" are we speaking of here? Certainly not the "natural reason" the natural rights theorists view as a superior norm to positive law. No, rather, the "reason" at play in the common law tradition is a form of "artificial reason": specifically, a form of reason acquired by effort and art that could in no sense be confused with the natural reason of a particular individual, even an individual who is intellectually superior to all others, because artificial law is nothing other than the very reason of the law itself. This is essentially Coke's argument in his famous exchange with James I: even if the king could naturally avail himself of some form of reason, as do judges, it is nonetheless the case that the king is not an expert of the laws of his kingdom, and therefore "the reason of the law is not the natural reason of any person but rather the artificial reason of the law itself."[24] For Coke, then, "the common law is nothing but reason; which is to be understood [as] an artificial perfection of reason gotten by long study, observation, and experience." In other words, the common law

> by many succession of ages. . . hath been. . . refined by an infinite number of grave and learned men, and by long experience grown to such a perfection for the government of this realm, [that] the old rule maybe justly verified of it, *Neminem opportet esse sapientiorem legibus*: no man out of his own private reason ought to be wiser than the law, which is the perfection of reason.[25]

We cannot understate the originality of this concept of reason. It is not that Coke doubted the existence of natural reason, nor some notion of natural law built upon the workings of natural reason. Indeed, the existence of natural reason was recognized by the scholastic philosophers of the twelfth and fourteenth centuries and the humanist philosophers of the sixteenth centuries, and Coke has no truck with such doctrines. Far from rejecting natural reason as such, Coke instead argues that natural reason is in fact incorporated into common law itself.[26] More accurately, Coke supplements natural reason with another type of reason we might call "historical reason." Historical reason, for Coke, was "the practical prudential reason of the experts, persons of experience, who have made a special study of their subject, who know their history, and who build on the learning and wisdom of many generations of other experienced persons."[27] We are thus dealing with a kind of "historical artificial reason" that alone can account for the profound continuity of English law *qua* common law. It is precisely in this sense that the first meaning of "common" overlaps with the second: if the law is "common" in that it applies to all the subjects of the kingdom, its commonality is also derived from the fact that it is an elaboration of an historical "common sense."[28] Common sense, then, denotes a form of moral judgment shared by an entire community – in this case a community of judges, lawyers, and experts in juridical matters, and by extension the entire English nation whose whole history is crystalized, so to speak, in the formation of these collective judgments.

Again, we cannot overemphasize the significance of the proposition implicitly advanced by Coke, and which has henceforth been referred to as the first principle of the historical school of legal thought: the law of a nation is first and foremost a product of its history. This is not merely to say that contemporary institutions stem from earlier institutions, which of course they do, but it is rather an admission that the past – and especially the distant past (in this case, the customs of the Anglo-Saxon era) – is more than just inert history: this past is a living part of the ongoing process of growth endowed with a finality and normativity as regards the present and future development of the law. Coke, in this regard, often recited a proverb from Chaucer: "out of the old fields must spring and grow the new corn."[29] What began as a doctrine uniquely suited to English history acquired – after Coke, to be sure – the singular force of a general principle that claims to supersede both natural law and positive law. The primary source of the law must be found in custom and judicial precedent, such that every other juridical source – such as universal notions of justice referenced by natural law, or by the will of a legislator in the case of legal positivism – should be subordinated to the historical development of the legal system.[30]

There are, however, several ways to understand the primacy of custom as the source of law. Berman, in this respect, forcefully distinguishes between "historicism" and "historicity": in the case of the former, established rules – as transmitted from judgments rendered in the past – must be "preserved and reiterated" in order to guarantee the continuity of law from one generation to the next. According to the latter, the history of law is viewed as "a process of adaptation of past experience to changing needs."[31] According to the terms of this distinction, Coke would be slotted on the side of "historicism," insofar as he stood by a "conception of an immemorial past and an unchangeable fundamental law."[32] The same cannot be said, however, for Coke's two great successors, John Selden (1584–1654) and Matthew Hale (1609–1676), both of whom saw the law from the perspective of "historicity." Selden, who directly witnessed the turmoil of the revolution, emphasized the profoundly evolutionary character of English common law, as opposed to its permanence and continuity. While he fully recognized the caesura or rupture introduced into the evolution of English law by the Norman invasion, he nevertheless persisted in considering the British, Saxon, and Norman periods "as three distinct phases of a single historical development."[33] Selden thus moved well beyond Coke's position by insisting that all legal systems, not merely English common law, must be grasped historically. For Selden, it is not antiquity in itself that is the core quality of a "people's" law – since this criterion applies to all legal systems – but the ability of the law to respond to the aspirations of a particular people.[34] From this perspective, the differences between national legal systems are derived from the diversity of different customs amongst different peoples, such that the relation between one people and another is analogous to relations between individuals. Selden, moreover, renewed the significance of the doctrine that made popular consent the cornerstone of political legitimacy. Indeed, for Selden, consent itself was "manifested in custom, that is, in the patterns and norms of behavior tacitly or expressly accepted by the community," as identified by experts or lawyers, "in response to changing circumstances."[35] On the basis of this definition, customary law is especially deserving of the appellation "common law," insofar as it implies the adhesion of all, through the generations and centuries, simply by virtue of the perpetuation of customs alone.

Yet of the three jurists, it was indisputably Matthew Hale who endowed this English philosophy of law with unparalleled scope. In addition to his criticism of Hobbes's theory of sovereignty, Hale is best known for his ideas about the historical development of the legal system and the associated concept of "artificial reason." Firstly, Hale understood common law as a customary law that evolves according to the logic of an adaptive movement designed to meet new ends through a process of progressive self-perfection; this is an idea Lord Mansfield later expressed with the phrase "the common law works itself pure."[36] Hale thus subscribes to a notion of identity through change, which he expresses through analogy with the famous dilemma of the Argonaut's ship: just as the ship was the same when it returned to port, even though it had undergone extensive repairs over the course of its long journey to the point at which "none of the original materials" remained, so too has English law undergone many "variations" and "accretions" throughout its history. Yet these changes were "only partial and successive" such that "they are the same English Laws now, that they were 600 Years since."[37] Berman explicates this analogous reasoning very clearly: "the nature of the historical development of the English legal system, according to Hale, is that the constitution as a whole—the ship of state—is itself constituted by the successive changes in its parts experienced over centuries."[38] Even more significant in terms of advancing the English philosophy of law as a whole, however, was Hale's response to Hobbes's criticism of Coke, in which he developed his own concept of "artificial reason."

Hale, in this respect, distinguishes between two concepts of reason: there is, on the one hand, "the reason in things," which is another way of saying "internal logic" – the relationship between the springs and hands of a watch would be one example of this. On the other hand, there is the "human faculty of reason," which is based on the connection between cause and effect, or the ability to perceive the proportions between lines and surfaces, etc. And while this capacity is found in all men, it is not the same as the first kind of reason: it is precisely because the internal or inherent reason of a variety of objects or activities differs from reason as faculty that the latter is compelled to differentiate itself by applying itself to these objects or activities, insofar as its application to specific objects requires specific methods and, consequently, prolonged exercise. This is especially true of the science of law, which is the most difficult of all the disciplines, because it does not deal with justice or the good in general, but in "the measure of good or evil as arising in concrete situations." The mere possession of reason as a general faculty (as in the second sense of the term) cannot therefore assure mastery over the science of law. To become a good lawyer, one must consider the manner in which rules might be applied under extremely varied circumstances, and thereby become familiar with the "reason" of the law as a practical activity (in the first sense of the word). The expertise of the jurist is thus the result of applying the general faculty of reason to the specific object of reason, which in this case is the law. "It is reasonable," writes Hale, "for me to prefer a law made by a hundred or two hundred persons of age, wisdom, experience, and interest, before a law excogitated by myself."[39] And for Hale, this conclusion is drawn from the nature of the law in general, not merely from the particularities of English law and common law: "in Hale's terms, what Coke called artificial reason is the combination of the reason inherent in law itself and the reasoning of experienced students and learned practitioners of law."[40]

We can now summarize the principle features of the concept of "common law" as it was shaped during the English Revolution of 1640–1689. Firstly, common law is rooted in a multinational history of the country, which means it has no singular or definable point of origin: as Geldart aptly puts it, the common law "grows, but it was never born."[41] Secondly, if it is true the common law "grows," it does so only in the sense that it evolves over the course of centuries without losing its fundamental identity. In other words, its organic growth ensures both its continuity and its gradual perfection. And thirdly, common law is primarily a law of judges, not legislators: common law is a "judge-made law," insofar as this term denotes the fact that the law is not "made" or "produced" by judges, but rather judges merely enunciate the law by acting as its spokespersons and interpreters. "*Judex est lex loquens*," as Coke would have it: judges are the law itself insofar as the latter speaks through them; judges speak the law (*jus dicere*), they do not give the law (*jus dare*).[42] In this sense, the judge subordinates himself to the law – for if he were the law's creator, he would be its superior. As such, the judge is no different from the king, parliament, or any other subject of the kingdom.

And lastly, the judge expresses his submission to the common law by referring to past judicial decisions in his judgments: the entire doctrine of "judicial precedent" takes shape here, and it is grounded in the notion that past judgments are not simply illustrations of the law, but are the source of the law itself. As Berman puts it, "the decisions are not only 'examples' of the principle or rule but also 'proof' of its reception by the judiciary and hence a source of its binding force." But since precedent itself refers to the continuity of custom, this "means that the source of law in precedent is itself linked to the source of law in custom."[43] Binding authority over future judgments is thus exercised by the *mos judiciorum*, which itself is bound up with a "filiation of judgments" emanating from the past experience of practitioners and legal professionals. The question we must investigate therefore concerns the extent to which this conception of common law, based on continuity, necessarily presupposes an illusory homogeneity of prior custom. And one of the easiest ways to determine the credibility and coherence of this presupposition is to examine what is arguably the most important legal reference in the entire English common law tradition.

A Foundational Referent: The Magna Carta

This referent is of course the 1215 text known as the Magna Carta. From the point of view of the "historicist" perspective adopted by Coke – according to which positive law and natural law are both part of common law – the "Great Charter" (*la Grande Charte*) is part of the historical laws of Parliament and, as such, was inscribed in the immemorial continuity of a legal tradition that pre-dated the Tudor era.[44] Yet the Magna Carta is not viewed as an absolute beginning, since one can always find a charter of some kind or another as far back in history as one cares to search. In 1235, for instance, the chronicler Roger Wendover reported that the archbishop Stephen Langton discovered a charter of "ancient freedoms" in 1213 that dated from the age of King Henry I (1100–1135). The archbishop then informed the barons that this charter might be a means for them to restore their past freedoms. According to this account, the 1215 charter was thus the result of the baron's struggle to re-establish these older freedoms guaranteed by Henry I.[45] This earlier charter, which dates back to Henry's ascension to the throne in 1100, was the model for the 1215 Magna Carta, and in between these two charters, there was also a charter associated with King Stephen in 1136, which we will discuss further below. And we could even go back further to 1100 and the Oxford Code of King Cnut (Knut, in Danish). This code dates to somewhere around 1018[46] – which takes us back before the Norman conquest – and this charter, in turn, was likely inspired by oral precedents that are all but lost in the mists of pre-history. In any case, what is essential for the whole common law tradition is the idea that every document always refers to a precedent of some sort or another. Of course, the challenge lies in determining the exact extent to which a preceding document actually served as a model for a subsequent text, and what the specific nature of the precedential relationship is.

There should be nothing at all surprising, then, in the fact that the opponents of James I (1603–1625) enthusiastically referred to the Charter of 1215 to justify their struggle against the Crown. Coke's personal commitment to the struggle against royal absolutism, under the reigns of both James I and his successor Charles I, was thus waged on behalf of the freedoms enshrined in the Magna Carta, especially Article 39 of the charter, which stipulates that no free man can be imprisoned except through the legal decision of his peers, or according to the laws of the country. During the debates in Parliament on this subject, Coke asserted, "the Magna Charta is such a fellow, that he will have no sovereign,"[47] and "the Great Charter is not a lady to be led by a sovereign."[48] Charles I, in particular, became increasingly aware of the political uses to which the 1215 charter was being put, and so when he learned in 1631 that Coke was working on a new book about the Magna Carta, he forbade its publication. While Coke was on his deathbed, his offices were ransacked and his manuscripts confiscated. Coke's work was, however, posthumously published in 1642 at the instigation of Parliament, under the title *Institutes of the Laws of England*. The book is a line-by-line commentary on the Magna Carta in both Latin and English, and contains voluminous explanatory notes. By publishing Coke's commentaries, Parliament's intentions were perfectly clear: the English reformers were keen to portray themselves as restorers of older customs, not as legal innovators.[49] Hannah Arendt draws the same conclusion:

> The fact that the word "revolution" meant originally restoration, hence something which to us its very opposite, is not a mere oddity of semantics. The revolutions of the seventeenth and eighteenth centuries, which to us appear to show all evidence of a new spirit, the spirit of the modern age, were intended to be restorations.[50]

But how, exactly, was this one text able to crystalize such opposition to royal absolutism? There are at least three known versions of the Magna Carta: a version from 1215, 1217, and 1225 respectively. In its original form, the text is comprised of sixty-three articles.[51] It was in mid-June 1215, on the Runnymede prairie along the Thames, that King John and the rebellious barrens signed the text and swore fidelity to its articles. A month earlier, in May, the barons had taken London by force and renounced their allegiance to the King, and so the charter was a concession forced on the King by the barons. In other words, the Magna Carta was a treaty that brought an episode of open conflict to an end. King John had just lost Normandy at the Battle of Bouvines in 1214, and in February of 1215 he vowed to lead a crusade to take back the Holy Lands from the infidels – the Fifth Crusade. In order to raise enough funds to re-conquer Normandy and finance the crusade, the King imposed a *scutage* on the barons, which was a tax paid in lieu of military service to the King. Given the contentious context in which the Magna Carta was created and signed, we would do well to heed Geoffrey Robinson's reminder about the historical nature of the document:

> The appearance of "rights" as a set of popular propositions limiting the sovereign is usually traced to *Magna Carta* in 1215, although that document had nothing to do with the liberty of individual citizens: it was signed by a feudal king who was feuding with thuggish barons, and was forced to accede to their demands.[52]

Beyond the contingent historical circumstances that led to the drafting and signing of the Magna Carta, it is worth noting how the document has been subject to starkly divergent political interpretation at various important moments in English history. For instance, some of the most radical revolutionaries during the constitutional conflicts in the seventeenth century drew inspiration from the Magna Carta. While Gerrard Winstanley, the founder of the famous community of "Diggers" in Surrey, thought the Magna Carta was problematic insofar as "the best Laws that England hath . . . are yoaks and manicles, tying one sort of people to be slaves of another," Thomas Tany, who considered himself to be a "Commoner of England," asserted in 1650 that the "Magna Charta is the being of our being."[53] And the same tendency to yield rival interpretations continues up to the present day. The Magna Carta is, on the one hand, a veritable Bible for proponents of rights discourses, including both classical liberals and the more recent neoliberals like Hayek. But it is perhaps less well known that the Magna Carta was also viewed as a powerful source of inspiration for opponents of neoliberalism. For instance, the recent return of arbitrary detention in places like Guantanamo Bay has given Article 39 new relevance, not to mention the doctrine of *habeas corpus* which Coke closely associated with the charter. Yet the Magna Carta's resurgent relevance is at least, if not more, due to the second message the charter supposedly delivers: political and legal rights "can only exist on an economic foundation," in the sense that "to be free citizens we must also be equal producers and consumers."[54] Of course most people are aware that the principle object of the text is the freedoms of political subjects, but as Linebaugh and other historians now insist, the text is also about the "economic foundation" of these political liberties, as if the text somehow anticipated the familiar Marxist *topos* on the inadequacies of "formal freedoms" and the need for economic and social rights to guarantee the "reality" of these formal political freedoms. For us, however, this interpretation is asking the text to do a little too much work on behalf of contemporary political concerns.

The truth of the matter is that the Magna Carta isn't a single text, but rather a document comprised of two texts: from its first uses in 1218, the expression "Magna Carta" was meant to distinguish the charter from another smaller text, namely the "Charter of the Forest" (*Charta de Foresta*). The first charter dates to 1215, at the end of the reign of King John (who died in 1216), while the second was adopted in 1225 under Henry III (the son of John and grandson of Henry II), before it was confirmed by Edward I in 1299. While the first charter is concerned with the "freedoms" of English subjects, the second deals with questions about the subsistence of the poorest of the kingdom's people. There is no persuasive rationale, in our view, to either ignore this second half of the charter or to dismiss it as a kind of appendix of lesser importance than the ostensible main text. In the preface to the second edition of his *Institutes of the Laws of England* (1642), for instance, Coke explains that the name "Magna Carta" is not due to the greater size of this charter relative to others, nor does the name suggest it is more important than the second charter (the Charter of the Forest). Rather, the name was merely meant to emphasize the importance of the Magna Carta's content, from Coke's retrospective vantage. Indeed, it is for the same reason that the Charter of the Forest was properly called the *Magna Charta de Foresta,* and likewise both of the charters were called *Magnae Chartae Libertatum Angliae*, the "great charters of English liberties."[55] In 1225, the two charters were actually re-issued together so that they could be confirmed together. In 1297, Edward I decreed the two charters become the common law of the country, and in 1369 Edward III ensured they were henceforth regarded as a single and uniform law. Both charters were printed together at the beginning of the English *Statutes at Large* which, according to Blackstone, marked "the final and complete establishment of the two charters."[56] Indeed, the second charter explicitly references the "End of Magna Charta" in its final sentence.[57] How unified, then, are these two charters? Is their unity an artificial assemblage designed to produce the retrospective illusion of a legal "foundation," or does an examination of the respective contents of these two texts in fact reveal a profound unity between the charters?

The first charter already contains two articles – 47 and 48 – that explicitly refer to the forest as royal domain. Article 47 reads as follows: "all forests that have been created in our reign shall at once be disafforested. River-banks that have been enclosed in our reign shall be treated similarly."[58] Firstly, we need to clarify the verb "disafforest": the verb does not have the same meaning as the contemporary notion of "deforestation." It does not refer to the destruction of trees or clear cutting, but rather designates the legal act of revoking the forest's status as incorporated by the Crown, and consequently removing legal censure from the forests. In other words, "disafforest" is the juridical opposite of "afforest," wherein the latter does not mean planting trees, but designates the legal act of converting the woods into a restricted royal "forest" or hunting grounds. Afforestation was a very common practice up until the Norman conquest. It endowed English kings with the exclusive right to freely hunt upon their own lands. But far from constituting a mere royal prerogative, a king was treated in this respect like any other owner of landed estate. According to the twelfth-century Anglo-Saxon historian Henry of Huntingdon, William the Conqueror used extremely brutal methods to afforest lands reserved for hunting – which he referred to as the "New Forest" – even going so far as to displace entire villages and their populations in order to create habitats for wild game. The new lands were added to the forests under the reign of Henry I (this is evident in the Charter of King Stephen in 1136, insofar as Stephen promised to restore the wooded areas incorporated by his predecessor).[59]

It is therefore necessary to distinguish between the physical forest – i.e., wooded lands – and legal "forests," which are royal domains used for the king's exclusive game. It is well known that King John took advantage of this practice to a much greater extent than those before him, and he reaped substantial revenues from the annexation of new areas. The grievances provoked by these excesses reached their climax in 1215, so much so that The Unknown Charter, which probably dates back to the spring of 1215, demanded all the lands added to the royal forests by Henri II, Richard, and John be immediately disafforested. Several months later, the Magna Carta of June 1215 adopted a more conciliatory approach: only the lands added to the Crown by John would be immediately disafforested. But a reprieve, due to the crusade, was granted to John concerning the lands appropriated by his father and his brother,[60] which explains the attenuated formulation of Article 47. Meanwhile Article 48 reads as follows:

> All evil customs relating to forests and warrens, foresters, warreners, sheriffs and their servants, or river-banks and their wardens, are at once to be investigated in every county by twelve sworn knights of the county, and within forty days of their enquiry the evil customs are to be abolished completely and irrevocably. But we, or our chief justice if we are not in England, are first to be informed.[61]

It is difficult to ascertain precisely what the text means by the expression "evil customs," and it is hardly illuminating to simply refer to the "common rights of the forest" without further precision. The act of "afforesting," or the placing of areas under the jurisdiction of the royal law – through which kings sought to strengthen their power against the barons, counts, and knights – involved subtracting the forests from the realm of common law. This is confirmed in the Dialogues of Scaccario (1176) by Richard Fitz Nigel, Lord Grand Treasurer of the English Exchequer:

> The whole organisation of the forests, the punishment, pecuniary or corporal, of forest offences, is outside the jurisdiction of the other courts, and solely dependent on the decision of the King, or of some officer specially appointed by him. The forest has its own laws, based . . . not on the Common Law of the realm, but on the arbitrary legislation of the King.[62]

Was the juridical act of disafforestation intended to make these wooded lands communal (or commons) and thereby abolish the various legal practices that had been introduced into the forests by virtue of their status as royal domains? What practices are we talking about here? The abuses committed by the barons and lords, or the collective practices that were developed by the poor? Or are we talking about abuses by royal officials themselves? In other words, was disafforestation meant to transform the wooded lands into commons or return these lands to their previous private owners? Or could it be both at once, given that common land was based on *use* rather than *ownership*, in the narrowest sense of the term. In 1215, when the first charter was adopted, there were 143 forests in England, about half of which were "wooded pastures."[63] The expression "wooded pastures" does not refer to wild forests but rather designates land used both for grazing animals and growing trees, which was a selective process carried out for centuries by local inhabitants. Old trees, mainly oaks, thrived, while livestock, such as goats and deer, ate the oak's competitors. This process produced a very unique landscape where commoners found and gathered what the English call "coppice" (small trees and thickets that are periodically cut), "sucker" (which grows again from the roots), and "pollard" (trees cut at a specific height, between six and fifteen feet, leaving a permanent trunk with branches out of the reach of livestock).[64]

Within these cultivated and structured spaces, what was called the "commons" was still someone's property, but it was collectively used by others (the "commoners"). The soil itself was usually owned by the lord, but the pastured areas were left to the commoners; similarly, the wooded areas were distinguished between "timber," which belonged to the lord, and the rest of the wood (particularly any wood that was separated from the trunk when a tree fell to the ground), which belonged to the commoners.[65] It would seem, therefore, since there is no reason to think otherwise, that Article 48 speaks in favor of transferring the incorporated forests back to their old owners *as well as* restoring the ancestral customary rights associated with these properties. In other words, it would be a mistake to anachronistically impose our modern concept of private property onto the communal lands of the medieval period. Thus, in sharp contrast to the account given by someone like William George Hoskins, who argued that every common is merely private property in that it is owned by someone (either an individual or corporate form),[66] E.P. Thompson rightly reminds us that "the central concept of feudal custom was not that of property but of reciprocal obligations."[67] The dominant land regime at the time was not that of exclusive property, but rather "fee simple," which is a real estate title unbound by time. We must be careful, therefore, not to overlook the relatively undefined character of this legal concept: "so long as wastes remained extensive and unstinted, landowners and commoners might co-exist without precise definitions of rights."[68]

In any event, it is clear that the formulation of the Charter of 1215 was extremely equivocal, such that by the eighteenth century it was difficult to agree on a dominant uniform interpretation. In his 1759 text on the two charters, Blackstone, for instance, remarked how the Bishops of Canterbury and Dublin feared that the generality of Article 48 would endanger the existence of all the forests. In their view, it could not have been the intention of the parties that the generalized wording of the charter should abolish all forest customs, given that the forests themselves could not have been preserved without these customs.[69] It would seem then that the text mutually agreed upon by King John and the barons sanctioned a somewhat precarious balance of power, and its provisions did little to solidify this balance, as became quite evident after the rapid resumption of war between these two antagonistic parties.

Yet it was precisely the painful and prolonged experience of war that led to a notable modification of the charter between 1215 and 1217. In Article 7, which concerns the situation of widows, the text was modified so that a widow may remain in her husband's house for forty days after his death, during which period she shall have "*reasonable estover in the common*."[70] The noun "estover" poses an almost insurmountable translation problem: the word comes from the old French *estovoir*, an impersonal verb similar to *faloir* that denotes something of vital necessity, such that the English nominalization of the term came to designate all manner of necessities permitted by the law. According to the *Oxford New English Dictionary on Historical Principles*, the term refers to timber that the tenant had a right to take so long as it was used to make necessary repairs to one's house, fabricate agricultural instruments – such as plows, hedges, or fences – or for firewood. The Old English word "bote" was often used to signify various kinds of "estovers": "housebote" was used to designate a tenant's right to furnish himself with wood from a landowner's property to repair his house; "ploughbote" analogously denoted the right to cut enough wood to make or repair a plow; "cartbote" referred to the right to take wood in order to make or repair a cart, etc.[71] The modification of Article 7 thus gives the widow the right to procure, from the common, what is reasonably necessary for her subsistence for a limited time.

In the same vein, Article 33 of the charter states, "henceforth all fish weirs shall be removed from the Thames and the Medway and throughout all England, except along the seacoast," which effectively granted the right to fish in another's water, in common with others.[72] Given the prior state of affairs in England, these concessions were far from negligible: in 1184, the Court of Woodstock placed strict conditions on the ability of the poor to collect estovers, particularly in terms of the satisfaction of the poor's three basic needs: food, firewood, and construction material. The charter, in this sense, can be interpreted as a form of social protection, especially against local tyranny.[73] At the same time, however, the scope of these concessions should not be exaggerated. As important as these concessions were at the time, they were far from guaranteeing substantive rights for the poor over the common, as many contemporary writers on the English commons often assert. The charters, according to its own terminology, outlined "freedoms and customs" more so than "rights" in the modern sense of the term.

What about the second charter, the Charter of 1225 or the Charter of the Forest, enacted by Henry III? The Charter of the Forest is an undeniably more precise document as concerns the articles relating to the commons. Of the sixteen articles, a few deserve particular attention, especially the first several. Article 3, for instance, does not merely stop at the demand to revoke King John's acts of afforestation, but those of his predecessors as well: "all Woods that have been made Forest by King Richard our Uncle, or by King John our Father, until our first Coronation, shall be forthwith, disafforested, unless it be our Demesne Wood."[74] Article 4 then returns the woods to all those whose land was afforested after the first coronation of King Henry II, the grandfather of Henry III – which includes archbishops, bishops, abbots, earls, barons, knights, and other freeholders – and reprieves them of any penalties incurred for "Purprestures, Wastes, and Asserts" since the coronation of Henry II, but they will be held accountable for any of the same infractions henceforth incurred.[75]

What is especially noteworthy, however, is the concern expressed in Article 1 for the preservation of the commons (which includes the commons inside royal domains as well):

> We will, that all Forests, which King Henry our Grandfather afforested, shall be view'd by good and lawfull men; and if he hath afforested any other Wood, more than his own Demesne, by which the Owner of the Wood hath damage, it shall be forth-with disafforested; and if he hath afforested his own Wood, then it shall remain Forest: saving the Common of Herbage, and of other things in the same Forest, to them who before were accustomed to have the same.[76]

In order to get a sense of the importance of this clause, it should be noted that the expression "Common of Herbage" refers to a law that allows animals to roam the forest. This allowance is similar to one called "agistment," which denoted the practice of opening a forest to cattle for a determined period of time. It is precisely this allowance that is established in Article 9, which states, "every Free-Man may Agist his own Wood within Our Forest, at his Pleasure, and shall take his Pawnage."[77] "Pawnage," here, refers to the food eaten by pigs in the forest – mainly beech nuts and acorns – and, by association, it designates the right to graze one's pigs in the woods, as the rest of Article 9 delineates: "Also, We do grant, That every Free-Man may drive his Swine freely; without Impediment, through our Demesne Woods."[78] Article 7 also forbids "Foresters" or "Bedles" from imposing a tax called a "Scotal," as well as forbidding them from taking wheat, oats, or corn, or from collecting lambs or pigs in lieu of taxes.

Articles 12, 13, and 14 are also of particular importance. Article 12 states: "every Free-Man from henceforth, without Danger, shall make in his own Wood, or in his Land, or in his Water, which he hath within Our Forest; Mills, Springs, Pools, Marsh-Pits, Dikes, or Earable Ground, without inclosing that Earable Ground; so that it be not to the Annoyance of any of his Neighbours."[79] Article 13 states: "Every Free-Man shall have within his own Woods Ayries of Hawkes, Sparrow-Hawkes, Falcons, Eagles, and

Herons; and shall have also the Honey that is found within his Woods."[80] And lastly, Article 14 deals with "chiminage," which refers to road tolls. It authorizes an appointed forester-in-fee to collect a certain toll from every carriage or horse. But at the same time it stipulates that "those who bear upon their Backs Brushment, Bark, or Coal to sell, though it be their Living, shall pay no Chiminage to our Forester, except they take it within our Demesne Woods."[81] This concession is not at all negligible given the fact that, in Somerset during this period, a six-pence sum was levied upon each man carrying wood on his back.[82]

As we can see, then, rights relating to "agistment," "pawnage," "chiminage," etc. all constitute a labyrinth of customary laws and rights whose contents are all very different, but which were all designed to help the poor of the kingdom attain the basic necessities of life. According to some medievalists, thirteenth-century England experienced many struggles around forest customs because these customs were progressively threatened by economic pressures that arose from the growth of cities and through increases in trade. The people of Stoneleigh in Warwickshire, for instance, sent a petition to the King in 1290 complaining about the loss of their estovers and pastures to manorial "assarts" (or "estates"). The trees had been removed for purposes of cultivation, which deprived the people of their forest customs.[83] But merely acknowledging all of these provisions does not mean we can isolate the Charter of the Forest from the patchwork of feudal and manorial rights to which the charter was consubstantially linked in the first place, as if referencing these rights alone enables one to wrap the charters in an ideologically and socially "progressive" envelope. Properly situated within the *longue durée* of English history, the charters must be viewed as inseparable from the manorial-agricultural regime that reached its apogee between the twelfth and the mid-fourteenth century. As Berman puts it, "under that system, peasants held parcels of land ('strips'), usually scattered in various parts of the manor, 'of' the lord of the manor, and the rights and obligations associated with such parcels, as well as rights in the commons, were based on manorial custom."[84] After the decline of this regime during the latter half of the fourteenth century, "especially after the Black Death of 1348–49," the peasants re-obtained their customary tenures, as written down in copies of old manorial records:

> But just as the gradual disappearance of the lord-vassal relationships changed the character of feudal tenures, so the gradual disappearance of lord-peasant relationships changed the character of manorial tenures. In the fifteenth century there emerged in the villages well-to-do peasants (yeomen), who acquired parcels of arable land from poorer peasants and who sometimes made inroads on the commons in order to obtain large areas of contiguous pastureland, chiefly for grazing sheep.[85]

The Magna Carta: An Unfulfilled Document

Examined in this light, Coke's interpretation – which, as we have seen, inscribed the Magna Carta into the organic continuity of an English law in the process of perfecting itself over the course of history – is endowed with a certain logic. He describes the charter as "a declaratory law restoring the subject to his former right."[86] Coke argues that "generally a man may common in a forest"; by using the term "common" as a verb, he interestingly emphasizes the manner in which the common is "a customary activity, not as a thing or resource."[87] Coke observes that customs traditionally belonged to the manorial courts – which he described as "little Commonwealths" – that by and large did a good job of protecting the poor. But, at the same time, Coke also points out some of the excesses produced by common use – specifically the excessive concentration of cattle on communal land – and so Coke stresses the importance of integrating the Charter of the Forest within the larger canon of English law. This was the basis for a proposal Coke made with others during the parliamentary session of 1624 that would suppress legislation designed to restrict the practice of enclosure (even as James I and Charles I tried to do the same). From Coke's point of view, there is no inconsistency in his proposal: common law was not frozen in time; it had to evolve and adapt to changing mentalities. For, indeed, change was already upon the English in the early seventeenth century. In 1601, for instance, Sir Walter Raleigh demanded the repeal of anti-enclosure legislation on behalf of the "English liberties" guaranteed by the Magna Carta.[88] We can thus see here how "common reason" is quite a pliable concept that can be adapted to very different situations and used as a means of legitimating a variety of different legal interpretations. The most we can say is that there is a certain tension between Coke's natural historicism and the recognition of the inevitable evolution of common law itself.

Is there an inconsistency here in the way in which Coke subordinates the Charter of the Forest to the rest of the common law? This, at least, is Linebaugh's view:

> On the one hand Coke recognized that the Forest Charter, like the Magna Carta, restored "the subject to his former right"; on the other hand he said that forest law was bounded by the common law and that it could not stand against laws enacted by Parliament. As he elevated Magna Carta to fundamental law, he subordinated the Charter of the Forest to statute and judges' law.[89]

Given that "statute law" designates prescriptive acts of parliament while "judges' law" denotes legal decisions rendered in the common law courts, it would appear as if Coke did not view the two charters as legal foundations in their own right, but as constitutive elements of English law that will eventually be replaced in the totality of its development, in accordance with his historicist position. Should we, then, sever the relationship between the Charter of the Forest and English common law, as well as statute law, in order to idealize these charters as the "germ form" of a future communism? Linebaugh's entire interpretation is based on the idea that this treaty did not resolve the conflicts it was designed to resolve – which is of course correct – and therefore it is up to future generations to more fully develop its latent principles. For Linebaugh, the whole of English history should be read in terms of either the development or the latency of one part or other of the Magna Carta: "over the great arch of English history some parts of Magna Carta, namely chapter 39, evolved in creative response to events while other parts, such as chapter 7 providing the widow with her reasonable estovers of common, and the entire Charter of the Forest, collected dust among the muniments."[90] We should thus bear in mind that while Article 39 "grew" and prompted further fundamental principles (*habeas corpus*, trial by jury, the prohibition of torture, etc.), most articles became nothing more than dead letters. For Linebaugh, then, it is now up to us to "nurture" these dormant aspects of the charters.[91]

Linebaugh's approach is a striking example of a reading that completely divorces the past from the future – and, indeed, we could say the same thing for his interpretation of the German Peasants' War in 1526. The uprising, according to Linebaugh, was "the first great proletarian revolt of modern history" insofar as it "demanded the restoration of customary forest rights."[92] In very Engels-esque fashion,[93] Linebaugh characterizes this demand to restore older rights as anticipating the proletarian revolution to come; indeed, he seems to suggest these uprisings constituted the first glorious episode of the larger revolution as such. It is indisputable that the leaders of the Peasants' War demanded "the return to the village of its woods and forests so that building timber and firewood could be collected by the peasants" and "the return of communal meadows and fields by people who had seized them," as was laid out in Articles 4 through 11 in a manifesto called the "Twelve Articles."[94] There should also be no doubt, however, that this revolt was little more than an episode of feudal reaction. In their grievances, the peasants referred to practices that were introduced as recently as the end of the fifteenth and the beginning of the sixteenth centuries, "[when] the economic situation of landed noblemen deteriorated and many of them resorted to measures that violated long-established peasant rights."[95] The peasants' activities were also greatly inspired by the new faith proclaimed by such religious reformers as Martin Luther, Huldrych Zwingli, and Thomas Müntzer. When viewed as an attempt to re-cast the juridical order, the Peasants' War of 1525 looks more like another episode of the larger German Reformation of 1517–1555. But what we can be sure of is that describing the Peasants' War as the "the first great proletarian revolt of modern history" is anachronism pure and simple.

Beyond the specific case of the German Peasants' War, however, what most interests us is the ongoing relationship between the 1215 charter and the contemporary demand for the commons. It is clearly impossible, in our view, to fulfill the promises of the two charters today, but it is an open question as to whether the two charters might still, in turn, help us to meet our own present-day demands. In order to answer this question, we need to first dispel all ambiguity on the matter. Making the common the principle of a new legal order, which involves turning our backs on the moribund juridical apparatus of state sovereignty, would undoubtedly benefit from clear-sighted understanding of these two charters. Firstly, it will not do to conceive of these texts as "waiting to be realized" in terms of their latent potentialities. We must therefore definitively abandon any attempt to produce a new legal regime by "cultivating" the charters' articles – which is merely a way of saying we must break with the continuist-organicist paradigm that fuels common law ideology (rather than trying to somehow return to this paradigm from within our neoliberal present). This is not to say that we should be inattentive to the ways in which "customary rights" (pawnage, estovers, chiminage, etc.) acquired new meanings in and through the struggles that punctuate English history, but we cannot let this evolutionary history distract us from the fact that our contemporary struggles cannot be won by reviving older notions of the commons, even if on a new social basis; nor can we succeed by establishing new commons based on old models, as if new political rights based on the actualization of the so-called "social message" of the two charters are all we really need in order to achieve our ends. The Magna Carta of 1215 is not a declaration of civil and political rights *avant la lettre*, and the 1225 Charter of the Forest is not a declaration of social rights that function like the universal rights of the poor that economically propped up the Magna Carta's more formal political rights. It is simply too easy to *a priori* reduce neoliberalism to "an economic doctrine of globalization and privatization," and then interpret the Magna Carta as a challenge to neoliberalism on the pretext that the former is all about placing "limits [on] privatization."[96] If, for instance, we think of neoliberalism as a mode of life organized around the principle of competition,[97] then the recognition of our singular historical situation should give us pause when it comes to hasty approximations with these kinds of quixotic legal paradigms.

We must stress, then, that any analogy between the dismemberment of the commons from the fifteenth to the seventeenth centuries and contemporary struggles is bound to be misleading, and even politically harmful. As we have already established, today's digital "knowledge commons" are not analogous to the agrarian commons during the period of primitive accumulation, and so today's race for patents should not be viewed as simply a "new wave of enclosures." Because the agricultural commons were an outgrowth of older manorial customs, they were embedded in a network of personal dependencies at the local level in which individuals were inscribed in a plurality of communities that overlapped in very complex ways. And while it is true that the Charter of the Forest historically preceded the ideological narrative of common law as undergoing an indefinite process of "self-perfection," we cannot detach the charter from its specific historical and social context, least we merely supplant the myth of the uninterrupted growth of common law with another myth. And finally, if only to confirm what we have just asserted, not all "customary" rights are "progressive": there are some customs (notably inheritance rights) that are in themselves obstacles to the constitution of a substantial law of the common, insofar as rights of inheritance contradict the necessity of communal practices (commoning). Ultimately, it is the double relation between common law and customs on the one hand, and customs and the common on the other, that needs to be re-examined with an eye to the histories and the practices they help bring to light.

Custom, Common, Common Law

What became immediately clear from the moment we began this genealogical examination is the frustrating ambiguity of the concept of "custom." As E.P. Thompson reminds us, custom is first and foremost the *law of place* (*lex loci*). Custom is always attached to a specific county or land, whether this space is a manor, a parish, a riverbank, a reserve of oysters in an estuary, a park, a mountain pasture, a forest, etc. We might then, in this respect, follow Thomas Paine's lead and deplore the absurdity of grounding rights in geography or in inanimate matter, rather than inscribing rights to people independent of their geographical location.[98] Yet, whatever our view on the matter, the fact is that custom and customary rights were first and foremost grounded in places, not people. And it is precisely for this reason that customs were so extremely variable. At one analytical extreme, we find customs that were rigidly defined and fixed as a result of the strong influence of various local courts. In the middle of the spectrum, we find customs that were less exact and whose definitions were variably reproduced through oral tradition (such as the annual or biannual process through which the boundaries of a common were re-assessed and confirmed). And at the other extreme, customs existed in a state of constant confusion, in which unwritten beliefs mingled with improvised rules and *ad hoc* practices that were never codified. Customs were also frequently subject to temporal as well as geographical conditions: a tract of land, for instance, might be open to common use at a certain date and only for a certain length of time.[99] In general, the commoners themselves developed a rich variety of temporal and geographical communitarian institutions and sanctions that created certain restrictions on the uses of the common – all of which, by the way, undermine Garrett Hardin's narrative of agrarian commons as an unregulated free-for-all.[100]

It would therefore appear that custom as *lex loci* is, at the same time, *praxis loci*, although it must be admitted that the latter always seems bound or restrained by the former to some extent. The best way to put it, then, would be to say that custom is situated at the interface of praxis and law – or, rather, custom is itself this interface insofar as custom is both praxis and law and the same time.[101] To get a sense of this overlap, Thompson gives us the following passage from S. Carter's *Lex Custumaria* (1696):

> For a custom taketh beginning and groweth to perfection in this manner. When a reasonable Act once done is found to be good, and beneficial to the People, and agreeable to their nature and disposition, then do they use it and practice it again and again, and so by often iteration and multiplication of the Act, it becomes a Custom; and being continued without interruption time out of mind, it obtaineth the force of law.[102]

As Thompson points out, this author identifies four "pillars" of custom: antiquity, continuance, certainty, and reason. Further along in his account, Thompson cites Coke (1641) on the topic of customs to the same effect: "customs are defined to be a law or right not written; which, being established by long use and the consent of our ancestors, hath been and is daily practiced."[103] "If Coke's definition be followed," as Thompson writes, "then in many parishes the exercise of minor rights of common might have been proved by antiquity, continuance, certainly, and reason as well as those of the landholders and customary tenants."[104] If we compare the two definitions, a distinction appears that sheds some light on the ambiguity of custom: Carter expressly made "reason" one of the determining elements in the formation of custom. Coke does not. The question this raises is whether custom is reasonable in itself or whether this only applies to specific customs; and, concomitantly, how is one to practically discriminate between a reasonable and unreasonable custom? For as we have seen, the Magna Carta was not confined to consecrating the ancient customs that prevailed at the time of

Henry II: it also stated, in Article 48, that all "evil customs" will be abolished without specifying whether the term "evil customs" was simply just another term for "new customs."

At the same time, however, this ambiguity clarifies (somewhat) the relation between custom and common law: rather than "allowing" or "confirming" customs that were deemed to be "reasonable" and "certain," common law could only "reject" a custom if the latter did not meet these standards – especially the standard of "reason" – and only if a case was brought before the common law courts. In his commentaries, Blackstone goes so far as to establish a list of reasons for identifying good customs: antiquity, continuity, peaceable use, unreasonableness, certainty, compulsory (not optional), and consistency.[105] The terms "reasonable" and "unreasonable" may well have been professional jargon ("legal terms of art"), but as Thompson puts it, "on a very brief view of case law they were gates through which a large flock of other considerations might come baaing and grunting onto the fields of the common law."[106] Thompson mentions the "Gateward case" (1607) as particularly exemplary of the attitude of the common law courts toward the customary use rights enjoyed by the poorest inhabitants. The court rejected the defense of a man who pleaded before the common law court in the town of Stixwold (Lincolnshire) to justify his occupation of a house on the grounds that he had no interest in the house. The court argued that the claim was "unreasonable" because it lacked both the "certainty" and "continuance" of custom, and so, on the ground of reasonableness, the court added, "no improvements can be made in any wastes, if such common should be allowed."[107] Thompson points out that this argument about "improvement," which formed the basis of many subsequent judgments, effectively "licensed a motorway to carry political economy across the commons."[108]

In the later decades of the seventeenth and eighteenth century, the courts increasingly argued that the land or soil of a lord was his personal property, and "if the Lord's access to any part of 'his' soil should be restricted, 'this will be a ready way to enable tenants to withstand all improvements'" – an example of the now-entrenched Gateward precedent.[109]

The interval separating Coke and Blackstone (about a century and a half) thus witnessed a hardening and sedimentation of the notion of land ownership and a reification of the uses of properties that could henceforth be rented, sold, and bequeathed. A good metric for the importance of this change is the title Blackstone gave to the second volume of his *Commentaries on the Laws of England* – namely, *Of Rights of Things*. It is not that the idea of the "rights of things" was itself a novelty, but the fact that the treatise's title reflects the growing importance of the market, which is again manifest in the fact that Blackstone referred not to the rights *to* things, but the rights *of* things. This title speaks volumes about the strange, hybrid character of the law in England in the eighteenth century. In effect, the rights and uses that were once attached to a function or a place were now considered to be attached to "things," whose rights often superseded the rights of people: for instance, the guardian function of a forest or park could now be sold, with the powers, advantages, and rights attached to it.[110] But, contrary to what a certain historical and documentary record has taught us, this evolution of the law was not without strife, and confrontation continued well into the seventeenth century. Rights linked to the uses of the common gave rise, especially during the first six decades of the eighteenth century, to multiform and continuous struggles, and riots were far from a rare occurrence. In 1724, for instance, a quarrel over the right to use wood in Rockingham Forest led to an armed encounter in the forest between the parishes of Weldon and Brigstock: men loyal to Lord Gowran of Brigstock pulled down several trees and the parish tenants were sent with carts to carry the wood away. More than two hundred men and women from Weldon suddenly appeared in the forest, armed with hatchets, axes, and sticks, shouting and threatening to overturn the carts, frightening the horses, and carrying off some of the "lops and tops."[111]

The history of the communal forests in the English countryside is full of anecdotes such as these. Jeanette Neeson's historical work on the resistance to the enclosures in Northamptonshire shows that these kinds of insurrection were just one part of a much wider effort that included lobbying, letter writing, petitions, inspectors, the destruction of archives and minutes, arson, the demolition of walls, and, of course, the efforts of the parliamentary opposition itself. These forms of resistance could last for years after enclosures were erected.[112] The relentless restriction of the commons also provoked disputes within the legal field during this period, and these disputes often gave rise to legal decisions that are difficult to reconcile. In 1689, for instance, the court in Chancery decided to allow the majority of landowners to regulate and restrict a common, even if one or two "humoursome tenants" refused to agree. A new case then arose in 1706 in Gloucestershire, in which landowners agreed to reduce the common by 5,000 acres, but the parish rector and nine other persons opposed it. This case obviously involved much more than one or two "humoursome fellows," since the court decided "a right of the common cannot be altered without the consent of all parties concerned therein."[113] Unfortunately, it is difficult to get an appreciation of the various forms of protest and resistance, since they were rarely mentioned in the archives of the central administration or the London newspapers. In this respect, the correspondence between estate stewards and their absent masters often tells us much more about these acts of resistance than do official reports. Robert Walpole, for example, who was the Secretary at War in 1710, received a letter from his steward, John Wrott, describing a major confrontation over common rights in the Bedingfield Common: in opposition to the High Sheriff of Northamptonshire, Lord Cardigan, and other mounted gentry, "the mob began to gather from all corners, some in disguise with masks, and in women's cloaks, and others with axes, spades, pickaxes, etc."[114] While the crowd was momentarily dispersed, according to the steward, "they still persist to say the Right of Common is theirs, & next year they hope to see the Hedges demolished."[115] All these cases, and many others, sufficiently show that the struggle of the poor to defend their common use rights was both obstinate and enduring. It was not until approximately 1850 that resistance was finally overcome and the last "open" fields were, almost without exception, enclosed.[116]

The "War in the Woods" and *The Black Act* (1723)

The so-called "war in the woods" was a paradigmatic episode of the resistance that arose in response to attacks on customary rights, and it shows us how forest laws incited protracted conflict throughout the eighteenth century. This particular moment of insurrection was a response to the adoption of the Law of 9, George I c.22, "which came to be known as 'The Waltham Black Act' or simply 'The Black Act.'"[117] The Black Act was put into force in May 1723 and it was met with lively and tenacious resistance until it was finally repealed in 1823. The law was extremely severe: in one stroke, The Black Act created fifty new capital offenses corresponding to a variety of different crimes. Amongst the principle offenses were "hunting, wounding or stealing red or fallow deer, and the poaching of hares, conies, or fish."[118] These offenses were punishable by death "if the persons offending were armed or disguised": the law selectively targeted any person "armed with swords, fire-arms, or other offensive weapons, and having his or their faces blacked" (hence the offenders were referred to as "Blacks") who were found in any "forest, chase, park, or enclosed ground 'wherein any deer have been or shall be usually kept,' or in any warren, or on any high road, heath, common or down."[119] And in order to expedite the legal process, other clauses were added that "overrode customary procedure and the defenses of the subject."[120]

The first question that immediately comes to mind is what could have possibly motivated the adoption of such a draconian law without debate, and with unanimous consent, in the House of Commons? In the early eighteenth century there was marked unrest in the Windsor Forest and in certain forest districts around Hampshire. In March of 1720, an official proclamation mentions the practice of night hunting while disguised in the Windsor Forest:

> Fourteen men on horseback, armed with guns, together with two men on foot with a greyhound, had coursed red deer in the late afternoon in Bigshot Walk, with their faces blacked, and some of them with "straw hats and other deformed habits." Four deer were killed, and a keeper was threatened.[121]

In February 1723 another, more sensational proclamation asserted that "great numbers of disorderly agitated and ill-designed persons" had associated under the name "Blacks" in the counties of Berkshire and Hampshire: "they were armed, broke into forests and parks, killed and carried off deer, rescued offenders from the constables, sent menacing letters to gentlemen demanding venison and money, and threatening murder or the burning of houses, barns and haystacks."[122] As Thompson observes, comparable encounters between keepers and poachers during the eighteenth and early nineteenth centuries, in many countries, were at least as bloody, if not bloodier, as these "blackening" episodes. But, as Thompson puts it, "this was not the point":

> What made the 'emergency' was the repeated public humiliation of the authorities; the simultaneous attacks upon royal and private property; the sense of a confederated movement which was enlarging its social demands, especially under "King John"; [and] the symptoms of something close to class warfare.[123]

The Blacks received the support of the forest communities "for a year or two," and it was the "displacement of authority, not the mere crime of deer theft" that made the passage of the new "emergency" law so urgent for state leaders. For Sir Robert Walpole and a hardcore faction of the Whigs, the situation created by these insurrectionists was an opportunity to turn property into an almost absolute value, and they would use terror to meet their ends if necessary.

If nothing else, the episode reveals some rather interesting conflicts internal to the law itself. The Windsor Forest – of which only a few manorial areas were owned by the Crown – housed a complex economy subject to forest law. Over the centuries, the interests of the high nobility and the local nobility clashed with the forest's customary occupants who made claims for the right of "unrestricted grazing, timber, and peat-cutting on their commons."[124] An imposing bureaucracy of forest agents was charged with enforcing the forest laws, but "the position of all of these officials was complex, since they operated half within forest law, and half within statute law."[125] Because "the existence of forest law provided an alibi for the infrequent use of statute law,"[126] forest court judges were reluctant to apply the state laws to offenses committed in the forest, and this resulted in a relative relaxing of forest authority. After 1716, however, forest law was applied much more strictly and forest courts were consequently re-activated. The emergence of "blacking" should therefore be seen as a "response to the attempted reactivation of a relaxed forest authority."[127] The Blacks, in other words, were "armed foresters, enforcing the definition of rights to which the 'country people' had become habituated."[128] In the forests of Hampshire, for instance, where the royal presence was weak, the Church controlled most of the property, and customary tenures or timber rights were the principle sources of conflict between the bishops and the tenants during the early eighteenth century. The tenants complained that prosecutors, who also acted as judges, diverted from and broke with custom to their advantage. In several cases, judgments were rendered against the tenants, who were then forbidden to cut wood without a permit (except for repairs). The poorest farmers and foresters thus responded with direct action in order to protect their rights, especially over common lands and chases. In 1729, the General Surveyor of Woods observed "that the country people everywhere think they have some sort of right to the wood and timber in the forests." It was difficult to determine, in his view, "whether the notion may have been delivered down to them by tradition, from the times when these forests were declared to be such by the Crown, when there were great struggles and contests about them."[129]

What was the outcome of these wars of the forests? When the commissioners came to inspect the state of the forests in 1809, the inhabitants of the Windsor Forest had succeeded in preserving many of their communal rights, such as "the right to turn cows, horses, sheep, and pigs on the forest without limitation as to numbers . . . the right to cut turf, fern, and heath, and to take gravel and sand, with little restraint [and they had even enlarged] their claims upon browse wood, fallen timber, 'lops and tops,' and rootage."[130] But the fact is these inhabitants only obtained a short "reprieve" concerning various "pre-capitalist use-rights over the land." The forest court, where these rights were upheld, were coming into increasingly direct confrontation with "the idea of absolute ownership" that was fast becoming the foundation of the English legal system in the eighteenth century.[131] Nevertheless, this history of resistance tells us much about the nature of law and its different uses. There is no doubt the Whig oligarchy used the law to strengthen its class rule, both by creating new laws and by bending older juridical forms to its advantage. But the reality is that several competing definitions of the law confronted each other on the juridical plane during this period: "for as long as it remained possible, the ruled – if they could find a purse and a lawyer – would actually fight for their rights by means of the law."[132] Thompson thus challenges the tendency of a "highly schematic Marxism" to reduce the law to a mere "superstructure":

> If we look closely in such an agrarian context, the distinction between law, on the one hand, conceived as an element of "superstructure," and the actualities of the productive forces and relations on the other hand, becomes more and more untenable. For law was often a definition of actual agrarian *practice*, as it had been pursued "time out of mind."[133]

For Thompson, the law is "deeply imbricated within the very basis of productive relations, which would have been inoperable without this law."[134] Viewed from this perspective, the various forest wars reveal "the immense capital of human struggle ... in the forms and traditions of the law" transmitted to the eighteenth century from the two previous centuries: "for in the sixteenth and seventeenth centuries the law had been less an instrument of class power than a central arena of conflict."[135] For Thompson, then, it is crucial to hold on to the distinction between arbitrary power and the rule of law. In Thompson's view, the latter is nothing less than "a cultural achievement of universal significance" and "an unqualified good."[136]

Custom as a Site of Conflict

What lessons can we draw from this historical and political analysis? Two closely connected conclusions seem to present themselves immediately. The first conclusion is the fact that national common law was never simply the "shaping" of local customs to meet common concerns. In this respect, the "reason" at play in the decisions of judges and legal experts was not merely a matter of codifying customs on the basis of their longevity or antiquity. Rather, the actions and decisions of legal experts were largely dependent on the ways in which various courts interpreted the standard of "reasonableness." And many judges, in this respect, shared the views of the landowners, especially the latter's concern for "improvement," which is precisely what gave them the air of "reasonable men."[137] Thus, contrary to the claims of common law ideology, legal expertise did not merely "discover" and "declare" a law already embedded in traditional culture and mores, but rather expertise actively shaped and produced common law by trampling, if necessary, upon the criteria of antiquity and by disqualifying commoners through imprecise terms like "occupants," "parishioners," "inhabitants," "residents," etc. The relationship between common law and custom was thus somewhat confused within the legal field. A case before the Court of the King's Bench in 1766 clearly demonstrates the kinds of confusion that could arise in this context. The case dealt with persons who had "gleaned" from a partially harvested field of barley. Lord Mansfield ruled that "stealing, under the color of leasing or gleaning, is not to be justified, while another judge ruled that "the right of leasing does appear in our books."[138] The same issue re-surfaced in 1788 when charges were brought before Mary Houghton, the widow of John Houghton, for gleaning in an enclosed field in Timworth (Suffolk). It seems the case was not argued according to custom but was rather tried on the basis of the universal recognition of right in English common law. But, as Thompson notes, even displacing the charges from the field of custom to that of common law did not rid the defense of the difficulties, since, "if this custom were part of the common law of the realm, it would prevail in every part of the kingdom, and be of general and uniform practice."[139] In any case, custom remained *lex loci* despite the judgments rendered by the courts: "while case law now decided that gleaning could not be claimed as a right in common law, the right might still be claimed as local right, by the custom of the manor or by village by-law."[140] Generally speaking, then, common law decisions did not immediately impact local customary practice.[141] In fact "communal aspirations" – such as common pastures – persisted well until the eighteenth century, where they "co-existed with the most scrupulous regulation of common rights and stints by village by-laws (and *lex loci* of manorial courts) and by rigorous definitions of common rights (appendant, appurtenant, of gross, and by vincinage) at national law,"[142] such that customs appeared to conflict with the law. We can see, then, that nothing could be more misleading than simply identifying common law with national customary laws, nor the self-representation of common law as essentially deriving from custom.

The second important lesson to draw from this analysis flows directly from the first: if this was indeed the relationship between common law and customary use rights, it is precisely because custom was always a site of latent or open conflict between social forces. Again, we are forced to agree with Thompson on this point:

> The uncodified English common law offered an alternative notation of law, in some ways more flexible and unprincipled – and therefore more pliant to the "common sense" of the ruling class – in other ways more available as a medium through which social conflict could find expression, especially where the sense of "natural justice" of the jury could make itself felt.[143]

As early as the thirteenth century, common rights were exercised according to a "time-hallowed custom," and they were disputed according to "time-hallowed ways."[144] Conflicts over "botes" and "estovers" were constant, such that by the eighteenth century there was not "a forest or chase in the country which did not have some dramatic episode of conflict over common rights."[145] Citing the complaints expressed by the tenants of the Cumberland Manor in Askham in 1803 – "violations of our *Antient Custni* has always felt very painfull to us, and embittered many hours of our lives" – a Dr. Searle offers the following remark:

> Custom, then, was not something fixed and immutable, carrying the same body of meaning for both social classes. On the contrary, its definition was highly variable in relation to class position, and accordingly it became a vehicle for conflict not consensus.[146]

The spirit of these customs in common is especially well summarized by Thompson, and so it is worth citing him again at some length:

> Agrarian custom was never fact. It was ambiance. It may best be understood with the aid of Bourdieu's concept of "habitus" – a lived environment comprised of practices, inherited expectations, rules which both determined limits to usages and disclosed possibilities, norms and sanctions both of law and neighbourhood pressures. The profile of common right usages will vary from parish to parish according to innumerable variables: the economy of crop and stock, the extent of common and waste, demographic pressures, by-employments, vigilant or absentee landowners, the role of the church, strict or lax court-keeping, the contiguity of forest, fen or chase, the balance of greater and lesser landholders.[147]

We must, therefore, recognize that the common as custom was always an activity that produced and confirmed the law, and that its conflictual character was not contingent but *constitutive*. Instead of trying to establish an erroneous parallel between the commons of yesteryear and the commons of today, based on the positive characteristics of their respective contents, we must rather fully recognize the antagonistic dimension of the commons in our present situation: *the common is never simply a matter of "managing" a "good" or a "resource," but is grounded in an activity that constructs the common in and through conflict*. This is why we prefer the word "common" as a verb rather than a noun,[148] or, if it cannot be avoided, to make the noun denote a *sui generis* form of activity. The question that now arises is how to discriminate amongst customs themselves, such that it is possible to submit customs to what we might call the "test of the common as practice." Neither the "common reason" of juridical expertise, nor common sense, in the sense of that which transcends the merely local because it is common to all members of the nation – which are the two meanings of the "common" that, as we have seen, exist side by side in common law ideology – are sufficient for constituting the common. The question, therefore, is to very precisely determine the nature of this necessary practice of the common: for only this type of practice can make common law a *law of the common* – i.e., a law founded on the principle of the common and therefore a law that is not reducible to the codification of custom solely on the basis of a custom's antiquity. Once it is recognized that longevity and antiquity are not the supreme basis of the law – which is to say the test of the common is not duration but social practice – what remains is only to determine the nature of this practice and the corresponding forms of subjectivity this practice produces.

8

The "Customary Law of Poverty"

In the autumn of 1842, Marx published a series of five articles (from October 25 to November 3) in the *Rheinische Zeitung* concerning a law passed by the Rhine Provincial Assembly that outlawed the collection of fallen wood. This was called, appropriately enough, the "Law on the Theft of Wood." These early Marxian texts are usually only referenced for their biographical relevance: they showcase Marx's unique ability to combine the virtuosity of the pamphleteer with the argumentative sophistication of a lawyer. But for us, these texts should be seen as more than merely an early stage in Marx's eventual political development. For these five articles directly touch on the problem we have identified in the previous chapter, namely the problem of knowing what makes a customary "common law" a true "law of the common."

In Article 1, Section 1, the Rhine law states:

> the regulations enacted in this law with respect to the theft of wood include the following:
>
> 1. Any wood in any forest not yet felled.
> 2. Any green wood, outside the forests, intended for exploitation.
> 3. Any wood accidentally cut or overturned in whole trunks whose adjustment has not yet begun.
> 4. Any tree cuttings in the forest or in underdeveloped wooded areas.[1]

What is at issue in the passage of this law is both the legal characterization of "theft" as pertaining to the practice of collecting fallen or dead wood (which was previously considered a collective right), as well as the associated notion of property as primarily grounded in private and exclusive enjoyment. In fact, the Rhine law characterizes the collection of twigs and wood from the forest as a premeditated activity that is not categorically different from the theft of someone else's wood.[2] It is worth noting from the outset that an attack on customary use rights such as this was far from unusual in Europe at the time. By way of comparison, the French Forest Code of 1827, enacted under Charles X, reduced or removed use rights for the inhabitants of France's forests, whether the forests were state-owned or communal. The code states that inhabitants "will no longer be able to collect or gather: grass, dead leaves used to smoke poor soils, heather and broom, fruits (blueberries, mushrooms ...) and even fawns and acorns from which the poor made oil and even a kind of coffee."[3] And the collection of wood was itself severely regulated: "the peasant cannot collect wood, dead or green, nor of course cut trees; all infractions will be severely punished."[4] The code also limited the range, in terms of both time and space, in which animals were allowed to graze on forest undergrowth. The application of these provisions, especially restrictions on the collection of firewood and wood used for construction material, meant that many of the essential needs of communities were no longer met. Peasants were also often completely bankrupted by the code's heavy fines, and municipalities were forced to bear the increased financial burden of paying guards to enforce the laws. In the mountains of l'Ariège, for instance, the peasants were so angered that they disguised themselves as women and violently confronted the guards and soldiers tasked with enforcing the law: "it was the War of the Maidens, and lasted from May 1829 to the summer of 1830."[5]

The legal re-classification of wood collection as "theft" was, for Marx, clear evidence that the law was crafted to benefit the private interests of the forest owners. The landowners wanted to profit from the dead and fallen wood by selling it on what was then a booming firewood market, but this of course meant they had to dispossess the poorest peasants who customarily collected this wood and sold it themselves to make a living.[6] For those interested in protecting the rights of the poor peasantry, the difficulty they immediately faced revolved around the clear temptation to appeal to older feudal laws as a means of critiquing these modern, private property statutes. On the one hand, Marx did not hesitate at all to approvingly cite the Order of the Criminal Court of the sixteenth century, which stated that the theft of wood involves only the "removal of cut wood and illegal felling," and that the removal of fruits that are eaten during the same day is liable for civil punishment, but not criminal prosecution. As Marx writes, "the supreme penal code of the sixteenth century requests us to defend it against the charge of excessive humanity made by a Rhine Province Assembly of the nineteenth century, and *we comply with this request*."[7] Marx thus challenged the legal distinction between collecting fallen wood and the theft of wood, and – his reference to the Order of the Criminal Court aside – he was determined to do so without any reliance on feudal nostalgia. In the first of the five articles he published in the *Rheinische Zeitung* on the theft-of-wood law, Marx denounced feudalism in general as a "*spiritual animal kingdom*," and he denounced the customary rights of the privileged in particular as merely an "animal form" of the law.[8] As anyone who has read these articles knows, it can be rather difficult at times to follow the twists and turns of Marx's argument: Marx works here upon several registers all at once and marshals support from opposing discourses in German philosophy of law (Hegel and Savigny specifically). It is more than likely that the complexity of Marx's approach stemmed from the difficulty he faced in terms of differentiating his critique from more mainstream positions. As Mikhaïl Xifaras recognizes, Marx was confronted with a very specific dilemma: "how to critique a law that was obviously passed in the sole interest of rich property owners in the forest, and which deprives the poor of an essential resource, without appearing to defend a feudal conception of property?"[9]

We can schematically distinguish two general positions amongst those in favor of the Rhine law. On the one side, Count von Trips was in favor of this re-categorization of "theft" on the grounds that it is precisely due to the absence of this criminal charge that wood is removed so frequently. On the other side of the debate, a liberal politician named Brust argued that the collection of wood should rather be categorized as an abuse of rights – in this case an abuse of co-ownership or a usufruct – which would have at least meant formal recognition of the fact that the peasants enjoy a "usufructuary right of usage."[10] In contrast to both these positions, however, Marx argued that the collection of wood should not be an offense at all, and this argument can be fully legally justified. In the first of his five articles, and just after positively referencing the sixteenth-century Order of the Criminal Court, Marx strenuously highlights the essential difference between the act of collecting twigs and the premeditated theft of wood. Indeed, he infers an important legal distinction from this opposition: "if it must be admitted that the two actions are essentially different, it can hardly be maintained that they are identical from the legal standpoint."[11] To make his case, Marx argues that we must distinguish not between *two* actions, but between *three*: the appropriation of green wood, the removal of cut wood, and the collecting of fallen or dead wood. The first action suggests the wood was violently torn from "its organic supports," and in this sense constitutes an attack on the owner of the wood insofar as it is an attack on the tree itself. The second act is a form of theft because the wood is already the product of the owner insofar as it was the owner who had already cut the wood. There is no question, then, that these two acts infringe on property. The third action, however, does not infringe on property at all: the dead wood or branches have already been separated from the tree – or separated from the object of property – and the accidental falling of the branches is not an infringement of property. In other words, the collector of fallen wood takes possession of that which no longer belongs to the tree and its owner. At the center of Marx's argument is a certain conception of the relationship between the law and the nature of things, or what Marx enigmatically refers to as the "legal nature of things" (*die rechtliche Natur der Dinge*): "the legal nature of things cannot be regulated according to the law; on the contrary, the law must be regulated according to the legal nature of things." The law, in this sense, is "the universal and authentic exponent of the legal nature of things."[12] Rather than conforming to the legal nature of things (as the very concept of the law demands), the law prohibiting the theft of wood contravenes it.

Two argumentative threads develop out of this conceptual architecture. First, Marx argues that the Rhine law merely codifies the private interests of forest owners, and so Marx denounces the law on account of its partiality and its incompatibility with the constitutive universality of true law. The second argumentative thread invokes a normative distinction between the customs of the "privileged" and the customs of the "poor," and Marx argues that only the latter is worthy of legal codification. What tends to prevail in Marx's critique, then, is not so much a rational concept of law or the state, but an argument about the specific relation between custom and "nature," and it is a rather original attempt to overcome the antinomy between public (or universal) law and customary law, which we briefly discussed at the beginning of the previous chapter. Let's then examine these two argumentative threads in order to map out the manner in which they overlap, and then we will try to ascertain the effects of this overlap in terms of the intelligibility of the law in its different forms.

A "Law" Contrary to "Rational Law"

It is not too difficult to identify the influence of Hegel within the first of Marx's argumentative threads. The speculative theory of law had already distinguished between "real" or empirically existing law, and "effective" or "rational" law: the latter denotes the concept of law proper as it exists within positive law, and it is what makes it possible to critique that which is "irrational" in actually existing laws as contradicting law's ideal universality.[13] For Marx, this is precisely the problem with the Rhine Province Assembly's law on the theft of wood. While it is undeniably a "real" law (in the sense that it actually exists), it nonetheless contradicts "effective" or "rational" law insofar as it does not fully embody the concept of law in its empirical manifestation. As Xifaras puts it, "the concept of law itself is based on universality, or in this case on the equality of all citizens insofar as they are members of the state, and thus a concept of law that *applies only to property owners* is irrational."[14] By punishing a "social *irregularity*" or, at most, a "*contravention of a police regulation*" as a crime, the law fails to realize that the "basis of the state is undermined if misfortune becomes a crime or crime becomes a misfortune," and, from this point of view, the Provincial Assembly "does not observe even the elementary rules of legislation."[15] By perceiving criminal malfeasance in "he who commits infractions within the woods," the law demonstrates the extent to which it is exclusively driven by private interest. As Marx puts it, "the petty, wooden, mean and selfish soul of interest sees only one point, the point in which it is wounded."[16] Contrarily, if the state is to live up to its concept, it will

> regard even an infringer of forest regulations as a human being, a living member of the state, one in whom its heart's blood flows, a soldier who has to defend his Fatherland, a witness whose voice must be heard by the court, a member of the community with public duties to perform, the father of a family, whose existence is sacred, and, above all, a citizen of the state. The state will not light-heartedly exclude one of its members from all these functions, for the state amputates itself whenever it turns a citizen into a criminal.[17]

But he for whom the "inhuman" has become a "supreme essence," in the form of an "external object" or an "alien material essence" (i.e., wood), can only himself be inhuman and only capable of "*legislation inspired by self-interest,* and therefore by *cowardice*."[18] This critique runs through all five of Marx's articles on the theft-of wood-law. In the last lines of the article from November 3, 1842, Marx ironically adopts the point of view of the "savages" of Cuba and channels their perspective on this debate (had they been seated in the Rhine legislature): "would they not have regarded *wood* as the *Rhinelanders' fetish*," just as the indigenous Cubans viewed gold as the Spaniards' fetish?[19]

Marx's fourth article on the law further describes the legislature's inability to achieve the impartiality demanded by the very concept of law as such. Specifically, Marx hones in on a section of the law that confers the task of evaluating the worth of stolen wood to the local forest ranger (as opposed to the French Code, for instance, which tasked the forest ranger with catching the thief, while evaluation of the stolen property was determined by an independent body).[20] The law specifically stipulates that if a theft of wood occurs more than two miles from a royal district, "the *warden who makes the charge* determine[s] the *value* according to the existing local price."[21] As Marx asserts on this point, "it is obvious from an examination of the qualifications of the warden who makes the charge how little he is objectively able to be at the same time the valuer of the stolen wood."[22] For how could the forest warden be both the protector of the wood and the agent charged with evaluating the wood? By imposing a value on the wood, is the warden not also imposing "*his own value*," which is to say "his own activity"?[23] And how could the warden, "as the guardian of wood," both "protect the interests of the private owner" and, "as valuer," "protect the interests of the infringer of forest regulations against the extravagant demands of the private owner?"[24] And since the warden is also the "denouncer," "the charge he draws up is a denunciation" and thus the "value of the object ... becomes the subject matter of the denunciation."[25] The warden therefore "loses his dignity as a judge" because of his "function [as] denouncer."[26] And finally, entrusting the warden-as-denouncer, who "is in the pay and service of the forest owner," with the task of evaluating the stolen timber amounts to "leav[ing] the valuation, under oath, to the forest owner himself."[27] And in true partisan spirit, the Rhine Provincial Assembly also undermined "the sole provision which constitutes the last semblance of the state's power in the realm of forest glory, namely *life appointment* of the denouncing wardens."[28] According to the deputies who spoke in favor of eliminating life appointments for guards, life appointments were too financially burdensome for small forest owners who could not afford to hire a permanent warden.

Marx then asks if the relation between the state and the accused (the forest offender) should be defined on the basis of the resources of the forest owner. If, argues Marx, "the state has a right against the accused" it is "because it confronts him as a state," and thus it is dutifully compelled to act toward the criminal as a state: "the state has not only the means to act in a way which is as appropriate to its reason, its universality, and its dignity as it is to the right, the life and the property of the incriminated citizen; it is its absolute duty to possess and apply these means."[29] However, instead of drawing this conclusion, the Assembly deputies inverted this rationale: "it was concluded that since private property does not have means to raise itself to the standpoint of the state, the latter is obliged to lower itself to the irrational and illegal means of private property."[30] In Marx's view, one could not imagine a more complete degradation of the state, insofar as this action is in complete contradiction with its concept: "private interest. . . is bound to degrade the state to the thoughts of private interests."[31] This "sophistry of private interest" reaches its apogee in the remarks made by an urban deputy, who declared "every *spur* to loyal fulfillment of duty is *paralyzed* by life appointment."[32] As Marx aptly argues, whenever the warden is tasked with evaluating stolen wood, private interest "puts on its rose-colored spectacles" and manifests a "naïve, excessive confidence"; but when it comes to evaluating the same warden's sense of duty, private interest now dons its "world-wise dark spectacles of practice" and manifests an "abusive, censorious distrust."[33] By demanding the warden be entirely subject to the arbitrariness of the forest owner, the owners in fact demonstrate that they really only have confidence in themselves, as is aptly attested by the logic that "turns the servant of the forest owner into a state authority, [and] *turns the authority of the state into a servant of the forest owner*."[34]

And thirdly, the law passed by the Rhine Provincial Assembly seriously questions "the notion of public punishment."[35] Article 14 of the law reads as follows: "all fines for the theft of wood, even if they are paid by several persons in the case of co-perpetrators, accomplices, or beneficiaries, all accrue to the forest owners, as well as any forced labour in the case of insolvent convicts." The law thus obliges the thief to pay fines in addition to reimbursing the amount of stolen value, value that of course is determined by the forest warden. These fines are therefore a punishment imposed on the thief by public law. As Marx writes:

> *Punishment* as such, the restoration of the law, which must certainly be distinguished from restitution of the value and compensation for loss, the restoration of private property, is transformed from a *public punishment* into a *private compensation*, the fines going not to the state treasury, but to the private coffers of the forest owner.[36]

For Marx, then, the law clearly enters into open contradiction with the demands of legal formalism. As Marx reminds us, public punishment is "a right of the state, but it is a right which the state can no more transfer to private persons than one person can hand over his conscience to another."[37] But the matter is more serious still. Article 16 of the law stipulates that if "the fine cannot be recovered due to the indigence of the perpetrator or the persons responsible in his place, the fine will be replaced by forced labour or a term of imprisonment that, under no circumstances, shall be less than 48 hours." And, further, Article 19 adds: "the forced labour which the condemned person must perform firstly consists of forestry labour for the forest owner." This last proposition is nothing but the capture of the state by the private interests of the forest owners. For even after Article 4, which allows the forest warden to determine the value of the stolen wood, and Article 14, which directs fines toward the coffers of the private forest owners (and which retrospectively confers on Article 4 its true meaning, since the evaluator effectively taxes on behalf of his employer), it is in Article 19 that "the mask is discarded and a claim is advanced not only for money, but for the criminal himself, not only for the man's purse, but for himself."[38] In other words, just as Article 14 revealed the truth of Article 4, so too does Article 19 reveal the true nature of Article 14, insofar as the fines themselves now become the forest owner's right to exact forced labor, which is to say the "*temporary serfdom of the debtor*." The "forest owner," writes Marx, "has [now] cleverly concealed that he has adjudged himself the right of *punishment itself*"; it is because the fines are not simply a sum money but a form of punishment that the owner can secure the condemned "body and soul." The forest owner has thus succeeded in "converting a public right into his private property" by using the wood thief to situate "himself in the place of the state."[39]

In his final article, then, Marx is thus perfectly justified in summarizing his critique in the following terms: "our whole account has shown how the Assembly degrades the executive power, the administrative authorities, the life of the accused, the idea of the state, crime itself, and punishment as well, to *material means of private interest*."[40] The core of Marx's critique thus lies in the clash between private interests and the principles of law: in this affair, it is interest that has ultimately been imposed on the law, such that "private interest lay down laws to the law where the law had laid down laws to private interest."[41] By sacrificing the "interest of right" to the "right of interest," the law adopted by the Rhine Provincial Assembly denounces itself as "of no value," or an "empty mask," since it amounts to giving the form of law a content that is in contradiction with the universality and objectivity that necessarily belongs to the rational concept of the law. Thus, for Marx, "the whole law was an *exception to the law*."[42]

The dialectical inversion of the existing law through an appeal to the concept of law undoubtedly owes much to Hegel. It should be noted, however, that Marx's line of argumentation diverges from its Hegelian orientation in one crucial respect. As Xifaras observes, the Rhine Provincial Assembly's attempt to elevate the contents of private interest to the form of law should not have been unexpected, given the fact that the Assembly is nothing other than "an *Assembly of the Estates of particular interests*."[43] Since 1832, in both Prussia and Austria, three social "estates" were represented in the provincial assemblies – the nobility, the city, and the countryside – and the number of representatives from each estate was determined by the amount of tax each estate paid. What this meant, in both Prussia and Austria, was that 25 percent of the population effectively chose 85 percent of the legislature. Now, we know for Hegel that legislative power must precisely represent different social states (*Stände*) in such a way as to mediate between the government and the people and, in theory, a Hegelian lower house functions as a "universal state" since the civil servants and deputies who sit there do so as representatives of the state, not as private individuals, even if they happen to be property owners.[44] But if the house is also designed to represent each of the three estates – the nobility, the city, and the countryside – are the representatives not also representing the "particular common interests" of their particular estate?[45] In light of the universality inherent in the concept of law as such, are not such interests really just purely private interests? And in the case of the Rhine Provincial Assembly, are these private interests not directly determined by the very particularistic criteria of representative eligibility itself (i.e., taxation)? As Marx argues:

> The Provincial Assembly, therefore, *completely fulfilled its mission.* In accordance with its *function,* it represented a definite *particular interest* and treated it as the final goal. That in doing so it trampled the law under foot is a *simple consequence of its task,* for interest by its very nature is blind, immoderate, one-sided; in short, it is lawless natural instinct, and can lawlessness lay down laws? Private interest is no more made capable of legislating by being installed on the throne of the legislator than a mute is made capable of speech by being given an enormously long speaking-trumpet.[46]

In other words, private interests, even if they are "common" to a large number of representatives, are still nothing more than private interests: "how can it fail to follow that a *body representing private interests,* the estates, will seek to degrade, and is bound to degrade, the state to the thoughts of private interest?"[47]

In two separate instances throughout the five articles, Marx articulates his critique of the political pretensions of private interest through the character of Shylock from Shakespeare's *The Merchant of Venice* (which should dispel any doubts about Marx's motivation on this matter). The first reference appears in Marx's second article on the

Rhine law, published on October 27, 1842: "the petty, wooden, mean and selfish soul of interest" tries to destroy that which obstructs it; it does not fear non-right but rather the consequences of right in the person who threatens the external object with which it identifies, as is verified in the words of Shylock: "Hates any man the thing we would not kill."[48] The second reference appears in Marx's fifth and final article, in the form of a much longer passage from Scene 1, Act IV of the same play. In this scene, Portia has just rendered her verdict, and she then adds the following words:

PORTIA
Tarry a little; there is something else.
This bond doth give thee here no jot of blood;
The words expressly are "a pound of flesh":

An astonished Shylock responds:

SHYLOCK
Is that the law?
PORTIA
Thyself shalt see the act.[49]

This extended quotation appears in the context of Marx's aforementioned discussion of Article 19, whereby the forest owner is granted the ability to effectively make the offender his serf. Marx argues here that the protection of the interests of the forest owners is directly opposed to the "sense of right and fairness in protecting the interests of those whose property consists of life, freedom, humanity, and citizenship of the state, who own nothing except themselves (*des Eigentümers von nichts als sich selbst*),"[50] all of which is to the say the humanity of the offender himself. The ownership of the self, which makes all humanity property owners of a certain kind,[51] is opposed to the ownership over another person as invoked by the forest owners; their material things have been aggrieved and, as a result of their fetishized notion of value, these material things have become their very essence. This, for Marx, makes the principle embodied in Article 19 clear enough: "the forest owner, in exchange for his piece of wood, receives what was once a human being."[52]

These two Shakespearean references give form to a certain conception of private interest that is worth emphasizing. The character of Shylock embodies private interest, in its very being, as fundamentally calculating: "interest does not think, it calculates."[53] Indeed there is, as Marx writes, an "argumentative mechanism of private interest" whose two principle categories are "*good motives*" and "*harmful results*."[54] Sometimes interest justifies its disregard for law by invoking the "shrewd, wise and good motives" of those in power, and sometimes it depreciates the value of law by invoking its "harmful and dangerous results."[55] In the first case, its motives are the "numbers" or "figures" with which private interest calculates with an aim to "abolishing the basis of law," and in the second case, its calculations concern the consequences of law, which is to say its "effects in the external world."[56] In either case, interest never conceives of law "as an independent object," but subsumes law with the "internal world" of its own ideas, and it assesses law according to its effects in the "external" world. If private interest can only attack the foundations of law, if the "right of interest," this new "saint," necessarily contradicts the "interest of right," it is because it denies any autonomy to the law. This is to say that the *autonomy of law constitutes the true principle of the critique of the sophistry of interest*. Viewed in this light, Marx's critique is diametrically opposed to that embodied by the character of the Bastard in another Shakespearean play, *King John*. The eponymous King John is none other than the same king who signed the Magna Carta in 1215 (though this is not mentioned in the play), and at the end of Scene 1, Act II, the Bastard, the illegitimate son of Richard I, paints a striking picture of an empire without shared "Interests" ("Commodity"):

BASTARD
With that same purpose-changer, that sly devil,
That broker, that still breaks the pate of faith,
That daily break-vow, he that wins of all,
Of kings, of beggars, old men, young men, maids.[57]

What is striking about this critique is that interest, in this case, is not at all reduced to a natural instinct, as it was in Marx's references to *The Merchant of Venice*. Here, rather, interest is now opposed to the natural march of the world:

BASTARD
That smooth-faced gentleman, tickling Commodity,
Commodity, the bias of the world,
The world, who of itself is peised well,
Made to run even upon even ground,
Till this advantage, this vile-drawing bias,
This sway of motion, this Commodity,
Makes it take head from all indifferency,
From all direction, purpose, course, intent:
And this same bias, this Commodity,
This bawd, this broker, this all-changing word . . .[58]

Shakespeare's term "Commodity" is meant here in the sense of profit and interest, rather than denoting an economic product. It is thus difficult to maintain, as Peter Linebaugh does, that Shakespeare anticipated the Marxist labor theory of value, much less that he "reduces the commodity to the sexually active female."[59] There is, however, much that can be gleaned from the way in which the term is used twice to qualify "Interest" in this monologue: commodity is first of all described as "the bias of the world," and then again described as "this same bias." This term very effectively differentiates the perspective adopted by Shakespeare in *King John* from that perspective Marx quoted from *The Merchant of Venice*: the world inhabited by King John is depicted as a medieval world in which the values of fidelity, loyalty, and faithfulness are still proclaimed loud and strong. Together, these values comprise the ideal of chivalry. But, at the same time, this medieval environment is uncompromisingly measured by the

Renaissance yardstick as a world internally wrought by the cynical calculations of self-interest. The picture the Bastard paints of this world – in which the world is collapsing and on the verge of chaos – is framed around opposites: the right and the twisted, straightness and deviation, the direct and the warped. The world "of itself is peised well" – i.e., is well built – and is "made to run even upon even ground" is subsequently diverted by interest from its natural course, and is, in a sense, decentered. In other words, the world is still perceived by the Bastard from the point of view of chivalry, even if his perspective is here devoid of illusions about chivalry's future and is held by someone who wants to worship in the interest of his own "master." The world of *The Merchant of Venice* is, however, very different: it is, at least partly, the world of sixteenth-century maritime commerce. The play takes place in a city run by doges who engaged in widespread speculation and interest-lending, and whose laws are pitiless when it comes to the poor because they are entirely designed to promote the development of trade. The Bastard and Shylock, in other words, are two very different personifications of interest: while the Bastard is the spokesperson for that polyvalent interest that vituperates the vice of wealth one day and the vice of wretchedness the next, Shylock embodies the cruelty of that interest that will go to any length to get what is rightfully its own. This is precisely why Marx references Shylock in his critique of law on the theft of wood. Marx does not condemn private interest on behalf of some natural course of the world, founded on faith and loyalty, but rather denounces private interest as a "natural instinct" capable of cunning and reason. And he opposes this conception of interest to the public law of a modern state that actually conforms to its concept, based on a Hegelian-inspired approach that turns against orthodox Hegelianism itself.

The "Customs of the Poor" versus the "Customs of the Privileged"

Given Marx's emphasis on the conflict between public law and private interest, could we not simply label Marx a "good liberal rationalist" who denounces the mystification of a "falsely universal and rational state" on behalf of this same universality?[60] Is not Marx's critique, in this case, merely a matter of opposing the true purposes of public right against its appropriation by private interest? To see why this interpretation is not tenable, we need to look at the second argumentative thread woven through these five articles on the theft-of-wood law. From the very beginning of his first article, Marx gives special consideration to the nature of custom as such, and he concludes this article with a fierce denunciation of the customs of the privileged as "*contrary to the law*" (*wider das Recht*).[61] Taken literally, this assertion claims that the customs of the privileged are, in fact, illegal. On the other hand, Marx "demands for the poor a *customary right* [*das Gewohnheitsrecht*] and indeed one which is not of a local character but is a customary right of the poor in all countries."[62] In other words, Marx calls for a universal customary right of the poor.

Marx's claim is striking in its originality, and needs to be carefully unpacked. For it is through this unusual claim that Marx endows customary right with a rather singular double determination, namely the unusual extension of a very localized social content onto a global scale. This assertion fundamentally breaks with the dominant view that such laws or customs can only be local in nature. We have already seen that custom is *lex loci*, while "common law" is extended to the national level, at least in England,[63] and so it should not be identified with customary right. And as widespread and perennial as the customary rights of the poor were, they were far from indiscriminately codified into common law. The "artificial reason" of judges and lawyers was, as we have seen, extremely reluctant to endorse any customs that might discourage "improvements." But Marx is not satisfied with this claim alone (which is already a little confusing). "We go still farther," asserts Marx, "and maintain that a customary right by its very nature (*seiner Natur nach*) can *only* (*nur*) be the a right of this lowest, propertyless and elemental mass (*dieser untersten besitzlosen und elementarischen Masse*).[64] We need to pay careful attention to move from one premise to the next in order to properly grasp what Marx is saying at the beginning of the second sentence. He first asserts "we go still further," and thereby indicates he wants to move beyond the premise "there must be a customary right of poverty" (as far as such a thing can be claimed), to a more ambitious proposition: "customary right is necessarily the customary right of the poor." In other words, Marx is saying that there can be no other customary law other than that of the poor, because any other customary right would in fact be a non-right, or the negation of right – meaning any conflict between the customary rights of the privileged and the customary right of the poor is *a priori* excluded. The assertion that the customs of the privileged are contrary to right thus finds its logical compliment in the assertion that customary right is by its very nature the customary right of the poor. And if it is implied that this right of the poor is necessarily a global right, we must then conclude that customary right can only exist as a global right of the poor.

The juridical form of customary right is not, therefore, understood by Marx as a merely formal phenomenon indifferent to its social content: it is rather the specific form through which poverty can and must assert its rights. Accordingly, then, the question posed above about what criteria allow us to discriminate between good customs and evil customs is resolved as soon as it is posed: the only customs capable of being elevated to the form of the law are the customs of the poor; the other customs, those of the privileged, are the negation of right, pure and simple. The dissymmetry between these two kinds of custom, in terms of their relation to law, could not be more complete. And since, moreover, the customs of the privileged are only "so-called" (*sogenannten*) customs, the whole question here turns on our understanding of what precisely allows Marx to ground this dissymmetry in the nature of custom *qua* custom.

The first part of Marx's argument is meant to show how the customs of the privileged are in fact the negation of law. The "customary rights of the aristocracy" prove that they are in fact "*customary wrongs*" by virtue of the inherent opposition between their content and the universal and necessary form of the law as such: "the customary rights of the aristocracy conflict by their content with the form of universal law. They cannot be given the form of law because they are formations of lawlessness."[65] It is at this point that the two argumentative lines of Marx's articles begin to intersect: if, on the one side, the law passed by the Rhine Provincial Assembly violates the universality of the concept of law, the customary rights of the aristocracy, on the other hand, are equally unable to satisfy the same norm of "legal right." Considered in terms of their content, both the Rhine law and the customs of the aristocracy enter into open contradiction with the universality of the law: the first by virtue of the fact that the law tries to make the private interest of the forest owners the measure of legal right, and the second because these customs are nothing more than an attempt to perpetuate privileges that pre-date the formation of legal right, privileges that were inherited from an epoch in which "animal right" and "unfreedom" reigned due to the fact that humanity was divided into unequal races (*races inégales*).[66] For Marx, then, there is no opposition in principle between customary law and legal right: "at a time when universal laws prevail, rational customary right is nothing but the *custom of legal right*, for right has not ceased to be custom because it has been embodied in law, although it has ceased to be *merely* custom."[67] Understood properly, then, we are not dealing with a situation in which legal right puts an end to customary right by uniformly consigning custom to a "barbaric past" (as the edifying history of modernity would have it); rather, custom is re-constituted as the "custom of the state"; or better put, it is merely pre-legal custom itself that becomes the custom of the state. There is no rupture, then, between customary law and legal right. However, this only applies to "rational" customary law: whereas rational customary law is law insofar as it "exists *alongside* and *in addition to law*," the customary rights of the privileged social estates are non-rational because they do not anticipate the law – not in the sense that the privileged castes have not succeeded in obtaining recognition from the law for "even their irrational pretensions," but in the sense that these estates "have no right of anticipation in regard to law."[68] That these rights continued to be claimed by these estates changes nothing; they are only the manifestations of "whims" and "pretensions" that extend beyond the limits of the law. The conclusion is thus self-evident: the "customary rights of the aristocracy" do not anticipate the law because they are "customs which are contrary to the conception of rational right."[69]

Contrastingly – and this is Marx's second argumentative thread – the customary rights of the poor are rights that conform to the concept of rational law in that they anticipate legal right. If they are contrary to something, it is not the rational concept of law, but rather the "custom of positive law." As Marx puts it, "their content does not conflict with legal form, but rather with its own lack of form. The form of law is not in contradiction to this content, on the contrary, the latter has not yet reached this form."[70] If there is an opposition, it is an opposition internal to the customary right of the poor, an opposition between its content and its lack of legal form, and not between its content and legal form itself: since it does not have legal form as such, its content obviously cannot be formally opposed to the form of law; on the other hand, the customary right of the poor strives to achieve legal form, and in this sense it can be said to anticipate a legal right to come. But how, then, are we to understand the opposition between the customary right of the poor and the "custom of positive law"? This unusual formulation requires some explication. We should not confuse this custom with the "custom of legal right" discussed above, nor with the "concept of rational law." Positive law may have the form of law, and it is in this sense codified as legal, but it does not conform to the "concept of rational law." Indeed, in most modern countries, positive laws take the form of "liberal laws" that "treated and have been compelled to treat" the customary rights of the poor very "*one-sidedly*," and it is precisely this one-sided character that prevents the "custom of positive law" from truly conforming to the concept of rational law.[71]

What then, more precisely, is one-sided about positive law, and why has liberal legislation treated the customs of the poor in this way? In other words, what compels this one-sided treatment? What we need to explain now is positive law's non-recognition of the customary right of the poor, rather than the latter's conformity to the rational form of law. Marx observes that, in the field of private law, liberal legislation successfully abolished particular customs by simply elevating their laws to the level of the universal without granting any new rights over and above those already in force. Since these already-existing laws were the rights of "social estates," which is to say the privileges of those who enjoyed customs in addition to the law, those who did not belong to any social estate – this "propertyless and elementary class"[72] – have no rights, only customs. Under these conditions, abolishing all customs was tantamount to depriving the mass of the most underprivileged the only protections they enjoyed, which were little more than "accidental concessions" that eventually acquired the force of custom.[73] Marx articulates this logic through the example of monasteries and the secularization of monastic property. Marx borrows this example from Hegel's *Philosophy of Right*, but he interprets the example very differently. In §3, Hegel attacked the "historical justification" of institutions produced from contingent circumstances to more clearly mark the difference between historical justification and universal or conceptual justification:

> Suppose, for example, that we accept as a vindication of the monasteries their service in cultivating wilderness and populating them, in keeping learning alive by transcribing manuscripts and giving instruction, and so on, and suppose further that this service has been deemed to be the ground and the purpose of their continued existence, then what really follows from considering this past service is that, since circumstances have now entirely altered, the monasteries are at least in this respect superfluous and inappropriate.[74]

As already observed by Xifaras,[75] whereas Hegel uses this example to deplore the narrowness and poverty of the historical school of legal philosophy, Marx uses it to better demonstrate the injustices wrought on the poor by liberal legislation:

> The monasteries were abolished, their property was secularised, and it was right to do so. But the accidental support which the poor found in the monasteries was not replaced by any other positive source of income. When the property of the monasteries was converted into private property and the monasteries received some compensation, the poor who lived by the monasteries were not compensated. On the contrary, a new restriction was imposed on them, while they were deprived of an ancient right.

Instead of denouncing contingency, as Hegel does, Marx shows how contingency itself should have been raised to the level of law, such that this "accidental support" is transformed into a legal guarantee. It is precisely in this sense that we should see modern positive law as "one-sided": instead of transforming "accidental concessions" into "necessary concessions," chance and contingency were abstracted and this "accidental support" provided by the monasteries was suppressed, while, on the other hand, the privileges of the social estates were legally codified. In short, the old abuses were legalized while the "positive side" of these abuses – i.e., the customs that emerged alongside these abuses that allowed the poor to secure subsistence during periods of scarcity – was suppressed. But why was this necessary, strictly from the point of view of modern private property? It was because of the entrenched distinction between public law and private law that, as we have already seen, formed the fundamental basis of modern legalism from the sixteenth century onwards. For the relationship between the customs of the poor and the law was very different during the medieval period. As we saw in the work of E.P. Thompson in the last chapter, the concept of property was not the central concept of customary feudal law, which embraced blurry zones of indistinction that modern law, at its core, tries to reduce and eventually eliminate. This is precisely what Marx is talking about when he explains the one-sidedness of modern legislation in matters of private law:

> These legislations were necessarily one-sided, for all customary rights of the poor were based on the fact that certain forms of property were indeterminate (*schwankenden*) in character, for they were not definitely private property, but neither were they definitely common property, being a mixture of private and public right, such as we find in all the institutions of the Middle Ages.[76]

Generally speaking, then, almost "every medieval form of right," not only in terms of property, "was in every respect hybrid, dualistic, split in two." Modern laws, however, are the product of "understanding": this means, especially after Hegel, that every object of law must be endowed with a fixed determination, and it must be isolated from other legal objects. This process invariably transforms objects one-sidedly – it is by definition required if a previously dualistic or indeterminate object is to be transformed into a definite and particular thing. While such legal uniformity may indeed be a "great and remarkable" thing, it nonetheless had the effect of "abolishing the hybrid, indeterminate, forms of property by applying them to the existing categories of abstract civil law, the model for which was available in Roman law."[77]

What we find lurking behind the one-sidedness of modern private law is therefore, once again, Roman law. And on this particular point, there is actually agreement between the otherwise profoundly discordant historical and speculative legal traditions: each tradition agrees on the central legal importance of the concept of property. More specifically, they both consider the law of property as a "subjective and exclusive right" over an unfree object, to put it in Kantian terms. This equally applies to Roman law (this notion is certainly present in Savigny's treatise on Roman law) and it applies to Hegel's discussion of property as an "abstract right" in the first part of his *Philosophy of Right*.[78] For Marx, however, if the customary rights of the poor are "contrary to the customs of positive law," it is precisely because the concept of "custom" is a concept of modern private law, which is of course a form of law that is incapable of grasping the hybrid nature of older conceptions of property.

We now are able to gain a better appreciation of the originality of Marx's argument. On the one hand, Marx's conceptual approach to the relationship between law and custom – i.e., incompatibility or anticipation – allows him to distinguish between good and evil customs, whereas Hegelian philosophy rejects all custom outright on account of the formless and indeterminate nature of custom as such.[79] Custom exists, for Marx, "*alongside* and *in addition to*" legal right, and so we must recognize that there is a certain positivity and even rationality to custom, even if custom is not explicitly codified in law. We must therefore refrain from strictly identifying positive law and legal right in a Hegelian fashion. This is to say that the rationality of customary right owes little to reason in the sense of "the conscious activity of the faculty of the thought,"[80] much less reason in the speculative or conceptual sense of the term. But does this mean that Marx is aligned with Savigny and the historical tradition of legal philosophy? One could be forgiven for coming to this conclusion, insofar as the positivity of law, for Savigny, is a form of underground or unconscious positivity, a positivity that operates outside the will of specific legal actors and outside the arbitrary will of sovereignty. It is a positive law that lives in the "common consciousness of the people" and which, for this reason, could be called the "law of the people." It is a law that is expressed in spontaneous, regular, and continuous customs and practices throughout history; it is law as the manifestation of the shared beliefs of a people, and is in this sense much like a language. For Savigny, however, this active but invisible "historical" law does not contradict or cancel out Roman law, but is actually the means of its actualization in German law: it is precisely the continuity of Roman law *qua* private law in the multitudinous German states that allowed the latter to function as a kind of default national law that was conspicuously absent in Germany.[81] If the law inherited from the past includes custom law, canon law, and Roman law, this means Roman law "constitutes the only continuous and common feature of Western history."[82] Savigny's project is not, therefore, the artificial re-activation of Roman law, but rather the "Romanization" of historical law, or the "patient and collective updating of historical law to make the latter conform ever more precisely to the older traditions of the Roman jurists."[83]

It is important, then, to be precise about Marx's critique of the historical legal tradition. On the one hand, Marx would certainly agree with Savigny, *contra* Hegel, that positive law does not coincide with legal right, simply because the historical school endows spontaneous practices with juridical positivity independent of legislative assent or sovereign will. But, on the other hand, Marx cannot abide the notion of a "law of the people," nor the affirmation of Roman law as a pan-European universality, especially when we are dealing with the law of property. The first point is self-explanatory given the cleavage between the customs of the poor, which exist "alongside legal right" without opposing the form of the law, and the customs of the aristocracy, which are in fact "non-legal customs" since they oppose the form of law by virtue of their arbitrary content. This means that the very notion of the "the unity of the people" is, for Marx, an illegitimate notion. The second point directly relates to the nature of the law prohibiting the theft of wood: the historical tradition is fundamentally incapable of recognizing the use rights of the poor because, like all modern liberal law, it inherited its concept of property from Roman law. What is ultimately at issue here, then, is the categorical inability of Roman law to adequately express or translate customary forms of property, which are "neither public nor private because they are collective and indeterminate: neither absolute nor even exclusive since the same object can have many simultaneous masters and rights can be superimposed in any given situation."[84] Thus, unlike Savigny – whose attachment to the categories of Roman law means he is no more equipped than is Hegel for carving out a place for the customary rights of the poor – Marx traces the lineage of these customary rights back into ancient Germanic law: "little thought is needed to perceive how *one-sidedly* enlightened legislation has treated and been compelled to treat the *customary rights of the poor*, of which the various *Germanic* rights can be considered the most prolific source."[85] Now there is no doubt Marx owes at least something to the German historical school, whose spokesman, Georg Beseler, broke with Savigny and the other "Romanists" in 1835 over the question of the sources of historical law.[86] But for Marx, historical genealogy alone cannot serve as the basis for the customary rights of the poor. For rather than valorize an older national custom – and hence a "local" custom – to combat the effects of a universalizing Roman law, Marx asserts a universal customary right – one that would be "valid in all countries" – to combat the "one-sided" legislation grounded in an ostensibly universal Roman law.[87] The question, therefore, is how Marx determines the legitimacy of universal customary right?

What is the Legal Basis for the Customs of the Poor?

A careful reading of Marx's article from October 27, 1842 in fact reveals a double foundation for the customs of the poor. Marx's first justification for the customary rights of the poor is based on the specific nature of certain objects. For Marx, the modern legislative understanding of custom "overlooked the fact that there exist objects of property which, by their very nature, can never acquire the character of predetermined private property … by their elemental nature and their accidental mode of existence (*durch ihre elementarisches Wesen und ihr zufälliges Dasein*)."[88] In addition to this naturalistic justification, however, Marx advances a second argument for legally justifying the customs of the poor. This second approach appears rather unexpectedly and abruptly in Marx's article, as if it were a completely independent justification unrelated to the first and, on the whole, sufficient in and of itself. As Marx writes, "it is by its *activity* (*in ihrer Tätigkeit*) that poverty acquires its right."[89] The problem raised by the duality of Marx's argument relates to the overall coherence of Marx's critique, especially in terms of the potential articulation of these two perspectives: if the activity of the poor is, in itself, considered sufficient in terms of providing a foundation for their collective use rights, why invoke the particular nature of the objects of this activity at all? Unless, perhaps, the connection between the nature of the activity and the nature of the object upon which this activity is based is so close that the object is in fact the true foundation, since it determines the activity through which the poor "find" their rights? In other words, poverty is only able to ground its legal basis in activity because this activity is, in turn, anchored in the nature of its object. But were this the case, Marx's use of the term "already" (*schon*) is somewhat puzzling. Moreover, Marx's text goes to some length to establish a very direct relationship between the mode in which objects exist and the mode in which the "poor" exist as a separate class, thus raising the specter of a highly problematic double "naturalness" that relates to both objects and class, insofar as it is one's class determination that puts one into contact with certain objects to begin with. For us, then, the simplest means of disentangling this complex argument is to separately examine each of these two attempts to legitimize the customary rights of the poor in the order in which they appear in Marx's text.

"Physical Poverty" and "Human Poverty"

To follow the first argumentative thread, we need to be clear that Marx's entire approach is based on a very direct understanding of the relation between the "propertyless and elemental mass" and the elementary nature of objects ("their elemental nature and their accidental mode of existence"). In Marx's article of October 27, this relationship is woven through an elaborate analogy that we will need to re-construct. While speaking of all those objects that inherently resist the Roman categories of property rights, and which accordingly fall within the definition of "occupation rights" (*Okkupationsrecht*), Marx writes:

> [These] objects which, by their elemental nature and their accidental mode of existence, belong to the sphere of occupation rights, and therefore of the occupation right of that class which precisely because of these occupation rights, is excluded from all other property and which has the same position (*die selbe Stellung*) in civil society as these objects have in nature.[90]

Of course, we know that the law concerning the theft of wood refuses to recognize any such "occupation right" as enshrined in custom precisely because it prohibits the poor from collecting fallen wood.

Obviously, Marx's invocation of an "occupation right" is not the same as the technical term found in Roman law.[91] In Roman law, the concept of "occupation" refers to the act of materially appropriating an object that is susceptible to appropriation, but which has not yet been claimed. More precisely, it refers to taking possession of a thing without an owner (*res nullius*) with the intent to acquire ownership over said thing. This act of appropriation may apply to things as different as immobile or mobile property formed by the force of nature, wild animals caught by hunting or fishing, a portion of the royalties the state grants an "inventor," objects appropriated during war, objects abandoned by their former owners, etc. "Occupation," in this sense, requires two distinctive elements: first, the *corpus*, which consists in materially acting upon a thing; and second, an intentional element or *animus domini*, which is nothing other than the will or intention to become an owner or to acquire property.[92] This Roman notion of an "occupation right" was more systematically developed over time, especially in the seventeenth century. For instance, in Chapters 3, 4, and 5 of his *De jure belli ac pacis* (1625), Hugo Grotius expressly distinguishes between three "original" modes of acquisition, which are the three ways in which one might acquire a thing without a previous owner: occupation, specification, and accession. Grotius defines occupation as the "right of first occupant," a definition in which possession is effectively equated with property. Grotius's intent here was to define original, exclusive property as issuing from the rights of the first occupant. Grotius's approach presupposes an originary state in which the world itself was a *res nullius* of some kind. He then imagined the fiction of universal consent, or the tacit agreement amongst all men, by virtue of which exclusive right over a thing would be conceded to the first occupant.

In 1842, however, during the debates in the Rhine Provincial Assembly, the term "occupation" referred to the act of gathering dead wood – it did not refer to the taking possession of something under the aegis of a well-defined notion of intentionality: the dimension of *animus domini* seems to be lacking here (at least in the sense of a desire for "property"), and of course the "undefined" character of the medieval category of property as such meant that the dead wood was not really a case of *res nullius*. But this unusual use of the notion of "occupation" aside, what is especially original in Marx's critique is the homology he evokes between this "occupation right" and the social position of the poor as enunciated in the passage cited above: the impoverished masses occupy the "the same position in civil society" as does fallen wood within nature, and it is this positional identity or homology that, in the final analysis, justifies the "occupation right" the poor exercise over these objects.

How should we understand this homology? As we have already seen, the position of the poor is, above all, characterized by their absolute destitution, which is manifest in terms of their complete lack of property – in the strict sense of the term according to modern legal categories. In the first of his articles on the theft of wood, written on October 25, Marx posits a universal customary right for "the poor, politically and socially propertyless many," or the same group he describes later in the article as the "propertyless and elemental mass." But now, significantly, he also introduces a dimension of conflict or war between what he refers to as the "natural animal kingdom" and the "spiritual animal kingdom":

> Under feudalism one species feeds at the expense of another, right down to the species which, like the polyp, grows on the ground and has only numerous arms with which to pluck the fruits of the earth for higher races while it itself eats dust for whereas in the natural animal kingdom the worker bees kill the drones, in the spiritual animal kingdom the drones kill the worker bees, and precisely by labour.[93]

While it is possible to interpret this opposition as borrowed from the very similar opposition between the workers and the idle parasites in Saint-Simon's *Parabola* (1819),[94] what is more interesting in this passage is how we begin to see the notion of a "universal class," which is at the same time a "non-class," begin to take shape, insofar as this universal class is the product of the dissolution of all the "particular estates" (*Stände*) in civil society. In other words, because this class is the victim of an absolute injustice, it possesses "a universal character because of its universal suffering."[95] Marx's article from October 27 then confirms and reiterates this negative universality of non-ownership and non-belonging by opposing "the wrong of the estates" (*das Unrecht der Stände*) to the "the right of those without social estate" (*das Recht der Standeslosen*).[96] The universality of the impoverished class is thus, strictly speaking, merely the counterpart of its "elementary" condition. It is its negative counterpart. Before Marx explicitly endows a sense of universal destiny upon the impoverished class – the idea that the task of universal emancipation falls to those who possess only themselves and their labor – the universality of non-ownership described by Marx in these texts rather constructs a certain "kinship" between the impoverished class and nature.

This kinship, however, does not concern nature as a whole – in the sense of all of its products – rather it only concerns that which is "elemental" or "accidental" in nature, which is precisely the case with fallen wood. In a striking and original manner, Marx directly links "physical poverty" with "human poverty," which is to say social poverty:

> Fallen wood provides an example of this. Such wood has as little organic connection with the growing tree as the cast-off skin has with the snake. Nature itself presents as it were a model of the antithesis between poverty and wealth in the shape of the dry, snapped twigs and branches separated from organic life in contrast to the trees and stems which are firmly rooted and full of sap, organically assimilating air, light, water and soil to develop their own proper form and individual life. It is a physical representation of poverty and wealth. Human poverty senses this kinship and deduces its right to property from this feeling of kinship. If, therefore, it claims physical organic wealth for the predetermined property owners, it claims physical poverty for need and its fortuity. In this play of elemental forces, poverty senses a beneficent power more humane than human power.[97]

This passage is remarkable in more ways than one. It is firstly remarkable in the way in which it articulates the opposition between the limbs and branches deprived of all organic life, and the living tree's direct connection to nature's organic elements, which Marx compares to the opposition between poverty and wealth: indeed, the opposition through which nature illustrates the analogous opposition between poverty and wealth is nothing less than the stark contrast between the living and the dead – or more precisely, the opposition of inert, organic matter shorn of its connection to nature, and the vigor and force of organic life itself. The passage is also striking, however, in the way in which the opposition between physical wealth and physical poverty expresses or "represents" the opposition between social wealth and social poverty. In this way, there is a determinate homology established between the elementary or base essence of the branches and the elementary or base essence of the impoverished masses. Social poverty, in other words, occupies the same position in society as physical poverty occupies in nature, insofar as the rupture of the organic link is socially translated as the exclusion of the poor from the system of social estates: the limbs and branches that have fallen from the tree physically signify the most impoverished masses who have fallen to the bottom of the social ladder. And lastly, this passage is striking in a third sense by virtue of the natural character of the affinity or kinship that, for Marx, is felt or registered between the socially poor and the physically poor: "Human poverty," writes Marx, "senses this kinship (*fühlt diese Verwandtschaft*) and deduces its right to property from this feeling of kinship."

The "Legal Instinct" of the Poor

Does this affinity on the part of the poor constitute a legitimate basis for claiming a right of ownership that was actually practiced by the impoverished masses? Is it solid enough to ground what Marx identifies as an "occupation right"? In the first instance, the basis for this claim is nothing like the conscious will or reason of the subject who wants to become the owner of something as of yet unowned. Rather, Marx's homology is more similar to a kind of "legal instinct" (*rechtlichen Trieb*) or an "instinctive sense of right" (*instinktmässiger Rechtssinn*) that makes the poor feel an immediate kinship between the physical poverty of the fallen wood and their own social poverty. We are now at some distance from the Hegelian concept of law: not only, as we have already seen, does Hegel distinguish in his *Philosophy of Right* between the rational form of law and the informal collection of customary rights, but he takes great care also to delineate how "only animals . . . have their law as instinct," whereas "human beings alone have law as custom."[98] Marx is undoubtedly closer, in this respect, to Savigny's insistence on the subterranean and invisible source of law,[99] with the proviso that Marx does not invoke the immemorial foundation of popular beliefs and practices (as Savigny does) but rather speaks of a naturalistic, almost animal-like "instinct" that discloses the inhumane conditions of those, in society, who are deprived of all property and legitimate social belonging – in other words, those for whom existence is based on "a *mere custom* of civil society" and is not recognized "in the conscious organization of the state."[100]

This recourse to a legal instinct of the poor offers another advantage in terms of justifying the all-important opposition between the customs of the poor and the customs of the privileged. The notion therefore helps resolve the thorny question about the conflict between the different kinds of customs. For if we are confronted on all sides with the undeniable fact of ancestral customs, then the criterion of seniority, as it were, is of no real value. If these two kinds of customs – "good" and "evil" – are radically opposed, it is because the customs of the aristocracy, while still customs, are not rights – in fact they are "wrongs" (*Unrecht*) and contrary to reason – while it is the customs of the poor that conform to "rational law." But despite their injustice, and despite their contradiction with the universality of law, the customs of the aristocracy have nonetheless been codified into existing law, even though they are fundamentally irrational, while the customs of the poor, on the other hand, are still waiting to be recognized by the law despite their complete compatibility with the universality of law as such. Worse still, the customs of the poor are daily threatened in their very existence by legislation dictated by the corrupt logic of private interest. However, contrary to all expectations, the customs of the poor are not in the final analysis derived from their "rationality," from the fact that they are elaborated by reason as human faculty or proceed from an act of will enlightened by reason, but rather they come from the immediacy and spontaneity of an "instinct."

One could argue against Marx's critique that the customs of the privileged are also the product of a certain "instinct." But if the customs of the aristocracy are based on a kind of instinct, it is nothing other than the "blind, immoderate, one-sided" and "lawless natural instinct" which, as mentioned above, is precisely the kind of private interest enshrined in the law on the theft of wood. It is therefore fundamentally different from the legal instinct attributed to the poor. For insofar as the instinct of the poor does not meet the criteria of intentionality enshrined in Roman law (*animus domini*), the instinct of the poor is rather "something like an instinctual *animus proprietarii* that, coupled with natural needs, makes it possible to speak of the juridical nature of things."[101] For if, as Marx puts it, human poverty "claims physical organic wealth for the predetermined property owners, it claims physical poverty for need and its fortuity."[102] It is revealing, here, that Marx's statement concerning the feeling of kinship between physical poverty and human poverty inspires in the latter a clear sense of separation between what belongs to the forest owner and what by chance relates to the needs of the poor: the physical-organic wealth of the living tree relates to the right of those who, through the formal intentionality of premeditation, are constituted as *dominus*, but the physical poverty of the fallen wood relates to the right of those who must satisfy a natural need imposed upon them by circumstance, the latter of which is all the more imperious inasmuch as the lowly condition of the poor deprives them of any power over the means to satisfy their needs.

What we are left with here is the idea that the affinity felt between social poverty and physical poverty is an affinity between two kinds of chance or hazard of a natural kind: the hazard of precarious need, on the one hand, and the hazard of fallen wood as determined by the force and direction of the wind, and the more or less exposed position of the tree in relation to this force, etc., or what Marx calls the "fortuitous operation of elemental forces (*der Zufall der Elemente*), which take away from private property what the latter no longer voluntarily forgoes."[103] If human poverty instinctively feels a "beneficent power" in this "operation of elemental forces," it is precisely because this unintentional and unpremeditated movement manages to triumph over the deliberate will of the *dominus* by snatching from the latter that which it has no intention of renouncing. For unlike the "alms distributed in the street," the "*alms of nature*" are not a product of charity. The fortuity of the elements thus lies before the fortuity of need to which poverty is enslaved, it and provides, unintentionally, the means to satisfy this need solely through the only violence the will of the private forest owner encounters. However, if the fortuity of the elements is perceived as a "benevolent force" by those who suffer the fortuity of need, the same cannot be said about the arbitrary nature of social privilege. While it is true that this arbitrariness is also a matter of chance, this "chance" is not natural, especially when it comes to the chance of birth that distinguishes the aristocracy from the commoners. Marx's formulation thus very carefully distinguishes between the two forms of chance and, consequently, opposes "social chance" to the two related forms of natural chance: "the fortuitous arbitrary action of privileged individuals is replaced by the fortuitous operation of elemental forces."[104] The term "arbitrary" here is a translation of the German *Willkür*, and the English word "arbitrary" unfortunately does not have the advantage of expressing the notion of *Will*, or "will," at the root of the German word. Were we to take this into account, however, Marx's assertion becomes much clearer: far from proceeding from a "legal instinct," the arbitrary pretentions of the privileged are a function of the *Willkür*, which means that the "chance" of their arbitrariness is really the caprice of their will.

The remarkable coherence of Marx's argument now becomes clear: if the instinct of the poor is legally justified, it is because it opposes the arbitrariness of a will – i.e., that of the private owner – and thus the poor rightly see in the "natural elements" a force that aids them in their struggle. In other words, the legal instinct of the poor is not a substitute for a failed or missing *animus domini*; it cannot even be said to be an "instinctual *animus*" at all – which of course is a contradictory notion insofar as the Latin term *animus* legally signifies an intention that proceeds from a will – but rather it legitimizes an "occupation right" that radically challenges the very merits of *animus domini* insofar as it shows how the latter is itself devoid of all *animus*. Thus the pivotal role played by this "legal instinct" comes into clearer focus: its function is precisely to adjust or modify the natural existence of a class subjected to need as a result of its radical deprivation through the very naturalness of the thing or object coveted by this need. In other words, the instinct is a mediating term that guarantees the compatibility between the customs of the poor and the "legal nature of things." It is therefore through the homology between the social position of the poor and the physical position of the fallen wood that the customs of the poor become most meaningful.

"Activity" as the Foundation of the Law of the Poor

But can this juridical naturalism be readily reconciled with Marx's assertion that "activity" is the second foundation of the customs of the poor? Does this kind of assertion not belong instead to something we might contrastingly call a "practical legalism"? Let's re-examine the misleadingly brief phrase in which Marx abruptly introduces this activity-based justification for the customs of the poor, but now in conjunction with the following phrase in which Marx again discusses the collection of fallen wood: "but it is by its *activity* (*Tätigkeit*), too, that poverty acquires its right. By its activity of *gathering* (*Sammeln*) the base class of human society imposes order (*ordnend*) upon the base products of nature."[105] On the basis of this second phrase, we are encouraged by Marx to understand the right of the poor as directly derived from the activity of gathering, as an activity that orders the products of nature. But what does Marx mean exactly by "gathering" (*Sammeln*)? In the first instance, this activity consists in simply separating dead wood from the living trees, which in turn prevents the putrefaction of the wood accumulated on the forest floor from hindering the growth of the forest. It thus contributes to the health of the forest, despite the fact that this is not the direct purpose or end pursued by the poor. Immediately after subsuming this "gathering" under the concept of "activity," Marx enumerates a number of other cases in which he uses the same terminology: "The same thing holds . . ." (*ähnlich verhält es sich*). He first mentions the case of natural products that grow in the wild and whose possession is purely a matter of accident; it is "only because of their unimportance [that they] are not an object for the activity of the actual owner (*keinen Gegenstand für die Tätigkeit des eigentlichen Eigentümers bilden*).[106] Marx illustrates what he means through the example of wild "bilberries and cranberries" later in the article, which reinforces his point about the absence of activity on the part of the owner in relation to these products. It is legitimate, for Marx, that objects that are not the activity of the private owner necessarily become the "property" of those who make them objects of their own activity (harvesting wild fruit, in this case).

The same rationale can be applied to cases of "gleaning," mentioned by Marx immediately afterward. It should be noted from the outset that gleaning is a traditional use right in relation to the products of agricultural labor: after the harvest has been completed, custom allows the most impoverished to collect what remains in the fields, such as straw, grains, etc. "Gathering" is therefore an activity and a right through which, in different forms (collecting dead wood, gathering wild fruits, collecting straw and grains, etc.), the customs of the impoverished acquire *legal unity*: neither the dead wood extracted from the living forest, the straw and grains left over after the harvest, nor berries growing in the wild are objects of the owner's activity. Rather all these "products" are the objects of the activity of the poor.

Do we not see, in this idea of legal justification through activity, a trace of the Hegelian theory of labor in which activity is viewed as a "constituent moment in the right of ownership"?[107] Not necessarily: for it would seem that the concept of labor in Hegel's theory is much narrower than the notion of activity we find in Marx's 1842 article. As Hegel writes in the first section of his *Outlines of the Philosophy of Right* devoted to abstract law, the concept of labor presupposes a relation between the subject and its object such that the subject, understood as embodying "free will," refers only to itself in its relation to the object. This concept is clearly too dependent on the categories of Roman law for it to apply to the situation analyzed by Marx. There is, however, a closer approximation to Marx's concept of activity here, one that is less surprising than it may at first appear: namely Johann Gottlieb Fichte. For Fichte advances a rather original theory of property rights in his *Foundations of Natural Right* (1796) and *The Closed Commercial State* (1800), according to which every property right is "*an exclusive right to a determinate free activity*" and, thus, by no means an exclusive right over the possession of things."[108] This free activity, as Fichte explains, can be determined "either solely through the object that it acts upon" or "only through itself, through its own form . . . without any regard to the object that it acts upon," or, finally, by both at the same time, which is to say "through its own form and through the object that it acts upon." Free activity, for Fichte, is thus understood as "the right to undertake exclusively a specific act upon a certain object, and to exclude all other men from the same use of the same object."[109] It is therefore only "figuratively and derivatively" that one can call the object itself – like a field, for example – "the property of the one who has been granted the title of right. The exclusive right of the farmer to cultivate grain on this certain piece of land is of such a kind."[110] Fichte thus offers an ingenious and powerful justification for the "right of grazing" on another's field: the right of the husbandman, according to Fichte, "does not curtail the right of another to put his herd to pasture on the same land."[111] A footnote clarifies that grazing rights "may be quite uneconomical, but a trespass of another's property it is not," insofar as "the property right depends only on treaties, and, where explicit treaties cannot be demonstrated, on acquired possession and established tradition."[112] The purely political character of this position is related to the fact that "in our theory there is no property of the land," at least insofar as one understands the phrase "a property of *land*" and not "a right that is exclusively one's own to a certain *use* of the land."[113] But since property rights are never anything but a use right proceeding from free activity, no class of society (landowners or the aristocracy) can claim to be "its true owners," least they be guilty of an inexcusable act of appropriation: "the earth is the Lord's; to man belongs only the ability to cultivate it and use it in a purposeful fashion."[114] As a result of his determination of property right as delineated by space and time within the sphere of activity, it is perfectly conceivable that the same object could give rise to different rights held by different persons, without becoming a source of dispute or conflict.

We can immediately see what a Marx familiar with Fichte[115] could draw from Fichte's uncompromising criticism of all the forms of property reification that characterize property as an exclusive right to things and over things. This criticism could easily be used to critique the views of Kant, Savigny, and even Hegel himself.[116] From the moment in which the right of property is transformed into a use right that does not prejudice the rights of other users, one can perfectly account for the multiplicity and overlapping character of rights enshrined in custom: insofar as they are the object of the forest owner's activity, the living trees indisputably belong to the owner. But this does not in the least prevent the poor from exercising their use rights over the fallen branches and other forms of dead wood, since these parts of the tree, which nature has already separated from the living tree, are not the objects of the owner's activity but the objects of the activity of the poor. And of course the same rationale applies to the wild fruits growing in the forest, or the straw and grain left over after the end of the harvest. Ultimately, it is the distribution of use rights according to the criterion of activity that justifies ownership, as opposed to the right of exclusive possession over a thing *qua* thing, an unintelligible right that brings us back to the figure of the absolute master (*dominus*).

In any case, this recourse to the Fichtean concept of "activity" is inscribed here within a complex argument aimed at revealing the *double* foundation of the customs of the poor: first, these customs are justified by virtue of the kinship the poor instinctively feel with nature, and secondly, the customs are justified by the exercise of activity over these objects. This double justification is, however, not without its difficulties. For instance, if it is relatively easy to understand how fallen or dead wood physically "expresses" human poverty, it is difficult to see how the same could be said about wild fruits growing in the forest or the objects of gleaning. For it would seem that "elemental chance" does not play a very large role in their existence, insofar as the wild fruits, for instance, continue to grow and no specific or determined intention has caused them to fall to the ground; and whereas the berries are an organic product, the straw and grain are the byproducts of agricultural labor. Is it still legitimate to invoke a "legal instinct" on the part of the poor, and the associated feeling of affinity between these products and their own experience of social poverty, in all of these diverse cases? In order to do so, we must profoundly modify the spirit of Marx's homology. For can we seriously maintain that there is always an identity between the position occupied by these products in nature and the position of the impoverished class in society?

This immanent difficulty of Marx's argument is particularly visible when Marx moves on to an account of the debate between certain deputies in the Rhine Provincial Assembly about the harvesting of wild bilberries and cranberries. A deputy from the towns argues against the provision in the law that equates the gathering of berries with theft by arguing that this activity allows the children of poor families to help provide for the household. Another deputy replies that the berries in his region have already been commercialized and are shipped by the barrel to Holland. Marx comments on this dispute in the following terms:

> In *one locality*, therefore, things have actually gone so far that a customary right of the poor has been turned into a *monopoly* of the rich. That is exhaustive proof that common property can be monopolised, from which it naturally follows that it must be monopolised. The nature of the object calls for monopoly because private property interests here have invented this monopoly.[117]

What first of all emerges from this passage is the obvious sophistry by which "some mercantile souls" allow themselves to deduce a "must" (*muss*) from "can" (*kann*) – i.e., we are able to monopolize a common good for the benefit of the rich since we have already in fact done it in one region, and therefore this common good must be monopolized everywhere. But stalking in the background of this argument we find the same juridical naturalism that inspired the first basis for justifying the customs of the poor. The fruits that grow wild in the forest constitute in themselves a "common good," a form of nature that would not be affected by the unnatural transformation that makes this good the monopoly of the wealthy. Consequently, any attempt to argue that the "nature of the object" requires private appropriation by a *dominus* in the person of a landowner, opens up the inverse claim that the same nature requires its recognition and defense as a common good. This is why a "wise legislator" should be concerned about depriving the legal instinct of its negative character by "giving the latter a positive sphere of action":[118] it is once again the legal instinct that is summoned to adjust the customs of the poor to the "legal nature of things." This form of justification thus borrows from Savigny and Beseler, but not from Fichte. But should we not reverse this justification in order to ground legal legitimacy on the fact that gathering, like collecting, is an activity of the poor, and not an activity of the private owners? In this case, the emphasis is placed on the very fact of the activity, independent of the heterogeneous nature of the products that are the objects of this activity (dead wood, wild berries, or the byproducts of agricultural labor). This is a form of justification inspired by Fichte, and not by Savigny or Beseler.

The Irreducible Heterogeneity of the Customs of the Poor

While Marx undoubtedly succeeds in introducing an important dimension of conflict into our understanding of the customs of the poor – in terms of their opposition to the customs of the privileged and the prerogatives of private property as sanctioned by modern law – he fails to ground his opposition on a solid legal basis. We must therefore conclude that Marx considers custom, in contradistinction from all legal naturalisms, as a "contradictory social construct."[119] In other words, Marx's 1842 articles on the theft of wood failed to clearly distinguish "naturalism" from "practicism." But Marx does help us ask a very important question: namely, how can we theorize customs in terms of both their conflicted and constructed character at the same time? For, on the one hand, what remains of the irreducibility of custom, in contrast to laws pronounced by a legislator, if the former are also "constructions"? Is it possible to conceptualize something like a "constructed custom" without voiding the concept of custom of all its meaning? For even without subscribing to the organicist ideology of common law, it is a little difficult to disregard the fact that one does not really decide to adopt a custom the same way one decides to adopt a law. Perhaps it is necessary to dissociate the idea of "construction" from that of decision or will? But in that case, is it not necessary to positively determine the mode (or modes) of this legal constructivism? For if it is merely a question of juridical construction then resolving the difficulty is not really much better than avoiding the question entirely. How practical, then, is Marx's call for a universal customary right of the poor? For what is also problematic here is not merely the legal opposition between the customs of the privileged and the customs of the poor, but also the juridical unification of different customs of the poor. It is difficult to understand how the radical heterogeneity of all these customs might be overcome, and to know to what extent Marx's notion of universality would be something other than simply the lowest common denominator.

For legal theorists, the notion of the "communal" effectively designates two legal difficulties that are sometimes hard to distinguish: on the one hand, it designates a right of community inhabitants to the ownership of certain lands, and on the other hand it refers to collective uses that are exercised on private property, but which give the inhabitants rights over certain products, the most important of which is usually the right to access private grazing pastures for all inhabitants once the harvest has been completed. It is not that the interested parties were incapable of distinguishing between these two sorts of rights, but rather that they refused to dissociate them practically whenever the commons were threatened. As Nadine Vivier notes, "the inhabitants knew very well how to dissociated these rights, but they tended to make them indissociable whenever they felt under attack."[120] Vivier's remark about these two notions of the term applies to both France and Germany. In Germany, however, the term differed insofar as *Allmende* was used in the north, and *Gemeinheit* was used in the south. But, as in France, the definitions constructed by jurists did not refer exclusively to land that belonged to a local community, nor exclusively to the collective enjoyment of the inhabitants of a community to land that was not theirs. This relative indeterminacy meant jurists had to take both aspects of the term into account at the same time. Appearing in Germany in the mid- to late Middle Ages, the "commune" (*communaux*) based its existence on the community's claim to regulate its members' exploitative relationship to the surrounding environment; relatedly, the concept of the "commune" included the right to participate in this exploitation on both private land and land owned by the community.[121]

The inherent duality of the legal concept explains why collective practices in the communes were so varied across different regions of the same country. In France alone there was tremendous regional diversity that persisted underneath the unifying legislation that blanketed the country, and these differences reflected different behaviors within the various communes. In the center of the Paris Basin and the Aquitaine Basin, for instance, communes were very small and did not constitute centers of collective life; in the regions of the west and in the Massif Central they were considered mere annexes of private property; in the north and north-east, in the Jura and the Alps, however, they were considered to belong to the entire community, and so the community established rules for managing common lands for the benefit of all.[122] Thus, whenever the communes were considered appendages of private property, the particular law of the land prevailed; but when the land was open to all inhabitants, it was the rights of the person that prevailed.[123] How, under these circumstances, could such diverse practices be unified under common rules, especially when it is not possible to resort to legislative activity to establish a universal customary law? More seriously, who would be the one or ones charged with the formidable task of "inventing the new juridical language" in which this law would be formulated? If the poor were dispossessed of rights established in their name whenever this task was left to professional lawyers, should it not be up to the poor themselves to "make and become the direct interpreters of their law?"[124]

Under these conditions, the hope of establishing such a customary right of the poor seems destined to be little more than a pious wish. For in the final analysis, it is the very notion of "poverty" that, in its indeterminacy, discourages the advancement of such a project: the poor were certainly excluded from the right of ownership, but this exclusion was itself capable of taking various forms. Soon, however, the figure of the proletariat began to compete with the category of the poor, sometimes even assimilating it, such that even the purely negative criterion of propertylessness would become itself insufficiently discriminating. As early as 1843, the expression "the universal class" would designate not only the poor but also the propertyless who, condemned to sell their labor power, were trained in the factory and learned about collective struggle beneath the merciless whip of accelerated technical and industrial progress. Within this new historical perspective, the "absolute poverty" of propertylessness will prompt the demand for collective ownership over the means of production, rather than the perpetuation of a collective use right that did not question private property itself. Retrospectively, the resistance of the poor in the face of the expropriation of their communes will eventually come to look like a desperate attempt to turn back the wheel of history, or at the very least hinder its forward movement.

The Communism of the Poor: Obstacle or Progress?

This arrival of the proletariat ultimately explains why Marx's 1842 critique remained relatively obscure in the tradition of historical materialism. Yet the reference to the Fichtean conception of right as activity may appear, from this perspective, to be philosophically promising for certain theorists of socialism. In Chapter 3 of his book *Les Origines du socialisme allemande* (*The Origins of German Socialism*), titled "Le collectivisme chez Fichte" ("Fichte's Collectivism"), Jean Jaurès underscores the potential of this conception in which all direct forms of ownership over things is subordinated to the sole right of applying one's activity to an object. From his reading of Fichte, Jaurès drew the following decisive conclusion: since it is impossible to reserve part of the land or of industry for each individual citizen, it is up to the state to guarantee everyone the right to activity, which is to say the right to work. In this fashion, ownership rights can only be conceived in terms of a right to work: "But since ownership is free activity applied to one object or another, toward one design or another, everyone who has stable and guaranteed work will be an owner; the right to work is the real property!"[125]

This promotion of the state as guaranteeing the right to work does not, however, prevent the author of the monumental *Histoire socialiste de la Révolution française* (*Socialist History of the French Revolution*) from making several critical assertions about older use rights, such as the right of gleaning or the right to grazing pasture, and all in the name of historical progress. In Volume 1 of the above-mentioned work, which was devoted to the Constituent Assembly, Jaurès comprehensively shows how the peasant proprietors were caught between "feudal suzerainty" and "a kind of elementary communism," between the powerful aristocratic nobility and the "weak and poor communism of the village." He clearly sees that the 1766 Edict of Closure, which granted owners the right to enclose their land, directly challenged the poor's right to glean, who were henceforth condemned to work as cheap laborers during the harvest.[126] But he also deplores the "perpetual invasion and occupation" of the lands of the peasant proprietors, who were compelled to abandon "ears of corn left to the ground and the thatch, more or less high, to the inhabitants of the communes."[127] Ultimately, Jaurès vigorously protests the confusion between "the magnificent modern communism of the socialist proletariat" and the "miserable and rudimentary communism" that found expression in the right to glean. He unequivocally condemns this communism of the poor as a brake on the progress of humanity:

> Modern communism will put all the forces of modern science in the services of all the free peasants: and I recognize, on the contrary, that the ancient customs, such as gleaning, that struggled at the end of the eighteenth century against the growing intensity and growing exclusivity of individual property, were often contrary to progress. Prohibiting the use of scythes, on the pretext that the sickle leaves higher stubble for the gleaner, prevents the extension of natural or artificial meadows, and hinders the raising of cattle, and all under the pretext that the gleaners have a right to a determined surface to glean, is to prolong routine and misery: thus the individualistic harshness of the lords, farmers, bourgeoisie, and wealthy laborers *better served the future of humanity than the quasi-mendacity and somnolent routine that the poor wanted to maintain.*[128]

This assessment is less categorical when it comes to the right of grazing pasture, insofar as the conflict no longer opposes the "poor of the village" to the "rich laborers of the third estate," but rather concerns the "increased egoism of the noble and the monk" or, in other words, "idlers." For Jaurès, the meadows and the forests seem, "on an earth now shredded by individual property, the supreme asylum of primitive communism."[129] But shortly afterward he emphasizes the weakness of the third estate as it takes part in restoring the communes to its inhabitants who were dispossessed by the greedy lords: "the individual, bourgeois, and peasant conception of property enable the Third Estate to maintain or even reestablish, against the monopolization of the nobles, the old, traditional, and rudimentary communism: it did not allow the Third Estate to obligingly study and organize, with zeal, the scientific and intensive exploitation of this vast common domain."[130] Jaurès's position does not waver: the past is always judged by its contribution to the preparation for the future, whether capitalist or post-capitalist.

Nothing could be more eloquent in this respect than Jaurès's assessment of the plan drawn up by the Committee for Agriculture for the definitive division of communal property, which was a prelude to the law passed on June 10, 1793. In Volume IV of his *Histoire*, titled *Le Gouvernement révolutionnaire* (*The Revolutionary Government*), this assessment immediately precedes an objection:

> Sometimes socialists who believe in the rehabilitation of *l'Ancien Régime* as a means of critiquing bourgeois society claim that the Revolution, by dividing the communal districts and subdividing common property into individual property, has robbed the poor.[131]

In contrast to this view, Jaurès argues that the communal regime was "absolutely oligarchic" insofar as it was the wealthy, "alone or almost alone," who benefited from this arrangement, and that "almost everywhere, the wishes of the poor, of the proletarians, was very clearly in favor of partition."[132] After noting the position of Souhait, the only deputy in the convention who resisted the committee's final plan, Jaurès states that Souhait only asked for the partition to be temporary, not definitive, for the sole purpose of the ensuring that the poor do not "fall into a state of total misery, despair, and revolt." It is through this debate, then, that Jaurès argues, "no one seriously proposed a truly communist use of communal goods."[133] Jaurès then concludes by speaking very favorably of the Committee of Agriculture's plan: at least this plan does not try to "disguise, under the semblance of communism, a kind of charitable foundation perpetuated through the ages" but wants instead to "multiply individual properties"; it is precisely in this respect that the plan is superior to Souhait's position, "*even from the socialist point of view.*"[134] Then, after invoking the "agrarian communism" of the future, Jaurès definitively writes:

> It will not be arrived at by the extension of a vague domain disputed over by the routine egoism of individual owners, or conceded as charity to the poor beneath the full rights of property. It would have been better, even for the great communism of the future, to have added to the immediate strength, independence, and revolutionary *élan* of rural democracy and the agricultural proletariat, *rather than try to prop up a sterile parody, or maintain a derisory sketch, of an inferior and degraded communism.*[135]

As we have seen, this perspective is nothing like that adopted by Marx in 1842. For Marx, it was not at all a question of judging customary practices by situating them within the horizon of historical necessity, nor of deciphering an activity-based right as guaranteed by the state, but of seeking a legal basis for these customs independent of established state law. However, the working class was soon after invested with an emancipatory mission that blunted this entire line of thought, and so the question we are left with now concerns the formation of a properly proletarian law under the conditions of a struggle from within the very interior of contemporary bourgeois society itself.

9

The Workers' Common

Between Custom and Institution

The question of a specific "proletarian law" has been massively repressed in leftist thought, but it once a occupied central position in the work of many socialists who were concerned with both the continuity of workers' customs – which were sometimes very old – and the scope of original institutional inventions. The reasons for this suppression are not very mysterious. We saw in the first chapter of this book how the Party form, with its oligarchic tendencies, prevailed in the labor movement. The domination of the party was justified by the ostensible political incapacity of the workers, which stems from their situation of alienation and dispossession in capitalist society. Since, from this point of view, the workers are not themselves able to develop autonomy in their works or their lives, nor develop a culture of their own, institutions were created by the party to give their activity and their relations new form, which would in turn allow workers to begin to develop the outline of another kind of society from within the crucible of the old system. The party was thus the sole repository of the historical interests of the proletariat; the party was the proletariat's essence and its most precious good. This path – the path of political fetishization – was extremely influential in terms of the later construction of Marxism as a *theory of the party*. In sharp contrast to much of what Marx had to say in the 1840s, which focused on the importance of criticism for articulating the nature of the class struggle, the doctrine of the party tried to guide this struggle, dictate its rhythms, map out its goal and its method, and all in the name of a science of history monopolized by the party. This doctrine of the Party was first manifest as Guesdism in France, and in many ways anticipated the bolshevism of the Communist Party. The history of party Marxism is a history of a movement that used orthodoxy to justify all sorts of practices and goals that were often far removed from what might be considered traditional Marxist or Leninist ends.

The hegemonic evolution of party Marxism was, however, formed against the background of another tradition that is – or should be – of increasing interest for contemporary explorations of the common. Rather than focusing on a revolutionary party whose goal is to seize political power and wield the state apparatus, this other tradition argued that the emancipation of the workers should begin with the invention of new forms of work and production, new rules for social life, and a new workers' law that would ensure the latter's autonomy. This other tradition, which includes thinkers like Pierre-Joseph Proudhon, Marcel Mauss, Georges Gurvitch, Jean Jaurès, and Maxime Leroy, argues that the emancipation of the working class involves the invention of new workers' institutions. This tradition is usually referred to by its proponents as "associationist socialism" or merely "associationism."[1]

Once we exclude the Party form as an adequate means of achieving worker emancipation, what is the workers' movement if not the institutionalization of new social relations and new practices specific to the proletarian world? From the outset, socialism – especially in Western Europe – inherited an older tradition of sociability and solidarity from the *Ancien Régime* that was articulated through networks of corporations, guilds, brotherhoods, trade groups, etc., all of which tended to be structured by certain religious beliefs or more or less bacchanalian rituals.[2] However, many of the institutional manifestations of this older form of worker solidarity were destroyed: Turgot's Edict of 1776 and the Le Chapelier Law of 1791 banned such organizations in France, as did the Combination Acts of 1799 and 1800 in England. However, the spirit or cultures of these organizations were not completely erased from history, and for much of the late eighteenth and early nineteenth centuries, workers' organizations were forced to operate in secret. Le Chapelier himself aptly summed up the philosophy upon which these repressive reforms were based: "there can no longer be any corporations within the state; there is only the particular interest of each individual and the general interest. No one is permitted to inspire the citizens with an intermediate interest and thereby separate them from public affairs through the spirit of corporation."[3] The advent of industrialism, however, significantly revived worker solidarity, and new organizations emerged on the basis of heterogeneous associationist doctrines – Leroux, Buchez, Fourier, etc. These ambitious cooperative projects were greatly inspired by both the communities created by Robert Owen and, in the second half of the nineteenth century, after the great repressive phrase, labor exchanges or councils (*les Bourses du travail*) and trade unions.[4] Within these emergent institutional forms, the common worker was not defined by a party that only ever promised to empower the worker after it seized political power; rather, the worker was viewed as an active participant in the exercise of associationist solidarity. In this chapter, we focus on how worker institutions and their potential for social change were theorized, and, more precisely, how solidarity and cooperation were conceived within associationism as both the underlying principle and the overall effect of autonomous workers' institutions.

Customs and Institutional Creations

The first question we need to ask about workers' institutions is whether the latter are true inventions or merely a prolongation of custom. We cannot overlook the importance of historical inheritance in this respect, but we also cannot deny that these institutions were re-created in a very different context. The new forms of organization, such as the emergence of *Bourses du travail* in France at the end of the nineteenth century, etymologically mark this contiguity with the past.[5] The French word *bourse* comes from old orders of journeymen, who maintained a common *bourse* – "purse" or "funds" – for relief, aid, or festivals and rites reserved for those working in trades. Archaeologies of the industrial trade unions almost always find that the historical foundation for contemporary rules, rituals, and controls were originally customary rights, and sometimes very old ones. For instance, Édouard Dolléans, summarizing Jean Vial's thesis in *La Coutume chapelière* (1941), suggests that these "customs consist essentially in practices of solidarity bequeathed by the journeymen to the older public companies (*sociétés ouvertes*) and latter to the unions."[6] The survival of not only terminology but also specific rules gives us some sense of the extent to which traditional trades and workers' organizations were adapted to new conditions. What was at stake in this process of adaption of tradition, in an age of hegemonic political liberalism, was the ability of workers to create workers' laws and rights in the new industrial world. For social institutions do not emerge spontaneously from the minds of men, but from their experiences, and the manner in which their experiences influence and modify the institutions and practices they inherit from the past. Yet, as Beatrice and Sidney Webb have shown, there is enough novelty in modern trade unions for us to question the extent that unions ought to be viewed as primarily modern extensions of the older guilds. Trade unions, for instance, are not organizations of masters or aspiring masters who belong to trade-specific institutions; rather, unions are made up of all kinds of wage-earners who try to forge relations of solidarity in order to counter the competition the bosses try to impose between workers, and thereby collectively fight for better wages and better working conditions.[7] To put it more specifically, the uniquely modern or industrial separation of the labor force from the means of production in turn gave rise to new forms of association that were not based on trade-specific solidarity between masters and journeymen whose intent was to ensure a just price for their products. Modern unions, in contrast, are fundamentally based on the structural antagonism between workers and employers as a whole, over and above any specific trade or industry.

None of this is to say that the transmission of customs and the creation of new institutional forms are mutually exclusive; in fact, the two activities overlapped greatly throughout the *longue durée* of worker struggle. Indeed, the industrial working class's ability to organize and create its own institutions was in large measure dependent on its ability to build on the symbolic and legal gains of its predecessors. For example, the first workers' struggles often made use of old guild regulations, especially in terms of apprenticeships or older customary tariffs, which the new class of industrial employers tried to suppress within the framework of free trade and free contract. But of course the great institutional innovation, that emerged first in England, was the idea of transcending the trade-specific guild framework in favor of a new transversal unionism – "One Big Union" – that strives to bring all the trades into a single workers' institution.[8] As William Thompson writes in his 1827 pamphlet *Labour Rewarded*: "against the competition of the underpaid of surrounding trades, the ready remedy is a central union of all the general unions of all the trades of the country."[9] It should be no surprise that this view comes from an organizer who, along with Owen, grasped how necessary it was to invent new rules, new relations, and new practices based on cooperation, if workers were to successfully counter the new institutional regime of competition. The cooperative movement that developed during the 1820s thus discovered that the productivity of industry, and hence the wealth of all societies, lies in what Proudhon would later call the "collective force." But we have already covered the principle elements of Proudhon's theory, and so the question we are now concerned with is how to transform this cooperative ethic into a principle of social re-organization. This, more or less, is the core problem that confronted nineteenth-century socialism and the doctrine of association in all its diverse forms. And again it is Proudhon, one of the socialists most interested in the idea of a workers' law or right, who developed this question to its fullest extent.

Institutionalizing the Collective Force

Not only does Proudhon "discover" the collective force at the origin of social wealth,[10] but he also systematically reflects on the problem of creating institutions that are neither private property nor state property, and he does so to a far greater extent than does Marx. Proudhon, in this respect, is one of the first "institutional" theoreticians of the common. Just as we tend to underestimate Proudhon's impact on the intellectual development of early socialism (including the union movement), we also tend to underestimate his influence on Marx. Even if Marx was always a proponent of revolution against the more reformist Proudhonians, we often overlook the fact that Marx too, at times, advocated for proletarian inventions, especially institutions based on cooperation. In his inaugural address to the First International, for instance, Marx explicitly contrasted the "political economy of property" with cooperation, or what he called the "political economy of labour."[11] It was only after Marx's death that Marxism hegemonized the workers' movement to the point of more or less effacing Proudhon's contributions from socialist history, such that we tend to underappreciate the role of his ideas in the Paris Commune or in revolutionary unionism in general up until at least 1914. This is one of the reasons why we argue that a reading, or rather a re-reading, of Proudhon is so important today.

While theorizing the future society from a resolutely juridical and institutional point of view,[12] Proudhon wrote: "civilization is the product of law."[13] In *La Capacité politique des classes ouvrières*, Proudhon argues that the inferiority of the workers is due to their ignorance of this great social fact – i.e., the central importance of creating new juridical institutional forms. In other words, Proudhon argues that it is only through the development of their own economic and social laws that the workers will carve a pathway toward liberation. Georges Gurvitch, a meticulous interpreter of Proudhonian thought, argued that if social life is indeed, first and foremost, a fabric composed of the most diverse relations, then law, this "central element of society," is the basis of all social reformation.[14]

According to Proudhon, the human relationship itself is a matter of law: "nothing takes place between men but in the name of *right*."[15] Social transformation, therefore, is a matter of constructing a non-statist legal order based on living in common that is capable of regulating relations between social individuals. In other words, a form of law that will not be imposed from above all at once, but one that will progressively develop from the grass roots of society:

> Beneath the governmental machinery, in the shadow of political institutions, out of the sight of statesmen and priests, society is producing its own organism, slowly and silently; and constructing a new order, the expression of its vitality and autonomy, and the denial of the old politics, as well as of the old religion.[16]

If a new world is possible, it can only be created by establishing institutions on the basis of a social right, that is to say a legal system created by society and for society. It must be very different from the Roman legal tradition, for which the legislator was the source of law. This idea of a social right must be an ethos produced by the workers themselves, if it is to become a legal science through which workers can prevail. As Gurvitch continually emphasizes, there is a juridical Proudhon whose defining idea is the "reconciliation of socialism and the idea of the law."[17] Succinctly summarized, the purpose of this Proudhonian project is to replace the sovereignty of the state with the sovereignty of social law. The state must submit to the law emanating from society, and the political constitution must be subordinated to the "social constitution," or at the very least be counter-balanced by the proper juridical organization of society. In his later work on the concept of a federal constitution, Proudhon suggested that the state is never, or should never be, anything but the coordination of local or functional units.[18] This legal federalism, which is grounded in the idea of a society as an ensemble of relations, must be considered superior to the public law of the state and the private law of the proprietor. The social law is anterior to these other forms of law, and emerges out of a social community that pre-dates all forms of political constitution. The juridical form of the new workers' democracy is thus based on a fundamentally customary social law that organizes society on the basis of three elementary groups: the family, the municipality (*commune*), and the workshop.

For Proudhon, a true workers' law is designed to return to society full possession of its collective force. This recuperation is the true goal of the socialist movement, yet most communists and socialists do not understand this. It was Proudhon's clear intention to put an end to the "juridical skepticism" of the socialists and the communists, for largely practical, rather than theoretical, reasons. The negation of law, in Proudhon's view, will only lead to communist despotism. Yet Proudhon is forced to fight this battle on two fronts simultaneously, since he also goes to some lengths to condemn the pervasive liberal individualism that, in his view, also perverts the law.[19] Proudhon thus pits his notion of social law against all forms of "universalism" – whether it is the universalism whereby the community is viewed as a kind of superindividual that absorbs all singular personalities within itself, or the individualist brand of universalism wherein the individual is conceived as an abstract being isolated from all social relations. Against both these views, Proudhon argues that it is necessary to view society as a complex set of relations, and so we must create a form of organization that corresponds to the specific nature of this social system: "humanity, like a drunken man, hesitates and staggers between two abysses: property on the one side, community on the other. How will humanity navigate this path with its head struck by vertigo and its feet wobbling beneath?"[20] In other words, how do we escape from this false dichotomy between private property and communitarian property, between the "individualist hypothesis" and the "communist hypothesis"? For Proudhon, it should be possible to use the law to organize the collective force without crushing individual initiative. The great task of Proudhonian socialism – which is sometimes called "mutualism" or "federalism," or even "positive anarchism" – is to recognize and then organize society as a specifically social reality. In this respect, Proudhon is often taken as a proponent of the spontaneous social organization of society, in the tradition of Saint-Simon.[21] While this assessment is not entirely correct, it is true that Proudhon is particularly interested in the capacity of society to generate, through freely established contracts, a law that produces equilibrium and harmony. Against the views of someone like Louis Blanc, Proudhon shows that it is not from above, through the state, that revolution takes place. As Célestin Bouglé writes in his interpretation of Proudhon's thought, "it suffices for the citizens to directly agree on the regulations governing equal exchange. A sort of molecular revolution, a self-regeneration of society will take place that will render obsolete all the reconstructions dreamt up by political society."[22]

For Proudhon, then, the "social constitution" must replace the "governmental idea." Not the "communist project," not the utopian ideal or the great moral principle – not the "passional attraction" for Fourier or "devotion" for Cabet or Louis Blanc – but the legal constitution of the collective force. It is a mode of governmentality that will be based on social relations and economic forces, such as the division of labor or competition, and it will be geared entirely toward social justice and the organization of work. This is precisely what Proudhon calls "scientific socialism" in *What is Property?* It is not a matter of inventing everything from scratch, but of cultivating and regulating the life of the social organism; it is a process that begins from the activities of work, production, and exchange, and proceeds to re-organize society on the basis of a new law that issues from the practices and the concrete relations between individuals, groups, and functions. In the same way that ideals are born from collective forces, a new kind of law will be developed that will justly regulate relations between individuals. And this law can only be created from the ashes of Roman law, which, as we know, is characterized by the bipolarity between public and private law. Roman law, in Proudhon's view, gave birth to such a profoundly anti-social version of individualism that only oppressive state command could act as a proper counter-weight.[23] For each legal entity, it was the *will* that was regarded as an absolute, whether it was the will of the individual or the will of the state. As Gurvitch puts it, "to remedy the individual egoism, the old Roman law, by virtue of its individualistic principles, was condemned to rely on the egoism of the state. The distance is not so great between *dominium* and the *imperium*, insofar as the will of the individual, small or large, is the nucleus of the law."[24]

Social regulation, for Proudhon, emanates from practice and structures social relations. If "moral facts are essentially social facts," this is because morality belongs to the "collective being that contains and penetrates us," as Proudhon wrote to Cournot.[25] The law thus expresses social being: through the law we come to see ourselves as more than individuals; we see ourselves as we truly are, namely both "a person and a collective" at the same time. To prevent society from devolving into an admixture of small, isolated egos, it is imperative that interindividual regulation achieves a balance or equilibrium. But this regulatory law cannot be imposed by a magistrate, with or without voluntary consent; it must be drawn up by individuals collaboratively, individuals who are free to negotiate contracts between themselves. But what kind of contract are we talking about here? For if there is one thing the past few decades of "third-way" neoliberalism has taught us, it is how ambiguous the relationship between "contract" and "law" can really be.

Proudhon argues for a "synallagmatic" and "commutative" concept of the contract. Under conditions of reciprocity, this conception of the contract will lead to equilibrium between all parties. For Proudhon, the contract is able to resolve any problem between natural persons as well as between legal persons. In Bouglé's reading, Proudhon's vision of a contract-based society closely resembles the commercial model of society proffered by political economists in the eighteenth century. For Proudhon, as for the bourgeois economists, the contract supplants politics and makes government obsolete. This is why Bouglé refers to Proudhon as a "contract socialist," or even an "exchange socialist," who espouses a liberal concept of civil society as a network of voluntary contracts. Given the problematic implications of such an interpretation, we think Proudhon's thoughts on this matter merit closer examination.

The first distinction to be drawn between Proudhon's approach and normative juridical liberalism is the manner in which the Proudhonian social law does not require a supplementary state apparatus. This is because Proudhon's conception of exchange is more than the mere legalization of injustice and theft. Proudhon's approach is based on the equality that is realized when everyone receives what they are owned, according to the "true value" of their labor. The contract, then, is not conceived, as it is for liberals, as a meeting between two independent wills or two atomistic individuals. The contract is rather the formal expression of a relationship between fully social beings; it is the juridical form of a social relation of exchange that cannot be isolated from what individuals are and what they do, since individuals are essentially relational beings. The entirety of social life is made up of relations of exchange of many different kinds, all of which involve heterogeneous activities. Society, for Proudhon, should be juridically and morally constituted as a multiplicity of contracts corresponding to all these exchanges. At base, these contracts are merely objectifications that formalize and institute relations that are already occurring. As a key element of the social constitution, the contract is thus merely the legal objectification of an informal communal law, as previously manifest in the customary laws of the European communes or in the traditional economic laws that organize professional practices and interpersonal relations. As Gurvitch puts it, the contracts are "technical procedures that merely formalize a preexisting law."[26]

This assertion gives rise to another distinction vis-à-vis liberalism: if the social law is the formal objectification of social relations governed by an informal law, this means the law cannot be the expression of the wills of particular individuals, no more than it can be the "general will" embodied by a legislator. Proudhon's goal here is to restrict state law by arguing that a "social constitution" must take precedence over the state's political constitution. For Proudhon, then, the sovereignty of the law supersedes the sovereignty of the state:

> Commutative justice, the reign of contracts, an economic or industrial regime . . . all these are synonyms of an idea that will abolish the old systems of distributive justice, and the more concrete reign of feudal, government or military laws: the future of humanity lies in this displacement.[27]

There is no returning to the past; we must have no nostalgia for a more primitive state. On the contrary, it is the law that, through its development, produces civilization; it weakens an increasingly obsolete government, as society passes from "distributive justice" to commutative justice (and for Proudhon, this passage happens first in the family).[28]

And lastly, the third difference between Proudhon's social law and liberalism is the idea that exchange must be equitable. To achieve this qualification, exchange must be governed by a principle Proudhon refers to as "mutualism" (*mutualité*), which he specifically opposes to communism. If the industrial division of labor and its corresponding increase in specialization is here to stay, it is therefore necessary to regulate exchange by using a principle of reciprocity that prevents the extraction of a "tribute" from the weakest by the strongest. Mutualism is the principle of action that re-balances private property by means of reciprocity while still respecting individual liberty, since everyone is always free in relation to their commitments to others. This is not a question of common work, but of the proper circulation between producers, and between producers and consumers:

> In order to ensure perfect mutualism, it is necessary for each producer, by making certain commitments to others, who in turn commit themselves to him in the same way, retain full independence of action, in terms of the style or manner of his work: mutualism, etymologically speaking, is more about the exchange of functions than the collectivization of forces or creating a specific community of work.[29]

By the "mutualistic constitution of the nation," Proudhon means both a guarantee of justly distributed incomes to everyone through a system of mutual insurance, and justice exchanged on the basis of equal costs and penalties between persons considered equal. This approach is designed to nullify profits that are accrued merely as a result of owning property.

The "Social Constitution"

The social constitution is nothing other than the juridical self-organization of society. Beginning with the recognition of the particular rights of different sectors, the constitution proceeds toward a formalized common law for all co-producers across the whole of society.[30] Groups of producers, consumers, co-owners, associations, and public services are each bound together by this one autonomous law that, in its entirety, is the social constitution. It is not an arbitrary or voluntarist "social re-construction" imposed from above by an external government. The social constitution is the recognition of the more or less organized and explicit legal forms that govern collective life, both inside particular groups and between them, according to the principle of mutualism. The activity of these collective forces leads to a set of regulations capable of resolving conflicts. It is a kind of complex commutative justice. It is immanent to social relations, and is entirely different from the individualistic and statist law of the Roman tradition.[31] This law is rather a "social law," according to Gurvitch's formulation, that issues from real economic and social practices. Its purpose is to organize the social division of labor and ensure justice – i.e., ensure the disalienation of collective forces, whether economic, social, or political (insofar as it is possible to distinguish between these domains in the first place). What is unique to Proudhon is his view that the social law can be entrusted to re-appropriate exploited and alienated social forces.

As Gurvitch pointed out, the idea of a social law goes back as far as Grotius, for whom the *jus natural sociale* was the primary and fundamental layer of natural law.[32] Grotius's core idea, according to Gurvitch, is that the "whole" – whether this is understood as part of the people, all of the people, or even relations between people – "possesses the capacity to legally and immediately bind its members together on the basis of its very essence."[33] For Grotius (and Gurvitch), then, natural individual right does not precede social right, but follows from it. The central idea found in the entire school of natural social law – of which Leibniz is the pivotal thinker – is that the state of nature is not a state of dissociation but, on the contrary, encompasses multiple social forms with their own autonomous juridical forms that are independent of state power. For proponents of natural social law, Grotius was what they called the first *socialistus*.[34]

But how does this social law emerge and develop? For Proudhon, it is the product of collective practice that, in turn, leads to the development of a kind of common reason that once more leads to the construction of social rules. Law is an intermediary phenomenon, or a form of mediation between practices and ideas. Society does not only produce goods, then, but it also secretes ideas and creates rules. It spontaneously generates its own collective reason and its own legal consciousness. This "collective reason" is the counterpart, on the ideational terrain, of the economic power that social relations themselves produce. It is through this specific kind of "reason" that society reacts to instances of alienation by trying to re-appropriate that which has been dispossessed. Thus the association of workers, their practical "co-participation" in the production of this collective force, compels these co-responsible partners to fight against competition by developing a specific class ideal. The "workers' ideal" is the principle of solidarity that arises through the co-productive practice of workers. And once the appropriate institutional form has been found, this ideal will regulate the distribution of the social product amongst them.

This new mode of regulation, or new regime, thus governs all social relations, since everyone contributes, in one way or another, to the collective force. The social law, that recognizes and organizes the collective force, must therefore adapt to the diversity of its practical modalities. Organizing these relations between individuals within productive units and within society cannot, therefore, proceed on the basis of a single formula, principle, or regulation. This new mode of social organization is necessarily pluralistic, since social relations are themselves differentiated and the collective force takes different forms. For example, Proudhon differentiates between two major modalities of social relation: a *directly cooperative* relation in organizations or groups, and a *commutative* relation made possible by the division of labor and the instruments of exchange. This commutative relation, or the relation of reciprocity, is an exchange of equivalents that guarantees economic harmony on a "true basis" – i.e., on the quantity of labor embodied in the products of labor. In this way, Proudhon believes he can establish, especially through the institution of the "People's Bank," what the liberals have failed to realize: a state of economic equilibrium based on fair contracts.

We may infer, then, that associationism is not imposed in the same way upon every kind of activity: "association as dogma is refuted," writes Proudhon. Association is an appropriate governmental form only for certain kinds of economic activities and certain forms of labor: it is compatible with industrial activity, but not in agriculture or artisanal work, nor any situation involving a lone worker who wants to exchange his products on a true and just basis, according to the principles of commutative justice alone. For artisans and agricultural peasants must be able to work outside the associationist form (if this is what they want), since for them, as individual owners, the collective force to which they contribute is based on exchange and therefore necessitates a fair contract between producers and consumers. For Proudhon, then, the social and democratic republic will therefore assume a plural form: the peasants will manage the soil; the artisans will enjoy independence, property, and their trade; while the wage workers will be (associational) owners of their respective industries.

Associationism is thus merely the legal form suited to the collective force manifest in spaces like workshops or industrial enterprises. For it is principally there, as Proudhon showed in his work in 1840, that the right of workers over the value generated by their cooperation is most intensely violated and where collective ownership needs to be primarily imposed. In cases where a combination of different specialties is required for collective work, where "man fits in with man as wheel with wheel; the whole group of workers forms a machine, like the fitting of the parts of a clock or a locomotive," then "association seems to me absolutely necessary and right."[35] This will lead, in Proudhon's view, to the birth of "industrial democracy," which will replace "industrial feudalism" and ward off the dangers of "industrial empire," as Proudhon argues in his 1857 *Speculator's Manual*. Such "workers' companies" will be particularly prevalent in mining, the railways, and large factories:

> In cases in which production requires great division of labor, and a considerable collective force, it is necessary to form an ASSOCIATION among the workers in this industry; because without that, they would remain related as subordinates and superiors, and there would ensue two industrial castes of managers and wage-workers, which is repugnant in a free and democratic society.[36]

"The great industries, terrible engines of aristocracy and pauperism, become, in their turn, one of the principle organs of liberty and public prosperity."[37] But, for Proudhon, it would be dangerous for each factory to isolate itself and reserve the surplus it generates for its own members. Society, in this instance, has a right of inspection and control, and even dissolution of an industry in cases such as these. This great industrial association would thus be bound by a double pact: much like a "colony," these associations would have duties and rights in relation to the mother country, as constituted in a pact between the associations. Internally, the jurisdiction of the associates within their particular groups will establish what Proudhon calls an "industrial democracy." This "institution, that has no precedent and no model,"[38] will provide its members with election rights, access to training, undivided ownership, and a progressive career:

> By participation in losses and gains, by the graded scale of pay, and the successive promotion to all grades and positions, the collective force, which is a product of the community, ceases to be a source of profit to a small number of managers and speculators: it becomes the property of all workers. At the same time, by a broad education, by the obligation of apprenticeship, and by the cooperation of all who take part in the collective work, the division of labor can no longer be a cause of degradation for the workman: it is, on the contrary, the means of his education and the pledge of his security.[39]

It is not difficult to see why those who wanted to renew the struggle for worker autonomy or self-management in the 1970s saw Proudhon as something of a pioneer.

Federalism as Social and Political Organization

For Proudhon, worker control must not only be imposed in the realm of economic production: it is the whole mode of social and political organization that must be overhauled by the social constitution. First and foremost, this new associational form must replace the state. In this respect, then, we find the great Saint-Simonian idea of replacing top-down authority, government, and state law with a new "horizontalist" re-structuring of society as re-formulated by Proudhon. Yet for Proudhon, it is around the primacy of labor, the true substance of society, that the whole of society can and should be completely re-organized: "the government will be dissolved by the workshop" in the future society, asserts Proudhon.[40] Proudhon's *general idea of the revolution* is thus aptly summarized in the concise phrase "absorption of government within the economic organism," which is the title of Proudhon's seventh study in his *General Idea of the Revolution in the Nineteenth Century* (1851). Yet unlike Saint-Simon, who distrusted the law and lawyers, Proudhon argues that social and political unity is not arrived at through the play of economic forces alone, but must include the law as well:

> In place of the ancient classes of nobles, burghers, and peasants, or of business men and working men, we will put the general titles and special departments of industry: Agriculture, Manufacture, Commerce, &c. In place of public force, we will put collective force. In place of standing armies, we will put industrial associations. In place of police, we will put identity of interests. In place of political centralization, we will put economic centralization.[41]

Proudhon's greatest distrust has always been reserved for the government, which he views as an essentially incompetent instrument for transforming society, as he made clear in his *La Solution du problème social* (1848). The new social law will not be statist in character: it will be the legal form of the workers' associations, mutualist organizations, and federative structure. But will this new society also include political organizations of some kind? Will the economy absorb politics entirely, or should the workers also create some kind of non-governmental organization? This is the question that is at the center of Proudhon's final works.

For a long time, Proudhon was opposed to the idea of a "political constitution" and argued instead for a "social constitution." Indeed, he often spoke about how these two constitutional forms were "incompatible."[42] The social constitution, for Proudhon, is nothing more than the contractual formalization of economic relations and the expression of the equilibrium of economic interests. A political constitution, however, is all about the centralization of economic force, the separation or reification of political power, and all of these tendencies arranged hierarchically. However, Proudhon's opposition between the "social" and the "political" superficially equates state institutions with politics as such; it is a reduction that is common to both the Saint-Simonian socialists as well as to Marx,[43] and so it should not be too surprising that Proudhon reproduces this theoretical limitation as well. For we must recognize, in this respect, that socialism emerged during a specific historical period in which worker emancipation was thought to turn on the ability to re-appropriate social forces that were seen to have been monopolized or captured by external or parasitic institutions. And so while Proudhon, for many years, spoke of the state dissolving into the workshop (like Saint-Simon and Marx), his thought did shift in his later years toward a somewhat different regime he called "industrial democracy." While this new model would still include both the workshop and municipalities, it was now thought to require specifically political institutions of a unique kind. If Proudhon initially thought the state and the government must be dissolved within the socio-economic domain, in a prototypically Saint-Simonian way, his later work tries to articulate the two processes or institutions. In this later work, he views the state as the site or form of a specific and indissoluble reality in its own right, a kind of collective force with its own *raison d'être*. But politics must never be thought of as either anterior or superior to society. (Gurvitch also emphasized the evolution of Proudhon's thought in this respect by observing how Proudhon initially viewed the state's political authority as nothing more than an extension of the right of war.) In *De la justice dans la révolution et dans l'Eglise* (1858), however, Proudhon "highlights the multiplicity of different groups that make up the framework of social life, by both limiting and collaborating with each other."[44]

But how are we to make the jump from the local workshop, farm, or municipality to a national political structure? What form will this national level take? What will be the relationship between the collective units that make up this political society? In his later work, Proudhon tried to answer these questions by combining a juridico-economic order with a political order, wherein the latter is effectively homologous (in terms of its operational structure) to the former. The solution he came up with was "federalism." Under a federal system, central power is always limited by the regulation and rights of the local units. Federalism thus acts as a brake on the centralization and alienation of a collective force that issues from local or professional groups. The problem that plagued Proudhon since the 1850s,[45] however, had to do with the two simultaneous levels upon which federalism had to function: there must be a federation of production units (economic) and a federation of communal units (political). Proudhon's later solution to this problem was to construct a universal federalism that not only encompasses every country, but which also penetrates into every aspect of society as well. In other words, the workers must construct a federated system that strikes a balance between two forms of democracy: the *political* democracy of the municipalities or communes and the *industrial* democracy of the workers' enterprises. And once again, the law is called upon to be primarily a balancing or regulatory force. The principle of federalism is meant to balance the conflict between two legal systems: the economic law of the workers' associations and the political law of the municipalities. And this is all possible, for Proudhon, because of a distinction he makes between two types of federation: a political federation and the agricultural-industrial economic federation.

In *Contradictions politiques*,[46] Proudhon argues that federalism is much more than mere "decentralization," which simply denotes the devolution of power away from the centralized state without ever fundamentally questioning the form of the state as such.[47] Federalism, for Proudhon, begins with the living unity of the natural group, meaning every other "unity" in the social order is artificial. This natural group, which is the wellspring of this new political force, is also called the "collective man," which of course refers to Proudhon's cherished idea of the "collective worker." It is not the family, as the counter-revolutionary conservative tends to believe, much less the individual, that is the basis of society. It is the union of many local families that makes up this elementary society, and this elementary society then "constitutes" itself as a discrete *polis* or municipality – the two terms are completely synonymous for Proudhon – thereby becoming sovereign. In short, political federalism for Proudhon is entirely *communalist*. This elementary social unit is defined by its natural cohesion and concomitant inviolability. For Proudhon, there is a law of nature that dictates the size of such units: if such units become too large, they will naturally divide and tear apart. This is why Proudhon thinks the children born in these elementary units would have to leave and create new families and found new colonies that would themselves become independent cities or municipalities. For Proudhon, the unity that large states artificially impose from the outside cannot respect the real autonomy of nature beings, and thus monarchies and republics are really just different forms of the same tyranny.[48] The self-direction of social life is essential for Proudhon,[49] and political autonomy depends on the capacity of a political unit to direct itself without outside interference:

> Whenever men, followed by their wives and children, gather in one place and live together, share in the same culture, develop common industries, nurture neighborly relations, and create spontaneously bonds of solidarity, they form what I call a natural group. This natural group soon becomes a city or a commensurate form of political organization, and asserts its unity, its independence, and its life, movement (Autokinèsis), and autonomy.[50]

Political organization must therefore be constructed, first and foremost, from the basis of this fundamental unit. Several of these units then enter into a more complex agreement based on "mutual insurance," whereby they are able to guarantee their interests and develop their collective wealth while, at the same time, avoiding a "process of self-immolation before this new Moloch."[51] This federation of indestructible elementary units is then connected through a legal agreement between cities that does not, however, deprive each city of its independence or sovereignty:

> The city or commune is in essence – like every man, family, individual or intelligent or moral collective – a sovereign entity. The commune thus has a right to govern

> and administer itself, which includes collecting taxes, distributing properties and income, creating schools, appointing intellectuals, staffing the police force, national guard, and reserve or civic guard, appointing judges, organizing its own newspapers and journals, creating civil society organizations, businesses, banks, etc. The community codifies decrees and statutes, but it does not go so far so as to legislate laws from above. Each commune has its own church, its own form of worship, and its clergy are freely chosen. Each commune openly discusses everything that concerns its interests and enthralls public opinion in city councils and in its newspapers and journals. This is what each commune is: everyone leads an active and full life, universally. It rejects all limitations; its only limit is itself, and all external coercion is deeply unpopular.[52]

This communalist type of political federalism, based on mutualist links between cities, does not annul economic democracy but supplements it. It works in tandem with the "agricultural-industrial federation," and thereby enables each economic group to overcome its local particularism without reducing its independence. But to what extent does the political federation of the municipalities and their various public services take precedence over economic organization? Is it not at the political level that the working class implements its policies and its "ideal"? Does democracy not itself develop within this political federation? Where once Proudhon was vehemently anti-government, he now seems to have adopted a more politically oriented concept of self-government. His democratic ideal now seems to be that "every multitude must also be a ruling multitude; society, under these conditions, is now identical and adequate to the state, just as are producers and consumers within political economy."[53]

The "Proletarian Law"

In *De la capacité politique des classes ouvrières*, Proudhon argues for the "reorganization of industry under the jurisdiction of all those involved in industry," and this is to be accomplished through the implementation of a "new conception of the law."[54] This is the basis of Proudhon's idea of the "workers' enterprise" and agricultural-industrial federalism. He very clearly argues that his aspiration in this respect involves nothing less than the creation of an entirely new "civilization." For Proudhon, however, this total re-organization will not be achieved through a political *coup d'etat*, much less an eventual or hypothetical electoral victory. Rather, workers must immediately disengage from economic and political subjugation. And in order to make this disengagement work, Proudhon argues that the proletarians need to develop their own "subjectivity and autonomy" on the basis of the workers' movement itself, wherein the logic of the collective force reigns unhindered. In order to establish its own law, the proletariat must become an organized collective force: it must develop its own ideas and reject the representative institutions within which the proletariat's interests always come last. In short, the proletariat must create its own institutions. This is Proudhon's final message. And, as we will see below, while it may have been largely forgotten, it was a message that greatly influenced the numerous communist insurrectionists of 1871.

This idea that the wellspring of emancipation is proletarian institutional creativity inspired numerous socialist thinkers after Proudhon, including Sidney Webb in England and the French historian Maxime Leroy, who, in 1913, documented and analyzed the institutional forms created by the French proletariat since the mid-nineteenth century. In *La Coutume ouvrière* (*The Customs of the Working Class*)[55] Leroy provides a detailed description of what he calls the "proletarian law" – i.e., "the set of written or verbal rules that govern proletarian life and sociability."[56] Leroy's guiding premise is that there is indeed a "spontaneous workers' law, a direct and original creation of a proletariat grouped in federalist form, but it is a law grounded in customs without assuming explicit juridical form."[57] This is why Leroy prefers to speak of "proletarian law" instead of "labor law": in conventional usage, "labor law" refers to the regulation of labor by public authorities, whereas proletarian law designates the non-juridical rules of the proletariat itself, completely independent of public or state regulation. However, the use of the term "custom" in the title of book is somewhat misleading. The term is problematic in Leroy's usage insofar as he understands it as "a habitual way of acting, fixed by use," as if the transmission of old customs was sufficient in itself for establishing the kind of proletarian law he talks about. Leroy, in this respect, seems to suggest that the working class had already accumulated a sort of customary right of its own, one made up of norms transmitted by tradition and passively adopted by those who currently respected and obeyed them. From this perspective, proletarian law is nothing more than a class-biased form of "common law" that is produced by workers and designed for their exclusive use. For Leroy, the term "custom" essentially designates authority derived from a rule grounded in antiquity and longevity, and whose force of obligation largely rests on its historical character. But what Leroy's actual investigation shows is the creativity of the working class, its capacity to invent and re-invent its own history and its own tradition, rather than merely perpetuating and updating a centuries-old tradition. For the modern proletariat is not merely an updated version of the old medieval guilds: it had to invent new institutions that did not exist prior to the industrial revolution, and it had to deploy regulatory practices that became the source of its newfound laws. In this sense, Leroy agrees with Pelloutier when he said that people are above all "creators and inventors."[58]

Despite Leroy's use of the term "custom" – which was of course derided by modern legal orthodoxy – it is worth asking whether Leroy's analysis is not actually based on a rather orthodox concept of the law, which, if true, would put considerable distance between his work and Proudhon's project. Leroy's ostensible aim is to denounce the artificial antithesis of an anarchic society and a well-ordered legal apparatus that is imposed on the latter from the outside, but it is precisely his conception of the law as the "demiurgic master of social chaos" that allows him to interpret proletarian law as "custom" (i.e., not law as such). Proletarian "custom" is described as a "rich and mobile system of customs whose obligatory character does not come from public authority but from the necessities that arise whenever men live together in common,"[59] precisely because it does not have the abstract nature that is characteristic of modern law. In other words, if it is immanent to society, rather than being imposed from above, this by definition means we are dealing with custom rather than law:

> Custom is not superimposed on society, or on the organization of society: it is society itself. There is no custom, on the one hand, and society on the other … From the moment there is a society, there is necessarily a collection of social attitudes, or customs.[60]

And there was a second reason why Leroy was hesitant to conceive of proletarian law as a genuine form of law: it is not the product of a public institution. A union is, for Leroy, a private association. What kind of law, then, does a union produce? Leroy argues as follows:

> In relation to the law, a union is a private association within a constitutional system: in the minds of its members, the union is a tax collector, a legislator, a judge, and an autonomous administrator. As the manager of the collective interests of the workers, and the guardian of their corporation, the union is conscious of being invested with genuine sovereignty over all things relevant to the profession. In practice, it has all the characteristics and all the ambitions of a public association.[61]

Leroy's description thus betrays his intent. "In practice," he argues, the union produces rules that, for its members, are indeed legally binding. It does, therefore, seem to produce and operate according to its own specific form of the law. Yet the orthodox view maintains that law must emanate from a genuine public authority alone. Law should have the seal of public authority, and not come from social life or from professional or productive sectors. Yet the facts of Leroy's analysis seem to come to a very different conclusion: the rules of the proletariat "effectively organize an allegedly unorganized part of society."[62] While Leroy's objective might have been to valorize a certain notion of "custom" at the expense of standard legal hegemony, his analysis actually renders this seemingly clear distinction rather ambiguous. For what his work actually shows is that workers' *practices* actually lead to the production of their own rules and their own law – and these rules are rendered authoritative once they are codified in proletarian institutions. This conclusion in fact substantively overlaps with the premises of Durkheimian sociology and, more especially, with the Maussian conception of socialism. Speaking to Webb's work on the history of trade unions, Mauss, for instance, argues that unions have actually produced a new social fact: "what is most manifest is the creation of a new law, a workers' law, and the birth of a new moral subjectivity, the union … the union movement, the cooperative movement, are the real facts of worker emancipation."[63]

Yet once Leroy outlines his work in a more detailed fashion, his underlying purpose becomes much clearer:

> To explain the statues of the workers' associations, article by article, as so many laws, to confront the rules of the workshop, the rules of the strike, the rules of cooperation between workers, is to study a legal system that is unique to the proletariat. It is law in formation, and thus law already partially formed and applied, the object of which is to regulate the relations between members of these

> societies, and between the societies and their employers. It is law unrecognized although written, and law unknown but nonetheless applied.[64]

Leroy constantly insists that we must not underestimate the importance of proletarian law. We have already discussed the false symmetry Marx established between the pre-capitalist past and the post-capitalist future, between the constitution of the bourgeois class from within the framework of feudalism and the development of the proletariat within the "envelop" of capitalism, despite the asymmetrical nature of each of these different moments of economic and political development. For Leroy, however, who not only follows Proudhon's lead but who also draws on the work of historian Pierre-Émile Levasseur,[65] there are indeed striking analogies between these two historical moments, at least when examined from a juridico-institutional point of view. For Leroy, proletarian law is indeed comparable to bourgeois law prior to 1789: worker solidarities established by proletarian law are not fundamentally different from the communal solidarities that played a determinate role in the bourgeoisie's ability to assert their power against the feudal integument:

> Long before the appearance of royal ordinances, the bourgeoisie empirically developed rules that were opposed to feudalism and specifically tailored to their interests. The Revolution gave these rules real existence, transformed them into laws, and the Empire then turned these laws into codes . . . We are spurred on by the class physically closest to work. It was the bourgeoisie, but now it is the workers.[66]

This is why Leroy argues that the workers' movement "is essentially constituted by a system of regulations that produces a discipline as clear as that produced by bourgeois civilization."[67]

The worker's movement, in sum, is an institution: it consists not only of common memories and historical traditions, but also – and above all – common rules. Its strength and place in society is not solely the result of anger, its instinctual hatred of the bourgeoisie. Rather, its position in society is based on rules and codes that have emerged out of past struggles and have been adapted to current practices. Far from merely a vague, generalized social custom, these codes are very precise and technical. As Leroy puts it:

> Union law is complex, forward-oriented, and abundant in terms of its constitutional and civil rules, its dictates on mutualism and assistance, its morality, and its discipline. None of it is simple, and the least of its precepts are the product of a long history. Union law is much more than a verbal and floating tradition of empirical and arbitrary rules. The texts on the matter are so numerous that they really form several codes, feature voluminous works of pressing necessities, and feature a consciousness whose methodological development is the result of collective deliberation at congresses and the concomitant uncertainties of political activity.[68]

Proletarian law is produced by and through the proletariat's struggle, and this legal codification alone is evidence that the proletariat is aware of its social position and its potential historical role: "it is through the union that the worker becomes conscious of himself; it is there that he reflects on his condition, that he seeks to improve it, that he learns to solve the problem of his inferiority, ignorance, and obedience by reflection and action.[69] We can clearly see here how Leroy's work diverges from numerous theoretical discourses that conceive of "class consciousness" as a phenomenon that is fundamentally separate from social institutions, or which situates class consciousness in a politically active vanguard. The collective force – i.e., the union and the association of workers – is nothing without the organizations that constitute it, and class consciousness – what Proudhon calls the "*idée ouvrière*," and which, for Proudhon, is fundamentally a matter of uniting in order to ward off the ravages of competition amongst workers – can only ever be embodied and extended through these organizations. There is no solidarity without corresponding moral and legal obligations. If workers are to insist on their rights to their employers, they must first recognize their duties toward each other, in Leroy's view.[70] This obligation of solidarity presupposes a collective discipline that the unions often describe in very precise terms: respect union statutes, attend assemblies, pay membership dues, respect the minimum wage, refuse piecemeal work, pay for overtime, respect the dignity of all workers, show solidarity with those on strike, etc. It is by virtue of these organized rules of mutual obligation that the workers form not only a class, but a *society*.[71] The general principle of solidarity and the struggle against interworker competition – which is the fundamental basis of proletarian law and union obligation – is also at the root of worker internationalism, which is merely conceived as a way to extend the principle of worker co-obligation as far as possible.[72]

The universe of the working class is thus one built from institutions and moral rules: it is an autonomous juridico-moral universe. Almost half a century after Proudhon's death, Maxime Leroy documented the unique form of "reason" behind the development of workers' institutions. Trade unions, workers' councils, and cooperatives and mutualistic societies of varying sorts are not only economic organizations designed to satisfy the material needs of their members; unions are not merely organizations that allow workers to receive greater value for their labor on the market. For Leroy, the significance of the union extends beyond economic rationale alone. While actions like strikes undoubtedly contribute to the constitution of the workers as a class, such actions are not momentary and impulsive irruptions but are actions that deploy a pre-existing form of discipline that is fixed within a specific institutional framework. The general strike is not therefore based on myth or some other mystical belief – as was often denounced – but, for Leroy, is based on the "culmination of a vast organizational creation … [and] the realization of confederal discipline."[73] To create this kind of society, to build a "workers' society" within the context of the larger bourgeois society – which is what proletarian organization is all about, after all – also entails political consequences. This emergent society within society, by disseminating its norms throughout the rest of society, might at one point rise to a position of dominance, at which point it will translate its moment of organizational maturity into a political platform. We can see, then, how substantive Proudhon's influence is, even if many of the details of his ideas and works have been abandoned or forgotten. After an initial period of mistrust, many socialists, until 1914, saw unions, workers' councils, and cooperatives as the germ form of a new society. The same hope for a new kind of society still drives proponents of what today is referred to as the "social and solidarity economy," which includes associations, cooperatives, and mutualistic institutions of all kinds. In both cases, it is the same basic logic at work: the new class trying to change society does not merely quantitatively increase within the old society, but rather it must first create its own collective institutions, rules of solidarity, even its own culture, and all initially to suit its class needs, much like the rising bourgeoisie within feudal society. Simply put, the union, the cooperative, or the mutual association must, in this view, fulfill the same historic role played by the medieval commune in the context of feudal law: namely, to create a new legal form within the framework of the old.

The Socialist Cooperation of Mauss and Jaurès

After the initial development of the cooperative movement around people like Robert Owens and William Thompson, the idea of creating autonomous workers' institutions was taken up and enriched by the dual contributions of sociology and socialism, until about the beginning of the twentieth century. Theoretical reflection on the social and political functions of workers' institutions was at the core of Émile Durkheim's sociology and was even more central to the work of his nephew, Marcel Mauss. The great sociological and political lesson to be learned from Mauss is that the logic of the gift – which is so often imbricated within (but never reducible to) market relations – is the underlying principle of a wide range of attitudes, practices, and institutions in various types of societies. Mauss, as we know, called for a "return to the archaic" in our social relations, but this archaic content must be housed within the context of radically new historical forms. In his famous essay on the gift (1924), Mauss argued that the symbolic representation of valued goods was a universal social fact, "one of the human foundations upon which our societies are built."[74] The social bond, in all societies, presupposes that at least some of the goods circulating amongst members are the signs and instruments of obligations we all accept in order to live in society, whatever the "profane" uses of these goods may be. Of course, Mauss never claimed to have isolated a "pure gift" through his research, but rather he differentiated amongst various modes of gift distribution across a diverse range of relations, including competition and the exchange of goods. And, just as many seemingly "disinterested" relations often still involve forms of profit, the converse is also true: monetary exchanges and relations of power are not devoid of gift-like qualities. Numerous sociological works have shown the various ways in which the logic of the gift functions in capitalist societies, whether in terms of direct interactions between individuals or the social functions of institutions in fields such as education or health, for instance.[75] And as Mauss emphasized in his famous essay, this is undoubtedly also true of workers' institutions of social solidarity created at the beginning of the twentieth century.

The Maussian thesis on the continuation of "the gift" in modern societies should be viewed in light of Mauss's political commitment to cooperative socialism, a commitment that long preceded his theory of the gift and which inflected his famous work with its historical and political significance.[76] As a young socialist activist, Mauss was a member of the cooperative society *L'Avenir de Plaisance*, and was one of the principle founders of the "Socialist Bakery" on the rue Barrault, in the thirteenth arrondissement of Paris. Like Jaurès, Mauss was a great admirer of the Belgian cooperatives and the "People's Home" in Brussels. And, also like Jaurès (whom he apparently influenced on this point), Mauss viewed cooperatives as an organized forced that could be expanded to become one of the pillars of a future socialist society.[77] The cooperatives, as well as the mutualistic societies, unions, and socialist parties, were, for Mauss and Jaurès, two levers of socialism, each with its own function. These institutions advance the cause of socialism or, more precisely, "they make their socialism," as Mauss wrote concerning consumer cooperatives.[78]

Socialism, for Mauss, is thus the political art of making it possible for specialized and differentiated individuals to work and live in common. In this respect, Mauss is squarely in the Durkheimian tradition: the disappearance of the clans, great families, or politico-domestic power in general, means scattered and isolated individuals are directly confronted with the central power of the state – as can be seen, for example, in Le Chapelier's attempt to suppress the formation of any intermediate group between the individual and the state. What lies in wait for modern societies is nothing less than the amorphism that was wrongly associated with archaic societies. Under the heel of both the state and private business, modern societies abandon masses of unorganized consumers to a state of *anomie*, a state shorn of any reciprocal bonds.

How can we properly address this situation of individual isolation without falling into the various forms of integrated communitarianism or without adopting violent practices aimed at re-establishing totalitarian state sovereignty over social activities, as in the example of bolshevism? Mauss's sociological intuition – which was greatly influenced by de Tocqueville's discussion of local civic associations, perhaps even more so than Durkheim's work on professional groups – is that these problems can only be addressed by the creation of collective institutions based on social cooperation. For Mauss, the solution requires a multiplicity of groups and subgroups (especially professional ones) that will revive society.

The true revolution can only be realized through the creation of an extensive social law or right supported by the creation of new institutions as well as older collective institutions that still play an important role in modern societies. In this way, the spirit of the gift will once again pervade our atomistic societies, though without succumbing to a naïve romanticism that would nullify the West's progression toward greater individual and collective freedom as well as greater social equality. Mauss's socialism is in this respect more similar to that of Pierre Leroux, who famously argued that the third term – "fraternity" – is too often neglected by republicans. Cooperative socialism and unionism, for Mauss, are new conjunctural forms linking material economies, the lives of groups, and the circulation of ideas. Through these new forms of organization, not only can the economy regain its profound and real inscription in the ensemble of networks and circuits that make up society, but workers who have been injured, weakened, or atomized as a result of individual wage labor can also recover, through cooperation and common action, the necessary collective force to enhance their work and their lives. As Durkheim already argued, socialism is not first and foremost a doctrine or ideology of material interests and economic needs: socialism is fundamentally about dignity and recognition. In this sense, Mauss's conception of socialism has very little to do with the notion of a perfectly unified and classless society.[79] Mauss's socialism is about building a society that is much more differentiated than modern nations already are. It imagines a society that is animated by the incessant agonistic struggle to balance exchanges in the direction of a greater and greater reciprocity between groups, under the coordination of a political center tasked with trying to guide the efforts of all subgroups according to a common course. Socialist cooperation, whether in terms of consumption or production, does not therefore imply the re-establishment of an archaic community without any state domination; rather, it calls for institutions of cooperation and a law of the common. And the purpose of cooperation is not only to create non-capitalist spaces within modern societies, but to construct a new legal framework and a new morality of solidarity based on the practices of collective work.

Transforming Subjectivity by Transforming Social Practices

Both Marcel Mauss and Jean Jaurès conceive of social struggle according to three "pillars," or three forms of activity: political activity, union activity, and cooperative activity.[80] In *Le Movement Socialiste* of October 15, 1899, Mauss writes:

> It is unnecessary to show here how essential and fundamental the workers' organizations are. French socialism is seriously weakened by failing to be sufficiently allied with them. Without these organizations, there is no solid basis for political action. But through them, the total emancipation of the proletariat becomes possible from within capitalist society. The socialist unions and cooperatives are the foundation of the future society. They will be its conservative forces, the guarantors against all reaction. They will be the powerful and legitimate heirs of capitalism; they shall be the legal persons to whom all current property will be transferred.[81]

Mauss thus rejects the illusion of cooperative and socialist phenomena existing on the margins of capitalist society. In Mauss we see the echo of several decades of debate within the workers' movement that lead to a schism in the 1870s, a schism through which an independent socialist, even anti-socialist, cooperative movement arose, led by Charles Gide. For Mauss, as for Jaurès, however, trade union or cooperative action is meaningless except within the context of large-scale socialist transformation. And while Mauss may have appropriated Gide's term "cooperative republic," Mauss did not mean, by this term, a kind of cooperative space carved out within the bourgeois republic, but rather he used to the term to signal the fact that the principle of cooperation must be the foundation of the social republic. As Mauss put it in *L'Humanité* in August of 1904, "what makes a cooperative socialist is the constant goal of abolishing wage labor through cooperation (amongst other means), and of working in the service of proletarian emancipation."[82] For Mauss, the goal is to introduce the principle of cooperation across a greater and greater swath of the economy, so that socialism spreads more and more each day. For just as capitalism is internally driven, socialism too has an internal motor, which is the systematic re-investment of profit into the society.[83]

This is the basis of Jaurès's commitment to socialism as well.[84] We know that the turning point for Jaurès, in terms of his conversion to cooperative socialism, was the cooperative formed by the glassworkers at Albi (France). From this point on, Jaurès conceives of cooperatives as "laboratories of social experimentation." For Jaurès (like Mauss), cooperatives are much more than institutions designed to supply cheap goods, and much more than a source of funding for political parties – which was the view of many socialists at the time. Cooperatives, above all, are concrete means of demonstrating the advantages of socialism by way of example, and thus an essential means of "practical propaganda for the Communist Party," not only in urban and industrial areas but in the countryside as well: "especially in the countryside, with its undeniable persistence of small holdings, it is only through socialist cooperation that communism will gain a foothold."[85]

At the Cooperative Congress in July 1900, Jaurès declared, "it is not enough for cooperatives to become socialist, socialism must become cooperative."[86] Jaurès continued, "I do not mean by this that socialism should abandon or subordinate every other form of action, or that it should undermine the primacy of political action aimed at realizing the general expropriation of capitalist property. What I do mean is that socialism should not work against cooperatives." For Jaurès, cooperation is the flesh and the body of the socialist ideal; it is the union of the ideal and the real, and it is also a crucial form of apprenticeship for the proletariat's future management of the means of production.[87]

Cooperation and trade unions are, above all, what Marx already called the "schools of socialism." Mauss is particularly explicit on this point. The unions "are not merely mutual savings accounts or organizations of corporatist greed, but are mechanisms of struggle, institutions of workers' law, and organs of the future society."[88] This is the great lesson Mauss learns from his reading of *The History of Trade Unionism*. As the Webbs show, cooperative unions are a space of "awakening, in the organization of the union, of a new form of social conscience":

> It is here we seen the emergence of a new juridical body, new principles of action, new motives for sacrifice and solidarity, and new means of growth and conquest. What is most evident is the creation of a new law, a new workers law, and the birth of a new legal person in the union. The union does more than merely improving the material lot of the individual worker; it asks everyone to subordinate and sacrifice, and it makes them part of a larger collectivity. It produces a new form of acting and thinking.[89]

Socialist activity is always a practice of transformation for those involved. It is in this sense, as Mauss insists, that this activity must not be seen as purely political or economic, but always profoundly "social." Cooperative institutions and unions engage in what we might call "total social activity." Indeed, Mauss argues that "the organized economic action of the proletariat includes a juridical and moral dimension of the highest and most beautiful novelty." More than anything, novelty of cooperative practice lies in the self-transformation of workers through the creation of "new forms of life," including new psychological dispositions. Mauss's conception of transformative cooperative is undeniably similar to the Marxian concept of "self-activity":

> Economic facts are themselves social facts (money, value, etc.) and thus psychological facts, just like all the other social facts connected to them, which they determine and which are in turn determined by them (property law, for example). What is unique to socialism is its claim to be concerned with the totality of social facts. If these social facts have a psychological dimension, socialist action will therefore also be psychological in nature. It will be a psychological effort. It will give rise to a new way of seeing, thinking, and acting in the minds of individuals and throughout the social group. It will create a new mental attitude and, consequently, a new form of practice. Socialist action must instill socialist consciousness wherever it is absent. It must arouse new forms of life, which will be those of the future society, in the individual and in the group at the same time: it must lead to a new way of behaving vis-à-vis facts, a new law, a new social hierarchy, a new set of values; a new moral system of penalties and rewards, one that chastises the idle that flourish in our present society. In a word, social action today forges the framework, the bold metallic structure of the society of tomorrow.[90]

It is practice that counts; practice allows us to modify mental habits. The practice of cooperation, which is what makes one a "good socialist,"[91] does not only have an effect on the economy, but it affects all dimensions of human life:

> Every society is a whole that includes moral, technical, economic, etc., dimensions. Politics, morality, and economics are simply elements of the social art, the art of living in common . . . Social practice is the only platform for connecting the action of the moralist, the economist, the legislator. Or, put differently, there is no room for three kinds of technicians in this particular art form. Those who wish to be experts in social practice should not overcome mores by laws, nor criticize, in the name of a universal morality, or in the name of a purely practical reason, the technical, economic, and mental habits of the people. Such things can only be corrected by substituting other habits in their place, habits inspired by other ideas and feelings and, above all, by other acts whose successes turn into precedents.[92]

It is indeed the human subject itself that is transformed by practice, and through practice alone that individuals may acquire "a more fixed, grand, and beautiful part of social, aesthetic, intellectual, moral, and material life," which is the ultimate goal of socialism, after all.[93] It is in the same spirit that Mauss insists that the cooperative must also be an educational institution for the proletariat, a popular university, the "dreamt of sanctuary for the purely educational propaganda of the proletariat."[94]

As outlined in the "Cooperative Manifesto" of French intellectuals and academics of 1921, of which Mauss was one of the principle architects, cooperation is a "general program of social reconstitution" and not only at the national level.[95] Cooperation can and should become the new basis of international relations as well. Written in the aftermath of the First World War, the manifesto recalls how the cooperative movement, before the League of Nations, aimed to "modify international trade from its current form, which is the struggle for profit, and re-instate its true from, which is the cooperation of peoples resolved to use their resources in the best interests of all."[96]

These ideas led Mauss, in his "Appréciation sociologique du bolchevisme" ("Sociological Assessment of Bolshevism"), to attack the "political fetishism" of the Bolsheviks, who wanted to govern society through the use of ukases. "The Bolsheviks, romantic Marxists ... are too enslaved to the old doctrine; they believe that political power, the law, the decree, so long it was they who did the promulgating, could forge a new society."[97] We can clearly see here how Proudhon's ideas live on in Mauss. Consider, for instance, this notable assertion by Mauss: "we must cease repeating that 'the taking of political power' is the panacea of all evils."[98] For Mauss, taking political power is not the only aim; we must also create new forms of life amenable to socialism; it is a matter of directly living the social life as much as possible. "Practical socialism" is not opposed to the political project of the party, but rather prepares its realization by "drafting the future law," as Mauss wrote in 1904.[99] Marxism and Proudhonism would thus seem able to be reconcilable in the synthesis of sociology and socialism: for the cooperatives, mutualist societies, and unions the task is to "suppress capitalism a little bit each day"; the Party's task, on the contrary, is to prepare the revolution.

What Remains of the Workers' Common?

It goes without saying that the expectations of the authors we have covered, whose analyses called for the construction of workers' autonomy and the rise of "practical socialism," were almost completely dashed. The vitality of workers' organizations was weakened by a number of converging factors: the forms of work imposed by Taylorist capitalism, the nationalization of social protection, the domination of parliamentary democracy in political life, and the development of mass, bureaucratized parties led by oligarchies, etc. The institutions of workers' emancipation were almost entirely converted into schools of subordination to political or trade union oligarchies, whether social-democratic or Stalinist. The cooperatives, for their part, "followed their own trajectory and became market enterprises, and mutual aid organizations were absorbed into the systems of state protection."[100] Market mutualism and "coopitalism" prevailed in the twentieth century over socialist principles. Forms of alternative production and consumption were subject to such constraint within their respective environments that they often ended up mirroring dominant economic forms.[101]

The weakened state in which the working class finds itself today, its ongoing deunionization, its "invisibility" within society, the destruction of its organizational frameworks, and the erasure of its symbolic expressions, are crushing the hopes previous generations held about the progressive extension of the institutional autonomy of workers.[102] We still have much to learn from these experiences in terms of re-thinking the common today. Yet the core lesson seems to us very different from that which the Marxist tradition has often drawn from these experiences, which is part of the problem we find ourselves in today. If, for Marx, everything depends on the class tasked with fulfilling its great redemptive mission, it is because of the total oppression of which it is the victim and which is, in turn, supposed to turn the working class into the "universal class." But history does not show us a class passively constituted by the objective logic of capital; rather, it shows a class that was consciously created, which is to say instituted by the creation of its own categories, its own organizational frameworks, and its own moral and legal rules. The contributions of sociologists and historians who, following Proudhon, emphasized the institutional construction of solidarity and the instruments of worker struggle are thus increasingly essential in our view.

The lesson to be drawn from these experiences also seems to us to be very different from the political conclusions drawn by the "new left," whether unionist or political (associated in France with the *Confédération française démocratique du travail* and the *Parti Socialiste*), that always praises "social dialogue" between "social partners" under any circumstance, even those most unfavorable to workers. The "third way" or "third sector" ideology that frames "civil society" as both an increasingly autonomous sphere vis-à-vis the state and the market, and a substitute for genuine democracy, has led a number of the advocates of "worker self-management" to simply agree to the statist management of social affairs. It is striking, in this respect, to observe how the theme of "self-management," that once articulated (like the concept of cooperation before it) worker modes of organizational management and general forms of social constitution, has been so suddenly and thoroughly replaced by the theme of the "social economy," which is completely detached from anything that even resembles socialism.

What was the fate of the workers' common in the twentieth century? While it is impossible to catalog the innumerable social experiments that grew out of the nineteenth century in any detail here, we can identify two general forms. There was, on the one hand, the revolutionary form that tried to impose radical social and political change. This mode came into full bloom at the beginning of the twentieth century in several phases, and new organs of political power were created in each phase: 1905 and 1917 in Russia, 1918–1921 in Germany, Hungary, and Italy, and continuing on past the Second World War. This form of worker self-management then re-emerged in 1956 until the 1980s in Hungary, Yugoslavia, Czechoslovakia, Poland, and in numerous forms within the capitalist countries in the wake of May 1968 (its most famous French manifestation remains the occupation of the LIP factory in the 1970s). The second form is more modest in terms of its transformational scope, but much more widespread and accepted today. The second form includes everything that falls under the "social and solidarity economy" and encompasses a range of mutualist and cooperative associations. For both Mauss and Jaurès, these two models were by no means mutually exclusive. For Mauss, the only truly socialist dimension of the Russian Revolution was the "failed attempt at factory management by the worker councils."[103] Mauss thus advocated for a plurality of economic forms, but always under the aegis of the socialist form, and always with a view to eventual revolution. Things are very different today. The social and solidarity economy is often reduced to the "third sector," and its success is measured by its synchronic "social utility" rather than as a form of preparation for the future democratic management of all social property.

While the history of workers' councils was not entirely foreclosed, its eruptive phases have been too brief and dispersed to produce any obvious lineages or major forms of historical continuity. The displacement of the entire revolutionary model in the latter part of the twentieth century makes it especially difficult to envisage the sudden establishment of new organs of workers' power. But, above all, under contemporary historical conditions, it would be futile to expect some sort of return of the "soviets" or the "workers' councils." As we shall argue in the final part of the book, we perceive a very significant displacement of the problem in terms of the manner in which the institution of the workers' common was theorized during the long phase of industrial capitalism. To get a sense of this displacement, it is useful to review Hannah Arendt's comments on the Hungarian Revolution of 1956. There are undoubtedly many reasons to object to Arendt's opposition between the political – which she views as the proper domain of human praxis – and the economic – which is for her enslaved within the animal kingdom of essential needs. But she hit the nail on the head when she emphasized the political functions exercised by the "revolutionary councils" as opposed to the management of economic life that was exercised by the "workers' councils."[104] Arendt's analysis is in fact a complete inversion of the old Saint-Simonian myth of the dissolution of the political into the economic, which we also find in Proudhon and Marx. While remaining faithful to the memory of Rosa Luxembourg and, at the same time, one of her most original interpreters, Arendt emphasized the fact that the workers' councils – which had not been theoretically articulated in any substantive way and so were almost entirely experimental – were the only political form ever invented that posed a serious alternative to the party system.[105] As Arendt remarks, not only did this Republic of Councils fail to abolish politics, it actually extended politics to all places and forms of common activity – to the neighborhoods, to the universities and the schools, to all institutions, not just the factories.

Thus, against the Saint-Simonian notion of politics dissolving within a highly managed apparatus of production – and also against the strict partition of the political and the economic upon which this model is based – the partial experiments and the wider political experiences of the workers' movement make it possible to sketch a general political form of the common. This history tells us that forms of association, cooperation, mutualism, etc. should not be understood simply as instruments of economic management and social regulation, but as entirely political institutions. This is what disables the "social and solidarity economy" or the "third sector" from becoming a genuine alternative in itself, instead of a marginal space of conflict continually subject to relentless pressure from the dominant logic.[106]

In his inaugural address to the International Association of Workers (1864), Marx strongly emphasized how the cooperative movement that grew out of Owenism was proof that the economy could function perfectly well without its capitalist owners:

> The value of these great social experiments cannot be over-rated. By deed, instead of by argument, they have shown that production on a large scale, and in accord with the behests of modern science, may be carried on without the existence of a class of masters employing a class of hands; that to bear fruit, the means of labour need not be monopolised as a means of domination over, and of extortion against, the laboring man himself; and that, like slave labour, like serf labour, hired labour

> is but a transitory and inferior form, destined to disappear before associated labour plying its toil with a willing hand, a ready mind, and a joyous heart.[107]

But *contra* the Proudhonians, who Marx viewed as reluctant to face the realities of the political struggle, he argued that the development of economic cooperation, far from being sufficient in itself, required radical political transformation to provide the crucial momentum toward cooperative forms of organization: "to save the industrious masses, cooperative labour ought to be developed to national dimensions, and consequently, to be fostered by national means."[108] "To conquer political power," as Marx concludes, "has therefore become the great duty of the working classes."[109] Marx did not oppose cooperation at the economic level, but he also did not reject the seizure of political power by the workers: he combined them, making the latter a condition of the former. This 1864 text later finds both its complement and its correction in a subsequent text Marx wrote in homage to the Paris Commune, *The Civil War in France*. In this text Marx asserts that "the working class cannot simply lay hold of the ready-made state machinery, and wield it for its own purposes,"[110] but must create its own political form, what he calls the "communal constitution." The goal of the Commune, in this sense, was not to "take power" but to destroy the old mode of power and construct a new and very different type of political power. Marx's injunction thus breaks with the false alternative to either "take power or renounce the revolution." In other words, Marx argues, *contra* Arendt, that there is not only political praxis but an "economic" praxis as well; or, more exactly, that political praxis needs to assert itself into the very field of economy, and that it must be governed by the same principles and must also aspire to the creation of self-governing institutions. But since we cannot create these institutions out of thin air, the central question we are now faced with concerns the specific types of practices, under the conditions of struggle we currently find ourselves, that might lay the groundwork for the kinds of self-governing institutions that can make the common today.

10

Instituent Praxis

It seems to us that the law of the common cannot be conceived exclusively in terms of a "customary law." It is not that custom is unable to produce law; rather, the problem lies in the fact that the production of customary law is fundamentally based on the unconscious transmission of very old rules. As we have already seen, the transmission of custom is essentially conformational and repetitive in nature, even if changes are gradually produced over time.[1] For this reason, customary law is, in itself, incapable of instituting the principle of unappropriability, since an instituent act of this kind has to be consciously undertaken: it is an act that very consciously opposes use rights to property rights (private or state-owned). As we have discussed already, the instituent act does not precede use but is only ever realized through use.[2] There is no doubt that so-called "customs of the poor" have played an important historical role in terms of use rights, and the importance of custom for extending use rights has by no means been exhausted. Without necessarily diminishing the utility of such customs, we need to recognize, however, that such customs were primarily designed to protect against the continuous encroachments of private landowners, and in this respect many older collective rights still served an important purpose. In short, these older collective rights were designed from the beginning to co-exist with private property: the same tract of land might very well be a form of individual private property and, at the same time, give rise to collective use rights (though usually under certain temporal and geographic constraints).

The time has arrived, however, for the creation of new use rights that impose limits on private property and even begin to rescind the institution of private property itself through the recognition of unappropriability as a hegemonic social norm. Our preliminary concern in this respect, then, is to determine what kinds of practices are able to invent rules of use that are themselves capable of becoming customs over time. It is this kind of innovation that is most essential, in our view. For without this first practical step, the question of establishing customs, in the sense of ways of doing and acting, is completely devoid of meaning. No one can unilaterally decide to establish a custom, for the simple reason that customs are not the product of legislative choice or edict. *Customs are not decreed.* The difficulty of establishing customs, in this respect, is nicely highlighted by Vincent Descombes, who conveys an illuminating anecdote about a director of a private English college preoccupied with the creation of custom:

> If an individual agent, even one endowed with the authority of a college director, cannot bring new tradition into existence by a declarative act, and if a collective agent comprised of the director, his staff, and his students also cannot, then who can? *How can one willfully create a custom*?[3]

As we can see from this anecdote, substituting a collective agent for an individual agent does not in any way allow us to skirt the problem of willfully trying to establish a custom. But if it is true that an agent, whether individual or collective, cannot willfully establish a custom, is it possible to create legal rules through collective practice that are not only independent of existing laws but which actively work against them? While it is not possible to decide in advance how such practices may or may not be translated into custom, it is at least possible to begin to act in a way that permanently re-activates the power that presides over the implementation of these rules, and which is probably the best means of "making" customs in the long run. For while it is true that one does not decree a custom, *one can nevertheless decide to establish rules that may one day become custom through the sheer force of practical repetition*. This is the core and formidable problem of activity-based institutionalization.

What is an institution? From the very birth of the field, this was the question sociology posed for itself in order to delimit its object and ground the specificity of the discipline. In an article in *L'Année sociologique de 1901* titled "La sociologie. Objet et méthode," Marcel Mauss and Paul Fauconnet, two disciples of Émile Durkheim, attempted to provide a rigorous definition of sociology by making the institution its fundamental concept.[4] It is worth wondering, however, whether the concept of the institution is first and foremost a sociological concept. To sow seeds of doubt about the appropriateness of this definition, one need only examine the act from which the institution, as a system of rules, ostensibly proceeds. According to the Latin etymology, the verb *instituere* designates an act that establishes or fixes a state of things, an act of making or undertaking, a gesture of posing or planting, as well as the activity of training or educating.[5] The preliminary question is not, therefore, "what is an institution?" but rather "what kind of activity produces an institution?" Or, more simply, "what is an instituent act"?[6] With the emphatic shift from the verb to the noun – as is the case with sociology's defining concept – it is the act's result, rather than the act itself, that now garners all the attention. What comes to the foreground is now is a notion of the institution as (a) the system of rules that governs a collectivity rather than the very act of legislating, (b) the social group whose cohesion is assured by a constraining power rather than the act of transmitting or conferring this power, and (c) the educational institution rather than the educational activity. Attempts have been made to remedy this problem of nominalization by relying on the term "institutionalization" to partially designate the active dimension of the Latin verb *instituere* (or *instituer* in modern French). In the work of Chaïm Perelman (1968), for instance, "institutionalization" is conceived as the legal act that creates new institutions.[7] However, Perelman's emphasis on creative activity is not enough to entirely dispel the ambiguity inherent in the expression "institutionalization," insofar as this phrase may also designate the act of formalizing something that already exists, as when something that, to date, has been only implicitly recognized is then subsequently endowed with the fixity of an explicit rule. It is often said, for example, that the change in status that occurs when an organization acquires legal personhood is precisely an instance of "institutionalization." What we see here, then, is an instance of *ex post facto* recognition that sharply contrasts with the kind of creative activity that produces something new. In any case, this solution only foists the entire analytical difficulty of the relationship between the act and its result onto the nature of the act itself: the latter now either consists in the official consecration of something that already exists or in the making of something entirely new.

The Sociological Reduction of the Institution to the Instituted

How has sociology dealt with this duality? Or, more precisely, has it ever really dealt with it at all? For Auguste Comte, sociology's central premise is the notion that human society, like physics, biology, and psychology, is subject to intelligible laws. In other words, social phenomena can be explained by social causes, and societies or social groups have specific features that are distinct from the multitude of individuals that comprise them, and these features, in turn, determine individual behavior. Society is thus an entity comprised of collective forms or habits that pre-exist the individual and, concomitantly, shape the ways individuals act, feel, and think. Languages, matrimonial rules, and religious beliefs are all perfect examples of this. In the preface to the second edition of his *The Rules of Sociological Method* (1901), Durkheim defines an "institution" in these terms: "one may term an institution all the beliefs and modes of behaviour instituted by the collectivity; sociology can then be defined as the science of institutions, their genesis and their functioning."[8] For Mauss and Fauconnet, the word "institution" is the most appropriate term for designating "all the ways of acting and thinking that the individual finds pre-established and whose transmission is more generally achieved by education."[9] The proper object of sociology, for Mauss and Fauconnet, is therefore any pre-established set of collective habits – i.e., "ways of acting or thinking – consecrated by tradition and which society imposes on individuals." The problem, of course, is that these habits are "incessantly transforming," and these transformations must also be accounted for by sociology. To be even more precise, the problem for sociology is that these social forms are not independent variables but are rather completely interdependent on each other and their environment. The object of sociology, therefore, is the larger system that constitutes all these forms that are irreducible to individual will or sentiment.

What makes the "social" the core object of sociology is its fundamentally supra-individualistic character. The social is both exterior and superior in relation to the individual, and for this reason the social takes on a certain obligatory character for all individuals. If, in so-called "traditional" societies, the obligatory dimension of the social seems particularly powerful – as per the religious values attached to all manner of mundane activities – the individual seems rather more autonomous in "advanced" societies. In advanced societies, in other words, the social is less linked to the compulsory character of habit and is more a matter of institutional organization. Education, accordingly, is crucial for the dissemination and penetration of pre-established, institutional habits and forms amongst individuals. It is the *pre-established* nature of the social fact, the fact of already being there *before* the individual, and correlatively the fact that the individual always "finds it already there,"[10] that led Fauconnet and Mauss to propose the famous definition of sociology as the science of institutions, wherein the institution is very broadly defined as the "ensemble of *instituted* acts or ideas that individuals find already there and which are more or less imposed on them."[11] We can see here how the central feature of Mauss and Fauconnet's definition of the institution is its institut*ed* character, the fact that it is *pre-established.*

This definition allows these two authors to posit a rather audacious and naturalistic analogy: "in sum, the institution is to the social order as function is to biology: and just as the science of life is the science of vital functions, the science of society is the science of institutions thus defined."[12] This naturalistic definition thereby opened the door to what would become – especially in the Anglo-Saxon world – the twentieth-century sociological tradition referred to as structural functionalism, in which the work of Talcott Parsons is entirely paradigmatic. For this sociological school, the institution is conceptualized as completely pre-established, if not frozen entirely. Nevertheless, even the authors of this rigid interpretation of sociology recognize that the definition of the social as instituted or pre-established is somewhat wanting. What are we to make of change, of history itself, if institutions are analogous to biological function? The analytic duality of the social fact as envisaged by Comte, whereby social facts must be examined as simultaneously static and dynamic, thus continued to nag sociology into the twentieth century.

Yet despite the obvious importance of this duality, the dynamic dimension of the social fact is always conceived as a variation on the more dominant theme of the pre-established. Change does not occur *ex nihilo*. Change can only occur on the basis of pre-established institutions: "all these changes are always, to varying degrees, modifications to already existing institutions."[13] The object of sociology is thus re-defined as the science of *living* institutions, the process by which institutions are "formed, function, and are then transformed at different moments."[14]

This conception of the institution crops up again in Fauconnet and Mauss's considerations of "sociological explanation." If we explain social facts by reference to other social facts, and institutions are explained by reference to other institutions, it is difficult to maintain the notion that the influence that social structures exercise on other social structures is direct. There is no transformative force in society except what Fauconnet and Mauss call "opinion," which is to say, more precisely, "collective representation." "Social facts are therefore causes because they are representations, or they act on representations. The immediate foundation of social life is therefore a set of representations."[15] This definition, however, makes it difficult for sociologists to escape from the analytic circle that makes representations the "expression" of certain social states, while these states are simultaneously understood to be the "effects" of representations. All that can be said is that representations are the necessary mediations, conditions, and factors of change. They symbolize material states, morphologies, and institutions. By transforming, confronting, and altering their environment, these representations allow us to modify states and institutions. Hence, for Fauconnet and Mauss, "sociological explanation thus understood does not, in any degree, merit the reproach of the materialist, as sometimes been the case."[16] We have thus gone from the instituted as pre-established to the institution as modifiable by virtue of the mediation of representations, but without ever really escaping the terrain of the institut*ed*, since representations, the source of institutional modifications, are themselves also expressions of institutions.

Of course, certain sociological schools and thinkers were more concerned with re-thinking the institution in all its differential features, instead of simply diluting the concept so as to make it the singular object of sociology. Max Weber, for instance, makes an important distinction between what he calls a "*voluntary association*" (*Verein*) and a "*compulsory organization* or *association*" *(Anstalt)*.[17] These two forms of groupings are similar insofar as they are based on "rationally established rules" – which is to say "methodically" based rules. The distinction, for Weber, is that "an association's enacted order may be established in one of two ways: by voluntary agreement, or by being imposed and acquiesced in."[18] In Weber's terminology, "an order is always 'imposed' to the extent that it does not originate from a voluntary personal agreement of all the individuals concerned. The concept of imposition hence includes 'majority rule,' in that the minority must submit."[19] As Weber continues:

> The order governing a compulsory association claims to be binding on all persons to whom the particular relevant criteria apply – such as birth, residence, or the use of certain facilities. It makes no difference whether the individual joined voluntarily; nor does it matter whether he has taken any part in establishing the order.[20]

The "imposed" character of the regulations means that, for Weber, the state and the church should be classified as compulsory organizations. We are thus dealing here with "polar types" that, as Weber makes clear, "are by no means exhaustive of all conceivable types of organizations."[21] The overall sociological concern preoccupying Weber here is the sociological ability to determine the degree to which the members of a group will submit to leadership or "imposed" authority."[22] From this perspective, it is less the act of decreeing rules that garners Weber's interest, and more the manner in which the rules, once enacted, are observed. It is thus for fundamentally methodological reasons that sociology continues to shy away from a more focused examination of the institution as act or verb.

Institution, Sovereignty, Authority

In contrast to the sociological approach – which, despite its claims, ultimately fails to grasp "living institutions" in the very process of their formation – Jean-Paul Sartre's *Critique of Dialectical Reason* (1960) tries to capture the specific moment in which the "institution" emerges out of that which immediately precedes it – what Sartre calls the "organized group." It is on the basis of the institution's genesis from that which preceded it that Sartre is compelled to stress the contradictory nature of the institution. For Sartre, the institution "has the contradictory characteristic, often remarked on by sociologists, of being both *praxis* and a *thing*."[23] On the one hand, the institution as praxis is and always remains an ordered space that can be both liberating and alienating – what Sartre calls "its teleological meaning"; but, on the other hand, "the institution, as such, has considerable force of inertia":

> Not only because it is part of an institutional whole and is incapable of being modified unless all the others are modified too, but also, above all, in itself, because it posits itself, in and through its inert-being, as essentiality and defines men as the inessential means of its perpetuation.[24]

What makes the institution unique, however, is that while it is characterized by an intrinsic inertial force, its being-inertness does not suppress its practical character, which would otherwise inevitably turn the institution into a "pure corpse." We can see how, according to this specific problematization of the being of the institution, the dual characterization of the institution as "praxis" and as a "thing" is not at all the same as the previously discussed distinction of the institution as "act" and "result." Indeed, taken in itself, the distinction between "act" and "result" does not privilege the permanence or the non-permanence of the act, nor does it privilege the result: since the act is a praxis – which of course, short of being an absolute decision, it must be – this does not imply that the result of the act is one thing only. On the other hand, praxis cannot be reduced to the inaugural moment of the institution's creation, since praxis continues to support the existence of the institution well beyond its initial establishment. Praxis continues on in the institution's day-to-day operations. In other words, it is the very result itself – i.e., the instituted – that we must understand as both praxis and a thing, instead of dividing these two aspects of the institution into two disjointed temporal moments ("act" and "result"). It is therefore necessary to understand how human praxis can itself, under certain conditions, acquire the inertia of a "thing" such that it becomes an institution, by differentiating it from those practices that are devoid of this "thingness" and produce institutions nonetheless.

To this end, it is important to get some sense, however limited, of the specific progression that, for Sartre, leads from an "organized group" to an "institution." Sartre begins his examination with what he calls "practico-inert ensembles," and he then moves on to examine different kinds of "groups," before finally arriving at the category of "social classes" which, through their struggles, shape the course of history. For their part, the practico-inert ensembles include the "serial" and the "collective": if the serial constitutes a plurality of solitudes – for example, people waiting in line for a bus who are distinguished from each other only by the number on their ticket – the collective is defined as "the two-way relation between a material, inorganic, worked object and a multiplicity which finds its unity of exteriority in it."[25] An example of this kind of collectivity might be workers employed in same factory: they constitute a multiplicity of interchangeable individuals agglomerated in a fundamentally passive mode.[26] The group, on the other hand, is formed through reaction against the practico-inert ensembles; the group is defined by a common praxis and ordered toward a common end. Group praxis is based on a struggle to overcome the powerlessness and dispersion that characterize seriality, and so the analysis of the group consequently follows that of the practico-inert. But we must not misunderstand this transition: if we agree with Sartre that "the inert gathering with its structure of seriality is the basic type of sociality,"[27] this is not at all "meant in a historical sense," nor "does it imply temporal priority," but only designates a "logical anteriority."[28] For example, the groups that "constitute themselves as determinations and negations of collectives" (a subset of the practico-inert) are groups that "transcend and preserve" the collective,[29] whereas the collective, even if it is the result of a disintegration of another group, retains nothing of the previous group in its new collective form. That the group is always threatened with fragmenting back into a collective does not, however, prevent it from continually constituting itself against the collective, and in a sense the group always presupposes the collective. We are thus dealing with a genetic re-constitution that works by dialectically progressing from the simple to the complex and which is not susceptible to reversal. Speaking of groups internally, Sartre also distinguishes between "fused groups," the "organized group," and the "institution." The essence of the fused group is to proceed exclusively on the basis of a common praxis without an organized apparatus, unlike the organized group, which implies "a distribution of tasks" and "*specialized apparatuses*"[30] that direct and control common praxis.

The question, therefore, concerns how the transition from an organized group to an institution takes place. For Sartre, it is the contradictions within the organized group that lead to the transformation of the group into an institution thorough a "petrification"[31] of practice and the reinforcement of the group's integrative logic: "the organization is transformed into a hierarchy, and pledges give rise to institutions."[32] The pledge is the means by which a group seeks to ensure its survival beyond the struggle through which it emerged. In other words, the pledge is the mechanism through which the institution endows itself with a certain measure of permanence. It is for this reason that the pledge is inseparable from terror, insofar as terror is exercised internally by the group upon each of its members: everyone swears to keep their pledge, but in doing so they justify their own liquidation as traitors if they break their word. But ultimately, the pledge is a way of protecting the group from the threat of the practico-inert by creating an "artificial inertia." The contradiction here is plainly visible, since recourse to terror only reinforces the inertia the terror is supposed to eliminate. It is this contradiction that allows us to understand the emergence of the institution as a moment in which sovereignty assumes the determination of authority. For sovereignty consists precisely in the absolute power a group wields over each of its members by virtue of the pledge. But insofar as each takes the pledge and receives pledges from others, all are in fact sovereign or, rather, "quasi-sovereign," as Sartre puts it, since the sovereignty of each is limited by the sovereignty of others. Sovereignty thus tends toward unification and totalization, but without ever being able to achieve this totalization by reason of this reciprocal limitation. And this, for Sartre, is precisely the foundation of internal terror: the group is founded on this inoperable totalization and everyone is defined on the basis of this non-existing totality. This leads to a sort of "inner emptiness," a "distance," or a "malaise" that merely expresses the powerlessness of all and only strengthens integrative practices.[33] It is in order to overcome this void or insurmountable distance that sovereignty then takes the form of authority. Authority emerges once "everyone's shifting quasi-sovereignty is immobilized and becomes *authority* as a specific relation of one individual to all," at which point a "third party receives and concentrates the internal violence of the group as a power to impose his regulation."[34] Far from achieving its expected and aspired totalization, the emergence of authority only accentuates the internal contradiction of sovereignty. As Sartre puts it, "the sovereign reigns through and over the impotence of all,"[35] in the sense that the living union of all members would deprive the sovereign of any organizational function; but, now, the function of the sovereign is precisely to struggle against tendencies that push the group toward dispersion and seriality, "that is to say, against the very conditions which make his office legitimate and possible."[36]

Sartre's dialectic ultimately conceives of the "institutional moment, in the group" as corresponding to a "systematic self-domestication of man by man"; it is an "ossified *praxis*" that "is due to our own impotence" and "constitutes for each and for all a precise index of *reification*."[37] The appearance of the institution is thus, for Sartre, a "moment of common degradation" in which "everyone aims to expel freedom from himself in order to realize the endangered unity of the declining group as a thing."[38] In our view, however, this conclusion is precisely the principal limitation of Sartre's analysis. While we are indebted to Sartre's dialectical analysis of the institution for its capacity to theorize the ontology of the institution in terms of praxis, in contrast to classical sociology's more rigid approach – and Sartre should also be credited with trying to account for the mode of inertia that is unique to institutions as a product of this same praxis, without recourse to an intervention on the order of a *deus ex machina* that is totally foreign to the institution as such – why must he deliberately reduce the institution as always tending toward inevitable reification? Why not theorize the institution on the basis of the struggling group's common praxis prior to this moment of common degradation and ossification? Had he taken this route, Sartre might have discovered another possible conclusion, a conclusion based on the common praxis from which the institution emerges in the first place, but which would not necessarily devolve the group into modes of sovereignty and authority. In the end, Sartre was compelled to sacrifice this possibility as result of an argumentative logic that was organized from the beginning to articulate the state as an "organ of integration" in relation to the different groups within society, or more precisely as a governing group that owes its power to the manipulation of inert collectives. In the final analysis, the ultimate *telos* of the institution, for Sartre, is the state. The larger question we are faced with, then, is whether it is possible to theorize the institution in such a way that the later does not inevitably result in the establishment of authority and sovereignty.

Institution and Constituent Power

If it is true that "*authority* necessarily depends on inertia and seriality, in so far as it is constituted Power,"[39] it is equally true that authority must inversely work to actively counteract the "invasion of the group by seriality," and this is precisely the function of the sovereign: "the institutional group, constituted reason, the dialectic imitated and already distorted by seriality, appears in the practical unity of the sovereign as constituent reason."[40] The distinction between "constituted reason" and "constituent reason" naturally corresponds to the distinction between "constituted power" and "constituent power," and it raises the question of how we might think about a group that is incapable of seizing its constituent power without simultaneously resorting to the kind of unity imposed by a sovereign. It also raises the question of the relationship between constituent power and sovereign unity. But the first question it raises is what exactly is meant by the term "constituent power"?

According to its classical political meaning, the distinction between constituent power and constituted power dates back to Sieyès: constituent power is the source from which a political constitution proceeds and, as such, it cannot be derived from some prior constitution, nor can it promise, in advance, not to modify the constitution it is tasked with enacting at some future date. Constituent power is thus a free will unfettered by any prior rule: it is an absolute will that would annihilate itself by agreeing to submit to a norm that pre-exists it or by complying in advance with a norm that only exists by virtue of the exercise of the will itself. Its exclusive subject is the "nation" or a "people" and all other governmental powers (legislative, executive, judicial) are "constituted" by the nation or people, as if the latter were simply their emanations. It is well known how Carl Schmitt radicalized this definition of constituent power as political will unfettered by any rule or norm – even constitutional norms – by grounding the entire political order itself on what he called a "founding political decision."[41] In fact, there is a whole tradition of political thought that conceives of constituent power as the very definition of sovereign power – i.e., constituent power as absolutely and literally "free with respect to laws." Theorized in these terms, it is particularly difficult to imagine a form of constituent power that both proceeds from common praxis and is non-sovereign.

Indeed it is precisely this difficulty that Hardt and Negri try to address in *Multitude* and *Commonwealth*, and they try to do so by theorizing the double relation between insurrection and institution: on the one hand, insurrection must challenge established state institutions in order to remove them, while on the other hand, insurrections always need to produce "alternative" institutions, otherwise the insurrection will not succeed in the long run. To overcome this difficulty, Hardt and Negri argue that we must refuse to think of new alternative institutions as homologous to state institutions: insurrectionary institutions must be institutions of a new kind. To theorize this radical novelty, we could, without much difficulty, follow Sartre and argue that state institutions are indeed subject to the logic of sovereignty, without necessarily agreeing that all institutions are inherently beholden to the same sovereign logic. Far from trying to achieve a state of unification and totalization through the "practical suppression of class conflicts" (Sartre), we need to make conflict itself one of the essential constitutive features of insurrectionist institutions. In *Multitude* and *Commonwealth*, Hardt and Negri draw on a diverse range of experiences to try to re-define the concept of the institution along these lines, and for them, three elements are particularly important: firstly, institutions are based on conflict, in the sense that they reinforce and extend the antagonistic force that is characteristic (by definition) of every insurrection by incorporating conflict within its institutional parameters – i.e., the institution as assumed conflictuality. Secondly, the institution consolidates the new forms of life that arose during the insurrection by turning them into habits and collective practices – i.e., institutions as the activity of institutionalization in continual process. And lastly, the institution is open to its own permanent transformation by the singularities of which it is composed – i.e., the institution as permanent process of self-transformation as a means of undermining institutional ossification.[42]

Yet even with the help of philosophers like Spinoza and Machiavelli,[43] Hardt and Negri's re-definition of the institution still runs up against certain difficulties. As the authors clearly perceive, their re-definition is subject to two major objections – one sociological, one political. The sociological objection derives from a rather functionalist conception of the institution: "individuals enter institutions and come out as identities."[44] The function of institutions, in this view, is precisely to transform individuals by making them conform to identitarian models. For Hardt and Negri, however, the whole question is to determine the "locus of agency": if the "conventional sociological notion [tells us] institutions form individuals and identities," Hardt and Negri's contrasting view is that "singularities form institutions."[45] The idea that individuals "enter" into institutions is based on the sociological presupposition we discussed at the beginning of this chapter: institutions always pre-exist individuals, and are independent of the latter's activity. The second objection, however, refers to a series of political and juridical theories that are just as "classical" as the sociological approach to the institution. According to these classical political theories, the political order is based on the transfer of rights and powers from individuals to a sovereign authority. From this perspective, the re-definition of the institution proposed by Hardt and Negri proves incapable of providing the necessary stability for the political order because it refuses to make the latter depend upon sovereignty. We see here, however, that if individuals also "enter institutions," they do not enter by silent constraint but do so through an act of voluntary, consensual transfer. What is most essential for this tradition is simply that individuals must "enter," and not the manner in which they enter: for if they are compelled to enter, in any way, they cannot then exercise a truly "formative" power over these institutions. Contrary to what the theories of the social contract claim, individuals are not really the sources of these institutions, since the latter can only be accepted into these by an act of renunciation on their part. "Institutions must serve as the foundation for the constituted power, that is, the constitutional order of sovereignty." Against this objection, Hardt and Negri posit the norms produced by an insurrectionary *constituent* power, as opposed to the rigid standards of *constituted* power: "according to our conception, in contrast, institutions form a constituent rather than a constituted power."[46] The originality of this constituent power is its ability to actively oppose the formation of a sovereign power: "the singularities that compose the multitude do not transfer their rights or powers, and thus they prohibit the formation of a sovereign power, but in their mutual encounters each become more powerful."[47] Instead of having to "enter" institutions that are already formed and are independent of them, these singularities reinforce their formative power through and to the extent of their common exercise or praxis. The difficulty now, however, lies in understanding precisely how this power can give rise to such a common exercise or praxis in the first place.

In Chapter 6.3 of *Commonwealth*, "Governing the Revolution," Negri and Hardt are not content to merely take up the notion of "constituent power" – they notably criticize all the "mechanisms that close down the development of constituent power in the structures of a constituted power" – and so they try to introduce the rather problematic notion of "constituent governance."[48] They are aware, of course, that the concept of "governance" originally referred to the "structures of regulation, management, and accountability of capitalist corporations" prior to designating forms of imperial domination.[49] Speaking to all those contemporary theorists who posit, somewhat classically, an opposition between government comprised of fixed legal structures and the reality of today's flexible and fluid processes of "global governance," Hardt and Negri argue that it is necessary to subvert the very concept of governance from the inside in order to re-formulate the latter as concept of democracy and revolution.[50] Drawing from the work of German theorists inspired by Niklas Luhmann's systems theory, they interpret the passage from "government" to "governance" as an attempt to promote a network logic capable of managing conflicts and realizing a normative compatibility within a highly fragmented global society.[51] From their point of view, then, a mode of "constituent governance" that inverts the old imperial forms now corresponds to a constitutional system in which the "sources of law" and the means of their legitimation are based solely on constituent power and democratic decision-making.[52]

What is striking about this account, however, is the difficulty of clearly distinguishing between "institution" and "constitution" as a result of the vagaries of their notion of constituent power. For Hardt and Negri, a "will to institution and constitution" traverses any revolutionary process, far beyond the duration of the revolt or insurrection itself.[53] This strange notion is analogized with the concept of *Kuntswollen* – or the "will to art" – that, according to Viennese historian of art Alois Riegl, was characteristic of later Rome. For Riegl, *Kuntswollen* should be understood as a "desire that articulates all the singular artistic expressions as a coherent institutional development." A revolutionary process, for Hardt and Negri, must likewise be governed by an "institutional and constitutional will," a kind of *Rechtswollen*, that can articulate the singularities of the multitude in a "powerful and lasting common process."[54] In short, Hardt and Negri's recourse to the notion of *Rechtswollen* is intended to overcome the conventional opposition between the "sociological" concept of institution and the "juridico-political" concept of constitution in order to better theorize the radical immanence of society's constituent power.

But what remains, then, of the very concept of constituent power? Does it not lose all its meaning once the concept of "constitution" simply designates the "process of forming political institutions and constitutions,"[55] and not the act of founding a new political body and the concomitant organization of the various constituted powers resulting from this foundational act? Does not the desire to refrain, at all costs, from theorizing the political specificity of the constituent act ultimately reduce the exercise of constitute power to the act of "constituting" in general, and which therefore already describes every social struggle, insofar as struggles or insurrections are always inventing new institutions *in situ* almost by definition? What conceptual or practical intelligibility is gained by uniformly designating the insurrections of the Arab Spring, the Indignados in Spain and Israel, or Occupy Wall Street as "constituent struggles" for the common? In Chapter 3 of *Declaration*, titled "Constituting the Common," Hardt and Negri define what they call "constituent struggles" in precise terms: "we consider to be *constituent* the struggles that are posed on the terrain of the common and that not only express the urgent need but also chart the path for a new constitutional process."[56] But how exactly are we to understand today's social movements through the use of expressions like "constituent action," "constituent decisions," constituent process," or "new constituent movements"?[57] Are these struggles not profoundly different, and are these differences not necessarily erased by subsuming them all within such uniform concepts? Should we not then re-submit a question to Hardt and Negri that they themselves believe they have answered, but which stubbornly remains, it seems to us, after reading their text: "why, then, should we consider these struggles part of the same cycle?[58]

What meaning is there in retaining the concept of constituent power if its purpose is to affirm how this power is "deeply embedded in [all] struggles"[59] to the point of erasing all distinction between these struggles? Is it not simply a way of designating that dimension of political inventiveness that is ostensibly the essential dimension of these movements in the first place? If this is the case, it is difficult to see how this constituent dimension would be able to account for the transformation of new forms of life into collective habits, in accordance with the second aspect of the institution as defined by Hardt and Negri. In other words, what do we gain by culling a concept from an older tradition of revolution whose singular purpose was to produce new political constitutions? Are we not ultimately forced to conclude that the old "concept of constituent power is obsolete"?[60] Or, inversely, if we think the concept is still relevant despite the intervening changes and experience we have gained since the age of the "great revolutions," would it not be better to return to the distinction between instituent power and constituent power, but on the condition that we reject the conventional division in which the former is understood as a sociological concept and the latter as a political concept?

Instituent Power and Social Imaginary

This was precisely the approach taken by Cornelius Castoriadis. While Castoriadis agrees that the study of the social should begin with the institution, he understands this "fact" in a completely different sense than that found in Durkheimian sociology. Castoriadis is especially interested in breaking with the causal and deterministic approach characteristic of the sociological conception of the institution. He cannot, and does not, passively accept Fauconnet and Mauss's proposition that historical changes, "from the daily variations of fashion to the world of great political and moral revolutions, are always, to varying degrees, changes in existing institutions."[61] Against this sociological reduction of the institution to the instituted, Castoriadis emphasizes the primacy of the *instituent* over the *instituted*: the latter is merely the result of the exercise of "instituent power," which is the true force of institutional creation.

It is therefore the creation of the "socio-historical" that, for Castoriadis, constitutes the primary and fundamental social fact, not the instituted as "pre-existing" in every society: "there is the social as instituted, but this always presupposes the social as instituting."[62] In other words, the object of Castoriadis's thought is the properly historical fact. Marx's famous phrase from "The Eighteenth Brumaire" – "men make their own history" – must therefore be understood in the sense that men create their own social word. But how does this creation occur? This question is Castoriadis's basic point of departure, but he cannot find a coherent and clear answer in Marx, particularly in terms of the inherent tensions arising from the revolutionary and naturalistic-evolutionary dimensions of Marx's view of social change. History, for Castoriadis, is the element of the new, the radically new. For Castoriadis, we must try to render this radical novelty intelligible, rather than always perceiving newness as a variation on what already exists. The institution, in other words, should no longer be regarded as primarily the "instituted" (i.e., that which already exists), but rather it is the instituent that shapes the instituted, and which, in time, will again be subverted by the radically new. The instituent moment testifies to the specifically human capacity to create entirely original meaning from scratch. Accordingly, representations are not an "image *of*"[63] but must be conceived as a radically new form that belongs to what Cornelius calls the "imaginary." This notion is introduced in Castoriadis's work through the concept of "social imaginary signification."[64] The concept runs entirely counter to the functionalist tendency to reduce social institutions to the functional role they play in fulfilling human needs. For Castoriadis, it is crucial to unearth the symbolic dimension of social life; we find this dimension of the symbolic not only in language but in every system of signification more broadly. All forms of symbolization proceed from the imaginary, insofar as the imaginary presupposes the capacity to "see in a thing what it is not" or "to see it other than it is."[65] For Castoriadis, the "imaginary" has two dimensions: the instituted (*l'institué*) and the instituent (*l'instituant*). While the former refers to established meanings and institutions, the latter designates the very source from which new meanings and institutions emerge in the course of history. What characterizes the human "socio-historical" is precisely the imaginary's instituent activity: "society is the work of the *instituting* imaginary."[66] The "imaginary," here, does not so much refer to the capacity to perceive something that is empirically absent (a capacity that belongs to the "reproductive" imagination), but, much more radically, to "the capacity to make arise as an image something which does not exist and has never existed,"[67] or "the originary faculty of positing or presenting oneself with things and relations that do not exist, in the form of representation (things and relations that are not *or have never been* given in perception)."[68] Castoriadis's theoretical valorization of the dimension of the imaginary is entirely related to his revolutionary posture. If it is true that "the instituted society is always subject to the subterranean pressure of instituting society," and "beneath the established social imaginary, the flow of the radical imaginary continues steadily,"[69] it is equally true that society tends to deny and repress this instituent dimension. For Castoriadis, then, the radical project of emancipation necessitates a society that is consciously self-instituting – which is another name for democracy. We can see, then, why a revolutionary political posture must begin from a definition of the social that grants primacy to rupture and to the emergence of entirely new historical meanings.

This perspective clearly conflicts with Durkheim's "causal" sociology (and its multiple offshoots). The latter is incapable of accounting for any changes in institutions or the status of social groups after the moment in which representations are "images *of*," i.e., mere expressions of the current state of things. But how can such reflective representations be transformed and thereby give rise to institutional change? In this regard, Castoriadis's critique is similarly aimed at Marxism, which also has a tendency toward causalism when it comes to the economy as the motor of society. Marxism, in Castoriadis's view, does not do a very good job of elucidating the concept of the institution, which is something of its *punctum caecum*, or its Achilles' heel. In the first instance, Marxism tends to relegate institutions to the juridico-political "superstructure" such that they are conceived as secondary "forms" determined by the primary economic "infrastructure." For this reason, institutions do little more than "express" the economy of infrastructure – usually institutional expressions "lag" behind the infrastructure, though at times they can also be anticipatory. And secondly, this Marxist paradigm articulates this infrastructure as a kind of "content" or "substance social life," that is structured prior to the creation of superstructural institutions, as if this kind of structuration was possible without institutions.[70] Against this mythical conception of a society without institutions,[71] we must remember that "the economy can itself exist only as an institution."[72] Generally speaking, then, the entire sociological tradition (including Marxism) only deals with reflection, repetition, reproduction, and reiteration, but is powerless before forms of radical historical novelty. But, as Castoriadis insists, "the social (or the historical) contains the non-causal as one of its essential moments."[73] In its strongest and most radical sense, the "non-causal"

> appears not as a simple deviation in relation to an existing type but as the *positing* of a new type of behaviour, as the *institution* of a new social rule, as the *invention* of a new object or a new form – in short, as an emergence or a production which cannot be deduced on the basis of a previous situation, as a conclusion that goes beyond the premises or as the positing of new premises ... History cannot be thought in accordance with the determinist schema (nor, moreover, in accordance with a simple "dialectical" schema) because it is the domain of *creation*.[74]

Instituent activity, in this sense, points to a dimension of life that is not only social, but also (at least in certain circumstances) fully political. Or rather, instituent activity coincides with the political itself, for it "amounts to the explicit putting into question of the established institution of society."[75] It is essential for such activity to strive for the "overall reinstitution of society," which Castoriadis defines as "explicit collective activity which aims at being lucid (reflective and deliberate) and whose object is the institution of society as such." During such dramatic revolutionary moments, this instituting activity asserts itself as "*a coming into light*, though certainly partial, of the instituting in person."[76]

To properly understand this definition of the political, we must pay careful attention to the decisive difference Castoriadis marks between conventional politics and *the* political.[77] While conventional politics is an activity concerned with the "overall institution of society," *the* political concerns the "dimension of explicit power,"[78] since this dimension is present in all forms of society, even those without the state form. Explicit power is present in "the existence of *instances capable of formulating explicitly sanctionable injunctions*" relating to jurisdictions (*dikê*) and decisions (*telos*). Explicit power thus refers to "juridical power" and "governmental power" in the broadest sense of these terms, since both are present "as soon as there is society," whether it is power exercised by the tribe, the elders, the warriors, the people, or the state.[79] No one, therefore, "invented" the political: "the Greeks did not invent *the* political, in the sense of the dimension of explicit power that is always present in any society. They invented – or, better, created – politics, which is something entirely different.[80] In contrast to the exclusive valorization of "explicit power," Castoriadis insists on a clear distinction between instituent power, or "implicit power," and constituent power (which is simply another instance of "explicit power"):

> For the fundamental "power" in a society, the prime power upon which all the others depend, what I have already called the ground-power, is the *instituting power*. And unless one is under the spell of the "constitutional delusion," this power is neither locatable nor formalizable, for it pertains to the instituting imaginary. Language, family, mores, "ideas," "art," a host of social activities as well as their evolution are beyond the scope of legislation in their essential part. At most, to the degree that this power can be participated in, it is participated in by all. Everybody is, potentially, a coauthor of the evolution of language, of the family, of customs, and so on.[81]

Castoriadis's insistence on the fundamental character of instituting or instituent power fundamentally deposes constituent power of the primacy it was granted by a whole philosophical tradition, a primacy neither Sartre nor Negri really knew how to question – the former for interpreting the institution as the site of sovereignty's emergence in the social, the latter for wanting to call all social struggles "constituent" and thereby emptying the term of any real meaning. Vincent Descombes rightly sees that Castoriadis's insight means breaking with what he calls the "circle of self-determination" (*le cercle de l'autoposition*) or the "philosophical prodigy of a normative self-determination": in the beginning, people come together to decide the constitutional rules and thereby create "a people" through this act, such that "a collective agent decides to create itself *ex nihilo* by fiat, thereby conferring upon itself authority over the lives of a group of people."[82] In order to move beyond the arbitrariness of a constituent power cut off from history, or to ward off the mythological Rousseauian legislator tasked with "instituting a people" by giving them their own constitution, it is crucial to insist on the pre-existence of social life, which is to say the historical depth of an already instituted social terrain, and, furthermore, that it is this social pre-existence alone that supports constituent power – i.e., assembled citizens who agree on the functional rules of political institutions. As Descombes put it, "we must not fail to see the exercise of instituent power behind the facts of constituent power."[83] As Castoriadis makes clear, the truly creative power is not "legislative power" – i.e., the power to make laws – which is but one form of constituent power amongst others (usually executive and judicial power). Nor is "constituent power" the truly creative power for Castoriadis, since the latter is merely that which outlines the roles and functions of legislative and executive power under constitutional forms of government. The truly creative power is the power to institute imaginary meanings that are the collective work of all, since they are "participated in by all." What the Greeks did by creating what we now understand as conventional politics was to make one part of instituent power explicitly "political" by creating institutions that "led to the equal participation of all the members of the body politic in the determination of *nomos*, of *dike* and of *telos* – of legislation, of jurisdiction, and of government."[84]

But how exactly should we interpret the proposition that instituting/instituent power is the truly creative power? Should we not distinguish these "imaginary meanings" from the act of creation in order to give primacy to the institution? Do we not risk reifying the imaginary – "which is creation *ex nihilo*" or "the unceasing and essentially undetermined (social-historical and psychical) creation of figures/forms/images, on the basis of which alone there can ever be a question *of* 'something,'"[85] – by conceiving it as merely the outcome or product of the *imagined*?[86] Moreover, what is the status of the creator in relation to both the act of creation and the thing itself created? On the acceded assumption that the creation of the social is not the act of one or more "subject-authors," and that "manifestly, the social-historical immensely transcends any 'inter-subjectivity,'"[87] are we forced to conceive of creation as a kind of emanation from an anonymous collective? Many of Castoriadis's formulations seem to tend in this direction. For instance, Castoriadis argues that instituting power could also be called "ground-power":

> This power itself is grounded upon the instituting power of the radical imaginary and of the whole preceding history which finds, each time, in the institution as it is posited its transient outcome. Ultimately, therefore, we are dealing with the power of the social-historical field itself, the power of *outis*, of Nobody.[88]

Of course, instituting power, for Castoriadis, is the power of no one particular person inasmuch as it is the power of all. But is it right to say that it is the power of nobody? How can the individual contribute, in his own way, to the creation of imaginary meanings if he is not in a position to exercise this power in any way? How are we to think of a collective creation in which the individual cannot participate as an individual? In fact, it is difficult for Castoriadis to articulate the instituting of the social imaginary in terms of the singular *psyche* as an individual imaginary, for as Aristotle well understood, imagination is the essence of the individual's soul. This formative and imaginative capacity, this faculty for producing phantasms (*phantasmatisation*), which precedes even the most primitive organization of our drives, is what Castoriadis calls the "radical imagination" or even the "unconscious." We must be clear about this: the "radical imagination" is not the same as the "radical imaginary." The radical imagination is a mode of being, or a manifestation of the radical imaginary; and the social imaginary is another mode.[89] One finds in Castoriadis a similarly important opposition between the singular psyche and society: the psyche is fundamentally asocial, to the point that the psychic monad is initially autistic.[90] The process of socialization consists precisely in internalizing the meanings produced by the social imaginary within the individual. The "radical imagination" and the "social imaginary" are therefore the two radically heterogeneous manifestations of the "radical imaginary," and it is difficult to see how they could be reconciled. Yet this is precisely what must occur, because it is the psyche's radical imagination that is "the source of the individual's contribution to social-historical creation,"[91] and the "psychic *sap*" that constantly nourishes creation.[92] It is therefore by virtue of this imaginative power that the individual participates in the exercise of instituting power, such as in the creation and growth of languages, manners, families, etc. Castoriadis maintains, however, that "the *ultimate* source of historical creativity is the radical imaginary of the anonymous collectivity."[93] What room is there then, under these conditions, for individual contributions to the "creation of meaning" (*Sinnschöpfung*) that constitutes the socio-historical? Is the individual's exercise of instituent power not ultimately assimilated to the individual's reproduction or modification of the organization of forces already at work in society? And is this not really just another way of talking about "custom" and the manner in which it is perpetuated, which seems rather distant from the ostensibly turbulent eruptions of the "radical imagination"?[94] And if this is indeed the case, how can we avoid reducing the emergence of new customs to the imperceptible modification of what came before, much like the manner in which classical sociology interprets the emergence of a new institution as a variation on an older institution?

To overcome this opposition, collective praxis must be prioritized through the recognition of its essential symbolic dimension. Thus understood, praxis would be something like the middle term through which the radical imagination of individuals could act upon the instituted meanings of the social imaginary. For it is only through collective praxis that a transformative project might take shape, one whose maxim is "where *No one* was, there *We* shall be."[95] But how can we connect the exercise of instituting power to praxis? Or, better, how might we think of this exercise as a form of praxis itself? What is problematic in this respect is Castoriadis's very conception of praxis. On the one hand, as we have seen, the creation of the socio-historical is a collective and anonymous work; it is an effort that escapes the control of consciousness and the will. On the other hand, praxis is an activity whose goal is autonomy, which is to say "activity [that] aims at others as (potentially) autonomous subjects and tries to contribute to their efforts to attain full autonomy."[96] This activity can, of course, take the form of a concrete relation between several individual subjects (as in pedagogical relationships or psychoanalysis), but it must also take a political form least it "lapse into total incoherence." Yet politics is by its very nature an "activity that aims at the transformation of society's institutions in order to make them conform to the norm of the autonomy of the collectivity"; it is the "*institution* of [the] social sphere that is the aim of politics," which is to the say "the institution as such."[97] Politics is therefore an activity that consciously pursues certain objectives, whereas the creation of new meaning is said to escape conscious activity. The question that now arises concerns understanding how a conscious collective praxis might contribute to the emergence of new collective meaning, if not bring it about directly.[98] It is therefore praxis that needs to be re-thought if we are to free up this possibility.

Praxis and Creation

Our most fundamental concern here is really about the relationship between *praxis* and *creation*. In the first instance, we might already expect the institution, as the product of the creation of meaning, to be praxis already. Yet according to Castoriadis's terminology, the category of "praxis" should only be applied to that activity that has autonomy as its goal, and not any form of human activity regardless of its end. The term is thus strongly charged with positive value, unlike the category of "creation," which is indifferent to the value of its content – i.e., it is axiologically neutral.[99] In other words, it is not possible to directly derive one term from the other:

> An ontological investigation oriented toward the idea of creation leaves room, in the most abstract way, for the possibility of the instauration of an autonomous society as well as for the reality of Stalinism and Nazism. At this level, and almost all others, *creation has no value content*, and politics does not allow itself to be "deduced" from ontology.[100]

The social is institution or creation, and whether this fact is recognized or denied changes absolutely nothing. Politics, on the other hand, is fundamentally praxis, otherwise it is not politics. It is therefore meaningless to speak of "Stalinist politics" or "Nazi politics," while Stalinist or Nazi "creations" are certainly possible insofar as these forms of society still belong to the socio-historical.[101] In short, while every form of authentic praxis necessarily entails the dimension of institution-creation as its conscious expression, and in this sense fully participates in it, every institution-creation does not necessarily fall under the category of praxis.

This constriction of the notion of praxis is somewhat puzzling, especially given Aristotle's discussion of the same term. And there is good reason to compare the two authors here (up to a certain point at least), since Castoriadis's formulation of praxis – an activity that takes autonomy as both its object and its end – resembles the Aristotelian idea of an activity that is its own end, rather than activity oriented toward an external end.[102] And while praxis is surely distinct from poiesis – that is to say, from technical activity – insofar as it is involves an end one gives oneself, this distinction is of no intrinsic moral significance to Aristotle: it is through repetitive activity that man acquires one virtue or another (courage, for instance), but it is also through repetitive activity that man acquires a range of vices (such as cowardice). Virtue and vice are both dispositions engendered by acts that fall within the parameters of praxis but not poiesis: for one does not become courageous or cowardly in the same way that one masters a technique. Thus when Castoriadis talks about autonomy, it is not the Aristotelian concept of praxis in general that Castoriadis references, but rather the Aristotelian definition of virtue as *hexis proairétiké*, "namely, the *habitus* that is dependent upon choice and that is the creator of choice."[103] Hence the parenthetical formulation found in Castoriadis's essay "Individual, Society, Rationality, History": "the term '*praxis*' therefore has here only a homonymic relation to the meaning Aristotle assigns to it."[104]

In our view, then, Castoriadis's entire conception of the relation between poiesis and praxis needs to be re-thought. The Aristotelian opposition is not really appropriate here insofar as the same activity, for Aristotle, can be both "poietic" and "practical." Psychoanalysis, accordingly, is not a "technique" in the sense that it does not consist in the implementation of prior knowledge and does not involve a code of positive prescriptions geared toward attaining a pre-determined result.[105] But on the other hand, psychoanalysis is undoubtedly a form of "practico-poietic activity" precisely because it simultaneously involves praxis and poiesis:

> I call it poetical because it is creative: its outcome is, or ought to be, self-alteration of the analysand – that is, strictly speaking, the appearance of another being. I call it practical because I call praxis that lucid activity whose object is human autonomy, an activity which can be reached only by means of this same autonomy.[106]

We can see here then how "poiesis" is associated with creation and "praxis" is defined by the fact that it has autonomy as its end. Psychoanalysis can thus be said to be both, insofar as its end (in the sense of its immediate outcome) is the appearance of a new being, while its more general purpose is human autonomy. Psychoanalysis is about "reciprocal transformation [and] creative self-alteration, which involves both the analysand *and* the analyst."[107] That the relation of the means to the end is no longer valid under these conditions was not meant to astonish readers of Aristotle. For Aristotle, the exteriority of the end in relation to the means is what characterizes technical production (poiesis), but it is precisely the suppression of this exteriority that defines praxis: insofar as praxis is its own end at every instant, it does not consist in using its means to attain an external end, as in the case of the construction of a house, for example. But what is more puzzling is that poiesis re-theorized as the creation of the absolutely new is itself irreducible to activities like "fabrication" or "production." Thus, for Castoriadis, "creation" in its theological sense – i.e., the creation of the world by God – is only a form of "pseudo-creation": it is merely a form of "manufacturing" or "producing," in the sense that the world is necessarily an effect of the essence of God and not something absolutely new. God did not invent the *eidos* (essence) of the world, but merely produced the world from his own essence.[108] This explains why, in the above citation, psychoanalysis is thought of as poiesis, but is absolutely not considered a technique in the sense of manufacturing. It fact, it would be meaningless to say that psychoanalysis produces a new being through the process of analysis,[109] since it is through the "*self*-modification" of the analysand that this new being appears. And so, whereas the two notions of "creation" and "fabrication" are related to each other in Aristotle, their dissociation is decisive for Castoriadis.

The stakes of this dissociation for Castoriadis are more apparent once we clarify the notion of "creation." One of the best definitions of the term comes from a passage in Plato's *Symposium* that Castoriadis is fond of quoting: poiesis is "when anything comes into being which did not exist before."[110] It consists in making something exist that did not exist whatsoever, even if only virtually. Interpreted rigorously, this definition means true creation is not the imposition of a form (*eidos*) already given to matter, but rather the invention of form itself, insofar as it is the creative act that brings a form into existence from nothing. If a craftsman truly creates a statue, it means he brings its *eidos*, or its essence, into being, as opposed to reproducing an *eidos* in a piece of bronze that already existed because it was created by someone else – in which case the artist does not "create," but rather "imitates" or "produces." In this strict sense, all creation is by definition creation *ex nihilo*: "the wheel revolving around an axis is an absolute ontological creation" because "the person who invented the wheel, or a written sign, was imitating and repeating nothing at all."[111] It is therefore necessary to invert Plato's definition of Platonism: the form is not, after all, something immutable that can only be imitated, but rather it is the form that comes into being from non-being through the creative act. Castoriadis is aware that the use of this theological notion for anti-theological ends might be a bit confusing, and so he qualifies its interpretation by focusing on the *ex* ("from"): "'creation *ex nihilo*,' 'creation of form,' does not mean 'creation *cum nihilo*,' that is to say, without 'means,' unconditionally, on a tabula rasa."[112] As Castoriadis continues, "all historical creation takes place upon, in, and through the already instituted (not to mention whatever surrounding 'concrete' conditions there may be."[113] And a passage from "Done and To Be Done" emphasizes the same point:

> Due to this very fact, it is clear that social-historical creation (as well as, moreover, creation in any other domain), if it is unmotivated – *ex nihilo* – always takes place *under constraints* (it does not occur in *nihilo* or *cum nihilo*). Neither in the social-historical domain nor anywhere else does creation signify that just anything can happen just anywhere, just any time and just anyhow.[114]

The essential point here, however, is that the pre-existence of the instituted in relation to the institution, while conditioning and shaping the institution, does not determine it.[115] If this were the case, meaning would be completely explained by the conditions that preceded its emergence, such that one would no longer have to deal with creation. In other words, the fundamental point here is the irreducibility of meaning to causation, as Philippe Caumières firmly defines it.[116] While all creation is of course influenced by antecedent conditions, these conditions are not the same as determinant causes of new emergent meaning.

Yet if recourse to the notion of "creation" is justified above all by the need to protect meaning from its reduction to a mere effect, what, in turn, justifies the provocative use of the theological expression "creation *ex nihilo*"? Indeed, what great difference is there between the *ex* of *ex nihilo* and the *cum* of *cum nihilo*? Why make this *ex* say something it doesn't say? Or, more precisely, why make *cum* refer to the means or conditions of an effect and *ex* refer to the cause, as if the shift from *cum* to *ex* could only be understood as an unfortunate embracing of causalism? Ultimately, *ex* only really means "from," and "from" does not necessarily mean "the cause of." In theological discourse, the expression has come to mean an act of creation that is not conditioned by pre-existing matter and, for this reason, does not apply to the artist's or craftsman's practice of shaping of matter. Divine creation, in this sense, is the paradigm of the pure, unconditioned act: *actus purus*.[117] In this doctrine, matter is not the cause of creation as such, in the sense that it is not the mere pre-existence of matter that compels God to create. It is merely the "form" through which the creation of the world takes place, which is to say it is precisely the *conditions* of the world's creation, but not its determinate cause (and, indeed, it is precisely this kind of conditioning that believers in the doctrine of divine perfection would rather not hear). It is therefore difficult to understand what justifies the use, even for polemical purposes, of this theological expression: whereas *ex nihilo* means God creates the world from nothing – without having to shape matter or take account of its possible resistance – Castoriadis interprets this expression as meaning that no form can be truly new if it acts upon pre-established matter (if matter is indeed the condition of possibility of form), as if the form was necessarily implied in matter already. But the mere presence of matter does not determine form, and does not, in itself, foreclose the production of the new. In fact, it seems like Castoriadis has fallen prey to the expression's cunning by assenting to the false opposition that "creation must be from nothing or it is no creation at all."

By rejecting this theological fiction, we can both do away this false alternative and maintain the irreducibility of creation to causal explanation. This allows us to arrive at the perfectly coherent idea of a "creation from something" (or creation *ex aliquo*) – i.e., a "conditioned creation" – which is in no way equivalent to a "caused creation," which is in itself contradictory. Or put differently, we arrive at the idea of creation *ex aliquo* but *sine causa*. The creation of form within the context of certain given conditions is therefore distinguished from causation of the form by these conditions themselves. Ultimately, then, wherever the relation between the act of creation and its conditions is concerned, the *ex* has exactly the same meaning as the *cum*: each merely signifies the impossibility of an unconditioned creation. But, once again, recognizing dependence on pre-determined conditions does not in any way mean we must reduce creation to a necessary effect of its conditions. This is precisely what is meant by the notion of "emergence," which is a term Castoriadis frequently uses in those texts in which he is trying to theorize the radical character of creation. The form that "emerges" comes from something that pre-exists and *ipso facto* conditions this emergence, but without necessarily causing it in the strong sense of this term. While speaking of the distinction between condition and cause, or between necessary and sufficient conditions, Castoriadis writes, "forms as forms are not caused by something – but they emerge given certain (in fact, numerable) conditions."[118] In other words, Greek mythology did not cause the *polis*, but the *polis* would have been impossible without Greek mythology.[119] Similarly, Freudian psychoanalysis, "however radically new, [did not arrive] in the void" but presupposed "the entire tradition of 'science' and, more generally, of Greco-Western thought."[120] In both of these examples, the instituted preceded the institution-creation as its condition, but it did not fully determine either of them. Why, then, do we even need to bother with the further idea of "creation from nothing"? Why should the creation of the new be on the order of an "absolute creation" that excludes all pre-existing conditions, given that such conditions are not causally determinate?

This question applies just as much to the concept of "praxis" as that of the "institution," given the precise meaning of these two terms in Castoriadis's work. On the one hand, we have the activity of an anonymous collective that does not pursue any specific end because its activity escapes the direct grasp of consciousness, but it nonetheless creates imaginary meanings (the institution); on the other hand, we have conscious activity that aims at and presupposes autonomy, but finds itself unable, in itself, to destroy old imaginary meanings and replace them with new meanings (praxis). The first activity, as we have seen, is morally neutral, whereas the second is inherently emancipatory. This only compounds the difficulty. The first difficulty concerns understanding how the institution, which is essentially unconscious, can become praxis. In other words, how does the institution become conscious of itself as part of a larger whole? The second difficulty we face concerns how the institution, which in itself is indifferent to the ideal of autonomy, can put itself in the service of this end. It is not by chance that Castoriadis chose the Greek *polis* and Freudian psychoanalysis as examples of self-conscious institutions. But are these institutions on the same level as the invention of the wheel or of writing, or the institution of language or manners? The first two examples – the Greek *polis* and Freudian psychoanalysis – undoubtedly belong to what Castoriadis calls "explicit power," inasmuch as the instituting act in this case originates from one or many "founders." These forms of praxis can rightly be called "instituting" or "instituent," though not in the sense that they arise from the unconscious transmission-modification of older practices, but insofar as they are gestures that establish new meanings and new ways of acting. Yet like instituted forms of "ground-power" or "implicit power," these examples of praxis are not free from certain constraining conditions. For the exercise of instituent power in society always involves, to varying degrees, the "resumption of the given" because it always "bears the weight of history": "the instituting society, however radical it may be, always works by starting *from* something already instituted, on the basis of what is already there. It is always historical – save for an inaccessible point of origin."[121] In the same manner, praxis as conscious institution, or instituent praxis, presupposes both certain pre-existing conditions and the act of "working on" these conditions in order to profoundly transform them. The emergence of the instituent in the form of politics, for example, is no more "absolute creation" than the unconscious activity of the anonymous collective that enables it, at least partially, to achieve conscious expression. Put differently, the emergence of the conscious autoinstitution always involves certain conditions inherited from the past, if only because it is always based on what has already been instituted below the surface of consciousness and will.

Instituent Praxis

What we are calling instituent praxis therefore manifests certain characteristics of praxis already theorized by Marx. The passage from "The Eighteenth Brumaire" already cited above – "men make their history"[122] – effectively condenses this entire conception of praxis as "conditioned self-transformative activity," and in turn helps us better grasp the originality of "instituent praxis." In essence, it tells us that this "making" is not on the order of technical fabrication, nor is it a case of "creation from nothing" or "absolute creation." If men "make" their history, it is always under circumstances and conditions they have not chosen. Men always find conditions simply "already there,"[123] inherited from previous generations. In the first instance, then, humanity's "making" is always conditioned by the results of the forms of activity of prior makers.

Yet far from foreclosing the creation of the new, this conditioning is precisely what makes the creation of the new possible. The conditions found by each new generation are not neutral environments to which the actions of men can only passively conform. By acting under certain specific conditions – and this applies to the second half of this "making" – men act on these same conditions precisely in order to create new conditions. In other words, men are driven to overthrow previous states of things and bring into existence that which has no historical precedent. They may be unaware of this, inasmuch as the crushing weight of all dead generations "weighs like a nightmare on the brain of living," and so in order to avoid the anxiety of the new, humanity dons borrowed masks and costumes (the trappings of the Roman Republic by the French Revolutionaries, for example). In other words, men are incapable of speaking the language of their actions directly, much like someone who is unable to shed their mother tongue while learning a new language. But this does not prevent men from "making" the new emerge through their actions. In his discussion of the actions of men in the midst of a revolutionary crisis, Marx spoke of how men "anxiously conjure up the spirits of the past" even though they "seem engaged in revolutionizing themselves and things, in creating something entirely new (*noch nicht Dagewesenes zu schaffen*)."[124] As the text indicates, the German verb "seem" (*scheinen*) does not refer to the act of creating something absolutely new, but to the state of being "engaged" or "occupied": while revolutionaries are *de facto* creating something absolutely new, they are not completely "engaged" or "preoccupied" with the creations they invariably produce through their activity. In other words, their consciousness is "occupied" with something else, which in the case of Marx's discussion is playing the roles that history seems to have assigned them in advance. We thus find a certain dissonance between the novelty of activities undertaken by historical actors, and awareness of the same actors, which is largely focused on playing a part already played out in the distant past (Brutus, Cato, etc.). And while this dissonance may surely obstruct the progress of said actions, it cannot in itself cancel out the novelty that is invariably produced through these actions.

What Marx's analysis of the conduct of men in the throes of revolution reveals is that their action always manifests two indivisible aspects. First, it is always conditioned by the given. Historical actors always find conditions already there without having produced said conditions, and so their activity (as much as it may displease idealists) is never "pure." At the same time, however, and notwithstanding tributes to past meanings they have inherited, their action is never simply a "resumption of the given" but rather brings forth something new (as much as this may displease the more passive materialists who view men as simply the product of their historical circumstances). And what is most remarkable is that this action does not only create novelty in terms of external circumstances, but it also creates newness within the actors themselves, who are invariably transformed by their actions, down to their innermost being. In other words, history does not give us "authors" who direct their action on the basis of a well-mapped-out "project." Rather, history gives us actors who emerge as subjects in and through their actions, which is a very different matter. The recognition of this dynamic helps us grasp what Marx's third thesis on Feuerbach calls the "coincidence" (*Zusammenfallen*) between "changing of circumstances" (*Ändern der Umstände*) and the human activity of "self-transformation" (*Selbstveränderung*),[125] a coincidence that is crucial for Marx's notion of "revolutionary practice." That the changing of circumstances by men is also, at the same time, the self-transformation of men themselves only makes sense if this self-transformation is at one with their own action, and not a simple "effect" of transformed external circumstances – which would of course imply a causal relation between these two kinds of transformations. Praxis, therefore, is the self-production of its own subject by the self-transformation in the actor in the very course of this activity.[126]

This conception of praxis is very different from that found in Castoriadis. There is no doubt that, here and there, Castoriadis is also dissatisfied with the Aristotelian cleavage between poiesis and praxis. Several formulations in *Crossroads of the Labyrinth* (relating to the practice of psychoanalysis) reveal, in this respect, a certain proximity to Marx, in particular the notion of "a practico-poietic activity" whose work (*ergon*) is not something external to the agent but a self-transformation of the agent itself.[127] But overall, for Castoriadis, praxis is always oriented toward human autonomy as its driving end: this applies to psychoanalysis as well as to pedagogy and the political. For Marx, however, praxis is independent of the particular end the actors in question are trying to meet: whether we look at the Lutheran Reformation or the French Revolution, the emancipatory value of the cause does not fundamentally alter the reality of praxis as the self-production of the human subject itself. In fact, Marx's notion of praxis is a little like the "institution" of the social-historical in Castoriadis, in terms of the neutrality of each actor as regards subjective ends. In either case, what is fundamentally at issue is the meaning of the verb "to make" in Marx's phrase "make history." In the first place, "making" is that form of praxis by and through which men continually re-make themselves as subjects; in the second instance, the "making" is a form of "instituent making" through which imaginary meanings are created, and as such "making" is co-extensive with the entire "socio-historical field" insofar as it is nothing other than that activity that brings newness into existence. Hence, we encounter two fundamental and interconnected difficulties. If the second difficulty involves transforming the institution into a project of autonomy, the first difficulty concerns theorizing the transformation of praxis into emancipatory praxis. If it is true that not every institution is concerned with autonomy, it is equally true that every praxis is not an emancipatory praxis. The self-transformation of the agent in the process of altering external circumstances is not inherently liberating, and can perfectly well produce "alienated" subjects. We must therefore explicitly indicate what differentiates emancipatory praxis from praxis that is not emancipatory, based on the understanding that all forms of praxis produce subjectivities through the self-transformation of the actors themselves.

In "The Eighteenth Brumaire," Marx seems to think a clean break with tradition is one of the distinctive features of emancipatory praxis: for the first time in human history, the proletarian revolution seems posed to free itself from the crushing weight of tradition that presses down on the "brains of the living" by turning its face toward the future as it readies itself for its world historical task – hence Marx's famous motif of "poetry" of the future.[128] In the first instance, Marx seems to perpetuate the illusion that praxis is capable of totally freeing itself from conditions inherited from the past, thereby producing men who are "fully engaged" in creating absolutely new conditions without adopting roles borrowed from the past. Subjects, in other words, who can learn to speak the language of their actions directly without translating their praxis into the "mother tongue" of tradition. But even more importantly, this belief that emancipatory praxis can be detached from any dependence upon tradition misrecognizes the extent to which a clear-sighted recognition of historical indebtedness is in fact the first distinctive feature of this praxis itself. The fact is that praxis is fundamentally grounded in the need to overcome the specific inertia of its inherited conditions (and, likewise, the notion of creating something absolutely new "from nothing" is absurd, simply because, as we have argued above, the creation of the "absolutely new" is never an "absolute creation"). If Marx overlooks this, it is because of his anti-historical conception of the proletarian revolution as the decisive rupture with "humanity's pre-history," which is a notion that is rather difficult to reconcile with the discordant notion of praxis as a fundamentally conditioned activity. It is important, therefore, to hold on to Marx's principle lesson while letting his secondary idea go. Every form of praxis has two faces: one that looks toward its inherited and invariably conditioning past, and the other that looks toward the future in order to create newness "with" (*cum*) and "from" (*ex*) this past. And emancipatory praxis cannot be an exception to this rule – in fact, emancipatory praxis must fully conform to it. It is in this respect, indeed, that the Marxian concept of praxis profoundly differs from the Fichtean concept of activity (as we have seen above) that undoubtedly inspired the young Marx's reflections on the legal basis of the customs of the poor.[129] "Activity," for Fichte, always proceeds from the ego's self-positing, which is by definition opposed to that which limits it. What is at issue here, in the final analysis, is the recognition or misrecognition of the relationship between instituent activity and that which precedes it. In other words, what we need to focus on now is the relation between the institution and the already instituted, and the pre-existent as really conditioning creative praxis.

Praxis as the Co-Institution of Rules

Let's get directly to the heart of things by frankly positing our thesis: *emancipatory praxis is instituent praxis, or the conscious activity of the institution*. Now, what do we mean exactly by the activity of the institution or instituent activity? Our definition begins with a doubly negative delimitation: to institute, which consists above all in the act of establishing legal rules, is neither to create rules *ex nihilo*, nor to formalize or consecrate *post factum* rules that already exist but which are not recognized in law. In this sense, then, instituent praxis perfectly aligns with what Marx said about praxis in general: it never starts from nothing, but is rather always undertaken *in situ*, "in" and "on the basis of" given conditions that said praxis has itself not produced. But, at the same time, praxis also creates new conditions and thereby achieves a real "subjectification" by producing new subjects through the self-transformation of the actors that have undertaken this instituent praxis.

Clarifying this point should be sufficient to dispel several competing conceptions of the institution. First of all, we will not be misled by the false symmetry between "instituent power/constituent power." As we have already seen, conflating these two expressions has given rise to multiple controversies and misapprehensions. In the interest of clarity, we should point out how the terms "instituent" and "constituent," both of which are present participle adjectives, come from the same root, namely the Latin verb *statuere*, which means to "erect" or "establish." Consequently, the terms only morphologically differ from each other in their prefixes: *in-* for "instituent" and *cum-* for "constituent." The latter prefix – *cum-* – suggests a foundational act, an act usually identified with the absolute punctuality of an origin. Yet Hannah Arendt has noted how the term "constitution" is equivocal insofar as it can just as easily refer to an act of government and an act by which the people establish a government.[130] Equivocal it may well be, but there is still no question that it is the second of these two meanings that has largely prevailed in our modern vocabulary: constituent power is the power to "constitute" the government insofar as it is vested in an assembly or a convention that is singularly authorized to exercise political power. And privileging the power to constitute (as opposed to the power of a constitution already given) is sufficient to render the former power sovereign. What this means is that sovereign power can only exist as the power of a political subject that is defined by a notion of will that is unmoored from all obligation – such as that of the nation, the people, etc. The difficulty involved in theorizing a non-sovereign form of constituent power lies in the confused thinking about what kind of subject might correspond to this modality of power – hence Negri's attempt to describe the actions of social movements as "constituent decisions." In this sense, the "instituent praxis" we are interested in here cannot be the exercise of a constituent power, not even the exercise of the "constituent micro-power" of a single institution: instituent praxis does not have the majesty of a solemn foundational act, and it does not need a subject that pre-dates it. In contrast to constituent power, instituent power has the initial advantage of dispensing with the need for a sovereign subject, at least insofar as it is understood as an "implicit power" situated below the surface of intention and will – as was the case with Castoriadis. The question, therefore, is to know whether the exercise of instituent praxis corresponds to the establishment of an instituent power or a constituent power.

But first, there is another important observation that warrants discussion. Castoriadis's notion of "ground-power" is in fact so participatory that it becomes almost non-participatory as it reaches its extreme limit, insofar as it starts to resemble the unconscious transmission-modification of habits and customs. It is not a trivial matter in this context that the example or model of ground-power Castoriadis most often invokes is language. The distinction between *language* and *code*, which he introduced in the late 1960s in a rough draft titled *L'Imaginaire comme tel* (*The Imaginary as Such*),[131] is constantly referenced whenever Castoriadis wants to think about the relationship between language and meaning. Effectively, language, for Castoriadis, is both a code and a language: as a code, it is a system of signs with fixed terms and relations; as a living language, it conveys meaning.[132] But there are no essential elements of meaning or determined operations that regulate the production of meaning; there are only signifiers and codified operations for generating new terms, or what we might call language's "lexical productivity." Yet the immanent power of language, at least as long as a language is "alive," is that which "makes the new emerge" through the self-transformation of the various elements or signs that already exist. This is the basis of language's exemplarity for Castoriadis: "language, in its relation to significations, shows us how instituting society is constantly at work and also, in this particular case, how this work, which exists only as instituted, does not hamper the continued instituting activity of society."[133] Interestingly, the caveat "in this particular case," when taken literally, forbids the careless extension of language's example to the socio-historical in general: in other words, Castoriadis seems to suggest that, in other cases, the already instituted may block the "the continued instituting activity of society." We are not, of course, unaware that "once an institution is established it seems to become autonomous [and] it possesses its own inertia and its own logic," which, for Castoriadis, is reason enough to explain the alienation of society from its institutions.[134] Castoriadis's prudent use of this caveat does not, however, prevent language from demonstrating certain similarities with instituent activity, and this brings us back, in the final analysis, to the emergence of new meanings through variations of use. Indeed, language's similarity to the instituting act brings us into the orbit of Wittgenstein, insofar as Wittgenstein drew a similar analogy between the rules of language and the rules of a game in order to undermine the reductive analysis of language as a form of calculation – though, at times, there is a temptation to re-absorb all the normativity of language into this Wittgensteinian immanence of "meaningful use" (*sinnvoller Gebrauch*), as if what occurs in meaningful practice was already on the order of an infinitely revisable rule.[135] In any case, what is certain is that theorizing linguistic rules of use as analogous to the kinds of rules created and modified during the playing of a game[136] makes it very difficult to conceive of a form of praxis that consciously creates the rules, which is precisely the prerogative of the concept of instituent praxis we are working toward here.

If we do indeed want to push things further and make the exercise of this "implicit power" coterminous with the establishment of new legal rules, it is difficult to see how this is all that different from simply making custom the source of new rules or laws – and this then leads us right back to the same problems we already discussed in relation to common law.[137] We could try to make an end run around this difficulty by replacing the Hayekian concept of cultural evolution (which is itself modeled on Darwin's notion of natural evolution) with a kind of "artificial selection" of rules that are already in place. This is largely the approach that has been taken by institutional economics – or at least that branch of institutional economics concerned with the common – which tries to theorize the rules of activity used in "active organizations" or "institutions" ("all the way from the family, the corporation, the trade union, the trade association, up to the state itself").[138] In this approach, the state functions as the model institution, and thus all organizations described therein are said to exercise a certain degree of "sovereignty" by enacting and sanctioning various rules of activity. The establishment of these rules follows the methodology of common law, which is to say "through an artificial section of unorganized rules" (or customs) that are then promoted to the rank of "organized rules."[139] Unlike Hayek, however, the institutional economics concerned with the commons does not interpret legally codified customary rights as issuing from a "spontaneous order," but rather as a kind of selection-formalization of certain customs as arbitrated through conflicts of interest. The establishment of new laws is not therefore essentially different from after-the-fact recognition of various rules of conduct "discovered" by judges (as in Hayek). In either case, however, the source of the production of laws is ultimately again rooted in custom.

In a more general manner, however, the whole concept of "rules" is prevalent throughout institutional economics, both old and new, and this analytic premise must be questioned insofar as the whole approach is based on the problematic model of the "game."[140] Following the work of Aoki, we can schematically distinguish between three approaches that rely on the analog of the "game." The first approach, which is essentially that of the political economy of the commons, perceives institutions and organizations as essentially the same: institutions are active organizations and it is their rules that keep them active. A second approach, which is taken by North[141] and Hurwicz, distinguishes between organizations, which are viewed as players, and the institutions, which are viewed as determining the rules by which the game is played. And the third approach, that of Aoki, Schotter, Greif, and Young, conceives of institutions as a kind of equilibrium.[142] According to this approach, the decisive element is the manner in which agents all share a certain number of beliefs, hence the definition of the institution as a "self-sustaining system of shared beliefs about how the game is played."[143] The indisputable merit of all these approaches is their denaturalization of the market through viewing the latter, as well as the economic agents therein, as "institutions of capitalism." That said, the principal limitation of this approach lies in an inability to use the game analogy to explain the genesis of institutions as such: "the 'rules' of the game [are] considered to be given from the start" rather than being the product of "pre-existing human institutions," as if such rules could be viewed as purely technical and ahistorical parameters.[144]

We must be careful to take this dimension of historicity into account not only when theorizing internal changes within institutions, or the transformation of an institution from one type to another, but also when we are considering the *creation* of a new institution. The first virtue of the concept of "instituent praxis" is precisely to make this kind of creation intelligible: to institute new rules is, in effect, to create a new institution, at least if by "institution," one means the system of *rules* that issue from instituent activity, and not simply this activity itself. Like all forms of praxis, instituent praxis is not simply a type of technique, but an activity that begins "from" the "already instituted" – i.e., the weight of the past. At the same time, instituent praxis is all about establishing new rules that retrospectively endow this inherited past with new meanings it would not otherwise have had. The second virtue of instituent praxis is, therefore, to demonstrate the absolute necessity of continuous instituting activity beyond the moment of its inaugural act: instituent praxis as "continuous institution." In their own distinctive ways, both Sartre and Castoriadis understood how institutions, once in place, tend to become relatively autonomous in relation to their founding act by virtue of their own inertia. This is why it is so crucial to continuously struggle against this institutional inertia. Instituent praxis is therefore both the activity that establishes a new system of rules *and* the activity that tries to permanently revive this inaugural activity so as to avoid the ossification of the instituent within the instituted. Instituent praxis is thus a form of praxis that, from the very beginning, consciously anticipates the need to modify and re-invent the institution it has posited in order to improve its chances in the long run. It is in this sense, then, that the concept breaks out of the reductive opposition between "constituent power" and "instituent power." Rather than being conceived as a kind of "implicit power," the concept of instituent power we are describing does not emanate from an "anonymous collective": it is both conscious and explicit. But unlike "explicit power" of the constituent type, instituent power is not the legislative activity of a subject defined by its sovereign will, since instituent praxis produces its own subject by the very fact of its activity. In other words, whereas the subject of constituent power pre-exists its exercise or activity of said power – and indeed, it tends only to intermittently exercise this power – instituent praxis produces its own subject through the continuity of an activity that continues on after the creative or generative act. More exactly, instituent praxis is the *self-production of a collective subject in and through the continuous co-production of the rules of law*.

In order to flesh this point out more fully, it is useful to learn some of the intellectual and political lessons of a specific social and political movement that, from its outset, inscribed the problem of the creation of the institution at the heart of its practice. The movement we are referring to here is *institutional psychotherapy* (*la Psychothérapie institutionnelle*).[145] The movement's founder, François Tosquelles, was greatly influenced by his military experience in the POUM (Partido Obrero de Unificación Marxista/Workers' Party of Marxist Unification) during the Spanish Civil War, and it was from this experience that he modeled his conception of a collective as defined by its "transversality" – i.e., a permanent articulation and re-articulation between an organization's vertical and horizontal axes.[146] It was, furthermore, on the basis of this idea of transversality that Jean Oury developed the idea of a "collective" in which the vertical structure of the psychiatric establishment is cross-cut by a horizontal reception structure in which patients participate in their own treatment (of the "club" type).[147] In Oury's writing, the dual character of praxis – as both a conditioned and transformative activity – is especially evident, particularly in his idea that institutional activity always implies a certain "sub-structure" (*sous-jacence*). "It does not seem possible to institute any form of structure without taking into account that which is already there. We do not believe in the creation of the institution pure and simple; there is always some sub-structure (*sous-jacence*) that already functions and from which the physician must bring forth any new constructs."[148] This idea – which is equally important for someone like François Tosquelles – led Oury toward the notion of an "institutional net" (*filet institutionnel*) composed of transitory constellations rather than rigid "codes" or "laws,"[149] and which oscillates between an "institution" and "permanent institutionalization": "one can only go so far in the treatment of psychotics by using a rigidly functioning system that gives priority to the institution without leaving space for institutional reinvention, and even permanent revolution: this is what we like to call *institutionalization*."[150] We can see here how the term "institutionalization" does not refer to the legislative creation of new institutions – as in the work of Perelman – much less the formalization of that which already exists but is not formally recognized. Rather, the term refers very precisely to the permanent re-invention of the institution through which the group that created the institution continually counter-acts its institutional inertia. The whole collective apparatus is oriented around this requirement to constantly revive the organization's instituent activity. If differentiation prevails within the institution between status and function – or between, for instance, the status of the chief medical officer and his or her medical function – or between different institutional sites, it is in order to stave off the suffocating effects of homogeneity and thereby give "everyone the ability to articulate something of their singularity, even within a collective environment."[151] Collective rules, therefore, do not have the rigidity of "codes" or "laws" and this makes permanent re-invention possible. And if it is possible to speak of the emergence of a "collective subject" as an effect of this kind of collective, we are undoubtedly dealing with a collective of a very different sort than that described by Sartre – which, as we have seen, is a modality of the practico-inert inasmuch as its subject is constituted in and through the imposition of social and psychological alienation.[152]

In the first instance, it would surely be a mistake to disregard or underestimate the influence Sartre's *Critique of Dialectical Reason* exercised in terms of the theorization of the institution as developed by the founders of institutional psychotherapy. That said, Sartre's influence was not so much felt in terms of his positive conception of the institution as much as it was manifest through continual reflection on the "institutional question" itself: more specifically, how to prevent the institution from constricting or even collapsing in on itself? This preoccupation testifies to the extent to which the real threat, for many of these psychotherapists, was not reducible to external conditions, such as unfavorable social, historical, or political realities, but was rather viewed as *internal* to the group itself. It is precisely from this perspective that Félix Guattari tried, early on, to combine the Sartrean theory of the group with psychoanalysis. Guattari's approach combined the psychoanalytic notion of the unconscious with Sartre's notion of the group, as well as introducing the dimension of the collective to Sartre's notion of subjectivity. Since every group is entirely capable of undermining itself, we must understand how the structuration of the group itself is always an intrinsic problem for the group's subjectification. It is at this juncture that the Sartrean theme of reification within the context of the practico-inert overlaps with the psychoanalytic concept of the death instinct. As Valentin Schaepelynck puts it:

> Within the framework of psychoanalysis, the death instinct seems to play a role analogous to that of the practico-inert in Sartre's *Critique of Dialectical Reason*, and it becomes something of a recurrent horizon for all collective formations: it tells us that the possibility of reification does not necessarily issue from an outside force that tries to capture and coopt an instituent dynamic, but that reification also comes from within the group itself . . . It is indeed from within the group, from its own interiority, that every new political subjectivity is continually threated with falling back into seriality, whether this is the effect of the "practico-inert" or the "death instinct."[153]

In the face of this problem, Guattari initially contrasted two types of groups: the "subjected group" (*groupe assujetti*) and the "subject group" (*groupe-sujet*). While the subjected group receives its law from the outside, the subject group is its own founder insofar as it "functions through an internal law." We can see how this opposition is not entirely dissimilar to Sartre's opposition between the "serial collective" and "fused group." In a 1966 text titled "The Group and the Person," Guattari returns to this theme and emphasizes the opposition between the activity of the "subject group" and the "object group":[154] the "subject group" is the group that wrests control of its internal rules, its project, and its action, while the object group is determined from the outside by other groups. We should note how this opposition is also related to the opposition between language (*langue*) and speech (*parole*): the subjected group is entirely gripped and petrified in a "code" (*langue*); it is no longer capable of new utterances, and is thoroughly compelled to repeat ready-made statements.[155] The institutional question raised here, then, is how a certain structure allows a group to "speak" (*parole*) in such a way as to disturb a coded order and thereby help the group dissociate itself from such codes. But for Guattari, this question was already articulated in psychoanalysis insofar as the code operates as a kind of "group fantasy" narrativized within an official and stereotypical history. The group's relationship to its unconscious is not at all, therefore, on the order of something "added on" or "supplemental"; on the contrary, it is by virtue of the unconscious that the group is able to break out of its self-imposed confines. This aspect of Guattari's thought is particularly evident in the concept of the multiple, differentiated, and heterogeneous "*collective agents of utterance*,"[156] which allows the multiple components of each subject to come into play. It is in this sense, then, that one can truly grasp Guattari's famous concept of "transversality" in all its scope: transversality is the dimension of the group that is neither its official vertical hierarchy, nor the contingent horizontality of people who, by chance, belong to the group. The transversal dimension thus enables the group to grasp the meaning of its praxis and its concomitant subjectivities in order to engage in effective forms of (self-) transformation. In other words, transversality designates the extent to which the collective is grounded in a praxis that makes it what it is, and it is this "transversal" praxis of enunciation that makes it possible to continually act on the institution and prevent its inertial foreclosure.[157]

Of course, directly transplanting this model of practice outside the psychotherapeutic domain is out of the question. Nevertheless, this example can help us grapple with some of the difficulties that have arisen with respect to the construction of collectives in other areas of social life. Let's look, for instance, at the example of the "recuperated" factories in Argentina in the early 2000s, as documented in the remarkable investigative work by Maxime Quijoux.[158] The case of Argentina is especially indicative of the diverse situations encountered by members of this recuperative movement and the diverse practices they adopted to confront the various situations they encountered. After the corporate abandonment of the workers in Argentina, the employees took over numerous factories and turned them into worker cooperatives. An initial glance at Argentina's legal framework (in 2003) as regards the organization of cooperatives seems to restrict employee freedom within each cooperative. It imposed a specific operational form that included a general meeting of associates acting as a sovereign body, an administrative board that could be recalled at any time, two distinctive assemblies ("ordinary" and "extraordinary"), and other institutional regulations. The fact was, however, that behind this legal framework a diverse array of practices were established, and these practices are demonstrative of a certain inventiveness in terms of the development of new rules. This was especially true in terms of the considerable tensions between these rules and the specific "work culture" the employees inherited from the employers, a culture that was often shot through with paternalism. What we find in the Argentinian recuperative factories, then, are forms of instituent praxis operating below the regulatory constraints imposed by state legislation. The specific tensions that arose from these cooperative experiments perfectly illustrates the kinds of obstacles this type of praxis must continually surmount – i.e., the tension between that which is "already there" and the self-managerial rules the cooperatives tried to promote in place of their older habitus. Two such examples – the cooperative factories of Brukman and Neuva Esperanza – amply highlight these difficulties.[159] The problems encountered in the first factory, Brukman, concern the priority this cooperative assigned to the dimension of horizontality and equality. In this cooperative, wages were equal and all power belonged to the weekly "extraordinary" assembly. This arrangement soon produced serious difficulties, however, particularly when it came to the length of the meetings (which were usually between two and four hours). The second factory, Neuva Esperanza, adopted different rules: the assembly met only once a month and these meetings were mostly informative (as opposed to participatory), such that the responsibilities and decisions about the factory's operations largely reverted back to a board of directors. The hierarchical character of the new administration largely mirrored the previous system, to the point that Quijoux describes the situation as a "superimposition of frameworks."[160] We thus have two divergent logics at work in these two worker collectives: in the first case, the horizontality of its worker democracy was essential; in the second collective, however, workers opted for a more vertical division of power. The originality of Quijoux's inquiry is that he does not limit himself to merely documenting this divergence, but he also emphasizes the tension within each logic in terms of their divergent value systems: "the 'new' value of equality in the workplace was forced to confront professional histories dominated by the values of social differentiation."[161] His analysis also showed how social precariousness tended to re-create "competitive situations that ran counter to the nature of the cooperative frameworks," and how these forms of competition soon led to "power struggles." Such difficulties were especially reflected in a strange embracing of "workplace self-sacrifice," or overwork, as if the old culture of "speedy production" became a kind of cultural defense used to deal with the difficulties encountered by the two collectives.[162] We can see, then, how instituent praxis is always faced with the risk of failing to adequately promote and instill new "social meanings." The contrast between these two cooperatives is a case in point: a constituent micro-assembly that sits almost continuously, on the one hand, and a renewed form of the old social hierarchy on the other. It is in this context that one of the lessons of institutional psychotherapy is especially useful: namely, the principle of differentiation and heterogeneity designed to accommodate each singularity within a collective. But beyond this question of institutional forms, we must also be attentive to the real challenges faced by these kinds of social experiments, which often relate to what Quijoux calls "community practices" (*bricolages communautaires*).[163] In this regard, the immeasurably valuable example of "Zanon 150"[164] stems from the type of relationship the factory established with the local urban community: the workers donated thousands of square meters of tile to hospitals, schools, and popular canteens, and turned to local movements of the unemployed when jobs at the factory became available. For what was at issue in this case was not solely about the politics of ownership and expropriation, nor the demand for a "workers' controlled state" as was advocated by certain groups. It was first and foremost a question of the institution of the common, and the degree to which the common is able to transcend the property form as such.

It is precisely in this sense that the common never emerges in the form of a ready-made, universal model, or a formulaic schema that can be transposed in any situation. As the experiences of institutional psychotherapy and the Argentinian cooperatives both show, it is crucial to think of the common in relation to the logic of institutionalization. The subjects who engage in instituent activity are not condemned to pass from "fusion" to petrification, from effervescence to ossification. Rather, it is from the very moment in which they refuse to separate the ends of their activity from the relations they have created amongst themselves in order to carry this activity that the forms of reflection on and modes of intervening in the institution they have themselves created provide the values and meanings that, "in the final analysis," guide their collective efforts. Only emancipatory instituent praxis is able to produce new meanings within the social imaginary, and it can only do this in the context of the common. This also means that the common, in the sense we have been giving it here, always presupposes an institution that is open to its history, open to the distribution of positions or functions, open to its internal statutes and regulations, open to the relations of domination and exclusion that may fester within, and open to everything that functions as its institutional unconscious. Are there, then, any broader political lessons can we learn from this investigation into instituent praxis and its relationship to the common? Or, more to the point, can these analyses provide the basis for producing the "politics of the common"?

Part III

Nine Political Propositions

We have argued in this book that the common is a *political principle*. This principle is not our invention, but has rather emerged out of ongoing challenges to the present order. The common marks out the front lines and zones of struggle where social transformation is currently underway. The political principle of the common thus reflects the aspirations of those hostile to capitalism and its machinations, and it fosters practices that help bring about the creation and governance of the commons.

The movements and struggles trying to realize the common, which we have seen emerge all over the world since the beginning of the twenty-first century, are the prototypes for new institutions: they are establishing new political form and content (or new means and ends) that largely bypass the party system and the dominant regime of representative parliamentary democracy. There is no question that this search for forms of self-governance is necessarily difficult and tentative. Yet the historical originality of these struggles against, for instance, the neoliberalization of the university, against the privatization of water, against oligarchic and state control of the Internet, against the appropriation of public spaces by the state or private authorities, etc., is undoubtedly due to their practical refusal to separate their democratic ideals from the institutional forms through which these struggles are fought out. In other words, the specific historical character of the politics of common is its drive to fight against capitalism while simultaneously turning its back on state communism. What is new in these democratic insurrections and social movements is not, as certain authors have suggested, the universal acceptance of "market democracy," but rather the refusal to use tyrannical means to achieve emancipatory ends. These movements are young, and everything is still to be invented or re-invented, but such struggles and insurrections against political dictatorship and neoliberal capitalism will only have lasting historical significance if they are able to invent new institutions, as was the case at the end of the nineteenth and the beginning of the twentieth century. This will be the crucial issue for large-scale instituent praxis today.

The heterogeneous axes of struggle against the existing order today, in all their infinitely varied forms and their incredibly diverse range of actors, compel some reflection on what the implementation of the principle of the common might look like in the fields of law, power, economics, culture, education, or social welfare. The possibilities are endless for those willing to try. Examining the common as the effective principle of institutional transformation thus presupposes an exercise in political imagination, even an exercise in historical prognostication, though an exercise that is of course subject to all the usual limitations of this specialized genre. But, for the moment at least, the creation of the common is a free and open endeavor for those bold enough to take the lead. We make no assurances whatsoever that the eventual historical transformation will correspond to the course we have outlined here, to the problems we have raised, or to the possibilities we have envisioned. We do not subscribe to any "laws of history," let alone any "revelations" of what the future ought to be. For us, it is more important to be adept at creating thoughtful and cautious forms of political experimentation and practice, at least so far as circumstances permit. That said, multiple examples can already be seen that illustrate the political propositions we offer below. Italy, for instance, is a country where quite a variety of such experiments have led to particularly interesting legal developments as well political initiatives in self-governance. The communal governance of water in Naples, or the construction of a common in the Teatro Valle (Valley Theater) in Rome immediately come to mind.[1]

It is precisely for this reason that we propose only a series of theoretical and practical propositions, propositions that take the form of brief overtures designed to invite reflection and, above all, intellectual and practical collaboration. In other words, these nine propositions do not constitute a fully worked-out "program." It is perhaps worth remembering, here, that the term "proposition" comes from the Latin *propositio*, which refers to both an enunciation and the major premise of an argument, which is a dual meaning that is also found in the Greek *protasis*: in both cases, we are dealing with a statement or enunciation that invites a response, much like a question or provocation that needs to be established and verified. The following propositions on the politics of the common should therefore be interpreted in this sense: they are declarative statements whose function is to invite further enunciations and responses, and their logic is such that they can only be verified and developed through practical efforts to build the common. Yet however fragmentary these propositions may be, they are interconnected by the red thread that weaves our present historical conjuncture together. To pose the principle of the common is one thing, but to imagine an actual politics of the common is something else, and so the logic of our propositions proceeds as follows: we begin by affirming the necessity of a politics of the common, which is to say a politics that makes the common the fundamental principle of social transformation (Proposition 1). This is followed by the necessity of undermining contemporary property rights with a new concept of use rights (Proposition 2). We then argue that the principle of the common must also be the principle of labor's emancipation (Proposition 3) and the governing structure of the worker-run industries (Proposition 4). We argue that associationism must prevail in the economic sphere in general (Proposition 5), and we affirm the necessity of re-building social democracy (Proposition 6), along with the importance of transforming public services into true institutions of the common (Proposition 7). And finally, we conclude with the need to make the common global (Proposition 8) on the basis of a federal model uniquely suited to the political principle of the common (Proposition 9).

POLITICAL PROPOSITION 1

We Must Construct a Politics of the Common

To escape from the unsustainable present in which we live, we cannot simply appeal to the creative spontaneity of society, as if it were sufficient, for example, to demand a universal basic income and then wait for the common to flourish through a thousand diverse activities or through the conjunction of a multitude of singularities. The common is a political construct – or better, the common is the institutionalization of the political at a moment when numerous dangers threaten humanity. To assert that the common is immediately political, as its etymology indicates, means that we are compelled to conceptualize the common as a new institutional power structure. The politics of the common is not "anarchist" in the sense of the simple negation of power or the contradictory refusal of all authority. Instead, the politics of the common demands, in the most systematic and profound manner possible, the widespread introduction of institutional *self-government*. We must be careful to distinguish this imperative from the many forms of *self-management* that arose during the twentieth century and which – if one wants to be true to the meaning of the term "management" – were limited to the function of organizing and which only concerned the administration of things. The common, as we understand it, is above all about the government of people, and the institutions and rules people create in order to coordinate their relations. The politics of the common is thus rooted in the political tradition of democracy, especially in the Greek experience. It is based on the Greek notion that there is no desirable human world except that which is explicitly and consciously founded on common action, a world where the source of laws and collective obligations is intimately linked to what the Greeks called justice and friendship. But, as Derrida argued, this concept of democracy will be even more prominent in the history of our incomplete or open democracies *to come*.[1] For the egalitarian dynamic identified by de Tocqueville does not issue from some mysterious, subterranean, or providential power at work within history; it is not unilaterally shaped by capital and the market, nor did it emerge after the Enlightenment tore back the veil of darkness that obscured the world. Rather, this conception of democracy insists that common action, in spite of its momentary repression and derailment, engenders new institutions, new projects, new relations, and new practices, especially during moments of democratic convulsion and subversion. A deliberate politics of the common will therefore strive to create self-governing institutions that enable the freest expression of common action as possible, within the limits societies give themselves based on the rules of justice they consensually establish.

The politics of the common we must construct today is therefore incontestably reminiscent of certain aspects of nineteenth-century associationist socialism and twentieth-century council communism. But today's politics of the common cannot be thought of in terms of artisanal or guild associationism or as a renewed version of the industrial workers' councils. Rather, the politics of the common today must touch on all aspects of social life, not just political activities (in the circumscribed parliamentary sense of the term) and not just economic activities. The politics of the common always cuts transversally across institutional separations, and it embodies a democratic demand that is both generalized and coherent: the politics of the common is literally "everywhere," in every single domain in which people interact and have the opportunity to participate in creating the rules that affect them, and in the governance of the institutions they create and in which they work and live. The politics of the common is not confined to small and isolated units of work and life, but cuts across the entirety of social space, from the local to the global (and passing through the national).

It is especially evident today that the global dimension, in particular, is in need of renewed political reflection. In the face of the ongoing ravages of cosmo-capitalism, there is an almost irresistible temptation to retreat behind the walls of the national state, to enclose ourselves in the nation-state's rhetoric of citizenship, identity, religion, etc. If we only look after our own, everything will be better. But it is precisely seductive injunctions such as these that spell the end of democracy, whether we are aware of it or not. On the other hand, however, it would also be a mistake to seek salvation in the creation of a world state. No global Leviathan will ever wrest control over global capital and bring order to today's economic chaos, nor prevent ecological disaster from befalling humanity. For if a global Leviathan were to arise (which is far from evident) it would almost certainly lead to more concentrated and intense forms of neoliberal governance.

We thus propose another direction here. A contemporary politics of the common must account for the profoundly global character of the struggles underway today, and conceive of all these struggles as so many interdependent expressions of the forces structuring our worlds of work and life, our imagination, and our intelligence. A *new internationalism* is already at work in the multiple alter-globalization organizations that coordinate actions, analyses, and slogans across global networks. Indeed, the very thematic of the "common," which is global in both scope and content, testifies to this. The imperative to give institutional form to these diverse efforts at self-government is thereby also an invitation to re-connect with philosophical and political ideas that form the basis of the *principle of federalism*. And if Proudhon's name is so often associated with the principle of federalism, it is undoubtedly because his articulation of this principle was arguably one of the most important advances of nineteenth-century socialist thought – indeed, Marx even seemed to have conceded as much when he eventually lent his support to the so-called "communal" constitution of the Parisian Communards in 1871. It goes without saying that this principle of federalism has nothing whatsoever to do with today's caricature of European pseudo-federalism, which is nothing but the minimum necessary political form needed to sufficiently "organize" generalized competition between citizens and workers. This form of federalism is in complete contradiction with the federalism we are advocating here.

Genuine federalism between commons, peoples, or activities is not possible except on the basis of cooperation, not competition. In other words, federalism properly understood implies the negation of capitalism's very foundation.

Convergence Rather Than Circumvention

Given the power capitalism has acquired over the past three or four decades, and the relative weakness of its opponents, it is tempting to imagine a kind of encirclement of capitalism from the outside, or to hope for its collapse from within. In the meantime, we make do with calls for improved public services, we put our faith in a cooperative "third sector," and we encourage the creation of isolated communities of life and work that might somehow escape the reach of the dominant order. Or we await the inevitable mass disengagement of workers who are exhausted by endless competition, a kind of generalized "dropping out"[2] that empties capitalism from within and deprives its engine of fuel, either by the mass exodus of intelligence ("brain drain") or sheer physical exhaustion. And all the while we quietly meditate on the ineluctable end of the capitalist system which, like the fall of the Roman Empire, will eventually lead to a new phase of history. The diversity of our denialism only testifies to the confusion that has resulted from the loss of our usual beacons of progressive thought. All these narratives, in one way or another, turn us away from the struggle rooted at the center of the economic system and allow us to *circumvent* the central feature of capitalism: private enterprise. *Yet it is here that the submission of labor to capital is still most evident.* It is the central node that yields vast inequalities and hierarchies, and it deeply shapes the ways in which we live and think. Any project that truly wants to transform capitalism must, therefore, squarely face the fundamental question of *property*. For us, the institutionalization of the common at the scale of society is simply not possible unless property rights, the absolute *dominium* of the proprietor over the earth, is subordinated to common use rights, which necessarily means property loses its absolute character. While we question some of their political strategies and conclusions, the first socialists were undoubtedly correct in basing their struggle on the problem of private property. They, at least, did not shy away from the central difficulty posed by the law of property, and they dared to imagine a fundamentally different kind of society.

It is therefore necessary to start thinking more transversally about the practices and institutions through which the most diverse resistant activities might *converge* toward the creation of the common. For the possibility of the convergence of the private, public, and associative spheres resides precisely in the fact that these activities lose their meaning if they are not contributions to the common, if they are not parts of the larger communal activity that produces society. If, as Maurice Godelier argued, "human beings, in contrast to other social animals, do not just live in society, they *produce society in order to live*,"[3] then the challenge we confront is the imperative to merely give democratic form to the already communal production of society. In other words, it is a matter of politically instituting society by creating, in all sectors of social life, self-governing institutions whose goal and whose operational rationale is the production of the common. Neither the dissolution of politics into the economy nor the bureaucratic and tyrannical statisization of the economy will suffice. Only the democratic institutionalization of the economic can produce the common. This was the basic political goal of socialism, which Jaurès inscribes in the long history of democracy going back all the way to the Greeks:

> The highest end to which men can aspire is to pass from a state of brutal competition to a state of cooperation, in which the masses escape economic passivity and embrace economic initiative and responsibility, and all the energies currently expended in sterile and savage struggle are coordinated toward a great common end. Less preoccupied with domination and the desire to defend themselves, and more sure of themselves and others, humans thus gain more leisure and more freedom to develop their physical and moral being; and it will truly be the first appearance of a civilization of free men – as if the brilliant and charming flower of ancient Greeks had not bloomed against a background of slavery but had given rise to a universal humanity.[4]

It is this political ambition we must re-kindle today.

The Common is the Principle of Social Transformation

To this end, it is crucial to first understand, as precisely as possible, the relationship between the political and this thing we call the "social." For this relation bears on both the *extension* and the *direction* of the politics of the common. By extension, we mean that the politics of the common cannot be limited to the "political sphere" or the state apparatus, in the sense of political science or political sociology. Rather, the politics of the common concerns everything we designate with the term "social." And by direction – recalling that the Latin term *directus* is at the root of the French term *droit* (law, right) – we mean the manner in which the politics of the common aims at the re-organization of the social by substituting use rights for the principle of property as the juridical lever of social and political transformation.

It is well known how Hannah Arendt identified the "rise of the social" – which is to say the emergence of the society "from the shadowy interior of the household into the light of the public sphere."[5] For Arendt, this was a considerable change that "not only blurred the old borderline between private and political,"[6] but transformed the meanings of these terms to the point that they became almost unrecognizable. Indeed, according to the "modern concept of government . . . the only thing people have in common is their private interests,"[7] and so it is the very distinction between the public domain and the private domain that is completely erased by "submersion of both in the sphere of the social."[8] The two constituent phenomena of the public – (a) "everything that appears in public can be seen and heard by everybody" and (b) "the world itself, in so far as it is common to all of us"[9] – are ultimately relegated to what was formerly the private domain, which for Arendt threatens the very existence of the "common world." In the face of this loss of the common, this "loss of world,"[10] Arendt favors the Greek relegation of the private to the "idiotic" – literally that which is "one's own" (*idiôn*)[11] – and the concomitant valorization of the public domain as the "proper place for human excellence."[12] But is Arendt's portrayal of this separation accurate? Is the social nothing more than a public that has been invaded and annexed by the private realm?

It is highly doubtful whether the Greeks conceived of these divisions in such a clear-cut manner – or, rather, it is doubtful if their understanding of their own societies was based on the principle of this separation. We are greatly indebted in this respect to Cornelius Castoriadis, who showed, *contra* Arendt, that the full deployment and articulation of Greek democracy was based on a partition of human activity into *three*, not two, spheres. In the first place, the strictly private or domestic sphere, or the *oikos*; secondly, a mixed "public/private sphere," the *agora,* the place where citizens met with each other outside the political realm"; and thirdly, the "public/public sphere," or the *ecclesia*, the place "where they debated and deliberated public affairs."[13] What is essential for our purposes is Castoriadis's distinction between the *agora* and the *ecclesia*. Of course the *agora* is public in the sense that "one engages in discussion with others," but this public space is also private in the sense that "no political decisions (legislative, governmental, or judicial) are arrived at here." While in the *ecclesia*, on the other hand, "which includes both the 'assembly of the people' as well as the 'government' and the courts, I am squarely in public space (public/public): I deliberate with others in order to arrive at political decisions, and these decisions are sanctioned by the public authority of the collective."[14] It is thus understood that the public dimension of the social does not refer to the common in the sense of "common affairs," but to the publicity of exchanges, almost as if this second sphere (*agora*) only refers to the first of the two meanings of the public as described by Arendt – i.e., that of "publicity" but not that of the "common world." This is why Castoriadis writes the following in the context of the public/private sphere and the public/public sphere: "the last two aspects of the public are often confused in current discussions, particularly since Hannah Arendt listed each under the concept of "public space."[15] In a passage concerning "experts and citizen," Castoriadis makes this even more explicit by revealing a paralogism in Arendt's analysis:

> While Arendt is correct that the political sphere excludes matters related to our biological interest, her reasoning falters when it comes to her concomitant exclusion of the social and the economic from the political sphere. Her rationale simply ignores that fact that from the moment a division of interests becomes sufficiently important in a society – which is practically always the case whenever a society transcends its archaic stage – it is perfectly utopian to imagine a political sphere operating this way, whatever the situation of the social and economic spheres.[16]

But beyond Castoriadis's critique of Arendt, it is worth asking in what sense this public/private sphere merits the label "public." Should we be satisfied with the thesis that the *agora* is considered public because it is a place of exchange and thus a place where citizens discuss with each other? By Castoriadis's own admission, the *agora* is very complex space. In the most literal sense, the term means the "market," but insofar as the term also designates the second of Castoriadis's three spheres, it then takes on a more general meaning. Specifically, it designates "the sphere where individuals meet and associate, not on the basis of explicitly non-political matters, but rather where they engage in multiple other activities and exchanges ... And of course these activities include 'economic' exchanges, i.e., production and the market, and discussions in the *agora* often concerned economic organization."[17] But, as we have already discussed in the context of the Hungarian Revolution,[18] self-governance must not stop at the doors of the shop floor and other spaces of production. Quite to the contrary, this principle must prevail everywhere: "here, as in properly political space, the same underlying principle must prevail: no execution of decisions without participation in the decision-making process."[19] We must recognize this principle to be none other than the principle of co-obligation based on co-decision and co-activity, which is the essence of the political principle of the common. And it is precisely in this respect that the second sphere must also be viewed as a "public" and not merely a place of "publicity," in the sense of mere discussion.

It would, however, be a mistake to conclude here that there should be no division or distinction at all between the political and economic spheres properly speaking, insofar as co-decisions involving one or many units of production should be distinguished from decisions involving a municipality (or commune) or a people *a fortiori*. In other words, the injunction to ensure that the principle of the common operates across all social spheres does not thereby abolish the distinction between these various spheres (social-economic, or public/private, and politics properly speaking). Rather, the principle's function is to organize the economic sphere in a manner that makes public deliberation possible, such that the former is not controlled by the interests of a specific socio-professional class. But, of course, this can only happen if the economic sphere is completely re-organized as a self-governing commons (including cooperatives, urban spaces, forest and water management, etc.). This is not to say that each unit should be entirely independent from all the others, as if they were separate, isolated productive units, for this would merely reproduce the atomization that is characteristic of private ownership, but at a more collective level. It is rather necessary to ensure that the self-governance of the economic commons accounts for all the "externalities" of its activities and, obviously, for the needs it is required to satisfy, all of which presupposes that the governmental organs of each unit are not merely open to users and citizens, but that the units are actually governed by the collective co-producers of the service or good themselves.[20]

In other words, the primacy of the common in both spheres – the political and the economic – which ensures that the social-economic domain is itself a training ground for quotidian co-decision-making, is what ultimately makes their reciprocal re-articulation possible. For the articulation between the spheres is especially important when we move on to more directly address the institutional forms of the commons themselves. The challenge here is to make sure self-governance in the "social-economic" sphere does not hinder the exercise of this same self-government in the "public/public" sphere.

POLITICAL PROPOSITION 2

Use Rights Must Challenge Property

At the outset, it is worth recalling how the articulation between the social-economic sphere and the public or political sphere was historically constituted by the double principle, stemming from Roman law, of the *dominium* and the *imperium*: private property was given the absolute power of *dominium* over what it possessed, and the logic of *imperium* endowed the sovereign with analogous power (at least originally) in the political realm. Classical political philosophy, however, strove to radically oppose these two notions by re-activating an important distinction in Roman law that separated property from political power: the power of command in the state sphere cannot be analogous to that of the proprietor, since the power to dominate implies a relationship of servitude between persons that is, in principle, excluded in the political sphere.[1] The fact remains, however, and this is essential in our view, that sovereignty still endows absolute power on its holder (or holders), and all forms of absolute power are always the power of domination, regardless of who wields it. Yet the history of the past few centuries in the West has been marked by a re-alignment of the relation between private rights, embodied in property, and public rights, exercised by sovereignty, as we see, for example, in the Bill of Rights in the United States and the Declaration of the Rights of Man and Citizen in France. The idea here is that the sovereign guarantee of unhindered enjoyment of property to those who own property presupposes that the sovereign has prerogatives in his own domain alone, and that he does not abuse his power at the expense of those he's obliged to protect. The politics of the common fundamentally challenges this specific logic of institutional separation, an articulation that continues to structure our collective existence and which is at the root of the separation of "civil society" from the rest of the state. The politics of the common thereby inscribes itself in a historical movement that refuses the double principle of absolutism embodied in both property and political sovereignty.[2]

Use and Property

Given the fact that the economic sphere, the sphere of production and exchange, is still largely organized on the basis of private property, an obvious question arises: how might the politics of the commons conceptualize use rights under conditions of economic unappropriability, and how could it make this concept of use rights the gravitational center of the economic sphere as a whole?

In order to answer these questions, it is necessary to begin with some legal definitions of the terms "ownership" or "property" and "use." In Article 544, the French Civil Code defines ownership as follows: "ownership is the right to enjoy and dispose of things in the most absolute manner, provided they are not used in a way prohibited by statutes or regulations."[3] The concept of "use" also appears several times throughout the code, across a range of different contexts: "in the Civil Code, the term 'use' appears in relation to the definition of property (Article 544), in relation to the right of use and habitation (Article 626), in the definition of common things (Article 714), in the obligations relating to a lessee (Article 1728), and in relation to loans (Articles 1874 and 1892)."[4] But if we concentrate on those articles concerned with "use rights," we can draw a few initial conclusions:

> The right of use is both very widespread and very vague in legal terminology. Apart from the right of use as succinctly regulated by the Civil Code, the term designates the faculty of taking advantage of the utility of a thing, whether in the context of the law or a contract . . . That said, the right of use tends to be defined negatively, insofar as what defines a use-right is the absence of the faculty of disposing of the thing to which it relates. It is thus the minimal faculty to which a good can be subject. It is often associated with the right to collect the "fruits" of a thing. In some cases, it obliges its holder to return the thing in the same state in which it was found, but more often, it allows its holder to return it in whatever state it happens to be in at the time of its return. It may be a real right or a right arising from a claim. In other words, the term is neutral and requires clarification.[5]

"Use" and "Usufruct": The Classical Model

In order to clarify this notion, we must take note of the classical distinction between a use right relating to a common object and a "usufructuary" right: according to the Civil Code, "a usufructuary right is a right over the enjoyment of a good (a usufruct), whereas one is naturally deprived of a common thing in cases of use."[6] In fact, Article 578 of the Civil Code states that a "usufruct is the right to enjoy things of which another has ownership in the same manner as the owner himself, but on condition that their substance be preserved."[7] On the other hand, the code also stipulates the following as regards common "things": "there are things which belong to nobody and whose usage is common to all. Public order statutes regulate the manner of enjoying them."[8] In the latter case, the rule of "common use" excludes any qualification that attempts to make the latter respect the characteristics of private property, since both property and the notion of a private good are lacking. Considered from this point of view, which is to say its relation to the use of common things, usufructuary rights appear to closely resemble the rights of the proprietor, to the point that they are often difficult to entirely distinguish from the right of ownership. Article 578, for instance, thus refers to the right to enjoy things one does not own "in the same manner as the owner himself." This is precisely how some nineteenth-century legal theorists understood usufructuary rights in relation to the thing the right allows one to enjoy. According to Demolombe and other authors, the usufruct is indeed a real right and of the same nature as the right of property, if somewhat reduced or lessened, but nonetheless real and absolute in its own right. In short, a usufruct is "almost" property, since it allows one to dispose of the property's fruits as the owner, but without being its owner.[9]

Since a usufruct presupposes "bare ownership" (*nue-propriété*), the whole issue of the usufruct revolves around whether the title of proprietor should be reserved for a single bare owner or shared between the bare owner and the holder of the usufructuary right, which would imply the title is sharable and the property is divisible.[10] There are two schools of thought that ought to be distinguished on this point. According to one view, the usufructuary holder enjoys a "real, immediate, and absolute right over the thing," such that we must admit there are two owners of one and the same thing. According to a second perspective, however, an absolute usufructuary right is not the same as an absolute right of ownership, which implies that the right of ownership is "full, complete, and undivided." In the case of a usufructuary right, then, we are dealing with an ownership right that is "absolute," in the sense of being "real," but also not "absolute" in the sense of being "full" or "complete." In contrast, the right of bare ownership is "absolute" in both senses of being "real" and "complete." This explains why a usufructuary right is only "almost" a right of ownership: it is "real" but not "complete." Viewed from this angle, then, the divisibility of property right doesn't oppose its absoluteness, but is in the fact the basis of absoluteness as such: "it is from the absolute freedom to dispose of a thing that the owner is justified in partitioning (*démembrer*) that which he owns."[11] We should also add here that this division of the *dominium* between two kinds of owners enjoying absolute title over a thing does not create a "community," in the legal sense of the term, insofar as it fails to establish any relation of personal obligation: if there is community, it is only objectively so, for it is devoid of any direct personal connection of mutual obligation or solidarity between its members.[12]

It is precisely for these reasons that we reject usufructuary rights as the *model* for conceptualizing the use of the unappropriable. That said, we can certainly see the utility of the duty of conservation incumbent on the holder of a usufructuary right, and this is something we may want to borrow and impose on those who use non-proprietary forms of common resources. According to Martine Rémond-Gouilloud, the holder of the right of "use and habitation" (Article 672 of the Civil Code) is not subject to the same specific constraints that apply to the holder of the usufructuary right. Accordingly, Rémond-Gouilloud suggests thinking about the usufructuary user as analogous to a modern user of a "natural resource": just as the usufructuary user has a duty to prevent its given object or resource from languishing, the "user who enjoys a natural resource is [similarly] charged with conserving its substance." The user of a natural resource thus resembles a "lifetime holder of a usufructuary right" who should be made accountable for any degradation of the resource by restoring the resource to the state in which it was found (such as with the "polluter pays" principle).

For us, however, the connection already established between the usufructuary user and the bare proprietor undermines this analogy, because the user of a common is not an owner of any kind, not even "almost." There is no place in the political practice of the common for "bare ownership," whether this owner is the God of the theologians or any of its subsequent derivatives – the human race, human society, nature, the earth, etc., all of which tend to be understood as agents pursuing their own specific ends – or "subjects of right" that can only be represented by particular associations who claim to speak on behalf of everyone through a suspect discourse of self-empowerment.[13] And lastly, whereas the usufructuary user tends to be portrayed as independent of any larger legal community, particularly in terms of personal obligations, the user of a common is fundamentally connected to other users of the common through the co-production of rules that govern the common's use. And this point is especially powerful, precisely because the users of a common do not divide the same piece of property, or the same resource, between two unequal subjects. Rather, the common is based on the co-obligation that prevails between all those who simultaneously make use of a non-proprietary resource

Access, Property, and Time Restrictions

But what of the reality of the law of property as it prevails in the world today? Is it true that the relationship between a usufruct and full ownership is always determined according to division of property between two unequal legal subjects? Or, more fundamentally, is ownership as exclusive mastery and control still hegemonic in contemporary capitalism, or is this entire model already in decline? And is not the whole question of use become increasingly central as a result of recent infrastructural transformations to contemporary capitalism?

In certain respects, it would seem that capitalism itself is undermining the centrality of property by making *access* to goods and services, rather than the outright ownership of these goods themselves, the principle means of meeting needs today. According to Jeremy Rifkin, "property" in all its forms is being replaced by "access": in the age of networks, the ownership of goods matters less than access to services. While access certainly still comes at cost, the acquisition of goods for the purpose of exclusive use is becoming an anachronistic model. Membership, in short, is replacing possession. Rather than seeing the extension of the logic of property into the immaterial domain, as is the view of many critical analyses of capitalism, Rifkin sees the erosion of property, especially in terms of the ownership of the physical means of production and consumption.[14]

But is Rifkin's account accurate? Is access really replacing ownership, or is ownership simply becoming more concentrated at the top? For one of the symptoms or effects of contemporary corporate concentration is not only the expropriation of the means of production, but, increasingly, the expropriation of the means of satisfying needs (or the means of consumption). This degree of concentration creates new forms of dependency based on membership and rent, and it makes it possible to both charge the user *ad vitam aeternam* and exercise temporal controls over consumption. If the first "enclosures" concerned space, today's concentration of property increasingly encloses time. And the growth of the Internet provides corporations with a formidable platform for extending this business model and accelerating the logic of capital accumulation in the cultural, educational, affective, and cognitive spheres.

For Rifkin, however, the most important aspect of communicative capitalism is the fact that goods are not primarily sold anymore – and neither, accordingly, are property rights over goods – but rather the *use* of goods and access to services are becoming commercially hegemonic. Yet this evolution toward what is often referred to as the "service economy," or sometimes the "economy of functionality," has prompted a wide range of interpretations. For instance, many proponents of "sustainable development" or the "green economy" view this as a positive development. They see it as a means, if not *the* means, of responding to the climate challenge and the energy crisis.[15] The companies that own, but rent, property would be responsible for the maintenance of this property throughout its lifetime, as well as for any associated waste management and recycling, and thus they would no longer have an interest in incorporating planned obsolescence into their business model. Ultimately, then, the consumer wins, since leasing rather than purchasing would necessarily include lifetime maintenance and service.[16] But on the other hand, we would be remiss to observe how this same trend is advocated by tech managers who want to develop new, highly profitable business models that extend into all manner of new domains on the basis of informational systems that track customer behavior.

It is abundantly clear that this new business model is particularly profitable for businesses that are able to recycle their inputs over a long period of time – as in the case of Xerox photocopiers – or generate significant profit margins (e.g., billing for truck tire mileage by Michelin).[17] But it cannot be stressed strongly enough how much this type of service capitalism favors monopolization and market control across entire commercial markets. This trend has been particularly noticeable in telecommunications and the IT sector. Far from abolishing and replacing property, this economic model produces ever more concentrated oligopolies that control access to all sorts of goods and services. These concentrated oligopolies wield an incredible amount of social, cultural, and political power by controlling consumer behavior through incentives and targeted advertising. As Rifkin himself lucidly observes:

> We are journeying into a new period in which more and more human experience is purchased in the form of access to multifaceted networks in cyberspace. These electronic networks, within which an increasing number of people spend much of their day-to-day experience, are controlled by a few powerful transnational media companies who own the pipelines over which people communicate with one another and who control much of the cultural content that makes up the paid-for experiences of a postmodern world. There is no precedent in human history for this kind of overarching control of human communications . . . It is a new form of global commercial monopoly – one exercised over the lived experiences of a large percentage of the human population on earth.[18]

The Theory of Property as a "Bundle of Rights"

Whatever the case may be, this trend toward a more "leasing-" and "access-" centered economy has, for our purposes, the great advantage of foregrounding the question of "use," which is increasingly essential from an ecological point of view in particular.

Whatever its shortcomings, Rifkin's analysis is useful for re-considering the role of property today and its subsequent evolution. For there seems to be a growing gap between the official doctrine of property and its actual practice, as is increasingly manifest by the accelerating complexity and a progressive fragmentation of property into multiple and differentiated forms of right.[19]

In the wake of property's "dismemberment" (as Mikhaïl Xifaras puts it) at the end of the nineteenth century, a new theory of property rights, referred to as the "bundle of rights" theory, emerged in the United States. This theory of rights, which has become the dominant paradigm in American law today, shifts the focus away from the exclusive *dominium* exercised by an owner and argues instead that there are a diversity of title holders and, consequently, a plurality of rights that exist over the same thing. The "bundle of rights" paradigm thus emphasizes the rules and restrictions imposed on the owner who holds "principle title." This approach undeniably places limitations on property rights, at least in terms of its classical orientation. For it is no longer simply a question of identifying degrees of so-called "servitude," but of identifying a range of different rights – especially rights of access, use, and control – that co-mingle under the category of "property rights." This shift in thinking was, first and foremost, due to the fact that property right was, in the nineteenth century, fragmented into many different forms of property rights: use rights, rights to the revenues derived from a piece of property, rights that permit the exchange of various other rights, etc.

This evolution of legal thinking is evident if we look at a variety of applicable properties. Land, which had been the model of property *par excellence*, was no longer the only object over which ownership rights had to be guaranteed. Rights were now being imposed over businesses, securities, trade secrets, trademarks, etc. In other words, the "dematerialization" of possession – or property's becoming intangible – invariably gave rise to a much more flexible concept of property. This evolution of the law was characteristic in common law, and it was particularly conducive to the ongoing extension of property to new forms of capitalist accumulation – i.e., the gradual market integration of what economists call "externalities."[20] But this new legal paradigm can also be viewed as a social evolution in the sense that land ownership was no longer simply a question of mastery (*dominium*) over discrete tracts of land, but came to be re-defined as a sedimentation of rights, or an overlapping of different rights over the same object or space. In a famous 1913 article, legal theoretician Wesley Newcomb Hohfeld argued that ownership was not a right of absolute independence, as Blackstone previously defined it, but was rather "a complex set of legal relations within which individuals are interdependent." This new approach led to a theory of "stakeholders" or "rights holders" in legal scholarship. And this was due to the simple fact that "absolute" property – in the sense of being both "real" and "complete" – was no longer the paradigmatic or hegemonic form of property: mortgages, loans, and traded stocks, for instance, are all examples of multiple different interests and rights that were now claimed over the same object.

Legal scholarship thus produced all manner of different lists enumerating these "rights" during the 1960s. One of the more prominent came from English legal theorist Anthony M. Honoré, who enumerates no fewer than eleven forms of ownership:

1. The Right to Possess – the right to exclusive physical control over a property or, if the property is immaterial, the right to exclude others from its use.
2. The Right of Use – understood as the right to the enjoyment or personal use of a property.
3. The Right to Manage – the right to decide how, or by whom, the property will be used.
4. The Right to Income.
5. The Right to the Capital – or the power to alienate, consume, spoil, or destroy a property.
6. The Right to Security – which provides immunity against expropriation.
7. The Incident of Transmissibility – the right to transmit property to someone else after one's death.
8. The Incident of Absence of Term – the indefinite duration of property title.
9. The Prohibition of Harmful Use – which prohibits owners from using their property in a way that would be harmful to others.
10. Liability to Execution – which implies that property can be expropriated as payment for a debt.
11. Residuary Character – the existence of rules governing the reversion to older property rights (determining, for example, who owns the property title if taxes are not paid).[21]

Such a flexible notion of property undeniably opens the door to various forms of government regulation, consumer protection, civil rights law, environmental law, etc. It emphasizes the fact that title owners not only have rights but also responsibilities. On the other hand, however, this approach is entirely integrated within the "law and economics" theory that re-defines property on the basis of market value: according to this approach, anything that is determined by the market to have value is *ipso facto* property. In any case, this re-definition of property rights truly endows the latter with an immense field of application. It is therefore hardly surprising that this notion of property, which is now commonplace in American law schools, has also been used to examine forms of "common property" or the "ownership of common resources." For instance, Schlager and Ostrom have shown that the classical definition of property (*dominium*) is of absolutely no analytical use in cases of common resources.[22] What is apparent here, then, is that there are now very different kinds of property rights that do not affect all stakeholders in the same way: rights of access and withdrawal, management rights, rights of exclusion, rights of alienation, etc. But what is essential here is that these different rights are all independent of each other.

Toward an Expanded Use Right *Against* the Law of Property

This independence and fragmentation of property rights seems, however, conceptually incoherent to us. Simply put, it seems rather naïve to imagine that multiple rights to the same thing could peacefully co-exist in order to facilitate the infinite expansion of the sphere of property. The illusive character of this proposition can be seen in the similarity between this notion and the hegemonic nature of rights in the feudal epoch. In the feudal period, the superimposition and entanglement of all manner of different rights was a function of the dense networks of relations of personal dependence that corresponded to a plurality of "legal communities" to which any single individual may simultaneously belong. It might seem tempting, then, to try to revive feudal collective use rights by invoking their compatibility with recent fragmentation of property rights. This, however, would blind us to how property rights really work in the world today.

The reality is that when one carefully examines these different rights, one realizes they are articulated in a specific hierarchical order that is far from incidental. In actual practice, for instance, it is clear that Honoré's Fifth Right – the Right to the Capital – is in fact the fundamental right to which all others are subordinated. For the power to "alienate" a thing – i.e., to sell or give it away, to consume it, spoil it, modify it, or destroy it – is the exclusive prerogative of the owner, or what is modestly referred to as the holder of the "principle title." The first and second of these rights (the Right of Use and the Right to Manage) do not carry nearly as much legal weight as the Right to the Capital. And it is precisely through the hegemony of the Right to the Capital that an owner – whether a private owner or the state itself – can always challenge older customs without worrying about the ground upon which his rights are firmly planted.

This is especially true for the ownership of land, which should not be hastily reduced to a residual form of property that has been surpassed by this supposed "pluralism" of property rights. To make this case, one need only consider the new agricultural order that has been established since the 2008 global economic crisis. In a matter of a few years, fifty million hectares of land have changed hands, such that many experts have begun to speak of a "new conquest of land." The stakes of this expansive land grab are considerable: it is a matter of feeding an increasingly large global population and controlling access to water. As already discussed,[23] the Ethiopian state, which owns all the lands within its borders, has authorized very profitable leases to foreign companies.[24] These are the lands that the poorest people on the planet cultivated to feed themselves and to graze their animals, but that are now under the control of transnational corporations (both private and public).

One might argue that this practice of land grabbing is in fact made possible by the absence of any substantive feudal-style use right. But even supposing the existence and recognition of such a right, its exercise is undermined from the outset by the fact that the use right is artificially dissociated from decisions about the rules governing resources: a right of use has no efficacy if it is cut off from the right to co-produce the rules of common use. Under these circumstances, the use right is a completely toothless right to consume one's individual part of a "good" whose overall fate depends on the goodwill of its owner or owners, or is, at best, a right to "manage" a "resource" under the control of a body that alone is empowered to make decisions. According to our thesis - namely, *the establishment of rules of common use through the exercise of instituent praxis, and its extension into a form of instituent use that is based on the ongoing revision of these rules* – common use must be linked to co-decision concerning the rules, and the resulting co-obligation that flows from this process. Without this link, common use cannot be considered truly common, or – what amounts to the same thing – the resource being used cannot be considered to be a true common. From this perspective, then, freeware or shareware licenses do not belong to a true common, at least not in terms of the concept we are discussing. There is no question these licenses authorize free and open use, but the software's proprietors do not ordinarily renounce their economic rights. While it is certainly admirable for a proprietor to authorize the widest use of his property as possible, this is not the same as a common.[25] In general, it is not enough to say use is the "right to use a thing according to its proper end."[26] For something to be truly common, use must involve collective deliberation and determination about its proper end by those concerned with its use. It is only under these conditions that use falls under what we have referred to above as "appropriation as convenience or purpose," which is the farthest thing from appropriation as a form of belonging.[27] And it is also under these conditions that we can spell out the full meaning of the double obligation that is part of the governance of the common: the negative duty not to infringe on the rights of other users, and the positive duty to conserve that which is collectively managed. Clearly, this is very different from the obligation of those who use or enjoy something that belongs to someone else, as in the case of a usufructuary user or a lessee.[28] Unlike these arrangements, which are ultimately based on the recognition of the property rights of others, the duty to conserve that issues from common use is derived from the co-obligation that unites the members of the same common, and this is a connection that is made without any reference to property whatsoever.

This brings us to an essential conclusion: *the older legal concept of the "common thing" must be rejected*, even if this results in a substantial re-organization whereby the common emerges through legal processes rather than on the basis of a purely naturalistic epistemology of the common. This natural conception of the common is fundamentally inadequate insofar as it leads to a dissociation of common use from the participatory establishment of the rules that govern this use. This natural notion of the common substance is also susceptible to the idea that it can be used by "all," effectively enlarging the circle of users to the whole of humanity.[29] For this approach effectively assimilates the common with the notion of the universal, which undermines the recognition that the universality of the common is of a *strictly practical type*: *its universality only includes those who take part in the common's governance*, those who co-produce the rules of use and who transform these rules when needed. Notions of abstract universality will only lead to a confiscation of the common by the only actors recognized by international public law, namely states.[30] We are thus left with something of a paradox: while certain resources, substances, etc. are "common" by virtue of the universal character of their purpose or end, they are nonetheless reserved in practice to a very limited category of "users."

This difficulty can only be overcome if we are willing to admit that there are only "commons," and not common "things," and that it is through the common, and not by an act of law cut off from any commitment to co-activity, that *makes* "things" common to "all," inasmuch as the latter term is understood to mean the group of practitioners associated with these commons. In other words, the notion of *res communis is intrinsically reifying*, which is why it must be challenged, not enlarged or even re-formulated. We must, therefore, move toward a re-definition of use right: rather than simply expand property rights to others, we must *turn away* from property rights as such, whether in private or statist form.[31] Two examples will suffice to underscore the full political significance of this conclusion.

The first example concerns the occupation of the Somonte Farm, in the province of Cordoba, Spain, by hundreds of agricultural workers in March 2012.[32] Since the 1980s, these lands have been owned by the autonomous government of Andalusia, and run by the Spanish Socialist Workers' Party, who bought tens of thousands of hectares from large landowners for the purpose of agrarian reform. Instead of re-distributing the land, the autonomous government left the lands under the responsibility of the Andalusian Institute for Agrarian Reform (IARA), and the lands were used for intensive cultivation or for research projects financed by European subsidies (the production of agro-fuels, for instance). In 2011, as financial difficulties mounted, the government auctioned off 22,000 hectares of the land managed by the IARA. This led to occupation of the Somonte lands by the agricultural workers and their union: the farm was slated to be sold to speculators, who already own more than 60 percent of the richest lands in the county and who soak up the majority of agricultural aid the region receives. But the workers' occupation suspended the sale of these farmlands. What makes this occupation particularly important for our purposes, however, is the fact that the workers do not claim *ownership* over the Somonte farm. Rather, their movement is based on the *right of use*: their occupation is motivated by the fact the farm's four hundred hectares have not been used to feed anyone for twenty years. As one of the occupiers puts it, "the land belongs to no one. It is not a commodity. It must remain in the hands of those who work it. We've occupied this land to feed our families and live with dignity." We can see here, then, how the whole occupation is ultimately based on the commons' end or purpose: to remain "in the hands" of the workers does not denote a form of property, but more precisely refers to the co-determination of the ends or purpose of the common by those who cultivate the land. If the workers decided to reject the practices of intensive agriculture that lead to the depletion of the land, it is because they believe these practices run counter to the social utility of the land – namely, satisfying the needs of the peasants and their families in the region. In the end, the workers' cooperative decided the land was to become a kind of ecological farming project: sowing traditional seed, re-planting trees, restoring clean water, etc.

The second example is Vandana Shiva's initiative for the sharing of traditional seeds. As already discussed,[33] her initiative vigorously opposed the patents filed by American agro-businesses to appropriate the fungicidal properties of a tree – neem – that was used for centuries by Indian peasants. Three major lessons can be drawn from this struggle. The first concerns the role of states as joint holders of patents alongside private corporations: the patents filed by US agro-corporations were often held simultaneously by a US corporation and the US Department of Agriculture, much like the patent on Monsanto's *Terminator*. These patents tended to prohibit farmers from re-using their seed, and so farmers were compelled to buy new seeds from Monsanto (and the US government). The role of the state in supporting transnational agro-business is especially problematic given the fact that the Nagoya Protocol on Access to Genetic Resources (2010) does not compel states seeking to appropriate traditional knowledge to procure the prior and informed consent of local communities, and so the only regulations that have the force of law are the domestic laws of the particular states. The second lesson relates to the intrinsic legitimacy of these patents as such. How can the research interests and expenses of a private corporation, which are what justify these patents, be compared to the cross-cultural work of local communities to keep and transmit ancestral knowledge? How does one evaluate the importance of traditional practices according to the quantified measures private businesses use to calculate their "return on investment"? It is certainly tempting to argue that local communities and organizations should compete with these businesses, such that we could discriminate between "good" local patents and "bad" transnational patents. But this course of action fundamentally misunderstands the importance of the uses and practices that have made collective knowledge "common" in the first place – namely, its resistance to any form of property whatsoever. It is one thing to publish the content of traditional knowledge in a scientific journal in order to demonstrate past usage and thereby protect a resource against private patents, but it is another thing entirely to subscribe to the illusion that patent filing could somehow be made "cooperative." And, finally, there is a third lesson to be drawn from Vandana Shiva's struggle that is perhaps the most valuable when it comes to understanding what a politics of the common might look like: namely, her creation of a traditional seed bank, the Navdanya, through which 10,000 peasants from India, Pakistan, Tibet, Nepal, and Bangladesh have rediscovered organic farming.[34]

What we have here is a perfect example of the institutionalization of the common through the creation of certain rules that are intended to both combat biopiracy and ensure the effective sharing of knowledge, particularly insofar as this knowledge is not merely local but *transnational* in nature. In contrast to the Global Seed Back in Norway, which is controlled by states and large multinational agro-business, Shiva's traditional seed bank is an institution that coordinates with other similar institutions from around the world in order to create the foundations of a true global seed common. What all these examples teach us, then, is that the "custody" of a common can only be entrusted to those who are its co-users, and not states, who should never be perceived as guardians who manage "common things" through the power to enact and enforce laws.[35] Instituent use of the common is not a right of ownership: it is the practical negation of property rights in all of its forms, and the only form in which the unappropriable can be properly managed.[36]

POLITICAL PROPOSITION 3

The Common is the Principle of Labor's Emancipation

When it comes to the problem of labor, nothing is easy or obvious. To be blunt, the current relations of force between labor and capital seem especially unfavorable. Private-sector unions have been decimated around the world, and wage labor is everywhere undermined by generalized conditions of precarity. Capital seems to have so successfully subsumed work and the subjectivities of workers that it hardly seems possible for labor to mount any effective opposition, with the possible exception of purely defensive struggles aimed at "safeguarding one's job." How, under these conditions, can labor find the strength to regain its representative autonomy and the power to struggle, given both the absence of powerful labor organizations and the declining public support and trust of mainstream political parties?[1] As we have already seen, many partisans are counting on a kind of spontaneous political self-development spurred on by the quasi-mechanical emergence of a "collective intelligence" out of today's digital technologies. This is a tempting but ultimately illusory hope. Based on the history of the working class since the nineteenth century, as described by E.P. Thompson and Jacques Rancière, autonomous political representation and activity is always built up through long processes of cultural, legal, and political invention. In other words, it is only through collective action and effort that a new collective consciousness might emerge amongst the working classes.

Despite their weakened state, working-class trade unions still have a major role to play in contesting the ideological hegemony of employers and their monopolization over contemporary forms of work, as well as the purpose of the productive process as a whole. The recognition that the class struggle is political – and, moreover, that it is the political dimension that gives trade unionism its true meaning – is of course not a new idea. Arguably Marx's greatest lesson was his insistence that the source of class struggle resides in worker resistance to the logic of accumulation, and in worker rejection of the forms of domination this logic imposes on their activity. This basic idea was also the inspiration for the Charter of Amiens (1906) that, it is often forgotten, conferred on unionism "this double task, daily and in the future."[2]

Of course, transforming the current organization of labor, which is now squarely under the expansive and meticulous control of capital, is no easy matter. But it is nonetheless a "moral imperative" (*ressort moral*), as Jaurès put it, that must not be neglected and which rests on the dual *collective* and *social* character of labor. This double dimension of labor is particularly manifest in its "conflictual" character, which is hidden but nonetheless constant, even in spite of the deterioration of organized labor today.[3] In our view, the collective (but often hidden) reality of labor is perhaps the most important means of transitioning from the reign of forced cooperation to emancipated common activity.

On the basis of the abstract logic of capitalism, labor is nothing more than a means to further accumulate capital. In its concrete context, however, work is a site characterized by multiple connections and – especially in the service sector – multiple relations between workers, clients, and users. The employee does not leave his moral values, his sense of justice, his relation to the collective, and his diverse social identities at the door of the workplace. From the capitalist's perspective, however, ethical and political values have no place in the compartmentalized world of economic relations. This is even truer today, as neoliberal management tries to more radically decouple labor from its underlying communal horizon. This new regime of workforce management individualizes every aspect of one's professional activities: it shatters all forms of collectivity and injects interemployee rivalry into the workplace (despite all the lofty rhetoric of "participatory management"), while still trying to motivate employees through a pseudo-patriotic corporate discourse. And, of course, the hegemonic narrative that contrasts the "real work" of the private sector to the ineffective and costly operations of the public or state service only further undermines the relationship between concrete work and one's sense of the common.

Yet it is always important to remember the most basic lesson the sociology of labor has to teach: we always work with others. This simple idea reminds us, for example, how workers' collectives deploy modes of resistance against capitalist rationality in all different forms. For the sake of simplicity, we will group the modes of resistance under two distinctive forms: *cooperative resistance* and *resistant cooperation*. For even practices such as slowing down the workday, sabotage, absenteeism, or appropriating work time or resources for personal ends can only take place under collective conditions.[4] Generally speaking, the cooperation of other workers is often required if workers are to bypass hierarchical injunctions and official rules to make these resistant activities possible. It is the workers or employees that collectively "make the workplace run," after all, and they always defend their autonomy against managers, in spite of explicit managerial tactics designed to disrupt this collective autonomy.[5]

But while we work *with* others, we also work *for* others. Danièle Linhart, working in the tradition of Durkheim, has written much about what she refers to as the "altruistic" dimension of work.[6] This moral component of work emerges through a sense of the social utility of the things we produce, the satisfaction gained by making something "beautiful," and the connections we make with others while working toward a common end, etc. It is a woefully under-researched dimension of work, largely because we have become accustomed to narrowly examining the behaviors of workers through the rigid utilitarian criteria of *quid pro quo* market exchange. Philippe Davezies offered perhaps the best description of the undeniably communal nature of ostensibly "individual" work:

> The development of work activity appears to us to be the dynamic movement through which the individual progressively integrates concern for the activity

> of others. The worker feels pleasure as he realizes he is capable, through the development of his work, of bringing more to the collective than that envisioned according to a narrow definition of his task. From this perspective, the autonomy that is produced through the development of this activity is very different from the closure of the individual within himself. On the contrary, it frees the worker from the tyranny of his own demands for immediate gratification and opens the worker to the possibilities of constructing a common world. The worker is thereby able to offer and realize free forms of activity that connect him with others.[7]

To work is always to engage in common action of a moral, cultural, and even aesthetic kind. However, it is precisely because this aspect of the common is not only misunderstood but actively repressed that work, under the domination of capital, is so profoundly frustrating and demoralizing. This is exactly what American sociologist Michael Burawoy discovered when he wondered why employees work as much as they do, even within the capitalist framework, while orthodox economic theory contrastingly views the worker as a perpetual shirker.[8] What mainstream economics fails to grasp is precisely the aspect of work that is common, which Thomas Coutrot aptly summarizes as follows: "the worker is deeply committed to his work not to increase profits for the firm, nor even to increase his own wages, but in order to assert himself as part of a community, or a group of peers."[9] The utilitarian faculties so readily ascribed to "economic man" are incapable of accounting for this often-gratuitous cooperation, which cannot simply be reduced to a matter of "interest" in any well-understood sense of the term.

Labor thus presupposes a "collective" dimension in order to be effective. This "collective" dimension, however, is much more than the mere grouping of workers in one place. We must therefore understand the *institution* of labor as a reservoir of tradition. The institution of labor is the vehicle through which all the words and gestures of a trade are transmitted through time, through which traces of past environments lost to memory are preserved, through which all those transpersonal and generic resources that do not belong to anyone in particular are maintained. Everything, in short, that cannot be reductively assimilated to the category of "human capital" comprised of personal skills, as is the norm in economic science and public and private management. What the sociology of labor identifies is nothing other than the unappropriable dimension of the professional common, and it is this alone that makes individual work possible.[10] When it is not completely prescribed and channeled, work is always creative, or as we would like to put it, *instituent*: it produces relationships of camaraderie, new gestures, new modes of coordination and cooperation, and, above all, tacit rules of mutual assistance and collusion between employees. Work creates and renews the milieu in which it takes place, and it implicitly and informally results in collective rules of cooperation. And as far as is possible, it produces its own criteria for evaluating performance and its own moral framework. It "makes a society" within the bureaucratic constraints and managerial imperatives to which it is subjected by capital or the state (or both). It is false, then, to say cooperation is forced upon labor by capital through a system of explicit rules. Rather, the co-activity that is inherent to all work is always accompanied by a sense of obligation, if only minimally, to the common. This relation to the common is reflected in the signs of recognition, familiar words, jokes, etc., all of which form, however fragilely or tenuously, the institutional and symbolic realities without which work would be impossible.

It is this symbolic relationship, woven by these connections of reciprocity, that business leadership is increasingly trying to exploit. As Thomas Coutrot puts it, "productivity very often depends on the ability of businesses to harness the interplay of social norms within working environments for their own benefit. This is the central issue of workforce management: how to channel this symbolic energy toward productivity and away from resistance."[11] The neoliberal firm, as Coutrot explains, also engages in forms of "coerced cooperation"; not in the direct, brutal, and despotic manner of the assembly line or other Taylorized industries, but through the mediation of financial markets: by defining the norms of productive efficiency and financial performance, the market operates as a kind of disciplinary force that compels workers to cooperate in order to keep their jobs.[12] The neoliberal firm makes the employee identify with competition: exposing oneself to all the risks of economic warfare is framed as a laudable or altruistic attitude, while public officials and welfare recipients are shielded from these risks, and are thus the true beneficiaries of the Great Cause of national competitiveness. As Danièle Linhart writes:

> modern work confines the individual within an circumscribed perimeter, one that encompasses the aims of one's firm and one's own ego to the exclusion and detriment of the rest of society. It attacks the link that connects the meaning and experience of one's work with the larger society. This causes everyone to withdraw inward and leads to a kind of incomprehension about the lives of others.[13]

This competition-based neoliberal policy, in concert with neoliberalism's more diffuse attack on solidarity and public services, only aggravates the loss of communal meaning and suffering in general. Under the constraints of corporate hierarchies and abstract norms, employees only have the impression of pursuing quantitative objectives that do not fit into any meaningful conception of their trade or their work. This leads to a whole range of physical and psychological pathologies of considerable human and economic cost.

However, despite all its efforts, the neoliberal firm is still confronted with the "fundamental contradiction of capitalism" that, according to Castoriadis, resides in the fact that the firm must motivate its employees and solicit their participation, while simultaneously reducing them to mere performers who must obey a logic that is exogenous to their activity.[14] Castoriadis argued that political activity in the sphere of labor should direct itself toward transitioning from coerced cooperation to a form of self-determining and self-organized activity based on the excess derived from the collective dimension of work that is not captured by the formal and proscriptive definition of one's individual job. Realizing this kind of common political activity under conditions of exploited and alienated wage labor is one of the central axes of struggle against today's modernized managerial apparatus, whose single purpose is to meticulously destroy the moral and collective dimension of work by transforming subjectivities from within. Of course, attacking the heart of capital's domination over labor is no easy task, especially under present conditions. Yet ongoing employee resistance to this regime continually shows us the potential force for a generalized opposition to capitalist domination that even wage labor's relative state of anesthesia cannot totally subdue. If workers are still attached to their work today – despite the conditions of employment and the often meager income they receive – it is not due to alienation, voluntary servitude, or pure economic coercion: it is because wage labor remains an activity through which individuals socialize and maintain connections with others.

The question of power thus remains central to private enterprise: private power is based on property, but it is also that which determines all the inequalities pervading the organization of labor. The hierarchy that reigns in the private firm even surpasses the most rigid forms of hierarchy found in the army or in the church. This structural subordination clearly has an effect on work itself, on the "motivation" of the worker and on worker creativity, but it also has an effect on social life as a whole. Atrophied or passive leisure time and a thirst for consumerist forms of compensation are all symptoms of this submission.[15] Re-composing the current organization of work, especially its distribution within this functional hierarchy, is thus a crucial political imperative for us. Workers must have the right to collectively participate in decisions that affect them. This is perhaps the most important aspect of the socialist tradition, and the cost of its abandonment by the trade unions and the political left has been considerable, as Bruno Trentin reminds us. This rejection has also played a decisive role in the fatal outcomes of the economies in the East. The inability of the communist ruling caste to introduce even the most modest dimension of democracy into the labor process all but ensured the collapse of these societies.

In the late 1970s, Rudolf Bahro produced a particularly lucid analysis of the defects of the Eastern bureaucratic systems of production. He argued that these defects could be corrected through the introduction of a limited number of creative groups, spaces and periods of free activity, and voluntary forms of productive association. While modern large-scale production still required, for the foreseeable future at least, routine, automatic tasks and a relatively high degree of formal procedures and prescribed techniques, Bahro argued that modern business was not condemned to be a purely vertical and hierarchical organization dealing only in specialized and standardized tasks. It was not, in other words, fated to become a Weberian bureaucracy. Bahro explained how workers could distribute work differently and set aside time for collective and creative work designed to at least partially overcome the atomization of their small and repetitive tasks. Not only is this free activity – in which workers take the initiative – necessary for endowing their work with meaning, but it is also beneficial in terms of scientific and technical invention. And it has the additional benefit of overcoming the fragmentation of daily life by creating some degree of transversality between the spheres of social life:

> The fragmentation of human activity into thousands of subordinate functions which are of little significance in themselves, leads to the atomization of individuals. Creative group work on unsolved problems can also be the point of departure from which the identity of cooperation and communication is re-established.[16]

As we know, this "alternative" to bureaucratic socialism never came to fruition. But this does not mean its underlying lesson is no longer current: the common, in the form of concrete cooperation within freely formed groups, is still one of the best ways to counter the effects of hierarchical domination in work and social life, and one of the best ways to allow everyone to freely develop in the context of truly collective work. Re-situating the question of the organization of labor at the heart of the political struggle is the only answer to the political strategies of neoliberal management.[17] It is not enough merely to "enrich" the work carried out by employees or "consult" workers from time to time concerning the conditions of their work. Workers must take part in the development of the rules and decisions that affect them. If it is important to continue to fight for employment standards, such as the rules that give employees legal status, it is also necessary to insist on the democratic transformation of the workplace in accordance with the cooperative content and social purpose of all workplace activity – in the capitalist private sector and in the public and voluntary sectors as well. Instituting the common in the sphere of production means that businesses, freed of the domination of capital, must become democratic institutions, and employees must organize themselves on an explicitly cooperative basis.

POLITICAL PROPOSITION 4

We Must Institute Common Work

Freeing labor from the grip of capital is only possible if workplaces themselves become democratic institutions, rather than an island of employer and shareholder autocracy. This is not a new idea: it was at the heart of the older notion of the "social republic." To "dissolve the Republic into the workshop" ("faire descendre la République dans l'atelier"), according to the expression from the 1830s,[1] was a rallying cry of republican and socialist workers who wanted to end the new feudalism that reigned in the factories and the workshops. Socialism was thereby conceived, from the outset, as the extension of democracy into economic life. This idea was later taken up at the turn of the nineteenth century by the Catholic social movement called Le Sillon ("the furrow" or "the path") and, as the movement's founder Marc Sangnier put it, "we cannot have a republican society while monarchy reigns in the workplace." "Political democracy," Sangnier argued, "is not enough: what we want is for the worker to not only be able to cast a ballot to appoint a political representative, but also be able to participate in the management of affairs in the factory and the industry in which he works.[2] And Jaurès, along with all the other socialists, made precisely the same claim when he accused the fanatical economic partisans of private property, who rejected the very principle of economic democracy, of being monarchical zealots.[3] And while the spirit of this idea has not entirely dissipated – traces of it can be still be found in the French Auroux Laws of 1982[4] – the more general ideological collapse of "social democracy" has almost completely erased this demand from the discourse and actions of today's so-called "socialists."

Capitalism, concomitantly, has remained completely inflexible in this respect. Its hatred for democracy is the crux of its domination and its defining institutional dogma. Any form of democracy in the workplace is in direct contradiction with the capitalist's domination over what he considers to be his exclusive property.[5] The sovereignty of the owner is the dominant principle of the employment contract, and its execution must reside under the capitalist's absolute command. Nonetheless, labor law has made considerable advances in a number of areas. Through the institution of collective bargaining, labor was at least partially able to realize the otherwise fictional notion that the employment contract is signed between two equal individuals. But the essence of capital's domination remains in place: subordination to the firm deprives the employee of rights while under the owner's control. The reality is that the ostensibly "free" worker loses a great deal of freedom by submitting to this sovereign authority. Articles 122–135 of the French Labor Code, for instance, stipulate that personal rights and individual or collective freedoms can be subject to all manner of restrictions, as can be justified by the execution of work. In other words, the private enterprise is *beyond the rule of law*.

In fact, the private corporation (*enterprise*) does not exist in French law. The latter only references the "firm" (*société*), a term used to designate an act of association and the new legal person this association produces. As Article 1832 of the French Civil Code puts it, "a firm is established by two or several persons which agree by a contract to appropriate property or their industry for a common venture with a view to sharing the benefit or profiting from the saving which may result therefrom."[6] The corporation, which is described as an action of several associated persons, does not belong to anyone. Capitalists are not the "owners" of this common activity (which does not really make sense anyway), but are rather the economic powers who are associated in the form of a firm (*société*) that is eventually represented (in the case of publically listed companies) by property titles traded on financial markets at prices that vary according to future bets made by investors. It is only through a misuse of language that the securities of the firm (*société*) held by shareholders are described as a "corporation" (*entreprise*). Employees, however, who also pool their qualifications, their knowledge, and their "industry," do not own anything: they have no special legal title and no right to appropriate the products of their common activity. They are simply subject to the domination of the owners of capital, to whom they have rented their labor power. Yet, in the final analysis, private enterprise is still fundamentally based on "labor power." Indeed, it might even be argued that this perpetual source of potential resistance has been strengthened to the extent that employees have injected increasing amounts of knowledge and experience into private firms, although this is not reflected in the rise and fall of share prices in the financial markets. Worker cooperation and collective intelligence have no autonomous legal existence: cooperation and intelligence are rather indirectly translated into financial forms that primarily benefit the incomes of owners and managers. Under the conditions of financial capitalism, even the most indifferent and ephemeral shareholder is an absolute sovereign, and everyone else becomes the shareholder's "agents," who are compelled through the perpetual threat of competition to produce ever more financial value.[7] The scandal of this ongoing exploitation is only exacerbated by the fact that private business produces much more than mere economic value for its shareholders: it produces and reproduces society itself.

Altering the institutional structure of this central social organ of society is thus one of the most important ways of countering the hegemony of capitalism in economic activity and social life. Institutions of production must also become political institutions devoted to a social purpose – namely the selling of goods and services on a market. Yet the difficulties that socialism has traditionally encountered in this respect are all too clear: "social" or "collective" property has too often been transformed into state property and thereby subjected to centralized, bureaucratic, and ultimately inefficient management. Marx, Engels, Lenin, and Trotsky all wavered in their institutional responses to these questions, and therefore tended to speak in obscure or even contradictory ways on this subject.[8] It has been rare for socialist thinkers to actually sketch out the economic organization of the future socialist society in any detail. One of the rare exceptions was Jean Jaurès. Jaurès was acutely aware of the tyrannical effects excessive centralization yielded, and so his plan for the socialist society clearly separated the administrative state from corporate forms of production managed by autonomous and decentralized professional groups:

> To give to the statesmen and governors – who already have control over the national army and national diplomacy – effective direction over the national labor force … would be to give a small cadre of men a power greater than that wielded by the Asiatic despots, whose power flows across the surface of society but did not regulate economic life itself.[9]

Jaurès's plan included geographically decentralized and co-administered political municipalities (*communes*), industries, trade unions, professional associations, and social property, and all were to remain under the general control of elected workers' representatives and elected political representatives, within the framework of a "national labor council" that determined national economic laws.

Of course, creating the common today is not a matter of imitating Jaurès – who favored the election of representatives over forms of direct democracy – but it depends on inventing new forms of common production. Between the older model of the "workers' cooperative" – which, despite its practical inventiveness, was always prey to capitalist competition – and nationalized industries that are run in virtually the same manner as their private-sector counterparts, there is plenty of room to come up with new models that privilege forms of cooperation organized by the workers themselves. Yet the cooperative dimension of production must not be confused with cooperative enterprise (*l'entreprise coopérative*). In France, for instance, the SCOPs (Société coopérative ouvrière de production, or Cooperative Workers' Corporation) are undoubtedly a model worth looking at, if only because they confirm the viability of productive organizations that depart from a strictly capitalist framework. In the SCOPs, the employees must always be the majority shareholder: they deliberate and decide on all the major business decisions – particularly regarding the allocation of profits – and they select their own leaders. Their principle of representative democracy – "one man, one vote" – is markedly different from the absolute power of the owner. This principle profoundly alters the status of capital in the workers' cooperative: *it is no longer a power in itself, but merely a means to an end*, in accordance with the initial principles of Owen and Thompson's cooperative movements. Labor makes all the decisions, and capital serves only an instrumental purpose. We must admit, however, that the SCOPs are only a small fraction of the French economy. There are just over 2,000 SCOPs in France, and they account for approximately 45,000 employees, which is barely one-tenth of the number of agriculture cooperatives in France. The SCOPs thus operate in an environment that hardly facilitates their expansion: distrustful banks create barriers to their growth, and political hostility can be fatal – this was the case with the LIP company, for instance, that was forced to liquidate in the 1990s after fifteen years of struggle. But there are nonetheless many success stories, such as the cooperative Mondragon Corporation of the Basque region. It is composed of 116 cooperatives, 70,000 employees (half of whom are "partners"), and has total revenues of over 10 billion euros.[10] But, as Daniel Bachet points out, the expansion of the cooperative to the global level actually tends to be detrimental for the company's ongoing cooperative operation, since the success of cooperatives tends to be a function of the local history and sociology of their founding regions.[11]

Substantive reform therefore depends on reaching the nerve center of the capitalist system, which remains the private enterprise. How do we establish an alternative to the Anglo-Saxon model of corporate governance that has so expanded its empire in recent decades? To help guide our efforts, let's first examine some recent thinking – or re-thinking – about the world of private work. In order to break out of the capitalist model, some authors, like Daniel Bachet, argue that decision-making should be situated in two distinctive entities: one entity made up of shareholders interested in a return on their investment, and another entity that represents the business or corporation as a specific entity.[12] The general idea here is to give the institution itself a more concrete existence, such that it becomes a reality unto itself that transcends the particular interests of its various parts. This would also theoretically prevent capitalists from simply liquidating the company for profit when it suited them. And it would also entail a complete re-thinking of the corporation's "social" interest or purpose, beyond its economic value alone. This is essentially a proposal to "decommodify" private enterprise and re-define it as primarily a "worker community." This is obviously in direct contradiction with the financialization of the economy and the concomitant denial of the institutional dimension of the corporation – as is evident, for instance, in the rise of stock prices after layoffs, the practice of leveraged buy-outs (LBOs), changes in asset evaluation methods, and the rise of new neoliberal instruments of managerial control.

Isabelle Ferreras has similarly argued that private businesses should be reformed in the same fashion as were the political democracies in Europe during the eighteenth and nineteenth centuries, namely by establishing a "bi-cameral" institution in which capitalists and workers are given control over each house or body – a chamber for the capitalist lords and another for the salaried commoners.[13] But how would these reforms manage the basic incompatibility between the "democratic governance of capitalism," on the one hand, and the competitive and conflicted nature of private enterprise on the other? When Ferreras asserts that "labor is the beating heart of firm,"[14] it makes us wonder if the institutional compromise she is envisioning might be rather short-lived: by agreeing to share power with labor, would capital's claim to appropriate the firm's revenues still be legitimate? It is true that there is still a House of Lords and even a monarch in England, but generally speaking, these proposals for democratizing the workplace by adopting the forms and institutions of representative democracy are not focused enough on the need to invent much more active, participatory, and permanent forms of democracy. And these proposals are always potentially waylaid by the inherent incompatibility between capitalism and democracy as such.

Thomas Coutrot, who is much more skeptical about the compatibility between capitalism and democracy, argues for a democratic transmutation of private enterprise that goes beyond the traditional Marxist paradigm of "worker control" over production. For Coutrot, this transmutation must account for all the enterprise's social interactions and "externalities" – i.e., not only the direct economic effects of production, but all the multiple indirect effects production yields within the larger environment. What he calls "citizen control" would be exercised by an administrative council of employees and the representatives of capital, but also various other stakeholders who are impacted by the company's activities. Such stakeholders may include an association of users or residents, NGOs, or representatives of local or regional councils.[15] This notion of a "citizen government" has the benefit of avoiding the strain of economism we find in much socialist thought all the way back to its beginnings (in which control over production was reserved for the "association of producers" alone). For Coutrot, the economy must be re-integrated back into social life and become enmeshed in democratic society by introducing a plurality of perspectives into the sphere of production, and we must construct a new system for managing these conflicting views through institutional rules.

Whatever the line of thought pursued by these various authors, it is clear that the question they are all trying answer, in a very practical way, is not simply about distributing resources more "justly," but about the very way power itself functions in the workplace. And of course this question only arises in the first place if the workplace is transformed and managed as a common institution. The denial of labor's common activity in favor of a financial reality in which capital reigns completely over the economy, a view in which money trumps human activity, is the main lynchpin that must be blown out of the capitalist system. It is effectively the very notion of the market itself that needs to be undermined. But transcending the reign of capital will not be achieved by merely "suppressing" the market through forms of bureaucratic planning and distribution. The market and capital must, instead, be re-integrated into society. It must be replaced with a system of individual consumer choice within the context of collectively determined frameworks (especially at the local level). The consumer must no longer be pitted against the worker, as is too often the case today. The goal must be to construct new "civic" market institutions that combine the self-governance of workers with the collective sovereignty of consumers.

POLITICAL PROPOSITION 5

Economic Associationism is the Pathway to the Society of the Common

The "social and solidarity economy" (*l'économie sociale et solidaire*, or ESS), as it is called in France, differs from the capitalist enterprise in terms of its operating statutes, social purpose, and internal organization of power.[1] The so-called social economy is, accordingly, often described as a "different economy" or even an "alternative to capitalism."[2] Yet the logic of this claim is rather ambiguous: is the goal to carve out a "social and solidary" sector within a pluralistic economy that includes capitalist and state actors? Or should the social and solidarity economy "contaminate" every sector of the economy, as the socialist advocates of associationism and cooperatism had initially hoped? In either case, the social economy is almost always framed as a major mechanism for democratizing the economy. For Jean-Louis Laville, the solidarity economy "is bound by a refusal to submit to the law of profit and a desire to democratize the economy . . . the guiding and empirically verified idea is that economic efficiency and democracy are not contradictory, especially in a knowledge and service economy where collective intelligence becomes a major asset."[3] The social economy is thus an attempt to expand democracy into the economic realm, and to nurture a voluntary social bond concerned with equality and solidarity. The social economy is proof that the economy is not reducible to the market/state binary, and that there is a legitimate place for collective action based on different principles and ends.

The first argument for the social economy as an alternative to standard capitalism simply emphasizes its share of the overall economy. In France, the social economy accounts for 10 percent of overall assets and 6 percent of GDP.[4] The second argument emphasizes the democratic nature of the social economy, which is an especially powerful idea at a time when capitalism seems especially morally and economically predatory. Such arguments, however, tend to portray the social economy as a relatively homogenous phenomenon, when the reality is rather more complex.[5] In the first place, each country has its own more or less formalized definition of the social or solidarity economy, and since these definitions vary from one country to another, comparisons are not a simple matter. Secondly – and we will focus on France as an example here – the term tends to encompass a rather diverse range of activities and institutions (associations, cooperatives, mutual aid societies, etc.). And while the social economy is an inherently composite and variegated phenomenon, it tends not to be diffused across the whole economy but is more often concentrated in specific sectors. In Brazil, for instance, it is mostly the agricultural sector in Nordeste that operates as a social or solidarity economy, while it is mostly found in the service sector in France. And in both countries, it is almost entirely absent in industrial production.

The social economy is therefore profoundly shaped by its national context, especially in terms of its orientation toward ancillary characteristics of the social economy, such as charity organizations, social integration, alternative forms of production, or social activism. Within the field as a whole, Philippe Frémeaux identifies two basic logics: an "associationist" logic that he traces back to the institutions that emerged during the nineteenth century, and whose purpose was to provide mutual aid and solidarity between members of a profession or social group, and a more charitable and religious institutional logic.[6] For the moment at least, the social economy is not a committed and mobilized social movement, either at the national or global level, despite the increasing visibility of some of the more prominent social economy NGOs. It is thus difficult to argue that such a diverse and unstructured phenomenon actually constitutes a real "alternative to capitalism," much less the only possible alternative. Such an assertion is all the more problematic given the substantial pressure these organizations and institutions face from both capitalist actors and the public sector: at the moment, there is simply no room for a full-fledged alternative to the market and the state. We have already discussed the strictly political limitations of economic associationism. Their freedom to develop is greatly limited, particularly insofar as these institutions tend to be placed under the control of state administrations. The state tends to become the sole arbiter of their public utility, and things do not seem fundamentally different today. Léon Duguit saw this danger quite clearly in 1901: "governments are always afraid freedom of association has become too great, and these free organizations might take over areas where the state wants to preserve its leadership, if not its monopoly."[7]

While many advocates of the social economy are completely dedicated in their attempts to change economic behavior by offering concrete examples of alternative economic forms, the reality of the social economy is not as promising. In this respect, Jean-Louis Laville cites the words of a particularly enlightening cooperative manager: "the cooperatives wanted to change the market, but it is the market that changed the cooperatives." This dynamic was especially prevalent for cooperative banks, but also many mutual aid organizations that have recently been isomorphically transformed into quasi-capitalist organizations:[8] they are immersed in the market, subject to competition from capitalist firms, forced to adapt to the utilitarian behaviors of consumers searching for the best price, and are continuously denounced by neoliberal politicians and private employers as "subsidized" institutions that distort the market. In addition, their overriding concern for "managerial respectability" invariably distances them from union and political struggles, and so social economy organizations tend, in the long run, to drown in the icy waters of the market economy. And even if these institutions manage to survive in this hostile environment, many fall into the orbit of state and local authorities by completing tasks for less money than would government institutions staffed by a unionized civil service. Far from promoting a "different economy," the social economy sector tends to become a low-cost subcontractor at the behest of the welfare state, which in turn has led to a rise in poorly paid precarious workers, while better-paid government positions have stagnated or even declined.[9]

Coping with the fiscal crisis of the welfare state and competition from low-wage countries runs into the persistent risk that the social economy will become little more than "a ghetto for poor workers who perform low-skill and low-qualification activities," in the words of Bruno Trentin.[10] Indeed, the very function of today's social economy may merely be to provide lower-cost substitutes to the welfare state. In fact, this is precisely the view taken by the Organisation for Economic Co-operation and Development (OECD).[11] And the social economy is often ill-suited when it comes to the delivery of public services: its recipients often do not play an active role in these organizations; many social economy organizations are dependent on public funding which compromises their organizational autonomy; and their "democratic" governance is often more rhetoric than reality, if not a masquerade entirely. In actual practice, employees of social economy associations tend not to be involved in decision-making, and in many mutualist societies and cooperative banks, members often lose interest in electoral rituals that are usually devoid of any substantive content in any case. In practice, the largely formal electoral procedure for appointing administrators gives ruling oligarchies a free hand to impose managerial practices that move social economy organizations farther and farther away from their original social aspirations. The social economy has thus been unable to substantially assert itself as a different economic format within the current state/market system, let alone the foundation upon which an entirely new economy might develop.

As a result of these shortcomings, neither employees nor members feel as if they are truly participating in a political project aimed at creating an alternative to the dominant economy.[12] In almost every case, it is the political dimension of the "third sector" that is undermined by an increasingly ubiquitous focus on managerial practices. This rather somber reality is a testament to what is ultimately a foreseeable strategic impasse. For the very notion that it might be possible to slide into the interstices of the dominant system and create micro-breaches little by little was largely viewed as a futile strategy by the first generation of socialist and cooperative thinkers. For these socialists, the cooperative struggle to provide a real alternative to the current economic system had to be fought in concert with union and political forces. The importance of the so-called "three pillars" of socialism, according to Jaurès and Mauss, was based on the understanding that the struggle for another economy must be total, not interstitial.

Insistence on total struggle should also guide the politics of the common, and so reviving the politics of the social economy is crucial. This is an indispensable tradition that must be recovered, and its aspirations must be fulfilled.[13] But this means ensuring that the principle of the common becomes an explicit matter of struggle. This is crucial because the fundamental principles of the social and solidarity economy, which were born out of protest against capitalist forms of production, are largely resonant with the principle of the common as we have described it. Thierry Jeantet, for instance, enumerates a certain number of the practical characteristics of this "other economy" that we already see, more or less realized, in the social economy: freedom of collective initiative, internal democracy, fair distribution of surpluses, the total or partial indivisibility of its assets, solidarity, individual promotion, and state independence.[14] Thierry sums up the spirit of the movement as follows: "a collective project driven by the cooperation of actors."[15] Speaking of economic associations, Philippe Chanial and

Jean-Louis Laville insist on the connection between the cooperative form and actual solidarity, and between concrete associative practices and civic purpose: "the power of associationist creation is the feeling that defense of the common good presupposed collective action."[16] To put it more directly, the ideal coherence of this alternative economy resides in the concatenation between a democratic institution of common activity, and the production of the common as the end to which this action it directed. This tradition can therefore only be revived if the connection between the association's "social objective," which belongs to the production of the common, and the democratic workings of the social economy is firmly restored – which is far from the norm today. Struggling against the financial takeover of social purpose, or against practices that undermine internal democracy, is thus indispensable. The outcome of this struggle will ultimately determine whether this sector of the economy is able to contribute to the creation of the common. And because increased state and local government support will be also be indispensable (especially in the interim) for offsetting pressures exerted by competitive markets, making democratic cooperation a criterion for state funding or tax exemptions is essential if the social economy is to make a meaningful contribution to changing society as a whole.

The struggle that must be carried out within the social economy also concerns the ability to establish democratic mechanisms (for employees, consumers, and other actors) and to determine the "social utility" of both the project as a whole and the internal activity of the association. And under certain conditions, the social economy may even challenge the state's monopoly over the definition of the general interest, and the market's hegemony over what counts as value. It is here, especially, that the social economy is, potentially, most subversive: it is increasingly difficult to measure the value of the wealth produced by the social economy according to strict market notions of value, or, as is often the case with state production, its equivalent market price.[17] By synthesizing a variety of diverse approaches since the 1990s, Jean Gadrey proposed a series of criteria for assessing the contributions social economy associations make to society. Organizations may be considered socially useful if they "contribute to a reduction of economic and social inequality, including the affirmation of new rights, if they increase solidarity (national, international, or local) and sociability, or contribute to the amelioration of the collective conditions for sustainable human development (including education, health, culture, the environment, and democracy).[18] Especially conspicuous in this list of criteria is the "production of the social bond." But "social utility" does not only concern the impact of some action or other on society; its evaluation must also be sensitive to the direct effects of those who participate in these organizations. It would be outright paradoxical to assess the contributions of these associations without including those volunteers, employees, and beneficiaries who are the co-producers of the organizations to which they belong.

Can the Social Economy Re-Make Society?

If political mobilization is necessary to emancipate the social economy from bureaucratic state tutelage and private competition, we must ask what kind of future society is latent in this type of economy. The advocates of the social economy often emphasize the merits of "economic pluralism." Transcending capitalism, in this case, is synonymous with the creation of a pluralistic economy that encompasses all the contributions of civil society. Giving more space and more visibility to these economic forms would already be an enormous step in the right direction, in this view, because it would prove that the profit motive is not the only possible form of economic incentive. It would show everyone that humans are not simply calculating, maximizing, and egoistical; it would show that social ties count more than commodities; and above all, it would make clear that democracy can be economically efficient. Economic pluralism, in short, would show, by example, that cooperation produces better social and economical outcomes than hyper-competition. The social economy, in other words, has many advantages and virtues: it would counter-balance the market and limit its scope, it would improve the quality of public interventions through its marked capacity for "social innovation," and it would fulfill an educative function by nurturing a spirit of solidarity and civic responsibility within the population.

Many theorists, however, imagine an even more strategically ambitious role for the social economy. According to Thomas Coutrot, the social economy is destined to play a major role in the transition to a post-capitalist society. In this scenario, "civil society" will mobilize and gradually organize itself in associative and cooperative forms at all levels until it constitutes a global force strong enough to counter the power of transnational financial capitalism. This is also the view of André Gorz, who envisioned a multiplication of collective initiatives that, little by little, would eventually form a coherent system. The social economy, in other words, prefigures an entire society of self-organized institutions that largely correspond to Fourier's nineteenth-century utopian phalanstery and his later idea of "sociocracy," (which in turn resembles the Zapatistas' strategy of refusing to "take power"). The creation of freely chosen, self-organized, and self-governing cooperatives and associations, apart from the market and the state, in the domains of food production, education, childcare, housing, or leisure, indeed seems to revive the great dream of building emancipated enclaves within the very heart of society. This strategy obviously depends on the desire "to live and work differently" on a mass scale. It presupposes material, institutional, and subjective conditions that, while not present at the moment, could be realized through a growing collective enthusiasm to make a meaningfully "different world," or perhaps through the refusal of capitalist and market forms that have become ecologically unsustainable and psychologically repulsive.

For Gorz, this whole transformative project is based on increasing amounts of free time and the introduction of a universal basic income. Such measures were not, as he argued, about some "right to laziness," but would rather create the proper conditions for a self-organized society. Local collectives would support this movement, and state intervention on behalf of the unemployed, the poor, and the precarious would lead to a kind of collective empowerment such that those excluded from the system could create their own forms of activity within associative and cooperative forms they would themselves organize. This strategy, as envisioned by Gorz, is part of a tradition that refuses to view socialism as a kind of "barracks economy" subject to central command. The future society should be no less based on the principle of economic freedom than was the market society. The difference, however, is that this would be a form of freedom open to all, not just the owners of capital, since it would be a collective product from the outset. Marcel Mauss insisted on this very principle in his criticisms of bolshevism. As he argued, "collective appropriation" does not mean state ownership: "there is room for another kind of commercial and industrial freedom: that of the collectivities themselves, such as the cooperatives, professional groups, etc."[19] It is worth bearing in mind, here, that Mauss is only repeating what was, in effect, the presupposition of all the nineteenth-century struggles against the individualistic conception of society that, since the Le Chapelier Law of 1791, prohibited the freedom of association to pursue what were otherwise perfectly legal objectives.

There is, however, a danger in Gorz's vision of an economic and social transition based on the principles of self-organization, cooperation, and self-activity: namely the risk that many of these experiments will be isolated and closed off from each other. Christian Arnsperger, who is especially interested in the question of a transition toward a post-capitalist society,[20] argues that the creation of a new political, economic, and social democracy "from below" implies choosing a simple, more autonomous, and convivial life, a choice that could lead to the creation of local communities that are more livable than the large metropolises dominated by the rhythms and structures of global capitalism. This conviviality, which offered a way out of capitalism for authors like Ivan Illich and André Gorz, would be characterized by a strategy Arnsperger calls "bio-regionalism" that is based on local connections and solidarities at the level of the village, the neighborhood, and the city. And while there are many virtues to these various neocommunalistic proposals (as listed above), we don't think these organizational forms will be sufficient, on their own, to create the politics of the common. Through a kind of revival of the Franciscan approach, these neocommunalisms seem to necessitate an almost spontaneous and widespread ethical conversion to post-capitalist ideology. This shortcoming is similar, in our view, to other leftist appeals that want to be radical, but which see no way out of capitalism except through a general retreat "out of power," through a kind of subtraction from domination. What this approach overlooks, however, is what the struggle for the common can bring to the sphere of associations and, more generally, to the field of alternative forms of production. For the gradual accumulation of practical alternatives has important educative and subjective effects that actually reinforce the political translation and generalization of these alternative practices. For what is most interesting about these practices is not their withdrawal from the world, but the far more stirring and arousing effects they can have upon subjectivities engaged in these practices. It is in this respect, then, that it is crucial to think about the various political and social constructs that enable these associations to become a means by which the population can actively mobilize and participate in decisions that concern them.

POLITICAL PROPOSITION 6

The Common Must Be the Basis of Social Democracy

For many progressives today – or at least those who have not resigned themselves to capital's absolute triumph – the objective of political struggle should essentially be to the restore the welfare state and protect it from further neoliberal incursions. From celebrating the legacy of Franklin Roosevelt to commemorating the anti-Nazi resistance, this brand of progressivism is dedicated to defending and even extending the undeniable achievements through which the working class and the population more generally gained access to important public services and programs, such as healthcare, education, pensions, etc. But given the increasingly uninhibited attacks on the welfare state from the right, in combination with the cynical concessions from the "socialist" left, this strategy risks blinding us to the very real limits of the welfare state as it was established at the end of the nineteenth century. For we must never forget that the common has been historically suppressed by the very welfare state that monopolizes much of the left's attention today. Thus any genuine politics of the common must, first and foremost, focus on the democratization of those social institutions currently under the control of a state administration bent on narrowing the welfare state's scope and adapting the latter to the "constraints of competitiveness."

Since the end of the nineteenth century, the so-called "social" or "welfare" state has been the guarantor of the "principle of solidarity." At the end of the nineteenth century, the prior liberal conception of civil society as an agreeable association of co-contracting proprietors, represented by wise and enlightened elected representatives, was shaken by the clear evidence of industrial pauperism and the concomitant emergence of socialism. Threatened liberal governments across the Western world were then compelled to establish various forms of income transfers and public services, without which a substantial part of the population would have been condemned to poverty. The "welfare" dimension of modern societies was thus organized as an institutional system, one that differed from one country to the next, that integrated the non-property-owning sector of the population into political society by guaranteeing it a modicum of security (i.e., "social security") through various forms of voluntary and obligatory insurance programs and other systems designed to re-distribute income through taxation.

The principle of the welfare state is to inject a certain degree of social "solidarity" within a capitalist system of private property regime in order to stave off the worst outcomes of capitalist accumulation. The welfare state can therefore be interpreted in two fundamental ways: first, as a program of partial deproletarianization and partial labor decommodification;[1] and second, as a "welfare" support system necessary for perpetuating an economic system in which the accumulation of private wealth is facilitated by universal wage labor. In other words, while the welfare state indeed mitigates the most negative effects produced by the private ownership of the means of production, it ultimately does so in order to protect the overall system by pacifying social relations.

The welfare state is thus the end product of a series of governmental strategies that responded to worker protest and were designed to quell the threat of revolution by undermining the strictly political aspects of social and economic conflicts. As Giovanna Procacci has shown, a new type of government, a "government of misery" (*gouvernement de la misère*) developed in France between the outbreak of revolution in 1789 and 1848 in order to deal with mass poverty and thereby "defuse the potential for antagonism"[2] linked to proletarianization. The concept of "welfare" therefore designates the methods by which the state turned to new administrative practices to deal with a series of problems relating to health, political discontent, and criminality arising from economic crises, and a more general state of revolt and public unrest. In other words, the state was forced to adapt older forms of governmental power to a political environment shaped by liberal doctrines. For neither classical political economy nor liberalism's legal conception of individual rights were effectively able to respond to these new forms of "modern misery" so aptly documented by Alexis de Tocqueville's *Memoir on Pauperism* (1835). Socialism, on the other hand, offered its own menacing response (from the perspective of the ruling classes, that is) by advocating for the "right to work" and the right for labor to assert its power through various forms of cooperation and associationism. By 1848, the republican bourgeoisie was compelled to come up with some means of reconciling the otherwise contradictory logics of the market, citizenry, property, and fraternity. Its sociological, legal, and political answer was "solidarity."

Léon Duguit perfectly summarizes the conception of welfare that gradually emerged in the latter half of the nineteenth century:

> Society is now a great cooperative in which everyone benefits from the advantages produced by the division of labor. If, however, this division of labor causes some members of the community to suffer a particular harm, if the cooperative malfunctions, or if circumstances are such that some experience greater losses than others, then the whole community must intervene in order to address these injuries. State revenues thus become a kind of mutual insurance program designed to benefit all members of society.[3]

This conception of society as a "cooperative" and the state as a kind of "insurance program" was, of course, met with fierce resistance from liberal economists and conservative legal thinkers. For what this new concept of welfare calls into question, as Duguit was well aware, was not only the principle of proprietary exclusionism, but the definition of the state's role as limited to the maintenance of public order and the integrity of the national territory. In any case, these two complimentary absolutisms were quickly eroded by the emergence of the "welfare" principle. For this was the long-term outcome of a contradiction that emerged in 1848 with the advent of universal suffrage, which was supposed to guarantee both popular sovereignty and the exclusive right of bourgeois property.[4] Hence the "strategic" re-interpretation of solidarity by republicans who strove to install welfare as the principle of a progressive republic by renewing Condorcet's remarkably anticipatory calls for universal education and social security.

Political sovereignty cannot exist without social solidarity between the classes. Thus, through the influence of proponents like Léon Bourgeois, social solidarity became the driving philosophy of the Third Republic in France and the governmental technique of state insurance became its *modus operandi*.[5] As the threat of shared or communal property (*des partageux*) increased, the response from the progressive factions of the bourgeoisie was the "the socialization of risk" and "equality of opportunity." These reforms justified the institution of private property by facilitating its more widespread attainment through education and work, and by protecting those deprived of property through the development of the "insurance society."[6] The new principle of welfare thus deflects criticism away from private property and makes the bourgeois proprietor seem financially responsible. It is, in any case, the price the bourgeoisie must pay if they want to keep and quietly enjoy their property.

If solidarity was initially a socialist ethic and a proletarian practice that was antagonistic to the institution of private property, it was now state policy and was used to stabilize capitalist bourgeois society. Even Pope Leo XIII admits its usefulness in his encyclical on *Capital and Labor* (1891): "the mass of the poor have no resources of their own to fall back upon, and must chiefly depend upon the assistance of the State." The state thus becomes pastoral: "and it is for this reason that wage-earners, since they mostly belong in the mass of the needy, should be specially *cared for and protected by the government*." Curiously enough, the French republicans, who consistently opposed the Catholic Church's hold over public affairs in France, pursued largely the same policies, even if their philosophical justification was very different from the Church's.[7] What ultimately unites these two otherwise heterogeneous concepts of social solidarity, however, is the assertion that a state-based welfare system owes nothing to any form of institutional practice "from below." Social solidarity, and its associated benefits, are dispensed by an administrative providence harmoniously adapted to the nature of the social world (in the case of French republicans) or as morally demanded by a natural law of divine origin (in the case of the Catholic Church). In either case, the modern welfare state is fundamentally grounded on the negation of the common as a form of social co-activity. It is not the members of society that construct the institutional rules shaping their relations, but rather the benevolent and beneficent state that determines the rules of reciprocity, mutual aid, and the distribution of production. Solidarity between employees and citizens is transformed into a debt we owe to the benevolent state.

What we call the "welfare state" is, of course, also a legal reality that has transformed the nature of work and workers, and its legal framework makes labor something more than a simple commodity negotiated on the labor market. Labor and labor relations in the welfare state are governed by laws, collective agreements, and insurance programs that are part of a more general development of "social law" designed to re-integrate labor back into the society (to borrow Polanyi's phrase). But has the welfare state not simply consolidated relations of domination and exploitation? What about the socialist promise to emancipate labor from exploitation?

The overall sociological consequence of these developments, according to Robert Castel, was the advent of the "wage society" by 1945, wherein social protections were extended to the majority of the population. This new form of society succeeded in "surmounting the gap between owners/non-owners" by constructing a whole continuum of comparable but different social conditions, and by replacing the class struggle with a more diffuse struggle for status within a generalized wage society built on bourgeois norms.[8] Under these conditions, however, welfare becomes detached from democracy, and socialism's earlier desire for collective self-organization gradually disappears from popular consciousness. The notion that society is the product of specific relations that can be overthrown thereby fades with the decline of the traditional labor movement. The role of unions in the management of welfare – which, in France, was already substantively weakened by the *paritarisme*[9] established in France after the Liberation – lost much of its influence with the growth of state administration and supervision. The welfare state thus increasingly became a providential state that distributed benefits according to exogenous economic constraints that always took precedence over the rights of citizens. In other words, the welfare state began to resemble what Tocqueville feared when he anticipated the emergence of a great, anonymous bureaucratic machine that operates according to universal principles, without the possibility of citizen intervention over the decisions that impact their lives. The socialist concept of "solidarity" was thus transformed by a state that undoubtedly protected workers from some of the intrinsic risks of the market, but which concomitantly excluded workers from political deliberation and decision-making through the strictly bureaucratic administration of public services and social protections. In short, democracy-based social solidarity, as imagined by the socialists, was only realized in the form of state-organized social protections. Welfare thus resembled a form of state property that was itself continually subject to potential political reversal.

Of course, the welfare state is now under almost constant attack by the combined forces of the right and the so-called "socialist" left on the grounds that the former lacks appropriate "competitiveness." The struggle against these forces thus presents the left with a new opportunity to revive the demand for the common in a new way. The principle of the common is not based on a simple defense of the achievements of the welfare state, because the notion of the social at work in the logic of the common is fundamentally different from that upon which the welfare state is based. Whereas the notion of the "social" in the logic of the welfare state is a mere object of insurance and assistance programs managed by state technocrats who distribute these benefits as individual commodities, the notion of the social in the logic of the common is based on a more fundamentally politically and historically original understanding of "social democracy"; it is a view of social democracy as a set of institutions that the members of society build for themselves in order to re-distribute a portion of what they produce based on what they think is most important. This presupposes that the members of society themselves are its democratic governors and that they both determine long-term strategic goals and manage everyday services. Of course, it is unrealistic to think that some level of bureaucratic management will not exist. Each local organization cannot completely re-invent and govern its own "social common," since most social insurance programs require large-scale participation. But the social institutions they create will not be state properties managed by dominant oligarchies subordinated to the global imperative of "competitiveness" or the European practice of "social dumping" – i.e., a process of competitive bidding in which labor contracts are awarded to the lowest-paid workers.

The logic of the common is based on direct political participation in the decisions and the management of that which is shared in common. The financial flows that circulate between contributors and beneficiaries do not belong to anyone "in particular," nor are they an "expense" borne by the employer. They are the collectively managed and individually allotted uses of production itself. The principle of the common, in other words, demands a complete revision of the meaning and organization of solidarity. Democratizing the social relations that govern these organizations is thereby a means to transform state administrations into the social institutions of the common.

Social and Economic Citizenship

The great practical question thus concerns the role of "citizenship" in society and in the economy. Yet the term "citizenship" is not really optimal here, since it refers to an individual who simply "belongs to a political community" without doing anything other than passively enjoying political rights, often without even defending them. There has been a fairly common diagnosis of the modern citizen going all the way back to Tocqueville: the citizen is little more than an "idiot" (in the Greek sense of *idiōtēs*, or a "private" person) immersed in the insatiable consumption of individual goods and the passive enjoyment of his subjective rights. Whatever the accuracy of this description, it is a negative view that ignores an entire range of other features that fall under the term "citizenship."

According to British sociologist Thomas Humphrey Marshall, "social citizenship" is the greatest invention of the twentieth century.[10] For Marshall, "social citizenship" refers to the ensemble of social rights related to social security, education, health, work, and the rights guaranteed by the state that are stacked on top of the first two sedimentary layers of rights: first, the civil liberties gradually acquired in Europe since the eighteenth century (personal freedoms, freedom of thought and expression, property rights, contract rights, and the right to sue, etc.); and second, the array of political rights that were expanded and strengthened during the twentieth century (suffrage, election laws, etc.). When he penned his analysis in 1949, Marshall had little doubt that the egalitarian dynamic that had enlarged and deepened citizenship in England and the other advanced Western countries would eventually lead to a "war" between the dynamics of citizenship and the dynamics of capitalism. This conclusion seemed obvious to Marshall, insofar as the history of the last few centuries was marked by struggles that tried to make active use of previously acquired rights. Social citizenship emerged out of the massive and prolonged exercising of the right to collective action, particularly union activism, and was therefore only conceivable as a result of the political activism of wage workers. Generally speaking, then, every form of citizenship was, for Marshall, based on some prior form of activity, on the rights and possibilities of political action, and this in turn explains the dynamic extension of rights as such. Social citizenship, therefore, only arose as a result of the prior institutionalization of forms of collection action in the sphere of labor. Marshall did, however, foresee a limit to this forward momentum. If collective action led to a significant change in the structure of social inequalities, there was no reason to think it would not eventually cease to be compatible with capitalism. Marshall's analysis was thus one of the earliest and most prescient discussions about the theoretical limitations of the compromise between the welfare sate and an economic system based on inequality. However, Marshall seems less prescient that the welfare state compromise would be one whereby the recognition of rights relating to social protection and economic re-distribution would be balanced by the renunciation of any real notion of economic citizenship in the workplace, and involve submission to the most ruthless standards of workplace organization, which would eventually lead to the weakening and near collapse of autonomous collective action by workers.

As Bruno Trentin showed,[11] the official European left (and even the global left), as well as the trade unions and the parliamentary movement, collapsed in on itself because it was unable to prolong and extend the workers' protests against Taylorism and Fordism during the 1960s and 1970s, such as the struggles of the Italian councils, the mobilizations of the French OS workers (*ouvriers specializes*, or semi-skilled workers), or the shop stewards' resistance in England. Instead, the left adopted the double principle of scientific management and social welfare. The so-called Fordist compromise, in which the left played an active role, tried to marry the progress of technical rationality with a dose of re-distributive solidarity. The Great Compromise meant workers would tolerate alienated productive activity for the security of the welfare state; oppression at work was traded for the bureaucratized protection of one's existence. One of the central goals of the politics of the common must therefore be to disrupt this compact and re-introduce communal activity into the workplace.

POLITICAL PROPOSITION 7

Public Services Must Become Institutions of the Common

Positing the common as a political principle is not a call for the state to protect and extend the common by indefinitely expanding public property, nor is it a call for the state to increase its bureaucratic hold over both the economy and society. Nineteenth-century associationist socialism and twentieth-century council communism explicitly differentiated socialism's institutional form from the bureaucratic management of the economy by the state.[1] But even these movements, rare exceptions aside, did not adequately account for the development of what, in France, we refer to as the 'public services.' Inversely, the development of public services in the interwar years modified the content of socialism itself by augmenting or reinforcing its statist and centralizing tendencies.[2]

Are public services social institutions or instruments of public or state power? Much like the welfare-state protections we discussed in the previous proposition, the state form does not exhaust the historical significance of public services. Accordingly, public services should not be viewed as merely the instruments of political domination but as communal services that have so far only been historically developed by state administrative power charged with public order and the general policing of the population. Hence the dual nature of these services: they are both instruments of political power and social institutions designed to satisfy use rights and the needs of the population. This means public services are always sites of tension and struggle, and should not be unilaterally viewed as being simply "state apparatuses" in the service of bourgeois domination, nor should they be taken as organs that are already fully serving the needs of society.

It is not obvious that the role of public services under conditions of communal production demands interrogation. On the one hand, there is a widespread and very understandable feeling that nothing is more urgent than defending public services against neoliberal reforms. What is referred to today as "public sector reform" is nothing more than a neoliberal attack designed to produce the usual outcomes: increased job precarity in the public sector, a reinforcing of arbitrary hierarchies, a weakened civil service, the virtual destruction of any resistant groups within the state apparatus, declining public healthcare, shrinking local governments, etc.[3] But we argue that it would be equally risky to oppose the democratization of public services on the basis of a reflexive need to "defend the state" against neoliberal attack. Indeed, the history of the public services in France is especially instructive on this point. French public services have retained an unusual degree of residual sovereignty, and this has led to a persistent attitude of superiority for the civil servant vis-à-vis the user of services. This has in turn produced confusion concerning older ideas of "public power" (*potestas publica*) and the relationship of the public service to the community. Jaurès quite rightly explained the arrogance of the French civil service as regards ordinary citizens by arguing that the former always imagined their "absolute power" to be an extension of the monarch under *l'Ancien Régime*.[4] The question, then – especially in France, but also across the Western world more generally – is how to transform public services into institutions of the common that are oriented toward use rights and democratically governed. We must cease conceiving of the state as a gargantuan, centralized administrator and more like the ultimate guarantor of the citizen's fundamental rights, as regards the satisfaction of needs collectively considered essential. Under these conditions, the administration of public services would not fall to the state, but would be entrusted to bodies that may include state representatives but also workers and citizen-users as well.[5]

On this matter, it is worth recalling Marx's argument that schooling is a form of the common *avant la lettre*. It is well known that Marx, in general, condemned governmental interference in the affairs of schools, especially the state's nefarious practice of ideology-based enrollment. Marx's opposition to this kind of state interference is amply documented in the various debates held during the period of the First International, before the Congress of Geneva in 1866 or the Congress of Basle in 1869, and even more so in the notes he made in the margins of the Gotha social-democratic program. On the subject of American schools, for instance, Marx argued before the International Workingmen's Association (IWMA) General Council in August 1869 that "national education had been looked upon as governmental, but that was not necessarily the case."[6] Using Massachusetts as an example, Marx showed how local municipalities provided the bulk of the funding for schools, and these schools were in turn managed by local councils. But even if education was not necessarily organized by the state, its local management, Marx argued, should nonetheless conform to a national educational framework guaranteed by national law, and inspections should be used to ensure the law is applied. The state should also provide a universal guarantee for equal funding amongst schools. For Marx, then, the state should "disappear," in the sense of a great centralized bureaucracy (the "boa constrictor," as he put it in *The Civil War in France*),[7] though it must still play an important legal and symbolic role in terms of guaranteeing the application of general legal principles. While Marx's analysis of the American educational system is rather underdeveloped, it is consistent with his more general view on the "self-government" of society that he will more fully develop in his commentary on the Paris Commune. And we find similar communalist tendencies in Jaurès's discussion of public services. For Jaurès, public services should be "citizenship services" (*services de citoyenneté*) that are determined by general political choices and co-governed at every level by actors directly concerned with their implementation. Early on, then, both Marx and Jaurès saw the importance of democratic public services: to effectively respond to "collective needs," public services need to be articulated, debated, and developed democratically. Without this kind of civic engagement, the user of public services is merely a subject or a client, and sometimes both at once. Either way, the general interest is diluted and citizenship becomes a superficial legalism.

But how do we transform the public service into a truly common service? The first step requires a considerable modification to our conception of the state. While the distant origins of the notion of the public service are rooted in ancient and medieval categories of "public utility" and the "general interest," we must not forget that a state that largely administers these public services is constructed as an *imperium* and not an *obsequium*.[8] That said, the "sociological" doctrine of public services may illuminate the shifting nature of the development of the public service as a function of, or even the definition of, the state. According to Léon Duguit, one of the major Durkheimian theorists of public law, public services are a positive obligation of the state. If we see society for what it truly is, namely a great cooperative that coordinates differentiated functions, public activities must be viewed as necessary functions facilitating the general interdependence that characterizes the social organism. The multiplication, extension, and diversification of public services is merely a manifestation of the great law of social evolution that leads society toward greater functional differentiation. This functionalist thesis is fundamentally opposed to the sovereign theory of the state, in which the latter is viewed as the "sovereign director of the common will," according to Otto Gierke's definition.[9] For Dugit, then, we should get rid of the false and reactionary liberal conception of the state as limited to "executive functions" (army, police, justice, etc.), which, for Duguit, should also be considered public services.

But there are, of course, many other public services that have since come into existence and whose justification is based on social function rather than the older idea of state *imperium*. To contest their existence and extension, as many orthodox economists did at the time, is thus to fundamentally misunderstand the modern conditions of social and economic life. For these services are born from the needs that arise from the modern division of labor itself, and are thus functions that are absolutely necessary for the maintenance of collective life. For Duguit, public services are

> any activity whose fulfillment must be regulated, ensured, and controlled by rulers (*les gouvernants*), since the fulfillment of this activity is indispensible for the realization and development of social interdependence. And these services are of such a nature that they can only be completely guaranteed by the intervention of a governmental force.[10]

Public services, for Duguit, are therefore an obligation of rulers, not a manifestation of their sovereign and commanding power: "rulers are no longer organs of a collective person in command: they are the daily managers of society's collectivity."[11] For Duguit, there is no governmental activity that is not subject to the obligation of public service: "public service is the foundation and the limit of governmental power."[12] Public services are necessarily organized by the state because these services create the common conditions for all social, collective, and individual activity. In other words, the public service is not a manifestation of sovereignty but the medium by which collective needs are satisfied. Nor are public services, in this view, a response to pre-existing subject rights, but the effect of an objectively valid rule of law that generates individual rights after the fact. From this sociological perspective, coordinating all the activities of modern society simply cannot be fulfilled by a transcendent and sacred sovereign power, a superior "*moi commun*" (Rousseau) that rules over individuals. Meeting the needs of a modern society requires social communication between the agents of the public services and the population (which is not something at which sovereignty excels), and this particular mode of communication must take place between organized groups, such as trade unions and other organizations, that exert moral authority over individuals and are capable of directing them toward the general interest.[13]

But who, in Duguit's view, determines the needs that are provided by the public service? How can the public service fulfill its function if it is an arm of the state, and its users and agents are not given any powers of initiative, control, or participation? The sociological approach argues that the state must be in contact with the population in order to be aware of its needs, and so it must trust its agents on the basis of their specific competences and their direct relations with the population. This is precisely the conclusion Duguit draws: he argues that the growth and diversification of public services demands their decentralization and deconcentration. For Duguit, the central state must manage the coordination of the public services and ensure their compliance with the law, but it also has to delegate these services to autonomous entities and allow regional and local organizations to implement the actual services themselves. And local agents must be granted protection from the arbitrary power of governmental rulers and be permitted sufficient freedom to assess the manner in which public services ought to be rendered.

For most theoretical accounts of the public service, the great "solution" to the problem resides in the organizational development and political recognition of the "professionalism" of public service agents. Only this professionalism can guarantee objective identification of the needs arising from social interactions, to which public services are then tasked with responding. And this in turn means the creation and training of civil service associations. Durkheim favored the organization of professional groups within state administrations, while Duguit supported the representation of professional interests by public service unions. But these professional associations and unions were not only conceived as corporate bodies, but also as organizations dedicated to social interaction and exchange. In other words, the figure of the "professional" was precisely designed to overcome the institutional opposition between the "social" and the "political." As Duguit writes, "only an active and politically viable organization can represent a social element and … on the other hand, every strong and coherent social element itself becomes a political force that exerts itself directly or through representation."[14] This perspective thus demands trade unionism assume its fully political function through continual contact and communication with the population: "from the moment in which unionism becomes one of the essential elements of the national structure, it becomes a political force, and its representation is spontaneously organized."[15] The "public service state" is thus the state whose central nervous system is informed of the needs of the population through specially trained professionals, who in turn respond as rationally as possible. This is exactly the view we find, for example, in Durkheim's *Leçons de sociologie*.[16]

This functional approach undoubtedly sees a central place for the "professionals" charged with ensuring communication with society.[17] Maxime Leroy even went so far as to speak of the rise of the "professional" as a fourth power.[18] This sociological interpretation of the public service helps expose the fragile equilibrium that has been established in French public law. The difficult recognition of union participation thus lends a state that is otherwise still defined by the traditional notion of *imperium* some modicum of democracy. But this equilibrium between democracy and *imperium* was precarious and fraught with tension, insofar as these professions were conceived as functional organs within an integrative organism, not as political agents struggling within a divided society – and this in spite of the fact that the trade unions were obviously organizations that propagated their own set of values, values that were often in direct contradiction to the values of the capitalist state.

In any case, it is clear that functionalist sociology was unable to view the state for what it is: the state is not an "organism," an "apparatus," or a "machine" defined by functionality alone, but it is rather a complex field of forces and struggles riven with conflicting interests and values. Generally speaking, the sociological conception of public services ignores the existence of social classes entirely and tries to imagine society as an organism that might very well be "dysfunctional," but is not constitutively divided or conflicted.[19] By conceiving society as a great, and already instituted, cooperative, Duguit could not imagine the state retaining its prior domineering attributes, along with all the potential dangers this form of state power entails – namely violations of freedom, unequal treatment, arbitrary police power, injustice, preferential treatment, and even the theft of the community itself through the sale of public domains or preferential treatment.[20] Duguit's positivistic optimism was simply unable to imagine that the state might still be viewed, in modern legal or political culture, as a sovereign form of public power.

From "Social Organism" to the Public Institutions of the Common

It was undoubtedly the great English political theorist Harold Laski who was the first to take the ethical conflict between the "public service professional" and capitalist ideology seriously.[21] Much to the discontent of the omnipotent masters of the Victorian economy, as Laski describes, a new stratum of "technicians" and "professionals" gradually emerged who conceived of their jobs as more than a means of merely making a living: they genuinely believed in disseminating social values. "As these sciences have developed," writes Laski, "they have become organized into professions; they have created within themselves a spirit of their craft, of which the essence is a refusal to be governed by the mere motives of private gain."[22] This is true of the engineer, the lawyer, the doctor, the teacher, and the soldier. These professionals, in short, developed a public service ethic that ran counter to the dominant values of capitalist society and became a political force that threatened the ideology of the businessmen.[23]

Subsequent analyses have shown how the state is a field of internal struggles along other axes, such as the antagonism between the "lower" civil servants – who belong to what Michael Lipsky refers to as "street-level bureaucracies" – and the "upper" civil servants – or the "state nobility," as Pierre Bourdieu put it – within a hierarchical state structure."[24] This struggle within the public service is not solely material, but it is about the very meaning of the work performed for the benefit of the public. Bourdieu, for instance, showed how this great state nobility, which mostly came out of the École nationale d'administration (ENA) and Sciences Po (Political Science Institute), sought the "destruction of the idea of the public service" under the pretext of trying to manage the public services like private businesses.[25] The war that has been waged between the "right hand of the state" – an "upper" administration converted to neoliberal doctrine – and its "left hand" – the civil servants devoted to "the management of social problems" – is not only about the control of public services (whereby professional bodies, with so-called "archaic values," have their autonomy curtailed or even eliminated), but is also about the social control of subjugated citizens, a population becoming increasingly impoverished, divided, atomized, and surveilled.

It is clearly insufficient to accept this entirely idealized discourse about protecting the state from neoliberalism. Rather than simply trying to defend the public services, we must try to transform them into truly democratic organizations that allow professionals and also citizens – the ultimate recipient of these services – the ability to intervene, deliberate, and make decisions about the public service in accordance with the general laws and ethical mission of the public service itself. Without this kind of transformation, the much-overused notion of "participatory democracy" has no real meaning. This expression of course gained worldwide renown after the experiments in "participatory budgeting" in Porto Alegre at the end of the 1980s, which were viewed as an attempt to "radically democratize democracy."[26] In practice, however, this exercise of participatory democracy often meant little more than simple consultations about depoliticized management issues at the local or micro-local level. The "neighborhood councils" (*conseils de quartier*) introduced by the Valliant Law in France in 2002 (described as a "local democracy") are but another example of how the concept of participatory democracy tends to be diluted in practice – in this case, the local forms of deliberation and decision-making were always subject to the controls of councillors and local administrators. What is sometimes framed, in France, as the collaborative creation of public policy in one city or another, and usually described as an attempt to "revive community," sometimes has the effect – and often the explicit aim – of effacing underlying social conflicts and political contradictions. In these practical experiments, however, we can still detect the rough outlines of a more substantive notion of democracy, one that strives to transform the relationship between local politics and public services. Whatever its practical flaws, this demand for direct democracy should not be dismissed; it opens up the possibility of establishing truly common services at the local level. By networking these efforts in order to involve the population in the creation of public policies, participatory democracy endows political and social citizenship with much-needed meaning and significance. And these experiments in participatory democracy need not be confined to the local, but should be expanded to the regional, national, and even supra-national levels as well. To better flesh out what this might look like, an example from Italy deserves some of our attention.

"I comuni per i beni comuni"

The re-municipalization of the water system in Naples is undoubtedly one of the most recent and striking examples of the creation of a local commons or, more precisely, the creation of a local public service that is governed as a commons. Following the national struggle over the privatization of water, which culminated in a victorious referendum vote on the fate of public water in June 2011, the mayor of Naples, Luigi De Magistris, and his deputy, Alberto Lucarelli, the "Councillor for the Commons and Participatory Democracy" (who is also a professor of public law), composed a remarkable practical synthesis on the problem of "common goods" and participatory democracy. In the wake of the referendum victory, and after a vote of the Naples city council in October 2011, they created a "special legal entity" (*azienda speciale*) within public law which is called the Acqua Bene Comune Napoli. The principle that guided their efforts was the insistence that common goods like water – but also knowledge, culture, education, the sea, or the Internet, etc. – require a form of governance (*governo*) that does not belong to classic public law and its associated forms of public property, but which is rather based on "active democracy," which they viewed as the only way out of the ongoing crisis of representative democracy. For De Magistris, society is at a crossroads: we are either moving toward a society in which citizens are excluded from public space, or we are moving toward a society based on the fully active participation in the "government of common goods." There is no middle ground. It is thus necessary, they argued, to move beyond mere denunciation and indignation, reject the "wait-and-see" attitude that has prevailed so far, and start changing society through concrete action.[27]

Participation is local, here, in the sense that it gives the municipality a determinate place in the government of the common good. The slogan "I comuni per i beni comuni," which plays on the two meanings of the word *comune* in Italian (both "commune" and "common"), aptly sums up the spirit of the movement: common goods are first and foremost the business of the citizens of the local municipalities. But, at the same time, this effort was also imagined as part of a more global struggle for "public water" being carried out in Italy, Europe, and across the rest of the world. The value of the experience in Naples thus far exceeds its local context. The battle for local control of water in Italy is a perfect example of the "recovery of common goods," to use the slogan popularized in the "antiglobalizzazione" movements in Genoa in 2001. Since the mid–2000s, the local councils in Naples and its surrounding region have played an important role in constructing an entire activist network that eventually became the Italian Water Movements Forum (Forum Italiano dei Movimenti per l'Acqua). The Prodi government then instructed the Rodotà Commission (chaired by Stefano Rodotà, an Italian jurist and politician) to draft a new article in the Civil Code, in the section on public property, that introduces the legal category of common goods alongside already codified articles on private goods and public goods. In 2007 and 2008,[28] Stefano Rodotà, Alberto Lucarelli, Ugo Mattei, and others put the debate on the commons at the center of public discourse. The movement collected millions of signatures, which then paved the way for a referendum in 2011. The referendum annulled the previous law (the Ronchi Decree) that authorized the privatization of local public services (which the Berlusconi government had passed in ostensible anticipation of a forthcoming European law).[29] The fact that millions of voters thwarted such a project was viewed by Lucarelli as "an event of revolutionary significance," because it challenged some of the most fundamental categories and institutions of public law and, in particular, the pernicious duality of state sovereignty and private property.[30]

There are two main lessons we should learn from this experience. First, Lucarelli clearly shows that the commons must be negotiated at two levels: locally and nationally. In addition to local participation, it is also crucial that "the right to common goods" be enshrined in a national constitution (or comparable document) as a fundamental right of all citizens. Codifying this right nationally protects against the fragmentation of the common along local and regional lines, which may expose the commons to forms of exploitation.[31] But it is equally important that the government of the commons be as close to the population as possible, which is precisely what Marx argued in the context of education. Lucarelli understood perfectly well that the relationship between citizens, the municipality, and the common "good" is not a relationship of appropriation in the classical sense, but is a relation between subjects who create rights through their activity, and not rights over a thing, but rights governing use.[32]

Secondly, Lucarelli understood that by defining the commons (despite the rather traditional list of "commons" the commission selected) through reference to the fundamental rights of the citizens of a community, the free development of the individual, and the respect for the rights of future generations, the Rodotà Commission tried to profoundly alter public law, to the extent that the common cannot be appropriated by any legal subject (public or otherwise).[33] Lucarelli, in this sense, suggests a break with the fundamentally reifying categories that Western law has begun, even if this rupture is only partially accomplished in this case specifically.[34]

This local and collective action not only succeeded in blocking certain domains of social life from the reach of the market, but it also struck a blow against a political system based on corruption, prevarication, and predation. For the rot in the system does not only issue from multinational privatization; it also comes from the uses made of public property as a result of the party system itself. We can see, then, why Lucarelli wanted to emphasize the revolutionary character of these Italian reforms: they undermined the very foundations of a system of "political representation" that feeds off public property through the distribution of governmental positions and other forms of patronage, nepotism, and even outright embezzlement.

This concept of "popular sovereignty over common goods through citizen participation" is therefore concretely manifest in the fact that public service institutions like ABC Napoli are governed by user representatives, ecological associations, social movements, and workers' organizations, who are all on the institution's board of directors along with various other experts and local representatives.[35] By contrast, a completely different strategy was implemented in Paris during its re-municipalization of water services. The citizens of Paris had virtually no direct input into the creation of Eau de Paris – indeed, many citizens were completely unaware that water services had been (since 2011) placed under public control at all. The "governance" of the autonomous board of Eau de Paris includes experts, a number of associations, and staff representatives, but the majority of the administrative board is made up of elected officials from various political parties.[36] In other words, it is the dual legitimacy of the expert and the elected official that comes first, and any notion of user participation is little more than an afterthought. Without downplaying the importance of this kind of re-municipalization of water in the capital of a country that is home to some of the largest water multinationals in the world,[37] this initiative remains, nonetheless, confined to a classical managerial form that is structurally incapable of transitioning from "the public to the common." Without any real citizen mobilization and participation, Parisian users remain little more than uninformed passive consumers.

The ability to transform the public service according to the politics of the common is, for us, the most important dimension of the policies pursued in Naples. By linking "common goods" with "participatory democracy," Italian activists concretely implemented what we have been calling the "common." However, by confining their activity to a very traditional framework of common "goods," these Italian legal innovators, like Lucarelli and Mattei, nonetheless fell prey to a form of theoretical self-contradiction. While they very correctly broke out of the long-standing duality of *dominium* and *imperium* – i.e., "public" and "private" – by attacking the exclusive and exploitative relationship between the *dominus* and the "good" in question, they nonetheless continued to rely on the legal category of the "good" as such, and this category, in our view, invariably interpellates an owner.

POLITICAL PROPOSITION 8

The Commons Must be Global

To what extent can the principle of the common become a legal axis that operates on a global scale, one that is capable of both imposing itself on states and structuring the activity of international and intergovernmental institutions? In particular, how can we make the common the political principle upon which the total re-organization of society is based in the context of an irreducible plurality of "commons" of all shapes and sizes, from the local to the global? How do we ensure coordination amongst these commons without jeopardizing the autonomy of each? For without autonomy there is no co-obligation, and without co-obligation there is no common in the truest sense. Or better, can this coordination be conceptualized in such a way that it is itself conceived as a form of co-obligation at a higher-level, one that logically proceeds from the levels beneath it?

It becomes more and more obvious with each passing day that the neoliberal orientation of both transnational capital and contemporary nation-states – coordinated by international organizations like the International Monetary Fund (IMF) or the World Trade Organization (WTO) – will only aggravate today's problems to the point at which they will eventually become impossible to solve. We are thus witnessing increasingly urgent calls for some form of global counter-measure equal to the perils we are facing. The rhetorical success of phrases like "global justice" and "environmental justice" testify to this need. But growing consciousness of the problems we face is not nearly sufficient to take us where we need to go. Activists in NGOs, progressive legal circles, and in ecological and alter-globalization movements who are searching for alternatives face the daunting task of reconciling very heterogeneous approaches to the same problems: some persistently invoke republican "universalisms," others cling to a more socialist brand of internationalism, while still others insist the solution lies in a more or less "deep" environmentalism. This dilemma seems to be most acute when religious traditions or other essentialist cultural "ontologies" are awkwardly combined in order to formulate some notion of the inalienable rights of humanity, nature, Mother Earth, etc. For instance, "Pachamama" – the Inca goddess of Mother Earth – and Western notions of subjective rights are not necessarily all that philosophically compatible. The TIPNIS 1 conflict in 2011,[1] which was a project to build a 350-kilometer road through a Bolivian national park, was a perfect example of the competing logics that must often interact within social movements: indigenous communities, who invoked the rights of "Mother Earth," were opposed by the peasant unions who argued for the economic benefits of opening the region to industry. This case is exemplary insofar as it highlights the very practical problem of constructing a common that transcends the dichotomy between worker productivism and religious deifications of nature. Given the realities of this dilemma, good feelings and grandiloquent rhetoric tend to merely hide these underlying political fissures.

Yet despite all these difficulties, the idea of creating a "global common law" that might break through this intergovernmental impasse is gaining ground. In the first instance, however, it is difficult to see how a "government of humanity" could impose such a right from above. The development of some form of "common right of humanity" can only be realized through the creation of new forms of political organization. Moreover, such efforts must contend with an "international law" that is currently – perhaps more than ever – a formidable terrain of struggle that does not merely pit nation-states against one another. Rather, confrontations increasingly pit transnational corporations in alliances with states, who are committed to defending an international order entirely dedicated to the imperatives of capitalist accumulation, and hostile to all social and ecological forces dedicated to promoting fundamental rights of access to "common goods." Under these geopolitical conditions, we are incredulous that new political rights could issue from a global sovereign of some kind any more than they issue from the multitude of powers competing in today's neofeudal global order.

Is Humanity a Legal Subject?

According to some legal theorists, like Mireille Delmas-Marty, political action on a planetary scale seems to be oriented toward the affirmation of some notion of the "rights of humanity." In other words, we seem to be tending toward a new global legal framework in which "humanity" itself is increasingly conceived as a "legal subject." "Crimes against humanity," the "world heritage of humanity" (i.e., the United Nations Educational, Scientific and Cultural Organization [UNESCO]), "the common goods of humanity," etc. are all examples of legal or economic doctrines that testify to the gradual emergence of humanity as a "legal subject," which we should not view as problematic but should rather embrace as a solution to the issues facing our world. These various doctrines sketch out the legal framework of a global society that is grounded in the symbolic figure of humanity *qua* political subject. This is the hope of many of today's more optimistic legal thinkers: a global common, a new *jus commune* for the twenty-first century, is already in the process of emerging by virtue of the "imaginative force of law."[2] Humanity thus becomes a kind of retroactive legal subject by virtue of all the fundamental rights ascribed to it by various treaties, pacts, and other legal conventions.

This right of humanity was first rooted in the designation of humanity as a victim, through the recognition of acts of genocide or apartheid as "crimes against humanity," wherein it was argued that an attack on one part of humanity is an attack on humanity as such. Since the Second World War, crimes against humanity have been based on universal "founding prohibitions." The institutional recognition of "international criminal justice," based on a system of courts, doctrines, and jurisprudence, marks one of the first important steps in the gradual constitution of humanity as a legal subject.

The most optimistic proponents of this new legal humanism continually point out how we are only in the earliest stages of the eventual development of global justice: the geopolitical relations between the world powers still play a major role in the definition of crimes, the application of the law, and the realities of criminal prosecution. But for these proponents, the arc of history is not in doubt. And perhaps they are right: there is no doubt that "humanity" is increasingly replacing "God" as our great symbolic reference – but, of course, this does not mean "humanity" is any more capable than "God" of becoming a coherent legal subject. That humanity has not yet acquired full legal personhood is hardly contentious,[3] but the idea that humanity inevitably must acquire it certainly is. In our view, however, there is simply no place for a "bare owner" of any kind.

The Limits to the Globalization of Law

The promotion of global or world justice, according to the usual formula, at least, does not presuppose the legal subjectification of humanity. After the failure of the League of Nations, renewed interest in legal cosmopolitanism then followed the Second World War, and was buoyed by the widespread commitment to avoiding similar disasters in the future. As Alain Supiot has shown,[4] it was precisely this idea of transcribing global social justice in a declaration of rights that inspired the Declaration of Philadelphia of May 10, 1944. The declaration re-defined the goals of the International Labor Organization by addressing "all the peoples of the world." The declaration states that a "lasting peace can be established only if it is based on social justice," and this must constitute "the central aim of all national and international policy." The declaration's fundamental aim was the institutionalization of labor on global scale, as its opening article indicates: "labor is not a commodity."

But of course this declaration, like the 1948 Universal Declaration of Human Rights, has never enjoyed the full force of law. Similarly, the raft of conventions signed during the 1960s concerning all manner of social, economic, cultural, civic, or political rights were severely circumscribed in terms of their scope and application. What we learn from these past attempts is that there are two fundamental obstacles to the emergence of a "common law of humanity."

The first obstacle is of course the long-standing principle of political sovereignty. This principle has not been abolished by neoliberal governance (as some contend) but has rather been integrated into new forms of power: by means of sheer force alone, sovereign states continually paralyze the development of any such common right by relentlessly asserting their own interests. The commonplace paralysis in the United Nations Security Council sufficiently demonstrates how *la raison d'Etat* – which is nationalistic by definition – always trumps *la raison d'humanite*. The United States, and several of its allies, continually impedes international law by refusing to recognize the legitimacy of the International Criminal Court, by supporting the global extension of commercial rights and standards in line with US domestic law, or simply by using its technological and economic superiority to its own advantage. By effectively denying the very existence of international law, the United States indemnifies itself against any sanction relating to targeted assassinations, torture, extraordinary rendition, widespread electronic communications surveillance, etc. As David Rose aptly put it, the US invasion of Iraq was really an American war against human rights under the pretense of a war on terrorism.[5] The reality is that the most powerful states are constantly waging an extensive and systematic war against the very notion of a "common humanity," whether in the economic or financial sphere, the realm of ideas and freedoms, or concerning climate change. While the major powers may occasionally sign international treaties, they always interpret the contents of these treaties in ways that undermine their power the least.

The second obstacle to the creation of a "common law of humanity" is closely related to the first obstacle, insofar as it concerns neoliberal policies that "organize" the world according to competitive norms, predatory strategies, and a general logic of war, as opposed to principles of cooperation and social justice. It could even be argued that, over the past thirty years, neoliberal policies have in fact been used to methodically undermine all the post-war attempts to empower workers and citizens, to the point of halting and even reversing the prior trend toward greater human rights that began in 1945. The neoliberal doctrine of "normative Darwinism,"[6] which puts national legal systems in competition with one another in an attempt to create the most advantageous environments for international investment, is now being used to deconstruct any legal barrier or social protection that hinders the realization of maximum profits. Accordingly, the market is now the principle source of legitimacy in international and European law, and it promotes a social "race to the bottom" around the world.[7] As Delmas-Marty shows, the bipolarity in international law between the "market" and "human rights" now almost completely favors the former term. In place of "human rights," neoliberal policies encourage a "market of rights" and the associated practice of "law shopping" in relation to corporate taxation, commercial law, and labor law. This generalized "market of rights" is leading us toward a form of "re-feudalization," as Alain Supiot puts it, that benefits the most mobile legal entities – namely transnational corporations – who are then able to exercise their "free choice" and select the norms that suit them best. As Antoine Garapon points out, "globalization puts systems of justice into competition, because litigants [i.e., capital] now have the choice of litigating wherever they want."[8] "Legal evasion" through international "forum shopping" is now as systematic as tax evasion. Private economic powers, through these forms of competition, thus become direct sources of commercial, economic, and social norms. It is understandable, then, why the *lex mercatoria* is much more advanced, at the international level, than the laws designed to protect people: if the pace of commerce has advanced much more quickly than the pace of rights, it is precisely because rights themselves are now commodified.[9] Whether we are dealing with health, culture, access to water, or pollution, the logic governing these domains is always free trade and absolute respect for the rights of property. The principle objective of the WTO and its Dispute Settlement Body (DSB) is for every state to internalize international neoliberal standards. And the faster these norms are internalized, the better equipped they are to hinder the extension of human rights.[10]

There is no doubt that heterogeneous power relations are shaping these various systems. International law, for instance, has been largely taken over by American legal firms through their extensive consulting and lobbying efforts. The global legal order – if one can use such an expression – is therefore the product of a kind of "judicial commerce" between judges who circulate within a system of informal gatherings and are hired to perform international commercial arbitration.[11] Common law judges are especially valued in the settlement of commercial disputes, insofar as they view the contract as a sacred object that transcends any policies designed to serve the public interest.[12] This "trade in justice," in which regulatory authorities use the threat of law to (paradoxically) avoid applying the law, has been increasingly commonplace and reveals how much the law is complicit in its own abdication.[13] It is this globalized and globalizing jurisprudence that has created a world order that is increasingly tailored to the needs of capital, and which produces the very institution we have referred to here as "cosmo-capitalism." Cosmo-capitalism is a rather paradoxical institution, insofar as the law itself is completely commodified and reduced to a set of technical mechanisms that are manipulated in order to manage the interests of various parties according to their financial means. This is all part of an ongoing and very real privatization of international law that affects societies and economies in far deeper ways than the various guarantees it offers to investors and financiers.

Global Public Goods, or, How Not to Change the Frame

Unlike this neoliberal discourse, there is another discourse that deploys the tools of classical economics, but this time in order to advocate for "global public goods." In the early 1990s, when the norms and mechanisms of neoliberalism were first being established, the United Nations seemed to be following a new, if not completely divergent, path. In 1990, the United Nations Development Program (UNDP) issued its first report, which was strongly influenced by the work of Pakistani economist Mahbub ul Haq and Indian economist Amartya Sen. The report proposed expanding the definition of "development" beyond the narrow criterion of quantitative GDP growth. The report advocated what would become the Human Development Index (HDI), which ranks countries on such criteria as well-being, life expectancy, literacy rates, access to health services, and education. In 1992, the Rio de Janeiro Conference on Environment and Development (UNCED), which was prompted by the Brundtland Report (1987), introduced the notion of "sustainable development" as a means of linking the satisfaction of present needs with the needs of future generations.[14]

It is in the context of these developments that the ideal of "good global governance" was linked to the production of "global public goods," which themselves are defined in terms of their beneficial effects for the planet as a whole. Armed with its distinctions between different types of goods, modern economics offered to rigorously define the composition of this new "global public domain." "Global public goods" – which no one can be excluded from, by definition – are goods that no national state itself has an interest in producing, and which therefore give rise to the familiar "free rider" problem.[15]

The UNDP economists have been further developing this approach since the 1990s.[16] According to Inge Kaul, Isabelle Grunberg, and Marc A. Stern:

> Global public goods [have] nonexcludable, nonrival benefits that cut across borders, generations, and populations. At a minimum, the benefits of a global public good would extend to more than just one group of countries and not discriminate against any population group or set of generations, present or future.[17]

While the total list of these objects is a matter of debate, there is no doubt that the issue of pollution and sustainable development (much like the role tax havens have played in the study of fiscal deficits or international terrorism) has considerably accelerated analysis of this issue.[18] The UNDP economists distinguish between three classes of global public goods. Class 1 are "natural global commons" (the ozone layer, climate stability, etc.), and the principle concern regarding these goods is "one of overuse." Class 2 are "human-made global commons," such as scientific knowledge, the Internet, etc., and the principle concern with these goods is "underuse." Class 3 deals with "global policy outcomes" – i.e., the collective results of integrated or coordinated global policies, such as peace, health, and financial stability – and the principle problem here is "undersupply."[19] In slight contrast to the UNDP economists, Joseph Stiglitz identifies five global public goods: global economic stability, international security, the global environment, international humanitarian aid, and knowledge. Stiglitz has even generalized his approach by arguing that the global economy itself should be a global public good and should therefore be subject to forms of democratic governance designed to account for political "externalities" and thereby avoid systemic crises.[20] As we can see, both these approaches tend to include very different kinds of goods. As we have argued in Chapter 4, this diverse amalgamation is of course ultimately due to the *negative* definition of public goods: their exceptional status in traditional economic theory derives from the fact that the market cannot spontaneously produce these goods without deliberate collective action.

But is a world state necessary for the production of these public goods? For most of these authors, the answer is no. Instead, accountability and incentive mechanisms should be created that will allow both private and state actors – who are themselves considered private actors given the global character of the goods in question – to participate in their production and protection. Yet fiscal coercion (i.e., taxes) or state regulation would not be appropriate here, according to these economists (over and above the fact that imposing forms of fiscal coercion on states would be impossible to implement at present). As defined by the UNDP theory since the late 1990s, these goods are best produced by private actors through various incentive mechanisms. This theory also has the "virtue" of completely depoliticizing public goods: this approach treats the problem of global public goods as primarily a technical or strategic problem, in the game theory sense of these terms (i.e., the prisoner's dilemma), and thus this approach fundamentally neglects the constitutive social and economic conflicts inherent to underproduction or overuse of public goods.[21]

The ozone layer, for instance, which is often taken as a global public good *par excellence*, is now at the mercy of a market for polluter's rights, so to speak, on the pretext that financial incentives are the best means to lead rational actors toward an optimal solution. In the same manner in which financial organizations are allowed to participate in the definition of the rules that will regulate them (according to the

Basel III Accord), we must also have "confidence" that private actors will come up with optimum policies in environmental matters as well. The Organisation for Economic Co-operation and Development (OECD) similarly intends to solicit the voluntary cooperation of tax havens based on their willingness to provide financial information when asked. In certain cases, it is actually argued that the best way to produce global public goods is to create and strengthen property rights, as in the case of a global CO2 market! As François Constantin has suggested, this new doctrine appears to be a means by which economists can procure a monopoly over good intentions, from which they can derive sometimes symbolic and sometimes very material profit.[22] In any case, the entire approach is clearly an attempt to deal with key problems facing the world without making any substantive changes to the dominant order. In other words, once we exclude the state form from possible solutions to the "tragedy of the commons," the only solution that remains is the privatization of "governance" on the global scale, either in the form of contractual arrangements between private actors or through "public–private partnerships" that involve minimum state engagement.

Despite these problems, the theory of global public goods and its corresponding policies are supported by many global organizations, including the United Nations. The World Bank supports these policies,[23] as does the IMF (for whom economic and financial stability is the premier global public good). This sentiment is also shared by the WTO, as expressed by former director Pascal Lamy, who flatly asserted, "the multilateral trading system is itself an international public good."[24] For the economic and political "elite," private enterprise is the best method for producing the "common good." Through "corporate social responsibility" and "sustainable development," private enterprise is encouraged to integrate social and ecological considerations into its management choices. Capitalism, colored pink and green, passes itself off as a system that is both "social" and "natural."[25] The reality is of course a little different and much more prosaic: in order to continue to extend its domain without inflicting too much social and ecological "damage," capitalism must take advantage of all the "externalities" provided by governments, charitable associations, or NGOs (free of charge, of course). Multinational businesses continually demand an optimum "environment" in which to do business, which includes political stability, urban infrastructure, top-ranked university systems, and even charitable support for the working poor and adequate prisons for offenders. Yet at the very same time, the most powerful multinationals do absolutely everything they can to avoid paying corporate taxes, either through the threat of capital flight or with the help of international tax havens. Regulation through competition only ever leads to non-cooperative solutions that directly threaten the climate, energy resources, living and working conditions for employees, as well as the most basic collective functions performed by public services. In short, the unique categorization of global public goods, whether we are talking about currency, counter-terrorism, free trade, or climate policies, does not in any way prevent social and fiscal "dumping." In fact, one could argue that the dominant global powers (with the United States in the lead) and other international organizations (such as the WTO, the IMF, and the World Bank) have carefully selected certain "global public goods" that accord with their specific political and economic interests, to the detriment of other potential public goods.

The "Common Heritage of Humanity": The Ambiguous Return of "Things in Common"

We must not, however, confuse this economic theory of "public goods" with the legal paradigm of the "common heritage of humanity": they do not entirely overlap and they do not obey the same precise logic. The legal reification at work in the concept of "humanity's common inheritance" is largely derived from a much older juridical tradition of "things in common" (*choses communes*). Since at least Grotius's *Mare liberum* (1609), modern law has used Roman law as a template for codifying certain common spaces or objects as unappropriable by sovereign states.[26] We find contemporary uses of this legal tradition in, for instance, the discourse of a "world heritage of humanity" used by organizations like UNESCO and the United Nations to identify and protect unique natural and cultural resources. In this discourse, the old Roman category of *res communis* achieves a rather surprising currency in contemporary international law: through the work of organizations like UNESCO, nation-states agree to renounce their absolute territorial sovereignty (in very small territorial pockets) and submit themselves to collective rules on behalf of the present and future well-being of humanity, and all because the nature or uses of certain objects designate them *extra commercium* – i.e., the common heritage of humanity and therefore unappropriable.[27] Yet, for us, the expression "common heritage" is problematic insofar as the very notion of an "inheritance" without an owner does not seem very coherent.[28] This deserves a closer look.

The concept of the "common heritage of humanity" first appeared in The Convention on the Protection of Cultural Property in the Event of Armed Conflict (1954). The convention was a response to the looting and destruction of museums by Nazi armies during the Second World War, and the preamble explicitly references "the cultural heritage of all mankind."[29] The legal category of "world heritage" was also adopted in the first Geneva Conventions on the Law of the Sea (1958). As Prince Wan Waithayakorn of Thailand points out, it was in the "general interest to clearly determine the laws of the sea and ensure the law fairly regulates the various interests at play and ensures the conservation of this inheritance for the benefit of all."[30] A decade later, the seabed was then legally codified through this category so that mineral resources, beyond the zones controlled by coastal states, would be protected from exploitation and placed under the control of the United Nations. At the same time, a series of treaties have extended this same classification to the celestial bodies of the solar system – with the exception of the earth itself, of course. The 1967 Outer Space Treaty makes use of the notion of the common heritage of humanity to delimit any attempt by specific states to appropriate natural celestial bodies. Once again, then, we find the concept of "common inheritance" is largely reserved for objects or resources that are viewed as naturally or intrinsically unappropriable. Yet Susan J. Buck has insightfully shown how fragile this notion of a "world commons" can be. Through such examples as the seabed, Antarctica, outer space, or the atmosphere, Buck shows that while many "world commons" may, at one point, have been protected by declarations of intent or even international conventions that limit or forbid the logic of property, these agreements are ultimately relative to a certain state of technological progress and are therefore easily reversible. For Buck, such international protections tend only to remain in force until a new exploitative technology is invented.[31]

In any case, the work of UNESCO and other NGOs has gradually widened the notion of a "common heritage of humanity" by expanding its definition to knowledge, beliefs, rituals, techniques, monuments, and languages. In 1970, the Convention on the Means of Prohibiting and Preventing the Illicit Import, Export and Transfer of Ownership of Cultural Property declared all states responsible for protecting the "cultural property of humanity." The convention defines "culture" as "property which, on religious or secular grounds, is specifically designated by each State as being of importance for archaeology, prehistory, history, literature, art or science."[32] A series of largely symbolic declarations have since extended this category to the human genome[33] and the ozone layer, while the status of territories like Antarctica continues to be disputed. Interestingly, environmental summits at Rio and Kyoto, for instance, did not use the terminology of "common heritage" as a means of combating global climate change.

In International Law, then, the category of "heritage" encompasses quite a diverse array of material and immaterial goods. What they share in common is the fact that states (or other individuals or entities) cannot appropriate these objects or resources for their exclusive enjoyment, nor can they remain indifferent to the effects of their use or their potential destruction. While many of these objects or resources are excluded from private or public ownership because of their intrinsic characteristics, this is not the only criterion. Some properties are excluded because international law deems them especially valuable on moral, historical, or intellectual grounds. The concept of "common heritage" therefore does not only apply to "things in common" in the traditional sense of Roman law. The current list of heritage objects is thus a strange mixture of resources that are excluded for natural reasons and other objects that are excluded for moral and religious reasons. The concept of "heritage" thus more closely resembles a contemporary "sacred treasure," or something similar to the *sacra* of ancient cultures and traditions. There is also the problem of removing some things from private and public ownership on the grounds that they "belong to humanity in common," while at the same time declaring these objects or resources the "common *property* of humanity," as if humanity was a kind of subject who enjoys an eminent right of property over goods that, according to positive law, are the exclusive property of individuals or states. In any case, however heterogeneous the legal category of the "common heritage of humanity" may be, it is quite different from the economic notion of "public goods," insofar as declarations as to whether some object or resource is part of this common "heritage" are entirely independent of assessments of exclusivity and rivalry. The category of "heritage" is thus much more expansive and flexible than those used in economics to determine whether or not something is a public good. This expansive and flexible logic demonstrates the extent to which these *declarative acts* are often largely symbolic actions that end up collecting the most diverse "things" under the capacious notion of the "common heritage of humanity." This category may therefore be extended whenever some right or need is considered fundamental, which amounts to turning these rights or needs into forms of quasi-property or immaterial assets, and thus a subset within the larger framework of the common heritage of humanity: "the inheritance of immaterial property of humanity."[34]

As we can see, it is clear that all manner of goods and rights are intermingled under this conceptual umbrella without any great concern for consistency or rigor.

In our view, this is due to the inherent ambiguity of the notion itself. On the one hand, this inherently *reifying* concept grants special status to only a limited number of objects or resources; on the other hand, the concept is relatively unlimited in the sense that its list of objects can be widened on the basis of changing social demands, political developments, and shifting public opinion. It is this second trait that especially leads us to believe humanity is becoming a legal category. The extension of "human rights" to include forms of "social rights" has actually shifted the former category from its victim-based orientation toward a subject capable of holding rights claims, and even a subject who enjoys property rights over common goods. For some, this shift suggests a possible breach in the continued domination of the logic of the market. If common goods are indeed related to fundamental rights, then political and social struggles may very well receive important support from influential sectors of society, for whom the defense and extension of this concept of "inheritance" relating to common goods lamentably becomes the first and last word of any future strategy.

Fundamental Common Rights: A Stalled Dynamic

It is no mystery why the dominant neoliberal logic wants to channel all claims of "common goods" toward a more economistic definition of "public goods." Whereas the dynamics of political struggle tend to broaden the domain of "common goods of humanity" by connecting them with fundamental rights, the economic logic of public goods is much more restrictive. For these so-called common "goods" do not only refer to finite "things," but also access to services or institutions: health, education, food, housing, work, etc., all of which are increasingly viewed as fundamental rights that must be universalized. The decisive point is this: according to this approach, fundamental rights and common goods are reciprocally defined. "Subjective rights" are re-defined in terms of access to the basic resources for life and dignity. In other words, water, health, and education are not common goods because of their intrinsic natures, but because they correspond to fundamental rights that are incompatible with the dual logic of markets and states (*dominium* and *imperium*) and thus constitute, virtually at least, a common law that supersedes both state sovereignty and property rights.

Critical economists fully understand the advantages to be derived from this notion, though this has often only led to more confusion. Jean Gadrey, for instance, defines common goods as "those collective resources or inheritances (natural, cultural, popular, knowledge-based, etc.) related to human life and activities both today and in the future; and, by extension, it also includes societal qualities and universal rights, because the latter must also be viewed as collective resources to be managed in common."[35] These sorts of definitions are nothing short of an open affront to the reifying discourse of standard economics: rights cannot be reduced to collectively managed "resources," and this is especially true when we are dealing with so-called "fundamental" rights. Strictly speaking, these rights are inseparable from the individuals attached to them. Transforming them into "resources" that are dealt in the same way in which economics deals with "natural common goods" is thus the surest way of canceling out their "fundamental" character.

This is not to say that such recourse to a fundamental right is new. Indeed, it would be more accurate, in this respect, to interpret the alter-globalization movement as merely extending and revising the "Spirit of Philadelphia." The call for fundamental rights in the immediate post-war years should thus be seen as merely the first step in a larger process. The Constitution of the World Health Organization (WHO) in 1946, for instance, asserts "the enjoyment of the highest attainable standard of health is one of the fundamental rights of every human being."[36] Similarly, the Universal Declaration of Human Rights (1948) sought to free humanity from "terror and misery" and to "create better living conditions" by asking signatory states to agree to guarantee a diverse range of human rights, including the "right to social security" (Article 22), the "right to work, to free choice of employment" (Article 23), the "right to rest and leisure" (Article 24), the "right to a standard of living" adequate to one's basic needs (food, housing, medical care, social services, and social protections) (Article 25), the "right to education" (Article 26), and the right "freely to participate in the cultural life of the community, to enjoy the arts and to share in scientific advancement and its benefits" (Article 27). It is clear, then, that the International Labour Organization (ILO), the WHO, and UNESCO all shared a similar vision in the post-war years. The International Covenant on Economic, Social and Cultural Rights (1966) similarly enshrined the right that "every member of the human family" must be recognized by their state.

And while this rights-based dynamic continues to be used, to some extent, by a handful of more or less legitimate organizations in the new global order – such as UNESCO or the ILO, for example[37] – it has been almost entirely abandoned by today's most dominant and powerful organizations, such as the WTO, the IMF, or any of the major powers. It is also clear that the imposition of the logic of the market over the past thirty years has been specifically directed against this augmentation of fundamental rights. Intellectual property agreements such as TIPS (1994) are, for example, clearly opposed to the "right to health." Even after mass protests in the Global South (South Africa, Brazil, India, etc.), pharmaceutical companies granted these countries only minor concessions: they could produce generic drugs for a very limited number of diseases, though their ability to export these drugs to countries that cannot manufacture them remains severely limited. The reign of the logic of property in fields like health and the environment is nothing less than criminal. And it is the height of cynicism whenever the market is described as guaranteeing humanity's survival through initiatives like a "polluter's market."

In any case, it is precisely this drive toward a more and more expansive understanding of fundamental human rights that a triumphant neoliberalism has halted and even reversed. It is worth recalling, in this context, how the most eminent members of the Mount Pèlerin Society, Hayek especially, ceaselessly denounced "totalitarian democracy" and the "illusion of social justice" that would only ever lead toward "serfdom." The political successes of the neoliberals in the 1980s thus produced policies aimed at brutally undermining any concept of "economic, social, and cultural rights." These policies have profoundly altered the state apparatus, along with the post-war subjective rights that largely depended on state largesse. Both have become increasingly unraveled in the capitalist countries, such that the neoliberal state, in the words of Wendy Brown, is nothing less than a "de-democratization" machine that has, by now, even begun to take aim at civil and political rights.[38]

It is understandable, then, why the alter-globalization movement has chosen to strategically circumvent the state. Under today's neoliberal conditions, the state has actually become one of the biggest threats to the fundamental rights it was supposed to guarantee: to ratify the rights of social citizenship, to recognize the "common goods of humanity," would mean adopting an operational norm other than the unlimited accumulation of private wealth. It would be a matter of "welding" the logic of the global commons onto the universal logic of the welfare state. And aside from the logistical problems that would inevitably arise from this rather artificial concatenation, would this endeavor not simply reproduce the same Western political structures, as if these structures were timeless frameworks that could be unproblematically transposed onto the fundamental new situation we are facing today?

The basic contradiction of the welfare state, as we have described above, is that the latter was realized within a formal apparatus that knows only two opposing logics: the logic of citizen rights, on the one hand, and the logic according to which the state is tasked with guaranteeing these rights, on the other. The problem arose, however, from the fact that there was no sure way to effectively guarantee these rights (especially as they began to expand in the post-war period), and so the welfare state deployed a combination of income re-distribution and national solidarity in the hopes that the rights of the citizenry could ultimately be compatible with a "civilized" version of capitalism. In fact, these "social, economic, and cultural rights" were theorized, like civil and political rights, as subjective rights that limited the power or reach of the state. In other words, these rights were not based on the kind of obligations and duties that produce the common, which is to say from the practical, political, and institutional conditions that enable the subject of social rights to be, at the same time, the co-producer of these very rights. Indeed, it is rather striking in this respect to observe that the concept of "duty" is only found in one article of the 1948 Declaration of Human Rights, namely Article 29: "Everyone has duties to the community in which alone the free and full development of his personality is possible." While we understand that these duties, much like civil and political rights, are greatly conditioned by the "nature of the community" in question, it is nonetheless surprising that nothing at all is said in this document about the underlying political and economic conditions or mechanisms that would enable each individual to fulfill their obligations to others. The reality of the matter is simply that the sovereign nation-state was the only possible mechanism for asserting rights against the reign of capital during the period in which these conventions were drafted. And it is precisely this difficulty that paralyzes the alter-globalization movement: the movement unhesitatingly asserts the fundamental right to access a range of goods considered vital or essential to human dignity, but it does not envision a corollary transformation of the global political system in order to realize these fundamental rights. It is hard to see how the current state system, dominated as it is by a pervasive capitalist rationality, could be transformed into the kind of political apparatus that could both support the "common good" and properly distribute "common goods," short of some miraculous ethical conversion. It is on this point that the alter-globalization movement, if it persists, will have to make a decisive leap and politically commit to transcending the international state system.

But before anything like this can happen, we must begin to acclimatize ourselves to the idea that the law is not simply a ruse of power or a figure of the "police," but that the law greatly contributes to the formation of modern subjectivity. This is precisely the issue Catherine Colliot-Thélène raises in her work when, for instance, she questions whether the left commands sufficient political and social force to defend our existing rights under today's conditions of capitalist globalization, much less bring about new political rights: "what will happen to the political subject, the subject of rights, when the state loses the monopoly it holds over guaranteeing these rights?[39] This is certainly an important question, but it is only partially developed. If we agree with Colliot-Thélène that the Western legal tradition has made us the subjects we are, and that it forces us to think in terms of subjective rights, we must also acknowledge that this whole system is in decline, insofar as the older Westphalian model is gradually being replaced by forms of neoliberal governmentality. Under these conditions, then, it is entirely insufficient to encourage citizens to "defend their rights" in the face of today's pluralistic world order. Instead, citizens must actively struggle for the right to co-produce the conditions through which their rights are recognized and their needs satisfied. In other words, it is no longer "social citizens" who must make the rights claims we need. What we need instead are politically and civically active citizens who build relations of responsibility through common production, and who are capable of inventing institutions that allow them to become co-producers of the common, rather than passive "consumers" of services.

While the future "global order" is of course uncertain, there are, nonetheless, trends that have begun to emerge and will continue to take shape unless the situation is reversed. We are skeptical that the most likely outcome will be a spontaneous march toward an "ordered pluralism," as Mireille Delmas-Marty imagines.[40] A more likely outcome is described by Alain Supiot, who argues that neoliberal globalization is leading toward a global "re-feudalization." For Supiot, this process is characterized by the decline of the state's social functions and the augmentation of its repressive functions, the possible break-up of nation-states into independent "state-regions," and the multiplication of regional and supra-national authorities based on a logic of multiple fragmentation in which each sector of society produces its own "mafia-like" norms. This depiction of normative chaos, in which the powerful reinforce their power and wealth by relying on state or para-state forms of violence, already in fact describes much of the world today, especially in the economic sphere. Should we respond, then, by simply clogging up the Westphalian system? Or maybe we should hope for a re-awakening of the republican spirit within a nationalistic framework? The greatest risk, in our view, of pursuing a course of "national re-nationalization" is that this strategy might inadvertently strengthen reactive, nationalistic, and xenophobic political movements that are already a global force. The question we must ask ourselves, then, is whether or not we have finally come up against the hard limits of the centralized state and the forms of subjectivity this system produces. And if this is the case, as we think it is, the final question we must deal with is what specific form of political organization is able to institutionally realize the co-production of the global commons if not the nation-state.

POLITICAL PROPOSITION 9

We Must Institute a Federation of Commons

Theorizing the possibility of instituting the commons ultimately means confronting what we call the "question of power." We have already argued how we think it is illusory to imagine a piecemeal expansion of the commons "from below" that will gradually erode and collapse the foundations of capitalism.[1] Accordingly, we have argued that it is indispensable to theorize the political construction of a new form of political power, given our absolute insistence on the inadequacies of merely "seizing power," in the sense of taking over the state apparatus. The so-called "lesson of the Commune" for us is thus exactly the opposite of that drawn by Trotsky: adherence to the principle of communal autonomy is not a "great error" that merely hides one's "cowardice in the face of revolutionary action,"[2] but rather testifies to a great lucidity concerning the profoundly authoritarian and anti-democratic character of a unitary and centralized state. Communalism proves its great coherence by forcefully asserting its hostility to the "one and indivisible" Republic."[3]

As we argue in our final political proposition, the only political principle that respects the autonomy of local governments is the *federal principle*. As Proudhon argues on this point:

> Federation, from the Latin *foedus*, genitive *foederis*, which means pact, contract, treaty, agreement, alliance, and so on, is an agreement by which one or more heads of family, one or more towns, one or more groups of towns or states, assume reciprocal and equal commitments to perform one or more specific tasks, the responsibility of which rests exclusively with the officers of the federation.[4]

The essence of federalism is its commitment to reciprocity and equality of obligation, and the absolute exclusion of any form of structural subordination. Thus understood, the federal principle is directly opposed to the nation-state principle of sovereignty, whose essence is the recognition of a supreme power that transcends all others and which is absolved (*ab-solutus*) of any obligation toward them.[5] The federal principle is the fulcrum upon which we must begin theorizing the necessary conditions for the political construction of the commons. Our discussion of federalism brings us back full circle to our etymological root *munus*, which, we might recall, denotes a relation of obligation built on reciprocity and mutualism.[6] That said, we must also recognize that there are many different kinds of federalism. We will begin then by schematically distinguishing between a federation of people-states (*peuples-États*) at the international level, a federation that unites several quasi-autonomous states within a larger state (an "intra-state" federation), and the internal organization of an entity that is not a state strictly speaking.

International Federalism

Our discussion of federalism begins at the international scale, and Immanuel Kant's "Toward a Perpetual Peace" (1795) is our point of departure. In this famous essay, Kant enumerates three definitive articles for achieving perpetual peace, and each article corresponds to a different level of "public law," so to speak. Kant's first article states, "The Civil Constitution of Every State Shall be Republican."[7] This article corresponds to what we might call the first level of public law, which is to say the level of civic rights within a state structure (*jus civitas*). Kant's second article asserts, "The Right of Nations shall be based on a Federation of Free States."[8] This article corresponds to the level of the law that deals with the reciprocal relations between states (*jus gentium*). And Kant's third article states, "Cosmopolitan Right shall be limited to Conditions of Universal Hospitality."[9] This article does not correspond to the level of international law exactly, but rather refers to what Kant calls "cosmopolitan right, in so far as individuals and states, coexisting in an external relationship of mutual influences, may be regarded as citizens of a universal state of mankind (*jus cosmopoliticum*)."[10] For Kant, the federalism of a free state first of all presupposes a republican constitution, which is to say a constitution based on the separation of executive power from legislative power. This form of federation thus constitutes a "federalism of peoples"; this is not "the same thing as an international state," which is to say a "world state."[11] Far from putting an end to the plurality of states within the international system, this version of federalism presupposes it, and Kant thereby precludes the possibility that this "peoples-state" plurality would function fundamentally differently from a federated state. Kant's federation would therefore be a "pacific federation" (*foedus pacificum*) in which republican states work toward a complete cessation of all wars. Kant's federation is not, then, based on "the positive idea of a *world republic*."[12] His federation of nations is therefore ultimately a means for states to protect themselves from war by renouncing the so-called "right to go to war."[13]

Unfortunately, this type of purely defensive interstate federation is of little help when it comes to thinking about the coordination of the commons on a global level based on the principle of self-government. Kant's sketch does not fundamentally challenge the principle of national sovereignty and accordingly precludes any internal federal structure with each state precisely because of his persistent attachment to the principle of sovereignty. It is also worth observing that Kant's version of federalism produces a cosmopolitan law in which the foreigner is granted the "right of resort," which should be distinguished from a "right of residence." Recognition of the right of resort compels every state to admit any foreigner onto their soil – without necessarily making this foreigner a permanent resident – so long as the foreigner does not threaten the state's existence. What Kant has in mind with this "right of resort" is in fact the necessary legal conditions for developing international trade. Kant rejects the "European argument about *terra nullius* in America and Africa that deprived indigenous populations of all their rights" and justified their colonization.[14] This is the true content of Kant's notion of the "right of world citizenship," in the sense that it too has no positive content: its function is exclusively to promote trade between nations, according to the widely held belief in Kant's age that sufficient trade is all that is required to pacify international relations.[15] Kant then confirms that the "universal state of mankind" (the third order of public law) refers only to a "transcendental" reality in the moral order of duty.[16] Kant's argument is also based on a rather singular re-interpretation of the idea of "originary communal possession" of the soil, which we have already seen at work in Locke. Yet whereas Locke evoked this notion of original communalism to justify the passage from undivided co-possession to exclusive private appropriation without relying on the artifice of a convention, Kant actually succeeds in making "originary communal possession" itself the basis of the right to private property. Far from referring to any kind of actual historical point of origin, Kant argues that the legal impossibility of *res nullius* is in fact an "idea of reason": nothing can be absolutely vacant since "all land belongs exclusively to the people (not collectively, but distributively)," and thus everyone must be considered equally entitled to appropriate a portion of land that has not yet been appropriated. In other words, the "common" of "originary communal possession" of the soil "is reduced to a license granted to all, which is to say to each individual, to declare for themselves a portion of the soil that has not yet been appropriated."[17] Kant's version of federalism is thus a purely defensive interstate alliance designed to guarantee peace and trade. For Catherine Colliot-Thélène, the system's defensive *telos* and its cosmopolitan insistence on the individual's "right of resort" both "flow from the same principle, namely the freedom of possession."[18] And of course Kant's articulation of the "common" as that which allows each individual to appropriate land for themselves has nothing whatsoever to do with the concept of the common, and the centrality of common use therein, that is at the center of our analysis.

The "Federal Republic"

Federalism does not only concern reciprocal external relations between states at the international level, but it also bears on the internal structure of the states themselves ("civic law"). Whereas Kant was our point of departure at the international level, our touchstone for intra-state federalism is Book IX of Montesquieu's *The Spirit of the Laws*. Chapters 1, 2, and 3, which are dedicated to a discussion of the "federal constitution" and the "federal republic," are especially pertinent to our present concerns. Speaking of the federal republic, Montesquieu writes:

> This form of government is an agreement by which many political bodies consent to become citizens of the larger state that they want to form. It is a society of societies that make a new one, which can be enlarged by new associations that unite with it.[19]

Montesquieu's famous definition ("a society of societies") broke with the previous correlation, as established by Pufendorf, between statism at the national level, on the one hand, and interstatism at the international level, on the other, which was a reinforcing homology rooted in the general principle of sovereignty. Montesquieu's conception of a union between several republics is not at all the same as the relation between states that prevails at the international level: the states bound by their federal pact constitute a single unit at the international level, and the citizens of each republic are, at the same time, citizens of the larger republic that emerges from the federation of all the smaller republics. The federal republic thus combines the internal advantages of the republic with the advantages of monarchy "with regard to the exterior."[20]

Unlike the hypothetical version of federalism advocated by Kant, Montesquieu's conception of federalism has been repeatedly tried throughout history. Montesquieu himself mentions the Republic of the United Netherlands, the Federal Republic of Germany, and the Swiss Leagues, and he is especially interested in the ancient Republic of Lycia, which was comprised of twenty-three cities.[21] Indeed, Montesquieu's emphatic praise for the federal republic inspired many of the leaders of the American Revolution. Madison, for instance, adapted Montesquieu's concept to arrive at his own notion of a "compound republic";[22] he also celebrated the "mixture" that characterizes the United States Republic, inasmuch as the latter "[partakes] both of the national and federal character." In an article from 1788 in the *Federalist Papers*, Alexander Hamilton also draws on the same chapters from Montesquieu's *The Spirit of the Laws*, especially Montesquieu's discussion of the Lycian Confederacy. Hamilton even suggested the twenty-three Greek *poleis* of the Lycian Confederacy prefigure the "states" of the American Union.[23] Interestingly, the anti-federalists also invoked Montesquieu, and they did so precisely to critique Madison and Hamilton's pro-federal arguments. In any case, the latter tend to describe federalism as a "technique for the vertical distribution of power" that effectively detaches the federal dynamic from any determinate social content. In other word, federalism, in the hands of the American Federalists, is little more than a "technical" solution to a "technical" problem.

The reality, however, is that this whole approach negates what is most essential in the federal principle. Strictly from the point of view of democracy (and all other things being equal), a crucial distinction emerges out of the American experiment in federalism between a "juridical federalism," in which it is the Supreme Court that acts as the guarantor of the constitution through its legal interpretations, and a "referendum federalism," in which the people are the ultimate guarantors of the constitution through their direct vote. This is why Hannah Arendt is clearly misguided in celebrating the American Revolution's decision to opt for a "legal" rather than a "political" *auctoritas*. The fact that a panel of judges is charged with exercising, as Woodrow Wilson put it, "a kind of Constitutional Assembly in continuous session" does not speak in favor of American federalism but is rather a mark against it.[24] Entrusting continual "constitutional control" to a "judicial branch of government" runs directly counter to the democratic conception of the separation of powers by granting the judiciary preeminence over the properly political organs of government. And the anti-democratic character of the court is exacerbated when the judges are appointed for life (in the dual sense that they are neither elected nor subject to recall). More generally, then, perhaps it is worth asking if the praise Arendt bestows upon the federal principle at work in the

Paris Commune is not in total contradiction with her valorization, in this very same text, of the "most important" innovations of the Americans. In the last chapter of *On Revolution*, Arendt cites Odyssée Barrot, who argues that as a "social revolution" the Paris Commune must "continue" and "complete" the revolutionary period of 1793. Yet as a "political revolution," Barrot argues that the Commune is a direct "reaction against" the 1793 phase of the revolution and a return to 1789."[25] Yet in the minds of many of the Communards, not only was there no contradiction between social and political revolution, but the federal principle they inherited from 1789 was the most appropriate political form for continuing to challenge the absolute right of property that the revolution initiated in 1793.[26] Arendt's interpretation of the French Revolution, however, goes in exactly the opposite direction: Arendt argues that the centrality of the "social question" was precisely the ferment from which the Terror was born, in the sense that the revolution's attempt to free people from misery necessitated recourse to the most unrestrained means of violence.[27] In this respect, we think Castoriadis offers a more accurate interpretation of the subject:

> The economic and social question was not, in fact, taken into account by those who established the first colonies in New England. And Arendt welcomes this, as if this reticence was not precisely one of the factors that lea d to the subsequent evolution of American society she so deplores.[28]

In other words, it was precisely its neglect of the social question that led the United States to increasingly accept the unitary logic of the nation-state and, consequently, turn its back on the federal structure of elementary "small republics" for which Jefferson argued at the end of his life. The "social" thus takes its revenge in the worst forms: in this case, it resulted in an oligarchic constitution that methodologically separated the people from direct participation in public affairs by making politics "a profession and a career," and by introducing all manner of advertising into politics "through which the relationship between representative and elector is transformed into that of seller and buyer."[29]

"Intra-State" and "Interstate" Federalism

In light of this institutional evolution, the issue we are confronted with is the extent to which federalism is able to endow the social with a form of institutional expression in order to prevent some of the more dangerous effects that arise whenever the social is unduly distanced from political institutions. Clearly, most existing forms of federalism do not correspond, in any direct way, to some specific social content or other (systems of social protection, for example). In this case, then, we will firstly want to distinguish between "interstate federalism" (Canada and Europe) and "intra-state" federalism (Switzerland, the United States, and Germany), in order to better differentiate an administratively decentralized unitary state, like the United States, from a "non-centered" federalism "with asymmetrical and multinational content" as can be seen in Canada, where the relationship between the federal government and various provincial governments is managed through a network of federal-provincial conferences.[30] The Canadian example is especially useful for reflecting on how the European Union (EU) could re-organize its own institutions in the spirit of enhanced social citizenship and monetary federalism. Examined from the perspective of the connection (or lack thereof) between institutional form and social content, the experience of the EU is actually a perfect counter-example, or an example of what not to do. The EU of course prides itself on the fact that its constitution is the combined product of very diverse intellectual sources, from Kant's reflections on perpetual peace to the market-based statism of German ordo-liberalism.[31] In terms of its actual institutional structure, the EU is neither a supra-national state nor a union of several states (as in the model of a federal republic). Nor is it a defensive alliance based directly and solely on the rights of "nations"; nor is it a little of all these at once. The crises currently afflicting the EU are therefore profound and penetrate all the way down to its very foundations. This is why neither the return of national sovereignty nor the opposing attempt to add a political constitution "on top" of the existing institutional infrastructure will be sufficient to deal with the problems facing the EU.

Júrgen Habermas has recently proposed an institutional re-arrangement of the EU as a means of remedying the technocratic drift of what he calls "executive federalism."[32] But Habermas's position, in our view, is based on an untenable reading of the Treaty of Lisbon. The fact is the treaty very nearly endows the EU with a form of "transnational democracy," insofar as it enshrines the division of constituent power between the citizens of the union and the peoples of the various member states. For instance, in Article 1, paragraph 1, the Treaty of Lisbon speaks of the "will of citizens and states of Europe." But what justifies this divisive "and"? Should we understand the citizens and the states as two distinctive political subjects? Of course, a citizen of the union is not qualitatively distinctive, legally speaking, from a citizen of a member state, simply because the treaty establishes an equivalence between a "citizen of the union" and a "citizen of a union member state": it is by virtue of being a citizen of a member state, and for no other reason, that one becomes a citizen of the EU. What escapes Habermas's attention – and is the reason why the technocratic drift of the EU's executive federalism cannot be remedied within the existing institutional architecture – is rather the internal connection between three aspects of the EU that are normally dissociated: a) the "executive federalism" that privileges intergovernmental bodies (the European Council) at the expense of parliament; b) the manner in which economic competition is enshrined in the constitution, which encourages speculation and leads to state indebtedness; and c) the EU's refusal to recognize social rights as fundamental rights.[33] In other words, the technocratic drift deplored by Habermas does not stem from a superficial or superstructural "democratic deficit" that could be somehow remedied in isolation from the rest of the system, but is the perfectly predictable outcome of the social content that was the EU's very purpose from the beginning. The primacy given to economic competition and the secondary importance of social rights is why the Commission and the Council of Ministers are the two institutional bodies charged with "promoting the general interest": their independence and distance from the citizens and from parliament are designed to ensure that social interests will not intrude and distort the EU's overriding principle of economic competition.

The True Scope of the Federal Principle

The real challenge we are facing, then, involves realizing the federal principle in such a way that it is directly linked to a substantive conception of democracy, one that does not exclude the very "social" sphere that has tended to be seen as foreign to the "public domain" of pure politics. We need a federalism that can generate two modes of politics for both the *agora* and the *ecclesia*, to borrow Castoriadis's phrasing of the problem. Indeed, it is precisely this concern for ensuring the continuity between the "social" and the "political" that has led many contemporary theorists back to the work of sixteenth-century German jurist Johannes Althusius. For many, Althusius's work is considered the crucible of an "original notion of federalism" that is starkly different from today's modern version of "statist" federalism.

In actual fact, the central doctrine articulated in Althusius's *Political Methodice Digesta* (1603) is not the federal principle at all, but the doctrine of *consociatio symbiotica*. Pierre Mesnard translates this doctrine as "symbiotic community" in order to clearly designate Althusius's conception of an organic union that "transforms members into *symbiotes* or "guests" (*convives*).[34] The concept describes a true community of life (*symbiosis*) whose cohesive force is entirely affective and spiritual.[35] Yet, despite the organic character of these communities, Althusius wants these communities to produce new communal forms of increasing complexity: from simple or private communities, followed by mixed or public communities, and ending with the highest communal form, the state. His method is based on the reproduction of an "exact genetic order" in which restricted communities lead to more integrated and complex forms. In this way, the simplest communal forms invariably give rise to more complex communities that incorporate the early, simpler forms into their subsequent permutations. The two predominant forms of simple or private communities are the family and the "college" or "brotherhood," which is a voluntary civil group whose members are "companions." The most extensive of such groups are what Althusius calls the different orders, the clergy, nobility, and the third estate. For Althusius, several of these private communities coalesce and create public communities or *Universitates*, whose members are called "citizens." Pierre Mesnard emphasizes the specificity of the term "citizen" for Althusius: one only becomes a citizen, in the sense of *symbiote*, by first becoming a member of a college or brotherhood, such that the elements of the civic body are not essentially comprised of individuals but of constituent communities.[36] For Althusius, there are two types of public communities – the municipality (a rural commune, village, parish, borough, urban commune, etc.) and the province – and the rules governing each are perfectly homologous. Above these public communities, and always proceeding through the movement of generative coalescence, is the final form: the state, or the "integral symbolic community."[37] This community is governed by a college of ephors and a supreme magistrate: the ephors are the supreme guardians of the constitution, and they represent the people and speak in their name; and the supreme magistrate is the administrator and agent invested with executive power. But this division of power must not obscure the superiority of the collective body over the supreme magistrate: the latter is only an agent or a *féal*, and it is always in the name of the integral community, its justice and its law, that the ephors and the magistrate are obliged to act. By virtue of the continuum connecting every community to those above it, the same organizational principle prevails at each level – namely a division of powers coupled with the superiority of the collective over its representatives: the superiority of the corporation over its president, the superiority of the municipality over its mayor, the superiority of the states (in the sense of the various orders) in each province over their respective leaders, etc.

What can we learn from Althusius's conception of political organization, in which complex entities are derived from simpler ones? On the one hand, this model offers an interesting means by which the state is constituted from the bottom, and not from a power center of some kind. On the other hand, however, the entire doctrine is grounded in a rather questionable conception of the social. By conceiving of the social as an almost evolutionary system in which an integrative logic allows simpler social forms to yield more complex forms, this approach might more accurately be described as a corporatist doctrine rather than a federal doctrine.

We find it difficult to imagine how this form of "federalism" could act as a model for coordinating the multitudinous networks that make up today's technologically immersed social movements.[38] Nor do we see how this approach helps us theorize the articulation of different commons at all levels of social life. At bottom, the principle of common use is radically incompatible with the principle of corporatist organization (least the common become a political form that is restricted to certain communities).

In order to properly identify the type of federalism that is most appropriate for the practice of common use at all levels of social life, we need first to return to the most basic definition of the federal principle. In *The Principle of Federation* (1863), Proudhon contrasts the "federal contract," in which the "political contract binding the citizen to the state [is] equal and reciprocal" to "the society of private property," or what Proudhon calls "the replica in miniature of all absolute states."[39] Federalism, for Proudhon, is based on a double imperative: the first imperative is the reciprocity between each side of the contract (the contract must therefore be "synallagmatic" or "bilateral"); the second requirement insists on equivalence between that which is exchanged between each party (the contract must therefore be "communtative"). Under these conditions, the parties to the contract "reserve for themselves more rights, more liberty, more authority, more property than they abandon."[40] The "society of common property" therefore compels its adherents "to give up their independence, and to devote themselves totally to an organization."[41]

Proudhon describes the difference between the federated municipality (*commune*) and a society in which all property is held in common in these terms:

> The authority responsible for its execution can never overwhelm the constituent members; that is, the federal powers can never exceed in number and significance those of local or provincial authorities, just as the latter can never outweigh the rights and prerogatives of man and citizen. If it were otherwise, the community would be communistic.

Proudhon then outlines what he considers to be the "fundamental law" of the federal system as such:

> In summary, the federal system is the contrary of hierarchy or administrative and governmental centralization which characterizes, to an equal extent, democratic empires, constitutional monarchies, and unitary republics. Its basic and essential law is this: in a federation, the powers of central authority are specialized and limited and diminish in number, in directness, and in what I may call intensity as the confederation grows by the adhesion of new states. In centralized governments, on the contrary, the powers of the supreme authority multiply, extend, and become more direct, bringing the business of provinces, towns, corporations, and individuals under the jurisdiction of the prince, as a direct function of territorial scale and size of the population.[42]

Proudhon's "fundamental law" of federalism is therefore very different from that contemporary European construct known as the "principle of subsidiarity." As Bruno Théret aptly remarks on this point:

> The principle of subsidiarity can, in effect, be used to both extend and limit the prerogatives of the Union and the domain over which it intervenes. As a dynamic principle of decentralization that allows power to be staggered across different political levels of a unitary superstate according to the specific competencies of the varying levels, this principle is clearly part of a functionalist and centralist conception of political order.[43]

In fact, this principle, as formulated in Article 3b of the Treaty of Maastricht, is perfectly compatible with a centralized union that is founded on the principle of competition, since union intervention is only possible on the condition that certain member states fail to "sufficiently" meet the objectives of some proposed action.[44] The principle is therefore very different from the federal principle according to which power decreases as one progressively moves up the institutional ladder.

To get a better appreciation of Proudhon's position on federalism, we must emphasize the continuity between his earlier critique of the very idea of "government" (1840) and his advocacy, twenty years later (1862), for federal relations between states. For the later Proudhon, federally related states at the international level are not, as they were in Kant, simultaneously unitary states in terms of the internal constitution, but are themselves comprised of federated municipalities. For Proudhon, the federal principle is not only concerned with relations between nations, then, but is also intended to ensure contiguity of power between the municipalities and the provinces, between the provinces and the state, and between the state and other international states.[45] To put it in Kantian terms, we could say the federal principle concerns both "civil right" (the first level of public law") and "international right" (second level of public law), though it is doubtful if this distinction has any meaning so long as one presupposes a centralized state. What is certain is that Kant's demand for a "republican constitution" (the first Kantian requirement for perpetual peace) must be replaced with the demand for a "federated constitution" within each state. What is more, this same internal federal principle must also operate at the international level in relations between states in order to forestall the creation of a world superstate, since the very idea of a superstate itself betrays the federal principle in which local forms of federalism are projected onto increasingly higher levels. And, of course, the more one rises from one level to another, the more power must be restricted and specialized in such a way that the lower levels retain maximum prerogative and power of initiative, which necessarily excludes the integration of various states into a world state. On the other hand, one could well imagine "conferences" (something like the federal-provincial conferences in Canada) between the states at a regional or continental level, which would then provide the platform for coordination at the global level. What we are describing here, then, is a radical form of non-state federalism, rather than an "interstate" federalism as we described above: the state does not disappear, strictly speaking, but is simply one stage in a larger institutional continuum that extends both below and above the state level as such. And while the "state" level may just happen to correspond to the historical and social content of a given "people" or "nation," this correspondence is of no particular importance, let alone privilege; a non-state federalism is, in this sense, also a *non-centered* federalism.

It was precisely this interpretation of the federal principle that the Paris Commune turned to in 1871. The proclamation adopted at its second meeting explicitly describes the prospect of a "federal constitution for the communes of France."[46] It is hardly surprising, then, that Marx felt compelled to revise his former position in order to recognize the originality of the 1871 communal constitution. In his earlier address to the Central Committee of the Communist League in March 1850, Marx and Engels vigorously opposed the democrats who favored a federal republic:

> The workers, in opposition to this plan, must not only strive for a single and indivisible German republic, but also within this republic for the most determined centralization of power in the hands of the state authority. They should not let themselves be misguided by the democratic talk of freedom for the communities, of self-government, etc.[47]

"Nor," as Marx asserts even more emphatically, "can this so-called free system of local government be allowed to perpetuate, side by side with the state civil law," at which point Marx speaks, in a very complimentary manner, of the centralization in France during 1793. Indeed, in a note added to an 1885 edition of Marx's address, almost fifteen years after the Commune, Engels argues that Marx has not given up on the idea of national political centralization as the primary political objective of the proletariat. Engels is here entirely preoccupied with dispelling any "misunderstanding" about the meaning of Marx's 1850 critique of communalism, and so he contrasts the virtues of the provincial or local self-government in France during the revolution (which he sees as similar to the United States) with the "narrow-minded cantonal or communal self-seeking which strikes us as so repulsive in Switzerland."[48] This facile opposition between the grandeur of American federalism and the narrow-mindedness of Swiss federalism is not so much designed to play one form of federalism against another as it to retrospectively justify the struggle against the "South German federal republicans" who, in 1849, wanted to model Germany after the Swiss system. The main function of this otherwise self-serving critique is to restrict communal self-government to very narrow conditions: provincial and local autonomy is admissible, for Marx, only if it is inscribed within a framework defined by national political centralization. In other words, Marx does not view local or provincial autonomy as a lever for higher forms of non-unitary and non-centralized political construction, and so any local autonomy is largely emptied of its substance. And thus we once again encounter the same Marxian limit: the proletariat's first objective is the conquest of state power. The proletariat must centralize its own power, and for this it needs a unitary and centralized state apparatus.

Against Marx's political idealization of 1793, Proudhon's *De la capacité politique des classes ouvrières* (1865) interpreted the year 1793 as but one moment in the long and varied evolution of French political unity, which was a process of successive annexation that both pre-dated and extended well beyond the 1789 revolution: "the reformers of 1789 continued the monarchical project of constructing a unity doctrine of the state with the total acclaim of all the people up until the present day."[49] Various French *départements* or municipalities resisted this gradual centralization of power, but their efforts were ultimately undermined by the Constitutions of Year II and Year III, which made municipal administrations mere subdivisions of the central national administration. The centralization of power was further entrenched by the creation of administrative prefects in 1800. This evolutionary centralization was completed with the law of May 5, 1855, which allowed the emperor or the prefects to appoint mayors and deputies: "as a result of the law of May 5 1855, municipalities became what the logic of unity – from 1789, 1793 and 1795 – decided they would be, namely a powerless branch of central authority."[50] While Proudhon commiserates the death of the "old spirit of the municipalities," he remains nonetheless convinced that "the moment is approaching when, after a final crisis, a call will be made on the basis of principles and a movement in the opposite direction will begin."[51]

Toward a Double Federation of the "Commons"

We now want to examine whether the federal principle might organize not only relations between local municipalities and the federal authority, or between the states and the federal authority – i.e., political relations *stricto sensu* – but also the relations between the various commons in the socio-economic sphere. And, more broadly, we need to examine whether the federal principle is able to organize not only the internal institutions of these spheres, but also their reciprocal interrelations. To this end, it is especially important to have a firm grasp of the content of the federal principle itself.

In the bourgeois world, according to Proudhon, two principles function as the "two pillars of society and the state": the principle of "political centralization" and the principle of "economic competition" – which he also refers to as "commercial and industrial anarchy" – and this "necessarily leads to the feudalization of society by capital" and thus functions as a counter-weight to the first principle or pillar.[52] For Proudhon, however, our aim should not be to oppose these two principles with two countervailing principles, but to oppose them with one and the same principle, namely "mutualism" (*mutualité*), a term that implies both municipal autonomy and economic solidarity. Why? "The French word *mutual*, *mutualité*, *mutuation*, and its synonym *réciproque*, *réciprocité*, comes from the Latin *mutuum* and signifies today as "loan" (*prêt*) or, in a broader sense, "exchange." If it is assumed that a borrower who consumes a loan makes an equivalent loan to someone else in one form or another, and that a lender in turn becomes a borrower at some subsequent point, then a situation of "mutual benefit" or "exchange" necessarily arises. But what is crucial to understand, for Proudhon, is "how we are able to substitute justice for authority, community, and charity through these values of mutualism, reciprocity, and exchange, and how we are then in a position, in politics and the political economy, to build a system of relations that will do nothing less than fundamentally transform the social order."[53]

One may object at this point that the principle of mutualism only concerns the commercial sphere, or the socio-economic sphere, and that it is connected to the federal principle we have been discussing above only with great difficulty. For Proudhon, however, federalism itself is nothing more than the extension of mutualism into the political sphere: "thus, transported into the political sphere, what we have been hitherto calling mutualism or guarantism is now called federalism. In this simple synonym, the whole political and economic revolution opens up in front of us."[54] What we have here then is a simultaneous *distinction* drawn between the economic and political spheres and the *identification* of a principle linking the spheres together. It was the awareness of this identity that led Proudhon to advocate the establishment of "workers' corporations" that were subject to neither the state nor capital, and it was for the same reason that the Paris Commune favored the creation of cooperative workshops rather than the development of large-scale industry: the extreme centralization of the latter was seen as largely incompatible with self-government in the sphere of production. It is in this sense, then, that we are able to conceptualize the federal principle as two-fold: it orients both the federation of productive units and the federation of municipal units. Federalism, then, as we have described above,[55] must become the basis of two forms of democracy: the political democracy of municipalities and the industrial democracy of the workers' enterprises. And this is precisely why the distinction between the two forms of federalism – political and economic – is perhaps better viewed as merely the extension of the principle of productive or economic mutualism throughout society as a whole.

This idea of a double federalism connecting the political and socio-economic spheres seems very promising to us. A question, however, remains as to whether the principle of mutualism is best suited to realizing this articulation. As Proudhon himself indicated, the *mutuum* of "mututalism" refers, above all, to the necessity of reciprocity between lender and borrower, the "exchange of good offices and products." But is a commercial relation the best model to be applied to all manner of social relations? Might the social not be impoverished if it is governed as nothing more than a contractual system linking independent individuals or units? This tendency to theorize the social in contractual terms – for example, Proudhon's proposition to substitute "contracts" for "laws" – is one of the more problematic characteristics of Proudhon's concept of federalism. But as we have pointed out in the beginning of the book,[56] if *mutuum* is indeed a derivative of *munus*, it is difficult to reduce the term to strictly economic forms of reciprocity insofar as its genealogical root denotes the holding and exercising of public office. We must therefore re-affirm the primacy of *munus* over *mutuum* and, consequently, make the principle of co-obligation (which links co-participants of the same activity) the central internal organizing principle of the two spheres, as well as the principle of their reciprocal articulation. For we must, at all costs, avoid organizing the federalism of the political sphere on the basis of the relations of exchange (*mutuum*) prevailing in the economic sphere: to orient the political sphere on the basis of the economic would be to repeat some of the same Marxist errors described in previous chapters, and we should be cautious about making the same mistakes with Proudhon. Proudhon rejects the notion of a centralized state that "corresponds" to the centralization of large-scale industry, and so he instead proffers the notion that the mutualism of the political sphere should be an extension of the mutualism organizing the economic sphere. Thus, in both cases – Marx and Proudhon – the political sphere is organized on the basis of the economic sphere, and this can only result in a compromised political sphere. The concluding logic of this strategy is the all-too-familiar dissolution of the state or of politics into the economy, an idea that haunted the early Proudhon, and an idea that Marx turned into the ultimate truth of history as such.

We must, instead, insist on the irreducible diversity of these two types of federalism while holding to the necessity of their democratic coordination: unlike the logic of *mutuum*, the common is not an economic principle that can "become" political by merely extending it to the political sphere. Nor can this economic logic serve as an ahistorical principle of moral justice. Rather, it is first and foremost a political principle that strives to govern the socio-economic sphere in the same manner as it governs the political sphere. The remaining question, then, is how to institutionalize the irreducible difference between the two spheres without hindering their interconnection.

In spite of her attachment to the absolute separation between these two spheres, Hannah Arendt indirectly furnishes us with a promising means of answering this pressing question in an interview from 1970 titled "Thoughts on Politics and Revolution." In her discussion of "a different state concept" that breaks with the principle of sovereignty (particularly in terms of the latter's "claim to unchecked and unlimited power in foreign affairs"), Arendt suggests, "the mere rudiments I see for a new state concept can be found in the federal system, whose advantage is that power moves neither from above nor from below, but is horizontally directed so that the federated units mutually check and control their powers."[57] Arendt then evokes the emergence of the council system as a new form of government, and she is careful to point out that history provides us with examples of such councils *of all different types*: "neighborhood councils, professional councils, councils within factories, apartment houses, and so on,"[58] all of which are participatory bodies concerned with public affairs. Arendt's evocation of the council system is especially interesting because it departs from the otherwise purely territorial or geographic division of the public sphere characteristic of almost all proposals aimed at reforming governmental systems. We might recall, in this regard, Jefferson's famous proposition near the end of his life: "the subdivision of the countries into wards."[59] There is no doubt Jefferson's "administrative subdivision" was designed to combat the danger of corruption emanating from the increasing expansion of the private sphere: to the extent that counties are organizational forms that are still too vast to allow every citizen the possibility of effectively participating in public affairs, the smaller "elementary republics," or wards, would devolve public space and place political power more directly in the hands of the ordinary citizen. Yet no matter how this "graduation of authority" may proceed (district, county, state, union), this strategy never departs from the notion that political organization is fundamentally *territorial* and geographic in nature. But Arendt's extreme diversification of the various types of councils induces a *radical pluralism of the public sphere*, particularly in terms of the councils formed on a *socio-professional* (rather than territorial) basis. But given the fact that these new councils must persist beyond the immediacy of the revolutionary effervescence from which they arise (at least historically speaking), it is difficult to see how councils so constituted would not introduce conflicting socio-economic interests into the public sphere itself. The radical pluralism Arendt envisages thus favors a substantial enlargement of the public sphere, whereby an essential dimension of the social now becomes part of the public sphere itself: namely a diversity of social and economic interests that are otherwise always in danger of breaking out into open conflict. And in the final lines of her interview, Arendt pushes her ideas on federalism even further:

> A council-state of this sort, to which the principle of sovereignty would be wholly alien, would be admirably suited to federations of the most various kinds, especially because in it power would be constituted horizontally and not vertically.[60]

This radical pluralization of federalism advanced by Arendt is largely irreconcilable with the schema proposed by Jefferson, according to which there is only one type of federation, namely one established along a vertical plane oriented according to a logic of "graduated authority." The very different horizontalism of which Arendt speaks, however, opens up the possibility of not only relating the lower levels of a federated structure with the higher levels, but it also suggests a means of relating various lower levels with each other, horizontally, without passing through the upper echelons of the institutional pyramid – districts with other districts, counties with other counties, etc. – and all independent of those in control of the upper levels. Arendt's conception of the council system also extends beyond the political sphere and includes socio-economic or professional councils. Arendt's council system is thus structured by means of a *double horizontality* or a transversal horizontality: there are federal relations between councils established on a socio-professional basis, but also federal relations between those economic councils and councils established on a strictly territorial basis. And, insofar as this double relation must also be reversible or reciprocal, there are also federal relations between various territorial councils, as well as between the territorial councils and the socio-economic or professional councils.

If we push the institutional logic of a double federal horizontalism as far as possible, what we arrive at is a complex institutional system articulated on the basis of a double federation: on the one hand, there is a federation of commons constituted on a strictly professional basis and, at the same time, a federation of commons established on a strictly territorial basis. Put differently, we have a socio-economic federation and a political federation. And these two types of commons are concatenated by a transversal horizontalism of the following type: first, the socio-economic commons (commons of production, consumption, seed banks, etc.) are independent of the logic of territoriality; in other words, they are solely constituted in order to take charge of the socio-economic resources or goods around which they were initially formed. Thus, for instance, a common river or a common forest may be granted its own institutional structure and rules. The river or forest may intersect many administrative territories, but it will not submit its institutional norms or rules to these administrative regions. Second, the political commons, on the other hand, are constituted according to a territorial logic: their integrative rules ensure, at the geographic level, the coordination of the various commons that fall within them. Whatever the extent of the territory, these rules are codified as a form of "political constitution." The basic unit of the political commons is the municipality – i.e., the elementary form of local self-government – which revives the older meaning of the Roman *municipium*. Its basic political constitution is therefore a communal constitution. And regardless of the territorial echelon within the institutional pyramid, the entire political constitution is based on the recognition of the individual's fundamental rights. Each political common must vigilantly protect these rights. Henceforth, then, the development of these constitutional rules means the political commons are bodies that are designed to be responsive to any individual, in any community, who believes their subjective rights are threatened or challenged. And, in our view, this double system of a federal commons must be global in scale.

Constructing a Transnational Political Citizenship

What type of citizenship might correspond to this form of global federation? In the first instance, we must immediately exclude any form of "global citizenship" that merely projects the nation-state model onto the global level: the global federation of the commons is in no way a form of world state, and therefore the mode of citizenship that corresponds to it must be plural and decentralized, like the very public spaces in which citizens live. Of course, achieving the objective we are aiming at here undoubtedly means working actively, in the present, to build new forms of citizenship that transcend national borders. But we must not downplay the difficulty of this task by merely evoking the joint crises of nationality and sovereignty. There is no question we are in the midst of a "denationalization of citizenship." But we must not deceive ourselves about the nature of this process. As Catherine Colliot-Thélène writes, "it is the mobility of capital, much more than the mobility of populations, that is undermining national citizenship."[61] Accordingly, there is no "transnational community"[62] that will spontaneously emerge from this dilution of national citizenship, and so it is up to us *construct form a transnational citizenship in the absence of any spontaneous appearance of a transnational community.*

Given today's great ecological peril, it is very tempting to revive the old cosmopolitan chestnut of "global citizenship": we should all be citizens of one and the same world, such that our common belonging alone is sufficient to make us act as responsible global citizens. But can the world really be a single *polis?* From what point of view would we be justified in calling ourselves citizens of the world, and what would be the meaning of this notion of citizenship? We have of course already broached the subject of global citizenship. Kant, for instance, understands the latter as a kind of superstate citizenship that is distinct from "state citizenship" as well as from "infrastate citizenship," i.e., "city citizenship."[63] It is indisputable, in our view, that contemporary state citizenship should not be considered the "norm" of citizenship in general. But, at the same time, there is no denying that the notion of citizenship loses much of its substance once it is diluted on the global scale. As we have seen in Kant, the right of global citizenship is transformed into a "right of resort" that is merely meant to facilitate commercial trade. In other words, this is not a right of residence or anything else we might consider comparable to citizenship. Under these conditions, it is difficult to see how this kind of "global citizenship" could retain any political content. Superstate citizenship thus seems threatened by a constitutive apoliticism, if it is not dissolved outright into a purely technical legalism.

The Stoics, at least, tried to ground the world *polis* on the basis of our common constitution as rational beings (gods and men): to be concerned with the common good (*koinônikon*) was, for them, to put oneself in the service of the whole, and for them one's *polis* was only a small part of this whole. For the Stoics, the universal city is what counts. *To be a human being* is that which makes one a citizen of the world.[64] The difficulty here again, however, is that whatever citizenship gains in extension it tends to lose in quality, such that notions of global citizenship tend invariably to merge, purely and simply, with the mere quality of being human, or with humanity in general (to turn the Stoic formula around). Cosmopolitanism is thus reduced to an apolitical form of citizenship – and is apolitical citizenship not a fundamental contradiction in terms? We cannot escape this difficulty by invoking vague notions of belonging to the "earth" as "a city of men and all living beings."[65] These concepts all subscribe to a notion of global cosmopolitan citizenship that, if not apolitical, is "metapolitical" and, correspondingly, tries to link the rights of global citizenship to the rights of "humanity" as such.[66] What we need to come up with is a form of citizenship that is capable of escaping from the closed alternative between an apolitical global citizenship, be it either infrapolitical or metapolitical, and some extension or other of contemporary state or national forms of political citizenship. What we need to construct, then, is a form of non-state and non-national political citizenship that also avoids all the one-dimensional forms of "legal," "commercial," or even "cultural" citizenship. For us, this creative activity of constructing a new form of citizenship can only arise through instituent praxis (for example, by encouraging the creation of citizen collectives comprised of many nationalities around a common issue, such as an ecological issue).

In addition to extra-national political experiments, we are also drawn to the notion of citizenship that James Holston has beautifully called *insurgent citizenship*. For Holston, the term refers to forms of citizenship practiced by citizens who belong to disadvantaged populations living in the peripheral neighborhoods of large Brazilian metropoles: through their struggle these underprivileged groups managed to win new rights that were hitherto reserved for privileged minorities, especially in terms of public services like health and education.[67] Holston's examples show us how non-state forms of citizenship can take many diverse forms, from the local to the transnational. These heterogeneous forms of citizenship challenge the neat, cumulative logic of citizenship envisioned by Thomas Marshall above (wherein civil rights lead to political rights, and political rights lead to social rights). Transnational citizenship must be decoupled from mere belonging and the rights that are granted on the basis of mere belonging; it must be thought of in terms of practices rather than formal rights granted from above. As Catherine Colliot-Thélène puts it, "citizenship is always a matter of rights, and rights are only ever actualized in practices: in their use, in their defense when they are threatened, and in the struggle to obtain new rights."[68]

But are the practices that produce this type of citizenship sufficient to bring about the creation of the global federation of the commons we need today? We will let Hannah Arendt answer this question for us: "but if you ask me now what prospect it has of being realized, then I must say to you: very slight, if at all. And yet perhaps, after all – in the wake of the next revolution."[69]

Post-Script on Revolution in the Twenty-First Century

Strange, according to Hegel, is our presentiment of a new world in the process of becoming:

> The Spirit in its formation matures slowly and quietly into its new shape, dissolving bit by bit the structure of its previous world, whose tottering state is only hinted at by isolated symptoms. The frivolity and boredom which unsettle the established order, the vague foreboding of something unknown, these are the heralds of approaching change. The gradual crumbling that left unaltered the face of the whole is cut short by a sunburst which, in one flash, illuminates the features of the new world.[1]

If we feel today that the old world is disappearing "bit by bit," the strangeness described by Hegel is re-doubled by the fact that we are unsure as to whether this process of dissolution will lead to the tyrannical and increasingly absolute reign of capital, or a new democratic and anti-capitalist revolution on a planetary scale. Naïve are those who see only the signs of a coming "sunburst" in this collapse, since it may very well introduce a night that will never end. We are well beyond the old certainties that made the nineteenth-century philosophers consistently view such ruptures in history as a re-birth that would invariably lead to a "superior" society. As we pass deeper into the twenty-first century, no one knows for sure what path history might take. But what we can be sure of is the long period of convulsions, confrontations, and upheavals awaiting us. Those who dream of a smooth transition toward a greener and more generous world, who think we can reform capitalism by adding a few more taxes, or who merely await the arrival of a new Keynes or Roosevelt, are gravely mistaken. They seem not to want to understand the ruthless dynamic through which neoliberalism has codified competition as the reigning law governing our world; they do not seem to want to understand the systemic character of today's global oligarchies, and the powers of financialization and state surveillance they wield; and so they refuse to recognize the near insurmountable constraints that neoliberalism's institutional framework imposes on our politics, our behavior, and our subjectivity itself. Under neoliberalism, we remain all but imprisoned.

In short, the impasse we face should be obvious, yet few are able to perceive the extent to which the "reforms" called for today have nothing at all in common with cause of "progress" championed by the struggles of yesterday. How can we fail to understand that the very term "reform" now means anything but social justice? How can we fail to observe, without exception, that the so-called "social democratic" left has condemned itself to political irrelevance by making itself another agent of capitalist globalization and market finance?[2] Hence the sometimes overpowering feeling that capitalism is completely victorious, that it has been installed at the center of our political systems, and that it has deeply penetrated into the very way we live our lives, such that it has changed our "hearts and souls," as Margaret Thatcher wished it would.[3]

It is true that it is not easy to fully grasp the logic governing these ongoing transformations. Out dominant discourses are contradictory, if not denied outright by the facts. The inconsistencies of the media and of politicians are especially striking in this respect: they sing the praises of competition in the morning, weep over unemployment and poverty at noon, and call for the liberalization of the labor market in the evening. Yet behind the contradictions and inconsistencies that petrify the mind and liquefy the will, there is a rationality at work, a "new way of the world" (to reference the title of our previous book). But this fact still seems lost on many. Certain critics reproached us for encouraging fatalism and disengagement. In their view, the financial crisis marked the end of the neoliberal phase and signaled the return of the welfare state and Keynesianism. We saw things differently: we were all told that after the crisis and collapse of this so-called "savage" version of capitalism, the earth would once again revolve in its proper direction after several decades of reversal, and it would be enough to merely "regulate," "revive," and "moralize" to make everything like it was again in 1945. We have seen what these "optimistic" and "voluntarist" prognostications are worth. And so we persist with our view: neoliberal reason has not ceased imposing itself on our lives, not only because it has not yet encountered sufficient counter-force, but also because the manner of its imposition is still not yet well understood. Disciplinary confinement in the context of universal competition is the principle lever that has transformed our societies into environments designed to (greatly) benefit a small but extremely powerful oligarchy who have gained the most from the generalized economic competition that rules our world today.[4]

But we nonetheless insist today's cosmo-capitalism is not destined to go on forever: a reversal of history is possible. Neoliberalism is not a force of nature: its success is a function of deliberate policies that have gradually built the institutional framework within which the merciless struggle between individuals and peoples is given free rein. It is the inflexible rigor of the overall framework – both macro-economically and micro-economically, materially and ideally, politically and socially, etc. – that has created this seemingly nightmarish and all-encompassing system. In fact, it is perfectly accurate, almost by definition, that whatever functions within the institutional framework of the competitive market is necessarily determined by the systemic constraints and goals of the very institutions of capitalism itself. In this sense, the neoliberals absolutely succeeded in their revolution – which was also, and maybe even primarily, a counter-revolution – by consciously creating a coherent system of capitalist institutions. From this strict point of view, the neoliberal institutional constructivists demonstrate a far greater level of consistency and coherence than the so-called social democratic "pragmatists" and "realists."

Disrupting neoliberalism therefore means disrupting today's existing institutional framework and replacing it with another. As Auguste Comte liked to say, in reference to Danton, "only what which is replaced is destroyed." It is necessary for the left, in turn, to re-invent itself in a fully revolutionary manner, as the neoliberals did before them. But the good news is resistance movements and democratic insurrections have been demanding the commons for over ten years, and so many of the first steps have already been taken toward the formation of an alternative form of reason: the common is the new political reason that must replace neoliberal reason.

Reviving the Grandeur of the Idea of "Revolution"

Today's neoliberal environment leaves little room for successfully reforming capitalism through the uses of public law and social protection in their current state. If we are to exit neoliberalism, it will only be through revolution. The concept of revolution can surprise, repel, or seduce. It is a word that is both overused and disquieting. On the one hand, we live in an era of incessant revolutions in the world of marketing and technology, and our political world has likewise been punctuated by "rupture" after ostensible "rupture." For the past thirty years, the "revolutionary" figure has been the innovative entrepreneur who disrupts old habits, or the "maverick" politician without taboos or scruples who dares to employ "courageous measures" against the population. Of course "revolution" is still spoken of on the left, but in a different sense, usually to refer to some partial rupture or other that is ultimately compatible with capitalism: for instance, some champion a "revolution" of our political institutions (a more democratic republic) or a "fiscal revolution" (a more progressive tax regime), while others speak of a "monetary revolution" (exiting the Euro). This manner of speaking testifies to symptomatic hesitation around the idea of a revolution that could reverse the direction of today's policies, change the logic of our institutions, and change the very meaning of collective life.

For the left, revolution seems to be simultaneously undesirable, dangerous, and impossible. Of course, revolution is always undesirable if one is convinced every revolution is intrinsically totalitarian, if not in its aims then at least in its consequences. This is arguably one of the more pernicious ways conservative thought has succeeded in making us believe that any change in the social order would be a mortal danger to our individual freedoms. One of the most common reactionary tropes today is the idea that too much democracy kills freedom, and thus it is consequently better to have the "soft" domination of oligarchies, which are supposedly respectful of freedoms, than a regime of popular sovereignty that might entirely suppress them.[5]

But desirable or not, revolution is in any case impossible in the "developed countries," according to the dominant conservative rhetoric. Revolution is only appropriate for politically backward countries who are naturally expected to repeat the same historical trajectory as the European and American democracies, while, if possible, avoiding some of the "excesses" that have characterized past revolutions. Neoliberalism, in this respect, is not only a counter-revolutionary discourse driven by a constant need to protect against persistent revolutionary threats. Its most radical novelty is its ability to entrench the eternal repetition of the same in our thought, and the concomitant idea that capitalism necessarily extends forever into the future. It is senseless to "defend" capitalism against its enemies, according to this logic, since capitalism *is* reality, or at least the only reality we can ever know. In the mid–1990s, François Furet offered one of the clearest examples of this rhetorical prestidigitation: "the idea of *another* society has become impossible to conceive of, and no one in the world today is offering any advice on the subject or even trying to formulate a new concept. Here we are, condemned to live in the world as it is."[6] Furet thus offers a minor revision of de Tocqueville's similar prediction of the end of revolutionary ideals. We might recall here that, during the 1830s, de Tocqueville argued that democratic individuals, bathed in the respectable materialism of their private interests, were forced to renounce social transformation as the object of their passions. The American and French Revolutions, in this sense, were less a new cycle of political convulsions, and more the beginning of a transformation that would enclose its citizens in an individualistic and utilitarian universe.[7] In a world of private individuals, there is no politics, no common good, and no history. As Furet puts it:

> Modern society however, is characterized by a lack of politics in relation to private, individual existence. It is blind to the idea of the common good, since the members of society, consumed with relativism, have their own individual notions of the common good, and modern society can conceive of it only in terms of a taste for well-being, which divides its members rather then unifying them and thus destroys the community supposedly being constructed in its name. The revolutionary idea is the impossible attempt to circumvent that calamity.[8]

It is not overly difficult to interpret analyses such as these as a continuation of Tocqueville's great insights on bourgeois society: the tendency for individuals to be confined to their private worlds, a certain predilection for compensatory and envious consumption, and the growing influence of bureaucracy. Yet the ultimate question remains: is the privatization of individuals, the culture of consumption, and bureaucratic society the last word of a disenchanted humanity resigned to its fate? This conception of a foreclosed history is the strictly symmetrical counterpart of the "progressive" belief that the human species would progress, surpassing threshold after threshold, by virtue of a providential ascension, or according to the logic of an ever-increasing "accumulation" (*épargne*), to borrow Péguy's term.

Since Furet penned his version of the end of history, as if it was the ultimate historical truth of the fall of the Berlin Wall, subsequent events have cruelly invalidated his thesis. The notion that revolution is a relic of the past seems itself rather out of date. It has already become commonplace to hear talk about some "economic model" or other that is no longer ecologically sustainable, about the explosion of inequality threatening democracy, or about our social fabric being in tatters. In short, it seems things cannot go on as they are, and there is widespread demand for the system to change. The state's inability to corral financial capitalism – even if state actors had the political will, which is far from certain – growing doubts about the possibility of effective social and ecological policies, the rise in ethnic hatred, etc., all suggest that a reversal of the existing order is desirable, and maybe it is even possible. And if revolution is indeed widely desirable, why would it not be possible? While there is no law of history guaranteeing the advent of revolution, and no law protecting us from regression into barbarism, there is likewise no law of history preventing the *possibility* of popular revolution either.

Revolution as the "Self-Institution of Society"

We insist it is both possible and desirable to re-connect with an idea of revolution that has nothing to do with either a millennial apocalypse or the inevitable triumphant march toward a brighter future. In a 1987 interview titled "What Revolution Is," Cornelius Castoriadis tried to dispel some confusion on this subject. "Revolution doesn't mean civil war or bloodshed," argued Castoriadis, "a revolution is a change in some of society's central institutions by the activity of that society itself: the explicit self-transformation of society."[9] Revolution must not be confused with changes to institutions like the family, language, or religions, etc., all of which change according to their own specific temporalities (which in the case of these institutions is usually decades or centuries long). Rather, for Castoriadis, "revolution means that most of the community enters a phase of *political* – meaning *instituting* – activity."[10] Revolution is therefore a moment of acceleration, intensification, and collectivization of the conscious activity we described here as "instituent praxis." *Revolution is the moment when instituent praxis, through a process of "self-instituting," becomes the institutional framework of society itself.* But how, exactly, should we understand this idea of revolution as self-institutional activity?

To answer this question, it is important to return to the alternative meanings of the concept of revolution in the modern world, as described by Hannah Arendt.[11] Arendt identifies the origins of the term's political meaning as deriving from its prior astronomical uses ("the regular, lawfully revolving motion of the stars"): the word initially designated "a recurring, cyclical movement" (which is of course very different from the idea of "novelty" and even "violence"), and its transposition into the world of human affairs initially referred to a "restoration" of an original state. Arendt cites the example of the Glorious Revolution of 1688 to show how the word revolution, employed for the first time in its modern political sense, referred to "a movement of revolving back to some pre-established point and, by implication, of swinging back into a preordained order" – which in this case was "a restoration of monarchical power to its former righteousness and glory."[12] In the subsequent context of the French Revolution, the word came to mean the inexorability of a process that no human power is able to stop, rather than the return to some prior state of affairs. From then on, the term revolution signified "a mighty undercurrent sweeping men with it," an "irresistible process" that was expressed through metaphors like "stream," "torrent," or "current."[13] From this perspective, revolution is not fundamentally the work of humans: "we did not make the revolution, the revolution made us," as Danton puts it in a play by Georg Büchner.[14] Hegel further modified the concept by theorizing the new "force" and the "necessity" of revolution as a "process" of universal history. In fact, the quotation that began our post-script suggests a quasi-natural process of maturation that is periodically interrupted by a sudden "sunburst." Indeed, Hegel uses the same metaphor of the "glorious sunrise" in his *Philosophy of History* in the context of the French Revolution, but now it is the revolution's distinctiveness from the orderly rotation of the planets around the sun that he stresses. Arendt famously opposed this particular sense of the term and preferred to adopt a concept of revolution that favored the American Revolution over the French. She preferred an understanding of revolution as a new "foundation of freedom" through the creation of institutions designed to inaugurate a *novus ordo saeculorum*.[15] The conclusion Arendt drew from her comparison between the French and American Revolutions is that the latter's refusal to pose the "social question" allowed the American Revolution to avoid the trap of the Terror. By focusing on "the foundation of freedom" in the public sphere rather than "the liberation of man from suffering," the American Revolution avoided doom, because "every attempt to solve the social question with political means leads into terror."[16]

Castoriadis responded to Arendt's criticism of the French Revolution in a 1989 interview titled "the Idea of Revolution."[17] Speaking of the "specificity of the historical creation of the French Revolution," Castoriadis emphasized the latter's radicalism in relation to the American Revolution. In North America, the institutionalization of society was limited to the public political sphere: the Founding Fathers did indeed inherit a social state from the past, namely the institution of "agrarian freehold." The Founding Fathers had no qualms with this social state of affairs, and therefore had no intention of changing it. In other words, "for the American Founding Father there was a social given" and "all that was to be furnished was the corresponding political structure."[18] In contrast,

> the grandeur and the originality of the French Revolution is to be found, in my judgment, in that very thing for which it is so often reproached, viz., that it tends to call into question, *de jure*, the existing institution of society in its *totality*. The French Revolution couldn't create politically if it did not destroy socially.[19]

Castoriadis is thus doubly critical of Arendt's assessment. First, Castoriadis argues that Arendt misunderstands (as we have already mentioned) the fact that "the social question *is* a political question" and thus "in contemporary terms: is not economic power *ipso facto* also political power?"[20] And secondly, Arendt neglects the fact that the *Ancien Régime* was a "total social structure" and not merely a political apparatus:

> It is the whole social edifice that was to be reconstructed, for without that a political transformation was materially impossible. The French Revolution could not, even if it wanted to, simply superimpose a democratic political organization onto a social regime that it would have left intact.[21]

And consequently, "where the American Revolution could build on the illusion of an 'equality' already existing in its social state," the French Revolution had to deal with an ancient past that compelled the revolution to "attack . . . the social edifice as such."[22] In France, the revolution thus took on the sense of a total self-institutionalization of society, and it is this sense of the term we need to re-connect with today in order to further the conscious self-transformation of society. Indeed, the limits the French Revolution encountered issued precisely from the dominant political imaginary – namely the state structure and the corresponding notion of sovereignty – and meant the logic of representation ultimately prevailed.[23]

Understood in its purest sense, revolution is the "explicit reinstitution of society" by "the collective and autonomous activity" of the society itself, or at least a large part of it.[24] It is this notion of revolution that must be the basis of our current attempts to develop a project of society's radical transformation. "Counter-conduct" alone will no longer suffice,[25] because neoliberal reason is itself another "total social structure," one that is very different from the *Ancien Régime*, no doubt, but one which nonetheless imposes the same suffocating totality on those who try to overthrow it. The radical character of this totality nullifies any conception of revolution as the mere restoration of a prior state of affairs before the advent of neoliberalism, just as it forbids us from thinking of revolution as an organic process of maturation or the manifestation of immanent historical necessity – whether it is conceived as a sunrise or a re-birth. Of all the different meanings associated with the term revolution, as examined by Arendt, only its sense of radical "novelty" remains useful to us, insofar as this meaning points us toward the creation of a new order through the invention of political institutions whose purpose is to overturn the entire structure of society. And a revolutionary process such as this can only be conceived as arising from very diverse economic, social, political, and cultural practices. On the condition that common lines of force eventually emerge through the links created between these diverse actors and practices, it is possible that an "imaginary signification" will crystalize and coalesce between what were otherwise merely dispersed, disparate, or even marginal practices.

Instituting the Unappropriable

The principle of the common is at the heart of this revolutionary project, as we understand it. We think it is necessary here, then, to spell out as precisely as possible our definition of this principle by condensing its core features as we have identified them throughout the course of this analysis. The following remarks have this purpose, and none other.

1. We have systematically argued throughout the book for the noun "common," rather than using its more habitual adjectival form. To this end, we have even gone so far as to remove the article from the title of the book itself. Our goal was to signify, at the outset, our understanding of the common as a *principle*, and not a thing, a substance, or a quality belonging to a thing or a group of things. But what do we mean by "principle"? A principle is not just what one starts with, and that which influences everything that follows. Nor is a principle a "beginning" that "fades away after its initial use," nor a simple "point of departure" that one leaves behind and never returns to. A principle is a true beginning, a "beginning that always begins," which is to say a beginning that governs and guides all that

follows.[26] The Greek *arche* has the double meaning of both "beginning" and "command": *arche* is the source from which all else derives.[27] The common is a political principle in the sense that it orders, commands, and governs all subsequent political activity. Or, if one prefers the logical sense of the term, a principle is the premise of a rational proposition or demonstration, and this also accords with the sense we have given the term in the third part of the book: the nine "political propositions" are meant to be viewed as logical principles in the sense that they are premises designed to guide a future rationality and, moreover, are enunciated in such a way as to indicate the manner in which the common itself should be viewed as a political principle.

2. If the common is indeed a political principle, it is not a principle like most others; it is a *political principle*, or better yet, it is *the* political principle. By "politics" we mean the deliberative activity in which citizens collectively determine what is just, and the decisions and actions that proceed from this collective activity. Politics is therefore not an activity reserved for a minority of professionals; it is not determined by the competence of the specialist, nor is it a trade or career. Politics is the business of any person, whatever their status or occupation, who desires or wishes to participate in public deliberation.[28] Politics, in its essence, is about "taking part" in public deliberation, and the activity of "collectively sharing one's words and ideas." While the dream of a politics founded on scientific proof, or on the model of evidence-based medicine,[29] is still alive and well, it is crucial to recall the elementary truth that a politics based on scientific truth would be no politics at all: without deliberation and the exercise of popular judgment, there can be no politics. A "scientific politics" is not therefore a form of politics, but at most the scientific negation of politics, if not its outright annihilation.
3. As a political principle, the common makes participation in the same activity the basis of political obligation: co-activity as co-obligation. We must recall how the term *munus* at the root of the term "common" signifies both obligation and activity. This means that no form of belonging – ethnicity, nationality, humanity, etc. – can itself constitute the basis of political obligation. Likewise, political obligation cannot be sacred or religious in character, which means that any transcendental source, any authority external to activity, must be rejected. Political obligation proceeds entirely from common action: it draws all its force from the practical commitments binding all those who collectively developed the rules governing their activity, and it is only valid in relation to the co-participants of this same activity.
4. Thus understood, the common cannot be an *object*, at least in the sense of an object of desire or of the will. It resists all forms of objectification: it cannot even be said to be the quality by which an object is perceived as desirable. The common is not an *end* after which one aims or strives; we must refrain from confusing the common with what is often called the "common good." In the discourse of political philosophy, the common good designates that which is sought after and defined together. The common good is therefore often confused with the just, insofar as it tends to coincide with the common benefit that all forms of collective deliberation

strive to achieve.[30] The common good, in this sense, is the desirable *par excellence*. This is not to say that a society, of whatever form, can dispense with the need to determine the content of the "common good" in some way or another, but it is simply to say that the good must always be determined in common. The common is thus the principle that orients the search for the "common good" *qua* object, since truly seeking the common good necessitates common deliberative activity. In other words, the common always precedes the "common good."

5. Insofar as the common is not an object, neither is it thing (*res*), nor the essential property or a characteristic of a thing. We must not confuse the common with something held in common by virtue of this or that natural or inherent property: light or air, for example, are undeniably "commons," but this is not the same as being the common. The common should also not be confused with various forms of legal commons, which can be material (the high seas, transnational rivers, sites designated as the common heritage of humanity, etc.) or immaterial (ideas, scientific information and discoveries, intellectual production in the public domain, etc.). The juridical category of "common things" (*res communis*) necessarily detaches common objects from activity, and it is only through activity that such things truly become common. This approach must be abandoned.
6. We can, on the other hand, speak of *the commons* in order to designate those objects that have been taken over by an activity of "sharing" or "pooling," which is to say rendered common through this activity. Again, nothing is inherently or naturally common: only collective practices determine the common character of a thing or a group of things. There are, therefore, a very diverse range of commons (rivers, forests, modes of production, seeds, knowledges, etc.) depending on the types of activities instituted by the actors in charge of managing and preserving such commons. The natural properties of the common object or resource will of course have much to do with the type of activity or activities that make such resources common, but in every case it is this activity that "communizes" the given object and inscribes it in an institutional space through the production of specific rules governing its maintenance.
7. The common is above all a matter of *institution* and *governance*. Whenever we have spoken about the institutionalization of the common, we have tried to stress the extent to which the common, in general, is always generated from an institutional act. For the mere fact that the common is a principle does not make it real: if the principle of the common did not need to be instituted, but only recognized, then all commons would be the common already. Rather, the common can only exist, which is to say instituted, by practices that define certain operational rules. And this institutionalization must be carried on beyond the initial act that creates the common. It must be sustained, in the long run, by practices that are able to modify the institutional rules that these practices themselves established. This is what we have called "instituent praxis." Instituent praxis is not a form of "management," in the sense of administrative power divorced from the power of decision. The managerial illusion is in fact linked to the naturalistic view of the common: if the common is a function of the natural

properties of things, its status as common is often determined by a managerial consensus divorced from the actual social conflicts that traverse social space.

Unlike "management," "governance" embraces social conflicts and explicitly deals with them through collective decisions about the rules governing the common. Instituent praxis is thus the *practical governance of the commons* by the collectives that establish the common in which they exist.

8. As a political principle, the common applies to the social sphere as well as the public political sphere. Limiting the commons to the political sphere is simply out of the question: the commons must not abandon the entire sphere of production and exchange to the war of private interests or state monopoly. However, the common should not be viewed as a "third way" that can be interposed between the market and the state, or a new "mode of production," a "third sector" of the economy that exists alongside the private and the public. The primacy of the common does not, therefore, imply the abolition of private property nor, *a fortiori*, the abolition of the market. On the contrary, the principle of the common demands the market's subordination to the common and, in this sense, implies the *limitation* of the right of ownership and the market – not by merely subtracting certain objects from the realm of commercial exchange and thereby preserving them for common use, but by abolishing the right of abuse (*jus abutendi*) that permits a thing to be entirely surrendered to the egoistic will of its owner.
9. If the *common* is a transversal political principle that cuts across these two spheres, and if the *commons* are institutional spaces opened up by certain practices relating to certain objects, whatever the type, it follows that there are political commons as well as social commons. The political commons are concerned with "public affairs" at all levels, from the local to the global, and by way of the national. The socio-economic sphere is solely organized by the criteria of social activity, wherever it extends, according to a federal logic. The political sphere is organized on a strictly territorial basis through a gradation of levels also organized according to a federal logic. The municipality constitutes the elementary form of self-government in the political sphere, and is in this sense the cellular form of the political common. The nation-state model – unitary, centralized, and ordered by the principle of sovereignty – is strictly forbidden by this logic. The political principle of the common is thus based on a double federation: a federation of socio-economic commons founded on a socio-professional basis, and a federation of political commons founded on a territorial basis. Together, these spheres form a *democracy of the commons*.
10. As a principle, the common enshrines the norm of *unappropriability*. The fundamental purpose of the principle of the common is to transform all social relations according to this norm. Unappropriation does not refer here to that which *cannot* be appropriated – i.e., what is factually impossible to appropriate – but rather what *should not* be appropriated – i.e., what is no longer *permissible* to appropriate because it is protected by the practice of common use. It therefore falls to instituent praxis to determine what is unappropriable. It may be objected

that what is unappropriable cannot be the object of an institution but can only be based on the recognition of the fact of unappropriability as such: the will to institute unappropriability is to make the latter depend on the act of one or many subjects who, by definition, are engaged in an act of appropriation. But this is to forget that the collective subject is in fact produced by the act of instituting the common itself, and does not precede this act. And, more importantly, it is to forget that there is an essential difference between two types of appropriation: appropriation-*belonging*, through which something becomes the object of ownership, and appropriation-*destination*, through which something is directed toward a certain end – specifically, the satisfaction of social needs. To institute unappropriability is to subtract something from appropriation-*belonging* in order to more effectively realize some form of appropriation-*destination*; it is, in short, to prohibit its "appropriation" in order to more effectively "appropriate" it for some social purpose – for example, appropriating land to address food insecurity. The principle of the common regulates use without creating property, and without granting itself the power to dispose of the commons as its master. This is why we prefer not to speak of "common goods," even if we understand the strategic benefits of this term as a rallying cry for ongoing struggles. There are no "common goods": there are only commons to be institutionalized, or commons to be made common.

Notes

Introduction

1 See Michael Löwy, *Écosocialisme, l'alternative radicale à la catastrophe écologique capitaliste* (Paris: Mille et une Nuits, 2011).
2 Isabelle Stengers, *In Catastrophic Times: Resisting the Coming Barbarism*, trans. Andrew Goffey (London: Open Humanities Press, 2015).
3 See one of our previous books, *The New Way of the World: On Neoliberal Society*, trans. Gregory Elliott (London: Verso, 2017).
4 Joel Kovel, *The Enemy of Nature: The End of Capitalism or the End of the World?* (New York: Zed Books, 2002).
5 UNDP, *Fighting Climate Change: Human Solidarity in a Divided World, Human Development Report 2007/2008*: http://hdr.undp.org/sites/default/files/reports/268/hdr_20072008_en_complete.pdf.
6 Harald Welzer, *Climate Wars: Why People Will Be Killed in the Twenty-first Century*, trans. Patrick Camiller (London: Polity, 2012), 6.
7 See John Bellamy Foster, "Ecology against Capitalism." *Monthly Review*, vol. 53, no. 5 (October 2001).
8 Ugo Mattei, "Rendre inaliénables les biens communs." *Le Monde diplomatique*, December 2011. See Ugo Mattei, *Beni comuni: Un manifesto* (Rome: Laterza, 2011), viii–ix.
9 We gladly defer here to Cornelius Castoriadis's wise words following the discontinuation of *Socialisme ou Barbarie* in 1967: "revolutionary activity will again become possible only when a radical ideological reconstruction will become capable of meeting up with a real social movement." See Cornelius Castoriadis, "The Suspension of Publication of *Socialisme ou Barbarie*," in *Cornelius Castoriadis, Political and Social Writings, Volume 3, 1961–1979,* trans. David Ames Curtis (Minneapolis: University of Minnesota Press, 1993), 121.
10 Moshe Lewin, *The Soviet Century* (New York: Verso, 2005), 379.
11 First Communiqué of the *Cordinadora de defensa del agua y la vida* (Cochabamba, December 1999).
12 Michael Hardt and Antonio Negri, *Multitude* (New York: Penguin, 2004) and *Commonwealth* (Cambridge: Belknap, 2009).
13 See Hervé Kempf, *How the Rich are Destroying the Planet* (Vermont: Chelsea Green Publishing, 2008).
14 This phrase comes from the manifesto *Our Commons, Who, Why?* See mustereklerimiz.org.
15 Ferhat Taylan, "Taksim, une place vitale." *La Revue des Livres*, no. 12, (July–August, 2013), 57.
16 See Zeynep Gambetti, "The Gezi Resistance as Surplus Value" (July 5, 2013. www.jadaliyya.com). Gambetti, professor of political theory at Bosphorus University,

shows how the "value" created by this movement is far in excess, in terms of meaning and praxis, of the individuals that participated in the event.

1 Archaeology of the Common

1 Auguste Blanqui, "Lettre à Maillard, 6 juin 1852." *Maintenant il faut des armes,* La Fabrique (Paris, 2006), 176. In 1852, after Louis Napoléon Bonaparte's coup d'état, Blanqui declared: "what then, I beg you, is a democrat? It is a vague, banal word, without precise meaning, a word made of rubber." He then added: "What opinion would not accommodate itself under this sign? Everyone claims to be a democrat, especially aristocrats."

2 Translator's note: Dardot and Laval conclude their prior book – *The New Way of the World,* trans. Gregory Elliott (London: Verso, 2013) – with the claim that only the creation of a new "reason of the commons" will be able to supplant today's dominant neoliberal reason (ibid., 321). This book is their attempt to provide a detailed account of this new "reason."

3 Émile Benveniste, *Dictionary of Indo-European Concepts and Society* (Chicago: HAU Publishing, 2016), 69.

4 Aristotle, *Politics,* trans. Ernest Barker (Oxford: Oxford University Press, 2009), 112 (1282b).

5 Aristotle, *Nichomachean Ethics,* trans. Terence Irwin (Indianapolis: Hackett Publishing, 1999), 150 (1170b). It is significant that *philia,* in the sense of civic friendship, is conceived by Aristotle as the affective outcome of participation in the same activity, and not as an affective community realized by a strict hierarchy of functions (as in the case of the Platonic community where friendship is always "diluted"). See Aristotle, *Politics,* 42 (1262b).

6 We offer a more detailed discussion of this topic at the beginning of Chapter 6.

7 See Aristotle, *Politics*: "it is clear from what has been said that the better system is that under which property is privately owned but is put to common use" (ibid., 47 [1262b]), and, "on our view, property ought not to be owned in common, as some writers have maintained – though it ought to be used in common and as friends treat their belongings, but none of the citizens should go in need of subsistence" (ibid., 274 [1329b]).

8 Ibid., 47 (1263b): "on such a scheme, too, moral goodness will ensure that the property of each is made to serve the use of all, in the spirit of the proverb which says 'Friends' goods are goods in common.'"

9 See, for example, Riccardo Petrella, *Le Bien commun. Éloge de la solidarité,* Éditions (Lausanne: Page deux, 1997) and *Pour une nouvelle narration du monde,* (Montréal: Écosociété, 2007), 17. And for a different perspective, see François Flahaut, *Où est passé le Bien commun?* (Paris: Mille et une Nuits, 2011).

10 It should be noted that the category of "common goods" has been susceptible to specific modifications throughout the course of various struggles against neoliberalism. The Italian movement against the privatization of water, for instance, which added the category of "common goods" to its Civil Code thanks to the remarkable work of the Rodotà Commission (2007–2008) interpreted the common in a legally innovative way by integrating it into its definition of "participatory democracy" (see Part 3, "Political Proposition 7"). On the other hand, the economists working for the United Nations Development Programme (UNDP) developed a

theory of "global public goods" that is a much clearer example of the logic of legal reification. See Part 3, "Political Proposition 8."

11 Cicero, *On Duties* (Cambridge: Cambridge University Press, 1991), 111 (Book III, v. 30).

12 Ibid., 109–110 (Book III, v. 27).

13 Ibid., 111 (Book III, v. 31). See the commentary in Jean Gaudement, "Utilitas publica," *Revue historique de droit français et étranger*, no. 29, 1951, reprinted in Christian Lazzeri and Dominique Reynié, *Politiques de l'intérêt* (Besançon: Presses universitaires franc-comtoises, 1998), 11.

14 Ibid., 116 (Book III, v. 47).

15 We will return to these two meanings of "public" in Chapter 6 and in Part 3, "Political Proposition 1."

16 In numerous other languages, including English and to a lesser degree French and Italian, the very substantial overlapping of these two notions continues to this day. See Elio Dovere, "Le discours juridique et moral de l'utilitas à Rome," in Alain Caillé, Christian Lazzeri and Michel Senellart, *Histoire raisonnée de la philosophie morale et politique* (Paris: La Découverte, 2001), 108–115.

17 Elio Dovere, "Le discours juridique et moral de l'utilitas à Rome," 115. The same applies for the term *jus publicum*.

18 Jean Gaudemet, "Utilitas publica," 21.

19 Augustine, *The City of God*, Book XIX, Ch. 21, vol. 25 (Washington, D.C.: Catholic University of America Press, 2008), 232.

20 Jean Bodin, *On Sovereignty: Four Chapters from The Six Books of the Commonwealth* (Cambridge: Cambridge University Press, 1992), 1.

21 Jean-Jacques Rousseau, *The Social Contract* (Oxford: Oxford University Press, 1994), 63.

The purpose of the institution of the state is, of course, the common good itself.

22 See Yves Sassier, *Structures du pouvoir, royauté et res publica* (Rennes: PUR, 2004).

23 Qtd. in Yves Sassier, "Bien commun et *utilitas communis* au XIIe siècle, un nouvel essor?" *Revue française d'histoire des idées politiques*, no. 32 (2010), 251.

24 John Marenbon, *The Philosophy of Peter Abelard* (Cambridge: Cambridge University Press, 1997).

25 Yves Sassier, "Bien commun et *utilitas communis*," 252.

26 Aristotle's *Politics* was translated into Latin in 1260.

27 Mathew Kempshall (*The Common Good in Late Medieval Political Thought,* Oxford: Clarendon Press, 1999) shows that the common good, for the theologians, borrowed much from the Aristotelian notion of *ordo*, which refers, as demonstrated by Benveniste, to a Indo-European category that designates "order, arrangement, the close mutual adaptation of the parts of a whole to one another" (see Benveniste, *Dictionary of Indo-European Concepts and Society*, 387).

28 Bénédicte Sère, "Aristote et le bien commun au Moyen Âge. Une histoire, une historiographie." *Revue française d'histoire des idées politiques,* no. 32 (2010), 281.

29 André Modde, "Le Bien commun dans la philosophie de saint Thomas." *Revue philosophique de Louvain,* vol. 47, no. 14 (1949), 230.

30 Ponitifical Council, "Justice and Peace," "Compendium of the Social Doctrine of the Church." See online at www.vatican.va. Observe the difference with Aristotle: whereas for Aristotle the private use of property ought to be rendered common through legislation, it is the good, in Thomasism, that tells us whether private usage should be directed toward the common. We thus pass imperceptibly from common use to

common good, which is not at all a neutral passage insofar as use is still governed within a purely private system.

31 Virgil, *The Aeneid*, trans. Robert Fagles (New York: Viking, 2006), 221.

32 Paul Veyne indicates in a note to his translation of *L'Énéide* (Paris: Albin Michel-Les Belles, 2012) that "the Trojans suggest that they require very little," which, from his point of view, justifies the use of the qualification "ne . . . que" in French.

33 Marie-Alice Chardeaux, *Les Chose Communes* (Paris: LGDJ, 2006), 1 (note. 4).

34 Ibid., 3–4.

35 Ibid., 16–17.

36 As put by Yan Thomas ("Res, chose et patrimoine. Note sur le rapport sujet-objet en droit romain." *Archives de philosophie du droit*, no. 25, 1980, 422), the word *patrimonium* "signifies the 'legal status of the *pater*,' while everything *matrimonium* designates the legal status of the mother' (the *-monium* suffix indicates the juridical condition of the name of the agent to which it aggregates)." The term eventually lost all its statutory meaning and began to denote the evaluation of goods by money, or the "objectification of the wrold of commodities."

37 For the distinction between *sanctum* and *sacer,* see Émile Benveniste, *Dictionary of Indo-European Concepts and Society*, 460. *Sanctum* is that which is defended and protected against the violations of humans through the use of sanctions. It is in this sense that one may speak of *leges sanctae*. That which is sacred, and denoted through the word *sacer,* means "consecrated to the gods."

38 Marie-Alice Chardeaux, *Les Chose Communes*, 135 (footnote 163). We will return to the importance of this qualification in Chapter 6.

39 Ibid., 17.

40 Ibid., 18.

41 Ibid., 135. The author refers to a text by Yan Thomas: "*Imago naturae.* Note sur l'institutionnalité de la nature à Rome," in *Théologie et droit dans la science politique de l'État moderne,* Proceedings of the Round Table organized by l'École française de Rome with the assistance of CNRS, no. 147 (1991), 201 and 203.

42 Ibid. The author refers to a text by Yan Thomas, cited above, 211.

43 The passage "*cunctis . . . patentem*" from the *Aeneid* cited above takes on its full significance.

44 Marie-Alice Chardeaux, *Les Chose Communes*, 134.

45 Ibid., 136.

46 Yan Thomas, "Res, chose et patrimoine," 425–426

47 Ibid., 416. We will return to this conceptualization of *res* in Chapter 6.

48 Ibid., 417.

49 Ibid., 425. "*Res, pecunia, bona*: these terms were developed during the turn of the third and second centuries B.C.E and were part of a language of goods situated on a completely different plane, and which corresponds to a mode of thought that is completely different from the traditional vocabulary. We are dealing here with abstract and universal terms totally divorced from their familial and social connotations. The 'object' is no longer inscribed within a statute, but it is viewed separately in a world of objects that now have their own values as determined through exchange and money."

50 Marie-Alice Chardeaux, *Les Choses communes,* 8.

51 Ibid., 11.

52 Ibid., 6–7.

53 Qtd. in Pierre-Joseph Proudhon, *What is Property?*, trans. Donald R. Kelley and Bonnie G. Smith (Cambridge: Cambridge University Press, 1994), 72.

54 Gilles Martin, *De la responsabilité civile pour faits de pollution au droit à l'Environnement*, (Nice: thèse soutenue, 1976), 115.
55 Marie-Alice Chardeaux, *Les Choses communes*, 116.
56 Jean Domat, *Les Lois civiles dans leur ordre naturel* (Paris: Nicolas Gosselin, 1713). It should be noted that if Domat distinguishes things in common from things public (rivers, streams, shorelines, highways), he nonetheless submits everything to the same juridical regime – i.e., common things – by subtracting things held in common from the domain of sovereignty (Marie-Alice Chardeaux, *Les Choses communes*, 34).
57 Hugo Grotius, *The Law of War and Peace* (New York: Bobbs-Merrill Company, 1925), 191.
58 J.L.E. Ortolon, *Explication historique des Instituts de l'empereur Justinien*, livre 2, (Paris: Joubert Libraire-Éditeur, 1840), 30. Qtd. in Marie-Alice Chardeaux, *Les Choses communes*, 112.
59 Marie-Alice Chardeaux, *Les Choses communes*, 116.
60 Ibid., 131.
61 See Chapter 4.
62 Proudhon's citation of Charles Comte reproduced above could easily pass as an example of the criterion of non-rivalry. A very similar sensibility is found in the words of the jurist Demolombe: "The creations of the intellect, of literature, science and art may, at the same time, profit each and all, entirely, completely, without the enjoyment of one preventing or diminishing the enjoyment of an other." Qtd. in Mikhaïl Xifaras, *La Propriété. Étude de philosophie du droit* (Paris: PUF, 2004), 380.
63 Marie-Alice Chardeaux, *Les Choses communes*, 191–228.
64 Ibid., 213–214.
65 Ibid., 225.
66 Judith Revel, "Produire de la subjectivité, produire du commun : trois difficultés et un post-scriptum un peu long sur ce que le commun n'est pas." From the seminar "Du public au commun," December 5, 2010, 6.
67 *Dictionnaire historique de la langue française*, Alain Rey (ed.) (Paris: Le Robert, 1992), 455.
68 Judith Revel, "Produire de la subjectivité, produire du commun," 6.
69 René Descartes, *Meditations on First Philosophy*, trans. Michael Moriarty (Oxford: Oxford University Press, 2008), 23. Translator's note: Dardot and Laval do not of course reference the English translation of Descartes's *vulgus* in their original text, but rather draw attention to its conventional translation into the French term *commun*.
70 Ibid., 24.
71 Descartes's celebrated formula "common sense is the most fairly distributed thing in the world" must not of course be taken literally to mean all men are endowed with it in equal amounts.
72 On this point, see Jacques Brunschwig, "En quel sens le sens commun est-il commun?", in *Corps et âme*, Gilbert Romeyer Dherbey (ed.), (Paris: Vrin, 1996), 208. One example of Aristotle's notion of "common sense" is movement: movement is not perceived by one sense in particular, but by different senses all at once, insofar as an object in motion has color, makes a sounds, etc.
73 Immanuel Kant, *The Critique of Judgment*, trans. Paul Guyer (Cambridge: Cambridge University Press, 2000), 173.
74 Ibid., 175.
75 Ibid.
76 Lord Shaftsbury, *Characteristics of Men, Manners Opinions and Times* (Cambridge: Cambridge University Press, 2000), 49.

77 Barbara Cassin (ed.), *Vocabulaire européen des philosophies*, 242. It is in this context that one should interpret the title of Thomas Paine's *Common Sense* (1776), which laid out all the arguments for rebellion in the American colonies.
78 Hans-Georg Gadamer, *Truth and Method* (New York: Continuum, 2004).
79 Hannah Arendt, *Lectures on Kant's Political Philosophy* (Chicago: University of Chicago Press, 1992), 44.
80 For more on this distinction, we refer you to Pierre Aubenque, *Le Problème de l'être chez Aristote* (Paris: PUF, 1972), 210.
81 G.W.F. Hegel, *Encyclopedia of the Philosophical Sciences in Basic Outline. Part 1: Science of Logic*, trans. Klaus Brinkmann and Daniel O. Dahlstrom (Cambridge: Cambridge University Press, 2010), 237.
82 Ibid., 238.
83 Rousseau, *The Social Contract*, 66.
84 Hegel, *Encyclopedia of the Philosophical Sciences in Basic Outline*, 238.
85 Hegel, *Outlines of a Philosophy of Right*, trans. T.M. Knox (Oxford: Oxford University Press, 2008), 230.
86 Hegel, *Encyclopedia of the Philosophical Sciences in Basic Outline*, 249.
87 Ibid., 250.
88 Ibid.
89 Ibid.
90 Catherine Collioyt-Thélène, *La Démocratie sans 'demos'* (Paris: PUF, 2011), 138.
91 Ibid., p. 137.
92 For the distinction between these three senses in Kant see ibid., 133–132.
93 Friedrich Nietzsche, *Beyond Good and Evil*, trans. Judith Norman (Cambridge: Cambridge University Press, 2002), 40.
94 In *The Making of the English Working Class* (published in 1963), Thompson discusses the example of shop looting during a period of rising prices. He subsequently defines the moral economy of the poor in these terms: "consistent traditional view of social norms and obligations, of the proper economic functions of several parties within the community" ("The Moral Economy of the English Crowd in the Eighteenth Century," *The Past and Present Society*, no. 50 [Feb, 1971], 79).
95 Karl Marx, "Letter to Pavel Vassilyevich Annenkov, December 28th, 1946," *The Letters of Karl Marx* (New Jersey: Prentice Hall, 1979), 45.
96 This turn of phrase comes from Chapter 1 of Peter Linebaugh's book *Stop Thief!* (Oakland: PM Press, 2014), 13: "Human solidarity as expressed in the slogan 'all for one and one for all' is the foundation of commoning. In capitalist society, this principle is permitted in childhood games or in military combat."
97 Léon Duguit, *Souveraineté et liberté: Leçons faites à l'Université de Columbia* (Paris: *Félix Alcan*), 167–168.

2 The Communist Burden; or Communism Against the Common

1 Leon Festinger, *A Theory of Cognitive Dissonance* (Stanford: Stanford University Press, 1957).
2 Domenico Losurdo's rehabilitation of Stalin, which employs terms like "objective context" and "comparatism," is indicative of how opposition to capitalism and neoliberalism has the potential to fuel supposedly demystifying "counter-histories" that are, in reality, narratives designed to trivialize the terrorism of bureaucratic

communism. See Domenico Losurdo, *Staline: Histoire et critique d'une légende noire* (Brussels: Aden, 2011) and *Fuir l'histoire? La révolution russe et la révolution chinoise aujourd'hui* (Paris: Delga, 2007). And while Alain Badiou concedes that criticism of Stalin is and remains necessary, he follows this assertion by claiming that the only rigorous critique of Stalin comes from Mao: "the political critique of Stalin and his terrorist vision of the State needed to be undertaken in a rigorous way, from the perspective of revolutionary politics itself, and Mao had begun to do as much in a number of his writings." Alain Badiou, *The Communist Hypothesis*, trans. David Macey and Steve Corcoran (London: Verso, 2010), 251. Later in the chapter, we will look more closely at Badiou's thoughts on Mao and the part he played in the Cultural Revolution.

3 Jean-Luc Nancy, "Communism, the Word." *The Idea of Communism*, ed. Costas Douzinas and Slavoj Žižek (London: Verso, 2010), 145.

4 Nancy, "Communism, the Word," 146.

5 We should also reference here Sylvain Maréchal's "Manifesto of Equals and the Fragment for a Project of Economic Decree," in Philippe Buonarrotti's *History of Babeuf's Conspiracy of Equality* (London: H. Hetherington Publishing, 1836), 314.

6 Buonarrotti, *Babeuf's Conspiracy for Equality*, 317.

7 See Philippe Riviale, *L'Impatience du bonheur. Apologie de Gracchus Babeuf* (Paris: Payot, 2001), 275.

8 Buonarrotti, *Babeuf's Conspiracy for Equality*, 315.

9 Ibid.

10 See Victor Serge, "Thirty Years After the Russian Revolution." *Critique*, no. 1, vol. 28 (May 2009): 239–258.

11 The denial of the gulags, for instance, was a lasting phenomenon. It took the publication of "camp literature," such as the admirable *The Kolyma Tales* (New York: Penguin, 1995) for the reality of the camps to be recognized by the communist parties. See Jean-Jacques Marie, *Le Goulag* (Paris: PUF, 1999).

12 According to Durkheim, "all communist theories formulated later derive from Platonic communism, of which they are hardly more than variations." See Émile Durkheim, *Socialism*, trans. Charlotte Sattler (New York: Collier Books, 1958), 68.

13 See Jacques Grandjonc, *Communisme/Kommunismus, Communism. Origine et développement international de la terminologie communautaire prémarxiste des utopistes aux néo-babouvistes 1785–1842*, vol. 2 (Trier: Karl-Marx-Haus, 2013), 332.

14 Durkheim, *Socialism*, 73.

15 Plato, *The Republic*, trans. Desmond Lee (New York: Penguin Books, 1987), 125 (417b).

16 Ibid., 188 (463b).

17 Ibid., 125 (416e). The term "syssitia" designates a common meal. It is revealing in this regard that Pierre Leroux sees a form of communism *avant la lettre* in the Spartan practice of communal meals.

18 See Chapter 6.

19 Aristotle, *Politics*, 41–43.

20 See Gérard Raulet's article "Communism" in *Grand Dictionnaire de philosophie*, Michel Blay (ed.) (Paris: Larousse, 2003). Engels' examination of the communist sects and the German Peasants War contrastingly emphasizes this religion dimension. See Friedrich Engels, "On the Early History of Christianity in Marx and Engels," in *On Religion* (New York: Dover Publications, 2008). This point is discussed at length in Pierre Dardot and Christian Laval, *Marx, Prénom : Karl* (Paris: Gallimard, 2012), 622.

21 Proudhon, who was to some extent anti-communist, emphasized in his strongly anti-clerical writings how much the Church exalted a certain form of communism,

both in its history and in some of its institutional forms, while nonetheless remaining a largely feudal organization: "through a contradiction all its own and which results directly from its dogma, the Church, as it relates to both the organization of labor and property, is both communist and feudal. It is communist, because it considers the pure community, shorn of any distinction between yours and mine, as the ideal model of human association; this ideal, according to the Church, which would have been realized as an earthly Paradise with the hopes and grace of Jesus Christ, can still be realized through coenobitic institutions. Yet the Church is also feudal, by virtue of the original sin that destroyed the law of charity, and forever inscribed inequality amongst men. Now that this inequality becomes unchangeable and, on the other hand, because not everyone is able to become part of a religious community, the Church found that the most appropriate way to regulate this inequality was by giving it hierarchical form, which was then counterbalanced by the various religious communities and by charitable institutions." Pierre Joseph Proudhon, *De la justice dans la Révolution et dans l'Église*, Vol. 1 (Paris: Fayard, 1989), 389.

22 It is not a matter of indifference that Babeuf, who did not use the word "communist," at least speaks, at times, of "communautists" to designate the followers of the "Community of Equals." See Jacques Grandjonc, *Communisme/Kommunismus, Communism*, 310–304.

23 In *De l'Humanite* (1840), Pierre Leroux argues that the Essenes are especially important in this respect. He sees them as Jesus's predecessors because of their practice of equality and brotherhood without restriction, as opposed to the other "Jewish sects," the Sadducees, which were very individualistic, in his view, and the Pharisees, who restricted their charitable activities within their own Church. See Pierre Leroux, *De l'Humanite* (Paris: Fayard, 1985), 160 and 460.

24 *Acts of the Apostles*, 2. 42, 44–46.

25 Ibid., 4.32–35.

26 For more on the communal meal as a sacrificial rite, see Georg Simmel, "The Sociology of the Meal." *Societies*, vol. 37 (1992): 211–216.

27 *The Rule of Saint Benedict*, ed. Timothy Fry (New York: Vintage Books, 1998), 36.

28 Ibid.

29 Michel Foucault, *The Hermeneutics of the Subject*, trans. Graham Burchell (New York: Palgrave-MacMillan, 2001), 216–217.

30 Michel Foucault, *Security, Territory, Population*, trans. Graham Burchell (New York: Palgrave-MacMillan, 2007), 175–185.

31 Qtd. in Jacques Grandjonc, *Communisme/Kommunismus, Communism*, 52.

32 Foucault, *Security, Territory, Population*, 202–216.

33 Ibid., 211.

34 Ibid., 218 (note 11).

35 Étienne Cabet, *Voyage en Icarie*, Part III.

36 Buonarroti, *History of Babeuf's Conspiracy of Equality*, 318, 321.

37 Claude Mazauric, "Introduction," *Babeuf. Écrits* (Paris: Le Temps des Cerises, 2009), 77.

38 Qtd. in Buonarroti, *History of Babeuf's Conspiracy of Equality*, 418.

39 Ibid., 69.

40 "The current progress and boundless power produced by steam and machinery assures equal abundance," in the words of Étienne Cabet. See *Voyage en Icarie*, Preface, Part III.

41 Translator's note: The Icarian movement was founded by nineteenth-century French philosopher and utopian socialist Étienne Cabet. The Icarians established a series of

egalitarian communes in Texas, Illinois, Iowa, Missouri, and California. The last of the Icarian communes was voluntarily disbanded in 1896.

42 Hence the insoluble problems the Icarian community faced as a result of the insurmountable internal conflict between its egalitarian principle and the "organization of everyday life ruled by the Father of the community." See Jacques Rancière, "Communists without Communism?" *The Idea of Communism*, 170.

43 Durkheim has a tendency to underestimate the associationist aspect of modern socialism in favor of its more statist conception.

44 The inventors of modern socialism are often explicit in signaling their opposition to the older model of communism. The Saint-Simonians, for instance, attacked anyone who reproached them for not distributing goods perfectly equally and for defending skill-based inequalities. See *Doctrine de Saint-Simon*, 1831 Edition (Paris: Au Bureau de l'Organisateur), 183 and Victor Considerant, *Exposition abrégée du système phalanstérien de Fourier* (Paris: Librairie sociétaire, 1845), 27–28.

45 The opposition between "community" (*Gemeinschaft*) and "society" (*Gesellschaft*) is the fundamental explanatory principle of a "pure sociology" for Ferdinand Tönnies in *Community and Society*, trans. Jose Harris and Margaret Hollis (Cambridge: Cambridge University Press, 2001). Whereas *Gemeinschaft* is viewed as a "living organism," *Gesellschaft* is a "mechanical aggregate and artifact" (ibid., 19). By situating community in the primordial past, Tönnies holds to a view of communism as "primitive." As for socialism, which "is already latent in the concept of *Gesellschaft*," it presupposes the development of individualism within the context of an urban environment and attempts to manage markets and labor through the state mechanism (ibid., 260).

46 Marx articulates this very well in *The Poverty of Philosophy* (New York: International Publishers, 1992), 126: "the working class, in the course of its development, will substitute for the old civil society an association which will exclude classes and their antagonism, and there will be no more political power properly so-called, since political power is precisely the official expression of antagonism in civil society."

47 Pierre Ansart, *Marx et l'Anarchisme* (Paris: PUF, 1969). 525–526.

48 Karl Marx, *Economic and Philosophical Manuscripts of 1844*, trans. Martin Milligan (New York: Prometheus Books, 1988), 114.

49 Ibid., 14.

50 Karl Marx and Friedrich Engels, *The German Ideology* (London: Lawrence and Wishart, 1938), 70.

51 For an analysis of this internal tension in Marx, see our *Marx, Prénom : Karl* (Paris: Gallimard, 2012).

52 Karl Marx, *Capital*, vol. 1, trans. Ben Fowkes (New York: Vintage, 1977), 929.

53 Ibid., 929.

54 Cornelius Castoriadis, "The Content of Socialism I," in *Cornelius Castoriadis: Political and Social Writings*, vol. 1, trans. and ed. David Ames Curtis (Minnesota: University of Minnesota Press, 1988), 303.

55 Ibid., 302.

56 Ibid.

57 Ibid., 303. While this assertion is insightful, it is not exactly accurate, insofar as capitalist transformation involves a kind of permanent revolution. Moreover, Castoriadis's account neglects the distinctive institutional forms, rules, and values created by the workers' movements.

58 This confusion is manifest in a passage about the "association [*assoziation*] of workers" realized in the factories as a result of the division of labor and cooperation, and the

"association [*Verein*] of free men" evoked in the first chapter of *Capital*. The same word (*assoziation*) also appears in the *1844 Manuscripts* to designate both an objective tendency of capital and a future form of society. See Dardot and Laval, *Marx, Prénom : Karl*, 627–629.

59 See Immanuel Kant, *Critique of Practical Reason*, trans. Mary Gregor (Cambridge: Cambridge University Press, 2010), 121. What Badiou calls the "subjective component" of the Idea of Communism corresponds to the effect produced on the will by Kant's postulate of practical reason.

60 Alain Badiou proffers the analogy of Fermat's theorem. See *The Communist Hypothesis*, 6.

61 Ibid.

62 Leon Trotsky, *Communism and Terror* (Ann Arbor: University of Michigan Press, 1963), 55.

63 In *State and Revolution* and the *April Theses,* Lenin still speaks of an explicitly anti-statist form of power.

64 Early on, Rosa Luxemburg criticized the Bolshevik policy of democratic suppression: "the tacit assumption underlying the Lenin-Trotsky theory of the dictatorship is this: that the socialist transformation is something for which a ready-made formula lies completed in the pocket of the revolutionary party, which needs only to be carried out energetically in practice." *The Russian Revolution* (Ann Arbor: University of Michigan, 1962), 69.

65 Serge, "Thirty Years After the Russian Revolution," 253.

66 See Marc Ferro, *The Russian Revolution of 1917* (London: Routledge, 1972).

67 The logic that substitutes the Party for the working class is central to the challenge of the "workers opposition," whose most famous representative is Alexandra Kollontaï. The movement was born in 1920 in opposition to the theory of a single industrial program defended by the leaders of the Bolshevik Party. In vain, the workers' opposition tried to defend the idea of the "creativity of the working class" in the development of communism and to uphold the "autonomous activity of the masses" in place of bureaucratic administration in economic and social development.

68 See Marc Ferro, *Des soviets au communisme bureaucratique* (Paris: Gallimard/Julliard, 1980). Ferro is one of the only historians to write a detailed institutional history of the 1917 revolution.

69 Ferro, *Des soviets au communisme bureaucratique*, 112.

70 See Cornelius Castoriadis, "The Role of Bolshevik Ideology and the Birth of Bureaucracy," in *Cornelius Castoriadis: Political and Social Writings*, vol. 3: 1961–1979. D.A. Curtis (ed.) (Minneapolis: University of Minnesota Press, 1993) and Claude Lefort, *Éléments d'une critique de la bureaucratie* (Paris: Droz, 1971).

71 Leon Trotsky, *Terrorism and Communism*, 168. Qtd. by Cornelius Castoriadis, "The Role of Bolshevik Ideology and the Birth of Bureaucracy." *Cornelius Castoriadis, Political and Social Writings*, vol. 3, 99.

72 Needless to say, the claim that such an interpretation stems from Hannah Arendt is nothing short of intellectual dishonesty and must be denounced. Arendt never ceased linking the phenomenon of totalitarianism to the question of conditions of *action*, which for Arendt always has the specific characteristic of placing humans *in relation* with others (*inter-ests*). And just as we should be cautious of this "liberal" reading of Arendt, it is equally important to reject, in the most forceful terms possible, the various conservative interpretations of Arendt (the work of Alain Finkielkraut being paradigmatic). For what unites these two interpretations is their failure to comment on, or their outright ignorance of, Arendt's attachment to the tradition of the revolutionary councils and her ruthless criticism of the principle of the nation-state.

73 Cornelius Castoriadis, "The Hungarian Source." *Political and Social Writings*, vol. 3, 267. Castoriadis references Marx's celebrated formula from Chapter 32 of *Capital*, vol. 1 (1977), which asserts that the working class is "trained, united and organized by the very mechanism of the capitalist process of production" (929).

74 Yves Cohen, "Administration, politique et techniques. Réflexion sur la matérialité des pratiques administratives dans la Russie stalinienne (1922–1940)." *Les Cahiers du monde russe*, vol. 44, no. 2–3: 269–307, and Yves Cohen, *Le Siècle des chefs. Une histoire transnationale du commandement et de l'autorité: 1890–1940* (Paris: Éditions Amsterdam, 2013).

75 For the relevant passages from Lenin and Trotsky mentioned by Castoriadis, see "The Role of Bolshevik Ideology and the Birth of Bureaucracy," 99–104.

76 Hannah Arendt, *The Human Condition* (Chicago: University of Chicago Press, 1958), 40.

77 Cornelius Castoriadis, "The Hungarian Source." *Political and Social Writings*, vol. 3, 252.

78 Ibid., 260, 261.

79 Ibid., 260.

80 Ibid., 264.

81 Ibid., 266.

82 Ibid., 270, note 14: "Unbelievable as it might sound, Lenin and Trotsky considered the organization of work, the management of production etc., as a purely *technical* question that had nothing to do, according to them, with 'the nature of the political power,' which remained 'proletarian' – since it was exercised by the 'Party of the proletariat.' To this corresponded their enthusiasm for the capitalist 'rationalization' of production, Taylorist, piecework, etc." For the primacy of the workers' perspective on production, see ibid., 266.

83 Jean François Billeter, *Chine trois fois muette* (Paris: Allia, 2010), 51.

84 Jasper Becker, *La Grande Famine de Mao* (Paris: Dagorno, 1998).

85 Billeter, *Chine trois fois muette*, 50. One might also consult the major study by Yang Jisheng, *Tombstone: The Great Chinese Famine, 1958–1962* (New York: Farrar, Straus and Giroux, 2013). Jisheng does not merely describe Mao's responsibility for the forced collectivization of the Chinese countryside, he also underscores the degree to which the Party functioned as a particularly efficient apparatus for hiding the actual effects of its policies. Those who dared to speak about what they saw were treated as "foreign elements within the working class," "degenerate elements," "right-wing opportunists," and other kinds of "unwanted elements," and they suffered repressive consequences (187).

86 Billeter, *Chine trois fois muette*, 52–53.

87 Hua Linshan, *Les Années rouges* (Paris: Le Seuil, 1987). For Jean François Billeter, Linshan's book is "the best book published on the cultural revolution in any language whatsoever" (Billeter, *Chine trois fois muette*, 53).

88 The questions were formulated in these terms: "Why is the Central Committee attacking us? What ideological errors have we committed? Is it not egregious for the preparatory group to be massacring the population? What is preventing us from fighting against them? What has happened to the principles of the Cultural Revolution? What does Chairman Mao think? And what, ultimately, is the Cultural Revolution?" (Linshan, *Les Années rouges*, 292).

89 On this point, see Roderick MacFarquhar and Michael Schoenhals, *Mao's Last Revolution* (Cambridge: Belknap Press, 2006), 168.

90 Billeter, *Chine trois fois muette*, 54.
91 Hua Linshan, *Les Années Rouges*, 367.
92 This is Alain Badiou's interpretation: Mao is simultaneously the "supreme name of the party-state" and "the name that which, in the party, cannot be reduced to the state's bureaucracy." *The Communist Hypothesis*, 103,153. This is Badiou's specious inference that the contradictory character of the Cultural Revolution actually comes from the "intrinsically contradictory" name of Mao himself, as if this name, in itself, accurately reflects the abrupt and convulsive course of the actual Revolution.
93 Ibid, 113.
94 Marx's view of Plato's *Republic* is also clear: "Plato's *Republic*, in so far as the division of labour is treated in it as the formative principle of the state, is merely an Athenian idealization of the Egyptian caste system" (*Capital*, vol. 1, 489).
95 Plato, *Republic*, 237 (501a–d). For more on this, as well as more on the general difficulty of articulating the three meanings of the notion of hypothesis, see Pierre Dardot's lecture, "Communism is not a Hypothesis," at the Paris VIII Conference, "Question Marx" (January, 2010): http://www.questionmarx.typepad.fr/.
96 It is important to speak of the "form *of the* party" and not just the "party-form": the latter expression gives the impression that the party is merely a neutral form in the sense of a "method" or a "means," whereas the party, from the very beginning, has always commanded a certain content – specifically, the counter-state (in the sense of a substitute state) in formation.
97 The bureaucratic capture of the common was never total. Societies continued to live and cultures continued to develop outside and often in conflict with official supervisory apparatuses. Neither the most brutal police violence, nor the forms of bureaucratic socialization used to create a "new man" were able to completely prevent the formation of public opinion, patterns of behavior, and an array of other practices designed to escape and resist the vertical logic of the state-party. See Alexandre Sumpf, *De Lénine à Gagarine: Une histoire sociale de l'Union soviétique* (Paris: Gallimard, 2013).

3 The Great Appropriation and the Return of the "Commons"

1 Vandana Shiva, "Water Democracy." *Cochabamba! Water War in Bolivia*, eds. Oscar Olivera and Tom Lewis (Cambridge: South End Press, 2004), xi.
2 We will return to this subject at greater length in Chapters 6 and 7.
3 See Donald Nonini, *The Global Idea of 'The Commons'* (New York: Berghahn Books, 2007).
4 For this distinction in Roman law, see Chapter 1.
5 Olivier Hoedeman and Satoko Kishimoto (eds.), *L'Eau, un bien public* (Paris: Éditions Charles Léopold Mayer, 2010).
6 This dimension of the common will be more thoroughly addressed in Chapter 4.
7 See Raúl Zibechi, *Dispersing Power: Social Movements as Anti-State Forces* (Oakland: AK Press, 2010). The expression "revolution in the revolution" comes from the title of Régis Debray's famous book *Revolution in the Revolution? Armed Struggle and Political Struggle in Latin America* (New York: Grove Press, 1967). The phrase refers to the "foco" strategy (guerilla warfare) that was supposed to supplant the strategy of the Leninist-type party. The book's new 2003 edition suggests the commons is, in turn, replacing the foco strategy.

8 See James Boyle, "The Second Enclosure Movement and the Construction of the Public Domain." *Law and Contemporary Problems*, vol. 66, no. 1 and 2 (2003). Also see James Boyle, *The Public Domain: Enclosing the Commons of the Mind* (New Haven: Yale University Press, 2008).
9 See David Bollier, *Silent Theft: the Private Plunder of our Common Wealth* (New York: Routledge, 2003).
10 See Jeremy Rifkin, *The Biotech Century: The Coming Age of Genetic Commerce* (New York: Penguin, 1998).
11 See Gilles Van Kote, "La course aux terres ne profite pas aux pays du Sud." *Le Monde*, April 27, 2012. Also see the remarkable documentary by Alexis Marant, *Planète à vendre* (France: Arte, 2012): http://planete-a-vendre.arte.tv. And in English, *Planet for Sale*: https://www.farmlandgrab.org/post/view/18542-documentary-planet-for-sale.
12 See the project "Land Matrix," which identifies financial transactions associated with "land grabbing": http://landmatrix.org.
13 See Riccardo Petrella (ed.), *Eau: Res publica ou marchandise?* (Paris: La Dispute, 2003).
14 Marc Laimé, "La marchandisation de l'eau s'accélère." *Le Monde diplomatique*, March 2008.
15 See Oscar Olivera, "Privatization." *Cochabamba! Water War in Bolivia*, eds. Oscar Olivera and Tom Lewis (Cambridge: South End Press, 2004). Also see Pierre Sauvêtre; *Crises de gouvernementalité et généalogie de l'État aux XXe et XXIe siècles*, 921.
16 Peter Linebaugh, *The Magna Carta Manifesto: Liberties and Commons for All* (Berkeley: University of California Press, 2009).
17 We will return to this assertion in greater length in Chapter 7.
18 David Bollier, "Growth of the Commons Paradigm." *Understanding Knowledge as a Commons*, eds. Charlotte Hess and Elinor Ostrom (Cambridge: MIT Press, 2007).
19 David Bollier, "Growth of the commons paradigm," 29.
20 We will return to this work in greater detail in Chapter 4 of this book.
21 David Bollier, *Silent Theft: the Plunder of our Common Wealth* (New York: Routledge, 2002).
22 David Bollier, "Les communs. ADN d'un renouveau de la culture politique." *Libres Savoirs: Les biens communs de la connaissance* (Paris: C&F éditions, 2011), 306.
23 Yochai Benkler, *The Wealth of Networks: How Social Production Transforms Markets and Freedom* (New Haven: Yale University Press, 2006).
24 Naomi Klein, "Reclaiming the Commons." New Left Review, no. 9 (May–June 2001): 81–89.
25 Klein, "Reclaiming the Commons," 82.
26 Ibid.
27 David Bollier, "Les communs. ADN d'un renouveau de la culture politique," 307.
28 Ernesto Laclau and Chantal Mouffe, *Hegemony and Socialist Strategy: Towards a Radical Democratic Politics* (London: Verso, 1985).
29 Philippe Aigrain, "Pour une coalition des biens communs." *Libération*, Aug 55, 2003. Access online at http://paigrain.debatpublic.net.
30 Pierre Bourdieu admired the same link between the local and the global in the activism of José Bové when he was the head of Peasant Confederation.
31 Amongst the partisans of the commons, not every position is this radical. David Bollier, for example, argues that the defense of the commons does not entail a questioning of the market as such, but rather aims at "equilibrium" between communal resources and the forces of capitalism. See David Bollier, *Silent Theft*, 3.
32 See Oscar Olivera, "Privatization." *Cochabamba! Water War in Bolivia*, eds. Oscar Olivera and Tom Lewis (Cambridge: South End Press, 2004). We will return with

greater precision to the political dimension of the commons' management in the following chapter.

33 See Jérôme Baschet, *La Rébellion zapatiste: Insurrection indienne et résistance planétaire* (Paris: Flammarion, 2005).

34 Franck Poupeau, "La Bolivie et le paradoxe des 'communs.' Sept thèses commentées sur le processus de transformation *politique* actuel," at the seminar "Du public au commun," December 15, 2010.

35 See "Reclaim the Commons": http://bienscommuns.org/signature/appel/index.php?a=du&c=nfg1de.

36 See online at: http://www.aefjn.org/index.php/archive-348/articles/Houtart_presentation_in_CETRI.html.

37 See Chapter 1.

38 For a re-construction of the main lines of this argument, see Chapter 6.

39 Milton and Rose Friedman, *Capitalism and Freedom* (Chicago: University of Chicago Press, 1982).

40 We will return to this argument in Chapter 4.

41 See Joseph Schumpter, *Capitalism, Socialism and Democracy* (New York: Harper-Perennial, 2008), especially Part II, titled "Can Capitalism Survive?"

42 See Blandine Laperche (ed.), *Propriété industrielle et innovation* (Paris: L'Harmattan, 2001).

43 Douglass C. North and Robert Paul Thomas, *The Rise of the Western World: A New Economic History* (Cambridge: Cambridge University Press, 1973), vii.

44 Ibid., 1–2.

45 Ibid., 2.

46 Ibid., 3.

47 Douglass C. North, "Institutions." *The Journal of Economic Perspectives*, vol. 5, no. 1 (Winter, 1991), 97. We will return later, in Chapter 10, to the decisive question of institutions.

48 North and Thomas, *The Rise of the Western World*, 132, 146.

49 Ibid., 152.

50 Ibid., vii.

51 Ibid., 155.

52 See Dimitri Uzunidis (ed.), *L'Innovation et l'Économie contemporaine: Espaces cognitifs et territoriaux* (Paris: De Boeck, 2004).

53 See Amy Kapzincski and Gaëlle Kirkorian, *Access to Knowledge in the Age of Intellectual Property* (New York: Zone Books, 2010).

54 See Mélanie Dulong de Rosnay and Hervé Le Crosnier synthesis, *Propriété intellectuelle: Géopolitique et mondialisation* (Paris: CNRS éditions, 2013), 13–14. Richard Stallman offers an uncompromising criticism of the amalgamations introduced by the notion of intellectual property: "If you want to think clearly about the issues raised by patents, or copyrights, or trademarks, or various other different laws, the first step is to forget the idea of lumping them together, and treat them as separate topics. The second step is to reject the narrow perspective and simplistic picture the term 'intellectual property' suggests. Consider each of these issues separately, in its fullness, and you have a chance of considering them well." Richard M. Stallman, "Did You Say 'Intellectual Property'? It is a Seductive Mirage": https://www.gnu.org/philosophy/not-ipr.en.html.

55 Interview with Maurice Cassier, *Nouveaux Regards*, no. 15 (Fall 2001).

56 Mikhaïl Xifaras, "Copyright and the Theory of Property." *Eurozine*, Sept. 16, 2010: http://www.eurozine.com/articles/2010-09-16-xifaras-en.html.

57 Interview with Maurice Cassier, *Nouveaux Regards*.
58 French Collective Against Biopiracy, "Biopiracy," *Libres Savoirs*, 143.
59 See Vandana Shiva, "Monsanto and the Seeds of Suicide." *The Asian Age*, March 27, 2013.
60 Many contemporary historians have expanded on these classic expositions. Notable examples include E.P. Thompson, *Whigs and Hunters: The Origin of the Black Act* (London: Allen Lane, 1975), Christopher Hill, *The World Turned Upside Down: Radical Ideas During the English Revolution* (New York: Pelican Books, 1975), and Ellen Meiksins Wood, *The Origin of Capitalism: A Longer View* (New York: Verso, 2002). Also see Michael Perleman, *The Invention of Capitalism: Classical Political Economy and the Secret History of Primitive Accumulation* (Durham: Duke University Press, 2000).
61 Thomas More, *Utopia*, trans. Robert M. Adams (Cambridge: Cambridge University Press, 2016), 19.
62 Ibid.
63 Ibid.
64 Karl Polanyi, *The Great Transformation: the Political and Economic Origins of Our Times* (Boston: Beacon Press, 2001), 37.
65 Marx, *Capital*, vol. 1, 874.
66 Ibid., 874.
67 Ibid., 885.
68 Ibid., 889.
69 Ibid., 875 (our emphasis).
70 Ibid., 899.
71 Ibid., 875.
72 Ibid., 927.
73 For a more detailed analysis of this sequence, see Dardot and Laval, *Marx, Prénom : Karl*, 641–647.
74 By "improvement" Locke referred to the increases in the yields from otherwise closed-off lands, which in his view justified private appropriation.
75 David Harvey is one of the more recent authors to sing the praises of primitive accumulation in this Marxian manner. See David Harvey, *The New Imperialism* (Oxford: Oxford University Press, 2005). Jean Jaurès was also very critical of customs-governed traditional commons. See Chapter 8.
76 See Dardot and Laval, *Marx, Prénom : Karl*, 648.
77 See, for example, Pierre Jalée, *The Pillage of the Third World* (New York: Monthly Press Review, 1968), André Gunder Frank, *Capitalism and Underdevelopment in Latin America: Historical Studies of Chile and Brazil* (New York: Monthly Review Press, 1967), and Samir Amin, *Accumulation on a World Scale. A Critique of the Theory of Underdevelopment* (New York: Monthly Review Press, 1974).
78 Rosa Luxemburg, *The Accumulation of Capital*, trans. Agnes Schwarzschild (London: Routledge, 2009). Also see the renewal of Luxemburg's analyses by Hannah Arendt: "Part Two: Imperialism," in *The Origins of Totalitariansim* (New York: Harcourt, 1976).
79 Luxemburg, *The Accumulation of Capital*, 335.
80 Luxemburg, *The Accumulation of Capital*, 367.
81 Louis Althusser, "Preface to Capital Volume One," *Lenin and Philosophy*, trans. Ben Brewster (New York: Monthly Review Press, 2001), 56.
82 David Harvey, "The Future of the Commons." *Radical History Review*, no. 109 (Winter 2011): 101–107.
83 David Harvey, *The New Imperialism*, 158.

84 Ibid., 148.
85 David Harvey, *The Enigma of Capital and the Crises of Capitalism* (London: Profile Books, 2010), 54.
86 Harvey, *The New Imperialism*, 149.
87 David Harvey, *The Enigma of Capital*, 249, and *The New Imperialism*, 178–179.
88 Harvey, *The New Imperialism*, 189.
89 John Holloway, *Change the World Without Taking Power* (London: Pluto Press, 2010).
90 Massimo De Angelis, "Marx and Primitive Accumulation: the Continuous Character of Capital's 'Enclosures.'" *The Commoner*, no. 2 (September 2001): 1–22.
91 See Karl Marx, *Theories of Surplus Value*, vol. 3, trans. Emile Burns (London: Lawrence and Wishart, 1969). Also see, on this point, Dardot and Laval, *Marx, Prénom : Karl*, 548.
92 This is what Marx called, drawing on his Hegelian background, "its own presuppositions." On this point, see Dardot and Laval, *Marx, Prénom : Karl*, 548.
93 See Robert Castel, *Les Métamorphoses de la question sociale. Une chronique du salariat* (Paris: Fayard, 1995), 268 and Donald Nonini, *The Global Idea of 'The Commons,'* 6.
94 See Sheldon Wolin, *Democracy Incorporated: Managed Democracy and the Specter of Inverted Totalitarianism* (Princeton University Press, Princeton, 2008).

4 Critique of the Political Economy of the Commons

1 The prize is actually called the Economic Prize of the Bank of Sweden "in memory of Alfred Nobel." Elinor Ostrom's work was developed within the framework of an interdisciplinary research group she founded with her husband, Vincent Ostrom, in 1973 at the University of Indiana, called the Workshop in Political Theory and Policy Analysis. For a historical overview of the group's work on the commons, see Charlotte Hess, "Is There Anything New Under the Sun? A Discussion and Survey of Studies on New Commons and the Internet," a paper presented at the Eighth Conference of the International Association for the Study of Common Property, Bloomington, Indiana, May 31–June 4, 2000: http://dlc.dlib.indiana.edu/archive/00000512.
2 This is why Ostrom settles on such a minimalist definition of the commons as "a resource shared by a group of people." See Charlotte Hess and Elinor Ostrom (eds.), *Understanding Knowledge as a Commons: from Theory to Practice* (Cambridge: MIT Press, 2007), 3.
3 André Gorz, "The Exit from Capitalism has Already Begun," in *Ecologica*, trans. Chris Turner (London: Seagull Books, 2010), 36, 38.
4 The economic distinctions on this topic can be traced back to Roman civil law and its division of goods according to their nature (see our analysis in the "Reification of the Commons" in Chapter 1).
5 For exegesis of this doctrine, see Luc Weber, *L'État acteur économique* (Paris: Economica, 1997).
6 See Richard Musgrave, *The Theory of Public Finance:* a *Study in Public Economy* (Columbus: McGraw- Hill, 1959) and Paul Samuelson's canonical *Economics* (Columbus: McGraw-Hill, 2009).
7 Mancur Olson, *The Logic of Collective Action* (Cambridge: Harvard University Press, 1971).
8 For instance, there are individualistic consumable goods – like education – that may be provided by the state or the market, just as a lighthouse can be public or private. Similarly, roads can be free of charge but users may also pay tolls.

9 See Elinor Ostrom, *Governing the Commons: the Evolution of Institutions of Collective Action* (Cambridge: Cambridge University Press, 1990).

10 Garrett Hardin, *Science*, no. 13 (December 1968): http://www.sciencemag.org.

11 Étienne-Gabriel Morelly, *Code de la nature* (Paris: La Ville brûle, 2011), 44.

12 Thomas R. Malthus, *An Essay on the Principle of Population*, 2nd ed. (London: J. Johnson, 1803), 531.

13 See Alfred North Whitehead, *Science and the Modern World* (New York: The MacMillan Company, 1946), 15. For Whitehead, the Greek conception of nature – "a drama in which each thing played its part" (11) – tends toward its proper end just as tragic art pushes destinies toward their completion, and this is the foundation of modern science: "their vision of fate, remorseless and indifferent, urging a tragic incident to its inevitable issue, is the vision possessed by science" (15).

14 Hardin, "The Tragedy of the Commons," 1244.

15 For further clarification on this point, see Matthew MacLellan, "The Tragedy of Limitless Growth: Re-Interpreting the Tragedy of the Commons for a Century of Climate Change." *Environmental Humanities,* vol. 7 (2015), 41–58: http://environmentalhumanities.org/arch/vol7/7.2.pdf.

16 Julien Bouissou, "Agriculture, surexploitation des nappes. L'Inde est menacée par une pénurie d'eau." *Le Monde*, August 10, 2013.

17 See Chapter 1, "The Reification of the Commons."

18 Private ownership also reduces bargaining costs by limiting negotiations to a small number of persons who settle neighborhood problems face to face, whereas every member is forced to negotiate with every other member in instances of common ownership – this is indeed a curious way of envisioning collective deliberation. See Harold Demsetz, "Toward a Theory of Property Rights." *The American Economic Review*, vol. 57, no. 2 (May 1967), 357.

19 Charlotte Hess and Elinor Ostrom (eds.), *Understanding Knowledge as a Commons*, 5, and Yochai Benkler, "The Political Economy of the Common." *Upgrade*, vol. 4, no. 3 (June 2003): 6–10: www.upgrade-cepis.org.

20 The translation of the "commons" into "biens communs" in French, or into the Italian "beni comuni," effaces Ostrom's groundbreaking work.

21 David Bollier, "Growth of the Commons Paradigm." *Understanding Knowledge as a Commons*, ed. Charlotte Hess and Elinor Ostrom (Cambridge: MIT Press, 2007), 29.

22 Elinor Ostrom, *Crafting Institutions for Self-Governing Irrigation Systems* (San Francisco: ICS Press, 1992), 19.

23 Ibid., 20, 19. According to Ostrom, two mistakes must be avoided: one must not confuse practical rules with formal rules, and one must not believe there can be no other institutions except those created by the state.

24 Benjamin Coriat, "Des communs 'fonciers' aux communs informationnels. Traits communs et différences." *International Seminar on "Propriété et Communs, les nouveaux enjeux de l'accès et de l'innovation partagés,* Paris, April 25 and 26, 2013. Also see, from the same seminar, Olivier Weinstein, "Comment comprendre les 'communs.' Elinor Ostrom, la propriété et la nouvelle économie institutionnelle."

25 Translator's note: Dardot and Laval use the phrase "'guichets' de l'État" here to denote the phenomenon of passive consumer citizenship. See Jean Marc-Weller, *L'Etat au guichet* (Paris: Desclée de Brouwer, 1999).

26 Ostrom, *Crafting Institutions for Self-Governing Irrigation Systems*, 24.

27 As North puts it, "institutions are the rules of the game in a society or, more formally, are the humanly devised constraints that shape human interaction." See Douglass C.

North, *Institutions, Institutional Change and Economic Performance* (Cambridge: Cambridge University Press, 1990), 3.
28 Ostrom, *Governing the Commons*, 35.
29 Ibid.
30 When North, following Ronald Heiner, argues that institutions are rational because they diminish the inherent uncertainty of human interactions, he believes he has discovered a profound truth. He forgets that classical authors like Hume already addressed this question.
31 See Jean Pierre Chanteau and Agnès Chanteau, "L'institutionnalisme méthodologique d'Elinor Ostrom au-delà des communs. Quelques enjeux et controverses." *Revue de la rægulation*, no. 14, (Fall 2013).
32 Ostrom, *Crafting Institutions For Self-Governing Irrigation Systems*, 41.
33 Ibid.
34 Establishing rules is conceived as an investment in social capital capable of generating revenue. See Elinor Ostrom, "Constituting Social Capital and Collective Action," in Robert O. Keohane and Elinor Ostrom (eds.), *Local Commons and Global Interdependence* (London: Sage, 1995), 125.
35 Ostrom, *Crafting Institutions for Self-Governing Irrigation Systems,* 14.
36 Olivier Weinstein, "Comment comprendre les 'communs,'" 15.
37 Significant, in this regard, is Mark Pennington's collaborative rehabilitation of Ostrom in a pamphlet released by the Institute of Economic Affairs. See Mark Pennington, "Elinor Ostrom, Common-Pool Resources and the Classical Liberal Tradition," in Elinor Ostrom, *The Future of the Commons. Beyond Market Failure and Government Regulation* (London: IEA, 2012).
38 Olivier Weinstain, "Comment comprendre les 'communs,'" 32.
39 J. Rogers Hollingsworth and Robert Boyer (eds.), *Contemporary Capitalism: the Embeddedness of Institutions* (Cambridge: Cambridge University Press, 1997), 2. These authors stress how "institutions are embedded in a culture in which their logics are symbolically grounded, organizationally structured, technically and materially constrained, and politically defended" (2).
40 Olivier Weinstain, "Comment comprendre les 'communs,'" 31.
41 Robert Boyer, *Regulation Theory: State of the Art*, trans. Carolyn Shread (London: Routledge, 1995), 2.
42 This typology can be found as early as 1977 in Vincent Ostrom and Elinor Ostrom, "Public Goods and Public Choices," in E.S. Savas, *Alternatives for Delivering Public Services* (Boulder: Westview Press, 1977).
43 Ellen Meiksins Wood, *The Origin of Capitalism: a Longer View* (New York: Verso, 2002).
44 Ibid., 244.
45 Pierre Bourdieu, *The Logic of Practice*, trans. Richard Nice (Stanford: Stanford University Press, 1990), 81.
46 The term "new commons" covers a much greater terrain than the commons of knowledge alone, as will be the focus of discussion for the rest of the chapter.
47 Hess and Ostrom, *Understanding Knowledge as a Commons*, 7.
48 Ostrom, *Governing the Commons*, 183.
49 David Harvey, "The Future of the Commons." *Radical History Review*, vol. 2011, no. 109 (2011), 102.
50 Hess and Ostrom, *Understanding Knowledge as a Common*, 4.
51 Ibid.

52 Thomas Jefferson, letter to Isaac MacPherson, August 13, 1813. Qtd. in Peter Levine, "Collective Action, Civic Engagement, and the Knowledge Commons." *Understanding Knowledge as a Commons*, ed. Charlotte Hess and Elinor Ostrom (2007), 250, and Lawrence Lessig, *Code: And Other Laws of Cyberspace* (New York: Basic Books, 1999), 182. Also see commentary on this letter by James Boyle, *The Public Domain: Enclosing the Commons of the Mind* (New Haven: Yale University Press, 2009).

53 Nancy Kranich, "Countering Enclosures: Reclaiming the Knowledge Commons." *Understanding Knowledge as a Commons*, ed. Charlotte Hess and Elinor Ostrom (Cambridge: MIT Press, 2007).

54 Coriat, "Des communs 'fonciers' aux communs informationnels. Traits communs et différences," 18.

55 Coriat, "Des communs 'fonciers' aux communs informationnels. Traits communs et différences," 10.

56 Michael Heller and Rebecca S. Eisenberg, "Can Patents Deter Innovation? The Anti-commons in Biomedical Research." *Science*, vol. 280 (May 1998): 698–701. Also see Michael Heller, "The Tragedy of the Anti-Commons: Property in the Transition from Marx to the Markets." *Harvard Law Review*, vol. 111, no. 3 (January 1998): 621–688 (see online at www.unc.edu).

57 Hess and Ostrom, *Understanding Knowledge as a Commons,* 15.

58 See Pierre-André Mangolte, "Le logiciel libre comme commun créateur de richessess." Presentation at the International Seminar, "Propriété et Communs: les nouveaux enjeux de l'accès et de l'innovation partagés," Paris, April 25–26, 2013.

59 Robert Braden (Network Working Group) "Who's Who in the Internet," Request for Comments 1251, 3. See online: https://tools.ietf.org/html/rfc1251. Qtd. in Patrice Flichy, "Comment Internet est devenu un marcheé." *Traité de sociologie économique*, ed. Philipe Steiner et François Vatin (Paris: PUF, 2009), 479. See online: www.ietf.org/rfc/rfc1251.

60 Robert K. Merton, "The Normative Structure of Science" [1942], in *The Sociology of Science* (Chicago: the University of Chicago Press, 1973), 267–278.

61 Hervé Le Crosnier, "Leçons d'émancipation. L'exemple du mouvement des logiciels libres," *Libres Savoirs*, 180.

62 See Richard Stallman, "The GNU Project": www.gnu.org. On the history of the free software movement, see Sébastien Broca, *L'Utopie du logiciel libre. La construction de projets de transformation sociale en lien avec le mouvement du free software* (Dissertation, Université Paris-I, January 2012).

63 According to Robert Stallman, new Xerox computers and printers introduced to his laboratory came with a new operating system that required non-disclosure agreements, which "meant that the first step in using a computer was to promise not to help your neighbor." A community based on cooperation was completely forbidden. The rule imposed by those who held the monopoly on proprietary software was: "if you share with your neighbor, you are a pirate. If you want any changes, beg us to make them" (The GNU Project: www.gnu.org).

64 Phillipe Aigrain, *Cause commune. L'information entre bien commun et propriété* (Paris: Fayard, 2005), 109.

65 After resigning his position at MIT, Stallman developed a computer operating system called UNIX, through his GNU project, that was compatible with the systems used in universities.

66 See Mélanie Clemente-Fontaine's study, "Sur la valeur juridique de la Licence publique générale de GNU." *Multitudes*, no. 5 (2001).

67 See Mikhaïl Xifaras, "Le copyleft et la théorie de la propriété." *Multitudes*, no 41 (2010).
68 For Mikhaïl Xifaras, copyleft is not, however, a global alternative to property: it is less a subversion of property than a neutralization of the deleterious political and moral effects of its exclusiveness.
69 Mangolte, "Le logiciel libre comme commun créateur de richesses," 4.
70 Chris Anderson, *Makers: the New Industrial Revolution* (New York: Signal, 2012).
71 Ibid., 5.
72 Eric S. Raymond carefully distinguishes between the "hacker" (which originally denoted a worker who manufactures furniture with an axe), who is a programming enthusiast, and the "cracker," who is an informational pirate. See Eric S. Raymond, *The New Hacker's Dictionary* (Cambridge: the MIT Press, 1996), 130. Raymond also describes the cracker as a "dark-side hacker" (142), which is of course a reference to George Lucas's character Darth Vader ("the dark side of the Force").
73 The culture of developers is actually more diverse than the hacking theorists often admit. There is a division between those who favor "free" software and those who favor "open" software; while this may seem esoteric from the outside, this division designates two very different attitudes, with the first being much more focused on the establishment of value structures within the digital environment.
74 Raymond, *The New Hacker's Dictionary,* 234.
75 Flichy, "Comment Internet est devenu un marcheé," 472.
76 Pekka Himanen, *The Hacker Ethic and the Spirit of the Information Age* (New York: Random House, 2001).
77 See Howard Rheingold, *The Virtual Community: Homesteading on the Electronic Frontier* (New York: Harper-Perennial, 1994), and more recently Yochai Benkler, *The Wealth of Networks: How Social Production Transforms Markets and Freedoms* (New Haven: Yale University Press, 2006).
78 Séverine Dussolier, "Open Source and Copyleft: Authorship Reconsidered?" *Columbia Journal of Law and Arts*, no. 26 (2002–2003).
79 For a critical analysis of this type of sociologically unfounded extrapolation see Sébastien Broca, "Du logiciel libre aux théories de l'intelligence collective." *Tic & société*, vol. 2, no. 2 (2008).
80 Gabriella Coleman, *Coding Freedom: the Ethics and Aesthetics of Hacking* (Princeton: Princeton University Press, 2013), 17.
81 Richard Stallman, "On Hacking": "it is hard to write a simple definition of something as varied as hacking, but I think what these activities have in common is playfulness, cleverness, and exploration. Thus, hacking means exploring the limits of what is possible, in a spirit of playful cleverness. Activities that display playful cleverness have 'hack value.'" See https://stallman.org/articles/on-hacking.html.
82 Pekka Himanen, *The Hacker Ethic and the Spirit of Information*, 89.
83 The hacker movement already plays a very active role in civic and political organizations devoted to the protection of freedoms in a number of countries. This was the case in Tunisia, which pitted militant hackers against the secretive government and which led to an "open gov" initiative. See Élodie Auffray, "Stallman et le 'libre' champions de Tunis." *Libération*, May 6, 2012.
84 Eric S. Raymond, "The Cathedral and the Bazaar": www.unterstein.net. For more on this point, see Pierre-André Mangolte, "Le logiciel libre comme commun créateur de richesses," 10–13.

85 For a synthesis of the scholarly literature on cooperative practices, see Broca, *L'Utopie du logiciel libre*, 131.
86 Lessig, *The Future of Ideas*, 23.
87 Ibid., 11.
88 Yann Moulier-Boutang, "Droit de propriété, terra nullius et capitalisme cognitif." *Multitudes,* no. 41 (2010).
89 Broca, *L'Utopie du logiciel libre*, 145.
90 Lessig, *The Future of Ideas*, 35.
91 Lawrence Lessig, *The Future of Ideas*, 40.
92 Lawrence Lessig, *Code and other Laws of Cyberspace* (New York: Basic Books, 1999).
93 See Lawrence Lessig, "Code is Law: On Liberty in Cyberspace": http://harvardmagazine.com/2000/01/code-is-law-html.
94 See Valérie Schafer and Hervé Le Crosnier, *La Neutralité du net. Un enjeu de communication* (Paris: CNRS éditions, 2011).
95 Eben Moglen, "The dotCommunist Manifesto": http://moglen.law.columbia.edu/publications/dcm.html.
96 Michael Hardt and Antonio Negri, *Multitude: War and Democracy in the Age of Empire* (New York: Penguin, 2004), 339.
97 Broca, *L'Utopie du logiciel libre*, 97.
98 See, for example, Maurizio Lazzarato, *Les Révolutions du capitalisme* (Paris: les Empêcheurs de penser en rond, 2004), 115.
99 We discuss this conception of the common in more detail in the following chapter.
100 André Gorz, *The Immaterial: Knowledge, Value and Capital*, trans. Chris Turner (New York: Seagull Books, 2010), 14.
101 John Hagel III and Arthur Armstrong, *Net Gain: Expanding Markets through Virtual Communities* (Boston: Harvard Business Review Press, 1997), and John Hagel and Marc Singer, *Net Worth: Shaping Markets When Customers Make the Rules* (Boston: Harvard Business Review Press, 1999).
102 Oliver Zara, *Le management de l'intelligence collective*: *Vers une nouvelle gouvernance* (Paris: M21 éditions, 20080:
103 Zara, *Le management de l'intelligence collective*, 26.
104 Zara, *Le management de l'intelligence collective*, 29 and 30.
105 Luc Boltanski and Eve Chiapello, *The New Spirit of Capitalism*, trans. Gregory Elliot (London: Verso, 2005).
106 Thomas Coutrot, *L'Entreprise néolibérale, nouvelle utopie capitaliste?* (Paris: La Découverte, 1998). These "new" managerial techniques should obviously be viewed as "trends" rather than completely normative.
107 Zara, *Le management de l'intelligence collective,* 229 (our emphasis).
108 Jeff Howe, "The Rise of Crowdsourcing." *Wired*, no. 14 (June 2006): https://www.wired.com/2006/06/crowds/. Qtd. by Broca, *L'Utopie du logiciel libre*, 117.
109 And speed is of the essence: "those who aspire to play the role of community organizer or owner will need to move quickly and aggressively to increase the likelihood of becoming the first to aggregate a critical mass of members in a target area" (Hagel and Armstrong, *Net Gain,* 75).
110 Ibid., 59.
111 Eric von Hippel, *Democratizing Innovation* (Cambridge: MIT Press, 2005).
112 Don Tapscott and Anthony D. Williams, *Wikinomics: How Mass Collaboration Changes Everything* New York: Portfolio Books, 2006), 1.
113 Ibid., 3.

114 Ibid., 12.
115 Yann Moulier-Boutang, "Droit de propriété, terra nullius et capitalisme cognitive," 167. For more discussion of this point, see the following chapter.
116 Though of course these forms of exploitation are superimposed and articulated. Even the most modern firms are still imposing drudgery on new generations of aspiring employees – the contemporary practice of "internships" is one obvious example.
117 Tapscott and Williams, *Wikinomics*, 3.
118 Ibid., 15.
119 For more on this point, see Antonella Corsani, "Éléments d'une rupture. L'hypothèse du capitalisme cognitif," in Christian Azais, Antonella Corsani and Patrick Dieuaide (eds.), *Vers un capitalisme cognitif. Entre mutations du travail et territoires* (Paris: L'Harmattan, 2001), 183–184. Also see Enzo Rullani, "Le capitalisme cognitif : du déjà vu?" *Multitudes,* no. 2 (2000).
120 Richard Stallman aptly summed up this prudent position as follows: "computers and the web make it much easier to work collaboratively and continuing to improve publications. I think that this will become even more true in the future, as people develop better ways to do it. The proprietary mindset might as well be precisely calculated to deprive us of this benefit of the Internet." "The Hacker Community and Ethics: An Interview with Richard M. Stallman": https://www.gnu.org/philosophy/rms-hack.en.html.
121 Benkler, *Wealth of Networks*, 15.
122 Benkler refers to Langdon Winner's work on technology in "Do Artifacts Have Politics?" in *The Whale and the Reactor: A Search for Limits in an Age of High Technology* (Chicago: University of Chicago Press, 1986), 19–39. According to Winner, some technologies lend themselves to a range of political uses, while others are more inflexible and their consequences for social organization are therefore determined *ab initio*. For Benkler, it seems that the older broadcast media were of the second kind, but when it comes to the Internet, things are less clear. This is what sets Benkler apart from the supporters of informational communism, for whom Internet technology is fundamentally and irrevocably democratic.
123 Benkler, *The Wealth of Networks*, 17.
124 Ibid., 22.
125 Ostrom, *Governing the Commons*, 3.

5 Common, Rent, and Capital

1 It is a universe Pierre Sauvêtre aptly calls "the historical ontology of the common." See Pierre Sauvêtre, *Crises de gouvernementalité et généalogie de l'État aux XXe et XXIe siècles*, 1015.
2 Hardt and Negri, *Multitude*, xv.
3 Ibid.
4 As Coccoli shows, the theme of "theft" is widespread today, even in Marxist literature, and it often trumps Marx's central idea that it is capitalism itself that initiates cooperation in order to exploit its benefits. It is all the more curious that this Marxian notion is more prominent in management literature, almost all of which recognizes the importance of this collective aspect of capitalism when it comes to the exploitation of "human resources." See Lorenzo Coccoli, "Property is (still) Theft! From the Marx-Proudhon Debate to the Global Plunder of the Commons." *Comparative Law Review,* vol. 4, no. 1 (2013): http://www.comparativelawreview.com.

5 Michael Hardt and Antonio Negri, *Commonwealth* (Cambridge: Belknap Press, 2009), 137.
6 As we saw in Chapter 2, this scheme is at the heart of the second discourse of communism.
7 Hardt and Negri, *Multitude*, xv.
8 Hardt and Negri, *Commonwealth*, viii.
9 Ibid., 250.
10 Ibid., viii.
11 For more on the "Production of the Common," see Hardt and Negri, *Multitude*, 196.
12 The concept of "biopolitics" is borrowed from Michel Foucault but is given a completely different meaning. It no longer designates a politics of normalization, but rather the production of "life," society, collective intelligence, and autonomous subjectivity. See Hardt and Negri, *Empire*, 22–41.
13 Hardt and Negri, *Multitude*, 113.
14 Hardt and Negri, *Commonwealth*, x.
15 This reference is to Hardt and Negri's analysis of the hegemony of immaterial labor in the context of "biopolitical production." See *Commonwealth*, 132–149. For a critical analysis of this aspect of their work, see Pierre Dardot, Christian Laval and El Mouhoub, *Sauver Marx? Empire, multitude, travail immatériel* (Paris: La Découverte, 2007).
16 Hardt and Negri, *Commonwealth*, 167–128.
17 For an earlier discussion of ours on the topic of this Proudhonism, see *Sauver Marx?*, 56.
18 For more on all these points see Stéphane Haber, *Penser le néocapitalisme. Vie, capital et aliénation* (Paris: Les Prairies ordinaires, 2013): 163–180.
19 Hardt and Negri, *Commonwealth*, 249.
20 See the special edition of *Multitudes*, "Capitalisme cognitif: la démocratie contre la rente," no. 32 (2008) and especially the article by Antonio Negri and Carlo Vercellone, "Le rapport capital/travail dans le capitalisme cognitif."
21 Hardt and Negri, *Commonwealth*, 230.
22 Karl Marx, "Value, Price and Profit." *Karl Marx and Frederick Engels: Collective Works*, vol. 20, 1864–1868 (New York: International Publishers, 1985), 125.
23 Hardt and Negri, *Commonwealth*, 140.
24 See Antonio Negri, *Marx Beyond Marx: Lessons from the Grundrisse* (London: Pluto Press, 1991). Also see "The Common in Capital and the Common Worker" in this chapter.
25 Yann Moulier-Boutang, *Cognitive Capitalism*, trans. Ed Emery (London: Polity Press, 2011), 77.
26 See Carlo Vercellone, "La nouvelle articulation salaire, profit, rente dans le capitalisme cognitif." *European Journal of Economic and Social Systems*, vol. 20 (2007): 45–64. Also see Carlo Vercellone, "Il ritorno del rentier." *Posse* (Nov. 2004): 97–114. And see Bernard Paulré, "Finance et accumulation dans le capitalisme postindustrial." *Multitudes*, no. 32 (2008): 77–89.
27 Hardt and Negri, *Commonwealth*, 140.
28 Hardt and Negri, *Multitude*, 150.
29 Karl Marx, *Capital*, vol. 3, trans. David Fernbach (New York: Penguin Books, 1991), 939.
30 As Vercellone continues: "the source of the 'wealth of nations' is increasingly based on a productive cooperation that develops outside the confines of businesses." See

Carlo Vercellone, "La nouvelle articulation salaire, profit, rente dans le capitalisme cognitif," 58.
31 See Antonio Negri and Carlo Vercellone, "Le rapport capital/travail dans le capitalisme cognitif,"
32 Ibid., 43.
33 Ibid., 44.
34 Vercellone, "La nouvelle articulation salaire, profit, rente dans le capitalisme cognitif," 57.
35 In a classic article, "The Nature of the Firm" (1937), Ronald Coase explains the existence of firms through the fact that firms make it possible to obtain "in-house" goods and services at a lower cost than they would be obtained "externally" on the market. See Ronald Coase, "The Nature of the Firm." *Economica*, vol. 4, no. 16 (Nov. 1937): 386–405.
36 Vercellone, "La nouvelle articulation salaire, profit, rente dans le capitalisme cognitif," 57.
37 Negri and Vercellone, "Le rapport capital/travail dans le capitalisme cognitif," 42.
38 Ibid., 42.
39 Vercellone, "La nouvelle articulation salaire, profit, rente dans le capitalisme cognitif," 59.
40 Negri and Vercellone, "Le rapport capital/travail dans le capitalisme cognitif," 45–46.
41 See Christian Laval, Francois Vergne, Pierre Clément and Guy Dreux, *La Nouvelle École capitaliste* (Paris: Découverte, 2011).
42 Negri and Vercellone, "Le rapport capital/travail dans le capitalisme cognitif," 47.
43 El Mouhoub and Dominique Plihon, *Le savoir et la finance: Liaisons dangereuses au cœur du capitalisme contemporain* (Paris: La Découverte, 2009).
44 See Chapter 2.
45 Pierre-Joseph Proudhon, *La Solution du problème social* (Paris: Lacroix, 1868), 131.
46 Pierre-Joseph Proudhon, *What is Property?*, trans. Donald R. Kelly and Bonnie G. Smith (Cambridge: Cambridge University Press, 1994), 181.
47 Pierre-Joseph Proudhon, *De la création de l'Ordre dans l'humanité*, in *Œuvres complètes*, vol. V (Paris: Marcel Rivière, 1926), 299.
48 Ibid., 300.
49 Ibid., 318.
50 Ibid.
51 Proudhon, *What is Property?*, 91.
52 Pierre-Joseph Proudhon, *La Capacité politique des classes ouvrières*, in *Œuvres complétes*, vol. 3 (Paris: Marcel Rivière, 1923), 185. For more on Proudhon's notion of the "economic forces," see *Les Confessions d'un révolutionnaire*, *Œuvres complètes*, vol. 7 (Paris: Marcel Rivière, 1927), 217.
53 Pierre Ansart, *Marx et l'Anarchisme*, 157.
54 Pierre-Joseph Proudhon, *De la justice dans la Révolution et dans l'Église*, 693.
55 Pierre-Joseph Proudhon, *Carnets*, March 11, 1846, vol. 2 (Paris: Marcel Rivière, 1960–1974), 3.
56 Proudhon, *What is Property?*, 111.
57 Ibid., 151.
58 See Pierre Ansart's commentary in *Marx et l'Anarchisme*, 152.
59 Proudhon, *What is Property?*, 93 (our emphasis).
60 Proudhon, *De la création de l'ordre dans l'humanité*, 312.
61 Ibid., 302.
62 Proudhon, *De la justice dans la Révolution et dans l'Église*, 706.
63 Ibid., 708.

64 For further discussion of the Proudhonian concept of law, see Chapter 9.
65 Proudhon, *What is Property?*, 196.
66 Pierre-Joseph Proudhon, *System of Economic Contradictions or, the Philosophy of Misery*, trans. Benj. R. Tucker (Boston: Benj. R. Tucker, 1888), 317.
67 See Chapter 9 and Part 3, "Political Proposition 9."
68 For more on all these points, see Lorenzo Coccoli, "Property is (still) Theft!," *Comparative Law Review*, vol. 4, no. 1 (2013).
69 Karl Marx and Friedrich Engels, *The Holy Family, or Critique of Critical Criticism*, trans. Richard Dixon and Clemens Dutt (Moscow: Progress Publishers, 1980), 41, 53.
70 Proudhon, *What is Property?*, 215.
71 Marx, *Capital*, vol.1, 929.
72 We know the circumstances of their final quarrel. In May 1845, Marx suggested Proudhon become the French correspondent of a communist information network. Proudhon refused, and this precipitated the rupture between the two. In 1847, Marx wrote a violently anti-Proudhonian text, *The Poverty of Philosophy*, which was a response to Proudhon's *The System of Economic Contradictions, or the Philosophy of Poverty* (1846). This was the beginning of a series of hostile remarks concerning Proudhon and a political battle that extended to the struggles against Bakunin and his supporters within the International. After calling him the "Socialist of Empire," Marx nevertheless acknowledged Proudhon's great courage in his obituary, especially when the latter faced a furiously hostile National Assembly on July 31, 1848.
73 Karl Marx and Friedrich Engels, "Manifesto of the Communist Party." *The Marx-Engels Reader*, ed. Robert C. Tucker (New York: W.W. Norton & Company, 1978), 485.
74 Max, *Capital*, vol. 1, 443.
75 Ibid., 447.
76 Ibid., 448.
77 Ibid., 449.
78 Ibid., 451.
79 Ibid.
80 Ibid.
81 Ibid.
82 There are in fact many passages in Marx's political writing that strikingly resemble Proudhon's work. In *The Eighteenth Brumaire of Louis Bonaparte*, for instance, Marx describes the French centralized state as an "appalling parasitic growth, which enmeshes the body of French society like a net and chokes all its pores." And he later discusses state centralization in the following manner: "every *common* interest was straightaway severed from society, counter-posed to it as a higher, *general* interest, snatched from the self-activity of society's members and made an object of governmental inquiry." See "The Eighteenth Brumaire of Louis Bonaparte." *The Marx-Engels Reader*, ed. Robert C. Tucker (New York: W.W. Norton & Company, 1978), 607. And for further commentary, see Dardot and Laval, *Marx, Prénom : Karl*, 273.
83 Karl Marx, "The Eighteenth Brumaire of Louis Bonaparte." *The Marx-Engels Reader*, ed. Robert C. Tucker (New York: W.W. Norton & Company, 1978), 606. This is the passage in which Marx cites Shakespeare's famous phrase "well grubbed, old mole!"
84 Marx, *Grundrisse*, 699.
85 Ibid., 692.
86 In his seminar dedicated to the *Grundrisse* (and published in *Marx Beyond Marx* [1991]), Antonio Negri emphasized the exceptional nature of Marx's 1857–1858 writings. While we do not necessarily ascribe to Negri's view that Marx was able to

invert his theoretical objectivism by assigning revolutionary subjectivity (both theoretically and practically) to the proletariat, we agree with Negri that the *Grundrisse* contains numerous original passages that are of great importance when it comes to understanding Marx's thought.

87 Marx, *Grundrisse*, 693.
88 Ibid.
89 Ibid., 699.
90 Ibid., 700.
91 Ibid.
92 Ibid., 694–695.
93 Ibid., 704.
94 Ibid.
95 Ibid., 700.
96 Ibid., 708.
97 Ibid., 709.
98 Ibid., 712.
99 Ibid., 706.
100 Ibid., 705.
101 Ibid.
102 Ibid., 706.
103 Ibid., 708.
104 See William Morris, *How We Live, and How We Might Live* (Nottingham: Five Leaves Publishing, 2015).
105 Marx, *Grundrisse*, 662.
106 Ibid., 705.
107 Ibid.
108 See Chapter 2, "Communism as 'Association of Producers.'"
109 See Chapter 9, "The 'Social Constitution.'"
110 Michael Hardt and Antonio Negri, *Declaration* (New York: Argo, 2012), 13.
111 Hardt and Negri, *Commonwealth*, 283–284.
112 Ibid., 301. See Patrick Rozenblatt, "Vers de nouvelles formes de coopération dans le travail." *Futur antérieur* (Sept. 1994).
113 Hardt and Negri sometimes play with words when they equate the extractive logic of the rentier in the context of intellectual cooperation to conditions of real subsumption of capital and society under capital in which there is no longer anything "organic."
114 In Hardt and Negri's words, "the distributed network structure provides the model for an absolutely democratic organization that corresponds to the dominant forms of economic and social production and is also the most powerful weapon against the ruling power structure" (*Multitude*, 88).

6 The Law of Property and the Unappropriable

1 Qtd. in Ostrom, *Governing the Commons*, 2. See Aristotle, *Politics*, 42 (1261b).
2 Ibid., 46 (1262b).
3 Ibid.
4 Aristotle, *Politics and the Constitution of Athens*, trans. Steven Everson (Cambridge: Cambridge University Press, 2012), 36 (1263a). Translator's note: for this passage, I have cited the Cambridge translation of Aristotle's *Politics*, by Steven Everson, because

it more directly translates Aristotle's *koinônein* into the English "common," and is therefore better suited to Dardot and Laval's purposes in this specific context.

5 See Chapter 2.
6 Aristotle, *Politics*, 36 (1263a).
7 Aristotle, *Nicomachean Ethics*, trans. Terence Irwin (Indianapolis: Hackett Publishing, 1999), 150 (1170b).
8 Pierre Aubenque, *Problèmes aristotéliciens. Philosophie pratique* (Paris: Vrin, 2011), 209.
9 For more on this, see Chapter 10.
10 Hannah Arendt, *The Human Condition*, 194–195.
11 Aristotle specifies, however, that the term *politikè* also applies to the "legislative," which should suffice to exclude this second space from being declared "pre-political" and ejected from the political as such: *politikè* is thus the generic name that encompasses both species *and* the specific name for the second species.
12 Aristotle, *Nichomachean Ethics*, 92 (1141b, 29).
13 Arendt, *The Human Condition*, 195.
14 Pierre Aubenque, *Problèmes aristotéliciens*, 81.
15 Ibid., 83.
16 See Chapter 1.
17 Aristotle, *Politics*, 112 (1282b). The Greeks distinguished amongst goods in terms of the useful or the suitable (*agathon*) and the good in the sense of acquisition and possession (*ktêsis*): the common advantage, which is not the same as the politico-philosophical notion of the general interest, constitutes a good in the first sense of the term but not the second (since it cannot be an object of possession).
18 We should point out, here, that deliberative power, for Aristotle, is the power exercised by the Assembly.
19 Pierre Aubenque, *Problèmes aristotéliciens*, 171.
20 Ibid.
21 Aristotle *Politics*, 12.
22 Pierre Aubenque, *Problèmes aristotéliciens*, 172. We must therefore not give *taxis* the sense of an order made by the political community and its instantiation, but the active sense of an ordering that constitutes the political community, a meaning that refers directly to the activity of sharing or pooling in common.
23 The evocation of "nature" here by Aristotle does not at all cancel out the necessity of intentionally instituting the political community. In this sense, his naturalism is the opposite of the naturalization of the common as discussed in Part 1.
24 As Hegel observes in his work on natural right, the Greeks used the verb *politeuein* to signify active participation in public affairs. It would be inaccurate to translate this verb as politics in the sense of the specialized activity of a minority of professionals within a pre-established constitutional order. *Politeuein*, rather, refers to the collective activity of all citizens in matters of public affairs, which implies something closer to sharing in common or *koinônein*.
25 This phrase is borrowed from Alain Testart's article "Propriété et non-propriété de la terre." *Études rurales*, no. 165–166 (January–June 2003), 1.
26 Marx, *Capital*, vol. 1, 171.
27 Ibid., 929. For further interpretation of this passage, see Dardot and Laval, *Marx, Prénom : Karl*, 641.
28 In 1855, Marx read Barthold Georg Niebuhr's *History of Rome*, which included a section titled "The Possessions in the *Ager Publicus*" that explains the origin and nature of the *ager publicus*. See Paul Sereni, *Marx, la personne et la chose* (Paris: Harmattan, 2007), 152–154.

29 This is the definition provided in *Ager Publicus* (vol. 4, 133) of the monumental *Dictionnaire des antiquités grecques et romaines* by Daremberg and Saglio (Paris: Hachette, 1887–1919), which cites Niebuhr in Footnote 16 concerning *deditio*, or the process through which foreign annexed territory could be rendered *ager publicus* (the other method being the use of force after the destruction of a city).
30 Paul Sereni, *Marx, la personne et la chose*, 144. In an 1841 letter to Blanqui on the subject of property, Proudhon discusses the example of the Roman Republic to justify his conception of "possession" as a form of appropriation that excludes an absolute right and an unlimited sovereignty over things. Ibid, 147–148.
31 Marx, *Grundrisse*, 476.
32 Ibid., 483.
33 Ibid.
34 Ibid., 484.
35 Paul Sereni, *Marx, la personne et la chose*, 159.
36 Marx, *Grundrisse*, 485.
37 Alain Testart, *Avant l'histoire: L'évolution des sociétés de Lascaux à Carnac* (Paris: Gallimard, 2012).
38 Ibid., 408. Testart cites the words of an Inuit anthropologist on this subject: "in principle, the situation is this: personal possession is conditioned by the actual use of property."
39 Ibid.
40 Ibid., 410.
41 Ibid., 417.
42 Ibid., 431
43 Ibid., 430, note 3. As Tacitus writes, "the great extent of the land makes the division easy. They plough different fields every year and there is still spare land available." See Tacitus, *Agricola and Germania*, trans. A.R. Birley (Oxford: Oxford University Press, 1999), 50. Testart states (in the same note) that Tacitus opposes *ager* (the earth in general) from *arvum* (the earth that is plowed and seeded).
44 Ibid., 431.
45 Ibid., 451–457.
46 Engels only uses the term once. He does not define the term precisely, nor does he reserve it for the Germans alone (ibid., 483, note 2).
47 Ibid., 482.
48 Ibid., 485.
49 Ibid., 488.
50 Ibid., 488–489.
51 Ibid., 511.
52 Alain Testart, "Propriété et non-propriété de la terre," 16–17.
53 Ibid., 3.
54 Ibid., 7.
55 Ibid., 14–15.
56 Ibid., 23–35. For more on the concept of *terra nullius*, see Chapter 1.
57 Ibid., 16.
58 Ibid.
59 See Chapter 2.
60 Thomas Aquinas, "Second Part of the Second Part, Question 66: On Theft and Robbery," in *Summa Theologica* (translated by Fathers of the English Dominican Province): http://www.documentacatholicaomnia.eu/03d/1225-1274,_Thomas_Aquinas,_Summa_Theologiae_%5B1%5D,_EN.pdf.

61 Leo XIII, *Rerum novarum*. "On the Condition of the Workers," May 15, 1891. The target of the encyclical is socialism, as can be seen in the following passage: "It is clear that the main tenet of socialism, the community of goods, must be utterly rejected, since it only injures those whom it would seem meant to benefit, is directly contrary to the natural rights of mankind, and would introduce confusion and disorder into the commonweal. The first and most fundamental principle, therefore, if one would undertake to alleviate the condition of the masses, must be the inviolability of private property." In this document, the Catholic Church unconditionally rallied in support of the ideological principles of capitalism. See: http://w2.vatican.va/content/leo-xiii/en/encyclicals/documents/hf_l-xiii_enc_15051891_rerum-novarum.html.
62 Aquinas, "Second Part of the Second Part, Question 66: On Theft and Robbery," in *Summa Theologica*: http://www.documentacatholicaomnia.eu/03d/1225–1274,_Thomas_Aquinas,_Summa_Theologiae_%5B1%5D,_EN.pdf.
63 Leo XIII, *Rerum novarum*: http://w2.vatican.va/content/leo-xiii/en/encyclicals/documents/hf_l-xiii_enc_15051891_rerum-novarum.html.
64 Leo XIII, *Rerum novarum*: http://w2.vatican.va/content/leo-xiii/en/encyclicals/documents/hf_l-xiii_enc_15051891_rerum-novarum.html.
65 John Locke, *Two Treatises of Government* (Cambridge: Cambridge University Press, 1988), 287 (§27).
66 For more on this point see Dardot and Laval, *The New Way of the World*, 129.
67 Locke, *Two Treatises on Government*, 298–299 (§44): "From all which it is evident, that though the things of Nature are given in common, yet Man (by being Master of himself, and *Proprietor of his own Person,* and the Actions or *Labour* of it) had still in himself *the great Foundation of Property*; and that which made up the great part of what he applyed to the Support or Comfort of his being, when Invention and Arts had improved the conveniences of Life, we perfectly his own, and did not belong in common to others."
68 Léon Walras, *Études d'économie sociale. Théorie de la répartition de la richesse sociale* (Paris: F. Pinchon, 1896), 214–215.
69 Adolphe Thiers, *De la propriété* (Paris: Paulin, Lheureux et Cie, 1848), 39.
70 Ibid., 22.
71 Ibid., 36.
72 Ibid., 28.
73 Ibid., 25.
74 Ibid., 95.
75 Locke, *Two Treatises of Government*, 302 (§ 51): "Right and conveniency went together."
76 See Christian Laval, *Les artifices du capitalism* (Paris: PUF, 2003) and Stephen G. Engelmann, *Imagining Interest in Political Thought: Origins of Economic Rationality* (Durham: Duke University Press, 2003).
77 Léon Walras, *Études d'économie sociale*, 237.
78 Robert-Joseph Pothier, *Traité du droit de domaine de propriété*, t. 1, Debures père, no. 21 (1777): 23–24, qtd. in Marie-Alice Chardeaux, *Les Choses communes*, 120 (note 81).
79 Xifaras, *La Propriété*, 378.
80 Ibid. Pierre-Joseph Proudhon also avails himself of this argument in his criticism of Charles Comte in *What is Property?*, 72: "thus the earth, like water, air, and light, is an object of prime necessity which each may use freely, as long as the rights of others are not infringed. Why, then, has the earth been appropriated? Monsieur Ch. Comte's reply is a curious one. Say pretends that it is because it is not transient; Monsieur Ch. Comte

assures us that it is because it is not infinite. The land is limited; therefore, according to Monsieur Ch. Comte, it is something that should be appropriated. It would seem, on the contrary, that he ought to say that it should not be appropriated."

81 Xifaras, *La Propriété*, 379.
82 Ibid., 381–382.
83 Ibid.
84 See Chapter 1.
85 Qtd. in Mikhaïl Xifaras, *La Propriété*, 385 (our emphasis).
86 See Marx, *Grundrisse*, 245 (Marx references the *Institutes of Justinian*).
87 Ibid., 246.
88 On this topic, we're relying on the thesis of Paolo Napoli in his lecture during the April 6, 2011 session of the seminar titled "Du public au commun," which dealt with various conflicts concerning different uses of the law. The term "pandectism" comes from the "Pandectists," which etymologically derives from the Greek *pandectai*, or "that which contains everything." For more on the "Pandectists," see footnote 91 below.
89 Reinhard Zimmerman, "Roman Law and the Harmonization of Private Law in Europe." *Toward a European Civil Code*, ed. Arthur Hartkamp et al. (Leiden: Kluwer Law International, 2004), 29.
90 Harold Berman, *Law and Revolution II: The Impact of the Protestant Reformations on the Western Legal Tradition* (Cambridge: Belknap Press, 2003), 4.
91 These two texts are referred to as *The Pandects* and *The Institutes*. *The Pandects* are better known as *The Digest*, since the Latin title under which they were promulgated in December 533 was *Digesta, sive Pandecta Juris*. Widely used in the Byzantine Empire but little known in the West, this summary of Roman law was re-discovered in Italy in the middle of the eleventh century and became the point of departure for legal scholarship in European universities.
92 Berman, *Law and Revolution II*, 126.
93 Ibid.
94 This phrase comes from Paolo Napoli, "*L'histoire du droit et le commun*," 2.
95 Ibid., 6.
96 Berman, *Law and Revolution*, 116. In note 52, Berman refers to Hans Mullejans's work, *Publicus und Privatus im römischen Recht und imalteren kanonischen Recht unter besonderer Berücksichtigung der Unterscheidung Iuspublicum und Ius privatum* (Munich, 1961), and talks about how "Mullejans concludes from his careful study of the sources that the Roman lawyers and the early ecclesiastical lawyers 'made no clear distinction' between a "*ius publicum*, that is, a law pertinent to the affairs of the state or of the ecclesiastical domain" and "a *ius privatum*, that is a law governing the private affairs of persons."
97 Ibid., 120.
98 Ibid., 126.
99 See Kant's tripartite division two centuries later in his *Doctrine of Right*.
100 See Chapter 1.
101 Yan Thomas, "La valeur des choses. Le droit romain hors la religion." *Annales: Histoire, Sciences sociales*, vol. 6 (2002): 1431–1462.
102 Ibid., 1444. For more on this, see Chapter 1.
103 Paolo Napoli, "*L'histoire du droit et le commun*," 6 (our emphasis).
104 Yan Thomas, "La valeur des choses," 1432.
105 Ibid., 1433.

106 Ibid., 1435 (our emphasis).
107 Ibid.
108 Ibid., 1436.
109 Ibid., 1444. Thomas discusses an example of a sacred building destroyed by an earthquake: the consecrated site did not become profane and it "continued to resist the grip of private sale."
110 Ibid., 1445.
111 Ibid., 1448. In legal history, the qualification *res nullius* "is traditionally related to abundance. If it belongs to no one, and if everyone can use it as they please, without constraint, it is primarily because no one is afraid of depleting it. It is profuse. The herring, for Grotius, writing in the seventeenth century, was thus symbolic of it." See Marine Rémond-Gouilloud, "Ressources naturelles et choses sans maitre." *L'Homme, la Nature et le Droit*, ed. Christian Bourgois (Paris, 1988), 222. The emergence of a shortage can thus bring a thing out of the sphere of *res nullius* and make it enter that of *res communis*, which demonstrates how the point at which a thing belongs to one category or another is always decided historically, and never on the basis of a supposed "essence."
112 Yan Thomas, "La valeur des choses," 1448.
113 Ibid. This point can also be found in Henri Allart's *De l'occupation en droit romain, des brevets d'invention en droit français* (Paris: Moquet, 1877) in the context of a legal development devoted to things without master but which are susceptible to acquisition by "occupation": "it is important not to confuse terms here: we have seen that things *divini juris* – sacrae, religiosae, sanctae – are called *res nullius* in the sense that they do no and *cannot* belong to anyone, insofar as their very nature is irreconcilable with the very idea of private appropriation. The *res nullius* we're describing do not yet belong to anyone, but nevertheless *can* be appropriated" (our emphasis).
114 Ibid.
115 Ibid., 1449. Also see Chapter 1 for more on this point.
116 Ibid., 1461.
117 Ibid., 1462. This meant, for instance, that someone who built his house in the middle of a sacred place was compelled to restore the place to the god.
118 Paolo Napoli, "*L'histoire du droit et le commun*," 7.
119 Ibid.
120 Ibid., 6.
121 Ibid., 8.
122 Rousseau is always eager to remind his readers about the etymology of the term *ministre*, which in French is linked to *serviteur*.
123 Giorgio Agamben, *The Kingdom and the Glory: For a Theological Genealogy of Economy and Government* (Homo Sacer, II 2), trans. Lorenzo Chiesa (Stanford: Stanford University Press, 2011), xi.
124 Ibid., 1. By the expression "economic theology," Agamben tries to indicate that the God of the Trinity (especially in the person of the Son) takes over the management of the world in an immanent way, while the term "economic" is meant etymologically (*oikos*) and designates the management of domestic space.
125 The concluding lines of the book are rather eloquent in this respect: "modernity, by removing God from the world, has not only failed to leave theology behind, but in some ways has done nothing other than to lead the project of the providential *oikonomia* to completion" (287).

126 Ibid., 285.
127 Ibid., 277.
128 This expression comes from the conclusion of Pierre Dardot's presentation at the first session of the seminar titled "Du public au commun" on November 30, 2010 ("Le passage du public au commun," 9). Equality is for us the product of participation in that which makes the *koinônein*.
129 According to Paolo Napoli's forceful expression, "L'histoire du droit et le commun," 9.
130 Ibid., 9. Napoli refers to the demand from the First Epistle of Timothy to "keep the deposit," which he argues should be understood in the sense of "watching over the common heritage of faith and to give an account of it at any time."
131 Ibid.
132 Ibid.
133 Ibid. On this subject, Napoli discusses how the jurists of the twelfth century attributed the ownership of ecclesiastical property to places rather than persons. Thus, the property of the monastery, after the deaths of all its members, belonged to the walls of monastery itself. He also discusses how this legal fiction was taken up by the Italian Court of Cassation in 1953 when it maintained that the walls of the houses of a village remained the owners of the common lands that ensured the subsistence of the inhabitants and which therefore remained depopulated for some time.
134 Marx makes a formal distinction between the two meanings of *Aneignung*, especially in terms of differentiating between "real appropriation" in the labor process and the juridical form of property.
135 Pierre Legendre, *De la Société comme Texte. Linéaments d'une anthropologie dogmati*que (Paris: Fayard, 2001).
136 Pierre Legendre, *Sur la question dogmatique en Occident* (Paris: Fayard, 1999), 106.
137 For more on this ontology, see Chapter 5.
138 Jean-Luc Nancy, *La Communauté affrontée* (Paris: Galilée, 2001), 34.
139 Nancy, "Communism, the Word," 149. Translator's note: Dardot and Laval add the following sentence, which was taken from Nancy's preparatory notes from his lecture at the "The Idea of Communism" conference in London, March 2009: ". . . where politics had before been precisely thought of as the assumption of the common, of a being that was supposedly common."
140 See Pierre Sauvetre, *Crises de gouvernementalité et généalogie de l'État aux* XX*e et* XXI*e siècles*, 183.
141 Nancy, "Communism, the Word," 147.
142 Martin Heidegger, *Being and Time*, trans. John Macquarrie and Edward Robinson (New York: HarperCollins, 1962), 155.
143 Pierre Sauvetre, *Crises de gouvernementalité et généalogie de l'État aux* XX*e et* XXI*e siècles*, 190.
144 Jean-Luc Nancy, *Being Singular Plural*, trans. Robert D. Richardson and Anne E. O'Byrne (Stanford: Stanford University Press, 2000), 34.
145 Nancy, "Communism, the Word," 151.
146 Ibid.
147 Ibid., 148.
148 Robert Esposito, *Terms of the Political: Community, Immunity, Biopolitics*, trans. Rhiannon Noel Welch (New York: Fordham University Press, 2013), 45. Esposito also draws on § 26 from Heidegger's *Being and Time*.
149 Ibid., 45.

150 According to the meanings of *munus* that are privileged by Esposito in his book *Communitas* (Stanford: Stanford University Press, 2009).
151 Esposito, *Terms of the Political*, 15, 18.
152 Ibid., 18.
153 Arendt, *The Human Condition*, 52.
154 Ibid., 55.
155 Ibid., 57–58.
156 Esposito, *Terms of the Political*, 91, 96.
157 Jean-Luc Nancy, *The Truth of Democracy*, trans. Pascale-Anne Brault and Michael Naas (New York: Fordham University Press, 2010), 25.
158 Esposito, *Terms of the Political*, 130.
159 Ibid., 110.
160 Ibid., 15.
161 Ibid., 121. This difficulty is aptly described by Frédéric Neyrat in the preface to the French edition.
162 See Pierre Dardot, Christian Laval, and El Mouhoub Mouhoud, *Sauver Marx?*, 253.
163 Gilles Deleuze and Felix Guattari, *A Thousand Plateaus*, trans. Brian Massumi (Minneapolis: University of Minnesota Press, 1987), 203.
164 Michel Foucault, "What is Revolution," trans. Lysa Hochroth, in *The Politics of Truth* (Los Angeles: Semiotext(e), 2007), 95.
165 Hannah Arendt highly praised the Americans' decision to entrust the US Supreme Court with authority over the US Constitution. See Hannah Arendt, *On Revolution* (New York: Penguin, 2006), 171–207. It is here, however, that we reach the limits of her political intervention, despite her very justified criticisms of the natural community as guaranteeing a "common world." As the site of judiciary power, the Supreme Court enjoys a monopoly in terms of the enunciation of the law, which is completely antithetical to the co-production of law in and through common use. In general, we think this entire political paradigm must be questioned (for a critique of this paradigm, see Chapter 10).
166 Translator's note: in the original French, Dardot and Laval prefer the term *homme du commun* (man of common) over *homme commun* (common man), insofar as the latter sounds more like a sociological or statistical average.

7 Law of the Common and "Common Law"

1 G.W.F. Hegel, *Outlines of a Philosophy of Right*, trans. T.M. Knox (Oxford: Oxford University Press, 2008), 199 (§ 211).
2 For more on this, see Mikhaïl Xifaras, "Marx, justice et jurisprudence. Une lecture des 'vols de bois." *Revue française d'histoire des idées politiques*, no. 15, (April 2002), 22.
3 F.A. Hayek, "The Legal and Political Philosophy of David Hume." *Studies in Philosophy, Politics and Economics* (London: Routledge & Kegan Paul, 1967), 107.
4 Ibid., 108.
5 See Dardot and Laval, *The New Way of the World*, 128.
6 See Pierre Dardot and Christian Laval, *La Nouvelle Raison du monde. Essai sur la société néolibérale* (Paris: La Découverte 2010), 6. We will return in the following chapter to the German Historical School of Savigny in the context of Marx's articles on the "theft of wood." Translator's note: the English translation of Dardot and Laval's

La Nouvelle Raison du Monde is an abridged translation, and accordingly some references to this work can only be found in the original French edition.
7 Ibid., 170.
8 In the analyses that follow, we rely on the second section of *Law and Revolution*, vol. 2, titled "The English Revolution and the Transformation of English Law in the Seventeenth Century," 199–372.
9 Berman, *Law and Revolution*, vol. 2, 461.
10 Ibid., 303.
11 Ibid., 264.
12 Ibid.
13 Ibid., 10.
14 Ibid., 229.
15 Ibid., 214. The Court of Common Pleas, established by Henry II in 1178, was the first permanent royal court.
16 Ibid., 213. Amongst the Prerogative Courts, Berman mentions the Court of the Star Chamber, the Court of Requests, the Court of Marches, and the Court of the High Commission. We should add to this list the High Court of Admiralty and the High Court of Chancery, which were not technically Prerogative Courts but which nonetheless contributed to the consolidation of royal power.
17 Ibid., 217. The suppression of the Prerogative Courts was confirmed by Charles II in 1660, which rendered the decision of the 1641 Parliament irreversible.
18 Ibid., 237.
19 Ibid.
20 Ibid.
21 Ibid., 239.
22 Ibid., 241.
23 *Dictionnaire de philosophie politique*, ed. Philippe Raynaud and Stéphane Rials (Paris: PUF, 2003), 108.
24 Ibid., 242.
25 Ibid.
26 Ibid., 244.
27 Ibid., 243.
28 Ibid., 243 and 465, note 37. Here, Berman points out the difficulty of finding terms in other languages that correspond with this English term.
29 Ibid., 245.
30 It is precisely this ideological conception of the law that Jeremy Bentham attacks in his ironic polemic, especially the belief in what he calls the "wisdom from ancestors." See Jeremy Bentham, *The Book of Fallacies* (Oxford: Oxford University Press, 2015).
31 Berman, *Law and Revolution*, vol. 2, 244.
32 Ibid., 246.
33 Ibid.
34 Ibid., 247.
35 Ibid., 248.
36 Ibid., 256.
37 Ibid.
38 Ibid., 257.
39 Ibid., 259.
40 Ibid., 260.
41 See Raynaud and Rials, *Dictionnaire de philosophie politique*, 108–109.

42 Ibid., 108.
43 Ibid., 274–275.
44 Ibid., 244.
45 Peter Linebaugh, *The Magna Carta Manifesto*, 78. Linebaugh's book is an indispensable source of information on the Magna Carta and provides a very illuminating, if sometimes reductive, approach to the subject. It will be referenced throughout this section of the chapter.
46 These two documents can be consulted at: www.earlyenglishlaws.ca.uk.
47 Linebaugh, *The Magna Carta Manifesto*, 78.
48 Qtd. in "Common Law," in Philippe Raynaud and Stéphane Rials (eds.), *Dictionnaire de philosophie politique*, 110.
49 Ibid., 79.
50 Hannah Arendt, *On Revolution* (New York: Penguin Books, 2006), 33. Berman comes to the same conclusion in his account: "the Puritan Revolution was conceived to be a restoration of the ancient liberties of Englishmen as laid down in the Magna Carta and other medieval statutes and judicial decisions prior to the usurpation of supreme power over church and state by the Tudor-Stuart monarchy more than a century earlier. The Commonwealth's Great Seal of 1649 was inscribed: 'The First Year of Freedome Restored.'" See Berman, *Law and Revolution*, 206.
51 For the 1215 version of the text, see Linebaugh, *The Magna Carta Manifesto*, 81–296.
52 Geoffrey Robertson, *Crimes Against Humanity: The Struggle for Global Justice* (New York: New Press, 1999), 2–3. Qtd. in Linebaugh, *The Magna Carta Manifesto*, 22.
53 Linebaugh, *The Magna Carta Manifesto*, 85.
54 Ibid., 6.
55 Ibid., 38.
56 Ibid., 39. The *Statutes at Large* were collections of Anglo-Saxon laws.
57 Ibid., 300.
58 Ibid., 290.
59 See Jane Winters, "Forest Law," *Institute of Historical Research*: www.earlyenglishlaws.ac.uk.
60 Ibid., 4.
61 Ibid., 291.
62 Jane Winters, "Forest Law": www.earlyenglishlaws.ac.uk. Also see John R. Maddicott, "Magna Carta and the Local Community." *Past and Present*, vol. 102 (1984). Qtd. in Linebaugh, *The Magna Carta Manifesto*.
63 Linebaugh, *The Magna Carta Manifesto*, 34.
64 Ibid., 32–33.
65 Ibid., 33. We tend to render the term "commoners" as both "common practitioners" and "common users," depending on the context; we also render the verb "common" as "practicing the common" and the progressive form "commoning" as "practice of the common."
66 See W.G. Hoskins and L. Dudley Stamp, *The Common Lands of England and Wales* (New York: Harper Collins, 1963).
67 E.P. Thompson, *Customs in Common: Studies in Traditional Popular Culture* (New York: the New Press, 1993), 127. We will refer to this essential work later in order to clarify the relationship between the law of the common and common law.
68 Ibid., 133.
69 Ibid., 37.
70 Linebaugh, *The Magna Carta Manifesto*, 284.
71 These terms can be found in the indispensable glossary at the end of Linebaugh, *The Magna Carta Manifesto*, 302, 306, 308, 309.

72 Ibid., 40.
73 Ibid., 41.
74 Ibid., 297.
75 Ibid. Perhaps the "bad customs" mentioned in the 1215 Charter refer to Purprestures, Wastes, and Asserts or similar legal infractions.
76 Ibid., 296–297.
77 Ibid., 298.
78 Ibid.
79 Ibid., 299.
80 Ibid.
81 Ibid., 300.
82 Ibid., 44.
83 Ibid., 44.
84 Berman, *Law and Revolution*, vol. 2, 332. We must be attentive here and differentiate between "feudal tenure," which characterizes a certain type of relationship between a lord and vassal (by virtue of which the vassal is, for example, obliged to render service of arms or pay a scotage), and "manorial tenure," which denotes the relationship between the manorial owner of a landed estate and its associated peasantry.
85 Ibid.
86 Linebaugh, *The Magna Carta Manifesto*, 79.
87 Ibid.
88 Berman, *Law and Revolution*, vol. 2, 499.
89 Linebaugh, *The Magna Carta Manifesto*, 80.
90 Ibid., 72.
91 Ibid., 45.
92 Ibid., 55.
93 This is in reference to Engel's pamphlet "The Peasant War in Germany." See: https://www.marxists.org/archive/marx/works/1850/peasant-war-germany/.
94 Berman, *Law and Revolution*, vol. 2, 56.
95 Ibid.
96 Linebaugh, *The Magna Carta Manifesto*, 11, 40.
97 See Michel Foucault, *The Birth of Biopolitics: Lectures at the Collège de France, 1978–79*, trans. Graham Burchell (New York: Palgrave-MacMillan, 2008), and Pierre Dardot and Christian Laval, *The New Way of the World* (London: Verso, 2013).
98 E.P. Thompson, *Customs in Common*, 98, 136.
99 Ibid., 124. In Nottingham during the Victorian era, a witness mentions that the opening of common lands usually happened on August 12, and he deplores the violence and abuse practiced by the local population on this occasion.
100 Ibid., 107–108.
101 Ibid., 97.
102 Ibid.
103 Qtd. in ibid., 128–129.
104 Ibid., 129.
105 Ibid., 129 (note 3).
106 Ibid., 129–130.
107 Ibid., 130.
108 Ibid.
109 Ibid., 134.
110 Ibid., 136–137.

111 Ibid., 99.
112 Ibid., 120–121.
113 Qtd. in ibid., 108.
114 Qtd. in ibid., 116.
115 Qtd. in ibid.
116 Ibid., 121. In Leicester, for example, the enclosure movement began in 1708 but wasn't completed until 1803 (ibid., 124).
117 We draw extensively in this section from E.P. Thompson's *Whigs and Hunters: the Origins of the Black Act* (New York: Pantheon Books, 1975). Ibid., 21.
118 Ibid., 22.
119 Ibid., 21–22.
120 Ibid., 22.
121 Ibid., 27.
122 Ibid., 27.
123 Ibid., 190. "King John" was the name of the leader of a band of poachers who stole deer in Hampshire between 1720 and 1723.
124 Ibid., 32.
125 Ibid., 36.
126 Ibid., 62.
127 Ibid., 64.
128 Ibid.
129 Ibid., 136.
130 Ibid., 239.
131 Ibid., 241.
132 Ibid., 261.
133 Ibid.
134 Ibid.
135 Ibid., 264.
136 Ibid., 265, 267.
137 Thompson, *Customs in Common*, 137.
138 Ibid., 139.
139 Ibid.
140 Ibid., 139–140, 143.
141 Ibid., 144.
142 Ibid., 128.
143 Thompson, *Whigs and Hunters*, 267.
144 Thompson, *Customs in Common*, 104.
145 Ibid.
146 Ibid., 110.
147 Ibid., 126.
148 Linebaugh, *The Magna Carta Manifesto*, 279.

8 The "Customary Law of Poverty"

1 See Pierre Lascoumes and Hartwig Zander, *Marx : du "vol de bois" à la critique du droit* (Paris: PUF, 1984), 175. In Edgar Reitz's 2013 film *Die andere Heimat – Chronik einer Sehnsucht* (*Home from Home*), the first scene takes place in 1843 and features a proclamation in a village square prohibiting the collection of dead wood from fallen trees.

2 Ibid., 135.
3 Nadine Vivier, *Propriété collective et identité communale. Les Biens communaux en France 1750–1914* (Paris: Publications de la Sorbonne, 1998), 217.
4 Ibid., 218.
5 Ibid., 218.
6 Ibid., 90 and 113. The list of forest-related offenses established by the Forestry Guard in 1845 gives us an idea of both the diversity and the extent of peasant needs the forest satisfied: theft of blueberries and other fruits of the woods, forest products necessary for the production of brushes and brooms, livestock feed, wood for roofing slats, hop poles (for crossing water), piles, stairs, trestles and scaffolds, pitch resin collected from damaged trees, etc. (Ibid., 95–96).
7 Karl Marx, "Debates on the Law on Thefts of Wood: First Part, October 25, 1842." *Karl Marx, Frederick Engels: Collected Works, Volume 1: 1835–43* (New York: International Publishers, 1975), 226 (our emphasis). Marx refers here to the *Constitutio Criminalis Carolina* adopted in 1532 by the Imperial Diet in Regensburg, which treats "theft by necessity" as a civil rather than criminal matter.
8 Ibid., 230, 231.
9 Xifaras, "Marx, justice et jurisprudence. Une lecture des 'vols de bois,'" 10.
10 Ibid., 11.
11 Marx, "Debates on the Law on Thefts of Wood," 227.
12 Ibid.
13 Xifaras, "Marx, justice et jurisprudence. Une lecture des 'vols de bois,'" 12–13.
14 Ibid., 13.
15 Marx, "Debates on the Law on Thefts of Wood," 235.
16 Ibid.
17 Ibid., 236.
18 Ibid., 236, 237.
19 Ibid., 262–263. This phrase is taken from Charles de Brosses' *Du culte des dieux fétiches ou Parallèle de l'ancienne religion de l'Égypte avec la religion actuelle de Nigriti* (1760), which was translated into German in 1785, and which Marx had just read before writing his articles on the theft of wood.
20 Xifaras, "Marx, justice et jurisprudence. Une lecture des 'vols de bois,'" 13. At the beginning of the October 30 article, Marx reminds us how, "in France, the warden's charge concerns the fact but not the value." Marx, "Debates on the Law on Thefts of Wood," 240.
21 Ibid., 237.
22 Ibid.
23 Ibid., 238.
24 Ibid.
25 Ibid.
26 Ibid.
27 Ibid.
28 Ibid.
29 Ibid., 240.
30 Ibid.
31 Ibid., 241.
32 Ibid.
33 Ibid., 242.
34 Ibid., 245.

35 Ibid., 251.
36 Ibid.
37 Ibid., 253.
38 Ibid., 255.
39 Ibid.
40 Ibid., 259.
41 Ibid., 261.
42 Ibid.
43 Ibid., 262.
44 Xifaras, "Marx, justice et jurisprudence. Une lecture des 'vols de bois,'" 15–16 (note 49).
45 According to Hegel, the particular common interests of all the members of a social estate are those which mediate between the particular interests of each individual and the general interests embodied in the state.
46 Marx, "Debates on the Law on Thefts of Wood," 261.
47 Ibid., 241.
48 Ibid., 236.
49 Qtd. in Ibid., 256.
50 Ibid., 256.
51 For more on this Lockean conception of self-ownership, which Marx never disavows and in fact borrows as the principle of "individual property" in communism, see Dardot and Laval, *Marx, Prénom : Karl,* 645 and 690.
52 Marx, "Debates on the Law on Thefts of Wood," 256.
53 Ibid., 249.
54 Ibid., 248.
55 Ibid.
56 Ibid., 249, 248.
57 See William Shakespeare, *King John*: http://shakespeare.mit.edu/john/full.html.
58 Ibid.
59 Linebaugh, *The Magna Carta Manifesto*, 67.
60 This is what Daniel Bensaïd argues in *Marx: Les Dépossédés. Karl Marx, les voleurs de bois et le droit des pauvres* (Paris: La Fabrique, 2007), 41. The label "liberal rationalist" is borrowed from Althusser's periodization, wherein Althusser designates a "liberal rationalist period" in Marx's intellectual development (ibid., 12).
61 Marx, "Debates on the Law on Thefts of Wood," 230.
62 Ibid.
63 The situation in Germany was very different. At the end of the fifteenth century, Germany was composed of several hundred provinces (*Länder*) united in a rather loose political assemblage called the Empire (*Reich*); each province was governed by imperial law in addition to local and feudal customary laws that differed from one region to the next, as recorded in various legal collections, such as the *Sachsenspiegel* (the "Mirror of the Saxons") or the *Schwabenspiegel* (the "Mirror of the Swabians"), etc. Additionally, customary rights often differed from city to city (see Berman, *Law and Revolution*, 34.).
64 Marx, "Debates on the Law on Thefts of Wood," 230.
65 Ibid., 231.
66 Ibid., 230.
67 Ibid., 231.
68 Ibid.
69 Ibid., 232.

70 Ibid.
71 Ibid.
72 Ibid., 139.
73 Ibid.
74 Hegel, *Outlines of the Philosophy of Right*, 23 (§3).
75 Xifaras, "Marx, justice et jurisprudence. Une lecture des 'vols de bois,'" 35.
76 Marx, "Debates on the Law on Thefts of Wood," 232–233.
77 Ibid., 233.
78 Xifaras, "Marx, justice et jurisprudence. Une lecture des 'vols de bois,'" 8–9.
79 See Chapter 7, and § 211 in Hegel's *Outlines of a Philosophy of Right* in particular.
80 Xifaras, "Marx, justice et jurisprudence. Une lecture des 'vols de bois,'" 25.
81 Ibid., 23–25.
82 Ibid., 29.
83 Ibid., 32.
84 Ibid., 43.
85 Marx, "Debates on the Law on Thefts of Wood," 232.
86 See Xifaras, "Marx, justice et jurisprudence. Une lecture des 'vols de bois,'" 45 (notes 114, 115).
87 Ibid., 46.
88 Marx, "Debates on the Law on Thefts of Wood," 233.
89 Ibid., 234. Translator's note: Marx, in the original German, uses the adverb *schon* (already) to qualify the verb "find" in this sentence, but this is lost in the English translation of the *Collected Works of Marx and Engels*. A more literal (and accurate) translation would thus read, "the poor *already* find their right in their activity." Dardot and Laval are especially interested in Marx's use of *schon*, as they subsequently elaborate.
90 Ibid., 233.
91 Xifaras, "Marx, justice et jurisprudence. Une lecture des 'vols de bois,'" 38 (note 101).
92 To get a precise sense of the concept of "occupation" at the end of the nineteenth century in relation to the concept of "possession," we relied upon the fourth volume of *Dictionnaire des Antiquités grecques et romaines de Daremberg et Sagli* and Chapter 3 of Henri Allart's *De l'occupation en droit romain, des brevets d'invention en droit français* (1877). For exegesis on the distinction between *corpus* and *animus* in relation to the category of possession in Roman law, see the entry on "Possession" written by Jean-Marc Trigeaud in the *Encyclopédie philosophique universelle*, II, *Les Notions philosophiques* (Paris: PUF, 1990).
93 Marx, "Debates on the Law on Thefts of Wood," 231.
94 See Dardot and Laval, *Marx, Prénom : Karl*, 53.
95 Karl Marx, *Critique of Hegel's 'Philosophy of Right'*, trans. Annette Jolin and Joseph O'Malley (Cambridge: Cambridge University Press, 1970), 141. Xifaras rightly emphasizes this "anticipation of the theme of the universal class that developed after 1843." See Xifaras, "Marx, justice et jurisprudence. Une lecture des 'vols de bois,'" 18 (note 57).
96 Marx, "Debates on the Law on Thefts of Wood," 232.
97 Ibid., 234.
98 Hegel, *Outlines of the Philosophy of Right*, 199 (§211).
99 "For Marx, as for Savigny, the principle of the intelligibility of the law (its reason) is not found in the conscious exercise of the faculty of thinking (reason)." Xifaras, "Marx, justice et jurisprudence. Une lecture des 'vols de bois,'" 39.

100 Marx, "Debates on the Law on Thefts of Wood," 234.
101 Xifaras, "Marx, justice et jurisprudence. Une lecture des 'vols de bois,'" 38.
102 Marx, "Debates on the Law on Thefts of Wood," 234.
103 Ibid.
104 Ibid.
105 Ibid.
106 Ibid.
107 This is one of Mikhaïl Xifaras's suggestions in "Marx, justice et jurisprudence. Une lecture des 'vols de bois,'" 38 (note 101).
108 Johann Gottlieb Fichte, *The Closed Commercial State*, trans. Curtis Adler (New York: SUNY Press, 2012), 130.
109 Ibid.
110 Ibid.
111 Ibid.
112 Fichte, *The Closed Commercial State*, 201 (footnote 1).
113 Ibid., 130–131.
114 Ibid.
115 We have every reason to think that Marx had indeed read Fichte, given his close intellectual relationship with the Fichtean Bruno Bauer during the years 1840–1841. Marx even collaborated with Bauer in the drafting of a pamphlet titled *The Trumpet of the Last Judgment.*
116 We should think in particular here of the position of the class in immediate relation to the land – i.e., the "substantive estate" of the landowners – and its status in the House of Representatives as Hegel conceives it.
117 Marx, "Debates on the Law on Thefts of Wood," 235.
118 Ibid.
119 We are in complete agreement in this respect with Mikhaïl Xifaras, in "Marx, justice et jurisprudence. Une lecture des 'vols de bois,'" 37.
120 Nadine Vivier, "Le rôle économique et social des biens communaux en France." *Les Sociétés rurales en Allemagne et en France, actes du colloque international de Göttingen* (Caen: AHSR, 2000), 195.
121 Reiner Pass, "Les communaux et leur usage dans l'économie domestique paysanne," 179.
122 Nadine Vivier, *Propriété collective et identité communale*, 299.
123 Nadine Vivier, "Le rôle économique et social des biens communaux en France," 205.
124 Mikhaïl Xifaras, "Marx, justice et jurisprudence," 47.
125 Jean Jaurès, *Les Origines du socialisme allemande* (Toulouse: Librairie Ombres Blanches, 2010), 57. The argument in this chapter is, actually, mainly concerned with the question of value measurement: Fichte's answer involves the creation of two measures of value: a "use" value and a "work" value, which he is ultimately unable to reconcile.
126 Jean Jaurès, *Histoire socialiste de la Révolution française*, t. I, La Constituante, première partie (Paris: Éditions Sociales, 1983), 283–284.
127 Ibid., 282. Note 17 then reads as follows: "the ears that escape the harvesters belonged to the poor; it was God's share; the wheat was traditionally gathered, and on the field there was a very high thatch that also belonged to the poor. Hence the hostility to the use of the scythe, on the part of these poor beneficiaries, which cut the wheat at ground level and left only a very short stubble."
128 Ibid., 286 (our emphasis).

129 Ibid., 295.
130 Ibid., 302.
131 Ibid., Volume IV, *Le Gouvernement révolutionnaire*, 142.
132 Ibid.
133 Ibid.
134 Ibid., 145.
135 Ibid (our emphasis).

9 The Workers' Common

1 Translator's note: in English, the term "associationism" also denotes a school of thought in theoretical psychology. Built successively on the work of philosophers such as John Locke, David Hume, John Stuart Mill, and Ivan Pavlov, psychological associationism conceives human consciousness as a series of successive and "associated" mental representations linked by an underlying principle. For an account of the history of socialist associationism, see Philippe Chanial, *La Délicate Essence du socialisme. L'association, l'individu et la République* (Bordeux, Le Bord de l'eau, 2009).
2 See Émile Coornaert, *Les Compagnonnages en France du Moyen Âge à nos jours* (Paris: les Éditions Ouvrières, 1966). For the historical relationship between these brotherhoods and fraternal societies, we make reference to the interesting remarks of André Gueslin, *L'Invention de l'économie sociale* (Paris: Economica, 1998), 146.
3 Speech from the Sitting of June 14, 1791. Qtd. in Henri Hatzfeld, *Du paupérisme à la sécurité sociale, 1850–1940* (Nancy: Presses universitaires de Nancy, 2004), 192.
4 See Henri Desroche, *Le Projet coopératif. Son utopie et ses pratiques, son appareil et ses réseaux* (Paris: Les Éditions Ouvrières, 1976) and "Sociétaires et compagnons. Des associations ouvrières aux coopératives de production (1831–1900)." *Archives de sciences sociales de la coopération et du développement*, no. 55 (1981), 51–73.
5 Translator's note: *Bourses du travail*, which translates most directly as "labor exchanges," were a form of labor council that emerged in France during the Third Republic. The councils were working-class (but also government sanctioned and surveilled) organizations built on the principles of mutual aid and self-organization.
6 See Édouard Dolléans, "Introduction." Jean Vial, *La Coutume chapelière. Histoire du mouvement ouvrier dans la chapellerie* (Paris: Éditions Domat-Montchrestien, 1941), III.
7 Beatrice and Sidney Webb, *The History of Trade Unionism* (New York: Longmans, Green, 1920), 1–64.
8 Ibid., 114.
9 Qtd. in ibid., 115–116.
10 See Chapter 5.
11 Karl Marx, "Inaugural Address of the Working Men's International Association." *Collected Works*, vol. 20 (New York: International Publishers, 1985), 11.
12 On the question of law, see Célestin Bouglé, *La Sociologie de Proudhon* (Paris: Armand Colin, 1911).
13 Pierre-Joseph Proudhon, "Letter to Clerc, March 16, 1863," *Correspondance* (Geneva, Slatkine), 309. Qtd. in Georges Gurvitch, *L'Idée du droit social. Notion et système du droit social. Histoire doctrinale depuis le XVIIe siècle jusqu' à la fin du XIXe siècle* (Aalen: Scientia Verlag, 1972), 353.
14 Pierre-Joseph Proudhon, qtd. by George Gurvitch, "Proudhon aujourd'hui," in *Écrits allemands II* (Paris: L'Harmattan, 2006) 51.

15 Proudhon, *What is Property?*, 23.
16 Pierre-Joseph, *General Idea of Revolution in the Nineteenth Century*, trans. John Beverley Robinson (New York: Gordon Press, 1972), 243.
17 Gurvitch, *L'Idée du droit social*, 339.
18 In this sense, Proudhon anticipates Duguit's theory of public services. See Léon Duguit, *Law and the Modern State: French and German Doctrines* (Hardpress Publishing, 2012) and *Manuel de droit constitutionnel. Théorie générale de l'État, organisation politique* (Paris: A. Fontemoing, 1907).
19 On these points, see Gurvitch, *L'Idée du droit social*, 346.
20 Proudhon, *Systèmes des contradictions économiques ou Philosophie de la misère*, 266.
21 Bouglé, *La Sociologie de Proudhon*, 186–187.
22 Ibid., 187.
23 Pierre-Joseph Proudhon, *De la justice dans la Révolution et dans l'Église*, 157.
24 Proudhon, qtd. in Gurvitch, *L'Idée du droit social*, 374. Proudhon seems to lean toward the absolutism of property, rather than the absolutism of the state, in his posthumously published book *The Theory of Property* (see: https://blog.proudhonlibrary.org/category/proudhons-works/theory-of-property/). Once the economic issue of *aubaines* (Proudhon's version of "surplus value") has been dealt with, property's only justification, for Proudhon, is political insofar as it opposes the absolutism of the state. "Property is egoism idealized, consecrated, invested with a political and juridical function." He goes so far as to say the "egoistic faculty . . . has rightly been designated by nature as the first representative and manager of the law."
25 Proudhon, "Letter to A.M. Cournot, Aug 31, 1853," *Correspondance*, vol. IV, 370.
26 Gurvitch, *L'Idée du droit social*, 335.
27 Qtd. in Bouglé, *La Sociologie de Proudhon*, 111.
28 Proudhon, *The General Idea of Revolution*, 110.
29 Proudhon, *De la capacité politique des classes ouvrières*, 113–114.
30 Gurvitch, *L'Idée du droit social*, 363.
31 Ibid., 38.
32 As opposed to a utilitarian conception of law, Grotius finds the source of law in humanity: "this Sociability . . . or this Care for maintaining Society . . . is the Fountain of Right, properly so called." Hugo Grotius, *The Rights of War and Peace*, Book 1 (Indianapolis: Liberty Fund, 2005), 85–86.
33 George Gurvitch, "La philosophie du droit de Hugo Grotius et la théorie moderne du droit international," *Revue de métaphysique et de morale* (1927). Gurvitch refers to the following passage from Grotius's *The Rights of War and Peace*: "in Matters for which each Association was instituted, the whole Body, or the major Part in the Name of the whole Body, oblige all and every the particular Members of the Society" (545).
34 As Gurvitch points out, the term "socialist," contrary to popular opinion, was not born at the beginning of the nineteenth century, but was used in the legal tradition of natural social law in the seventeenth century to refer to Grotius. See Gurvitch, "La philosophie du droit de Hugo Grotius et la théorie moderne du droit international," 377 (note 3).
35 Proudhon, *General Idea of the Revolution in the Nineteenth Century*, 219.
36 Ibid., 216.
37 Ibid., 221.
38 Ibid., 223.
39 Ibid.
40 Pierre-Joseph Proudhon, *Correspondance de P-J Proudhon*, ed. Jérôme Langlois, vol. 14 (Paris: Librarie Internationale, 1975), 290.

41 Proudhon, *General Idea of the Revolution in the Nineteenth Century*, 246.
42 In *Les Confessions d'un révolutionnaire* Proudhon wrote, "in every society, there are two types of constitutions: I call one the social constitution, the other is the political constitution." Whereas the latter is based on authority, the former is based on the organization of economic forces and the "balance of interests based on free contracts." The social constitution, for Proudhon, is the outcome of a process of discovering principles and rules "that are still today the subject of much socialist controversy" (217).
43 On this point, see Isaac Joshua, *La Révolution selon Karl Marx* (Geneva: Pages 2, 2012).
44 Georges Gurvitch, *Éléments de sociologie juridique* (Paris: Aubier-Montaigne, 1940), 58–59.
45 Voyenne, *Le Fédéralisme et Proudhon*, 148.
46 This work was written in 1864 and published posthumously in 1870 under the title *Contradictions politiques. Théorie du mouvement constitutionnel au XIXe siècle* (Paris; Lacroix, Verboeckhoven et Cie, 1870). It features a preface, written by M.L. Boutteville, explaining the conditions under which this posthumous text was published.
47 Proudhon often critiqued the liberals of his age for wanting to give more power to local government without completely renouncing state centralization; this kind of liberalism undermines true federalism. The prototypical liberal, for Proudhon, is Édouard Laboulaye. He is "one of those 'soft geniuses' who always wants to find a 'happy medium.'" See Proudhon, *Contradictions politiques*, 245.
48 Ibid., 226.
49 Ibid., 225.
50 Ibid., 237.
51 Ibid., 237.
52 Ibid., 245–246.
53 Ibid., 237.
54 Pierre-Joseph Proudhon, *De la capacité politique des classes ouvrières*, 123.
55 Maxime Leroy, *La Coutume ouvrière. Syndicats, bourses, fédérations professionnelles, coopératives, Doctrines et institutions*, 2 volumes (Paris: CNT-RP, 2007).
56 Ibid., vol. 1, 25.
57 Ibid.
58 Qtd. by Leroy, *La Coutume ouvrière*, vol. 1, 293. See Fernand Pelloutier, *L'Organization coopérative et l'Anarchie* (Paris: L'Art Social), 18.
59 Ibid., 28.
60 Ibid., 29.
61 Ibid., 201.
62 Ibid., 28.
63 Marcel Mauss, "L'action socialiste." *Le Mouvement socialiste*, October 15, 1899. See Marcel Mauss, *Écrits politiques* (Paris: Fayard, 1997), 79, 79.
64 Leroy, *La Coutume ouvrière*, vol. 1, 26.
65 Émile Levasseur, *Histoire des classes ouvrières en France depuis la Révolution jusqu'à nos jours* (Paris: Librairie de Guillaumin et Cie, 1867).
66 Leroy, *La Coutume ouvrière*, vol. 1, 26.
67 Ibid., 200.
68 Ibid., 39.
69 Ibid., 57.
70 Ibid., 194.
71 Ibid., 196. The *jaunes* must therefore submit to the *rouges* when the latter are in a majority position on a strike vote because they all share a collective fate.

72 While composing his work in 1913, Maxime Leroy was still optimistic about the development of systems of obligations that might constitute an international workers' society. See Leroy, *La Coutume ouvrière*, vol. 2, 825.
73 Ibid., 530.
74 Marcel Mauss, *The Gift: the Form and Reason for Exchange in Archaic Societies*, trans. W.D. Halls (New York: W.W. Norton, 1990).
75 See Jacques Godbout and Alain Caillé (eds.), See *L'Esprit du don* (Paris: La Découverte, 1992) and Philippe Chanial (eds.), *La Société vue du don. Manuel de sociologie anti-utilitariste appliquée* (Paris: La Découverte, 2008).
76 On all these points, see Sylvain Dzimira, *Marcel Mauss, savant et politique* (Paris: La Découverte, 2007).
77 On the eve of the First World War, there were more than 3,000 consumer cooperatives in France.
78 Marcel Mauss, "La coopération socialiste." *L'Humanité*, August 3, 1904, in *Écrits politiques*, 142.
79 On this topic, see the texts Mauss dedicated to the Russian revolution and bolshevism, especially "Appréciation sociologique du bolchevisme," in *Écrits politiques*, 537.
80 For more on this, see Henri Desroche, "Marcel Mauss 'citoyen' et 'camarade': ses incursions écrites dans le domaine du normative." *Revue française de sociologie*, vol. 20 (1979), 221–237.
81 Marcel Mauss, qtd. by Henri Desroche, "Sociétaires et compagnons."
82 Marcel Mauss, "La coopération socialiste," 147.
83 In the July 16, 1906 edition of *L'Humanité* Mauss argued, in the context of a plan for a "national cooperative" state: "voilà the two ideas of ancient communism and modern individualism; voilà the rivalries are suppressed; voilà the benefits made uniform; voilà widespread safety everywhere ; voilà equalized purchasing power for everyone ; voilà the unlimited possibility of accumulating funds ; voilà the indefinite extension of cooperation in all districts where it has been difficult to penetrate."
84 See Henri Desroche, "Jean Jaurès ou l'économie sociale comme économie collective." *Pour un traité d'économie sociale* (Paris: Coopérative d'information et d'édition mutualiste, 1983), 115–128.
85 Jean Jaurès, "Coopération socialiste," *La Petite République*, September 19, 1900.
86 Qtd. in Jean Gaumont, *Au confluent de deux grandes idées. Jaurès coopérateur* (Paris: Fédération nationale des coopératives de consommation, 1959), 71.
87 On Jaurès's conception of social property, see Philippe Chanial, "La propriété sociale contre l'État. Jaurès, le collectivisme et l'association." *Contretemps*, no. 5 (2002). Also see Philippe Chanial, *La Délicate Essence du socialisme*, 141.
88 Marcel Mauss, "L'action directe." *Écrits politiques*, 187.
89 Marcel Mauss, "L'action socialiste," *Écrits politiques*, 78.
90 Ibid., 76–77.
91 Mauss, "Les coopératives et les socialistes." *Écrits politiques*, 115.
92 Mauss, "Appréciation sociologique du bolchevisme," 557.
93 Mauss, "L'action socialiste," 80.
94 Mauss, "La coopération socialiste," 146.
95 Marcel Mauss, "Manifeste coopératif des intellectuels et universitaires français," *Revue des études coopératives*, October–December (1921), 7. See Henri Desroche, "Marcel Mauss, 'citizen' and 'comrade,'" 231.
96 Mauss, "Manifeste coopératif des intellectuels et universitaires français," 8. In his address to the first National and International Congress of Socialist Cooperatives in

July 1900 in Paris, Mauss called for a national and international federation of cooperatives: "when we have founded immense cooperative workshops on the model of communist production; when we have completely overrun the branches of production, either by regulating prices by wholesale purchase, or by blacklisting the factories that exploit the workers and fight against unions, or by producing goods ourselves; when we have created, through a whole network of solidarity institutions, a close and intimate union between all the members of the workers' cooperatives; when we have established our own relations with diverse workers' organizations: producer cooperatives, professional unions, and the international workers party, then we can think of organizing ourselves internationally in a complete way."

97 Mauss, "Appréciation sociologique du bolchevisme," 555.
98 Ibid., 554.
99 Mauss, "La coopération socialiste," 146.
100 Jean-Louis Laville, *Politique de l'association* (Paris: Le Seuil, 2010), 82.
101 Ibid., 237.
102 See Stéphane Beaud and Michel Pialoux, *Retour sur la condition ouvrière* (Paris: La Découverte/Poche, 2012).
103 Mauss, "Appréciation sociologique du bolchevisme," 541.
104 Hannah Arendt, "Reflections on the Hungarian Revolution," *The Journal of Politics*, vol. 20, no. 1 (Feb 1958): 5–43. While Arendt argues that the revolutionary councils were "primarily the answer to political tyranny," the workers' councils were a "reaction against trade unions that did not represent the workers but the party's control over them" (29).
105 Ibid., 30: "Under modern conditions, the councils are the only democratic alternative we know to the party system, and the principles on which they are based stand in sharp opposition to the principles of the party system in many respects."
106 See Part 3, Proposition 5.
107 Karl Marx, "Inaugural Address of the Working Men's International Association." *The Marx-Engels Reader*, ed. Robert C. Tucker (New York: W.W. Norton & Company, 1978), 518.
108 Ibid.
109 Ibid.
110 Karl Marx, "The Civil War in France." *The Marx-Engels Reader*, ed. Robert C. Tucker (New York: W.W. Norton & Company, 1978), 629.

10 Instituent Praxis

1 See Chapter 7.
2 See the end of Chapter 6.
3 Vincent Descombes, *Les Embarras de l'identité* (Paris: Gallimard, 2013), 245 (our emphasis).
4 See Marcel Mauss, *Essais de sociologie* (Paris: Le Seuil, 1971).
5 "Institution," *l'Encyclopédie philosophique universelle*, vol. 2, *Les Notions philosophiques*.
6 The active significance of the word is retained in the French verb *instituer*, which designates the establishment of a standard of action, the establishment of a legitimate power, the delegation of a title or power to someone, or the act of training or educating a natural being in the art of self-regulation. It is precisely this last meaning that Montaigne adopts in his essay titled "On Educating Children." See Michel de

Montaigne, "Chapter 26: On Educating Children," *The Complete Essays* (London: Penguin Classics, 2003).

7 See Chaïm Perelman, *Droit, morale, philosophie* (Paris: LGDJ, 1968).

8 Émile Durkheim, *The Rules of Sociological Method*, trans. W.D. Halls (New York: The Free Press, 1982), 45

9 Qtd. in *Dictionnaire de la pensée sociologique* (Paris: PUF, 2005), 360.

10 The German verb *vorfinden*, which belongs to the language of Hegel and Marx (as we will discuss later in this chapter), is especially apt in this context.

11 Mauss, *Essais de sociologie*, 16 (our emphasis).

12 Ibid., 16–17.

13 Ibid., 17.

14 Ibid.

15 Ibid., 26.

16 Ibid., 28–29.

17 Max Weber, *Economy and Society: an Outline of Interpretative Sociology*, vol. 1, trans. Ephraim Fischoff et al. (Berkeley: University of California Press, 1978), 52.

18 Ibid., 50.

19 Ibid., 51.

20 Ibid., 54.

21 Ibid., 53.

22 Ibid., 92. Weber here introduces the concept of "constitution" in a non-juridical sense to signify "when, for what purposes, and *within what limits*, or possibly under what special conditions (such as the approval of gods or priests or the consent of electors), the membership of the organization will submit to the leadership."

23 Jean-Paul Sartre, *Critique of Dialectical Reason*, trans. Alan Sheridan-Smith (London: NLB, 1976), 600.

24 Ibid.

25 Ibid., 269.

26 This example is borrowed from Alphonse De Waelhens, "Sartre et la raison dialectique." *Revue philosophique de Louvain*, 3rd Series, vol. 60, no. 65 (1962), 88.

27 Sartre, *Critique of Dialectical Reason*, 348.

28 Ibid.

29 Ibid (in the sense of Hegel's notion of *aufheben*).

30 Ibid. 446, 447.

31 Ibid., 600.

32 Ibid., 583. For Sartre, it is not by accident that this emphasis on hierarchy leads, in the case of the army, to "the archetypal institutional group" (ibid., 604).

33 Ibid., 599.

34 Ibid., 608.

35 Ibid., 628.

36 Ibid.

37 Ibid., 606.

38 Ibid.

39 Ibid., 608.

40 Ibid., 620.

41 Carl Schmitt, *Constitutional Theory*, trans. Jeffrey Seitzer (Durham: Duke University Press, 2008).

42 For their definition of these three elements, see Hardt and Negri, *Commonwealth*, 357.

43 Specifically the Spinoza of the *Tractatus Politicus* (1677) and the Machiavelli of the *Discourses on Livy* (1531). For Hardt and Negri, these two authors constitute a "minor line" of political theory that conceives of institutions in terms of social conflict, as opposed to the "major line" that is based on the social contract tradition (ibid., 355).
44 Ibid., 358.
45 Ibid.
46 Ibid.
47 Ibid.
48 Ibid., 371.
49 Ibid., 372.
50 Ibid., 373.
51 Ibid. It is in this respect that Hardt and Negri argue that the global governance of empire has "the merit" of "registering the increasing autonomy of the network of singularities, the overflowing and unmeasurable forms of value produced by the multitude, and the ever greater power of the common" (ibid., 372).
52 Ibid., 374.
53 Ibid., 375.
54 Ibid.
55 This was a definition given by Negri during the seminar "Du public au common" on March 21, 2012.
56 Hardt and Negri, *Declaration*, 51.
57 Ibid., 51–56.
58 Ibid., 65.
59 Ibid., 53.
60 This, at least, was what Negri said in his presentation on his and Hardt's book *Commonwealth* during a seminar titled "Du public au commun" on November 28, 2012.
61 Paul Fauconnet and Marcel Mauss, "La sociologie, objet et méthode." Marcel Mauss, Essais de sociologie, 17.
62 Castoriadis, *The Imaginary Institution of Society*, trans. Kathleen Blamey (Cambridge: Polity Press, 1987), 112.
63 Ibid., 3. "The imaginary of which I am speaking is not an image *of*." One of Castoriadis's most consistent criticisms of Lacan is the latter's reduction of the imaginary to the "speculatary," "the mere image of," and its consequent association with "deception" and "illusion." See Cornelius Castoriadis, *Crossroads in the Labyrinth*, trans. Kate Soper and Martin H. Ryle (Brighton: Harvester Press, 1984), 58–59.
64 Cornelius Castoriadis, "Institution of Society and Religion," in *World in Fragments: Writings on Politics, Society, Psychoanalysis, and the Imagination*, trans. David Ames Curtis (Stanford: Stanford University Press, 1997), 311.
65 Cornelius Castoriadis, *The Imaginary Institution of Society*, 127. On this point, see Arnaud Tomès, "Introduction à la pensée de Castoriadis." Cornelius Castoriadis, *L'Imaginaire comme tel* (Paris: Hermann Philosophie, 2007), 48–50.
66 Cornelius Castoriadis, "Power, Politics, Autonomy," trans. David Ames Curits, in Cornelius Castoriadis, *Philosophy, Politics, Autonomy*, ed. David Ames Curtis (Oxford: Oxford University Press, 1991), 145.
67 Castoriadis, *The Imaginary Institution of Society*, 388 (note 25).
68 Ibid., 127 (our emphasis). Arnaud Tomès is right to observe how Castoriadis distinguishes the "first and radical" imagination from the second imagination, which is

"reproductive or combinatorial." See Arnaud Tomès, "Introduction à la pensée de Castoriadis," 59 (footnote 2).

69 Castoriadis, "Power, Politics, Autonomy," 152–153.
70 Castoriadis, *The Imaginary Institution of the Social*, 124.
71 Ibid., 110. Castoriadis is referring here to the "higher phase of communism" in orthodox Marxism.
72 Castoriadis, *Imaginary Institution of Society*, 125.
73 Ibid., 44.
74 Ibid., 44–45.
75 Castoriadis, "Power, Politics, Autonomy," 159.
76 Ibid., 160.
77 Translator's note: in the original French, Dardot and Laval mark this difference as "*la* politique et *le* politique" respectively.
78 Castoriadis, "Power, Politics, Autonomy," 157.
79 Ibid., 155.
80 Ibid., 159.
81 Ibid., 168.
82 Vincent Descombes, *Les Embarras de l'identité*, 244.
83 Ibid., 244.
84 Castoriadis, "Power, Politics, Autonomy," 169.
85 Castoriadis, *The Imaginary Institution of Society*, 3. On these points, see the indispensable book by Nicolas Poirier, *Castoriadis. L'imaginaire radical* (Paris: PUF: 2004).
86 Castoriadis warns against potential categorical confusion here: "one might attempt to distinguish in the accepted terminology between what we term the ultimate or radical imaginary, that is the capacity to make rise as an image something which does not exist and has never existed, and the *products* of this imaginary, which could be designated as the *imagined*." See Castoriadis, *The Imaginary Institution of Society*, 127 (note 25).
87 Castoriadis, "Power, Politics, Autonomy," 144.
88 Ibid., 150.
89 "The radical imaginary exists as the social-historical and as psyche/soma. As social-historical, it is an open stream of the anonymous collective; as psyche/soma, it is representative/affective/intentional flux. That which in the social-historical is positing, creating, bringing into being we call social imaginary in the primary sense of the term, or instituting society. That which in the psyche/soma is positing, creating, bringing-into-being for the psyche/soma, we call radical imagination" (Castoriadis, *Imaginary Institution of Society*, 369).
90 Castoriadis, *The Imaginary Institution of Society*, 294. Castoriadis uses the psychoanalytic term "autism" to refer to a state of non-differentiation between the self and the outside world.
91 Cornelius Castoriadis, "Psychoanalysis and Politics," in *World in Fragments: Writings on Politics, Society, Psychoanalysis, and the Imagination*, trans. David Ames Curtis (Stanford: Stanford University Press, 1997), 133.
92 Castoriadis, *Crossroads of the Labyrinth*, 95.
93 Castoriadis, "Psychoanalysis and Politics," 134 (our emphasis).
94 Vincent Descombes interprets Castoriadis's notion of "implicit power" in this sense: "Castoriadis' 'implicit' power corresponds fairly well to the French word 'custom' as used by writers such as Montaigne or Pascal. As in these authors, the word designates a

habit, a second nature, and consequently an expressive power of the individual" (*Embarras de l'identité*, 247).

95 Castoriadis, *Crossroads in the Labyrinth*, 40 (our emphasis). This expression is a play on Freud's famous phrase "where id was, there ego shall be." See Sigmund Freud, *New Introductory Lectures on Psychoanalysis* (New York: W.W. Norton & Company, 1965), 100.

96 Cornelius Castoriadis, "Individuality, Society, Rationality, History," in *Power, Politics Autonomy*, ed. David Ames Curtis (Oxford: Oxford University Press, 1991), 76. Also see Castoriadis, *The Imaginary Institution of Society*, 75: "we term praxis that doing in which the other or others are intended as autonomous beings considered as the essential agents of the development of their own autonomy."

97 Ibid., 76, 78.

98 This difficulty is clearly perceived by Habermas, who argues, *contra* Castoriadis, that emancipatory praxis cannot impact the institution of social meaning since it cannot proceed from intentional collective action: how are we to consciously work to overthrow instituted meanings? For an illuminating re-construction of Habermas's critique, see Philippe Caumières, *Critique sociale et émancipation* (Paris: Texteul, 2011), 45–46.

99 Castoriadis, *Crossroads in the Labyrinth*, 34: "indeterminacy and creation do no in themselves bear value."

100 Cornelius Castoriadis, "Done and To Be Done," in *The Castoriadis Reader*, trans. David Ames Curtis (Oxford: Blackwell, 1997), 362 (our emphasis).

101 Castoriadis, "Psychoanalysis and Politics," 136: "heteronomous societies accomplish a *Sinnschöpfung* for everyone, forcing upon all the internalization of this meaning."

102 Similarly, the idea that praxis, while still a conscious activity, "is something quite different from the application of prior knowledge" seems to be directly inspired by Aristotle, since technical activity (poiesis) proceeds from prior knowledge. See Castoriadis, *Imaginary Institution of Society*, 76.

103 Castoriadis, *World in Fragments*, 167. As Castoriadis adds: "Autonomy is not a habit – that would be a contradiction in terms – but autonomy is created by the self-exertion of autonomy, which presupposes, in a certain manner, that it preexists itself." For Aristotle, this "definition" (insofar as one agrees to translate *hexis proairétiké* as the "disposition to choose") applies equally to vice and virtue (which is why, moreover, one is responsible for one's own vice or virtue).

104 Cornelius Castoriadis, "Individual, Society, Rationality, History," 76.

105 Castoriadis, *Crossroads in the Labyrinth*, 72.

106 Castoriadis, "Psychoanalysis and Politics," 129. Also see Castoriadis, *Crossroads in the Labyrinth*, 13. By describing psychoanalysis as a "*practico-poietic activity*," Castoriadis explicitly rejects the Aristotelian opposition between ends that are immanent to the activity and the external work of the agent.

107 Castoriadis, *Crossroads in the Labyrinth*, 83.

108 Castoriadis, *The Imaginary Institution of Society*, 196. In this sense, the Christian God is not dissimilar from the demiurge in Plato's *Timaeus*, in the sense that both are manufacturers rather than creators; the former because it produces the world from its own essence, and the latter because it imitates a pre-existing intelligible model.

109 "Free associations, for instance, are not just a means." Castoriadis, "Psychoanalysis and Politics," 129.

110 Plato, *The Symposium*, 42 (205b–c).

111 Castoriadis, *Imaginary Institution of Society*, 196 (footnote).

112 Castoriadis, "Individual, Society, Rationality, History," 64. And in *The Rising Tide of Insignificancy*, 292, Castoriadis argues: "when I say that history is creation *ex nihilo*, that does not signify in any way that it is creation *in nihilo*, or *cum nihilo*. The new form emerges; it takes up what it finds lying about. The rupture is in the new *meaning* it confers upon what it inherits or utilizes."
113 Castoriadis, "Individual, Society, Rationality, History," 64.
114 Cornelius Castoriadis, "Done and To Be Done," 370.
115 Ibid., 37.
116 Philippe Caumières, *Castoriadis. Le projet d'autonomie* (Paris: Michalon, 2007), 58.
117 Consider, for instance, the text of Genesis 1 that is usually invoked to support this dogma: in this book it is not a matter of creation from nothing, but the creation of heaven and earth from a deserted and empty land, and from the darkness on the surface of the abyss. What we have here, then, is creation from pre-existing matter (the Hebrew verb *bara*, which appears in this text, can also mean "create," "make, "model," or "form"). As early as the fourth century, Emperor Julian the Apostate observed that Moses did not say that the abyss, the water, or the darkness were produced by God in the same manner as light: "of them he says not a word to imply that they were not already existing at all, though he often mentions them." See Julian the Apostate, *Against the Galileans* (remains of the three books, excerpted from Cyril of Alexandria, *Contra Julianum* [1923, 319–433]): http://www.tertullian.org/fathers/julian_apostate_galileans_1_text.htm.
118 Cornelius Castoriadis, "Time and Creation," in *World in Fragments: Writings on Politics, Society, Psychoanalysis, and the Imagination*, trans. David Ames Curtis (Stanford: Stanford University Press, 1997), 397.
119 Ibid., 397–398.
120 Castoriadis, *Crossroads of the Labyrinth*, 75.
121 Castoriadis, "Power, Politics, Autonomy," 150. We emphasized the "from" (*à partie de*, or the famous *ex nihilo*) because it shows how working from the already given does not prevent the creation of radical being.
122 For a detailed explanation of this phrase, see Dardot and Laval, *Marx, Prénom : Karl*, 202.
123 We indicated in a note at the beginning of this chapter that this expression is best rendered by the German verb *vorfinden*, which belongs to the language of Hegel and Marx. This verb more precisely signifies the necessary anteriority of the instituted in relation to institution as an activity, an anteriority that classical sociology abusively detaches and isolates from its counterpart, namely instituent activity.
124 Karl Marx, "The Eighteenth Brumaire of Louis Bonaparte," *The Marx-Engels Reader*, ed. Robert C. Tucker (New York: W.W. & Norton, 1978), 595.
125 See Karl Marx, "Thesis on Feuerbach," *The Marx-Engels Reader*, ed. Robert C. Tucker (New York: W.W. & Norton, 1978), 144
126 On this point, see Dardot and Laval, *Marx, Prénom : Karl*, 201–202.
127 Castoriadis, *Crossroads in the Labyrinth*, 13.
128 Marx, "The Eighteenth Brumaire of Louis Bonaparte," 597.
129 On this point, see Chapter 8: "activity" as fundamental to the rights of the poor.
130 Hannah Arendt, *On Revolution*, 136.
131 For commentary on this text, see Arnaud Tomès, "Introduction à la pensée de Castoriadis," 89–142.
132 Castoriadis, *The Imaginary Institution of Society*, 217.
133 Ibid., 218
134 Ibid., 110.

135 For more on the analogy between language and a game, see Philippe de Lara, "Le paradoxe de la règle et comment s'en débarrasser," *Wittgenstein, métaphysique et jeux de langage*, eds. Sandra Laugier (Paris: PUF, 2001), 97–127; on the notion of "use-based meaning," see Jocelyn Benoist, "Sur quelques sens possibles d'une formule de Wittgenstein," ibid., 153–179.
136 Ludwig Wittgenstein, *Philosophical Investigations*, trans. G.E.M. Anscombe (Oxford: Blackwell Publishing, 2001), 33 (§ 82–83).
137 See Chapter 7.
138 Qtd. In Bernard Chavance, *Institutional Economics*, trans. Francis Wells (London: Routledge, 2009), 26.
139 Ibid., 23.
140 Usually in the sense of economic game theory, but sometimes in the sense of sports (as in North).
141 North's definition of institutions, given in the context of the genesis of property rights, was discussed in Chapter 4.
142 Equilibrium is understood here in the sense of Nash equilibrium, "in which no player can improve his situation by acting on his own (without cooperating with others) as the other players maintain their previous strategy" (ibid., 84).
143 Ibid., 56.
144 Ibid. We should note that Elinor Ostrom, as outlined in Chapter 4, also established a typology of rules based on game theory.
145 Institutional psychotherapy is, today, a discipline that finds itself embattled by adherents of both behavorialism and neuroscience.
146 Patrick Chemla, "Transmettre le mouvement de la PI, c'est récuser l'arrêt sur image." Lecture given at the "Europsy" colloquium, 2012. For Tosquelles, transversality was not a strictly political concept, but was rather a "source of *Gestaltung*, a form in motion that gives way to vectors of singularity supporting the political dimension." For more on the POUM, see the classic work by Victor Alba, *Histoire du P.O.U.M* (Paris: Ivrea, 2000).
147 See Jean Oury, *Le Collectif. Le séminaire de Sainte-Anne* (Nîmes: Éditions Champ social, 2005).
148 Jean Oury, *Psychiatrie et psychothérapie institutionnelle* (Nîmes: Éditions Champ social, Nîmes, 2001), 48.
149 Ibid., 234.
150 Ibid., 235. Oury cites here an article by Hélène Chaigneau published in *L'Information psychiatrique* of October 1970 titled "Psychanalyse et psychothérapie institutionnelle."
151 This is what Oury calls the "diacritical function." For more on this notion and its articulation within the collective, see Oury, *Le Collectif*, 108–109, 117.
152 At the commencement of the September 19, 1984 meeting of the seminar "*Le Collectif*," Oury talked about how he used the word "collective" twenty-five years earlier in a different sense than its usual meaning: "it did not accord with the meaning of the term in Jean-Paul Sartre's book, *Critique of Dialectical Reason*" (ibid., 11).
153 Valentin Schaepelynck, *Une critique en acte des institutions. Émergences et résidus de l'analyse institutionnelle dans les années 1960*, Doctoral Thesis in Education, Paris-VIII, December 2013), 162. We are indebted to this work for the insight it provides on Félix Guattari's contribution to the institutional psychotherapy movement.
154 Félix Guattari, "The Group and the Person," in *Psychoanalysis and Transversality: Texts and Interviews, 1955–1971* (Los Angeles: Semiotext(e), 2015): 206–234.
155 Despite some terminological differences – for Guattari, *langue* is identified with "code" – this opposition is reminiscent of Castoriadis's opposition between fixed sign systems ("code") and the transformative invention of meaning ("language").

156 Guattari, "The Group and the Person," 234.
157 We should note that this theme of permanent recreation through praxis will, in Guattari's later work, tend to fade in favor of the opposition between the "machine" and "structure," as demonstrable in a 1969 text titled "Machine and Structure," intended for *l'École freudienne de Paris* but which was instead published in *Change*: in its opposition to structure, the machine thus occupies a place analogous to that which Marx assigned to the productive forces in their opposition/relation to the relations of production. Guattari thus seems to increasingly adopt a certain "economism" that leads him to ultimately abandon the question of the institution.
158 Maxime Quijoux, *Néolibéralisme et autogestion. L'expérience argentine* (Paris: Éditions de l'IHEAL, 2011).
159 Both examples are from Quijoux's book.
160 Ibid., 223.
161 Ibid., 266.
162 Ibid.
163 This is a frequent expression of Quijoux's.
164 This is the collective name given to a recuperated factory in the city of Neuquén, in the south of Argentina.

Part III Nine Political Propositions

1 See *Teatro Valle Occupato. La Rivolta culturale dei beni comuni* (Rome: Derive Approdi, 2012).

Political Proposition 1 We Must Construct a Politics of the Common

1 Derrida spoke often of this "democracy to come" (*a démocratie à venir*). See Jacques Derrida, *Rogues: Two Essays on Reason*, trans. Pascale-Anne Brault and Michael Nass (Stanford: Stanford University Press, 2005), 78–94.
2 English in the original.
3 Maurice Godelier, *The Mental and the Material*, trans. Martin Thom (London: Verso, 1986), 1.
4 Jean Jaurès, *L'Armée nouvelle*, vol. 2 (Paris: Imprimerie nationale, 1992), 459.
5 Arendt, *The Human Condition*, 38.
6 Ibid.
7 Ibid., 69.
8 Ibid.
9 Ibid., 50, 51.
10 Ibid., 115.
11 Ibid., 38.
12 Ibid., 49.
13 Cornelius Castoriadis, *Quelle démocratie?*, t. 2, *Écrits politiques 1945–1997*, 402–403
14 Ibid., 403.
15 Ibid., 352.
16 Ibid., 240–241 and 358.
17 Ibid., 361.

18 See Chapter 2, "The Democratic Common versus the Common of State Production."
19 Castoriadis, *Quelle Democratie?*, 391.
20 Hybrid managerial forms, such as those found in non-profit organizations and local government, are all avenues to be investigated and explored.

Political Proposition 2 Use Rights Must Challenge Property Rights

1 Catherine Colliot-Thélène, *La Démocratie sans "demos,"* 15.
2 On this point, see Alberto Lucarelli, *La democrazia dei beni comuni* (Rome: Laterza, 2013).
3 Article 544, French Civil Code. See: http://www.fd.ulisboa.pt/wp-content/uploads/2014/12/Codigo-Civil-Frances-French-Civil-Code-english-version.pdf.
4 Marie-Alice Chardeaux, *Les Choses communes*, 274 (note 5).
5 Martine Rémond-Gouilloud, "Ressources naturelles et choses sans maître," 232–233.
6 Marie-Alice Chardeaux, *Les Choses communes*, 273. For a distinction between a use right (*jus utendi*), the right to levy the fruits of a thing (*jus fruendi*), and the right of abuse (*jus abutendi*), see the clarifications made by Alain Testart, *Propriété et non-propriété*, 4–15. See Chapter 6, The "Illusion of Archaic Collective Property."
7 Article 578, French Civil Code. See: http://www.fd.ulisboa.pt/wp-content/uploads/2014/12/Codigo-Civil-Frances-French-Civil-Code-english-version.pdf.
8 Ibid.
9 Mikhaïl Xifaras, *La Propriété. Étude de philosophie du droit*, 99, 104.
10 Ibid., 105 (it is in this context that Xifaras re-constructs the terms of this nineteenth-century legal debate).
11 Ibid., 105–106.
12 Ibid., 107–108.
13 We will return to this point in our discussion of the "global commons" in Political Proposition 9.
14 Jeremy Rifkin, *The Age of Access: the New Culture of Hypercapitalism, where all of Life is a Paid-For Experience* (New York: J.P. Tarcher/Putnam, 2000).
15 Fabrice Flipo, Michelle Dobré, and Marion Michot conversely emphasize the environmental impact and cost of the new technologies underpinning the service economy. See Fabrice Flipo, Michelle Dobré, and Marion Michot, *L'impact environnemental des nouvelles technologies* (Montreuil: L'Échappée, 2013).
16 We are thinking in particular here of the recent promotion of bicycle and electric car rentals in big cities. But, of course, this is not a new phenomenon: laundromats and public telephones already operate according to the same principle.
17 See Nicolas Buclet, "Concevoir une nouvelle relation à la consommation. L'économie de fonctionnalité." *Annales des Mines. Responsabilité et Environnement*, vol. 39 (2005): 57–67.
18 Rifkin, *Age of Access*, 11.
19 One need only consider the example of the franchise, which does not own its concepts, brand, workplace operation, or marketing strategies (Rifkin, *The Age of Access*, 83).
20 According to Denise R. Johnson, "property law could not remain stuck in a physicalist, land-centered theory that was irrelevant to or inadequately accounted for new forms of property." See Denise R. Johnson, "Reflections on the Bundle of Rights," *Vermont Law Review*, vol. 32, 255.

21 See Anthony M. Honoré, "Ownership," in *The Nature and Process of Law: An Introduction to Legal Philosophy*, ed. Patricia Smith (Oxford: Oxford University Press, 1999): 370–375.
22 Edella Schlager and Elinor Ostrom, "Property-rights regimes and natural resources. A conceptual analysis." *Land Economics*, vol. 68, no. 3 (August 1992): 249–262.
23 See the Introduction.
24 According to the documentary *Planète à vendre* (*Planet for Sale*) (2013), which we referenced in Chapter 2, Ethiopia has sold 1.6 million hectares of land to foreign investors, even though 80 percent of the country's population are farmers. In the case of an Indian company mentioned in the documentary, the state sold each hectare for only ten dollars!
25 Marie-Alice Chardeaux, *Les Choses communes*, 237. While the work of this author has taught us a great deal in field of law, we disagree with her identification, or lack of distinction, between the "common" and the "thing" in common that flows from it. Without this distinction, it is impossible to free ourselves from what we call the reification of the common.
26 Ibid., 274.
27 On this distinction, see Chapter 6, "From Statism to the Creative Practice of Law-Making."
28 Marie-Alice Chardeaux, *Les Choses communes*, 237.
29 Ibid., 313–314. "'All' is a plurality of non-individualized subjects, it is the 'universal community of the human race,' 'humanity' in its entirety."
30 Ibid., 314. Chardeaux invokes here the relativity of public international law in order to show how norms such a right, whose acceptance is subject to the goodwill of the states, "very rarely has universal scope."
31 It is revealing, in this respect, that the prefect of Rome responded to the occupiers of the Teatro Valle after a notary recognized the status of the Teatro Valle Bene Comune foundation as having no title for the disposition of a legal seat "without the authorization of the legitimate owner." There could not be a better example of the law of property's refusal to recognize the right of use.
32 All the information on this occupation and its objectives was taken from the website www.bastamag.net.
33 See Chapter 3, "The Demand for the Commons Against 'Intellectual Property'."
34 See *Actes des premières rencontres internationales contre la biopiraterie* (Paris: June 15, 2009), 31.
35 This is what Chardeaux recommends in *Les Chose communes*, 344.
36 For a very different conception of what prevents use from becoming a right, but a conception that is still completely outside the law, see Giorgio Agamben, *The Highest Poverty: Monastic Rules and Form-of-Life*, trans. Adam Kotsko (Stanford: Stanford University Press, 2013).

Political Proposition 3 The Common is the Principle of Labor's Emancipation

1 The problem of political action in the context of today's "destabilized" party system is not just a problem for labor, but a broader concern of all citizens.
2 On this point, see Dominique Mezzi (ed.), *Nouveau siècle, nouveau syndicalisme* (Paris: Syllepse, 2013), 113.

3 Sophie Béroud, Jean-Michel Denis, Guillaume Desage, Baptiste Giraud, and Jérôme Pélisse, *La lutte continue? Les conflits du travail dans la France contemporaine* (Bellecombe-en-Bauges: Éditions du Croquant, 2008).
4 See Robert Linhart, *The Assembly Line*, trans. Margaret Crosland (Amherst: University of Massachusetts Press, 1981).
5 See Michel Lallement, *Le Travail. Une sociologie contemporaine* (Paris: Gallimard, Paris, 2007), 251.
6 Danièle Linhart, *Travailler sans les autres ?* (Paris: Le Seuil, 2009).
7 Philippe Davezies, "Une affaire personnelle," Laurence Théry (ed.), *Le Travail intenable* (Paris: La Découverte, 2006), 256.
8 Michael Burawoy, *Manufacturing Consent: Changes in the Labor Process under Monopoly Capitalism* (Chicago: University of Chicago Press, Chicago, 1979). Also see Michael Burawoy, *Politics of Production* (London: Verso, 1985).
9 Thomas Coutrot, *Critique de l'organisation du travail* (Paris: La Découverte, 2002), 63.
10 See Yves Clot, *Travail et pouvoir d'agir* (Paris: PUF, 2008), 147.
11 Thomas Coutrot, *Critique de l'organisation du travail*, 70–71.
12 See Thomas Coutrot, *L'Entreprise néolibérale, nouvelle utopie capitaliste ?* (Paris: La Découverte, 1998), 220. Also see Norbert Alter, *Donner et prendre. La coopérationen entreprise* (Paris: La Découverte/Poche, 2010).
13 Danièle Linhart, *Travailler sans les autres?*, 213.
14 Cornelius Castoriadis, "Le mouvement révolutionnaire dans le capitalisme modern." *Capitalisme moderne et révolution* (Paris: 10/18, 1979), 105.
15 On this point, see Rudolf Bahro, *The Alternative in Eastern Europe* (London: NLB, 1978), 269.
16 Ibid., 298.
17 See Danièle Linhar, Robert Linhart, and Anna Malan, "Syndicats et organisation du travail. Un rendez-vous manqué." *Sociologie et sociétés*, vol. 30, no. 2 (Fall, 1998): 175–188.

Political Proposition 4 We Must Institute Common Work

1 Qtd. in Pierre Rosanvallon, *La Démocratie inachevée. Histoire de la souveraineté du peuple en France* (Paris: Gallimard, 2003), 340.
2 Marc Sangnier, qtd. in ibid., 342.
3 Jean Jaurès, "Esquisse provisoire de l'organisation industrielle." *La Revue socialiste*, vol. 22, no. 128 (August 1895), 144.
4 Jean Auroux, France's Minister of Labour from 1981 to 1983, wrote, "just as citizens are in the city, so must workers be in their workplace." See Jean Auroux, *Rapport au président de la République et au Premier ministre* (Paris: La Documentation française, 1981), 4.
5 All efforts in this direction in France have met with the most determined opposition from employers, from the François Bloch-Lainé report in 1963 up to the Pierre Sudreau report in 1975, not to mention the timid Auroux reforms in 1982, which recognized the rights of workers' representatives to be consulted via the works council (*comité d'entreprise*).
6 French Civil Code, Article 1832. See: http://www.fd.ulisboa.pt/wp-content/uploads/2014/12/Codigo-Civil-Frances-French-Civil-Code-english-version.pdf.
7 See Baudouin Roger (ed.), *L'Entreprise. Formes de la propriété et responsabilités sociales* (Paris: Collège des Bernardins, 2012).

8 See Antoine Artous, Henri Maler, and Jacques Texier, *Marx et l'Appropriation sociale*, (Paris: Syllepse, 2003).

9 Jean Jaurès, "Esquisse provisoire de l'organisation industrielle." *La Revue socialiste*, vol. 22, no. 128 (August 1895), 136.

10 Daniel Bachet, *Les Fondements de l'entreprise. Construire une alternative a? la domination financière* (Paris: Éditions de l'Atelier, 2007), 195.

11 Ibid., 196.

12 Ibid., 211. Also see Daniel Bachet (in collaboration with Gaëtan Flocco, Bernard Kervella, and Morgan Sweeney), *Sortir de l'entreprise capitaliste* (Belle-combes-en-Bauges: Éditions du Croquant, 2007).

13 Isabelle Ferreras, *Gouverner le capitalisme?* (Paris: PUF, 2012), 10.

14 Ibid., 20.

15 Thomas Coutrot, *Démocratie contre capitalism* (Paris: La Dispute, 2005), 171.

Political Proposition 5 Economic Associationism is the Pathway to the Society of the Common

1 In other countries, the ESS is referred to as the "third sector" or the "non-profit" sector, but these terms are not purely synonymous. For comparative work on the non-profit sector, see the Center for Civil Society Studies at Johns Hopkins University: http://ccss.jhu.edu/the-center/about-the-center.

2 See Thierry Jeantet, *L'Économie sociale, une alternative au capitalism* (Paris: Economica, 2008). For a more critical approach, see Philippe Frémeaux, *La Nouvelle Alternative? Enquête sur l'économie sociale et solidaire* (Paris: Alternatives économiques/Les Petits Matins, 2013).

3 Jean-Louis Laville, *Agir à gauche. L'économie sociale et solidaire* (Paris: Desclée de Brouwer, 2011), 15.

4 In 1999, an international study by the Center for Civil Society Studies at Johns Hopkins University showed that the non-profit sector in the twenty-two countries it studied represented one trillion dollars in revenue, which is equivalent to the GDP for the world's eighth largest economy. See Lester M. Salamon, Helmut K. Anheier, Regina List, Stefan Toepler, S. Wojciech Sokolowski, et al., *Global Civil Society: Dimensions of the Nonprofit Sector* (Baltimore: The Johns Hopkins Center for Civil Society Studies, 1999): http://ccss.jhu.edu.

5 See David Hiez and Éric Lavillunière, *Vers une théorie de l'économie sociale et solidaire* (Brussells: Larcier, 2013).

6 Philippe Frémeaux, "L'évaluation de l'apport de l'économie sociale et solidaire." *Rapport de mission à monsieur Benoît Hamon, ministre délégué en charge de l'Économie sociale et solidaire et de la Consommation* (September 2013), 20.

7 Léon Duguit, *Manuel de droit constitutionnel* (Paris: Éditions Panthéon-Assas), 286.

8 Laville, *Agir à gauche*, 48–49.

9 Ibid., 25. Also see Matthieu Hély, "L'économie sociale et solidaire n'existe pas": www.Laviedesidees.fr (2008) and Matthieu Hély and Maud Simonet (eds.), *Le Travail associatif* (Paris: Presses universitaires de Paris-Ouest, 2013).

10 Bruno Trentin, *La Cité du travail. Le fordisme et la gauche* (Paris: Fayard, 2012), 422.

11 See the OECD report, *The Non-Profit Sector in a Changing Economy* (2003): http://www.oecd.org/leed-forum/publications/The%20Non-profit%20Sector%20in%20a%20

Changing%20Economy.pdf. Also see Thomas Coutrot's commentary in *La Démocratie contre le capitalisme*, 102–103.

12 Frémeaux, *La Nouvelle Alternative?*, 111.

13 As Jean-Louis Laville emphasizes, "the solidarity economy, which is often described as a new phenomenon, is in reality of form of resurgence rather than emergence" (*Agir à gauche*, 23).

14 Thierry Jeantet, *L'Économie sociale, une alternative au capitalism*, 31 and 33.

15 Ibid., 55.

16 Philippe Chanial and Jean-Louis Laville, "Associationnisme." Antonio Cattani and Jean-Louis Laville (eds.), *Dictionnaire de l'autre économie* (Paris: Gallimard, 2006), 47.

17 The economic measure of "growth" is not compatible with the wealth produced by these various associations. Wealth is generally measured in terms of the stock of appropriable goods, and by the production of goods as quasi-commodities – i.e., non-market goods whose value is estimated based on production costs. But a large part of the indispensable value the social economy provides to society falls outside this narrow mode of evaluation, hence the utter stupidity of quantitative estimates of the social economy as a measure of GDP. Numerous authors (Alain Caillé, Jean Gadrey, Dominique Méda, Patrick Viveret) have shown that growth in GDP no longer corresponds to increases in well-being in a large number of countries. In strictly economic terms, it is not possible to measure the "social utility" of the social economy or other forms of activity that participate in what economic jargon refers to as "environmental and social health." It is an illusion to believe that it is possible to objectify relational and subjective phenomena that are inherently difficult if not impossible to quantify.

18 Jean Gadrey, "L'utilité sociale en question. À la recherche de conventions, de critères de méthodes d'évaluation." Jean-Noël Chopart, Guy Neyret, and Daniel Rault (eds.), *Les Dynamiques de l'économie sociale et solidaire* (Paris: La Découverte, 2006), 278. Also see Jean Gadry, "Utilité sociale." Antonio David Cattani and Jean-Louis Laville (eds.), *Dictionnaire de l'autre économie*. For a synthesis of these ideas, see Diane Rodet, "Les définitions de la notion d'utilité sociale." *Économie et Solidarités*, vol. 39, no. 1 (2008).

19 Marcel Mauss, "Appréciation sociologique du bolchevisme," *Écrits politiques*, 544.

20 For a discussion of these "critical existential communities," see Christian Arnsperger, *Éthique de l'existence postcapitaliste* (Paris: Le Cerf, 2009), 246.

Political Proposition 6 The Common Must Be the Basis of Social Democracy

1 See Gosta Esping-Andersen, *The Three Worlds of Welfare Capitalism* (London: Polity Press, 1990).

2 Giovanna Procacci, *Gouverner la misère. La question sociale en France (1789–1848)* (Paris: Le Seuil, 1993), 24.

3 Léon Duguit, *Souveraineté et liberté*, 167–168.

4 Jacques Donzelot, *L'Invention du social. Essai sur le déclin des passions politiques* (Paris: Fayard, 1984).

5 Ibid., 75. Also see François Ewald, *L'État Providence* (Paris: Grasset, 1986).

6 This phrase, la "société assurantielle," comes from François Ewald.

7 Alain Supiot, "À propos d'un centenaire. La dimension juridique de la doctrine sociale de l'Église." *Droit social*, no. 12 (December 1991): 916–925.

8 Robert Castel and Claudine Haroche, *Propriété privée, propriété sociale, propriété de soi. Entretiens sur la construction de l'individu modern* (Paris: Fayard, 2001), 83 and 96; and Robert Castel, *Les Métamorphoses de la question sociale*, 363.
9 Translator's note: *paritarisme* refers to a principle of co-management that includes an equal number of employee and employer representatives.
10 See Thomas H. Marshall, *Class, Citizenship and Social Development* (Garden City: Anchor Books/Doubleday, 1965).
11 Bruno Trentin, *La Cité du travail.*

Political Proposition 7 Public Services Must Become Institutions of the Common

1 See, for example, Anton Pannekoek, "Public Ownership and Common Ownership," *Western Socialist* (1947).
2 Such was not the case early on: the main proponents of public services in the 1880s were the "possibilists," according to the derisive term used by the statist Jules Guesde. For these proponents of communal socialism, who were truly the heirs to Proudhon, the local extension of public services was strategically central. See Paul Brousse, *La Propriété collective et les services publics* (Bordeaux: Le Bord de l'eau, 2011 [1910]).
3 Earlier critics of the state have, in this respect, tended to become the instruments of private power. A significant portion of the decentralized, self-governing left of the 1970s was converted to new ideals of capitalist management in the 1990s. We therefore understand how delicate a matter it is to advocate for public service reforms, given the existing state of power relations.
4 Jean Jaurès, "L'État socialiste et les fonctionnaires." *La Revue socialiste*, vol. 21, no. 124 (April 1895), 392.
5 This decision about the "fundamental" nature of rights and what needs are "essential" is, of course, a historical matter determined by political struggles, social mobilization, local values, etc., and is not determined by the nature of the goods in question themselves (as dominant economic theory would have it), or the objective nature of needs (as is the sociological view). See Jacques Fournier, *L'Économie des besoins. Une nouvelle approche du service public* (Paris: Odile Jacob, 2013).
6 See "Record of Marx's Speeches on General Education," in *Karl Marx, Frederick Engels: Collected Works, Volume 21: 1867–71* (New York: International Publishers, 1985), 398.
7 Translator's note: the most common English translation of this phrase is "ubiquitous organ." See Karl Marx, "The Civil War in France," in *The Marx-Engels Reader*, 629.
8 The Justinian Code uses the phrase *obsequium civilium munerum* to designate the charge of someone who holds a public office.
9 Qtd. in Léon Duguit, *L'État, le Droit objectif et la Loi positive* (Paris: Dalloz, 2003), 2.
10 Léon Duguit, *Manuel de droit constitutionnel*, 73.
11 Ibid., 77.
12 Ibid., 74.
13 One of the worst consequences of neoliberal public service reform is the destruction of the "spirit of public service" as encouraged by the New Public Management. The destruction of this spirit is largely based on the hyper-utilitarian approach favored by Public Choice theorists who see individuals in the most rudimentary egotistical terms.
14 Léon Duguit, *Manuel de droit constitutionnel*, 185.

15 Ibid., 186.
16 Émile Durkheim, *Leçons de sociologie* (Paris: PUF, 1990), 117.
17 Ibid., 136.
18 Maxime Leroy, *Syndicats et services publics* (Paris: Librairie Armand Colin, 1909), xi. Leroy favors a Saint-Simonian approach in which the state is reduced to the role of technical "manager" run by professional unions.
19 Duguit's idealism is never more obvious than when he is scandalized by the fact that the state does not provide work for all able-bodied adults, or when he demands state protection against exploitation: "it is unacceptable that one who works for another should be exploited by his employer and be obliged to accept starvation wages or perform work beyond his capacity. It is the state's duty to create laws that protect labor. By enacting such laws, it merely fulfills its obligation to ensure the free development of each individual's physical activity (*Manuel de droit constitutionnel*, 299).
20 Thus, when Duguit argues that the products of the state should not be regarded as the property of the state, he mistakes his wishes for realities: "what we call state property (*le patrimoine de l'État*) is legally and socially protected because it is assigned to the public services," as he puts it. What he overlooks is the fact that governmental authorities are only ideally obliged to act in the interest of the collective. As we have seen over the course of the past few decades, the state can also prey on public wealth through forms of privatization in which state actors are the first beneficiaries. See ibid., 79.
21 Harold Laski, *Democracy in Crisis* (London: George Allen & Unwin Ltd., 1933).
22 Ibid., 59.
23 Ibid., 60.
24 Michael Lipsky, *Street-Level Bureaucracy: Dilemmas of The Individual in Public Services* (New York: Russell Sage Foundation, New York, 2010).
25 Pierre Bourdieu, "The Abdication of the State," in *Weight of the World: Social Suffering in Contemporary Society* (Stanford: Stanford University Press, 1999), 182.
26 See Marion Gret and Yves Sintomer, *Porto Alegre. L'espoir d'une autre démocratie* (Paris: La Découverte, 2005).
27 Luigi De Magistris, "Prefazione." Alberto Lucarelli, *Beni comuni. Dalla teoria all'azione politica* (Vairegfio: Dissensi, 2011), 13.
28 It was the Rodotà Commission for the Reform of Public Property Standards that proposed introducing the distinction between three kinds of property: common, public, and private.
29 See Ugo Mattei, *Beni comuni. Un manifesto* (Rome: Laterza, 2012), 77–88 and Alberto Lucarelli, "L'Europa: La leggenda dell'obbligo di privatizzare." *Il Manifesto*, May 1, 2010.
30 Alberto Lucarelli, *Beni comuni*, 21 and 23.
31 Ibid., 45.
32 Ibid., 25.
33 Ibid., 53.
34 Ibid., 58. It is doubtful whether the introduction of the category of common goods into the Italian Civil Code will be the last word on the politics of the common in Italy. The Rodotà Commission's ambiguous definition of "common goods" – which was undoubtedly due to the balance of power within the Commission – undermines the coherence of the Commission's efforts. For it is impossible to reconcile the naturalistic definition of common goods, from which the Commission generated a rather traditional list of "common goods," with the definition of the new category's objective, which is the realization of the fundamental rights and the free development of each person, in the service of future generations.

35 Alberto Lucarelli, *La Democrazia possibile. Lavoro, Beni comuni, Ambiente, per una nuova passione politica* (Viareggio: Dissensi, 2013), 31.

36 See Agnès Sinai, *L'Eau à Paris. Retour vers le public* (Paris: Eau de Paris, 2012). Also see Alberto Lucarelli's commentary on the Parisian situation in *La Democrazia possibile*, 151.

37 See Anne Le Strat, "Préface," in Agnès Sinai, *L'Eau à Paris*, 7.

Political Proposition 8 The Commons Must be Global

1 TIPNIS is an abbreviation for the "Isiboro Sécure National Park and Indigenous Territory." It is a 12,000 km^2 protected natural park, and the conflict that emerged in relation to the construction project in the park revealed the antagonisms within the Morales government's electoral base. See Franck Poupeau's discussion of these tensions within the Latin American left in *Les Mésaventures de la critique* (Paris: Raisons d'agir, 2012), Chapter 3.

2 This is the phrasing offered by Mireille Delmas-Marty.

3 On this point, see Chapter 1, "The Reification of the Common."

4 Alain Supiot, *The Spirit of Philadelphia: Social Justice vs. the Total Market* (New York: Verso, 2012).

5 David Rose, *Guantanamo: America's War on Human Rights* (London: Faber and Faber, 2004).

6 Supiot, *The Spirit of Philadelphia*, 64.

7 From this perspective, wages are "burdens" and social rights are "hindrances" to competition. The World Bank's program for comparing national legislation, entitled "Doing Business," tries to encourage the most worker-unfriendly, but investor-friendly, standards and practices.

8 Antoine Garapon, *La Raison du moindre État. Le néolibéralisme et la justice* (Paris: Odile Jacob, 2010), 189.

9 Mireille Delmas-Marty, *Le Pluralisme ordonné* (Paris: Le Seuil, 2006).

10 Mireille Delmas-Marty, "Vers un droit commun de l'humanité" (interview with Philippe Petit), *Textuel*, Paris (1994).

11 Julie Allard and Antoine Garapon, *Les Juges dans la mondialisation. La nouvelle révolution du droit* (Paris: Le Seuil, 2005), 11.

12 See Garapon, *La Raison du moindre État*, 190–191. This development further illuminates our discussion in Chapter 7 on the ambiguities of common law.

13 Antoine Garapon and Pierre Servan-Schreiber (eds.), *Deals de Justice. Le marché américain de l'obéissance mondialisée* (Paris: PUF, 2013).

14 Jean-Marie Harribey, "Le bien commun est une construction sociale. Apports et limites d'Elinor Ostrom." *L'Économie politique*, no. 49 (January 2011): 98–112.

15 For a halfway-correct critique of this assessment, see François Lille, *À l'aurore du siècle, où est l'espoir? Biens communs et biens publics mondiaux* (Brussells: Tribord, 2006). While Lille does a good job of critiquing the neoliberal use of the category of public goods, he also thinks it is possible for the category to be used progressively. We think this is a mistake; it is the category itself that must be rejected.

16 See Inge Kaul, Isabelle Grunberg, and Marc A. Stern (eds.), *Global Public Goods: International Cooperation in the 21st Century* (Oxford: Oxford University Press, 1999).

17 Ibid., 452.

18 See "Biens publics mondiaux," Antonio Cattani and Jean-Louis Laville, *Dictionnaire de l'autre économie*, 66–75.

19 Kaul, Grunberg, and Stern, *Global Public Goods*, 453.
20 See Joseph Stiglitz, "The Future of Global Governance." *Initiative for Policy Dialogue: Working Paper Series*, Colombia University: https://www8.gsb.columbia.edu/faculty/jstiglitz/sites/jstiglitz/files/The%20Future%20of%20Global%20Governance.pdf.
21 See Jean-Jacques Gabas, Philippe Hugon, Étienne Le Roy, et al., *Biens publics à l'échelle globale* (Brussels: Collophon, 2001) and Jean-Jacques Gabas et Philippe Hugon, "Les BPM: un renouveau théorique pour penser l'action publique à l'échelle mondiale?" *Politiques et management public*, vol. 21, no. 3 (September 2003).
22 See François Constantin, "Les biens publics mondiaux, un imaginaire pour quelle mondialisation?" François Constantin (ed.), *Les Biens publics mondiaux, un mythe légitimateur pour l'action collective ?* (Paris: L'Harmattan, 2002), 2.
23 See, for example, the World Bank's "Millennium Development Goals": http://www5.worldbank.org/mdgs/.
24 Pascal Lamy, "Vers une gouvernance mondiale?" *Institut d'études politiques de Paris*, October 21, 2005: www.wto.org.
25 See, for instance, the United Nations Global Compact and its Ten Principles: https://www.unglobalcompact.org/what-is-gc/mission/principles.
26 Monique Chemillier-Gendreau, *Humanité et souverainetés. Essai sur la fonction du droit international* (Paris: La Découverte, 1995).
27 See Mireille Delmas-Marty, *Vers une communauté de valeurs?*, 207.
28 On this topic, see Marie-Alice Chardeaux, *Les Choses communes*, 221–222. According to Chardeaux, the notion re-connects with the original meaning of the term *patrimonium* (as that which derives from our fathers and their forefathers, etc.), and is therefore more of a metaphorical or allegorical term than a technical legal concept.
29 See: http://portal.unesco.org/en/ev.php-URL_ID=13637&URL_DO=DO_TOPIC&URL_SECTION=201.html.
30 Sompong Sucharitkul, "L'évolution continue d'une notion nouvelle: le patrimoine commun de l'humanité": www.fao.org.
31 Susan J. Buck, *The Global Commons: an Introduction* (London: Earthscan Publications, 1988), 1.
32 See: http://portal.unesco.org/en/ev.php-URL_ID=13039&URL_DO=DO_TOPIC&URL_SECTION=201.html.
33 The first article of the Universal Declaration on the Human Genome and Human Rights (1997) states, "the human genome underlies the fundamental unity of all members of the human family, as well as the recognition of their inherent dignity and diversity. In a symbolic sense, it is the heritage of humanity": http://unesdoc.unesco.org/images/0012/001229/122990eo.pdf.
34 See Sompong Sucharitkul, "L'évolution continue d'une notion nouvelle: le patrimoine commun de l'humanité."
35 Jean Gadrey, "Les biens publics et communs des économistes." *La Vie de la recherche scientifique*, no. 393 (May/June/July 2013), 23.
36 Constitution of the World Health Organization: http://www.who.int/governance/eb/who_constitution_en.pdfhttp://www.who.int/governance/eb/who_constitution_en.pdf.
37 The 2008 ILO Declaration on Social Justice for a Fair Globalization, for instance, describes "full employment" and "decent work" as fundamental rights.
38 Wendy Brown, "American Nightmare: Neoliberalism, Neoconservatism, and De-Democratization." *Political Theory*, vol. 34, no. 6 (Dec. 2006): 690–714.
39 Catherine Colliot-Thélène, "Pour une politique des droits subjectifs. La lutte pour les droits comme lutte politique." *L'Année sociologique*, vol. 59, no. 1 (2009), 252.

40 See Mireille Delmas-Marty, *Le Pluralisme ordonné. Les Forces imaginantes du droit*, vol. 2 (Paris: Le Seuil, 2006).

Political Proposition 9 We Must Institute a Federation of Commons

1 See Chapter 3. This is what we call "diffusion from the outside."
2 See Dardot and Laval, *Marx, Prénom : Karl*, 318–319.
3 Hannah Arendt, *On Revolution*, 66.
4 Pierre-Joseph Proudhon, *The Principle of Federation*, trans. Richard Vernon (Toronto: University of Toronto Press, 1979), 38. Drawing on the same etymology, Daniel Elazar combines *foedus* and *convent* (pact) to argue the combination of self-rule and shared rule is the defining characteristic of federalism. See Daniel Elazar, *Federal Systems of the World: a Handbook of Federal, Confederal and Autonomy Arrangement* (Harlow, UK: Longman Publishing, 1991), xv.
5 Bruno Théret, *Protection sociale et fédéralisme*, 46 (note 9). Théret cites Thomas O. Hueglin, "New Wine in Old Bottles? Federalism and Nation States in the Twenty First Century: a Conceptual Overview." Karen Knop, Sylvia Ostry, Richard Simeon, and Katherine Swinton (eds.), *Rethinking Federalism: Citizens, Markets, and Governments in a Changing World* (Vancouver: University of British Columbia Press, 1995), 203.
6 See Chapter 1.
7 Immanuel Kant, "Perpetual Peace: a Philosophical Sketch," in *Political Writings*, trans. H.B. Nisbet (Cambridge: Cambridge University Press, 2010), 99.
8 Ibid., 102.
9 Ibid., 98.
10 Ibid., 99.
11 Ibid., 102.
12 Ibid., 105.
13 Ibid.
14 On this point, we are drawing from the very convincing explanations provided by Catherine Colliot-Thélène in her essay "Pour une politique des droits subjectifs," 118–119.
15 For Michel Foucault, Kant's "guarantee for perpetual peace is therefore actually commercial globalization." See Michel Foucault, *The Birth of Biopolitics*, 58.
16 See Chapter 1, "Between the Vulgar and Universal."
17 Catherine Colliot-Thélène, "Pour une politique des droits subjectifs," 135. Colliot-Thélène also references Durkheim's interpretation of Kant (*Leçons de sociologie*): "the right of mankind to live on the earth implies the right of individuals to occupy small portions of the surface of the earth."
18 Ibid., 137.
19 Montesquieu, *The Spirit of the Laws*, trans. Anne M. Cohler, Basia Carolyn Miller, Harold Samuel Stone (Cambridge: Cambridge University Press, 1989), 131.
20 Ibid., 132.
21 Ibid., 133.
22 James Madison, "Federalist No. 62, February 27, 1788," in *The Federalist Papers* (New York: Tribeca Books, 2011), 178.
23 Alexander Hamilton, "Federalist No. 9," in *The Federalist Papers* (New York: Tribeca Books, 2011), 24.

24 Qtd. in Arendt, *On Revolution*, 192.
25 Ibid., 258. Later in the chapter we will see that Proudhon saw no fundamental contrast at all between 1789 and 1793, but rather viewed the latter as a continuation of the unitary and centralist trends begun during the former period.
26 In fact, in their Declaration to the French People on April 19, 1871, the Communards specifically referenced the commune movement that had begun during the twelfth century. See Dardot and Laval, *Marx, Prénom: Karl*, 308.
27 Ibid: "it was out of necessity, out of the pressing needs of the people that unleashed the Terror and led the Revolution toward its destruction" (377). "From the outset, or nearly the outset, the French Revolution's trajectory diverged from its original course because of the immediacy of the suffering: it was guided by the demand for freedom from poverty, not tyranny, and was driven to act by the limitless immensity of the misery of the people, and the pity it provoked" (406).
28 Castoriadis, *Quelle démocratie?*, 241.
29 Arendt, *On Revolution*, 268.
30 See Donald V. Smiley, *Intrastate Federalism in Canada* (Toronto: University of Toronto Press, 1985).
31 For an analysis of German ordo-liberalism, see Michel Foucault, *The Birth of Biopolitics*, 79–179, and Dardot and Laval, *The New Way of the World*, 75–100.
32 See Jürgen Habermas, *Zur Verfassung Europas: Ein Essay* (Berlin: Suhrkamp Verlag, 2011). The expression "executive federalism" is borrowed from politicians in the Canadian province of Quebec, who use the term to criticize the federal government's increasing use of intergovernmental conferences to bypass the will of the people as expressed in provincial legislatures.
33 For more on this, see Gérard Raulet, "La crise de l'Union européenne : une crise de légitimité démocratique." Yves Charles Zarka, *Refaire l'Europe avec Jürgen Habermas* (Paris: PUF, 2012), 98–102.
34 Pierre Mesnard, *L'Essor de la philosophie politique au XVIe siècle* (Paris: Vrin, 1977), 578.
35 Ibid., 581. According to Mesnard, Althusius's entire lexicon is dedicated to signifying the warm collective feeling that endows every community with its unity.
36 Ibid., 587.
37 Ibid., 593.
38 Indeed, it was through an opposition between the "network" and the "pyramid" that Antonio Negri introduced Althusius's federalist thought in a session of the March 21, 2012 seminar "Du public au commun."
39 Proudhon, *The Principle of Federation*, 38, 39.
40 Ibid., 39.
41 Ibid. Rousseau's characterization of the contract ("the total alienation of each associate, together with all of his rights, to the entire community") is, for Proudhon, the perfect definition of a "unitary republic."
42 Ibid., 41.
43 Bruno Théret, *Protection sociale et fédéralisme*, 41.
44 Ibid., note 1.
45 In a letter from November 2, 1862, during the period in which he was working on his theory of federalism, he summarized the fundamental idea in these terms: "if I began in 1840 with *anarchy*, which was the logical conclusion of my critique of the governmental idea, then I finished with *federation*, the necessary basis of right among the European peoples and, later, of the organization of all States." See *Property is Theft!*

A Pierre-Joseph Proudhon Anthology, Iain McKay (ed.) (Edinburgh: AK Press, 2011), 686.

46 Gustave Lefrançais, *Le Mouvement communaliste à Paris en 1871* (Cœuvres-et-Valsery: Ressouvenances, 2001), 197.

47 Karl Marx and Frederick Engels, "Address of the Central Authority to the League, March 1850," in *Karl Marx and Frederick Collected Works, Volume 10: 1849–51* (New York: International Publishers, 1978), 285. Hannah Arendt cites this passage in her essay "On Revolution" (249, note 64), but she was mistaken in her assertion that this text was drafted two years after *The Civil War in France* (though this does not detract from the relevance of her criticism of the text).

48 Ibid., 286 (note).

49 Proudhon, *De la capacité politique des classes ouvrières*, 288.

50 Ibid., 293.

51 Ibid., 298.

52 Ibid., 287.

53 Ibid., 90.

54 Ibid., 83.

55 See Chapter 9, "Federalism as Social and Political Organization."

56 See Chapter 1, "Co-Activity as the Basis of Political Obligation."

57 Hannah Arendt, "Thoughts on Politics and Revolution," *Crises of the Republic: Lying in Politics, Civil Disobedience on Violence, Thoughts on Politics and Revolution* (New York: Harcourt Brace Jovanovich, 1972), 229, 230.

58 Ibid., 232.

59 Qtd in Arendt, *On Revolution*, 245.

60 Arendt, "Thoughts on Politics and Revolution," 233.

61 Catherine Colliot-Thélène, *La Démocratie sans "demos,"* 179.

62 According to Soysal Yasemin Nuhoglu, *Limits of Citizenship* (Chicago: the University of Chicago Press) 1994, 3 (qtd. in ibid., 175), this type of transnational community is, in fact, already constituting itself.

63 "City citizenship" refers to the historical experience of the bourgeoisie who took part in the management of public affairs in medieval towns. For the emergent bourgeoisie, this form of citizenship preceded national citizenship. For more on the Kantian distinctions between various forms of citizenship, see Catherine Colliot-Thélène, *La Démocratie sans "demos,"* 120–121.

64 Pierre Hadot, *La Citadelle intérieure* (Paris: Fayard, 1997), 227–228. Hadot quotes Marcus Aurelius: "as the Emperor, Rome is my homeland; *but as a man*, I am a citizen of the world" (our emphasis).

65 Yves-Charles Zarka, *L'Inappropriabilité de la Terre* (Paris: Armand Colin, 2013), 45. Zarka's essay tries to deduce a norm of unappropriability from a phenomenological conception of the earth as "soil" (*sol*) that necessarily ties us to a relation of belonging. Yet it is precisely the foundational character of this relation that seems problematic to us. Nevertheless, we do agree with Zarka that "one does not depart from the logic of appropriation by opposing one form of appropriation with another, i.e., public appropriation rather than private appropriation (individual or collective) (ibid., 49).

66 Ibid., 86, 48.

67 James Holston, *Cities and Citizenship* (Durham: Duke University Press, 1999), qtd. in Catherine Colliot-Thélène, *La Démocratie sans "demos,"* 183.

68 Catherine Colliot-Thélène, *La Démocratie sans "demos,"* 182.

69 Arendt, "Thoughts on Politics and Revolution," 233.

Post-Script on Revolution in the Twenty-First Century

1 G.W.F. Hegel, *The Phenomenology of Spirit*, trans. A.V. Miller (Oxford: Oxford University Press, 1977), 6–7.

2 Paul Krugman, the American Nobel Prize-winning economist, lucidly articulated this state of "intellectual collapse" as entirely evident once a president of France, and leader of the Socialist Party, endorsed the dogmatic "Say's law" – the two-centuries-long foundation of liberal belief in self-regulation of the market, which states that "supply creates its own demand." This is only one symptom amongst the thousands of "collapses" we observe everywhere around us – in public discourse, in the comments of journalists and the editorials of the "serious" news outlets, in our businesses and governments, and even amongst some of our closest colleagues. See Paul Krugman, "Scandal in France." *The New York Times*, January 17, 2014.

3 We are hardly reassured by recent reports or position papers that warn us about how exploding economic inequalities are threatening global equilibrium and economic stability, especially when these reports come from the International Monetary Fund (IMF), the Vatican, the Organisation for Economic Co-operation and Development (OECD), or the Davos Economic Forum. See World Economic Forum, *Global Risks 2014* (Ninth Edition), January 2014: http://www3.weforum.org/docs/WEF_GlobalRisks_Report_2014.pdf.

4 Joseph E. Stiglitz, *The Price of Inequality* (New York: W.W. Norton & Company, 2013).

5 The main argument along these lines can be found in the work of American historian Jacob Talmon, *The Origins of Totalitarian Democracy* (Hammondsworth: Penguin, 1952). Albert O. Hirschman has also shown how reactionary rhetoric is always manifest in three great schemes: *perversity* ("any purposive action to improve some feature of the political, social, or economic order only serves to exacerbate the condition one wishes to remedy"), *futility* ("attempts at social transformation will be unavailing"), and *jeopardy* ("the costs of the proposed change or reform is too high as it endangers some previous, precious, accomplishment"). See Albert O. Hirschman, *The Rhetoric of Reaction: Perversity, Futility, Jeopardy* (Cambridge: Harvard University Press, 1991), 7.

6 François Furet, *The Passing of an Illusion: the Idea of Communism in the Twentieth Century*, trans. Deborah Furet (Chicago: University of Chicago Press, 1999), 502.

7 But we also know that on the eve of the 1848 revolution, Tocqueville, who had become aware of the strange dissemination of socialist ideas in Europe, reversed his forecasts. He even sounded the alarm to right-thinking Europeans: "danger de l'avenir: guerre de classe" ("danger of the future: class war"), as he put it in 1847. See Alexis de Tocqueville, *Œuvres complètes*, III, 2. (Paris: Gallimard, 1985), 727. Later, at the height of the crisis in his famous address to the National Assembly on September 12, 1848, he stressed the extent to which the stakes of the February Revolution were rooted in property and the demand for equality.

8 Furet, *The Passing of an Illusion*, 57.

9 Cornelius Castoriadis, "What Revolution Is," *Society Adrift: Interviews and Debates, 1974–1994*, (eds.) Enrique Escobar, Myrto Gondicas, and Pascal Vernay (New York: Fordham University Press), 144.

10 Ibid.

11 Arendt, *On Revolution*, 32.

12 Ibid., 33.

13 Ibid., 39–40.

14 Georg Büchner, *Danton's death/Leonce and Lena/Woyzeck*, trans. Victor Price (Oxford: Oxford University Press, 2000), 28.
15 Arendt, *On Revolution*, 51, 47.
16 Ibid., 102.
17 Cornelius Castoriadis, "The Idea of Revolution," in *The Rising Tide of Insignificancy*, trans. from the French and edited anonymously as a public service (Electronic publication date: December 4, 2003), 288. See: http://agorainternational.org/index.html.
18 Ibid., 290.
19 Ibid., 290 (our emphasis).
20 Ibid., 290–291.
21 Ibid., 291.
22 Ibid.
23 Ibid., 198.
24 Ibid., 202.
25 We have, on occasion, made use of this Foucauldian concept in order to theorize resistance against neoliberal governmentality. Without speaking to the value of this concept as such, it seems to us that only a revolutionary project is capable of achieving what Foucault called "the strategic codification of these points of resistance that makes a revolution possible." See Michel Foucault, *The History of Sexuality, Volume 1: An Introduction*, trans. Robert Hurley (New York: Vintage Books, 1977), 96.
26 Pierre Aubenque, *Problèmes aristotéliciens: Philosophie théorique* (Paris: Vrin, 2009), 124.
27 Aristotle, *Metaphysics*, trans. Hugh Lawson (London: Penguin Books, 2004), 12–13 (983b).
28 This is what the Greeks called *ho boulomenos* – or "the first comer" – in the sense of "anyone who wishes may speak, whenever he wishes." See Bernard Manin, "Direct Democracy and Representation: Selection of Officials in Athens," in *The Principles of Representative Government* (Cambridge: Cambridge University Press, 1997), 15.
29 The current expression "evidence-based policy" is derived from the expression "evidence-based medicine."
30 We must not forget Aristotle's formulation: "the good in the sphere of politics is justice, and justice consists in what tends to promote the common interest" (*Politics*, 112 [1282b]).